Android in Practice

Android in Practice

CHARLIE COLLINS
MICHAEL D. GALPIN
MATTHIAS KÄPPLER

MANNING

SHELTER ISLAND

For online information and ordering of this and other Manning books, please visit
www.manning.com. The publisher offers discounts on this book when ordered in quantity.
For more information, please contact

    Special Sales Department
    Manning Publications Co.
    20 Baldwin Road
    PO Box 261
    Shelter Island, NY 11964
    Email: orders@manning.com

Manning Publications Co.   Development editor: Cynthia Kane
20 Baldwin Road   Copyeditor: Benjamin Berg
PO Box 261   Typesetter: Gordan Salinovic
Shelter Island, NY 11964   Cover designer: Marija Tudor

ISBN 9781935182924
Printed in the United States of America
1 2 3 4 5 6 7 8 9 10 – MAL – 16 15 14 13 12 11

brief contents

v

contents

preface

There was a lot of buzz in late 2007 about a forthcoming Google-backed open source mobile phone venture, but there weren't a lot of details. We were interested from the outset because we were all involved with open source projects in one way or another, and we were Linux users with a Java background. The new Google-backed "Java/Linux phone platform," as several blogs and pundits termed it at the time, was exciting and it seemed to suit us perfectly.

Then several official press releases from the Open Handset Alliance came out and the word *Java* was absent from all of them. At the same time it supposedly ran a "custom virtual machine" and several people who we knew to be Java guys were tapped to work on various parts of it. Was this thing Java or not? This was the first of the ways Android intrigued us, before we were even sure what it was.

When more details about the platform emerged, it became clear that it would use Java "the language" but would avoid the Sun (at the time) virtual machine, and it would deviate from the standard Linux kernel/distribution approach. Google and their OHA partners were using a lot of existing and open tools and components, but were wiring them up in a new way and mixing in parts of their own.

We thought the platform had solid engineering, great timing, and a lot of potential. As soon as the first betas dropped, we grabbed the SDK and tools and started tinkering. We then bought the first Android devices available so we could put the early applications we wrote on our own phones, and we haven't stopped tinkering since.

We now know Android as a unique platform that's both open and extremely popular. There isn't a single device that runs Android anymore; now there are hundreds.

And the platform hasn't been standing still either. There have been many new releases and improvements. Android has grown by leaps and bounds and isn't showing any signs of slowing down yet.

Still, in all the excitement and growth of Android, one thing has become apparent to us, as developers. It's extremely easy to start building applications for the platform, because it's Java-based and familiar to so many, but it's also easy to get into trouble. Android is a powerful laser gun from the future, but a lot of us still have it aimed at our own feet. Beyond the idiosyncrasies of some of the APIs and the new capabilities such as GPS, cameras, and hardware sensors, there's also a constrained environment with limited resources. It's not enough to craft a new UI, get a web service working to talk to the network, and be able to use the GPS, for example. You need to do all that within a lifecycle that restarts your code when the device orientation changes, while supporting different screen sizes, without blocking the UI thread, playing nicely with system resources, and more. It's easy to create Android applications, but it's hard to create *good* Android applications.

This is where *Android in Practice* came into being. We've written Android apps downloaded by millions of users and have learned much along the way. As we learned from both our successes and failures, we published articles and wrote blog posts about Android. We collected a tip or a recipe here and there and tried to share it. We even read a few good introductory Android books, or smaller books that covered several topics well but left other things out. We realized there was a gap. There wasn't a book that started with the basics and then went into more depth with nontrivial examples and covered everything we thought was important—from background and development to building and testing and more. We got together and shared our ideas and collected our articles and a new book project was born.

What you're now holding in your hands is our effort at sharing our experiences and knowledge in trying to craft a book that both beginners and advanced users can learn from and use as a reference. We hope you'll find advice and techniques in this book that are truly useful, and we hope it helps you become aware of how to build *great* Android applications that are successful on the Android platform for years to come.

acknowledgments

It takes an entire cast of people to write a book. Without the tireless efforts of the crew at Manning, our friends who helped with several sections, and all of our technical reviewers and early access subscribers who provided feedback along the way, this book would never have happened.

Michael Stephens at Manning got the entire project off the ground and got us into the capable hands of Troy Mott, who directed us through the remainder of the project. Along the way Cynthia Kane was our development editor and main advisor on many topics. She helped us with just about everything, from grammar and usage to style and format and more. Mary Piergies kept everything organized and led the way into production. Once there, Benjamin Berg did a fantastic job of formatting and copyediting, while Gordan Salinovic did the typesetting. And publisher Marjan Bace made the whole thing possible.

Outside of Manning we managed to convince a few of our friends and colleagues to pitch in too. Tamas Jano and Robert Cooper provided code examples and text to help us create the 2D and 3D drawing chapter. And, Logan Johnson worked on several of the ContentProvider examples that became part of chapter 8, "Sharing data between apps." Without their excellent contributions we would've lacked coverage of those important aspects of Android programming.

Our other outside help came from our technical reviewers. Jerome Baton took the time to download and build and review all of our example projects, and he found several issues that we'd missed. As well, we got many suggestions and corrections from the other reviewers of our book, including Steve Prior, Nenad Nikolic, Kevin McDonagh,

Mark Ryall, Peter Johnson, Al Scherer, Norman Klein, Tijs Rademakers, Michele Galli, Sivakumar Thyagarajan, Justin Tyler Wiley, Cheryl Jerozal, Brian Ehmann, Robby O'Connor, Gabor Paller, Dave Nicolette, Ian Stirk, Daniel Alford, and David Strong. The Early Access subscribers also provided valuable feedback.

All of these people made this book much better than it would've been without them, and we're truly grateful for their contributions.

CHARLIE

Writing a technical book is a long and difficult process, but it's ultimately very rewarding when you can hold the finished product in your hands and be proud of it. I'd like to start by thanking my coauthors Michael and Matthias for that pride. These guys both not only really know their stuff, but they also kept going even when things took longer than planned, and they took on more than they had signed on for. In all it was a great experience working with them.

I'd also like to thank the Android team and the Android and open source community. All of the people who work to make Android better either directly, or with bug reports and patches, help on forums and question and answer sites, participation in user groups and conferences, and creating libraries and tools are a big reason the platform works and thrives. In addition to thanking everyone who contributes to Android, I'd be remiss if I didn't mention the open source community at large. Those who've worked on Linux, or a library like WebKit, or SQLite, or Apache HttpClient, or many more, and those who've worked on tools like Eclipse and Maven, are also key to the success of Android and to the everyday work that I get to do using the platform.

Finally I'd like to thank my family and friends. My wife Erin, and my daughters Skylar and Delaney were always supportive and encouraging, even when "the book" took time away from my participation in one family event or another. And my parents, Earl and Peg Farmer, have always been there for me and have always encouraged me to do the best that I can in whatever I attempt.

MICHAEL

I'd like to first and foremost thank my beautiful wife Crystal. It takes a lot of time to write a book and time is one thing in short supply for a developer working at a startup and for a father with two young sons. Without an amazing wife, there's no way this book could've happened. I'd also like to thank my high school English teacher, Dr. Ed Deluzain. He's the person who taught me how to write, and that skill has opened up many opportunities for me. Writing a book has been a dream that's finally coming true, but it's a dream that started in Dr. Deluzain's class. Finally, I'd like to acknowledge Troy Mott, who has worked with me for many years on various technical writing endeavors. It has pleased me greatly to work with him once again on this book.

MATTHIAS

First, I'd like to wholeheartedly thank the Android developer community, of which I am in highest appreciation. I'm an open-source enthusiast, and I fully believe in the idea of contributing back whenever you take. I have taken lots from the open source community: answers, ideas, code, and this book is my way of contributing back to you all. Thanks especially to everyone who has contributed ideas and code back to Signpost, Droid-Fu, and Calculon, my pet projects.

Personally, I'd also like to send a big kudos to Kevin McDonagh and Carl-Gustaf Harroch of Novoda, for all the effort they put into making Android not just a platform, but a community. Special thanks also go to Manfred Moser, Hugo Josefson, and Renas Reda, authors of the Android plugin for Maven and the Robotium library respectively, for reviewing those chapters in this book. Big thanks also go to Julian Harty, Carlos Sessa, Nenad Nikolic, Jan Berkel, Thibaut Rouffineau, and all the other great people who either reviewed this book, or with whom I had insightful discussions about Android and building amazing open source software. You guys are all rockstars!

It should not go unnoted that this book was a team effort; that's why I want to thank Charlie and Michael for continually driving this project forward and for the uniquely enjoyable ride!

Last, and definitely not least, I thank my dear parents for supporting me all the way through this book and for keeping me going whenever I was about to get stuck.

about this book

Android is an open source mobile device platform created by Google and the Open Handset Alliance. Android powers smartphones, tablets, set-top boxes, TVs, and more. *Android in Practice* is a book dedicated to helping developers build applications for the Android platform.

This book is intended to provide some background information and coverage of the basics of developing applications for Android for beginners and also goes into depth on many topics for intermediate to advanced developers. The overall goal of *Android in Practice* is to collect and organize helpful Android programming techniques over a variety of topics and explain those techniques in the context of the overall platform. We're going for the *why* as much as the *how.* You will find 91 techniques in the book, each consisting of a problem, solution, and discussion section.

Who should read this book?

This is a book about developing applications for the Android platform, from key components and application basics to advanced techniques, testing, building, project management, and more. We hope this book will appeal to Android developers of varying skill levels, from beginner to advanced; Android testers; and managers and team leaders looking to better understand Android development.

This book is intended for people who already have some programming experience and are at least familiar with Java. Therefore, we assume that most readers are somewhat familiar with Java and related technologies (working with IDEs, compiling and writing Java code, XML, basic networking, and so forth).

Roadmap

Chapter 1 introduces Android, the platform and talks about the progression that led to it, the companies behind it, and what sets it apart. It also introduces the core Android APIs and tools and includes a "hello world" programming example.

Chapter 2 covers all of the key components needed in a basic Android application, including resources, layout, views, activities, adapters, and intents.

Chapter 3 discusses the details of the lifecycle of an Android application and of activities. We discuss both the stack of activities an application includes and how activities are grouped into tasks.

Chapter 4 focuses entirely on the user interface. This includes how views are created and rendered, how they're arranged in layouts, how adapters are used to manage them, how they can be styled and reused, working with drawables, and handling devices with different screen sizes.

Chapter 5 provides details on multitasking using services. This goes from what a service is and why it's necessary to how they can be created, how they can be started automatically or scheduled with alarms, how they can be used to cache data and send notifications, and how to push messages from the cloud to devices.

Chapter 6 details where threads and asynchronous tasks can be used to make Android applications more responsive and performant. The topics covered include communicating between threads, managing threads, using handlers and timers, message loops, and more.

Chapter 7 deals with working with external and internal storage to store data. This includes using the filesystem and preferences files and working with SQLite and databases.

Chapter 8 deals with sharing data between different applications. This includes consuming data from other applications on the platform and providing data to other applications, both using a content provider.

Chapter 9 extends the concepts of storing and sharing data by using the network. This means using HTTP from several different clients, working with web services using XML and JSON, understanding how to detect and switch between different network data sources, and recovering gracefully from networking problems.

Chapter 10 deals with location-related services. This includes determining what location providers are present and what resources each requires, obtaining location data from different sources, and building map-based applications.

Chapter 11 features multimedia. The topics here include detecting multimedia capabilities, working with resources and files, using media related content providers, and working with audio and video, including using the camera, displaying animations, and controlling audio playback.

Chapter 12 delves into 2D and 3D drawing. This is where we learn about drawing shapes and lines on the canvas, creating effects, building custom views, and working with 3D programming using OpenGL ES.

Chapter 13 covers automated testing of Android applications. This includes working with different types of tests and several different test approaches and frameworks.

Chapter 14 discusses project management and build automation. This includes an overview of all the steps required in an Android build, coverage of working with build tools such as Ant and Maven, and continuous integration of Android builds with Hudson.

Chapter 15 targets developing for Android tablets. This includes using existing code libraries, targeting different devices, working with activity fragments, and different user interface components for tablets.

Appendix A picks up several questions involving debugging Android applications and gives some useful advice on how to effectively use the Android Debug Bridge. It also covers a recent addition to Android called StrictMode, which allows you to detect performance smells in your applications.

Appendix B presents Android application development from an entirely new perspective, as it explores two alternative approaches to native Android development: using WebViews and programming in alternative languages like Scala.

Appendix C covers use of the ProGuard byte code optimizer and obfuscator, something you should have on your radar for any production-quality application.

Appendix D covers monkeyrunner, a scripted tool used to instrument Android applications. This is our attempt to shed some light on a useful but underdocumented tool.

Code conventions and downloads

This book contains many example projects, all of which are based on multiple code listings. We've tried to be as thorough as possible in the listings and yet keep them concise, but this isn't always easy with Java and XML. Many of the listings also include code annotations that highlight important concepts and explain portions. These annotations are discussed in the text.

In some listings we've omitted the more verbose or boilerplate portions of the code where we feel it makes sense to do so. For example, after we've introduced one concept, we typically don't keep repeating the same technique in the code listings. We know it can be frustrating to not have complete examples, but it's also impossible to include all of the code this book covers in its entirety and still adequately discuss the related concepts. We've tried to strike a balance and indicate in the listings wherever code is omitted for brevity, and we've also included every line of code as a complete working project available for download as either source or in working binary form at the *Android in Practice* Google Code hosting site: http://code.google.com/p/android-in-practice/. The code is also available from the publisher's website at http://www.manning.com/AndroidinPractice.

Author Online

The purchase of *Android in Practice* includes free access to a private web forum run by Manning Publications, where you can make comments about the book, ask technical questions, and receive help from the authors and from other users. To access the forum and subscribe to it, point your web browser to http://manning.com/AndroidinPractice. This page provides information on how to get on the forum once you are registered, what kind of help is available, and the rules of conduct on the forum.

Manning's commitment to our readers is to provide a venue where a meaningful dialogue between individual readers and between readers and the authors can take place. It isn't a commitment to any specific amount of participation on the part of the authors, whose contribution to the forum remains voluntary (and unpaid). We suggest you try asking the authors some challenging questions lest their interest stray!

The Author Online forum and the archives of previous discussions will be accessible from the publisher's website as long as the book is in print.

About the authors

CHARLIE COLLINS is the director of development at MOVL, where he helps create apps that allow connected TVs and mobile devices to interact. Charlie has worked on several open source projects and has a strong background in web applications and web services. Charlie was also the coauthor of Manning's *GWT in Practice* and *Unlocking Android*. When he's not coding Android apps or writing server logic, Charlie can often be found playing tennis or mountain biking. Charlie lives in Atlanta, Georgia, with his wife and two daughters.

MICHAEL GALPIN is a developer at Bump Technologies where he works on Bump, one of the most popular social networking apps on the Android Market. Prior to that, he was at eBay for four years where he worked on eBay Mobile for Android, one of the most popular shopping apps. He frequently writes articles about open source technology for IBM developerWorks. He lives in San Jose, California, with his wife and two sons.

MATTHIAS KÄPPLER is a developer at Qype.com, Europe's largest community portal for local reviews, where he leads development in Qype's mobile products division, the "A-Team" (Android and API). He has been all over Android from its early alpha day and has founded or contributed to several well-received open source projects, including Signpost OAuth, Droid-Fu, Calculon, and Gradle's Android plugin. In his spare time he's a music, movie, and coffee addict, and when not busy discovering new locations and reviewing them on Qype, he's probably practicing Taekkyon, a Korean martial art. Matthias lives in Hamburg, Germany.

about the cover illustration

The figure on the cover of *Android in Practice* is captioned "Habit of the Grand Seigneur's Body Guard in 1700" and is taken from the four-volume *Collection of the Dresses of Different Nations* by Thomas Jefferys, published in London between 1757 and 1772. The collection, which includes beautifully hand-colored copperplate engravings of costumes from around the world, has influenced theatrical costume design ever since it was published.

The diversity of the drawings in the *Collection of the Dresses of Different Nations* speaks vividly of the richness of the costumes presented on the London stage over 200 years ago. The costumes, both historical and contemporaneous, offered a glimpse into the dress customs of people living in different times and in different countries, bringing them to life for London theater audiences.

Dress codes have changed in the last century and the diversity by region, so rich in the past, has faded away. It's now often hard to tell the inhabitant of one continent from another. Perhaps, trying to view it optimistically, we've traded a cultural and visual diversity for a more varied personal life—or a more varied and interesting intellectual and technical life.

We at Manning celebrate the inventiveness, the initiative, and the fun of the computer business with book covers based on the rich diversity of regional and historical costumes brought back to life by pictures from collections such as this one.

Part 1

Background and fundamentals

This first part of *Android in Practice* will explain the core concepts surrounding the Android platform and its key components. In chapter 1, you'll learn what Android is, who created it, and why it was created. We'll also introduce you to the basics of developing applications for it. In chapter 2, you'll take the basics further and build a foundation for later examples by completing your first nontrivial example. This will involve the application manifest, activities, views, resources, layouts, and adapters. Chapter 3 will build upon this foundation by helping you understand and work with the well-defined lifecycle of components such as activities, as well as overall Android applications.

Introducing Android

Reality is that which, when you stop believing in it, doesn't go away.

—Philip K. Dick

Today, mobile phones are everywhere. They're more prevalent than personal computers. They've replaced our watches, calculators, cameras, MP3 players, and often our means of internet access. They also provide capabilities such as GPS navigation, motion and gesture interfaces, social networking, and an indescribably broad array of "apps" that mix and match many features. With all of this, it's easy to see why mobile devices are popular.

The technology behind mobile devices has advanced rapidly. It wasn't all that long ago that voice calls were routed through a completely wired network with human switchboard operators and all phones were attached to physical wires. The "plain old telephone system" (POTS), as it has become known, matured, and manual switchboards were replaced with computer controlled switches. Then features such

3

as voicemail and caller id were added. Eventually, the wires were cut. At first, wireless phones had home base stations and bulky antennas. Then, carriers built extensive wireless networks that made even that unnecessary. Next, crude applications began to appear alongside the telephony capability, and mobile devices and networks were pushed to provide more and more functionality. Today, we've come a long way, but we're still pushing. With impressive hardware and network speeds, we have incredibly powerful wireless handheld computers.

Making use of all this computing and networking power is the tricky part. Until recently, the software in many mainstream mobile devices was proprietary. This typically meant several things, all of which were hurdles for developers:

- The source code wasn't available to see how things ticked.
- There may have been formidable licensing fees or other development costs.
- There were restrictive terms and opaque policies even if you were licensed.
- There weren't easily approachable programming languages or software development kits (SDKs).
- There weren't easy ways to get applications in front of users and installed on devices.

A consortium of companies known as the *Open Handset Alliance*, led by Google, looked at the landscape several years ago and asked the question "What would it take to build a better mobile phone?" By *better* they meant a phone that could overcome the hurdles holding back widespread collaboration, innovation, and adoption on other platforms. The answer they came up with was Android. Android is a powerful and open platform that anyone can use and extend. Figure 1.1 shows a montage of screen shots that demonstrate a few of the platform's capabilities.

Android's power and capabilities make it appealing to users. Those same features combined with the open nature and impressive engineering make it attractive to developers. Android is the way forward. The potential is there; what's needed now are more innovative developers to write quality applications. Android needs you.

Being both Android users and developers ourselves, this is what inspired us to try to pass on some practical knowledge about the platform, and about how to write applications for it. That's where *Android in Practice* comes into play. This book is about building applications for Android and it brings real-world tips from the trenches.

PREFLIGHT CHECK   One thing we need to get out of the way up front is that *Android in Practice* is intended to be a recipe-style book of practical examples that tackle many different aspects of the platform (some of them advanced). Part 1 of this book, including this chapter, is a whirlwind introduction to the basics. Once we get past this, we'll advance quickly. If you're already familiar with Android and have already written Android applications, you may want to go straight for the deeper dive and skip ahead to parts 2 and 3. These are each focused on a particular area of the platform and go into much more depth than this introduction. You're welcome to stay with us and revisit the fundamentals if you prefer as well.

Figure 1.1 Several Android screen shots demonstrating some of the capabilities of the platform, including a customizable interface, phone, application market, full-fledged browser, mapping, and navigation.

In this first chapter, we'll start by sharing some background information and dealing with the basics. That means we'll first talk more about what Android is, and why it matters. From there we'll build a simple "Hello Android" application to get the lay of the land. Through that exercise, we'll introduce you to the *Android Software Development Kit (SDK)* and the main parts of an Android application. Then we'll move on to cover the key aspects of the specialized Java runtime Android uses, *Dalvik*. We'll also examine some of the details of the Linux-based operating system (OS) that powers all of it. After that, we'll discuss Android's overall architecture, including its native middleware libraries, its applications and application framework, and further developer tools and SDK details.

At the end of this chapter, you should have a basic understanding of the Android platform and development process. With that foundation, you should be ready to move on to tackling more detail in chapter 2 and beyond.

1.1 Android in a nutshell

If we were to ask one of the millions of Android device owners "What is Android?" we'd get a variety of responses. Some might say it's a kind of phone, or it's a place to get apps for their phone, or maybe a cute little green robot. As developers, we go further—we understand it's a broad platform for creating and running applications.

Before we jump into the code, we need to define what we mean when we say "Android," touch on what sets it apart, and discuss the key components of the platform.

1.1.1   *Defining Android*

The marketing tag line is that Android is a "complete set of software for mobile devices: an operating system, middleware, and key mobile applications." It's that and more. It goes beyond mobile, and arguably, the development framework and SDK aren't captured in that description—but they're essential too.

Android truly is a complete stack, from boot loader, device drivers, and libraries, to software APIs, included applications, and SDK. Android isn't a particular device, or even class of devices; it's a platform that can be used and adapted to power different hardware configurations. Mobile phones are the main class of Android powered devices, but it's also currently used on electronic book readers, netbooks, tablets, and set-top boxes.

1.1.2   *What sets Android apart*

Even though it's open and powerful, Android isn't perfect. Android doesn't get everything right, but we think it's a big step in the right direction. Android avoids many of the issues surrounding proprietary systems by being open source and being licensed in an open manner (with no licensing fees whatsoever). Android provides an approachable and accessible (free) SDK and other development tools. And, Android deals with getting applications in front of users with a built-in market application that allows users to easily download and install apps right from their phones.

> **THE MARKET AND INSTALLING APPLICATIONS**   The Android Market is the main way users find and install applications on their phones. Anyone who registers and agrees to the terms can submit applications to the Android Market. Once in the Market, applications are available to users immediately (without any review process). Applications can then be rated and commented upon by users. This technique is different because it's ultra-convenient and it brings a social aspect directly to the mix. Application ratings are a sort of artificial selection for the app ecosystem. The fittest apps survive and thrive. In addition to the official Android Market, users can also use (if their carriers permit it) third-party markets and direct downloads to install applications.

Beyond the users and the market, Android also runs on a plethora of devices. In fact, there are so many different devices now that it can be difficult to develop and test applications that work on every one. This is one criticism that has been leveled at Android. But there are many ways to mitigate the associated problems, and Android was designed to help cope with this. We'll learn more about creating applications that work on multiple devices, even with multiple screen sizes, in several later examples in the book.

Android didn't pioneer the open source mobile operating system concept. Others have come before it, and there surely will be others after. Android also didn't invent the market approach that it uses to provide easy and socialized access to applications for users. Yet, Android has combined all of these things in new ways, with the backing of a consortium of successful commercial companies and solid engineering, and this has made it one of the most popular and successful mobile operating systems on the planet today.

With a description of Android in hand, and some understanding of the motivation for its creation, we'll next turn to the key components that make up the platform.

1.1.3 Key platform components

Like any technology stack, the Android platform can be broken down into areas of responsibility to make it easier to understand. The main divisions of the Android platform are depicted in figure 1.2.

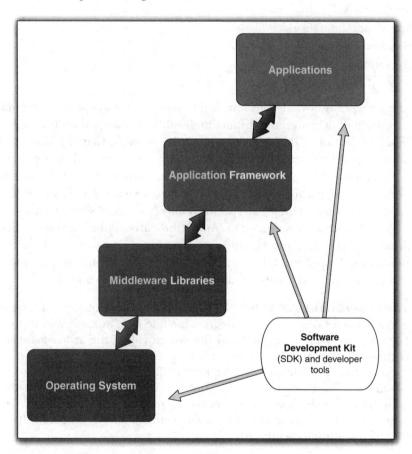

Figure 1.2 An overview of the major components of the Android platform: OS, middleware, application framework, applications, and developer tools

QRCODES AND URLS   Throughout the book, in cases where it might be useful on a mobile device, instead of providing only a text URL to an online resource, we're also going to provide a *Quick Response (QR) code* (2D bar code). These codes can be scanned by many bar code scanners, such as several available on Android, and resolved to URLs for quick and easy browsing.

The preceding QR code decodes to the official "what is Android" documentation: http://mng.bz/Z4Le. There you can find more information about what Android is, including the official architectural "layer cake" diagram.

The architectural diagram in figure 1.2 shows that the Android platform can be broken down into five sections:

- Applications
- Application framework
- Middleware libraries
- Operating system
- SDK and developer tools

Applications are pretty obvious. But several different types of applications are available on most Android devices, and the distinction is subtle. Core open source applications are included as part of Android itself, such as the Browser, Camera, Gallery, Music, Phone, and more. These are typically included with every Android device. There are also non–open source Google apps that are included with most official builds, including Market, Gmail, Maps, YouTube and more. Many carrier or handset manufacturer-specific applications are included on specific builds (such as AT&T's own music player, Verizon's own Navigator, or Sprint's TV). And, third-party applications are available in the Android Market, which can be either open source or proprietary. These include independent Google applications such as Goggles and Listen, official apps from popular services like Twitter and Facebook, and thousands of other choices.

WHY CAN'T I UNINSTALL SOME APPS?   Many handset manufacturers and service carriers, and even Google to some degree, include certain applications on a special read-only part of the Android file system called the *system partition*. Applications that are installed here can't be easily uninstalled (you need to have administrative privileges, and/or mount the partition as read-write to remove them). This is often annoying, but also understandable. Part of the power of Android is that manufacturers and carriers can customize it the way they want to. This is part of the reason why many of these companies have adopted the platform to begin with.

Supporting applications, the Android platform includes a framework to run them in. The application framework provides a tightly integrated part of the platform SDK and APIs that allow for high-level interaction with the system from within applications. When your application needs access to hardware sensors, network data, the state of interface elements, or many other things, it gets to that information through the application framework. We'll learn more about the SDK and the application framework in section 1.6.

Beneath the application framework sits the software collectively referred to as the *middleware*. As the name suggests, middleware is software components that sit *in between*—in this case between the operating system and the applications/application framework. The middleware includes libraries for many functions (data storage, graphics rendering, web browsing, and so on) and it also contains a special subsection called the *Dalvik runtime*. This is Android's special nonstandard virtual machine (VM) and its core application libraries. We'll learn more about Dalvik in section 1.3.

At the bottom of the Android stack is the operating system. Android's OS is Linux-based and performs much the same tasks you'd expect from any conventional desktop computer OS. This includes interfacing with the hardware through a set of device drivers (such as audio or video drivers), processing user input, managing application processes, handling file and network I/O, and so forth. We'll learn more about the Android Linux OS in section 1.4.

With Android's layered design, each level is an abstraction of the one beneath it. Don't worry—as a developer you won't have to deal with lower-level details directly. Rather, you'll always access subsystems by going through simple interfaces exposed in Android's application framework (unless you're doing native development work with the *Native Development Kit* or *NDK*, but that's getting ahead of the game).

Android is a vast system; we neither can nor want to cover everything here. Instead, as we progress through this chapter, we'll focus on the important parts, the parts we think you should know about and have a basic understanding of. As we go, we'll share more details about the layers we've introduced, within the context of building applications and understanding the platform from a developer's perspective. To do that, we'll start by getting the prerequisites in order and writing our first Android application, "Hello Android."

1.2 *Hello Android!*

Our first Android application will display a single line of text and one image on a single screen. It isn't impressive, but we're keeping it simple on purpose. We want the components of the application, and the process, to take center stage. The application we'll build, "Hello Android," is seen in completed form running in the emulator in figure 1.3.

Figure 1.3   The Hello Android application being run from an emulator instance and showing some simple onscreen elements: text and an image

To build *Hello Android* we'll use a few tools that we need to get in order first. These include the Android SDK, the *Eclipse Integrated Development Environment (IDE)*, and the *Eclipse Android Development Tools (ADT)* plugin.

1.2.1   Getting the SDK and Eclipse

If you've never worked with Android before, to get started you need to check the system requirements and then download and set up a Java development kit (JDK), the Android SDK, and the Eclipse IDE. We won't spend a lot of time on describing the processes for installing these prerequisites because they're well documented online. Table 1.1 includes a description of the related online resources, and links to where they're located.

Table 1.1   Prerequisites and online documentation for Android development

Description	URL
System requirements	http://developer.android.com/sdk/requirements.html
Java—JDK5 or JDK6	http://www.oracle.com/technetwork/java/javase/downloads
Eclipse IDE for Java Developers	http://www.eclipse.org/downloads/
Android SDK	http://developer.android.com/sdk/index.html
Android Development Tools (ADT) Eclipse Plugin	http://developer.android.com/sdk/eclipse-adt.html

The Android ADT plugin works in conjunction with Eclipse's *Java Development Tools (JDT)*. The fact that an Android application's source code can be written in Java (the language) and Android development is supported by Eclipse isn't an accident. Java has strong tooling support (like Eclipse) and a large active community of developers. Eclipse provides convenient Java development features such as syntax highlighting, code completion, error detection, build support, and an excellent debugger. Eclipse also provides wizards for creating and running Android applications, managing and manipulating Android Virtual Devices (AVDs), and specialized editors for creating user interfaces and managing application metadata.

DO I HAVE TO USE ECLIPSE?   The short answer is no, you don't have to use Eclipse. You can use the Apache Ant Java-based build tool and the command line if you prefer. Or, you can integrate the Ant-based tools supplied with another IDE if that's your preference. Our recommendation is to use Eclipse. The Android team has chosen Eclipse as the main IDE to support, and the Android Development Tools (ADT) plugin for Eclipse is useful.

FOR THAT MATTER, DO I HAVE TO USE JAVA?   For those out there who don't prefer Java, Android hasn't forgotten you entirely, and neither have we. We'll touch on using alternative languages such as Scala in an appendix. And, we'll also look at building web applications (using JavaScript and CSS, for example) for Android too. These are broad topics so we can't cover them in depth, but we want to at least introduce them and make sure you know there are options. That said, Java is the main development language of Android, and it'll be the main language we use throughout this book.

Though we aren't going to spell out how to install Eclipse and the Android SDK and ADT plugin here (as previously noted), we'll mention a few tips. Even if you already have Eclipse, if you don't have Android, you might want to reinstall Eclipse in a new location, and install the ADT plugin there. That way you'll have a shiny new Android-specific Eclipse install (or maybe also include the Google plugin for AppEngine and GWT and make it a Google Eclipse install). This helps on a few fronts: first, Eclipse can get bogged down when too many plugins and extras are installed; and second, this new installation will be out of the way of any existing projects and plugins you have, so it might be easier to troubleshoot any plugin issues or configuration problems should they arise. Also, even though you're likely to use Eclipse a lot, you'll want to make sure the Android tools are in your PATH and that you have the command line handy. A few tools only work from the command line (they aren't exposed in the plugin), and it's a good idea to know what the underlying tools are and how to use them. We'll cover the tools specifically in section 1.6, and as related topics come up in later examples and topics.

Once you get set up, the next step is to fire up the Eclipse IDE and create an Android project.

1.2.2 Creating an Android project with Eclipse

You're probably already familiar with Eclipse, or at least with the concept of creating a new project in a GUI tool. To create our *Hello Android* project we'll follow the well-worn path from File, to New, to Android Project, as seen in figure 1.4.

The next dialog that pops up in the IDE is the initial project properties screen. We'll enter some basic information for our project, as seen in figure 1.5. The project properties you'll need to create a new project include a Project Name (the name used to identify the project within Eclipse), and then a series of Android related inputs: Build Target, Application Name, Package Name, and Activity Name (labeled Create Activity in figure 1.5).

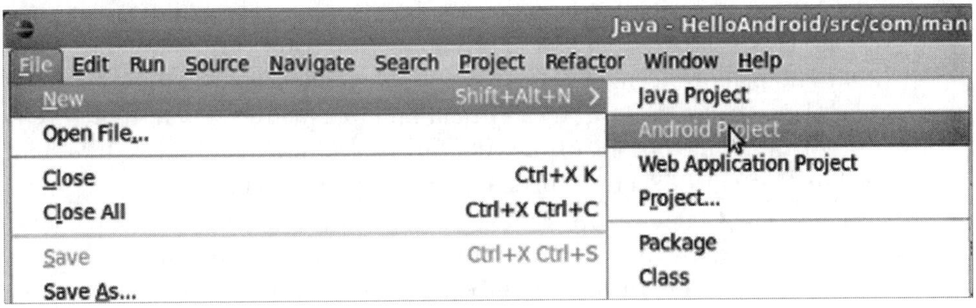

Figure 1.4   Creating a new Android project in Eclipse

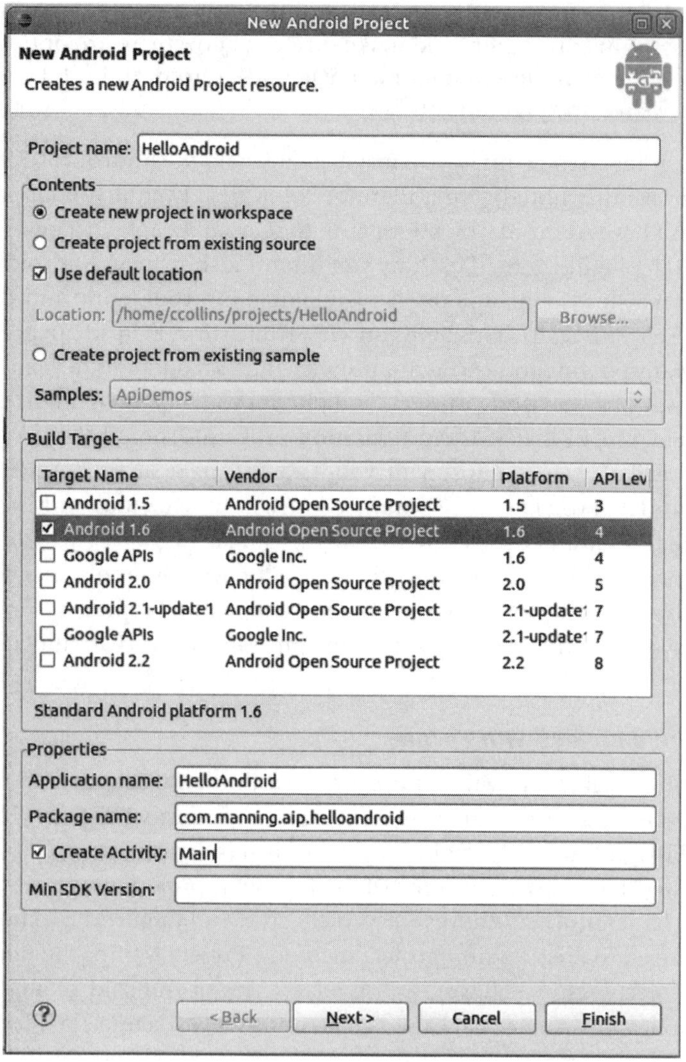

Figure 1.5 Set proper-
ties for the HelloAndroid
project in Eclipse using
the ADT plugin

The names are straightforward, as is the Java package. The Build Target is more interesting. This is the Android SDK Platform that you had to install when you installed the
SDK. The platform contains the particular dependencies and tools for a specific version of the Android API. You can install multiple platforms, and therefore build and
test for different versions of the API, but you're only required to have one. (We've
picked Android 1.6, but for this simple project it doesn't matter; any Target/platform
will do.) The Create Activity setting is also worth touching on. If you check this, the
ADT will create a template "Hello World" class and screen for you.

Before we go any further, let's take a look at the structure we now have after we click
the Finish button and let the Eclipse ADT plugin create our initial Android project.

1.2.3 Project structure

Android projects rely on a predefined project structure to allow different components to be located, and to provide some convention over configuration. Java source code, layout files, string resources, image resources, and more have their place in the hierarchy. Figure 1.6 depicts the complete structure for our Hello Android project, including the source (and generated source), resources, and manifest.

As figure 1.6 shows, Java source code for an Android project is placed in a top level src directory. From there a parallel gen directory is also present for generated source. This is where the Android tool chain will create autogenerated sources for you, including R.java.

R is an internal class that's used to wire resources. As for resources, they're noncode items (such as externalized strings) that are included with your project. Resources are placed in the res directory. Within the res directory are several subdirectories that determine the type of resource, and when it should be used. Lastly, within the top level directory is the Android configuration file for the project, AndroidManifest.xml.

Now that we've seen the structure and know where things go, in the next few sections we'll focus on what each of these items is, and how you build and use them, as we

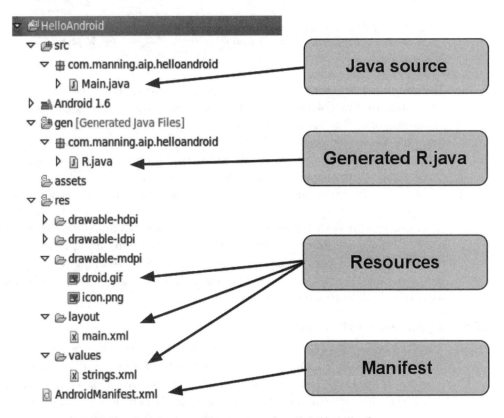

Figure 1.6 An overview of the basic project structure of an Android application

create the Hello Android application. We'll start with Main.java file in the src directory. This is our first look at an Android `Activity` class.

1.2.4   Introducing the Activity class

In Android terms, an *activity* is a Java class that creates a default window on the screen and allows for placement of the user interface (UI) elements. Simply put, an `Activity` class roughly correlates to a screen in an Android application (most of the time: there are some subtleties, which we'll learn as we go). Because we started our project using the ADT plugin and we enabled the Create Activity option, we already have our first `Activity` class, `Main`.

Listing 1.1   Main.java Android `Activity` class as generated by the ADT plugin

```
package com.manning.aip.helloandroid;

import android.app.Activity;
import android.os.Bundle;                              ❶ Extend
                                                          Activity
public class Main extends Activity {           ⬎
    /** Called when the activity is first created. */
    @Override                                          ❷ Override
    public void onCreate(Bundle savedInstanceState) {  ⬎  onCreate
        super.onCreate(savedInstanceState);
        setContentView(R.layout.main);          ⬅—❸ Set layout
    }
}
```

The generated `Activity` class the ADT plugin provides is simple, which makes it a great place to start poking around. First, we see that this class extends `Activity` ❶. This is important. `Activity` brings a lot along, including lifecycle methods such as onCreate ❷. As the comment in the code (which the plugin also generated) indicates, this is called when the `Activity` class is first created. We'll learn much more about `Activity` in chapters 2 and 3. `Activity` is one of the most important classes you'll use in day-to-day development, and it has many more facets we won't touch on here.

For now, think of this as the first screen, where you can hook into the lifecycle and tell the framework how to configure the visual elements using a separate layout resource ❸. In this case our layout resource is `R.layout.main` and we set it as the content *view*. The R class is a special generated class that hooks names with resources, something we'll learn more about shortly.

1.2.5   Setting the Activity layout

A *layout resource* is a special configuration file for the design and arrangement of visual elements on the screen. One handy aspect of Android development is that a lot of the time the UI can be declared in XML with a layout resource. This separates the presentation from the code (somewhat), and makes many UI elements reusable. The first layout resource we're using for our `Main Activity` screen is shown next.

Listing 1.2   Main.xml layout resource used to declare UI elements for the Main Activity

```xml
<?xml version="1.0" encoding="utf-8"?>
<LinearLayout
    xmlns:android="http://schemas.android.com/apk/res/android"
    android:orientation="vertical"
    android:layout_width="fill_parent"
    android:layout_height="fill_parent"
    android:background="#FFF"
    >
<TextView
    android:layout_width="fill_parent"
    android:layout_height="wrap_content"
    android:layout_marginTop="25dp"
    android:gravity="center_horizontal"
    android:textColor="#000"
    android:textSize="50dp"
    android:text="@string/hello"
    />
<ImageView
    android:layout_width="fill_parent"
    android:layout_height="wrap_content"
    android:src="@drawable/droid"
    />
</LinearLayout>
```

❶ LinearLayout parent element

❷ TextView for text

❸ Modify TextView settings

❹ Set TextView contents

❺ ImageView for images

❻ Droid image for ImageView

The layout we're using for Hello Android is basic, but we've modified it from the default generated layout the ADT plugin creates. The first thing to note here is the xmlns:android namespace. This is an XML shortcut. We define it this way so we can refer to the Android schema elements throughout the rest of the file using only the android: prefix. Next we see that we're using a LinearLayout ❶. LinearLayout refers to an Android layout class, in this case, one that puts the child elements it contains in a line (either horizontal or vertical; see the orientation attribute). A layout in Android is a specialized type of View (specifically, a ViewGroup, but we're getting ahead of ourselves). Several different layouts are available in Android, all of which we'll meet in chapter 4. View is the base class of elements that are capable of dealing with screen layout and are intended to be seen or interacted with by the user. Android is loaded with many different types of views, such as the TextView ❷ we see next in our layout.

A TextView, you guessed it, displays text. View elements often have attributes that can manipulate their properties. Here we've set the margin, gravity (position on the screen relative to other elements), color, and size of the TextView ❸. Also, we see that the android:text attribute, which determines what text to display is set to @string/hello ❹. This usage of @string means we're referring to a string resource. We could have hard-coded some text here, but externalizing resources like this keeps our layout and our content nicely separated.

After the TextView, we next have an ImageView ❺. For it, we're specifying the src attribute as @drawable/droid, another external resource reference, this time to a *drawable* named droid ❻. We'll discuss drawables in chapter 4. For now, we need to understand that we've included a *droid.gif* image file in the `res/drawable-mdpi` direc-tory of the project and that way Android can find and use it (this file is available with the code download for the book; we initially grabbed it from the Android goodies page: http://www.android.com/media/goodies.html). With our layout out of the way, let's take a closer look at how the resource references work.

1.2.6 *Referring to resources*

As we've seen, the @ sign in a layout file (which itself is a type of resource) is a refer-ence to another resource. In the case of `@string/hello` we're referring to a strings.xml file. It's always a good idea to keep different types of entities in your proj-ect separate from the code. This goes for layouts, strings, images, XML files, and any-thing that Android refers to as a resource.

With strings and images, this is obvious. If you want to have different resources based on different settings, such as language or location, you can. The @ sign tells Android to parse these values as resources. Android has many resource types, which we'll learn more about in the next few chapters, but for now let's take a look at what's in our strings.xml file.

Listing 1.3   The res/values/strings.xml resource file

```
<?xml version="1.0" encoding="utf-8"?>
<resources>
    <string name="hello">Hello Android!</string>
    <string name="app_name">HelloAndroid</string>
</resources>
```

This externalized string file is in an XML format, and it holds key/value paired data. In the layout we referred to the `hello` resource, which will ultimately display the "Hello Android!" string. Strings, as well as more complex data types such as colors and drawables (an Android type for shapes), can all be represented in XML and used as resources.

> **WHY ALL THIS XML?**   XML isn't all bad. For Android it makes a lot of sense. XML gives the tooling a rigid structure and strong types to work with, but it can often be bloated and slow to parse. Don't worry—these resources are compiled into a binary format by the platform and not parsed as XML at runtime.

Android can also use other components that aren't XML as resources. For example, our droid picture is a binary image file. When such binary files are placed in the cor-rect place in the project's path for their type, they're automatically made accessible as resources. Next, let's take a quick look at how resources are named and resolved.

All Android resources are identified by the Android application framework as con-stants in Java through the auto-generated R class. The R class is comprised of multiple internal classes, as shown in the next listing.

Listing 1.4 The autogenerated R.java class showing internal classes and constant names

```
/* AUTO-GENERATED FILE.  DO NOT MODIFY.
 *
 * This class was automatically generated by the
 * aapt tool from the resource data it found. It
 * should not be modified by hand.
 */

package com.manning.aip.helloandroid;

public final class R {
    public static final class attr {
    }
    public static final class drawable {
        public static final int droid=0x7f020000;
        public static final int icon=0x7f020001;
    }
    public static final class layout {
        public static final int main=0x7f030000;
    }
    public static final class string {
        public static final int app_name=0x7f040001;
        public static final int hello=0x7f040000;
    }
}
```

❶ R class is auto-generated

❷ Subclass for drawable types

❸ Subclass for layout types

❹ Subclass for string types

The comment at the top of the R source file makes it clear: this class is automatically created for you, and shouldn't be modified by hand ❶.

ECLIPSE AND R   If Eclipse complains about the R class not being present, or not compiling, don't panic. This class will be regenerated if you have a gen directory, and you clean (Project -> Clean) or recompile/build your project. The Android Asset Processing Tool, or aapt, is invoked by Eclipse when you rebuild your project, and it regenerates the R source file.

Inside the R source file is a separate subclass for each type of resource your project contains. For our purposes with *Hello Android* we've used drawables (images) ❷, a layout ❸, and some strings ❹. When an Android project is compiled, it goes through some special steps, one of which is to identify and label resources (and compile them, if they're compilable). The constants in the R class allow you to refer to resources later by name, rather than by the integer that defines the location of the item (in the resource table Android uses to look up resources).

Again, we'll learn more about resources in chapter 2, and throughout the book. At this point, keep in mind that noncode entities are stored as resources, and referenced via R.java. With some background on R, we now have Java source that's tied to a layout resource, and our layout resource itself refers to several other resources. The next thing we need to cover is how all of these different elements are brought together and wired up to make an application. This is why we need an application manifest.

1.2.7 *Project wiring: the manifest*

Every Android application must have a manifest file named AndroidManifest.xml. This file, as seen in the following listing, wires up the different components of the application and defines properties such as label, version, and a lot more.

Listing 1.5   The AndroidManifest.xml file used to define configuration

```xml
<?xml version="1.0" encoding="utf-8"?>
<manifest xmlns:android="http://schemas.android.com/apk/res/android"
     package="com.manning.aip.helloandroid"
     android:versionCode="1"                            Manifest definition  ❶
     android:versionName="1.0">
  <application android:icon="@drawable/icon"         ❷ Application element
       android:label="@string/app_name">
       <activity android:name=".Main"                  ❸ Activity definitions
              android:label="@string/app_name">
          <intent-filter>
             <action
                android:name="android.intent.action.MAIN" />
             <category
                android:name="android.intent.category.LAUNCHER" />
          </intent-filter>                                 Intent-filter  ❹
       </activity>
  </application>
</manifest>
```

The manifest file that our Hello Android application is using is basic. This file hasn't been modified at all from what the ADT plugin generated. It includes an opening manifest element with version properties, package name, namespace ❶, and an application element with icon and label ❷. Both of these elements support more attributes, and we'll explore the manifest further in chapter 2.

Inside the application element we see an activity element, with name and label ❸. You guessed it, this is where the single `Activity` class in our Hello Android application is defined. Each `Activity` within a particular application must be defined here in order to be resolved and used by the platform.

The next item, the intent-filter element, represents an important concept ❹. *Intent filters* are the way Android manages activities (and other components such as services and broadcast receivers, which we'll discuss in chapter 5) and decides what each is capable of. Other activities don't need to know the exact name of an `Activity` class to use it (though they can use it that way). Instead, activities can specify what they want to accomplish—*their intent*—and the system will check for any registered activities that fit the bill. These will be resolved and used at runtime.

Intent filters can get complicated. At this point we aren't going to veer off course and get into the finer points; we'll leave the topic for chapter 2. For now, it's important to understand that an intent filter with an `action` of Main, and a `category` of Launcher makes an `Activity` show up on the default Android application selection screen (which is a platform provided application called Launcher).

With our project in place, and our understanding of the basic structure complete, the next step is to run and debug our application from Eclipse.

1.2.8 *Running and debugging Hello Android*

Running and debugging an Android application from Eclipse is straightforward. It's done the same way you would any project in Eclipse, except that you have the option in the configuration to run via an emulated phone or another device. To create a launch configuration and run or debug Hello Android do the following:

- *Run*—Right click project -> Run As -> Android Application
- *Debug*—Right click project -> Debug As -> Android Application

Once your application has been launched once, you'll have a launch configuration that you can edit (under Run -> Run Configurations in Eclipse). From this dialog you can set the Target (which device or emulator instance to use) to manual or automatic, and you can tweak other emulator options. We'll go into more depth concerning the Android emulator and Android Virtual Devices (AVDs), Eclipse and the ADT plugin, and other tools in section 1.6.

Before we get to those details though, let's step back and examine how the platform and architecture work together to make Android tick now that we have a working application. To begin with, we need to explain the way Android deals with Java.

1.3 *Java, but not Java Java*

Any Java runtime environment (JRE) consists of two things. First, the core library bundles all classes that are part of the Java platform, including language utilities, networking, concurrency, and so forth. Second, the Java virtual machine (JVM) runs Java programs by interpreting the Java bytecode contained in a set of class files produced by a Java compiler.

Android's runtime environment follows this pattern, but the similarity with Sun/Oracle's JRE ends there. Android's Java core library doesn't bundle the same packages (although there's significant overlap) and the JVM can neither load .class files nor interpret Java bytecode. At first, this sounds bad. Don't panic—you'll still be able to reuse many Java libraries with your Android application and you usually won't even notice that Java bytecode isn't a part of the picture.

If Android Java isn't regular Java, what is it? In the next few section, we'll discuss just that. We'll cover the Java core library implementation, which is based on the Apache Harmony project, and which standard packages are or aren't included. Additionally, we'll address the virtual machine, named Dalvik, that runs all Android applications written in Java.

1.3.1 *Built on Harmony*

As we've already noted, Android is an open source project. This includes its Java core library implementation. You might assume that Google either created their own open source implementation of Java or took the source code from Sun's OpenJDK project

(Sun started to turn the Java platform into open-source several years ago). Neither is the case. Instead, Android is based on Apache Harmony, an alternative implementation of the Java 5 Standard Edition released by the Apache Software Foundation.

When mentioning Harmony, it's important to understand that even though it's the basis for Android's core Java library, they aren't exactly the same. The Android core library implementation is trimmed down to include only packages that are useful on a mobile device or those that aren't replaced by an Android-specific Java technology. In all, what's included, and what isn't?

1.3.2 Packages and libraries included

Let's say it one more time: not all of Java's runtime library is implemented in Android. Understanding what is and isn't there lets you know how much of your Java programming knowledge you'll be able to reuse and determines if you'll be able to leverage existing Java libraries (because those libraries are likely to rely on the core Java runtime library). Figure 1.7 shows a breakdown of which parts of the Java standard runtime library are implemented on Android.

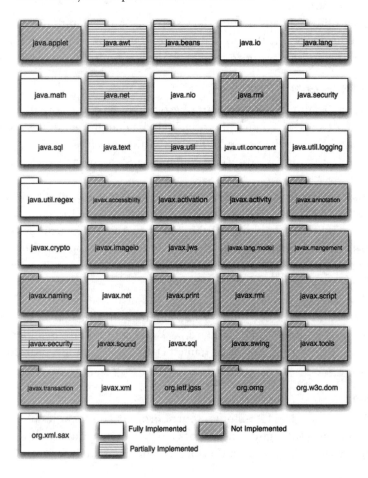

Figure 1.7 A graphical representation of the top-level packages in the standard Java runtime and their status in the Android runtime

As seen in figure 1.7, Android implements much of the Java standard runtime library. For most of the unimplemented packages, it's fairly obvious why they were omitted from the Android runtime. For example, Java's desktop user interface libraries, AWT and Swing, aren't implemented and this is sensible. Android provides its own user interface components (based on Views as we saw earlier), so there's no need for AWT or Swing. Java also supports some legacy technologies such as CORBA and RMI that would make little sense as part of Android (these often make little sense as part of standard core Java as well, but we digress).

If you look at what Android does implement, you see the majority of the Java runtime that most developers regularly use. You see most of the essential java.lang package. You also see most of the java.util package, which has all of the key data structures you might need, such as linked lists and hash tables. You see all of java.io and java.net, the packages for reading and writing data from files, the network, and so on. You also see all of the java.nio package for reading and writing data asynchronously.

In fact, some of the packages included with Android might surprise you. For example, Android includes the java.sql and javax.sql packages. That's right: Android includes classes for connecting to relational databases. (Because Android supports such things doesn't mean you'd want to connect to a remote database from a phone.) Android also provides most of the many XML support classes in Java. For example, it supports both Document Object Model (DOM) and Simple API for XML (SAX) parsing of XML documents, and includes all of the core Java classes that those parsers require. Nevertheless, not all of the XML options offered by Java are supported in Android. For example, the Java API for XML Binding (JAXB) is missing completely. Also, Java's Streaming API for XML (StAX) is notably absent, although Android does include a library with similar functionality. This library, the XML pull-parser (org.xmlpull.v1) has been popular on the Java ME platform because of its small memory footprint.

The XML pull-parser library used in Android is an example of an open source, third-party library that's included with the Android runtime and is therefore available to any Android application. Several other similar, notable libraries are included with Android. The one that you'll most likely use is the Apache HttpClient API. This is a popular open source library that has been around for a decade, and as the name suggests, can be used to greatly simplify HTTP communication. You can use Java's java.net package directly, but if you need to deal with things such as cookies, redirects, authentication, and the like, then you'll want to consider HttpClient. Another notable third-party library bundled with Android is the JavaScript Object Notation (JSON) API from json.org. The Android JSON API is a stripped down version of that popular library, with only the essential classes needed for parsing JSON strings, and serializing Java objects into JSON strings. (We'll discuss all the networking and XML/JSON options in detail in chapter 9.)

Knowing what's available, both in terms of standard and third-party libraries, will save you a lot of time when building Android applications. Beyond these basic Java libraries, Android also provides a rich set of APIs for accessing Android specific parts of the platform. This includes device hardware, media, graphics, location, local data, and more.

We'll learn more about these APIs when we focus on the SDK in section 1.6. Another key aspect of Android Java is understanding the virtual machine it provides, Dalvik.

1.3.3   *The Dalvik virtual machine*

Dalvik is Google's own Java virtual machine, and as such is in charge of executing Java applications running on Android. It was designed and developed from scratch, and has been optimized to run on embedded systems such as mobile phones. Dalvik isn't bound to the Android platform; it works on any UNIX-based operating system, including vanilla Linux, BSD, and MacOS X.

When talking about running applications on mobile phones, what we mean is running applications in an environment that's low on both resources and power. Dalvik therefore has been designed around three basic requirements:

- It must be fast, even on weak CPUs
- It must run on systems with little memory
- It must run in an energy-efficient way

When we said Dalvik is a Java virtual machine, that's not completely true (but we find that it's easier to understand when thinking of it as the part of Android that runs applications written in Java, which certainly is true). That's because as we touched on earlier, Dalvik can't interpret Java bytecode, which is what you get when compiling a Java program using `javac`. Instead, Dalvik uses a memory efficient, custom bytecode language, into which the .class files produced by the Java compiler get converted.

The Dalvik bytecode format differs from Oracle/Sun Java bytecode in several significant ways. First, the code isn't spread over multiple self-contained `.class` files, but is aggregated into a single `.dex` file (short for *Dalvik executable*). This helps reduce duplication of internal data structures and cuts down significantly on file size. (To put this into perspective, an uncompressed DEX file is about half the size of a compressed JAR file.) Second, unlike the Oracle/Sun JVM, which is a stack-based virtual machine, Dalvik is based on registers. This implies that its instruction set is slightly more complex (it needs a bigger vocabulary than a stack-based VM to represent and interpret programs), but at the same time can perform the same tasks using less code. The result is fewer instruction dispatches and smaller program size. Fewer instructions means less CPU cycles and therefore less battery consumption. Smaller program size means less memory consumed at runtime.

Even though DEX isn't Java bytecode, one key thing to understand is that `javac` and Java bytecode are still part of the equation. This is because Java source code written for an Android application is first compiled into Java class files. There are several excellent reasons for building on top of the Java compiler, instead of replacing it. The compiler does a lot of optimizations for us, and Java bytecode is a much simpler programming language to work with from a tooling perspective. The other nice thing about this design is that you can use anything that you have class files (or a jar) for. It's not necessary to have the source code for a library to use it in an Android application.

After the source code is compiled into class files, they're then dexed (compiled) by the Android dx tool. We'll touch more on tools, and dx, in section 1.6.

In addition to using the streamlined DEX format, Dalvik also performs a host of other optimizations, such as utilizing shared memory to allow objects being used by more than one application. This results in less memory consumption and fewer garbage collector cycles (again saving computing time and therefore battery). To achieve this, Android starts a special Dalvik VM instance on system boot, called Zygote, which preloads data into the shared memory that will likely be used by all applications (such as the core libraries). The Zygote VM then forks a new Dalvik instance from itself for each new application that's about to start. Each child process (which is also a separate Linux process, as we'll discuss in the next section) can then access the shared data. An overview of the VM and Zygote application-spawning process is depicted in figure 1.8.

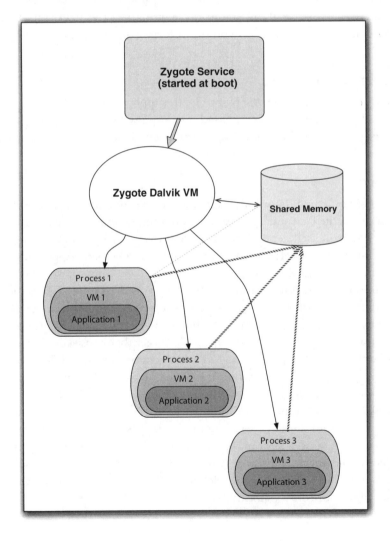

**Figure 1.8
An overview of the
Android Java Dalvik
VM and application
initialization process
through the initial
Zygote VM**

Dalvik is therefore intentionally different from a standard Java VM. Dalvik has optimizations that were designed for better performance and resource usage on an embedded device. The Zygote Dalvik VM is also intended to make copies of itself for each application process. An Android device ultimately runs many virtual machines, many separate instances of Dalvik.

> **DALVIK AND JUST IN TIME COMPILATION (JIT)**   As of Android 2.2, Dalvik also includes a *just-in-time (JIT) compiler*. Using a JIT, the Dalvik VM can automatically recognize and optimize portions of code at runtime, and compile them into native code. This further helps improve the performance of code running on the Dalvik VM (code that would otherwise always have to be interpreted and run as bytecode).

Android provides a Java runtime that's (almost) as powerful as on the desktop, and better yet, super-fast. Next, we'll talk about the next part of the stack: the operating system the virtual machine runs on. In Android terms, that means a specialized version of Linux.

1.4   *Linux, but not Linux Linux*

Underneath the Java source code, the bytecode, the application platform, and the Dalvik VM, Android is powered by a Linux-based operating system. Operating systems are complicated beasts, but you have nothing to fear. Even if you don't know much about them, as a programmer you'll be able to understand the core concepts involved.

1.4.1   *Is Android Linux?*

There is some disagreement about whether the Android operating system should be referred to as *Linux*, the free and open source operating system invented by Linus Torvalds in the 1990s. Truth is, it depends both on what you mean by Linux, and how picky you are. Traditionally, Linux refers to the Linux kernel, the OS core stripped of any additional applications. Often, when people refer to an OS as Linux, they mean a GNU/Linux distribution. A GNU/Linux distribution comprises the Linux kernel, the set of standard operating system applications from the GNU project (which aren't exclusive to Linux), plus any additional applications specific to that distribution. Ubuntu, Red Hat, and OpenSUSE are examples of GNU/Linux distributions: they consist of a Linux kernel (often modified), the GNU applications, and other vendor-specific applications.

That being said, Android is based on the Linux kernel. It has been forked from the 2.6.x mainline, yet it's *not* a GNU/Linux distribution because it lacks many of the applications that all GNU/Linux distributions share (especially the X11 windowing system). In fact, Android doesn't even contain the GNU standard C language library (glibc). Rather, it contains a custom, much slimmer implementation optimized for mobile devices called *Bionic*. This means that programs written for x86 GNU/Linux distributions won't work on Android by default—if at all. Instead, they first have to be compiled against Android's C library (Bionic).

OF ANDROIDS AND PENGUINS When Android development began, the Android operating system kernel started out as a true branch of the 2.6.x Linux kernel tree. The Linux community had high hopes for the future of Linux, with a player like Google actively working and improving on the source code and contributing changes back upstream. But due to heavy modifications to the driver architecture (partially caused by Android's custom security system), code contributions from the Android kernel branch were impossible to merge into the Linux kernel mainline. This upset the Linux community, because it locked out vendors who developed Android device drivers by keeping them from contributing code back to the Linux kernel. As a result of this, any code contributions made by Google to the Linux kernel project have been completely removed from kernel.org as of February 2010, and both projects are now being developed independently of each other.

Despite these sometimes pointed discussions, the Android OS always has been—and for the most part still is—Linux. Don't let Linux's prankish mascot Tux the penguin fool you. Linux is a serious player in the operating systems market and is deployed on millions of systems worldwide. Its flexible architecture, security, speed, and stability make it an excellent choice for many purposes.

If you don't have any experience with a Linux-based OS, again, don't worry. You'll rarely have to access the Android OS directly, because most tasks that involve the OS are either wrapped in a framework interface (when talking about application development), or can be performed by means of specialized tools provided with the platform SDK (when talking about user-level interaction such as accessing the command prompt). Still, we think it's a good idea to know about certain aspects of a typical Linux system, because a few key points are vital to understanding how Android applications work and interact (and why the Open Handset Alliance, the consortium of companies behind Android, chose Linux to base the platform on). We'll start with Linux's file and device handling, continue with its security model, and finally have a brief look at its process model and how it affects application development.

1.4.2 Storage devices and the file system

In contrast to Microsoft Windows, storage devices such as hard-drives, memory cards, and so forth aren't assigned letters on Linux. Instead, Linux uses a single directory tree, called *root* or /, where each directory (including the root directory itself) can be mapped to a storage device (or more precisely, to a partition on a storage device, but for simplicity we'll ignore this subtlety hereafter).

A NOTE ABOUT PATH SEPARATORS Unlike Windows, file and directory paths on Linux use forward slashes. For example, the file readme.txt in directory help, which is located under the root directory, would be addressed using the following absolute path:

```
/help/readme.txt
```

If you're already in the root directory, you can address files using a relative path:

```
help/readme.txt or ./help/readme.txt
```

The period (.) in a Linux path always refers to the current directory.

A directory mapped to a storage device, is called a *mount point*. We furthermore say that a device is being *mounted* to some directory. You may have already come across the term mounting when plugging your Android phone into your computer. When you do this, you'll see a notification asking whether you'd like to mount the phone's SD card. This means that the SD card storage device will be bound to a directory through which you'll be able to access its contents.

The root directory must always be a mount point; it typically points to the boot partition. Other directories may refer to other devices, such as a memory card or a DVD drive. These devices can be mounted and unmounted at runtime, making this a flexible approach to managing multiple devices and access paths. Let's look at the directory tree of an Android emulator instance, as seen in figure 1.9 (you'll learn more about the emulator and the adb tool used to launch the shell in section 1.6).

The # symbol on the second line of figure 1.9 indicates that this is a command line prompt for the *superuser,* or *root user.* This is the administrative account on a Linux system, and the default on the Android emulator. For normal users, this symbol would change to $. The ls / part is a command. ls is a GNU application which lists the contents of the directory or path given to it, in this case /, which is the root directory. Everything following that line, up to the next # symbol, is the output of the ls command.

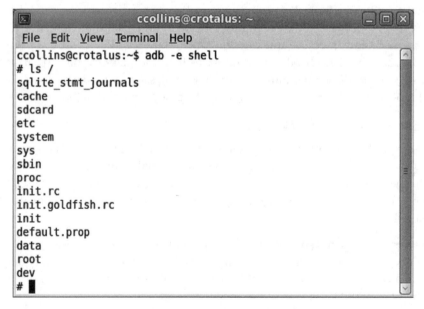

Figure 1.9   Emulator shell instance showing the top-level directory structure by using the ls command

Usually, you don't have to deal with most of the files and directories, but for some of these, it's helpful to know where they are, and what they're for. Table 1.2 lists some of the most important locations on the Android filesystem.

Table 1.2 Important locations on the Android filesystem

Location	Description
/sdcard	This is the mount point for the Secure Digital (SD) mass storage card that you can stick in many Android devices. If you want to browse its contents, or copy files from/to it, this is where you'll want to look.
/data/app	This is where Android saves all installed applications, in their bundled form (as APK files).
/data/data	This is where Android saves application specific data. If, for example, your application uses a preference file or bundles custom libraries, you can find them here.

When talking about files and directories, one question that inevitably arises is what about security and privacy? How can you prevent another user from accessing your private data? As it turns out, Linux uses a simple but effective permission system to handle that.

1.4.3 *User accounts and file permissions*

One thing Linux is popular for, especially in multiuser environments, is its user account management and—closely related—its permission and privacy model. Permissions in Linux are handled on a per-file basis. This may sound restrictive, but it isn't, because we didn't yet mention a rather curious aspect about Linux (in fact, any UNIX-based OS): everything in Linux is a file. Disks and processes are represented and controlled through files, applications and their settings are files, even directories are files. Hence, you can control access to almost anything by looking at one or more files. This is reflected in Linux's security model; permissions are stored directly in the filesystem. Every file permission mask controls three security realms: user, group, and others (corresponding to the file's owner, the file's user group, and everyone else, respectively). For each of these realms, you can set read, write, and execute permissions separately. A file could for instance be writable by its owner, but not by anyone else. Running the ls -l command on a file or directory, as seen in figure 1.10, shows the permissions, and a few other notable things.

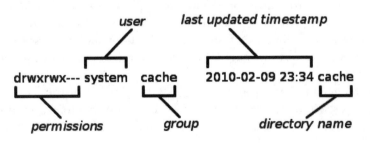

Figure 1.10 Annotated diagram of the output produced by the ls command

There are several important parts to the output seen in figure 1.10. We'll touch on each section from left to right. The leftmost letter in the permissions group indicates the type of file (in this case d for directory). The three groups of read-write-execute permissions (rwx) correspond to user, group, and others. A dash indicates the absence of a permission. Next is the user. In this case, the system user owns this resource. Following that is the group, cache. The last-updated timestamp is next, followed by the name of the resource. Here we have a directory named cache. In all, this output shows us that the user and group have full access to the directory and everyone else has no permissions at all—they can't even list the directory's contents.

This system enables fine-grained control over resources (files, directories, and other resources that are treated as files). This has an important implication for Android. When a user installs an application on their Android phone, a new user account is created for the application, and only that account can access the files. The application is thereby sandboxed. It can't access sensitive system files, files of other applications, or the user's private data—it can only access its own files and data. This isn't to say that Android applications can't interoperate or access each other's data, or that users and permissions can't be explicitly controlled. All of those things are possible, and we'll learn about them, but the default settings are one locked-down user per application.

1.4.4   *Processes and multitasking*

Android's rigorous security model continues with system processes. Every Android application starts in its own Linux system process, isolating its state from any other process running at the same time—in particular from other applications. That's because an application process on Linux (in fact, any modern OS) is only allowed to access the memory it's been assigned, not the memory reserved by the OS or another application.

We'd like to mention one more aspect briefly, and that's multitasking. Even though all modern operating systems can execute many processes in parallel, you may be used to running only one application at a time on your phone. That limitation isn't present on the Android platform; you can run as many applications in parallel as you like.

Multitasking offers the huge benefit of not having to exit an application when launching another, improving the overall user experience. This is important on platforms where interaction between applications is part of the system's overall design, which is the case for Android. Android balances the potentially significant cost of multiple applications running simultaneously in a limited environment with some design choices. Specifically Android gives preference to applications the user is currently interacting with, or has used most recently, and all applications are run in a stack. We'll learn more about the lifecycle of Android applications, and processes and tasks, in chapter 3, but the platform manages the system resources by balancing the most relevant applications.

That is all you need to know about Android's Linux lineage. If you want to learn more about Linux itself, there are plenty of good books on that topic, but now that you're equipped with the fundamentals of Linux's file management, and have been introduced to its account, security, and process model, you're good to venture into the Android native libraries that run on top of it.

1.5 *More capabilities with native libraries*

We're now going to look at the system libraries bundled with the Android platform. Welcome to the world of C/C++ and native libraries! These libraries are also exposed to the Android SDK via JNI, and therefore you don't have to deal with native code (unless you want to), but it's important to understand the relationships.

Well cover these libraries briefly, to describe the Android middle tier. Our intention is to give you an idea of what's possible with Android by looking at some of the technologies that ship with it. We'll begin with the stuff that gets your attention first: audio and video from OpenCORE. Then we'll check out the database storage option, SQLite. From there we'll look at the browser rendering engine, WebKit. And finally we'll wrap it up with a discussion of hardware sensors and the camera.

1.5.1 *Audio and video processing*

Android has rich support for multimedia, sporting advanced 2D/3D graphics rendering using SGL and OpenGL ES (which we'll cover in chapter 11), as well as audio and video playback and recording in various formats. For the latter, Android builds on PacketVideo's OpenCORE system, a sophisticated media framework optimized for mobile devices that supports a host of common file formats and codecs, including MP3, MIDI, Ogg Vorbis, PCM, and AAC for audio; and H.263, H.264, and MPEG-4 for video playback. The 3GPP container format is supported too.

With these audio and video libraries, Android applications have access to a some serious multimedia capabilities. Beyond recoding video and playing 3D games, another important library Android provides is its SQLite data storage engine.

1.5.2 *Storage engine*

If you need to persist data from your application to the device, then Android has you covered. Android ships with SQLite, a fully transactional database engine based on the SQL-92 standard. SQLite is a relational storage engine. It stores data in tables (called *relations* in database theory), much like MySQL, Oracle, or DB2. But its architecture dramatically differs from conventional database management systems (DBMS) like the ones mentioned.

First, SQLite doesn't require a client-server architecture. With a client-server DBMS, a server process listens for incoming requests from one or more client processes, transferring data back and forth using interprocess communication (IPC—typically via sockets). This is required for a client to query a remote database, for example over the Internet. SQLite can be embedded directly with the application that uses it, communicating with it via simple function calls instead of complex IPC mechanisms.

Second, SQLite is simpler in almost every aspect. It uses a much simpler approach to data storage, storing a database's schema, indices, and tables in a single, cross-platform portable file. This makes database backups ridiculously simple; you copy a single file from A to B. It's also self-contained and extremely small. SQLite is deployed as a single library file of about 200-300 kilobytes (depending on the configuration at compile time), with only minimal dependencies to the C language library. It also requires literally zero configuration. SQLite doesn't require configuration files or installation procedures; you drop it somewhere and use it. This makes it a perfect candidate for embedded systems such as mobile phones.

Despite these simplifications, SQLite is powerful. Its storage engine supports ACID (atomic, consistent, isolated, durable) compliant transactions, and supports B-tree indexing for fast data access. It also has its limitations though. Writing to a database table will lock the entire database, resulting in reduced throughput where high concurrency is desired. That's typically not the case in a mobile application, making this less of a drawback than it may sound. Much worse is SQLite's limited support for ALTER TABLE statements, making schema migrations painful to handle. This can be a serious problem when deploying updates to your application. Persisting data using SQLite will be covered in chapter 6.

Along with having data covered, Android also includes another library that's of paramount importance in the modern web-enabled world, a full-blown browser rendering engine based on WebKit.

1.5.3   *Web integration*

Android comes equipped with WebKit, a complete HTML rendering engine also used in Apple's Safari and Google's Chrome. WebKit supports CSS Level 3 stylesheets (scoring an impressive 100 out of 100 points in the important Acid3 web standards test) and also sports a performant JavaScript engine (Google's V8, which outperforms most other JavaScript VMs in many head-to-head comparisons). The Browser application that comes preinstalled with every Android handset is as powerful as any desktop browser out there. This is a key point. The browser engine Android provides isn't stripped down. It's not exactly the same as your desktop browser, but it's close.

Also, it's important to understand that use of WebKit isn't constrained to the Browser application. In fact, you can embed HTML backed by WebKit directly into your applications by using a UI widget component called a WebView (which we'll see in several examples in the book). This will allow you to seamlessly integrate your applications with content from the World Wide Web.

The next area of native library integration we need to visit is the impressive array of hardware drivers and support for sensors and cameras, and more.

1.5.4   *Sensors, camera, and more*

In addition to multimedia, database support, and web browsing capabilities, Android also comes with support for a wide array of sensors to scan the phone's environment, plus support for built-in digital cameras. The latest version of Android has support for the following sensor types:

- GPS location for accurate device position detection (network-based positioning using cell triangulation is also possible; see chapter 9)
- Device orientation and movement detection through gyroscopes and accelerometers
- Magnetic field detection
- Ambient light and proximity detection
- Temperature sensors
- Pressure sensors

Note that not all sensor types are supported by all devices. Google's first Android phone, the G1 (a.k.a. HTC Dream), only has GPS, accelerometer, magnetic field, and orientation sensors. Newer Android phones such as the Motorola Droid (called Milestone in Europe) also have light and proximity sensors. All Android phones at the time of this writing are equipped with a camera. We'll leave it to your imagination how you can leverage these technologies to build truly innovative applications, but table 1.3 outlines a list of applications that already do.

Table 1.3 List of notable applications that make innovative use of sensors on the Android platform

Application name	Description
Hoccer	Uses location and throw/catch gestures to exchange items like contacts, images, or files between two phones—data exchange has never been funnier!
Locale	Manages your phone settings such as ringer volume based on location and time—automatically silence your phone when at home!
Coin Flip	Uses flick gestures and gyroscopic positioning data to toss a virtual coin—let the bets come!
Bubble	Uses orientation sensors to realize a virtual bubble level—never have skewed pictures on your wall again!
The Android phone app	Uses the proximity sensor to determine whether you're holding the phone to your ear—this will automatically turn off the display during calls to preserve battery!
Compass	Uses magnetic field data to render a virtual compass—never get lost again!
Barcode Scanner	Uses the camera to read 1D and 2D barcodes—never type lengthy product codes again!

There are more examples, but table 1.3 should give you an idea of what's possible with sensors on Android. In total, it's an impressive combination of hardware and software that makes for some unique and exciting user experiences.

Now that we've covered the basic background of Android itself—from what it is and why it was created to application fundamentals, key platform components, and native libraries—it's time to take a closer look at the day-to-day developer tools from the SDK and Eclipse ADT plugin.

1.6   *Tools of the trade*

We know you're eager to get into more Android application details, but software development is like a craft; a good carpenter must know their nails and timbers (the materials) as much as their drill and hammer (the tools). Now that we have a taste of basic development, and have learned a bit about the materials involved, we'll take a closer look at the tools.

Android provides many different tools for creating, maintaining, debugging, profiling, and more. Among them, the SDK provides libraries for accessing everything on a device from sending SMS to determining latitude and longitude, and a rich application framework that's designed to make application development straightforward and keep boilerplate code to a minimum. Along with APIs, the SDK also includes a wide array of extremely useful command line programs. And, there's a helpful GUI wrapper for both in the form of the Eclipse IDE and the ADT Eclipse plugin.

1.6.1   *Android-specific APIs*

The Android SDK provides about all of the core Java functionality you're likely to need through the Apache Harmony–based core JVM libraries we discussed in section 1.3. The main `java` and `javax` packages, and general use third-party libraries for networking and XML parsing and the like are all available. But what about libraries for accessing Android-specific constructs? What about interacting with device hardware, working with audio and video, using local networking, and more? The answers to these questions take us to the next level of the Android SDK, the `android` package namespace.

Within the Java realm, beyond the core libraries are the Android specific constructs in the `android` package. Want to play an MP3? Look at the `android.media` package. Need to get the user's geolocation? Check out the `android.location` package. Maybe you need to connect to another Android device using Bluetooth? Take a look at the `android.bluetooth` package. Most phones have a camera, and you can access that using the `Camera` class in the `android.hardware` package (where you can also find other hardware-related APIs). Speaking of phone features, what about making phone calls or sending text messages? The `android.telephony` package exposes those traditional mobile phone features.

Along with media and hardware support, another compelling feature of Android is its stunning graphics. This is obviously important for game developers, but what application doesn't benefit from some gratuitous eye candy? The `android.graphics` package contains a lot of easy-to-use APIs for working with graphical primitives such as images, colors, and polygons. For more intense 3D graphics, the `android.opengl` package is where you'll find Android's implementation of the OpenGL ES library for 3D graphics.

> **WHAT ABOUT GOING NATIVE?**   Like the vast majority of Android application code, the SDK's core libraries and application framework are written in pure Java. But the SDK also has a C/C++ counterpart, the NDK. The NDK is an add-on to the SDK and works in conjunction to it. With the NDK, you can write code directly in C or C++ and bypass Java and the Dalvik virtual machine

altogether. As you might guess, this is usually done for performance reasons. The NDK includes all of the headers you'll need to link to your native code, as well as tools for building your native libraries and embedding those libraries in an Android application.

The Java side of the Android SDK comes into full view when you combine the android APIs with the core Java libraries with key third-party components also present. The sum of these parts is a powerful foundation to build applications on top of. Beyond APIs, the Android SDK also provides some important command-line tools.

1.6.2 SDK tools and components

Speaking of tools, the SDK comes packed with them. Among them, it includes tools for compiling your application source code into the dex class files understood by the Dalvik VM, packaging your code into an APK file for use on an Android device, running an Android emulator, logging, live debugging, performance profiling, and more.

In fact, we used some of these tools when we worked with the Eclipse ADT plugin in section 1.2 and created the Hello Android application. Here we'll go into a bit more detail. The plugin wraps many of the tools and incorporates them automatically. This is a nice feature: you can manually use the tools we're about to introduce, and they're often extremely useful, but you don't have to. We encourage you to get to know the tools and understand what they do, because doing so will give you a better understanding of Android overall. That knowledge will make it easier for you to identify and troubleshoot any issues, if you prefer you can stick to the Eclipse plugin.

Before we delve in, we have to explain that Android tools come in two different varieties: core tools and platform-specific tools. One complexity of developing for Android is that you must deal with multiple supported versions of Android APIs or platforms. The SDK accounts for this, and you can install multiple platform components within the SDK. This is definitely better than having to install multiple SDKs!

Once you install the SDK and a platform or two, you'll find the tools in a couple of locations. The core SDK tools can be found in the `<sdk>/tools` directory (which can be added to your PATH to make the tools convenient to use from anywhere). Platform-specific tools can be found in the `<sdk>/platform-tools` directory. Table 1.4 lists some of the key tools and describes what they do.

Table 1.4 Some of the key Android command-line tools

Tool	Location	Description
aapt	`<sdk>/platform-tools`	Android Asset Packaging Tool—Used to compile resources into binary assets, and to package archives (APK files).
aidl	`<sdk>/platform-tools`	Android Interface Definition Language—Compiles .aidl files that are used to define interfaces for Android Inter-Process Communication (IPC).

Table 1.4 Some of the key Android command-line tools *(continued)*

Tool	Location	Description
dx	\<sdk\>/platform-tools	Used to read .class bytecode and transform it into Android bytecode (which is stored in .dex files).
adb	\<sdk\>/platform-tools	Android Debug Bridge—A client/server application used to interact with and manage devices and emulators. Provides many subcommands.
android	\<sdk\>/tools	Used to create and delete Android Virtual Devices (emulator instances). Also used to create and update projects from the command line. Also used to manage SDK platform components.
ddms	\<sdk\>/tools	Dalvik Debug Monitor Service—Used for debugging and inspecting running Android applications. Provides an interface to logging, memory statistics, thread statistics, state information, and more. Also used to send mock call, SMS, and location data to a device or emulator instance.
draw9patch	\<sdk\>/tools	Used to draw Nine Patch images.
emulator	\<sdk\>/tools	QEMU-based mobile device emulator.
hierarchyviewer	\<sdk\>/tools	Used to view and optimize UI layout hierarchies.
layoutopt	\<sdk\>/tools	Used to quickly analyze and recommend layout optimizations.
mksdcard	\<sdk\>/tools	Used to create images to be used as external storage (SD card) by emulator instances.
sqlite3	\<sdk\>/tools	Used to explore and interact with SQLite databases.
traceview	\<sdk\>/tools	Used to analyze trace files, which are profiling snapshots of Android applications.

In addition to the overview we've provided here in table 1.4, which isn't comprehensive, you can quickly see a description of each available tool and its usage instructions by invoking it from the command line with no arguments (or in some cases using --help as the sole argument). You can also find detailed documentation for each of these tools in the online SDK documentation. We'll go over some of the more essential tools here to give you an idea of what tools fits what job (and we'll revisit other relevant tools in other areas of the book). We'll start with compiling code using the dx compiler tool.

Android uses the Java programming language (most of the time), as we've discussed, but the binary files that are deployed to a device aren't Java class files that run

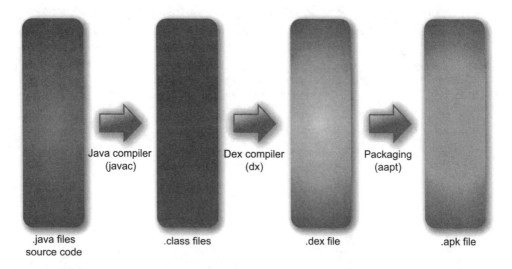

Figure 1.11   The Android compiling and packaging process from source files, through compilation steps, and finally into an APK file

on the Java VM. Instead, as we noted in section 1.3, they're .dex files that run on the Dalvik VM. Java developers are used to using the Java compiler, javac, to compile Java source code files into Java class files. Even though the Dalvik VM doesn't use Java class files, we still need the Java compiler, as you can see from figure 1.11.

The dx tool is a platform-specific tool, as you'd expect. It takes all of the class files in your application and produces a single .dex file. This file is the input to the last step in the larger process of packaging an application. Packaging is handled by the aapt tool we noted in section 1.2.6 when exploring the R file.

The aapt tool handles all of the building and compiling of an application, but what about running and debugging? First, before you can run an application, as we noted in section 1.2, you need to create an Android virtual device (AVD) to run it on. This is an emulator image that runs a specific version of the Android OS and has specific hardware (mainly its visual display). To create an image, you can use another tool, the Android SDK and AVD Manager.

The android tool is used to manage AVDs and to update/install platforms and update the SDK itself (remember, the SDK is modular). You can create a new AVD with the following command:

```
android create avd -t <PLATFORM> -n <NAME>
```

For example, android create avd -t android-7 -n avd21 would create an AVD called avd21 that targets the android-7 platform. The string android-7 identifies an Android platform (also called *API level*). To get a list of available platforms, you can use the command android list target. Typing android -help will display all of the many options with the android tool. If you don't want to remember all of this, you can

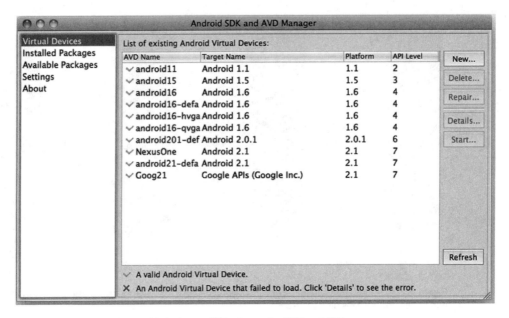

Figure 1.12   The android tool interface, which shows the SDK and AVD manager

invoke the `android` tool with no arguments and it'll launch a graphical interface that lets you execute any of the commands. Figure 1.12 shows the `android` GUI.

As you can see from figure 1.12, the `android` tool GUI is also used to start an AVD— to launch an Android emulator. From the GUI, you can do this by selecting an AVD and clicking on the Start button in the right column. You can also start an emulator from the command line using another tool, the `emulator` tool:

```
emulator -avd <AVD NAME>
```

For example, `emulator -avd avd21` would launch the AVD called `avd21`. There are many more options to the android tool, and to the emulators you can create with it. For complete details see the help output or the documentation. Figure 1.13 shows the emulator running an Android 2.1 image.

Now that you've seen the tools for creating and running an AVD, to query for available devices and get your application installed on an emulator you'll use a tool that you'll get to know well, the Android debug bridge, `adb`. The `adb` tool is your main access point into a running AVD. It has numerous capabilities, and you're encouraged to explore them. As with other tools, you can get a list of the options by typing `adb -help`. To check for devices that are connected or running (which you've created and started) you can use the `adb devices` command. To install an application (after you've confirmed an emulator device is running), you can use this command:

```
adb install <app>
```

For example, `adb install MyApp.apk` will install MyApp.apk to a running emulator (this will only work if one emulator is running; if more than one are running, specify

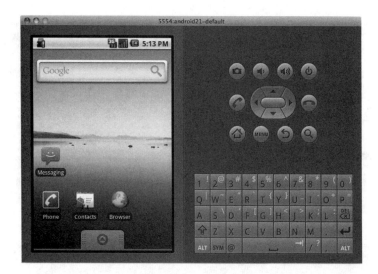

Figure 1.13 The Android emulator running an AVD image configured to work with version 2.1 of the Android platform

which emulator to run on). You can use the same adb command to install the application on a physical device as well. A handy way to direct adb commands back and forth between a single emulator and a single physical device is to use the -e and -d switches, respectively (adb -e install or adb -d install).

You can also use the adb tool to connect to the device using the adb shell command and explore the virtual system. Remember, as we saw in section 1.4, the Android kernel is based on Linux and the shell will give you a command prompt. The shell itself has many other useful subcommands; again we encourage you to explore it. We'll see the shell again in several other areas of the book where it's relevant. Once you have an emulator running and your application is installed on it, another use for the adb tool is to trace log files or dump debug information.

For a more detailed inspection of a device, you'll need another indispensable SDK tool, the Dalvik Debug Monitor or ddms. This graphical application shows various types of diagnostic information from an emulator or device. Figure 1.14 shows the ddms tool in action.

Figure 1.14 gives you an idea of the capabilities of the ddms tool. It can attach to the Dalvik VM of your application and show you detailed logging information, as well as data about memory allocations and garbage collection. This is valuable because mobile applications are often memory challenged, so understanding memory usage is key. The ddms tool can also be used to tweak the behavior of an emulator. For example, with it you can change the speed of the emulator's network connection. Your development computer is probably enjoying a LAN or broadband connection, and that's much faster than the typical data connection on a mobile phone. You can also simulate incoming phone calls, text messages, and even give the device mock GPS coordinates. Depending on what your application does, these can make testing with an emulator more realistic and therefore, more valuable.

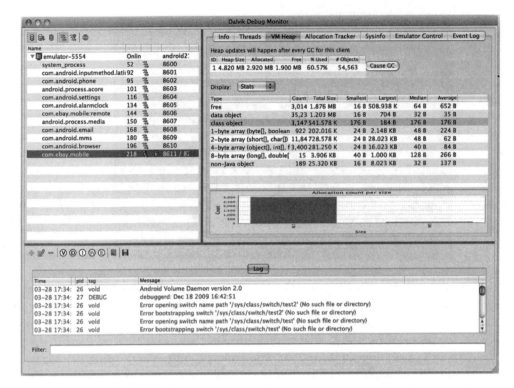

Figure 1.14   Using the Dalvik Debug Monitor (DDMS), which has many capabilities, to inspect the heap of a running application

We'll see more of these tools as we progress through the book. We'll also touch on others we haven't singled out here. For instance, we'll talk specifically about draw9patch, layoutopt, and hierarchyviewer in chapter 4, and we'll use the adb tool in several later examples. The key is to understand where these tools are and what they offer. Though the command-line tools aren't mandatory, they can help with diagnosis and troubleshooting, and they do offer some advanced options that the IDE plugins may not expose.

1.7   Summary

Welcome to Android. We hope that our rapid-fire introduction here has whet your appetite and that you're more eager than ever to learn and create. After all, developers building quality applications is what the Android ecosystem is trying to empower, and what drives the entire platform forward.

At this point in our journey, you should have a solid understanding of what Android is and some of the motivation behind its creation. Android has a recurring theme, as we've seen—it's open. The platform is open and can be used by anyone. Its code is open and can be tailored to meet different needs. Even its tools are open and give developers the freedom of choice when it comes to how they'll develop their applications. The importance of this aspect can't be understated; it's what sets Android apart.

Along with understanding the bigger Android picture, you should also now have an idea of what the Android architecture is. You've seen that Android is based on Java and Linux, but it's not the typical out-of-the-box variety of either. You've also seen that Android provides a capability-packed set of middleware that sits between the specialized Dalvik VM (and core Java libraries and application framework) and the operating system layer. All of this architecture is in place to optimize the operating environment of a mobile device for running applications.

For applications themselves, you've also now seen what it takes to create a basic application, from source code, layouts, resources, manifests, and more. Along with those application constituents, you've seen the Android SDK tools and components, as well as the Eclipse IDE and ADT plugin. Again, all of this is the foundation of Android application development. Now it's time to reinforce and build upon that foundation and go further into the details surrounding the fundamentals of Android application development.

Android
application fundamentals

In this chapter

- Core building blocks
- The application manifest
- Working with resources, layouts, views, and widgets
- Adapters, intents, and intent filters

I'd take the awe of understanding over the awe of ignorance any day.

—Douglas Adams

To build solid Android applications you need to start with the basics. It's the same with learning any technology, skill, or sport. This is the point where a basketball coach would give the speech about learning to dribble and pass, before trying to perfect the alley-oop. Advanced techniques will come, but they're built on a basis of mastering the fundamentals.

To that end, in this chapter we'll focus on the core building blocks of Android application development. This means we'll revisit and expand upon the fundamental concepts we introduced in chapter 1, and we'll fill in more detail too. Specifically, we'll take a closer look at the entire scope of an Android application. We'll start with the manifest and resources, and then we'll explore layout and views, then activities and intents, and the use of Adapters to bind data to widgets. Finally, we'll also touch on passing internal data between activities using the Application object. All of these concepts relate to common ways to accomplish basic tasks with the Android platform, and they're all part of the foundation we need to build before diving deeper in later parts of the book.

With the wide array of topics to address in mind, we're going to build another sample application that pulls in all of these parts. Though the application we'll be building isn't trivial, it's not overly complicated either. This is because we want to cover a wide variety of the essential programming techniques found in many Android applications, and we want to keep things relatively straightforward at the same time. This application isn't going to be intricate or pretty, but it'll get the job done. If you want your application to look good, you'll have to wait until chapter 4, and if you want to add more features, we'll come to those in later chapters too. Until then you'll have to live with a homely application that only a developer could love. Without further ado, let's meet the DealDroid.

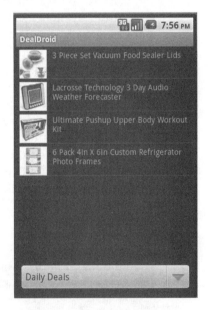

2.1 *The DealDroid application*

DealDroid is a nice application that displays the "Daily Deals" from eBay. More importantly, it also illustrates a lot of the basic components and common techniques used in many Android applications. So what's DealDroid? Well, let's start with eBay's Daily Deals.

Daily Deals is a popular application on the eBay web site that shows limited-time sales for savvy e-commerce shoppers. You can view it at http://deals.ebay.com, but who wants to view this in a boring web page when you could instead check it out in a convenient Android application? Do you see where this is going? Figure 2.1 shows the opening screen of the DealDroid application, which displays the eBay Daily Deals.

Figure 2.1   The main screen of the DealDroid application shows the featured deals of the day in an Android ListView.

 GRAB THE PROJECT: DEALDROID You can get the source code for this project and the packaged APK to run it at the *Android in Practice* code web site. Because some code listings here are shortened to focus on specific concepts, we recommend that you download the complete source code and follow along within Eclipse (or your favorite IDE or text editor).

Source: http://mng.bz/r560, APK file: http://mng.bz/ARip

The opening screen of DealDroid, aptly named `DealList`, displays a list of the featured Daily Deals for the current day. This is dynamic data from eBay that changes, well, daily. It can change more frequently than daily, as deals often sell-out and are replaced by new deals. Not only will this application show the current Daily Deals, it can also show other deals in various categories of more specific interest, like gadgets and fashion. When you find a deal that you like, you can view more detail by clicking on it and drilling down into the `DealDetails` screen, as seen in Figure 2.2.

That about does it for the core UI of the Deal-Droid. As we said, it's simple and somewhat ugly. Beyond the UI though, what if you want to do more than look at a deal? DealDroid lets you email the deal to a friend, by leveraging the bundled Android mail application. Also, if you want to share the deal by another means, such as via FaceBook or Twitter (or any other application wired in by the framework to allow sharing), Deal-Droid lets you to do that too. If instead you love the deal so much that you want to buy it, then DealDroid uses Android's excellent browser and sends you to eBay's mobile website. Figure 2.3 shows the sharing menu, and what each menu option launches.

Figure 2.2   The DealDetails screen of the DealDroid application shows specific deal information. Selecting a deal on the `Deal-List` screen will take you to this screen.

Additional DealDroid features

DealDroid is capable of running a background `Service` to keep an eye out for new deals as they show up (maybe a deal ran out and a new one replaced it, or you had the application running when the day's new deals were revealed) and issuing a `Notification`. We aren't including those features in the discussion in this chapter, because `Services` have their own focus in chapter 5, and we want to stay on track here. For this reason, the source code download for the book includes two versions of DealDroid: basic as we'll build here, and *DealDroidWith-Service,* which includes several broadcast receivers and a background `Service`.

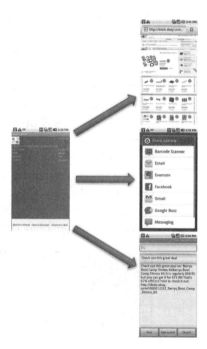

Figure 2.3   DealDroid likes to share with other apps. Tapping the phone menu button displays the sharing options from the detail screen.

Now that we've seen what this application can do, let's tear it apart and see how it works. This is your red pill/blue pill moment: if you don't want to see the android behind the curtain revealed, then stop reading now! Otherwise, keep going and get ready for the gruesome details of Android applications.

2.2 Core building blocks

One of the most valuable aspects of a platform like Android is its application framework. Not only does it provide access to the GPS sensor on a device, or let you make HTTP requests, it gives you a structure to fit your application into. It makes a deal with you. If you put certain kinds of files in certain kinds of places, it'll use those files in a well-understood, predefined manner. You're given a blueprint to follow. A lot of boilerplate tasks are stripped away, and you can focus on your application. This can be liberating for developers. You have less to worry about because of what the platform takes care of for you. This is a key, but often-ignored reason for the success of native mobile application platforms such as Android, over mobile web applications. A mobile web application developer may have more freedom in many ways, but they may also have more tedious things to deal with and worry about. In several ways it's easier to develop on a native platform such as Android.

Figure 2.4 shows the main components that Android provides for building applications.

We've already seen a quick tour of a basic Android application in chapter 1, but now it's time to define the components, and then in the upcoming sections we'll look at each in more detail. First, Android applications are mainly built with several core entities:

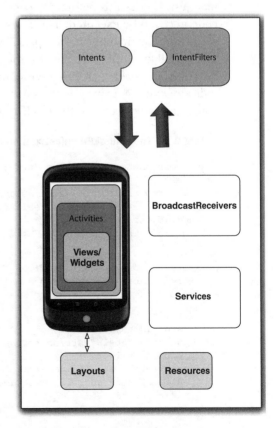

- `Activity`—The foreground; they dictate the UI, and handle events and interaction
- `Service`—The background; they can perform long-running tasks or poll
- `BroadcastReceiver`—Handlers that can wake up and respond to broadcast events (intents)
- `ContentProvider`—Allows you to expose a data API to other applications

These entities are what you'll use to build user interface screens, create background processes, and react to

Figure 2.4 The essential application components provided by the Android platform

certain types of events. Additional components are used in the construction of these entities, their logic, and wiring between them:

- Views—UI elements that are drawn onscreen
- Layouts—View hierarchies that control screen format/appearance
- Intents—Messages wiring components together
- Resources—External elements, such as strings and drawables (pictures)
- Manifest—Configuration for applications

We'll learn about all of these concepts in the upcoming sections as we review the sample DealDroid application step by step. We'll begin with the bottom layer, the manifest file that defines the relationships, capabilities, permissions, and configuration of every Android application.

2.3　*Application manifest*

As we saw in chapter 1, the application manifest is the starting point for any Android application. This isn't some platitude—it's literally true. When a user launches an Android application, the first thing that the Android OS does is read the application's manifest. It does this before any code can execute, because the manifest tells it what code needs to be executed. This follows the traditional executable application model of Java, where an application is packaged as a jar file, with a manifest file that tells the Java virtual machine what class (in the jar file) is the entry point to the application. In the Android world, activities are the units of work; an application's manifest file must indicate which Activity is the entry point of the application. Let's look at a more concrete example of this: the DealDroid manifest file in the following listing.

Listing 2.1　The AndroidMainfest.xml manifest file of the DealDroid application

```xml
<?xml version="1.0" encoding="utf-8"?>
<manifest
    xmlns:android="http://schemas.android.com/apk/res/android"
    package="com.manning.aip.dealdroid"
    android:versionCode="1"
    android:versionName="1.0">

<application
    android:icon="@drawable/ddicon"              ❶ Application
    android:label="@string/app_name"                with icon,
    android:name=".DealDroidApp">                   label, name

    <activity                                              ❷ DealList
        android:name=".DealList"                              Activity with
        android:label="@string/app_name">                    intent filter
        <intent-filter>
            <action android:name="android.intent.action.MAIN" />
            <category android:name="android.intent.category.LAUNCHER" />
        </intent-filter>
    </activity>

    <activity
```

```
          android:name=".DealDetails"                              ❸  DealDetails
          android:label="@string/deal_details" />                     Activity
    </application>

<uses-permission android:name="android.permission.INTERNET" />
<uses-permission android:name="android.permission.ACCESS_NETWORK_STATE" />
<uses-sdk android:minSdkVersion="4" />
                                                            Permissions defined  ❹
</manifest>
```

If you've programmed in Java for long, then a manifest file is probably a familiar concept to you. This file, always named AndroidManifest.xml for Android applications, provides internal configuration and metadata about your application to the Android runtime. In the manifest element, the package name and version identifiers for your application are listed. The application element then tells the runtime what the name, icon, and label are for your application ❶. Finally, the child elements of application define all of the things your application can do.

This includes the entry point Activity class with the name .DealList, and an IntentFilter that declares action MAIN and category LAUNCHER ❷. The activity class name is relative to the application's package. The IntentFilter tells the runtime that it should register this application and make it selectable from the phone's home screen (also known as the Launcher application). More generally, an IntentFilter is an expression of capability. Other components then use an Intent to declare an action to be completed. These concepts are important in Android because they allow different components to be combined and used in conjunction with each other at runtime (late binding). We'll learn more about this in section 2.9.

Along with the entry point, all other activities must be declared in the manifest ❸. The same is also true of other components such as BroadcastReceiver, Service, and ContentProvider (though we don't have any here). A BroadcastReceiver is a special filter that listens for intents that are broadcast through the system, and a Service is a background process. We'll focus on these concepts in chapter 5. A ContentProvider allows you to expose a data API to other applications; we'll learn about this in chapter 8. Back to the manifest: after the main components are declared, we then also have permissions ❹, which rounds out our DealDroid configuration.

2.3.1 Permissions

DealDroid declares that it should be allowed to use the Internet (it parses an RSS feed from eBay to get deal information), and that it should be allowed to check the status of the network state. Android's permissions system labels each protected action declared this way, and then displays them to the user when they elect to install an application. This detail is important. There are no checks at runtime. The user sees what an application wants to do when they install it, and if they allow it, the permissions are *permanently granted.* If an application tries to perform an action for which it doesn't have permission, a SecurityException is thrown.

Along with Internet and system events, you can also declare things such as whether your application will read or write to the filesystem, whether it'll read or write user contact data, whether it can wake up the phone when it's sleeping, and much more. The constants class `Manifest.permission` in the SDK is where you can easily see all the built in permissions available.

A less common use case is the need to declare and enforce your own permissions, going beyond the system declarations. If you need to, you can declare custom permissions in the manifest, and enforce them within components (activities, services, broadcast receivers and so on).

Moving past the manifest, the next step concept we need to address for DealDroid are the noncode elements it includes, namely resources.

2.4   Resources

Resource is a broad term. It can mean images used in your application, internationalized text, or any type of static value that you want to externalize from your application code, as we discussed in chapter 1. Resources are defined by placing files in the `/res` directory of your project. Resources can then be accessed either in code or through references in XML.

2.4.1   Defining resources

Everything declared in the `/res` directory will not only be packaged up as part of your application, but will also be programmatically accessible in your application code. Resources have a few key properties it's important to remember:

- Every resource has an ID
- Every resource has a specific type
- Resources have a specific location and file they are defined in

You'll typically define resources of a few different types, such as strings or layouts, using XML. This is by far the most common usage of resources. Resources don't end there though. You can define shapes, colors, drawables, styles, themes, menus, static data arrays, and a lot more as XML resources. Resources that you don't define in XML can either be placed in specified locations, such as `res/drawable` for images, or placed in the `/res/raw` directory and accessed as direct streams (such as for audio and video files). Once you define a resource by placing an item in the `/res` folder, the platform automatically parses it (unless it's raw) and uses the `aapt` tool to link the ID through the R class we saw in chapter 1. The R class maps each resource ID to its location or compiled content.

> **WHY RESOURCES?**   Android goes to a lot of trouble to define resource types and make support of resources available through the API. You might wonder why this is necessary. There are several reasons. First, they separate code from external entities such as images and strings. Such separation is a good thing because it keeps the code focused and uncluttered. Second, resources are efficient and fast. XML resources are compiled into a binary format. This makes them friendly at development time, without being slow at runtime.

Third, resources enable the support of dynamic loading at runtime based on various environment properties such as language, screen configuration, and hardware capability. This enables internationalization and localization, which we'll learn more about later, and other environment specific changes.

The resources that we'll deal with for DealDroid are simple: they're strings, plurals, and layouts. *Plurals* are a special type of resource that allow the system to automatically deal with plurality for strings; we'll come to those in a moment. First, let's look at the strings DealDroid uses in the following listing.

Listing 2.2 The res/values/strings.xml resources file showing values for named strings

```
<?xml version="1.0" encoding="utf-8"?>          ◁——❶ Top-level resources element
<resources>
    <string name="app_name">DealDroid</string>     ◁——❷ Define each string as element
    string name="deal_list_missing_data">
       No data to display, please try again later.</string>
    <string name="deal_list_retrieving_data">Getting deal data ...</string>
    <string name="deal_list_network_unavailable">
       No network connection, cannot retrieve data.</string>
    <string name="deal_list_reparse_menu">Re-parse Feed</string>

    <string name="deal_details">Deal Details</string>
    <string name="deal_details_price_prefix">$</string>
    <string name="deal_details_mail_menu">Mail</string>
    <string name="deal_details_browser_menu">Browser</string>
    <string name="deal_details_share_menu">Share</string>
    <string name="deal_details_msrp_label">MSRP:</string>
    <string name="deal_details_quantity_label">Quantity:</string>
    <string name="deal_details_quantity_sold_label">Quantity Sold:</string>
    <string name="deal_details_location_label">Location:</string>
</resources>
```

As promised, the strings we use in the DealDroid application are externalized and defined in an XML file. This XML file is strings.xml and it's placed in /res/values. The file starts off with the typical XML stanza and then has a root element named resources ❶. Each string is then defined in its own element with an attribute for the name ❷. The name will be the ID for the resource, as well as the constant identifier in the generated R class.

All of the strings we defined in strings.xml will be present as constants in the R class with hexadecimal values. The values are pointers to where the initial values have been compiled and stored in the internal resource table. You shouldn't ever need to dig into the resource table unless you're doing serious Android hacking, but it helps to understand that this is how compiled resources work.

NONRESOURCE RESOURCES—ASSETS If you need to access normal files that aren't preprocessed as resources and assigned an ID, you can use the /assets directory. Any file placed in /assets is available to your application. An example of an asset might be HTML source file for use with a WebView.

The other notable resources DealDroid uses are the XML screen layouts and the mysterious plurals file we mentioned previously. Plurals are an obscure but useful Android resource type that allow you to easily, and in an internationalized manner, deal with plural values. This next listing shows how plurals are defined in XML.

Listing 2.3   The res/values/plurals.xml resource file using the XLIFF format

```
<resources xmlns:xliff="urn:oasis:names:tc:xliff:document:1.2">          Special
    <plurals name="deal_service_new_deal">                               OASIS
        <item quantity="one">1 new deal!</item>        ❷ Quantity       XLIFF
        <item quantity="other">                           definitions    XML
            <xliff:g id="count">%d</xliff:g>           Use String        ❶ format
            new deals!                                 ❸ formatting
        </item>
    </plurals>
</resources>
```

Plurals are different from most other XML resources in that they use a special format, OASIS XLIFF ❶. You don't have to know a lot about this to use it. You define at least two text labels—one for items with a quantity of one, and another for items that are plural in quantity (a quantity of other) ❷—and the framework will return a proper value. Android string resources support String.format style arguments too, as we've done with %d ❸ (this marker will be replaced with the digit we supply when we get the resource later).

Why are plurals important? Why not say "10 new deal(s)" and be done with it? Well, you could do that, but it's arguably ugly, and it's not internationalized. Things can get tricky in a hurry with multiple languages and plural values. For example, there is no plural in Japanese and several plurals in Slovakian (for 1, 2, 3, 4, 5, or more). The plurals format alleviates that. The next thing we need to discuss is how to access resources.

2.4.2   *Accessing resources*

Once you've defined resources you'll then refer to them either in code or in XML by using their IDs. We'll learn more about this as we step through our DealDroid Activity classes later in this chapter, and when we start using styles and themes in chapter 4, but for now let's touch on the basics.

To access a resource in code, you use the R-defined constant's ID, such as R.string.deal_details. From this ID notation, you can tell that it's a local resource and not a system resource, and that it's a string. System resources are distinguished from local resources by the android namespace prefix, such as android.R. string.yes. You can use the ID with various methods, most notably with the Resources class as follows:

- For standard strings use Resources.getString(R.string.deal_details)
- For plurals use Resources.getQuantityString(R.plurals.deal_service_ new_deal, 1);

Making references to resources in XML is even easier. To do this you reference the resource ID you're interested in with the @ prefix. For example, you'd refer to the `deal_details` string as `@string/deal_details`. To include the `android` namespace you use a colon, such as `@android:string/yes`.

> **TYPES OF RESOURCES** There are many different types of data you can externalize as resources on Android. We've seen strings, plurals, and a few layouts at this point (more of those coming up), but you should know that menus, styles, animations, shapes, arrays of data, and more can also be defined as resources. We'll see more resources and different resource types as we progress through the book. For a complete and up-to-date guide of all the supported types, see the Android resources documentation at http://mng.bz/aLRy.

You need to be aware of a few more subtleties with XML resource access, such as how to define new IDs in XML and how to work with layouts. This takes us into designing the screen for an `Activity`, and working with view hierarchies, views, and widgets.

2.5 Layout, views, and widgets

A special resource known as a *layout* is what you'll use to design screens, items for lists, and other UI elements in Android. We introduced layouts in chapter 1, but here we'll clarify how you declare them as XML, and we'll touch on the components that comprise them: views and widgets.

We won't be done with layout, views, and widgets with one short discussion here, but we'll add detail as we keep the focus on the basics of Android development. Then, in chapter 4 we'll come back to these topics and take the deep dive.

2.5.1 Declaring layouts

When it comes to creating the basic UI elements in an application, Android separates the presentation into layout resources that resemble an HTML-like approach. This is in contrast to typical Java UI frameworks such as Swing. The basic idea is to statically declare the UI for a given view as an XML resource and then use IDs to refer to UI elements in code. Let's look at an example. The following listing shows the layout XML for the first screen in the DealDroid application.

Listing 2.4 The res/layout/deallist.xml layout resource file, showing views and widgets

```xml
<?xml version="1.0" encoding="utf-8"?>
<LinearLayout                                                    ① Top-level LinearLayout
    xmlns:android="http://schemas.android.com/apk/res/android"
    android:orientation="vertical" android:layout_width="fill_parent"
    android:layout_height="fill_parent">
    <ListView android:id="@android:id/list"                      ② ListView with
        android:layout_width="fill_parent"                         reserved ID of "list"
        android:layout_height="fill_parent" android:layout_weight="1" />
    <Spinner android:id="@+id/section_spinner"                   ③ Spinner
        android:layout_width="fill_parent"                          widget
        android:layout_height="wrap_content"
        android:layout_margin="5dp" />
</LinearLayout>
```

A layout file is an XML file. It's a different set of elements, but the concept is similar to the kind of HTML that would be used to create a web page. Whereas HTML elements tend to be low-level, Android's layout elements are more sophisticated. The root element of this layout file is a container of `View` classes known as a `LinearLayout` ❶. `LinearLayout` puts all of its child views into either a single row or column. Other layout types are provided, such as `FrameLayout`, `RelativeLayout`, and `TableLayout`, and you can create your own, but for now we're going to stick to `LinearLayout` and we'll meet the other types in chapter 4.

In our example, the orientation of our `LinearLayout` (defined as an attribute of the element) is vertical. This means all of the child views will be laid out in a single column, top-to-bottom in the same order as they are specified in the layout file. Inside the layout, we include two child elements: a `ListView` with a special reserved ID of list ❷, and a `Spinner` ❸. We can also see that we're defining attributes for these elements, such as `layout_width`, `layout_height`, and `layout_weight`. These control the size and positioning of the view elements, and again we'll get to the specifics surrounding these and other layout attributes in chapter 4.

As seen in the screenshot in figure 2.5, which our deallist layout produces, a `List-View` is a widget that shows a list of items, and a `Spinner` is a widget that displays a selection of choices with one element at a time showing (we'll learn more about each of these when we see the code that corresponds to this layout in the next few sections). Going back to listing 2.4, note how both widgets have resource IDs, like you'd assign to an HTML element.

One thing you may have noticed is that the `Spinner` resource ID is declared with a + sign in front of it: `@+id/section_spinner`. This special notation means go ahead and create the resource ID in the resource table (and R.java file) if it doesn't already exist. If you reuse a resource ID, or otherwise refer to one that already exists, you don't need to include the plus.

Figure 2.5 This DealDroid `DealList` screen shows the two components, a `ListView` and a `Spinner`, defined in the deallist.xml layout.

XML ISN'T THE ONLY GAME IN TOWN XML-based layouts are convenient and arguably a solid design choice that separate responsibilities, but it's important to note that you don't have to use XML at all. Layouts, other XML resources, and all other views and widgets can also be defined within Java code. All of the XML layouts that Android uses are representations of framework Java classes that are parsed and inflated into Java objects. We'll learn more about writing raw views later in the book, and more about layout inflation later in this chapter, but keep in mind that XML isn't the only way to define UI components in your Android application.

IDs in XML layouts let us refer to widgets in code, so we can populate them with data, attach event listeners, and so on. Also note that the elements' XML layouts correspond to much richer components than the low-level elements in HTML.

We aren't done with our discussions of layouts yet, because we have one more screen (the detail screen) to build for DealDroid, and we'll focus on the UI in chapter 4. Nevertheless, this gives us a good foothold into what they are; now we need to define the other terms we are bandying about: views and widgets.

2.5.2 Views and widgets

As we touched on in chapter 1, the class `android.view.View` is the base class for UI objects in Android. This is where every onscreen element in any Android application begins. There are three major types of views:

- `SurfaceView`
- `ViewGroup`
- `Widget`

The first and most basic view type is `SurfaceView`, which provides a direct drawing surface. We won't deal with these directly in this chapter, but you'll learn more about them when we talk about drawing and graphics in later chapters. The next view type is `ViewGroup`. These are an abstraction of layouts and other view containers (views that contain other views). We've already seen a few simple layouts, and we'll learn more about them and how they relate to view hierarchies and groups coming up. Finally, the last view type is `Widget`. These are the classic UI components you'll use most often.

Widgets, which are part of the `android.widget` package, are views that often interact with the user and can be backed by a data source. This means simple form elements such as text input boxes and buttons are widgets, and are more involved components like `ListView` and `Spinner`, as we've seen.

Now that we've declared views and widgets in layouts and touched on what these terms mean (knowing there's more to come), the next thing we need to do is link to these components in code and bring them to life with activities.

2.6 Activities

An `Activity` is a single focused thing that the user can do. Typically each screen in your application will be defined with a layout, and made up of views and widgets that are controlled by a corresponding `Activity`. Each `Activity` creates a window for UI, manages lifecycle and state, provides an endpoint for intents (which we'll learn about in section 2.8), handles interface events, controls menus, and more.

A SINGLE FOCUSED THING Typically an `Activity` will correspond to a screen in an application, but note the careful wording of the definition from the documentation. A "single focused" thing isn't a screen. The screen abstraction works most of the time, and it's a useful analogy, but keep in mind that an `Activity` can also be a floating window on top of another `Activity`.

To create an Android screen in an application you'll extend the `Activity` class or one of its specialized subclasses (and you'll usually define the UI for that screen with a layout resource, as we've seen). We'll cover some of the trickier parts of dealing with the `Activity` class, including lifecycle subtleties and how activities relate to tasks, in chapter 3. Here we'll address the basics of working with the `Activity` class, and we'll see our first use of a specialized `Activity` subclass for dealing with lists, `ListActivity`. We'll start with the most important parts of the `Activity` class, the methods that you'll implement often.

2.6.1 Activity basics

The Android platform performs an intricate juggling act to manage resources. With limited CPU power and memory available, Android uses a stack of activities that the system controls to try to keep the most relevant things a user is interested in running, and push other things into the background.

What's most relevant, and how does the system perform this juggling act? Most relevant is any application the user is using. An application is typically composed of a set of components, including activities, services, and broadcast receivers, that are run using the same user ID and process on the platform (as we noted in chapter 1). As users click on buttons or respond to notifications to open new activities, the system shuffles existing activities to the background. To do this, the system pushes activities through their lifecycle methods. The most common `Activity` lifecycle methods are:

- `onCreate`—Called when an `Activity` is first created
- `onPause`—Called when an `Activity` is going into the background
- `onResume`—Called when an `Activity` is being resumed after having been in the background

There are more lifecycle methods (we'll discuss all of them in the next chapter), but `onCreate` is where things are initiated, `onPause` is where they should be cleaned up or persisted, and `onResume` is where things are reloaded or reset. You'll override `onCreate` with every `Activity` you build, and in most (but not all) `onPause` and `onResume`.

In addition to the lifecycle phase hooks, `Activity` also extends `Context` and provides a host of event, state, menu, and other helper methods. The lifecycle methods of `Activity` are essential to understand and use correctly. Using these methods properly will result in a responsive and error-free application. Because these methods and the related concepts are important, we'll focus on this topic and related things such as managing state and using some of the other `Activity` methods in the next chapter. Before we get into those details, we're first going to look at the `Activity` implementation to create the deal list screen for DealDroid.

2.6.2   *List-based activities*

Lists in Android are a great place to start digging into views and activities, and a good example of the Model-View-Controller (MVC) design pattern. It's important to understand how data and its representation are decoupled from each other and how this is reflected in the framework interfaces.

Recall from figure 2.6 that DealDroid displays lists of deal data using a `ListView`. `ListView` is a scrolling container that may have an arbitrary number of child views, which we call *list items*. A list item can be any kind of view, and not all list items have to be of the same kind, which enables you to create lists of varied complexity. `ListView` does all the heavy lifting for you: it takes care of recycling and redrawing all visible list items if the underlying data changes, it handles touch events, and so on.

Even though it's perfectly fine to use `ListView` directly (and sometimes you need to), it's typically used indirectly by going through Android's `ListActivity` class. What `ListActivity` does is manage a `ListView` for you, and hence saves you from writing the boilerplate code required for setting it up and responding to events, and so on.

Here we'll take the `ListActivity` approach and build out the code that provides the `ListView` for DealDroid. The `DealList` class is our first nontrivial piece of code. We're going to break it into separate sections to discuss, starting with the biggest part: the declaration and `onCreate` method, as shown in the following listing.

Listing 2.5   Start of the DealList.java `Activity` class, from declaration through `onCreate`

```
public class DealList extends ListActivity {                      ← ❶ Extend
                                                                       ListActivity
    private static final int MENU_REPARSE = 0;

    private DealDroidApp app;
    private List<Item> items;
    private DealsAdapter dealsAdapter;
    private Spinner sectionSpinner;
    private ArrayAdapter<Section> spinnerAdapter;
    private int currentSelectedSection;
    private ProgressDialog progressDialog;

    @Override                                                     ❷ Override
    public void onCreate(Bundle savedInstanceState) {             ←   onCreate
        super.onCreate(savedInstanceState);
        setContentView(R.layout.deallist);                        ← ❸ Set layout as
                                                                       content view
        progressDialog = new ProgressDialog(this);
        progressDialog.setCancelable(false);
        progressDialog.setMessage(
                        getString(R.string.deal_list_retrieving_data) );

        app = (DealDroidApp) getApplication();                    ← Instantiate
                                                                     ❹ Application
        items = new ArrayList<Item>();          ❺ Set up Collection    object
        dealsAdapter = new DealsAdapter(items);    and Adapter

        setListAdapter(dealsAdapter);                             ← Set Adapter
                                                                  ❻ for ListView
        if (app.getSectionList().isEmpty()) {
```

```
        if (app.connectionPresent()) {
          new ParseFeedTask().execute();                        ← ⓻ Parse data from
        } else {                                                     the network
          Toast.makeText(this, getString(
            R.string.deal_list_network_unavailable),
              Toast.LENGTH_LONG).show();                        ← Show quick
        }                                                         ⓼ message with Toast
      } else {
        resetListItems(app.getSectionList().get(0).getItems());
      }

      sectionSpinner = (Spinner) findViewById(R.id.section_spinner);
      spinnerAdapter =
        new ArrayAdapter<Section>(DealList.this,
          android.R.layout.simple_spinner_item, app.getSectionList());
      spinnerAdapter.setDropDownViewResource(
        android.R.layout.simple_spinner_dropdown_item);    Set up Spinner ⓽
      sectionSpinner.setAdapter(spinnerAdapter);             and Adapter

      sectionSpinner.setOnItemSelectedListener(
                    new OnItemSelectedListener() {           ← Implement
        @Override                                              Listener
        public void onItemSelected(AdapterView<?> parentView, ⓵⓪ for Spinner
          View selectedItemView, int position, long id) {
          if (currentSelectedSection != position) {
            currentSelectedSection = position;
            resetListItems(
              app.getSectionList().get(position).getItems() ); ← React to
          }                                                     Spinner
        }                                                       click
                                                              ⓵⓵ event
        @Override
        public void onNothingSelected(AdapterView<?> parentView) {
          // do nothing
        }
      });
  }
  // ... continued in subsequent listings
```

The first thing to note with listing 2.5 is that, as promised, we're extending ListActivity ❶. From there, we see what almost every Activity will start out with, overriding onCreate ❷. This is part of the all-important Activity lifecycle that we'll focus on
in chapter 3. For now, we need to understand that onCreate is where we set things up
when our Activity is created. Inside of onCreate, we associate the layout file we built
in listing 2.4 as the content view using setContentView ❸. We'll learn more about
what exactly this is doing when we talk about *inflating* layouts in chapter 4. For now,
keep in mind that this method is how we associate our XML layout with our Activity.

After the initial setup, we're instantiating an Application object ❹, which we'll use
later to store some global state and define some utility methods. The code for this class,
and more discussion about Application objects in general, will be in section 2.9. Next,
we get to the heart of the ListView matter, using an Adapter to provide data for our list.

In this case, we're using a regular Java Collection (a List), and passing it into a
DealsAdapter class ❺. The DealsAdapter is a custom class that extends Adapter and

supplies the deal items for our list. In general terms, this is what adapters do: they provide data. Adapters come in various forms. They can be backed by arrays, collections, or even files or database cursors, and they can be trivial or complex. We'll learn more about adapters, and see the code for DealsAdapter, in section 2.7. For now, trust that the adapter will supply deal items to the ListView. We make the association between the Adapter and the ListView with setListAdapter ❻.

One important thing to note is that we haven't directly referenced a ListView anywhere. This is one of the conveniences ListActivity provides. We can imagine you frowning. How does this work, considering we haven't done any additional setup? We did, but it was subtle. Remember how we passed a reserved ID to the <ListView> element in the layout in listing 2.4? The trick is that whenever you inherit from List-Activity, it'll look for a <ListView> declaration in the activity's layout that carries the android:id/list resource ID. It'll then automatically connect this widget with the operations in the setListAdapter method (and other helper methods, such as getListView). No rocket science involved.

> **RESERVED RESOURCE IDS** Android uses predefined reserved IDs not only for lists, but also in some other places. One other example of this is TabActivity, which will look for the tabhost, tabcontent, and tabs IDs in your layout. You can also use them to access views defined in some of Android's predefined layouts. For instance, Android ships with default layouts for list items, such as simple_list_item_1 and simple_list_item_2 for single- and two-line text-based list items.

Getting past the adapter setup for our ListView, we then come to a method call that checks whether the current deal section list of items is already populated. If it's not, we check whether the network is available, and we then issue a mysterious call to ParseFeedTask.execute ❼. This is an invocation of an AsyncTask implementation. An AsyncTask lets us perform a long-running operation on a separate Thread from the UI (in this case, make a network call and parse the eBay deals RSS feed). We aren't going to step into this code here because it's off the fundamentals track, but don't worry; we'll cover threading, and AsyncTask in detail, in chapter 6 (and if you're interested in jumping ahead now, you can see this code in the download for the Deal-Droid project). The takeaway here is that we don't want to do any long-running and/or blocking work in our onCreate method (or anywhere on the main UI Thread for that matter). Also, if we can't run our AsyncTask because we can't connect to the network, we show the user a pop-up message on the screen using a Toast ❽.

After our data retrieval is out of the way, we then get to our Spinner widget ❾. As we saw in figure 2.6, the Spinner provides a stacked list of choices, much like an HTML select tag. The Spinner also uses an Adapter as a data source. This time it's a standard ArrayAdapter that gets data from our Application object (again, we'll get into the adapter details in the next section).

After the data is set up via the Adapter, we're then attaching an OnItemSelected-Listener to our Spinner ❿. This allows us to receive an event anytime an item in the

Spinner is selected. For this case, we get the clicked item, determine whether it's different than what we're already working with, and if so, call resetListItems with the selection **⓫**. We'll see what this method does in our next listing; first let's expand on how an Android View component reacts to an event. There are many listeners like this in the Android framework for all kinds of events: items being clicked, items being long clicked, scrolling, flinging, focus changes, and more. Listeners are interfaces. Here we've created an in place implementation of the OnItemSelectedListener interface with an anonymous inner class.

> **ANONYMOUS INNER CLASSES**   You could define a class in a separate file that implements a listener interface when you need it, then create an instance of that class, and then use it for the adapter's listener. Alternatively you could declare that the current class you're working on implements the interface and you could include the required method locally (and if you have multiple listeners, you can use the same method and filter for the correct component within it). There are several approaches to dealing with this situation, and which one to choose depends on the situation to some degree, and your personal preference. We find anonymous inner classes convenient and capable, and that's why we've chosen them, although they aren't easy to understand at first. One of the advantages of anonymous inner classes is that they have variable scope access to the enclosing method and class variables through a feature known as *lexical closure*.

That's it for the onCreate method of DealList. It's not trivial, so don't worry if you don't completely understand it yet. As we flesh out the details of the Adapters and work through the remaining listings, things will come into focus. We'll start with what happens when we have a new list of items to display in our ListView, such as when a selection is made from the Spinner. This takes us into the aforementioned resetListItems method, which is seen in the following listing.

Listing 2.6   Resetting the ListView adapter in the DealList.java Activity class

```
private void resetListItems(List<Item> newItems) {        ❶ Reset member
    items.clear();                                              Collection
    items.addAll(newItems);
    dealsAdapter.notifyDataSetChanged();          ◁──┐  Notify Adapter that
}                                                    ❷  data set has changed
```

The resetListItems method is short and sweet. In it, we take in a new List of Item, and we use it to repopulate the class member variable we've assigned for items ❶. Recall that this same instance of items is what we passed into DealsAdapter when we constructed it. It's the same instance, and after we change it, we call notify-DataSetChanged ❷ on DealsAdapter, and our list is updated and the views are redrawn. We'll see the code for our custom adapter, and learn more about adapters in general, coming up.

Now that we've seen how our ListView will get updated when we want to reset the data, the next thing we need to handle is how to respond when a user clicks a specific item in the list. This is done with the aptly named `onListItemClick` method in the following listing.

Listing 2.7 Handling a click event for an item in the `ListView` of DealList.java `Activity`

```
@Override
protected void onListItemClick(ListView listView,          ❶ Override
    View view, int position, long id) {                         onListItemClick
    view.setBackgroundColor(android.R.color.background_light);
    app.setCurrentItem(app.getSectionList().
        get(currentSelectedSection).getItems().get(position));
    Intent dealDetails = new Intent(DealList.this, DealDetails.class);
    startActivity(dealDetails);                    Respond with Intent ❷
}
```

The `onListItemClick` method, which is part of `ListActivity`, is an event-handling callback. If a user selects an item in a `ListView`, this method is fired, and we override it ❶ to do whatever we want ❷. Within it we set some global application state on the previously noted `Application` object, and then we launch the `DealDetails Activity` using an `Intent`. As we've touched on, intents are the wiring of Android applications; we'll learn more about them in section 2.8.

> **THE POWER OF LISTVIEW** As we've seen, `ListView` presents a scrollable list of selectable items. `ListView` is one of the most useful and powerful widgets Android provides. Though we aren't using more advanced features here, you should know that `ListView` could also support filtering, sorting, complex item views, custom layouts, headers, footers, and more. We'll see `ListView` again in many later examples in the book, and we'll exercise more of it as we go, but check the documentation for a comprehensive outline of the capabilities: http://mng.bz/2LZM.

After the `ListView` and the `Spinner`, we need to expand on one more aspect to the `DealList` screen: the options menu. The options menu is shown if the user presses the device's Menu button. For this version of DealDroid, our options menu only has one choice: reparse the data feed (because we aren't using a `Service` to do that for us, we have a menu choice to do it). Setting the options menu up, and reacting to menu events, are both accomplished in the following listing.

Listing 2.8 Setting up the menu for the DealList.java `Activity` class

```
@Override                                          ❶ Override
public boolean onCreateOptionsMenu(Menu menu) {         onCreateOptionsMenu
    menu.add(0, DealList.MENU_REPARSE, 0,
                R.string.deal_list_reparse_menu);          Add MenuItem
    return true;                               ❷ to Menu
}

@Override                                          ❸ Override onOptions-
public boolean onOptionsItemSelected(MenuItem item) {     ItemSelected
    switch (item.getItemId()) {
```

```
        case MENU_REPARSE:
            if (app.connectionPresent()) {
                new ParseFeedTask().execute();
            } else {
                Toast.makeText(this,
                    getString(R.string.deal_list_network_unavailable),
                        Toast.LENGTH_LONG).show();
            }
            return true;
    }
    return super.onOptionsItemSelected(item);
}
```

Any `Activity` can choose whether to include an options menu. To create one, you can override `onCreateOptionsMenu` ❶ and then append `MenuItems` to the passed-in `Menu`, as we've done here. The `Menu.add` method lets us specify a group ID, item ID, order, and a `String` to display ❷ (among other options, although we aren't using anything else here). The options menu can hold as many items as you want, although only the first six can be shown on what's called the *Icon Menu*. Beyond six, the *Expanded Menu* can be accessed by selecting More from the Icon Menu. Because we only have one item here, we aren't too worried about the group and item IDs, but they're useful when you have more items. We return true in `onCreateOptionsMenu` because we want the menu to be displayed (you can return false if you don't want the menu to be displayed).

To respond when a user selects an item from the options menu, we've also overridden the `onOptionsItemSelected` method ❸. Here, the selected `MenuItem` is passed in, and we use the item ID to tell which one we're dealing with. Once we have the specific `MenuItem` we're concerned with, we can perform whatever action we need to (in our case, reparse the daily deals feed, again using the `AsyncTask`).

> **OPTIONS MENU AS AN XML RESOURCE**   You can define your options menu in code, as we've done for DealList, or you can use an XML menu resource (/res/menu). There are many possibilities and options; for complete details on the options menu, see the current documentation: http://mng.bz/h8c0.

With the menu out of the way, the final piece of main `Activity` code we need to address for `DealList` is the all-important `onPause` method, which is shown in the next listing.

Listing 2.9   The onPause method in the DealList.java `Activity` class

```
@Override
  public void onPause() {
      if (progressDialog.isShowing()) {
          progressDialog.dismiss();
      }
      super.onPause();
  }
```

The `Activity` lifecycle, which we've already mentioned and will cover in detail in chapter 3, is managed by overriding lifecycle methods, such as `onCreate` and `onPause`.

onCreate was where we built up the components our Activity needs, and onPause is where we need to perform any necessary cleanup. For DealDroid we're using a ProgressDialog to indicate to users that something is happening at certain points (such as when we make the network call to get deal data). A ProgressDialog is an interactive pop-up dialog that can show progress, such as a horizontal bar filling up, or a spinning circle. If this dialog is showing when our Activity is stopped, it'll effectively be leaked, and that can cause force close (FC) errors. This is why we need to dismiss it, if it's showing, within onPause.

Now that we've touched on how Activity lifecycle methods are used (as a primer to chapter 3), and seen how a ListActivity works, the next step is to finish up and see how the adapters backing our views are implemented.

2.7   Adapters

When you have to feed data from a data source to a view, you'll use an Adapter, as we've seen. As the name suggests, an Adapter adapts a certain data source and hence lets you plug in different kinds of data sources into a view (an AdapterView) that can then render this data to the screen. ListView and Spinner are AdapterView views. Android ships with several predefined adapters, most notably ArrayAdapter, for serving data from a Java array object or Collection, and CursorAdapter for fetching data from a SQLite database (we'll learn more about databases and cursors in chapter 7). You're by no means restricted to the built-in adapters; you can, for instance, implement an adapter that wraps a web service and fetches data from the Internet directly into your views. Anything's possible!

2.7.1   Adapter basics

The most basic way to use an adapter is to leverage one of the existing implementations Android provides, such as ArrayAdapter (which, despite the name, also works with collections). To see how this works, let's take a quick look back at how we provided data for our Spinner in listing 2.5:

```
spinnerAdapter =
    new ArrayAdapter<Section>(DealList.this,
    android.R.layout.simple_spinner_item, sectionList);
```

To instantiate this ArrayAdapter, we're using DealList.this for the Context, then a layout resource to tell the Adapter how to display each item, and finally the data itself in the form of a List of Section objects. Section is a simple JavaBean-style class (getters and setters) with a title and a collection of Items that comes from our own model. Item is another simple bean that represents a particular deal with an ID, title, price, location, and so on (for the complete source on these classes, see the code download for this project). The layout we're using for the Spinner item is set using the reserved ID android.R.layout.*simple_spinner_item*. By default, ArrayAdapter expects a layout that represents a single TextView. As we can tell by the android name prefix, we're using a layout provided by the framework for this purpose. Our Spinner is simple, we'll use this built-in layout. If we wanted, we could change this layout and define our own. The default behavior of an `ArrayAdapter` is to call the `toString` method on each piece of data it has and render it using the specified layout. If you want to do something different, you can override the `getView` method of `ArrayAdapter` as we'll see in the next section.

> **ANDROID AND CONTEXT**   If you look through the various Android APIs, you'll notice that many of them take an `android.content.Context` object as a parameter. You'll also see that an `Activity` or a `Service` is usually used as a `Context`. This works because both of these classes extend from `Context`. What's `Context` exactly? Per the Android reference documentation, it's an entity that represents various environment data. It provides access to local files, databases, class loaders associated to the environment, services including system-level services, and more. Throughout this book, and in your day-to-day coding with Android, you'll see the `Context` passed around frequently.

A basic adapter provides a quick way to pour data into a view, but what if we need to customize the views, or moreover, what if we need to reflect changes in the data to the view, or vice versa? To deal with either or both of those conditions, we often need a custom adapter.

2.7.2 *Custom adapters*

Creating your own adapter means creating a class that implements the `Adapter` interface. There are several convenience classes such as `ArrayAdapter` or `BaseAdapter` from which you can inherit, and you need to override or add those parts that are relevant to you. The `getView` method is called whenever a list item must be (re)drawn. This happens frequently, for example when scrolling through the list. If the list data changes, you must tell the list view that it should redraw its children by calling `Adapter.notifyDataSetChanged`, as we saw in listing 2.6.

The `DealsAdapter` we referenced in listing 2.5 is a custom adapter that extends `ArrayAdapter`. In listing 2.5 we instantiated this `Adapter` and set it as the backing for the entire `ListActivity` using `setListAdapter(dealsAdapter)`. The `DealsAdapter` code is shown in this next listing.

Listing 2.10   The DealsAdapter.java custom Adapter for supplying views to the `DealList`

```
private class DealsAdapter extends ArrayAdapter<Item> {         ◁─── ❶ Extend ArrayAdapter

    public DealsAdapter() {
        super(DealList.this,
                R.layout.list_item, new ArrayList<Item>());       ◁─── ❷ Define constructor
    }

    @Override
    public View getView(int position,
                        View convertView, ViewGroup parent) {      ◁───
        if (convertView == null) {                                Override getView ❸
```

```
        LayoutInflater inflater = (LayoutInflater)
           getSystemService(Context.LAYOUT_INFLATER_SERVICE);
        convertView = inflater.inflate(R.layout.list_item,
                                parent, false);          ◄──   Use
    }                                                     ❹  LayoutInflater

    TextView text =
    (TextView) convertView.findViewById(R.id.deal_title);      ❺  Populate
    ImageView image =                                              convertView
    (ImageView) convertView.findViewById(R.id.deal_img);
    image.setImageBitmap(
        BitmapFactory.decodeResource(getResources(), R.drawable.ddicon));

    Item item = getItem(position);        ◄──❻  Get data item

    if (item != null) {
        text.setText(item.getTitle());
        Bitmap bitmap = app.getImageCache().get(item.getItemId());
        if (bitmap != null) {
            image.setImageBitmap(bitmap);      Apply data values to view  ❼
        } else {
            image.setTag(item.getItemId());
            new RetrieveImageTask(image)                  ❽  Use task to
                .execute(item.getSmallPicUrl());   ◄──       retrieve bitmap
        }
    }
}                              ❾  Return
                                   View
    return convertView;      ◄──
    }
}
```

The `DealsAdapter` class has a lot happening in it. This is the first custom `Adapter` we've seen, but it won't be the last. This concept is important when you want to do anything beyond the defaults with widgets. We need to go beyond the defaults because our `ListView`, as seen in figure 2.6, has a custom layout with a small picture and the title of the deal for each `Item` in the list. Recall that the default for `ArrayAdapter`, as we saw with our `Spinner`, is to display the `toString` value of the each data item. We need more than that.

`DealsAdapter` begins by extending `ArrayAdapter` ❶. This is important because `Adapter` is an interface with quite a few methods, and we only want to override the `View` being drawn, not all of the other plumbing. You can implement your own `Adapter` from scratch, or extend `BaseAdapter` to start from a lower level, but we want to reuse as much of the framework as we can, so we're extending `ArrayAdapter`.

The first thing our `DealsAdapter` class does is define its own constructor that passes along the required elements to `ArrayAdapter` ❷. To use an `ArrayAdapter` you need the `Context`, a layout resource ID, and an array or `Collection` of data. After the constructor, we override the `getView` method ❸. This is where the Android framework steps up and does something clever to help draw `ListView` screens faster: it uses a `convertView`. A `convertView` is an existing `View` that if present, and if of the right type, can be reused. Because a `ListView` can scroll many items on a screen, and often they can be represented by the same views with different contents (a new name and picture in our case), reusing views rather than re-creating them for every position is a major optimization. Even if the list has 1,000 items, they aren't all on the screen at the same time. We're effectively paging through the data, and paging through the UI elements and repurposing them, by using a `convertView` View. For our example, if the `convertView` passed in is null, we establish it by inflating the layout we want to use, `R.layout.list_item` ❹.

This is another static layout that we've declared in XML, and we're using the system *LAYOUT_INFLATER_SERVICE* to "inflate" it into code. This layout, which we've placed in the /res/layout directory in our project, is a simple `RelativeLayout`:

```
<RelativeLayout xmlns:android="http://schemas.android.com/apk/res/android"
        android:layout_width="fill_parent"
        android:layout_height="fill_parent">
    <ImageView android:id="@+id/deal_img"
        android:layout_width="50dp"
        android:layout_height="50dp"
        android:layout_margin="5dp" />
    <TextView android:id="@+id/deal_title"
        android:layout_toRightOf="@id/deal_img"
        android:layout_width="fill_parent"
        android:layout_height="wrap_content"
        android:layout_margin="5dp" />
</RelativeLayout>
```

A `RelativeLayout` works differently than the `LinearLayouts` we've seen up to now. Rather than lining up elements horizontally or vertically, it lays them out in relation to one another as you specify. Again, we'll find out more about this and all layouts in chapter 4.

Once the layout is established we use `findViewById` to get a handle to the `View` elements it references ❺. After we have the references, we then get the current data Item ❻ and apply the data values to the views ❼. The title comes right from the `Item` data class we're using, and the image we set first as a default using a resource drawable named `ddicon` (the file for this is located at res/drawable-mdpi/ddicon.gif). After the default image is set, we then try to get the image for the deal from the Internet using the item's URL ❽ (if it isn't already cached in our `Application` object). We do this using another `AsyncTask`, `RetrieveImageTask`, which makes an HTTP call over the network (the code isn't shown here so we can stay on topic, but again it's available with the project download if you're interested). Finally, `getView` returns the `View` it has worked to build ❾, and the `AdapterView` displays it.

In all, our custom adapter is drawing custom views and reflecting data model changes to those views. We're using the adapter's `notifyDataSetChanged` method within the earlier `resetListItems` method we saw in listing 2.6 to initially prime the adapter (and also when a user picks a different deal-type section from the `Spinner` selection listener). Again, this causes the views to be redrawn to reflect the current data.

The other side of this coin would be updating the data model based on actions in the user interface. This could be users selecting items in the list (and needing to keep track of what's selected, and what isn't), or more complicated interface elements in each list item that allow users to fill in form fields or otherwise interact with the data (you can make each item as detailed as you need). We don't need this for DealDroid, but it's important to note that this type of two-way data binding can be done with a custom adapter (we'll see examples in later chapters that include this).

> **A PATTERN EMERGES: MODEL-VIEW-CONTROLLER** You may have noticed a familiar pattern here: we have a view that renders data from a data source (the *model*), and we have an `Activity` that dispatches user input to the view and notifies it about changes in the underlying data so that it can redraw itself (the *controller*). That's MVC all right! If you look closely, the framework is full of object interaction that follows the MVC pattern. Keep this in mind: it's a flexible and powerful design pattern commonly found in widget frameworks (as is the Adapter pattern, by the way).

Think about how flexible the adapter solution is. If we were to store our data in a database, or retrieve it in a paged fashion from a web service, we could replace our adapter object with one that iterates over the data source we need. We wouldn't have to change a thing about our list view. That's loose coupling and object orientation par excellence.

Beyond the way activities can use views that are loosely coupled from their data sources via adapters, Android also provides another type of loose coupling between activities and other components: intents.

2.8 Intents and IntentFilters

One area where Android shines is the flexibility it provides in communicating between components, and sharing data between them. Android makes this possible using `Intent`- and `IntentFilter`-based events. As we've noted, an `Intent` is a description of an action you want to happen, and an `IntentFilter` is a means for a component to declare it's capable of handling a specific `Intent`. Intents themselves don't do any work; rather, they describe something that needs to be done.

If a component wants to perform an action, it declares that intention with an `Intent` and hands it off to the system. The system then decodes the `Intent` and decides which other component, `Activity`, `Service`, or `BroadcastReceiver`, can handle the job.

Also, if an `Activity`, `BroadcastReceiver`, or `Service` wants to offer some action to be available to other components, it declares an `IntentFilter`. The Android platform keeps track of all the `IntentFilter` declarations that the current running system is capable of handling, and then resolves intents as they come in to the most suitable component dynamically, on the fly, at runtime. Figure 2.6 looks at this another way, using interlocking shapes as an analogy to depict the `Intent`/`IntentFilter` relationship.

To see how the `Intent` process works, we'll implement the DealDetails part of DealDroid, which will involve declaring several different types of intents and talking a bit more about intent filters.

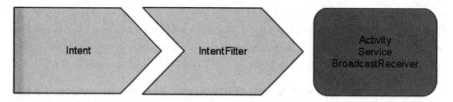

Figure 2.6 **Intents** and **IntentFilters** combine to filter and respond to events by dispatching them to registered components.

2.8.1   *Using intents*

To see what goes into an Intent object, we're going to build the final Activity of the DealDroid application, DealDetails. If you recall from section 2.1, the DealDetails screen displays the details of a deal after a user clicks on it from the DealList screen. Along with displaying information, the other major thing DealDetails does is allow the user to share the deal in several ways using intents and menu options, as seen in the following listing.

Listing 2.11   The first part of the DealDetails.java Activity **class**

```
public class DealDetails extends Activity {             ◁── ❶ Extend
                                                              Activity
   private static final int MENU_MAIL = 1;
   private static final int MENU_BROWSE = 2;
   private static final int MENU_SHARE = 3;

   private DealDroidApp app;
   private ProgressBar progressBar;

   @Override
   public void onCreate(Bundle savedInstanceState) {    ◁── ❷ Override
      super.onCreate(savedInstanceState);                      onCreate
      setContentView(R.layout.dealdetails);

      app = (DealDroidApp) getApplication();

      progressBar = (ProgressBar) findViewById(R.id.progress);
      progressBar.setIndeterminate(true);

      Item item = app.getCurrentItem();

      if (item != null) {
         // population of view items omitted to shorten listing
         // see code download
      }
   }

   @Override                                         ❸ Override
   public boolean onCreateOptionsMenu(Menu menu) {  ◁── onCreateOptionsMenu
      menu.add(DealDetails.NONE, DealDetails.MAIL,
         DealDetails.NONE, R.string.deal_details_mail_menu);
      menu.add(DealDetails.NONE, DealDetails.BROWSE,      ❹ Add
         DealDetails.NONE, R.string.deal_details_browser_menu);  MenuItem
      menu.add(DealDetails.NONE, DealDetails.SHARE,            choices
         DealDetails.NONE, R.string.deal_details_share_menu);
```

```
        return true;
    }
    @Override
    public boolean onOptionsItemSelected(MenuItem item) {
        switch (item.getItemId()) {
            case MAIL:
                shareDealUsingChooser("text/html");
                return true;
            case BROWSE:
                openDealInBrowser();
                return true;
            case SHARE:
                shareDealUsingChooser("text/*");
                return true;
            default:
                return super.onOptionsItemSelected(item);
        }
    }
}
...
```

Override onOptionsItemSelected ❺

Share with text/html MIME ❻

Open in browser ❼

Share with text/* MIME type ❽

Within the DealDetails class we see the standard pattern of extending Activity ❶, then overriding the onCreate lifecycle method ❷, and setting our layout using set-ContentView (the layout for DealDetails isn't shown here because it's simple and doesn't add to the discussion at this point). After those familiar steps, we come to onCreateOptionsMenu ❸, where we set up the option menu items ❹ for performing actions with a particular deal. This method returns true to make sure the menu is shown (it won't be shown unless the return value is true).

After the option menu items are defined, we then override the onOptionItem-Selected method that'll be called when an option item is selected ❺. Here we respond to the different option items: share a deal using a chooser with the text/html MIME type ❻, open the deal in the Browser application ❼, or share it using a chooser with the text/* MIME type ❽ (which offers more options than text/html). In each case that we explicitly handle here, we return true, which indicates that the menu processing should stop. In case any menu items are passed in that we don't handle, the default case passes off to the super implementation.

A *chooser* is a dialog of choices of how to handle an Intent, as we'll see momentarily. The following listing fills in the detail of exactly how we're performing these actions through intents, by diving into the shareDealUsingChooser and openDealIn-Browser methods.

Listing 2.12 The sharing actions of the DealDetails Activity, handled through Intents

```
private void shareDealUsingChooser(String type) {
    Intent i = new Intent(Intent.ACTION_SEND);
    i.setType(type);
    i.putExtra(Intent.EXTRA_SUBJECT, "Subject:");
    i.putExtra(Intent.EXTRA_TEXT, createDealMessage());
    try {
```

Intent with action ❶

MIME type ❷

Extra data ❸

```
        startActivity(Intent.createChooser(i, "Share deal ..."));
    } catch (android.content.ActivityNotFoundException ex) {
       Toast.makeText(DealDetails.this,
          "There are no chooser options installed for the "
             + type + " " + type.",
                Toast.LENGTH_SHORT).show();
    }
}

private void openDealInBrowser() {
    Intent i = new Intent(Intent.ACTION_VIEW, Uri.parse(
       app.getCurrentItem().getDealUrl()));
    startActivity(i);
}

private String createDealMessage() {
    Item item = app.getCurrentItem();
    StringBuffer sb = new StringBuffer();
    sb.append("Check out this deal:\n");
    sb.append("\nTitle:" + item.getTitle());
    sb.append("\nPrice:" + item.getConvertedCurrentPrice());
    sb.append("\nLocation:" + item.getLocation());
    sb.append("\nQuantity:" + item.getQuantity());
    sb.append("\nURL:" + item.getDealUrl());
    return sb.toString();
}

// AsyncTask inner class and closing of DealDetails omitted
// to shorten listing
```

Activity with Intent chooser ❹

openDealInBrowser

Intent with action and URI

❺ **createDealMessage**

Inside the shareDealUsingChooser method, where we do a lot of Intent-related work, we first set up an Intent with the action set to ACTION_SEND ❶. This step is small but key. Action is one of the primary pieces of information an Intent can contain, along with data (as we'll see in a second), and MIME type ❷. A Bundle of extras can also be included. The extra data can be simple types (strings, primitives, and so on), or custom types that are made Parcelable (serializable across processes). Here we're including a subject header and deal details in the form of a String ❸ (which is built by the createDealMessage method ❺). Once the Intent is ready, we then use startActivity with createChooser to fire it ❹. The chooser shown when we press the Share menu option in DealDroid (on an device, not the emulator, which has fewer capabilities) is seen in figure 2.7.

The chooser seen in figure 2.8 demonstrates that many registered components can handle a SEND text/* type Intent (which the DealDetails

Figure 2.7   The DealDroid details screen Share deal menu option chooser shows the many ways one particular type of Intent can be handled.

share button creates). By using a chooser, we're specifically indicating that we want the user to make a choice each time. If we hadn't used a chooser, the user would still have a choice to make, but they'd also have the option of selecting a default action. By changing one line in `DealDetails`, we can see how this works. If we edit the `share-DealUsingChooser` method and change the `startActivity` line from the following:

```
startActivity(Intent.createChooser(i, "Share deal ..."));
```

to

```
startActivity(i);
```

Then we can invoke the Share button again, and we'll get the choices seen in figure 2.8.

If we control the chooser (figure 2.7), we can set the title, and we can require the user to make a choice each time they perform the action (if more than one component can handle the action). If, on the other hand, we let the system present the choices (figure 2.8), we can't control the title, and the user is offered the choice of setting a default for the `Intent`. Either way, the more generic the `Intent`, the more choices. As we can see, `SEND text/*` is generic, and results in a long list of choices (there are more not seen in the screenshots, if the user scrolls).

Getting back to listing 2.12, in the `openDealIn-Browser` method, we see a different way to create an `Intent`. Here we're setting the action to `VIEW`, and the data to a `Uri` (in this case the HTTP URL to the deal). This is a far more specific `Intent` because we want to view the item, and the URI indicates a more particular type of data (it contains a URL with the protocol—HTTP—and a hostname and path). When we indicate that we want to view an HTTP URL in this manner, only one type of component should respond, a web browser. If there are multiple browsers on the system (which is possible, if the user has installed additional browsers), then this still could result in a choice, but that's far less likely than sharing `SEND` action.

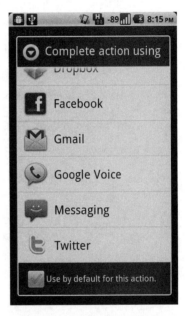

Figure 2.8 The same set of choices, without specifically using a chooser, shows that the user can set a default preference.

To see how we can create even more specific intents, and how the parts of an `Intent` affect what component will be able to respond to them, we need to discuss the different types of intents.

2.8.2 Intent types

Going back to listing 2.7, to get from the `DealList Activity` to the `DealDetails Activity` we used the following `Intent`:

```
Intent dealDetails = new Intent(DealList.this, DealDetails.class);
    startActivity(dealDetails);
```

In this case, the `Intent` doesn't have an action, a type, or data, like the ones we used in the previous section did. Instead this `Intent` points directly at a specific class, `DealDetails.class`, and says "you're it." This is an *explicit* `Intent`. Explicit intents are fairly common inside of a single application, where you know exactly what each component does, and you know the class name (they're simple and direct).

If, on the other hand, you want to reach out across application boundaries and/or use features that are described in a more abstract way (show this web page, dial this phone number, display this map, and so on), you use an *implicit* `Intent`. Implicit intents are resolved to components that can handle them using a combination of the available optional attributes present. These include action, data, type, and a few other things, as defined in table 2.1.

Table 2.1   Attributes that can be defined and used when declaring and resolving `Intents`

Intent attribute name	Description	Examples
action	The action to be performed.	ACTION_VIEW, ACTION_DIAL, ACTION_SHARE, ACTION_EDIT
data	The data to operate on.	content://contacts/people/1, http://www.reddit.com
type	The MIME type for any Intent data. Optional, can also be inferred from the data itself.	text/*, text/plain, text/html, image/png
category	Additional hints about the action to execute.	CATEGORY_LAUNCHER, CATEGORY_ALTERNATIVE
extras	A Bundle of additional information	putExtra("KEY", "VALUE")
component	The component class to use, bypassing all other Intent evaluation.	MyActivity.class

The action, data, type, and category are used to map an implicit `Intent` to a component that declares it can handle it. Alternatively, explicit intents hard-code the component that'll be invoked. The explicit part is easy to understand; the implicit approach is more complicated, and it involves a process of `Intent` resolution.

2.8.3   *Intent resolution*

`Intents` declare what you want to do. You use them to invoke other components. The other piece of the puzzle is declaring what actions, types, and categories your components support so that they can be used to fulfill intents from others. To do this, you declare and use an `IntentFilter`.

We saw an example of declaring an `IntentFilter` in the DealDroid application manifest in listing 2.1. That filter had an action of `MAIN` and a category of `LAUNCHER`. This declares that our `DealList Activity` can be made available on the Home screen (the platform Launcher application). Another example of an `IntentFilter` is one of the many declared in the platform built-in Messaging application, as shown:

```
<intent-filter>
    <action android:name="android.intent.action.SEND" />
    <category android:name="android.intent.category.DEFAULT" />
    <data android:mimeType="text/plain" />
</intent-filter>
```

As we can see from the `IntentFilter` declared in the Messaging application, it says make me available when something wants to use the `SEND` action, with the `DEFAULT` category, and a data MIME type of `text/plain`. In listing 2.12, the `shareDealUsingChooser` method created an `Intent` with similar parameters. We didn't declare a category there, but that's okay because categories only have to match if they're declared in the `Intent`. More specifically, if the `Intent` has a category defined, the `IntentFilter` must contain it for there to be a match. If the `Intent` has no categories defined, it matches any category.

One caveat to this can be tricky. Anytime the `Context.startActivity` method is called with an implicit intent (the component isn't set), it *automatically* adds the `DEFAULT` category to the `Intent`. This means any `IntentFilter` that wants to handle implicit intents should declare that it supports the `DEFAULT` category (like the Messaging `IntentFilter` does).

Because the Messaging `IntentFilter` matches the `Intent` we created in `shareDealUsingChooser`, the `ComposeMessageActivity` from the Messaging application shows up on our list of choices in figures 2.8.

We'll see many more examples of intents and intent filters as we proceed through the book, but the main thing to realize here is that Android is keeping track of all of the intent filters available and matching intents as they come to the components that can handle them at runtime. Android keeps track of the registered `IntentFilter` declarations with the `PackageManager` (which you can also query if you need to; it can tell you what is and isn't available at any given time). When a new application is installed, its declarations are added, and when an application is uninstalled, its declarations are removed.

At this point, we've created a good bit of the DealDroid application. We've constructed the `DealList` layout and `Activity`, and the `DealDetails` `Activity`. We've also explored setting up the manifest, declaring and using resources, declaring and invoking intents, working with views and widgets, and dealing with adapters. Now, the final thing we need to do to wrap up the DealDroid application is build and understand the `Application` object we've previously referred to in several listings.

2.9 *The Application object*

We've seen a lot of code in this chapter, and in several places we've seen a reference to an app object. If you recall, this object was a reference to a `DealDroidApp` class when we assigned it. `DealDroidApp` extends Android's `Application` object. An `Application` object has a well-defined lifecycle, and can be used as a data structure for holding an application's global state. We'll talk more about lifecycle in chapter 3, but the important thing to keep in mind with the `Application` object is that it's created when the process for your application is created, and it isn't bound to a particular `Activity` or `Service`. This means it's a great and extremely simple way to hold onto and share nontrivial and nonpersistent data between activities and services within your application. By nontrivial and nonpersistent, we mean data that your application needs which would be cumbersome to pass around as `Intent` extras everywhere, and also isn't appropriate for a file or database.

ANOTHER WAY TO SHARE IN-APP DATA   Another good choice for nontrivial and nonpersistent data is a static singleton object. You have to be careful with statics, though. They don't have a well-defined lifecycle, and it's easy to hang onto a reference that could cause a memory leak. If you prefer statics over the `Application` object, that's fine, but consider setting up and tearing down your static classes *from* the `Application` object, which does have a well-defined lifecycle, for the best of both worlds.

In the following listing we finally see the `DealDroidApp` object that we've used from several previous activities.

Listing 2.13   DealDroidApp.java file provides the shared `Application` object for DealDroid

```
public class DealDroidApp extends Application {            Extend Application
                                                       ①  object
    private ConnectivityManager cMgr;
    private DailyDealsFeedParser parser;
    private List<Section> sectionList;                    Include data members
    private Map<Long, Bitmap> imageCache;             ②   shared by application
    private Item currentItem;

    public DailyDealsFeedParser getParser() {
        return this.parser;
    }

    public List<Section> getSectionList() {
        return this.sectionList;
    }

    public Map<Long, Bitmap> getImageCache() {
        return this.imageCache;
    }

    public Item getCurrentItem() {
        return this.currentItem;
    }

    public void setCurrentItem(Item currentItem) {
        this.currentItem = currentItem;
    }

    @Override                                           ❸ Override onCreate
    public void onCreate() {                               lifecycle method
        super.onCreate();
        this.cMgr = (ConnectivityManager)
           this.getSystemService(Context.CONNECTIVITY_SERVICE);
        this.parser = new DailyDealsXmlPullFeedParser();
```

```
        this.sectionList = new ArrayList<Section>(6);
        this.imageCache = new HashMap<Long, Bitmap>();
    }

// retrieveBitmap and connectionPresent helper methods
// omitted to shorten listing
}
```

Like most custom `Application` instances ❶, the `DealDroidApp` object includes several data members we've used in various places in the application, and a few utility methods (which we aren't showing here). For the `DealDroidApp`, the data members we've included are ❷:

- The `ConnectivityManager`
- A `DailyDealsFeedParser` `XMLPullParser` implementation for parsing RSS
- The list of Sections, if any
- A `Map` to cache small images
- The currently selected Item, if any

After the member variables are declared, we then override the `onCreate` lifecycle method ❸ to set up our `Application` instance. Within `onCreate`, we see that we instantiate a few interesting things. First we create the `ConnectivityManager`, which is a system service that we can use to check network state (we'll learn more about this in later examples). Second we create an instance of the `DailyDealsFeedParser` class, which we used from the `DealList` `Activity` to parse the daily deals RSS feed (we'll discuss XML parsing in chapter 6). Then we instantiate a few standard Java `Collection` objects to hold data.

The final step is to make sure our application will use our custom `Application` object, which we already handled in the manifest. Back in listing 2.1 we did this by using the `name` attribute for the application element (without this, the default `Application` object would be used):

```
<application android:icon="@drawable/ddicon"
    android:label="@string/app_name"
    android:name=".DealDroidApp">
```

And that does it! The DealDroid application is complete now that we've placed some global state and provided utility methods via the `Application` object. This final part of DealDroid is also the final stop on our tour of the Android application fundamentals.

2.10 Summary

In completing the DealDroid application we've covered a lot of fundamental Android application development ground. We took this journey in order to work on the basics, to make sure you know what the core components of Android applications are and how they're used outside of a trivial example. That said, we've still tried to keep things at a relatively high level to this point.

We've learned that the main Android application-building blocks are the application manifest, resources, layouts, views, activities, and intents. The manifest is the configuration for your application, and resources are externalized elements (such as strings and images). The code begins with activities, which pull in resources and layouts. Layouts are groups of views that organize the UI of a screen or component. Often layouts are described in XML and inflated at runtime, which further helps separate responsibilities. Activities use views and widgets to create elements that are displayed to the user, or the user interacts with. Intents are the wiring between components, and even between different applications.

With DealDroid, and the basics of the components involved behind us, the next area we need to focus on is overall application and component lifecycle.

Managing
lifecycle and state

3

Each thing is of like form from everlasting and comes round again in its cycle.

—Marcus Aurelius

All Android applications are created equal. This isn't some ideological ideal; it's a truth born out of necessity. Many Android devices—as we've already noted a few times but will hammer home again even at the risk of repetition—have limited memory, CPU power, and other resources. Because of these factors, when the platform was created, the design had to include a way to give the most important processes the resources they needed, and at the same time subdue or kill other processes that might get in the way.

Android handles this by managing application processes within a hierarchy where the current and most recently used components are at the top. When resources get scarce, the platform will kill the least-relevant processes. In addition, Android components use a series of lifecycle methods that act as callbacks—the platform hooks into these methods to create and destroy components (and move them through other stages as well).

This all sounds well and good, but here's the rub: users don't care about any of this. They want applications that work quickly and efficiently without losing state data or crashing every time they rotate the device. That's not much to ask, right? It isn't, but you'd be surprised how many Android applications, even corporate offerings, fail at coping well within the Android environment. Here we hope to equip you with the knowledge you need to ensure that your applications don't fall into the same traps.

This journey will take us through defining what an Android application is and seeing how separate user IDs and processes are used for each (most of the time). From there we'll also discuss how Android decides which processes are eligible to be killed. Then we'll step down a level and talk about application components, most notably the `Activity` class. Activities (and other components such as `Service` and `BroadcastReceiver`, which we'll cover in later chapters) have a series of lifecycle methods, such as `onCreate` and `onPause` that allow you to control how they're created, destroyed, and recreated.

In addition to lifecycle, it's also critical to know how to deal with and maintain `Activity` instance state. Instance state is nonpersistent data that you need to pass from one instance of an `Activity` to the next (a new activity instance is recreated when screen orientation changes), so the user's selections and the like aren't lost. You can work within the lifecycle to maintain this data, once you know the right places to pass it along.

After we have the process-application-component picture down, we'll touch on the concept of tasks in Android. A task is a group of activities that are related based on what business action the user is trying to accomplish. Such activities may come from different Android applications, but to the user, they appear as one. Knowing a bit about activities, the activity stack, and how they relate to tasks, will help you understand the platform and build better applications.

3.1   *Defining an Android application*

One tenet of the Android platform is that an application can use components from another application, easily and transparently to the user. That blurs the definition of an application. To a user, an application consists of activities from all over the place (maps, browser, email, contacts, and camera, to name a few built-in options). The user's objective becomes important, regardless of the multiple components involved. Android labels this cross-application application a *task*.

We'll discuss tasks later in section 3.3. We mention them here to disambiguate the term. Our focus here will be on the technical definition of a single application. An Android application, the technical kind, corresponds to all the components run under the same user ID and process and linked by an overarching `Application` object. The `Application` object serves as a central context for all of the components (activities, services, broadcast receivers, and content providers). All of these items are rolled up into an APK file and can be deployed to the Market as an app.

Here we'll focus on this technical application definition. We'll discuss the `Application` object lifecycle and how an application relates to a process and user ID. We'll also see the priorities Android gives to different processes when it needs to reclaim resources.

3.1.1 *Application lifecycle*

Every Android application is hosted by an `Application` object. We used this object to share state and house utility methods in chapter 2, but even when you don't extend it and create your own, the default is there. The `Application` object has its own lifecycle, which is thankfully easy to understand, as you can see:

1 `onCreate` is called when the `Application` is started.
2 `onLowMemory` is called when the system requests that applications try to clean up what they can.
3 `onTerminate` is *sometimes* called when the `Application` is stopped.
4 `onConfigurationChanged` is called when the device `Configuration` changes while the application is running (see http://mng.bz/LJGK).

As you can see, there are four straightforward methods. Out of these, the most common ones you'll deal with are `onCreate` and `onLowMemory`. The other methods can be used, but `onTerminate` isn't guaranteed to be called, and `onConfigurationChanged`, at the application level, is typically only needed for advanced situations.

You'll use `onCreate`, as we saw in chapter 2, to set up any initial internal or global state for the `Application`. The Android framework will automatically create the `Application` object for you the first time your application is started, and it'll invoke `onCreate`. There's one caveat here: make sure this happens quickly. You don't want any long-running operations inside `onCreate`, because it affects overall application startup time. As for `onLowMemory`, this can be used to purge caches or otherwise release any memory that you can, in case the system requests that you do so. The benefit here is that if you implement this, and if enough other applications do as well, the system might be able to recover enough memory so that it doesn't have to start terminating currently unused applications, or worse yet, killing processes.

The significant thing to keep in mind with the `Application` object is that it's created when your overall application starts, and it's not killed until the application stops. It outlives your activities, services, broadcast receivers, and other components.

As to processes themselves, we briefly noted the fact that Android uses a separate process and user ID for each application in chapter 1, but you might be wondering how these relate to the `Application` object, and how you can control the arrangement, should the need arise.

3.1.2   *Application user ID, process, and threads*

When a user first requests any component of your Android application (`Activity`, `Service`, `BroadcastReceiver`, or `ContentProvider`), it's started with a unique user ID and kicked off inside a new system process running under that ID. We discussed Android's Linux OS in chapter 1 and touched on the fact that using separate processes for each application isolates memory and state, and therefore helps with security and true multitasking.

Another key thing to understand is that each process, by default, runs one main `Thread`. This main `Thread` is often called the UI `Thread`, but that's a misnomer because in addition to activities, broadcast receivers, content providers, and services also use it. Any component that needs to do so should start its own separate `Thread` from the main `Thread` in order to do any concurrent or background work (we'll learn more about threading in chapter 6). This hierarchy—process, application, main thread, and the components therein—is depicted in figure 3.1.

Typically, and by default, the process/application/thread/component arrangement is repeated, with a separate user ID and within a separate process, for each application. The OS manages the multiple processes, and the Android interprocess communication (IPC) mechanism is used to pass data between processes. If you run the `ps` command from the ADB shell, or use Device -> Show Process Status from the DDMS tool (which runs `ps`), you can examine the currently running processes, as seen in figure 3.2.

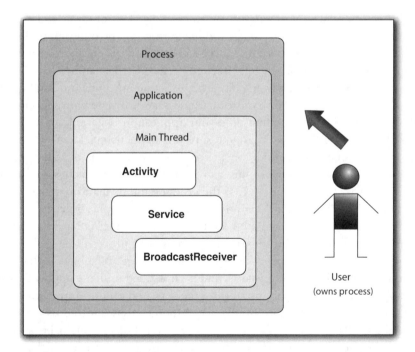

Figure 3.1   Each application runs in its own process, with its own unique user ID, and has its own main thread (by default).

```
●  ○  ○                   Terminal — adb — 87×48
                  adb
Last login: Tue Mar 22 14:50:03 on ttys000
Charlie-Collinss-MacBook-Pro:~ charliecollins$ adb —e shell
# ps
USER     PID  PPID  VSIZE  RSS    WCHAN     PC        NAME
root     1    0     296    204    c0093b98  0000c86c  S /init
root     2    0     0      0      c004bb50  00000000  S kthreadd
root     3    2     0      0      c003d428  00000000  S ksoftirqd/0
root     4    2     0      0      c00487a4  00000000  S events/0
root     5    2     0      0      c00487a4  00000000  S khelper
root     6    2     0      0      c00487a4  00000000  S suspend
root     7    2     0      0      c00487a4  00000000  S kblockd/0
root     8    2     0      0      c00487a4  00000000  S cqueue
root     9    2     0      0      c0174bf4  00000000  S kseriod
root     10   2     0      0      c00487a4  00000000  S kmmcd
root     11   2     0      0      c0068318  00000000  S pdflush
root     12   2     0      0      c0068318  00000000  S pdflush
root     13   2     0      0      c006cb08  00000000  S kswapd0
root     14   2     0      0      c00487a4  00000000  S aio/0
root     21   2     0      0      c01723f4  00000000  S mtdblockd
root     22   2     0      0      c00487a4  00000000  S hid_compat
root     23   2     0      0      c0187478  00000000  S mmcqd
root     24   2     0      0      c00487a4  00000000  S rpciod/0
root     25   1     740    296    c014c8dc  afe0c27c  S /system/bin/sh
system   26   1     808    244    c0193774  afe0c51c  S /system/bin/servicemanager
root     27   1     852    376    c0093b98  afe0c644  S /system/bin/vold
root     28   1     672    248    c019f514  afe0ceac  S /system/bin/debuggerd
radio    29   1     5420   676    ffffffff  afe0cb8c  S /system/bin/rild
root     30   1     75564  21704  c0093b98  afe0c644  S zygote
media    31   1     18500  3092   ffffffff  afe0c51c  S /system/bin/mediaserver
root     32   1     800    304    c02023c8  afe0c27c  S /system/bin/installd
keystore 33   1     1708   452    c019f514  afe0ceac  S /system/bin/keystore
root     34   1     740    316    c003b100  afe0d14c  S /system/bin/sh
root     35   1     840    340    c00b1308  afe0d29c  S /system/bin/qemud
root     38   1     6588   284    ffffffff  0000ecc4  S /sbin/adbd
root     44   34    796    292    c02023c8  afe0c27c  S /system/bin/qemu-props
system   52   30    208856 29088  ffffffff  afe0c51c  S system_server
radio    93   30    113732 21560  ffffffff  afe0d4a4  S com.android.phone
app_1    95   30    106888 22224  ffffffff  afe0d4a4  S android.process.acore
app_11   118  30    108972 17064  ffffffff  afe0d4a4  S com.android.mms
app_0    137  30    97464  16404  ffffffff  afe0d4a4  S com.android.alarmclock
app_4    139  30    103888 17440  ffffffff  afe0d4a4  S android.process.media
app_16   199  30    96864  15344  ffffffff  afe0d4a4  S com.svox.pico
app_24   219  30    103144 21128  ffffffff  afe0d4a4  S com.manning.aip.mymoviesdatabase
app_1    229  30    99520  16676  ffffffff  afe0d4a4  S com.android.inputmethod.latin
app_25   266  30    105428 18072  ffffffff  afe0d4a4  S com.manning.aip.lifecycle  ◁━━━
root     275  38    740    312    c003b100  afe0d14c  S /system/bin/sh
root     276  275   884    316    00000000  afe0c27c  R ps
# █
```

Figure 3.2 The output of the `ps` command from the ADB shell shows the currently running processes.

As you can see in figure 3.2, the `ps` command provides a good deal of information about the running processes. You can check the `ps` documentation for information about optional switches to control the output, and the meaning of all the columns it can display. The main things you'll want to note here are user ID (column 1), process ID (column 2), and name (column 8). For the most part, the user IDs are *app_n*, where *n* is incremented for each application. (Some special built in applications use special user IDs, such as *radio* for the phone, or *system* for settings.) And, the process names are the names of the application packages.

CHOOSING WHICH PROCESSES GET THE AX

The Android platform does its best to keep every application process around as long as it can. It can't keep everything around forever, because resources are limited. So, when it's time to start killing off processes, how does it decide which to keep and which to kill? It uses a five-level hierarchy, as seen in table 3.1.

Table 3.1   The five levels the Android platform uses to prioritize processes

Process status	Description	Priority
Foreground	A process that's running an `Activity` that the user is interacting with, hosting a `Service` that's bound to an `Activity` that the user is interacting with, hosting a `Service` that's executing one of its lifecycle methods, or is hosting a `BroadcastReceiver` that's executing.	1
Visible	A process that isn't used by the foreground, but is still hosting an `Activity` that can affect what's shown on the screen, or hosting a `Service` that's bound to another visible `Activity`.	2
Service	A process that's hosting a `Service` started with the `startService` method (and doesn't meet the criteria for foreground or visible by any other means).	3
Background	A process that's hosting an `Activity` that has been stopped. Many such processes may exist, and they're kept in an LRU list.	4
Empty	A process that doesn't host any current application components.	5

Android tries to make sure the highest-priority components, as defined by the hierarchy in table 3.1, are kept around, and it allows other processes to be killed to reclaim system resources. One notable thing about the way the platform uses the hierarchy is that a process hosting a `Service` is ranked higher than one hosting any background activities. This means for long-running background tasks, you should favor a `Service` (we'll learn about services in chapter 5).

> **Other component lifecycles**
>
> Much like `Activity` components, `BroadcastReceiver`, `Service`, and `ContentProvider` components are also tied to the main application's process (by default). Even though they use the same process, these components have a different lifecycle (with different methods). `BroadcastReceiver` is simple; it exists during the `onReceive` method it defines, and that's it. `Service` has its own more involved lifecycle we'll see in chapter 5, and we'll discuss `ContentProvider` in chapter 8.

FINE-TUNING PROCESS SETTINGS

Though the process arrangement we've described here is typical, it's not always the case. In advanced situations, if you need to, you can fine-tune the knobs and dials to control the setup. You can set the process that your application should run under, and you can optionally control the process that each component runs in.

These are advanced settings, and we don't want to get too far off track here, but you should be aware that you can choose to either run multiple applications in the same process, under the same user ID, or run a single application under multiple processes. Android has sensible and easy-to-use defaults, but it also gives you full control. To change the process, you set the `android:process` attribute in the manifest (which can be applied to applications and individual components).

Now, why might you want to manipulate these settings? If you want to run multiple applications and easily access the same files (or other resources, such as database), and still keep things private from other applications, you could run in the same process. Alternatively, if you want to do super multitasking, and you want to take on the responsibility to manage it correctly, you could run each activity in its own process. (we'll learn about services in chapter 5).

Knowing the way that system-level elements such as user IDs and processes affect your Android application comes in handy, but the components themselves also have their own lifecycles. Understanding `Activity` lifecycle is one of the most important, and unfortunately potentially most confusing, aspects of Android development.

3.2 Knowing the Activity lifecycle

Much like processes, activities don't get to hang around forever and suck up memory and CPU cycles. Even within a process, with multiple activities associated to the same application, some activities will be in the foreground and others won't. Those in the foreground, the ones the user is working with, get the priority. Other activities may be stopped when the platform needs to reclaim resources (or killed if the process hosting them is itself killed, based on the hierarchy we discussed in the previous section).

Users aren't supposed to notice any of the process and activity swapping that the platform does. To them the entire workflow of any task they want to perform should be seamless. If some activities are created new, and some are restored from an inactive state, the user doesn't care and shouldn't notice.

To developers, it's more complicated. We get stuck with the bill of knowing when to create and destroy resources, and how to maintain state as our activities are constantly created, destroyed, and recreated. It's our job, with the help of the framework Android provides, to make things appear seamless, and to keep our activities responsive and well behaved at the same time. This is where it's key to understand the `Activity` lifecycle phases and methods.

3.2.1 Lifecycle phases and methods

To tackle this, we'll begin with the big picture, the lifetime phases, and then we'll discuss the most important lifecycle methods. Activities have three nested lifetime phases:

- Entire lifetime (created to destroyed)
- Visible lifetime (restarted to stopped)
- Foreground lifetime (resumed to paused)

These lifetime phases correspond to relative importance to the system, and allow logical points to hook in and create, use, or destroy resources (views, system services, database cursors, network requests, and more). First, the *entire lifetime* phase is the super set. This encompasses everything from the time an `Activity` is created until it's destroyed. Next, the *visible phase*, is where an `Activity` is onscreen and can be seen, but it might not yet be in the foreground (it may be in transition, or it may be behind another floating `Activity`). Finally the *foreground phase* is the most important: this is where an `Activity` is interacting with a user.

To control the transition through these phases and manage the setup and tear down of resources, we'll use *lifecycle methods*. We've already worked with a few of these (such as `onCreate` and `onPause`), and you're no doubt at least vaguely familiar with them, but here we'll spell them out more because using these methods correctly is essential to building robust Android applications. The most important of these methods are seen in table 3.2 (which is taken directly from the Android documentation).

Table 3.2   Lifecycle methods

Method	Description	Killable	Next
onCreate	Called when the activity is first created. This is where you should do all of your normal static setup: create views, bind data to lists, and so on. This method also provides you with a `Bundle` containing the activity's previously frozen state, if there was one. Always followed by `onStart`.	No	onStart
onRestart	Called after your activity has been stopped, prior to it being started again. Always followed by `onStart`	No	onStart
onStart	Called when the activity is becoming visible to the user. Followed by `onResume` if the activity comes to the foreground, or `onStop` if it becomes hidden.	No	onResume or onStop
onResume	Called when the activity will start interacting with the user. At this point your activity is at the top of the activity stack, with user input going to it. Always followed by `onPause`.	No	onPause
onPause	Called when the system is about to start resuming a previous activity. This is typically used to commit unsaved changes to persistent data, stop animations and other things that may be consuming CPU, and so on. Implementations of this method must be quick because the next activity will not be resumed until this method returns. Followed by either `onResume` if the activity returns to the front, or `onStop` if it becomes invisible to the user.	Pre-Honeycomb	onResume or onStop

Table 3.2 Lifecycle methods *(continued)*

Method	Description	Killable	Next
onStop	Called when the activity is no longer visible to the user, because another activity has been resumed and is covering this one. This may happen either because a new activity is being started, an existing one is being brought in front of this one, or this one is being destroyed. Followed by either onRestart if this activity is coming back to interact with the user, or onDestroy if this activity is going away.	Yes	onRestart or onDestroy
onDestroy	The final call you receive before your activity is destroyed. This can happen either because the activity is finishing (someone called finish on it, or because the system is temporarily destroying this instance of the activity to save space. You can distinguish between these two scenarios with the isFinishing method.	Yes	nothing

Though we generally will try to avoid repeating information from the Android documentation, table 3.2 is an intentional exception. The Activity lifecycle methods are a big source of potential confusion, and this information is a key reference. Table 3.2 shows where the lifetime phases stop and start, along with a quick description of what each lifecycle method does, whether each method is killable, and the order of the methods.

To add a bit more to the descriptions of the most common lifecycle methods you'll override and to provide some notes, we've included table 3.3.

Table 3.3 The most commonly overridden Activity **lifecycle methods, when they're invoked, and what you'll typically use them for**

Method	When invoked	When to override	Description/Notes
onCreate	Invoked when an Activity isn't around in any form, and must be initially created.	You'll always override onCreate (making sure to call the super method, which is true for all overridden lifecycle methods).	This is where all initialization code should be placed. If it's the first time an Activity has been started, it won't have any saved instance state (the Bundle passed to it will be null). If an Activity was previously destroyed and is being restarted, it may have state (the Bundle will be what was last saved in onSaveInstanceState).

Table 3.3   The most commonly overridden `Activity` lifecycle methods, when they're invoked, and what you'll typically use them for *(continued)*

Method	When invoked	When to override	Description/Notes
onResume	Invoked when an `Activity` has come to the foreground and will start interacting with the user.	It's common to override `onResume` to update views, but it shouldn't be used to reinstantiate components. This is where you might refresh views based on a web service call to retrieve data that may have changed in between the time the `Activity` was stopped and resumed.	When this method is called, it means the `Activity` is being displayed and handling user events. This is the last nonkillable method in the lifecycle.
onPause	Invoked when an `Activity` is going to the background, but hasn't been killed yet.	You'll often override `onPause`. This is where you'll clean up anything your `Activity` has created.	This is where you'll store *global persistent state*, or state that relates to the task/application that outlives the `Activity` instance (data that needs to be saved in files or databases, and so on). This is also where you'll want to release any resources. For example, this is where you'll often unregister intent receivers, unbind services, remove location and sensor listeners, stop background threads, and so on.

The three methods you'll use most commonly are the ones we've noted in table 3.2: onCreate, onResume, and onPause. Still, as we've seen from figure 3.3, these aren't the only `Activity` lifecycle methods. Some of the others, such as onStart, onStop, and onDestroy, can be useful if you need more fine-grained control.

Now that we know what these methods are, and have an overview of what they do, let's take a look at a real example that reinforces these concepts.

3.2.2   *The lifecycle in action*

To get a more concrete idea of what causes an `Activity` to move through the lifecycle methods—when it's paused and resumed versus when it's killed—we're going to walk through an example that will log and notify us at each stage. Then, we'll poke and prod it and see what happens. Doing so will show us how activities are placed in a stack. It'll also allow us to see firsthand what happens when an `Activity` is initially launched, and then what happens when the Back or Home key is pressed. Also, we'll discuss killing the process that hosts the `Activity` to simulate the system reclaiming resources and doing the same.

The application we'll build to do this contains an abstract parent `Activity` that logs and optionally issues a `Notification` message for each lifecycle method that occurs. We'll extend this `Activity` with three others so we can explore the lifecycle

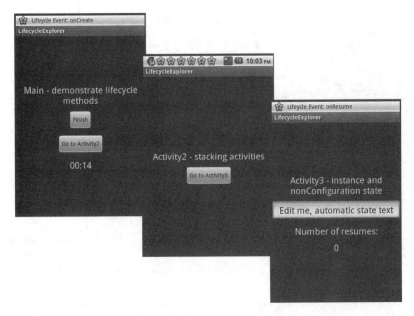

Figure 3.3 The three LifecycleExplorer activities display lifecycle method events as notifications, stack activities, and work with instance state.

methods, see how the stack responds, and later work with instance state. The completed application, which we'll call LifecycleExplorer, is seen in figure 3.3.

The LifecycleExplorer `Activity` screens can be accurately described as sparse and ugly, but that's okay. Here we're focusing on function over form. The first screen, `Main`, includes a few simple UI elements and buttons to go to the next `Activity` or finish the current one. The second screen, `Activity2`, is a placeholder in the `Activity` stack. The third screen, `Activity3`, we'll use later in the next section to work with instance state.

GRAB THE PROJECT: LIFECYCLEEXPLORER You can get the source code for this project, and or the packaged APK to run it, at the *Android in Practice* code website. Because some code listings here are shortened to focus on specific concepts, we recommend that you download the complete source code and follow along within Eclipse (or your favorite IDE or text editor).

Source: http://mng.bz/Hbuq, APK File: http://mng.bz/vUQO

The important part of the LifecycleExplorer `Main` screen isn't what it displays so much as how we can visualize the lifecycle methods with the notifications it generates, as seen in figure 3.4.

The notifications that LifecycleExplorer generates, as seen in figure 3.4, show the class name, method name, and a timestamp. When we initially launch the application,

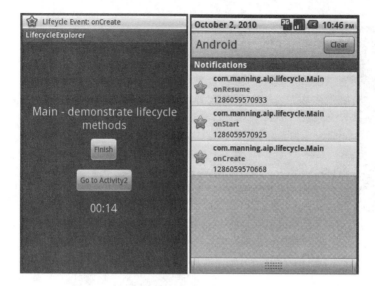

**Figure 3.4
The LifecycleExplorer
Main Activity screen
generates notifications.**

which invokes the Main Activity, we see that onCreate, onStart, and onResume are
involved. Here's the code for this screen.

Listing 3.1 The Main.java Activity of LifecycleExplorer overriding the lifecycle methods

```
public class Main extends LifecycleActivity {                    Extend
                                                              1  LifecycleActivity
    private Button finish;
    private Button activity2;
    private Chronometer chrono;

    @Override
    public void onCreate(Bundle savedInstanceState) {            Override
        super.onCreate(savedInstanceState);                     onCreate to
        setContentView(R.layout.main);                          instantiate
        finish = (Button) findViewById(R.id.finishButton);      resources
        finish.setOnClickListener(new OnClickListener() {    2
            public void onClick(View v) {
                finish();
            }
        });
        activity2 = (Button) findViewById(R.id.activity2Button);
        activity2.setOnClickListener(new OnClickListener() {
            public void onClick(View v) {
                startActivity(new Intent(Main.this,             Start Activity2
                    Activity2.class));                       3  via Intent
            }
        });
        chrono = (Chronometer) findViewById(R.id.chronometer);
    }

    @Override
    protected void onResume() {                         Override onResume to
        super.onResume();                            4  reset when resuming
```

```
      chrono.setBase(SystemClock.elapsedRealtime());
      chrono.start();
  }

  @Override
  protected void onPause() {                          ◁──┐   Override onPause
      chrono.stop();                                     ❺   to clean up
      super.onPause();
  }
}
```

For the Main screen, we first extend LifecycleActivity ❶. We'll see the code for that class, which sends the notifications, next. After that, we see the basic overriding pattern that we always use to manage an Activity class. We set up views in onCreate ❷, then we reset anything that needs to be reset in onResume ❹, and we cleanup in onPause ❺. To demonstrate something you might stop when pausing and reset when resuming, we're using a Chronometer widget. This is a fancy TextView that counts seconds. We don't want this to keep counting while our Activity is paused. We admit it's a contrived example, but we want to keep this simple. More realistically you'll do things such as update data in onResume, and you'll save data and release resources like listeners in onPause.

The only other notable thing here is that we include a Button to fire an Intent to take us to the second screen in the application, Activity2 ❸. There isn't any special code in Activity2, just a TextView and Button as we saw in figure 3.5, so we'll skip the code (though you can browse or download the complete application). We include Activity2 so that we can have several activities in the stack to see how the Back key works in a moment.

The next part of the LifecycleExplorer code we want to look at is the LifecycleActivity we're extending (which could be extended by any Activity). The following listing generates the logging and notifications for the lifecycle methods.

Listing 3.2 The LifecycleActivity.java class sends Notifications for each lifecycle method

```
public abstract class LifecycleActivity extends Activity {

   private static final String LOG_TAG = "LifecycleExplorer";

   private NotificationManager notifyMgr;
   private boolean enableNotifications;
  private final String className;

   public LifecycleActivity() {
      super();
      this.className = this.getClass().getName();
   }

   public LifecycleActivity(final boolean enableNotifications) {
      this();
      this.enableNotifications = enableNotifications;
   }

   @Override
```

```
public void onCreate(Bundle savedInstanceState) {                    ◁─────┐
    super.onCreate(savedInstanceState);
    notifyMgr = (NotificationManager)
        getSystemService(Context.NOTIFICATION_SERVICE);
    debugEvent("onCreate");
}

@Override
protected void onStart() {                                           ◁─────┤
    debugEvent("onStart");
    super.onStart();
}

@Override
protected void onResume() {                                          ◁─────┤
    debugEvent("onResume");                                          ◁─────┤
    super.onResume();
}

@Override
protected void onPause() {                                           ◁─────┘
    debugEvent("onPause");
    super.onPause();
}

    // remainder of lifecycle methods, such as onStop,
    // onDestroy, and more
    // omitted for brevity - they do the same thing as previous:
    // debug, super

private void debugEvent(final String method) {
    long ts = System.currentTimeMillis();
    Log.d(LOG_TAG, " *** " + method + " " + className + " " + ts);
    if (enableNotifications) {
        Notification notification =
            new Notification(android.R.drawable.star_big_on,
                "Lifecycle Event: " + method, 0L);
        RemoteViews notificationContentView =
            new RemoteViews(getPackageName(),
                R.layout.custom_notification_layout);
        notification.contentView = notificationContentView;
        notification.contentIntent =
            PendingIntent.getActivity(this, 0, null, 0);
        notification.flags |= Notification.FLAG_AUTO_CANCEL;
        notificationContentView.setImageViewResource(
            R.id.image, android.R.drawable.btn_star);
        notificationContentView.setTextViewText(
            R.id.lifecycle_class, getClass().getName());
        notificationContentView.setTextViewText(
            R.id.lifecycle_method, method);
        notificationContentView.setTextColor(
            R.id.lifecycle_method, R.color.black);
        notificationContentView.setTextViewText(
            R.id.lifecycle_timestamp, Long.toString(ts));
        notifyMgr.notify((int) System.currentTimeMillis(), notification);
    }
}
}
```

❶ Each lifecycle method invokes debugEvent

❷ debugEvent logs at debug level and sends Notification

The `LifecycleActivity` includes an override for each `Activity` lifecycle method. Inside these it calls the local `debugEvent` method with the method name ❶. The `debugEvent` method itself logs the method name, class name, and a time stamp at the debug level, and optionally sends a `Notification` with the same information (you can use `logcat` to see the output, which is faster, or view the notifications in the UI) ❷. The notification details are included here for completeness, but aren't part of the scope of this example (we'll learn more about notifications when we work with services in chapter 5).

Now that we've seen how simple this is and we know how it works, it's time to put our `Main` `Activity` through its paces. First, recall from figure 3.4 that launching our `Activity` the first time resulted in `onCreate`, `onStart`, and `onResume` being invoked, in that order. What happens if we press the Home or Back keys? After trying it, we get the notifications shown in figure 3.5.

Curiously, as we can see from figure 3.6, pressing Home or Back (after clearing previous notifications and restarting our VM) results in a different lifecycle path. When we press Home we see that the path is `onSaveInstanceState`, `onPause`, `onStop`. Instance state, which we'll discuss in the next section, is what's passed in the `Bundle` to `onCreate` if our `Activity` is ever destroyed by the system and then resumed. The `onSaveInstanceState` method does the saving. It's not a true lifecycle method, but it's related and important, so for now we've included a `Notification` for it as well. The path for Back is `onPause`, `onStop`, `onDestroy`.

Why does Back not save the instance state and end up destroying the `Activity`, whereas Home saves the instance state and doesn't destroy the `Activity`? The default behavior of the Back key is to pop the current `Activity` off of the activity stack by calling the `finish` method, which destroys it without saving any state. If an `Activity` is finished, it doesn't need to save state (it's done). Home, on the other hand, doesn't finish the `Activity`; it moves it to the background at the top of the activity stack.

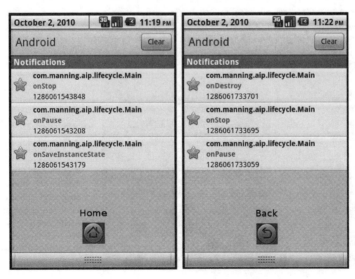

Figure 3.5 The lifecycle methods fired when pressing the Home and Back keys respectively.

> ### The activity stack
>
> As users navigate from one activity to the next, each activity is pushed onto a linear stack known as the *activity stack*. Users can go back to previous activities, which will pop the current activity off the stack and resume the previous one, by using the Back key. The home screen (Launcher) is the end of the stack. We'll talk more about the activity stack in section 3.4 when we discuss tasks.

The activity stack can be confusing at times, but it's how the platform can easily keep track of where the user has been and allow them to go back to the previous `Activity`. It's a great feature for users. We can see more of how this works by pressing the Go to Activity2 button from our `Main Activity` and navigating to `Activity2`, as seen in figure 3.6.

When we press Go to Activity2, the `Main Activity` isn't destroyed. Instead it goes through `onSaveInstanceState`, `onPause`, and `onStop` (like when we pressed Home), and ends up in the background. At the same time, `Activity2` is created (`onCreate`, `onStart`, `onResume`) and then displayed. At this point (at the `Activity2` screen) if we press Back, `Activity2` is destroyed, and then `Main` is what's left at the top of the stack, so it's resumed from the lifecycle event notifications as seen in figure 3.7.

So those scenarios demonstrate the happy path. They show how the stack works, what happens when an `Activity` is initially created, when it's resumed, and when it's destroyed with `finish`. What happens when we get off that path and into the weeds? What happens when memory is low and the process hosting an `Activity` is killed? There are several ways you can find out. You can log in to the `adb` shell and kill the process of the application, or you can use `ddms` to halt the target VM.

In either case, the `Activity` has to make it to the `onResume` method before it can be killed (or it wouldn't have shown up anyway). Once there, the process can be killed at

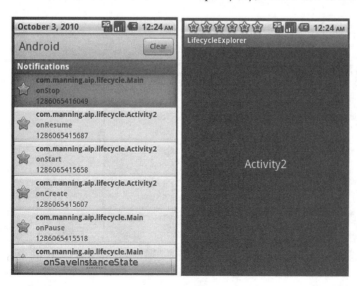

Figure 3.6 Navigating from `Main` **to** `Activity2` **in the LifecycleExplorer application shows the lifecycle events that are invoked for each** `Activity`.

any point. To describe this in fine Yogi Berra style, you'll only get as far as you've gotten. Combining this knowledge with an understanding of which items the Android system kills first when it needs to reclaim resources (see table 3.1) will help you identify where activities will typically be killed. Background activities are on the chopping block first, and by definition they'll have gotten to onStop. Visible but non-foreground activities are next, and they've already been to onPause.

Speaking of the rough patches off of the happy path, the final thing we need to address with regard to Activity and lifecycle is what happens on configuration changes.

Figure 3.7 Pressing the Back key displays the lifecycle events when navigating from Activity2 back to Main.

3.2.3 Configuration changes

The Configuration class defines all of the device configuration information that's returned to an application in the form of resources. This includes information about hardware configuration, device orientation, screen size, locale settings, and more. Some configuration elements rarely change at runtime, such as the locale of the device. Others, such as orientation, happen frequently.

A special gotcha to look out for with Android is that by default, when a Configuration change occurs, Android destroys and recreates the current Activity. Because orientation changes (portrait versus landscape) are a type of configuration change, this means a lot of tearing down and re-creating activities. Whenever a user tilts the phone, or slides out the keyboard (depending on the device, and settings), this occurs.

To see this happen, try rotating the screen while running our sample Lifecycle-Explorer application. To rotate the screen in the emulator, you can press CTRL+F11 on your keyboard. If you do this, you can easily see the lifecycle path from the log output using logcat (adb logcat from the command line or from Eclipse Window -> Show View -> Android -> Logcat), as shown in figure 3.8.

On a configuration change, an Activity goes from onPause to onDestroy, and then from onCreate to onResume. Additionally, instance state is saved and restored (onSaveInstanceState and onRestoreInstanceState). This is significant. Activities aren't paused and resumed, because they can't be. The configuration is different. They need to restart to respond to any potential differences. But, they do get to hold on to the instance state, and restarting should be fast (not noticeable to users). We'll talk about instance state and special nonconfiguration instance data in the next section, but the point to take away here is that activities *will* be created/destroyed/recreated frequently.

Understanding the Activity lifecycle and the stack of activities is the key to a responsive and robust Android application. You can create well-behaved activities by

```
D/LifecycleExplorer( 266): *** onCreate com.manning.aip.lifecycle.Main 1300820501730
D/LifecycleExplorer( 266): *** onStart com.manning.aip.lifecycle.Main 1300820501988
D/dalvikvm(   52): GC freed 9620 objects / 727664 bytes in 176ms
D/LifecycleExplorer( 266): *** onRestoreInstanceState com.manning.aip.lifecycle.Main 1300820502196
D/LifecycleExplorer( 266): *** onResume com.manning.aip.lifecycle.Main 1300820502208
D/dalvikvm(   52): GC freed 4030 objects / 219792 bytes in 97ms
I/WindowManager(   52): Setting rotation to 1, animFlags=1
I/WindowManager(   52): onOrientationChanged, rotation changed to 1
I/WindowManager(   52): Config changed: { scale=1.0 imsi=0/0 loc=en_US touch=3 keys=2/1/1 nav=3 orien=2 layout=18}
D/LifecycleExplorer( 266): *** onSaveInstanceState com.manning.aip.lifecycle.Main 1300820506548
D/LifecycleExplorer( 266): *** onPause com.manning.aip.lifecycle.Main 1300820506559
D/LifecycleExplorer( 266): *** onStop com.manning.aip.lifecycle.Main 1300820506597
D/LifecycleExplorer( 266): *** onRetainNonConfigurationInstance com.manning.aip.lifecycle.Main 1300820507097
D/LifecycleExplorer( 266): *** onDestroy com.manning.aip.lifecycle.Main 1300820507107
D/LifecycleExplorer( 266): *** onCreate com.manning.aip.lifecycle.Main 1300820507137
D/StatusBar(   52): updateResources
D/LifecycleExplorer( 266): *** onStart com.manning.aip.lifecycle.Main 1300820507375
D/LifecycleExplorer( 266): *** onRestoreInstanceState com.manning.aip.lifecycle.Main 1300820507394
D/LifecycleExplorer( 266): *** onResume com.manning.aip.lifecycle.Main 1300820507403
```

Figure 3.8   A logcat output demonstration of the lifecycle methods an activity undergoes after an orientation change

> **Controlling configuration change settings**
>
> If you don't want your `Activity` to be destroyed and recreated in its entirety when a configuration change occurs, you can set the `android:configChanges` attribute in the manifest. This allows you to list the individual types of configuration changes you'll have the `Activity` handle itself. It's good to be aware of this advanced setting, but you generally shouldn't use this as a substitute for correctly handling configuration changes and properly passing instance state (you don't want to fight the framework).

knowing the `Activity` lifecycle phases and methods and understanding where to create and destroy resources (and also not to leave things like static references hanging around). The next important part of working with activities and the lifecycle is knowing how to handle instance state and getting your activities to resume with it intact.

3.3   *Controlling Activity instance state*

If you've ever filled out a web form and then submitted it, only to have all of your form fields cleared because of one failed validation, you know how frustrating it can be to use an application that doesn't manage and restore state. It's maddening. Now, take that same scenario and magnify it by putting it on a mobile platform, pecking out a lot of data on a small virtual keyboard, and accidentally rotating the device. What, where did my data go?

What if it's an Android application and it loses the data it had for a large `ListView` and starts to re-retrieve the data from the network? Ouch, that's expensive, and it's sucking battery juice. Or, more subtly, what if the application still has the `ListView` data but it's 1,000 items long and it loses its place and drops the user back to the top? Ugh.

Fortunately you can prevent these types of issues and maintain a smooth and sane user experience if you know a bit about how to manage instance state in your Android activities.

3.3.1 Saving and restoring instance state

Instance state can be a confusing topic, so we'll start with some clarification of terms. *Instance state* refers to the state your activities need to reset themselves to where the user left off. This means things like current nonsubmitted form values, selections, the index in a ListView, and so on. Instance state doesn't mean information that should persist like the entire list of choices in a form, or your contacts, or your application preferences. Those things are *persistent state*. So we have two types of state:

- *Instance state*—Lives as long as the instance of your Activity
- *Persistent state*—Outlives your Activity (files, preferences, database, network)

The confusing part here is that by instance, Android doesn't mean the exact same Java instance. Instead, Android is referring to a new instance of the same object type with the same stuff so that it seems to the user like the same instance. Here's the key: instance state is saved whenever the system, and not you, destroys your Activity, as follows:

- *Instance state saved*—System destroys an Activity (config change or otherwise)
- *Instance state NOT saved*—finish is called (default for Back key)

Armed with that knowledge, Activity behaviors you've seen or troubleshoot before might make more sense. We touched on this in our discussion of the Back and Home keys in section 3.2, but the onSaveInstanceState method is what the system will use to try to save instance state. It calls this when a configuration change occurs, or any other time it's forced to destroy your Activity (if it can; if the memory situation is critical, it may not be able to get around to saving instance state). Instance state is saved in a Bundle. This is a package of Parcelable (interprocess passable) data that can include primitives, strings, and arrays of the same. (Other Parcelable types can be passed too, but these are beyond our scope for now.)

The system will save reasonable defaults for instance state, but you can override onSaveInstanceState and either take over or supplement it. For example, for each View the system will call through to View.onSaveInstanceState. This means Edit-Text elements will keep their contents and will be restored automatically, and so on.

Things are restored either in onCreate, which takes a Bundle as input, or in onRestoreInstanceState. The most common way to restore values is to use onCreate, but onRestoreInstanceState can be used if you want to separate this function from the initialization of other components.

To get an idea of how all of this creating, saving, destroying, and restoring, works, let's go back to our sample application and try a few things. For this we'll first look at the code for Activity3, which dabbles in instance state, as seen in the following listing.

Listing 3.3 The Activity3.java class saves and restores state

```
public class Activity3 extends LifecycleActivity {

    private static final String COUNT_KEY = "cKey";

    private TextView numResumes;
```

```
    private int count;                                    ┌──  Include class
                                                          ❶   instance variable
    @Override
    public void onCreate(Bundle savedInstanceState) {
        super.onCreate(savedInstanceState);
        setContentView(R.layout.activity3);
        numResumes = (TextView) findViewById(R.id.numResumes);
    }

    @Override
    protected void onResume() {
        super.onResume();
        numResumes.setText(String.valueOf(count));        ┌──  Set number of
        count++;                                          ❷   resumes to count
    }

    @Override
    protected void onRestoreInstanceState(Bundle savedInstanceState) {
        if ((savedInstanceState != null) &&
            savedInstanceState.containsKey(COUNT_KEY)) {
            count = savedInstanceState.getInt(COUNT_KEY);       Override
        }                                             onRestoreInstanceState ❸
        super.onRestoreInstanceState(savedInstanceState);
    }

    @Override
    protected void onSaveInstanceState(Bundle outState) {     ❹  Override onSave-
        outState.putInt(COUNT_KEY, count);                        InstanceState
        super.onSaveInstanceState(outState);
    }
}
```

The first interesting thing we start out with in the `Activity3` class in listing 3.3 is the count instance variable ❶. We use this inside `onResume` to set the value of a `TextView` to the count ❷. Because this overall application is dealing with lifecycle, we're using this example to keep track of how many times this activity has been resumed.

To maintain this instance variable even when our Java instance is destroyed and re-instantiated, we have to implement the instance state methods. We use `onSave-InstanceState` to store the count in the `Bundle` created ❹, and we use `onRestore-InstanceState` ❸ to retrieve the same `Bundle` and reestablish the previous count. Obviously, this is a simple example, but if we didn't do this our count would never show more than 0 (it would be cleared when the `Activity` is destroyed, and wouldn't be updated when paused and resumed). By going to `Activity3` and then rotating the screen (which causes a configuration change that destroys and recreates the `Activity`), we can demonstrate that this works as seen in figure 3.9.

As we can see in figure 3.9, our `Activity` was destroyed and then recreated after an orientation change. Still, it was able to maintain the previous text value we set for an `EditText` automatically, and it was able to keep track of its previous internal count state as well. This all went smoothly, and the user didn't lose any information or have to re-enter any values because we used `onSaveInstanceState` and `onRestoreInstanceState`.

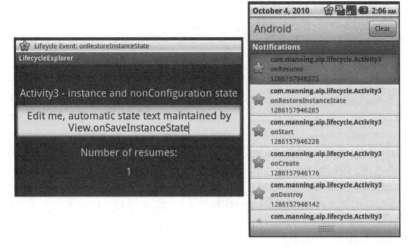

Figure 3.9 The `Activity3` screen shows the instance count has been maintained, and the lifecycle- and instance state-related methods involved via notifications.

Before we leave the discussion of instance state, there's one more special type of instance state you may find useful that goes even further: the potentially confusingly named nonconfiguration instance state.

3.3.2 Using nonconfiguration instance state

Nonconfiguration instance state refers to any extensive state you need to pass from the current instance of an `Activity` to its future self that will be created as the result of a configuration change. This special optimization Android can be incredibly useful at times. The caveat is that it applies *only* to the current instance, and the one that's created immediately after that previous instance is destroyed and recreated.

So how does this work, and what data can you pass? In the following listing, we've added the related code to the LifecycleExplorer `Activity3` class so we can see it firsthand.

Listing 3.4 Adding code to an `Activity` to work with nonconfiguration instance state

```
. . .
@Override
public void onCreate(Bundle savedInstanceState) {         Retrieve ❶
    super.onCreate(savedInstanceState);                  nonconfig
    setContentView(R.layout.activity3);                    state
    numResumes = (TextView) findViewById(R.id.numResumes);

    Date date = (Date) this.getLastNonConfigurationInstance();
    if (date != null) {
        Toast.makeText(this, "\"LastNonConfiguration\" object present: "
            + date, Toast.LENGTH_LONG).show();          Show previous
    }                                                 ❷ data, if present
}
```

```
. . .

@Override
public Object onRetainNonConfigurationInstance() {
    return new Date();
}
}
```

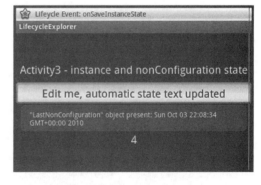 Save nonconfig
❸ state

Inside a revised onCreate method for Activity3, we see that we're grabbing an Object from the getLastNonConfigurationInstance method ❶. Specifically we're casting the Object to a Date, and then displaying it with a Toast ❷, but the important thing here is you can use whatever you want. This isn't a primitive or a special Android Parcelable type anymore; it's a plain old Object. Here we could cast to an image, Thread, Map, or to our own bean that contains all of the above—anything we want.

That is, anything that we've explicitly made available to getLastNonConfigurationInstance by putting it in onRetainNonConfigurationInstance. In this case, when we override that method, we return the Date ❸. Android will map the data from the current instance of your Activity to the next instance of the same Activity class that's immediately recreated.

> **Big Fat Warning**
>
> Even though you can put any type of Object into nonconfiguration instance state, you need to be careful not to ever retain anything that holds a strong reference back to the Activity that's about to be destroyed (a View, an entire Adapter, and so on). If you do, the Activity can't be completely destroyed, and you'll have a memory leak (you'll keep creating instances that can't be destroyed).

After we add the code in listing 3.4, we can relaunch the LifecycleExplorer application, navigate to Activity3, and rotate the screen. Doing so will then trigger a configuration change and show us that the Date gets passed as nonconfiguration data, as seen in figure 3.10.

The great thing about nonconfiguration instance state is that it's flexible and fast. There are a few concerns though. First it only works for the current-to-immediate-next Activity, so you can't use it haphazardly (it's an optimization, but can't be solely relied upon). And you have to be careful not to pass things such as strings, drawables, or any other resource that could change on a configuration change. After all, we're talking about "nonconfiguration" related state.

Figure 3.10 Passing nonconfiguration state from the current Activity to the immediately created instance of the same class, as a state optimization

With nonconfiguration state and regular instance state, you have some powerful tools for creating a seamless and nearly instantaneous user experience with Android activities. Next, to round out our lifecycle tour, we'll be focusing on groups of activities from one or more applications, also known as *tasks*.

3.4 Getting things done within a task

One additional concept in Android relates to processes, applications, and activities—the *task*. A task isn't something you instantiate via a Java object or define in the manifest; instead it's a framework concept that groups activities. This group is important because it relates closely to the activity stack and affects how users navigate groups of components.

3.4.1 Defining a task

We've already discussed the technical definition of a group of components in the same root package bundled into an APK file—that's an Android application. Still, as we noted previously, that's not what a user considers an application. To a user, an application consists of all of the activities they need to get something done. To Android this group of activities is a *task*.

One `Activity` always kicks off a task, and it's known as the *root activity*. Most of the time the root `Activity` is started via the Home screen (the Launcher application). From there, each `Activity` involved in the task is added to the task activity stack and the entire task is treated as a unit, as depicted in figure 3.11.

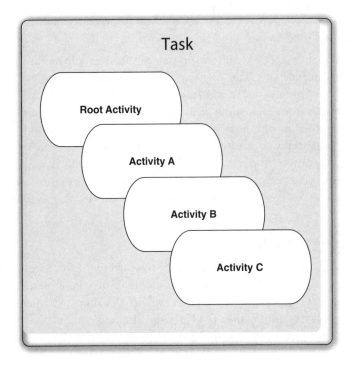

Figure 3.11 Diagram of a task and a stack of activities within it

Figure 3.12   **The recent tasks switcher shows the tasks a user can navigate back to displayed using the root activity's icon.**

Another way to see how activities are grouped into tasks—and to see the current running tasks on a device—is to long press on the Home key. This will bring up the Recent Tasks switcher, which shows an icon and name for each task, based on the root `Activity`, as seen in figure 3.12.

Beyond the root `Activity`, any other activities that are related to the application by being invoked via an `Intent` are (by default) placed on an activity stack *for that task*. We discussed an activity stack in section 3.2, and we saw how an activity can be pushed and popped from the stack. We've returned to this concept because multiple activity stacks are floating around, one for each task.

3.4.2   *Stacking activities within a task*

A group of related activities is a task, and within that group the activities are placed in a stack that the user can navigate. The user can push activities onto the task stack by starting them (using an application), and can pop them off with the Back key. When the user selects one task, the stack shows only activities related to that task—not all activities jumbled together in one large bunch. You can't go back through multiple tasks; that would be potentially confusing. Instead the navigation is per task.

Allowing parts of multiple applications to work together is extremely powerful. Grouping the different parts of multiple applications that are needed to accomplish an objective into a task makes them more manageable (and controls the activity stack navigation).

3.4.3   *Understanding activity task affinity*

Tasks provide powerful leverage for users, and they're convenient for developers too. We don't have to rewrite an activity that can send an email or take a picture; we can use the built-in applications via intents. When we do this, the activities that are invoked are linked with the application that invoked them as part of that task. The activities your application invokes are said to have an *affinity* to the task.

Much of the time you won't need to worry about controlling this affinity. If your application is started via the Launcher, the main `Activity` will start a new task (and run in a new process with its own user ID), and it'll be the root activity. Most other activities that are touched by your application will be associated with the task, and have affinity to it, automatically.

Affinity matters when you want fine-grained control. As usual, Android is willing to do the task/activity association for you, but it also allows you to step in and change the settings if you desire. Specifically, you can explicitly set the task affinity, change the launch mode behavior of activities (how they're related to tasks when launched via intents), control how and when the task/activity stack is retained or cleared, and more. For full details on these advanced settings you should check the current documentation.

Tasks are important because they're the final step in bringing together intents, applications, and activities, and they provide a logical grouping for navigation. Tasks are also the last part of our foray into the world of the lifecycle and state of Android applications.

3.5   Summary

Congratulations, you've conquered part 1 of *Android in Practice*, and you should now have a good background to prepare you for developing applications on Android!

Here we've focused on what an Android application is, and on the lifecycle of the `Activity`. Activities are the primary component of any Android application, and working within this lifecycle to control how components are created and destroyed is essential. Parallel to lifecycle, it's also critical to know how to maintain and restore instance state for activities. This can make or break the user experience. And it can be tricky to manage this in an environment that doesn't guarantee your application will run until you shut it down, and instead destroys and creates components on demand.

Another key thing we've discussed here is how Android groups activities together according to the user's *objective*, regardless of the applications involved, and treats them as a task. Tasks are important because they're logical navigation points for users, and they bring things full circle to with the stack of activities they contain.

These concepts—applications, activities, tasks, processes, and maintaining state—complete our final venture into building the foundation of your Android understanding. This chapter rounds out part one of the book, and is the final cornerstone of the basic information you'll need to get started with the more involved practical examples in parts 2 and 3 of the book.

Part 2

Real world recipes

In the second part of *Android in Practice*, you'll move beyond the basics and build many complete example applications that will cover, in depth, many of the most common application features and requirements. In chapter 4, you'll start with the user interface. This will cover resources and views, and additional concepts such as using styles and themes, and supporting different screen sizes. Chapter 5 will show you how to effectively multitask on Android using background services. Chapter 6 will continue the theme by presenting an overview of threads and concurrency including working with threads and handlers, asynchronous tasks, and more. Chapter 7 will then change gears to focus on storing data locally. Here, you'll use the file system, the internal and external storage, shared preferences, and a database. Chapter 8 will shift to sharing data between applications using content providers. Here, you'll both consume content from other applications, and learn how to create your own provider and expose data to others. Chapter 9 will take your data beyond the local device and delve into networking. Here, you'll learn how to cope with the instability that is inherent in mobile data connections, as well as how to work with HTTP and web services using JSON and XML. Chapter 10 will then navigate into location-based services and working with location providers. Here, you'll learn how to determine what providers are available and how to switch between them, and how to work with map based data and activities. Chapter 11 will bring in multimedia, where you'll work with audio and video, and learn a little about files, resources, and animation too. Chapter 12 will extend the animation and visual elements to teach you about 2D and 3D drawing, including working with the canvas, and using OpenGL.

Getting the pixels perfect 4

I don't know answers, I just do eyes. You Nexus, huh? I design your eyes.

—Blade Runner

This chapter is about all things visual. We'll see how views are laid out in a hierarchy and drawn to screen in several passes. We'll also explore more about the layout managers Android provides, and how layout parameters are applied. We'll then learn how to use themes and styles to customize an application, how to draw custom buttons and other window elements, and how to make user interfaces scale to different devices. Finally, most importantly, we'll see how to deal with common problems arising in all of these areas along the way. Be aware that this is one of the longest chapters in this book, but don't fret! It's also one of the most fundamental and widely applicable, so you'll find plenty of material here that'll make your Android developer life easier.

4.1   *The MyMovies application*

To carry us through the examples in this chapter, we'll be starting a new sample application, *MyMovies*. The DealDroid application we introduced in chapter 2 served us well to demonstrate most of Android's core elements, but in fairness wasn't the prettiest Droid to look at. Smartphone users are humans, not Androids, and humans are visual beings—we love a bit of bling in our applications! That's why this time around, we'll focus on presentation and deal less with functionality.

 GRAB THE PROJECT: MYMOVIES You can get the source code for this project, and/or the packaged APK to run it, at the *Android in Practice* code website. Because some code listings here are shortened to focus on specific concepts, we recommend that you download the complete source code and follow along within Eclipse (or your favorite IDE or text editor).

Source: http://mng.bz/7JxQ, APK File: http://mng.bz/26DZ

The task is to write a simple application that keeps track of your personal movie collection. To achieve that, we'll present the user with a list of movie titles, each of which can be flagged as *have* or *don't have* by tapping the list entry. As mentioned earlier, we'll keep it simple featurewise. In later chapters, we'll make it truly useful by extending the feature set introduced here. Using the example application, we'll learn how to create highly customized user interfaces, which not only work and scale well, but also look good. To whet your appetite, figure 4.1 shows a screen shot of the application you'll complete by the end of this chapter.

As you can see, the list of movies that are known to the application takes the majority of the screen. We'll accomplish this by using a `ListView` (which we met in chapter 2) that has been customized to add a translucent background and a gradient list selector with rounded corners that changes color when it's clicked. We've also added a background image and a title image that automatically scale with the screen width and orientation. These changes are by no means specific or limited to this particular application. Anything you learn in this chapter can be applied to your own applications. But first things first: let's make sure we understand what's happening under the hood when Android renders a user interface. Therefore, before discussing the MyMovies implementation, we'll discuss view rendering, layouts, and layout managers in detail.

Figure 4.1   The MyMovies application title screen. Note how we've customized the user interface to use features such as a translucent list selector.

4.2 View hierarchies and rendering

View rendering is an integral aspect of any application that involves a UI. We all love nifty-looking applications, but your application will spend a lot of time drawing its various interface elements. Therefore, it's important to understand what happens under the hood so you can avoid performance pitfalls. It's bad if your applications are beautiful, but slow. Though we've already introduced and used views, we're going to expand on their features. Specifically, we'll explain how they're organized, how they're drawn, and what sort of things you should keep an eye on in order to keep the UI snappy.

4.2.1 View hierarchies

We know that views in Android are typically defined in a declarative fashion using XML. XML structures information into trees; all nodes extend and branch from a single root node. It's no coincidence that Android employs this kind of representation, apart from XML's general popularity. Internally, the user interface of any Android application is represented as a tree of View objects. This is known as the *view hierarchy* or *view tree*. At the root of every view tree—and every application UI—sits a single DecorView. This is an internal framework class that you can't use directly; it represents the phone window you're currently looking at. The DecorView itself consists of a single LinearLayout, which branches into two FrameLayouts: one to hold the title section of the currently visible Activity, and one to holds its content (FrameLayouts block out an area on the screen to display a single item). *Content* here means anything that's defined in the current activity's layout XML. To illustrate, let's examine the XML layout for the MyMovies main screen (res/layout/main.xml):

```
<?xml version="1.0" encoding="utf-8"?>
<LinearLayout xmlns:android="http://schemas.android.com/apk/res/android"
    android:orientation="vertical"
    android:layout_width="fill_parent"
    android:layout_height="fill_parent">

    <ListView android:id="@android:id/list"
        android:layout_width="fill_parent"
        android:layout_height="fill_parent"
        />

</LinearLayout>
```

To understand how the hierarchy of view elements works for this screen, we'll use the *hierarchyviewer* tool that comes with the SDK. You can launch this tool either from the command line, or if you're using the latest version of the ADT, via the Hierarchy View perspective in Eclipse. Either method will connect to a running emulator instance or connected device and then present multiple options about your layouts. Figure 4.2 shows the view hierarchy for the main layout seen earlier.

The single dark box sitting in the center of figure 4.2 is the LinearLayout with which we began the XML file. As you can see from the hierarchy, LinearLayout has a FrameLayout parent for the content node (identified by the android.R.id.content resource ID). This is Android's way of representing the content area of the screen—the area

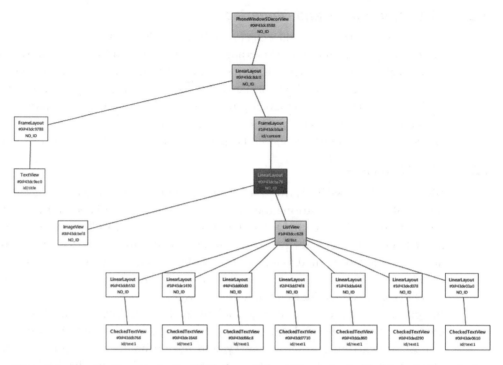

Figure 4.2 The view hierarchy for the MyMovies main layout created using the hierarchyviewer tool. The left branch represents the window's title bar, the right branch the current activity's contents.

which will make up most of your application's user interface. The majority of the time, you'll only be concerned with this branch—anything extending from the content node. The sibling `FrameLayout` for the title node (to the left) is also shown; this layout makes up the window's title bar. Underneath MyMovie's root `LinearLayout`, we see the `List-View` we defined in listing 4.1, which in turn has a child `LinearLayout` for each item in the list.

Whenever an `Activity` is started, its layout view tree is inserted into the application view tree by a call to the `Activity`'s `setContentView(int layoutId)`. This effectively replaces everything beneath the current content node with the view tree identified by `layoutId`, which, as we've seen, is a layout as defined in a layout XML file. The process of loading a layout and merging it into the current view tree is referred to as *layout inflation*. This is done by the `LayoutInflater` class, which resembles a tree growing in nature. Once in a while, a new branch grows, and from that branch grows another branch, and so on. Layouts aren't directly inflated from XML because Android converts XML into an efficient binary format before compilation (you'll learn about Android's build logic in chapter 14).

When a `View` has been inflated, it becomes part of the rendering chain, which means it can be drawn to the screen, unless it's obscured by another view. Android uses a two-pass algorithm to do that, which we're going to look at briefly now.

4.2.2 *View rendering*

Once a view tree is in memory, Android must draw it. Each view is responsible for drawing itself, but how the view is laid out and positioned on the screen can only be determined by looking at it as part of the whole tree. This is because the position of every view affects the position of the next. In order to figure out where to draw a view and how big it should be, Android must do the drawing in two separate passes: a *measure pass* and a *layout pass*.

MEASURE PASS

During the measure pass, each parent view must find out how big their child views want to be by calling their `measure` method. This includes pushing a measure specification object down the tree that contains the size restrictions imposed by a parent view on a child. Every child must then find out how big it wants to be, while still obeying these restrictions.

LAYOUT PASS

Once all views have been measured, the layout pass is entered. This time, each parent must position every child on the screen using the respective measurements obtained from the measure pass by calling their `layout` method. This process is illustrated in figure 4.3.

The layout and measuring of views happens transparently to the developer, unless you're implementing your own `View`, in which case you must override `onMeasure` and `onLayout` and hence actively take part in the rendering passes. Knowing about the complexity of view rendering makes one thing obvious: drawing views is expensive, especially if many views are involved and the view tree grows large. Unfortunately, your application will spend a fair amount of time in Android's drawing procedures. Views are invalidated and redrawn all the time, either because they're obscured by other views or they change state. There isn't much you can do about this, but what you *can* do is be aware of the overhead when writing your code and try to reduce unnecessary

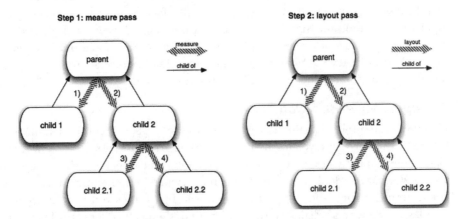

Figure 4.3 Views are rendered using a two-pass traversal of the view tree. Pass one collects dimension specifications (left); pass two does the positioning on the screen (right).

rendering. Table 4.1 lists some best practices for trying to optimize performance when working with views.

Table 4.1 **Best practices when working with Views**

Advice	Why
The cheapest View is the one that's never drawn	If a View is hidden by default, and only appears in reaction to a user interface event such as a tap/click, you may want to consider using a ViewStub instead (a placeholder view). You can also dynamically add/remove a view from the rendering chain by setting its visibility to View.GONE.
Avoid View cluttering	Along the lines of the previous advice, think twice about using a view and simplify your UI when you can. Doing so will keep screen layouts clean, and improve performance.
Try to reuse Views where possible	Often you can avoid extra inflation and drawing by caching and reusing views. This is important when rendering lists, where many items are displayed at once and state changes frequently (like when scrolling the list). The convertView and ViewHolder pattern can help here, and is covered in technique 1 of this chapter.
Avoid excessive nesting of layouts	Some developers use nested LinearLayouts to arrange elements relative to each other. Don't do that. The same result can usually be achieved by using a single RelativeLayout or TableLayout.
Avoid duplication	If you find yourself copying view definitions in order to use them in more than one layout, consider using the <include> tag instead. Similarly, nesting layouts of the same kind is in most cases useless duplication, and can be avoided using the <merge> tag.

View performance should always be on your mind when working with views and layouts. Some things may be obvious to you if you already have experience with Android, but we wouldn't have mentioned them if we didn't see applications violating these rules on a regular basis. A good idea is to always double-check your layouts for structural weaknesses using the layoutopt tool that ships with the SDK. It's by no means the only thing you should rely on, but it's fairly clever about finding smells in your layouts.

Mobile applications are all about user interaction: your application will likely spend most of its time in drawing its various interface elements and reacting to user input, so it's important that you have a solid understanding of what drives your UI. Now that we've seen how views and layouts are organized in memory, and what algorithms Android uses to measure and position views before it draws them on the screen, we'll next turn to more detail about layouts themselves.

4.3   *Arranging views in layouts*

Whenever you implement the user interface for an Activity, you're dealing with that Activity's *layout*. As we've already noted, layouts arrange views on screen. A layout is like a blueprint for a screen: it shows which elements the screen consists of, how they're arranged, what they look like, and so on. Hence, when implementing a screen for your application, thinking about layout is one of the first things you should do. Knowing your layout managers is crucial if you work with designers. You'll probably get mockups or wireframes for each screen, and you should know how to map a design to Android's layout managers.

> ### Layout versus Layout Manager
>
> When speaking of *layout,* we mean the set of all views for a single `Activity` as arranged by its layout XML file located in the `res/layout` folder. This is not to be confused with a certain layout class, called a *layout manager.* An `Activity`'s layout may involve more than one layout manager at a time, depending on its complexity. As we've already discussed, a layout manager is another `View` (a `ViewGroup` more precisely) that serves as a container and arranges views in a specific manner.

In the next section, we're going to give you a detailed rundown of general layout anatomy, plus a complete overview of the layout managers Android supports.

4.3.1 Layout anatomy

You've already seen several layouts at this point, such as the Hello Android layout from chapter 1 and the `DealList` layout from chapter 2. We've discussed the basics of these layouts, but we haven't specifically addressed which elements can be placed in layout files and how they're structured overall. We also haven't touched on the parameters and attributes layouts support. We'll look at these aspects now.

COMPOSITION OF LAYOUT FILES

Every layout file starts with an XML preamble, where you can define the file's encoding, typically UTF-8. Like any other XML document, a layout consists of a single root node with zero or more children, depending on whether the root node is a `View-Group`, which is the case for all layout managers, or a simple `View`, in which case it must be the only view defined in the layout. Node names correspond to class names, so you can put anything in a layout that's a concrete class inheriting from `android.view.View`. By default, class names are looked up in the `android.view` (`SurfaceView`, `ViewStub`, and so on) and `android.widget` (`TextView`, `ListView`, `Button`, and so on) packages. For other views that aren't part of the framework, such as those you define yourself, you have to use the fully qualified class name instead (such as `com.myapp.MyShinyView`). This becomes particularly important if you want to embed a Google Maps `MapView` (we'll learn about location and `MapView` in chapter 10). This class contains Google proprietary code and isn't distributed along with the core framework. Therefore, you have to use `MapView` using its fully qualified name:

```
<com.google.android.maps.MapView
    android:id="@+id/mapview"
    android:layout_width="fill_parent"
    android:layout_height="fill_parent"
    android:clickable="true"
    android:apiKey="Your Maps API Key"
/>
```

LAYOUT ATTRIBUTES AND PARAMETERS

Every `View` in a layout can take two different kinds of attributes: those that are specific to the view class and its parent classes, and those that are specific to the layout manager it's being placed into. Which attributes a view can take may be obtained from the view's documentation (or Eclipse's completion). A TextView, for instance, defines the android:text attribute, which allows you to define its default text value. It also understands the android:padding attribute, because that attribute is inherited from Android's View base class.

> **AVAILABLE VIEW ATTRIBUTES** You can look up all view attributes exposed by Android in one place in the documentation of the android.R.attr class.

Layout parameters are different: you can tell them apart from normal attributes by their layout_ prefix. They define how a View should be rendered while participating in the layout. Unlike normal attributes, which apply to the View directly, layout parameters are hints to the view's parent view in the layout, usually a layout manager. Don't confuse a view's parent *view* in a layout with a view's parent *class*; the former is a separate view in the layout in which the view is embedded, whereas the latter refers to the view's type hierarchy. All layout managers, and also some other views such as the Gallery widget, define their own layout parameters using an inner class called LayoutParams. All LayoutParams support the android:layout_width and android:layout_height attributes, and all layout manager parameters further support the android:layout_margin attributes.

> **MARGIN AND PADDING** Margin and padding can also be defined separately for each edge. In that case, define any of these attributes for a view:
>
> - android:layout_marginLeft
> - android:layout_marginTop
> - android:layout_marginRight
> - android:layout_marginBottom
>
> The same approach works for the android:padding attribute.

Any other parameters are specific to the various LayoutParams implementations found across the framework. The width and height parameters are special in two ways: they must *always* be present on any view or Android will throw an exception. Moreover, they can take not only numeric values (pixels), but also two reserved values:

- fill_parent—Indicates that the View would like to take up as much room as possible inside its parent view. It'll try to grow as big as its parent (minus padding and margins), regardless of how much room its own children occupy. If, for instance, the parent is a square of 100px and neither margins nor padding were defined, the child will be a square of 100px, too. Note that fill_parent has been deprecated and is now called match_parent. You'll likely want to support older versions of Android, so stick to fill_parent until older platform versions disappear.
- wrap_content—Indicates that the View would like to take only as much room inside its parent, as it needs to fully render its own content. If for instance, the parent is again a square of 100px, and the view's own children only occupy a 50px square, then the view itself will only be a square of 50px.

Now that we've seen several layout files in action, and have touched on how they're composed and the attributes and parameters they support, our next step is to dig further into layouts while we also examine the available layout managers in more detail.

4.3.2 Layout managers

Android currently defines four different layout managers that you can use to arrange views on the screen. You're free to implement your own if you need something more elaborate, but we won't cover that here. They can be divided into structured and unstructured, or by complexity, as summarized by table 4.2.

Table 4.2 Available built-in Android layout managers

Complexity	Unstructured	Structured
Lower	FrameLayout	LinearLayout
Higher	RelativeLayout	TableLayout

There's also a fifth layout manager, AbsoluteLayout, but it has been deprecated and shouldn't be used, because it doesn't scale to different screen configurations (which is important, as we'll see in section 4.7). With the exception of AbsoluteLayout, we're now going to visit each of these types briefly. Let's start with the simplest, FrameLayout, and work our way up to RelativeLayout, the most complex.

FRAMELAYOUT

This is the simplest of all layout managers. FrameLayout doesn't do any real layout work, but serves as a container (a *frame*). FrameLayout displays a single child element at a time. It supports multiple children, but they're placed in a stack. Child elements are slapped to the top-left corner and drawn on top of each other in their order of declaration. Does that sound useless to you? To be frank, FrameLayout is rarely useful for anything beyond a mere container or box-style layout. One case where it *is* useful is for fitting floating views next to a screen layout (for instance, the ignition library, which is a useful set of Android utilities and enhanced components, uses this technique to render "sticky notes" that can be attached to any widget). The following listing shows how to define a FrameLayout holding two TextView views.

Listing 4.1 An example FrameLayout containing two TextViews

```
<?xml version="1.0" encoding="utf-8"?>
<FrameLayout xmlns:android="http://schemas.android.com/apk/res/android"
    android:layout_width="fill_parent"
    android:layout_height="fill_parent">
  <TextView
      android:layout_width="150px"
      android:layout_height="150px"
      android:background="@android:color/darker_gray"
      />
  <TextView
      android:layout_width="75px"
```

```
    android:layout_height="75px"
    android:background="@android:color/white"
    />
</FrameLayout>
```

You may wonder how these two text views are being rendered as part of this layout. Have a look at figure 4.4, where you can see how they're laid out on top of each other, with the topmost view being the last rendered.

It goes without saying that `FrameLayout` isn't only the simplest, but also the fastest layout manager, so always think twice before jumping to more complex ones! Let's move on to a more useful layout manager, one that we've already seen used a few times, and one that you'll probably spend some quality time with: `LinearLayout`.

LINEARLAYOUT

`LinearLayout` is the most commonly used (sometimes overused) layout manager. It's simple, easy to use, and serves many purposes. As we've noted, in a `LinearLayout`, all views are arranged in lines, either horizontally or vertically, depending on the value of the `android:orientation` attribute. If you don't explicitly

Figure 4.4   Two views arranged using `FrameLayout`. Note how one view lays on top of the other and both are pinned to the top-left corner.

specify the orientation, it'll default to horizontal. `LinearLayout` has two additional layout parameters to be used by its children, as seen in table 4.3.

Table 4.3   Layout parameters specific to LinearLayout

Attribute	Effect
`android:layout_weight`	Tells the layout manager how much room this `View` should occupy relative to its siblings. The size of the `View` will be determined based on the relation of all weights to each other. If, for example, all views define the same weight, then the available space will be distributed equally among them. Which axis (width or height) should be affected can be controlled by setting the respective size to a value of `0px`.
	Note that weights don't have to add up to 1, although it's common to distribute layout weight over all children as fractions of 1 (percentage semantics). The relation between all weights is what matters.
`android:layout_gravity`	Tells the layout manager in which direction the `View` likes to be floated inside its container. This attribute is only meaningful when the `View`'s size on the same axis is either fixed to a constant value or set to `wrap_content`.

In the listing 4.2, we define a layout similar to what we did with FrameLayout in listing 4.1, but this time using the LinearLayout layout manager. You can also see how we use the weight attribute to distribute the available space equally among the two text views in the next listing.

Listing 4.2   An example LinearLayout with weighted children

```xml
<?xml version="1.0" encoding="utf-8"?>
<LinearLayout xmlns:android="http://schemas.android.com/apk/res/android"
    android:layout_width="fill_parent"
    android:layout_height="fill_parent">
  <TextView
      android:layout_width="0px"
      android:layout_height="100px"
      android:layout_weight="0.5"
      android:background="@android:color/darker_gray"
      />
  <TextView
      android:layout_width="0px"
      android:layout_height="100px"
      android:layout_weight="0.5"
      android:background="@android:color/white"
      />
</LinearLayout>
```

Figure 4.5 shows how this layout is rendered. Note how the two views take up exactly the same space across the horizontal screen axis. Again, the relation of the weights is all that matters: setting both to 1 would have the same effect, because 0.5 / 0.5 = 1 / 1 = 1.

LinearLayout is simple but effective. It's well suited to solving typical layout problems such as arranging buttons next to each other. You can also use it to create grids and tables, but there's a more convenient way to do this: TableLayout.

Figure 4.5   Two views arranged using LinearLayout. You can see how both views are sized to take the same amount of space and are aligned horizontally.

TABLELAYOUT

TableLayout is a LinearLayout (it inherits from it) with additional semantics that make it useful for rendering tables or grids. It introduces a special View class called TableRow, which serves as a container for table cells. Each cell must consist only of a single View. This View can again be a layout manager or any other ViewGroup. The following listing shows a simple TableLayout with a single row.

Listing 4.3 An example TableLayout with a single row

```xml
<?xml version="1.0" encoding="utf-8"?>
<TableLayout xmlns:android="http://schemas.android.com/apk/res/android"
    android:layout_width="fill_parent"
    android:layout_height="fill_parent">
  <TableRow>
    <TextView
        android:layout_width="150px"
        android:layout_height="100px"
        android:background="@android:color/darker_gray"
        />
    <TextView
        android:layout_width="150px"
        android:layout_height="100px"
        android:background="@android:color/white"
        />
  </TableRow>
</TableLayout>
```

Figure 4.6 illustrates what our table definition looks like onscreen. The differences to the LinearLayout example are marginal, for the aforementioned reasons.

From figure 4.6, you can see how each TableRow child View becomes a column in the table. You'd need significantly more code to arrive at the same layout using LinearLayout, so remember to use this layout manager whenever you need cells for tables or grids.

At this point, we've seen the first three layout managers Android provides out of the box, and we still don't know how to create truly complex layouts. The layout managers so far are performing simple tasks; at best, they line up views next to each other. If you need more control over how views should be arranged on the screen, then you need to turn to what's arguably the most useful Android layout manager: RelativeLayout.

Figure 4.6 Two views arranged using TableLayout. It differs from Linear-Layout only in the way you set up the layout, because TableLayout is merely a specialized LinearLayout.

RELATIVELAYOUT

RelativeLayout is the most sophisticated of the four layout managers. It allows almost arbitrary placement of views by arranging them relative to each other. RelativeLayout exposes parameters that allow its children to reference each other by their IDs (using the @id notation). To boil this down, let's look at another sample to see how this works.

Listing 4.4   An example RelativeLayout showing the use of relative attributes

```xml
<?xml version="1.0" encoding="utf-8"?>
<RelativeLayout xmlns:android="http://schemas.android.com/apk/res/android"
    android:layout_width="fill_parent"
    android:layout_height="fill_parent">
  <TextView android:id="@+id/text_view_1"
      android:layout_width="150px"
      android:layout_height="100px"
      android:background="@android:color/darker_gray"
      />
  <TextView android:id="@+id/text_view_2"
      android:layout_width="150px"
      android:layout_height="100px"
      android:layout_toRightOf="@id/text_view_1"
      android:layout_centerVertical="true"
      android:background="@android:color/white"
      />
</RelativeLayout>
```

❶ Attribute for relative positioning

In listing 4.4, `text_view_2` declares that it should be drawn "to the right of" `text_view_1` using the `layout_toRightOf` attribute ❶. This demonstrates how `Relative-Layout` views reference each other to define their positions. This is an effective and scalable way of positioning views, but it has a subtle side effect: because you can only reference views using `@id/view_id` that have already been defined, you may find yourself in a situation where you need to shuffle around `View` definitions to reference them. This can quickly become awkward with complex layouts. To solve this problem, you can use a special ID notation to tell the framework to create any IDs that don't yet exist.

HANDLING IDS IN LAYOUTS

Consider again the example from listing 4.4. If `text_view_1` were to reference `text_view_2` instead, you'd have to swap their definitions, or you'd get an error about `text_view_2` not being defined. To avoid this problem, you can use the special `@+id` notation when declaring an ID. When you add the +, Android will create a new ID for any `View` that doesn't exist yet.

> **NOTE**   Though it may sound awkward, because IDs are used to identify resources, IDs themselves are also resources. This means that as with any other resources such as strings, you can create an ids.xml file in `res/values` and use it to predefine blank IDs (IDs that have a name, but don't reference any other resources yet). The `@+id` notation is then no longer needed to use these IDs, because they already exist (but using it doesn't hurt, either). To define an ID in an `ids.xml` resource file, use the `item` tag:
>
> ```xml
> <item type="id" name="my_id" />
> ```

What `@+id` does is create a new ID in Android's internal ID table, but only if it doesn't yet exist. If it does already exist, it references the existing ID (it doesn't cause an error). You may use + on the same ID as often as you like, but the ID will only be created once (we say it's an *idempotent* operation). This means you can use this notation to reference a `View` that's defined further down in a layout XML file. Android will create any such ID when you use it for referencing the `View`, and when the `View` is finally defined, it'll reuse it.

To complete our discussion about layout managers, figure 4.7 shows the two `TextView` views from the previous examples arranged using `RelativeLayout`.

With the four built-in layout managers Android provides, you should be able to create almost any layout you need, even fairly complex ones. Once you start building more involved layouts, it's also a good idea to go back to the `layoutopt` tool and let it guide you with any issues it might uncover (we noted this previously, but it's easy to use, and often overlooked, so it bears repeating).

That covers our views and layouts 101. We feel that we've equipped you with enough background knowledge that you should be able to understand what makes an `Activity` in Android, including the layout containing its

Figure 4.7   Two views arranged using RelativeLayout. Note how we can arrive at almost arbitrary arrangements by specifying all positioning attributes using only relative values.

visual elements, and even how it's drawn to the screen. It's time to get our hands on some techniques now. We want to show you advanced techniques that will likely become good companions in your day-to-day Android UI development. Let's wrap up our discussion of layouts with our first technique: merging and including layouts.

TECHNIQUE 1   The merge and include directives

A handy optimization for your own sanity, and for layouts, is to not repeat yourself. As your layouts get more and more complex, you'll increasingly find yourself duplicating parts of your layout code because you want to reuse it elsewhere. A good example of this is a `Button` bar with Ok and Cancel buttons. Here's an example of such a layout.

Listing 4.5   A layout with a button bar for Ok and Cancel actions

```
<?xml version="1.0" encoding="utf-8"?>
<LinearLayout xmlns:android="http://schemas.android.com/apk/res/android"
    android:orientation="vertical"
    android:layout_width="fill_parent"
    android:layout_height="fill_parent">
  <TextView android:text="An activity with a button bar"
      android:layout_width="wrap_content"
```

```
            android:layout_height="wrap_content"
        />
    <!-- a button bar -->
    <LinearLayout android:orientation="horizontal"
        android:layout_width="fill_parent"
        android:layout_height="wrap_content">
        <Button android:text="@string/ok"
            android:layout_width="wrap_content"
            android:layout_height="wrap_content"
            />
        <Button android:text="@string/cancel"
            android:layout_width="wrap_content"
            android:layout_height="wrap_content"
            />
    </LinearLayout>
</LinearLayout>
```

Things are well and good if you only need these buttons in a single `Activity`, but what happens if you need them in multiple places? As we've seen, every `Activity` defines its own layout file. You can copy the layout section you need into multiple files, but as a good programmer, you know that this is a bad idea. Code duplication leads to programs that are brittle and difficult to maintain.

PROBLEM

You want to share certain parts of a layout with other layout files to minimize code duplication resulting from copying the same code over and over to other layout files.

SOLUTION

When you notice repetitive sections across different layout files, like this one, it's time to check into the special layout `<merge>` and `<include>` elements. These elements allow you to extract commonly used `View` snippets into their own layout files (think of view or layout *components*) that can then be reused in other layouts.

To see how this works, we can extract the button bar related section from listing 4.5 into its own file called button_bar.xml (and put it in `res/layout`) as shown in the following listing.

Listing 4.6 A reusable button bar component defined in its own layout file

```
<?xml version="1.0" encoding="utf-8"?>
<LinearLayout xmlns:android="http://schemas.android.com/apk/res/android"
    android:layout_width="fill_parent"
    android:layout_height="wrap_content">

    <Button android:text="@string/ok"
        android:layout_width="wrap_content"
        android:layout_height="wrap_content"
        />
    <Button android:text="@string/cancel"
        android:layout_width="wrap_content"
        android:layout_height="wrap_content"
        />
</LinearLayout>
```

In order to pull one layout section or component into another file you can then use the <include> element:

```
<include layout="@layout/button_bar" />
```

That's it! The include element doesn't take any specific parameters other than the layout. Nevertheless, if you want, you can pass it custom layout parameters or a new ID to override the attributes defined for the root view of the layout you're including.

> **INCLUDE AND LAYOUT ATTRIBUTES GOTCHA**   When overriding layout_width or layout_height using include, remember to always override both. If, for example, you only override layout_width, but not layout_height, Android will silently fail and ignore any layout_* overridden settings. This isn't well documented, and somewhat controversial, but easy to work around once you know what's going on.

One question remains: what happens if you want to include views that don't have a common parent View or you want to include a layout in different kinds of parent views? You'd think that you could get rid of the parent LinearLayout and redefine button_bar.xml from listing 4.6 as follows:

```
<?xml version="1.0" encoding="utf-8"?>
<Button android:text="@android:string/ok"
    android:layout_width="wrap_content"
    android:layout_height="wrap_content"
    />
<Button android:text="@android:string/cancel"
    android:layout_width="wrap_content"
    android:layout_height="wrap_content"
    />
```

Unfortunately, that's impossible, because that's not a valid XML document. Remember that XML documents are trees, and a tree always has a root. This one doesn't, so it'll fail. Android has a solution: the <merge> element is a placeholder for whatever parent View the views in the (partial) layout will be included into. This means we can rewrite the previous snippet as follows to make it work:

```
<?xml version="1.0" encoding="utf-8"?>
<merge xmlns:android="http://schemas.android.com/apk/res/android">
  <Button android:text="@android:string/ok"
      android:layout_width="wrap_content"
      android:layout_height="wrap_content"
      />
  <Button android:text="@android:string/cancel"
      android:layout_width="wrap_content"
      android:layout_height="wrap_content"
      />
</merge>
```

Think of <merge> as a wildcard: it's a glue point, and whatever the layout it wraps will be inserted into (a LinearLayout, RelativeLayout, and so on) will replace the

`<merge>` node at runtime. You can use this technique anytime you'd otherwise have to include a `View` under another `View` of the same kind (which is duplication, and hence discouraged).

DISCUSSION

We urge you to internalize this technique and apply it to your layout code whenever you can. It'll keep complex layout files clean and easy to read, and significantly reduce code duplication and hence maintenance work. A fundamental engineering principle is to never encode the same information more than once in your application, commonly known as the *DRY principle* (don't repeat yourself). That being said, `<merge>` and `<include>` help keep your layouts DRY.

One disadvantage of chopping up your layouts like this is that Android's graphical layout tool in Eclipse will sometimes get confused and not render the preview correctly. On the other hand, it should be a question of time until Android's tool support improves enough to preview even layouts that are merged together in complex ways.

With this first little technique, we conclude our discussion about layouts in Android. Remember how we promised to code a full application—one that manages movie titles and that looks good? We keep our promises. Because MyMovies, like the DealDroid, is made up from a list view, we're going to come back one more time to list views and adapter. There's more to them then you may have expected.

4.4   *Expanding on ListView and Adapter*

We've already seen how a `ListView` can be used with an `Adapter` in chapter 2. That example was simple: we showed a list of deal items, but the data behind that list was static. Once it was put behind the list, it didn't change. For MyMovies, we'd like to be able to tick off Movies that are in our collection. For this to happen, we need to expand on list views and adapters. We now need a stateful list that includes elements that can be in two states: checked or not checked. Moreover, we're going to spice things up by showing you how to add header and footer elements to lists. Along the way, we'll also explore a few optimizations, such as the ViewHolder pattern, which will make your list render significantly faster and hence scroll more smoothly.

First things first. In order to maintain the checked state we'll need for MyMovies, we have to store that the user owns a movie when it's selected from the list, and remove it when it's unselected. For this example, we won't bother to persist that information to a database or file because we haven't yet introduced the mechanisms to do so. This means that for now, all movies we'll add to the "collection" by tapping them will be lost when we restart the application. This is intentional at this point, so we can stay focused on understanding how adapters can maintain state. Don't worry—we'll learn about saving information to files and databases, and more, in chapter 7.

To see how the views for our `ListView` are bound to the data source we'll use a static movies file, via our `Adapter`. For now, we need to return to `ListActivity` and review the code for MyMovies.

Managing a stateful list

Recall from listing 4.1 that the main MyMovies screen is composed of a `ListActivity` that takes up the entire screen with a single `ListView`. Also, each movie in the list contains a check box that can be toggled. This toggle is a simple example of maintaining state between our model and our views. The question is: where do we store this state? And how do we reflect updates to this state in the `ListView`?

PROBLEM

You have a list that's backed by data coming from an adapter, and you want either changes coming from the view (such as from a list item click) to be written back into the data source, or changes to the data reflected back to the view.

SOLUTION

When having to maintain dynamic data that can change in reaction to view events (or any other event), you'll have to create your own adapter implementation that performs the following tasks:

- If the data wrapped by the adapter changes, it must inform the view about these changes so it can redraw itself.
- If the user interacts with the view in a way that's supposed to update the data, we must inform the adapter about this and make the according changes to the data source.

To see how this works, we'll start with the seemingly sparse code for the main MyMovies screen, as shown in the following listing. Then, we'll move on to the custom adapter.

Listing 4.7   The MyMovies.java ListActivity class file

```
public class MyMovies extends ListActivity {          ◄─── ① Extend ListActivity

    private MovieAdapter adapter;                      ◄───   Include
                                                         ② Adapter
    public void onCreate(Bundle savedInstanceState) {
        super.onCreate(savedInstanceState);

        setContentView(R.layout.main);

        ListView listView = getListView();

        this.adapter = new MovieAdapter(this);         ③ Set Adapter
        listView.setAdapter(this.adapter);             ◄──┘ on ListView
        listView.setItemsCanFocus(false);
    }

    @Override
    protected void onListItemClick(ListView l, View v,
                             int position, long id) {
        this.adapter.toggleMovie(position);
        this.adapter.notifyDataSetChanged();
    }
}
```

Our MyMovies main screen works similarly to the other activities we've seen up to this point, including the fact that it extends `ListActivity` ❶ (which we first saw in chapter 2). Also similar to chapter 2, this `Activity` includes an `Adapter` ❷. Before going further, remember that we use `ListActivity` because it takes care of many of the details of managing a `ListView`. This includes things such as easy access to `ListView` via `getListView`, and easy click handling with `onListItemClick`. Also, we again set our `Adapter` into our `ListView` to provide the data source for the items the list will handle ❸.

Next, we need to visit the data source and custom `MovieAdapter` our `ListView` will be using. Before setting up the adapter, let's look at the source of our movie data. We could fetch data from the Internet (some web services do that kind of thing, as we saw with the DealDroid, and will see in even more detail in chapter 9), but let's keep it simple for this example. We'll take IMDB's top-100 movies and store them as an array resource in our application. To do that, we create a new file called movies.xml in res/ values with the following structure:

```xml
<?xml version="1.0" encoding="utf-8"?>
<resources>
  <string-array name="movies">
    <item>The Shawshank Redemption (1994)</item>
    <item>The Godfather (1972)</item>
    <item>The Godfather, Part II (1974)</item>
    <item>The Good, the Bad, and the Ugly (1966) (It.)</item>
    ...
  </string-array>
</resources>
```

Recalling what we learned about resources in chapter 2, we can now reference this array in our application as `R.array.movies`. Note that we could've hard-coded the list as a plain old Java array in one of our application classes. But using Android's resource mechanism gives us the advantage of both having full control over when we want to load the data into memory, and at the same time keeping our application code clean. After all, application code is supposed to contain logic, not data.

The next step is to get this data to show in the `ListView`. Because we're dealing only with an array, Android's `ArrayAdapter` class is a perfect choice to implement our `MovieAdapter` (which we assigned to the `ListView` in listing 4.7). `MovieAdapter` is where we'll track the movies a user adds and provide an interface to its state so the check box view can update accordingly. The following listing shows how this is implemented.

Listing 4.8 The MovieAdapter keeps track of selected movies

```java
public class MovieAdapter extends ArrayAdapter<String> {          ⬅ ❶ Extend ArrayAdapter

    private HashMap<Integer, Boolean> movieCollection =
            new HashMap<Integer, Boolean>();                      ⬅ ❷ Include HashMap

    public MovieAdapter(Context context) {
```

```
        super(context, R.layout.movie_item,
            android.R.id.text1, context                          ❸  Use super
                .getResources().getStringArray(R.array.movies));     constructor
    }

    public void toggleMovie(int position) {                ◁──┐   Toggle
        if (!isInCollection(position)) {                   ❹  movie state
            movieCollection.put(position, true);
        } else {
            movieCollection.put(position, false);
        }
    }

    public boolean isInCollection(int position) {
        return movieCollection.get(position) == Boolean.TRUE;
    }

    @Override
    public View getView(int position, View convertView,        ❺  Override
        ViewGroup parent) {                                 ◁──    getView

        View listItem = super.getView(position, convertView, parent);

        CheckedTextView checkMark = null;                      ❻  Try to get
        ViewHolder holder = (ViewHolder) listItem.getTag();  ◁──  ViewHolder
        if (holder != null) {
            checkMark = holder.checkMark;
        } else {                                               ❼  Establish
            checkMark = (CheckedTextView)                         view
                listItem.findViewById(android.R.id.text1);
            holder = new ViewHolder(checkMark);              ❽  Set up
            listItem.setTag(holder);                            ViewHolder
        }

        checkMark.setChecked(isInCollection(position));

        return listItem;
    }                                                          ❾  Implement inner
    private class ViewHolder {                              ◁──  ViewHolder class
        protected final CheckedTextView checkMark;

        public ViewHolder(CheckedTextView checkMark) {
            this.checkMark = checkMark;
        }
    }
}
```

The first thing to note about MovieAdapter is that it extends ArrayAdapter ❶. By doing this, we need only implement the adapter methods we're interested in, and we don't have to reinvent the wheel. From there we also see that MovieAdapter includes a local HashMap for storing movie state data ❷. The user's movie collection is modeled as a mapping from positions in the movie list to Boolean values (true meaning the user owns the movie). Again, this state is transient, so once the user exits the application it'll be lost, but you can see how we could reference a database, the filesystem, or any other storage mechanism here if we wanted to.

Next, we see that the constructor makes a call to the `ArrayAdapter` super constructor, like any good Java subclass, and there provides the context, layout to use for each item, the ID of a `TextView` to populate for each item, and the initial data collection ❸. The first method we see is `toggleMovie`, which is used to update the model's state ❹. Next is the all-important `getView` method that we first saw in chapter 2. This method returns the view needed for each item, and is called whenever a list item must be (re)drawn ❺.

Redrawing of the list items happens frequently, for example when scrolling through the list. Because this behavior can have a lot of overhead, we use the ViewHolder pattern to optimize the way our `ListView` gets and populates list items. The idea is to eliminate extra calls to `findViewById` because that's a relatively expensive method. To do so, we cache `findViewById`'s result in a `ViewHolder` object. `ViewHolder` is an internal class that we've created to hold the `CheckedTextView` we need ❾.

But how do we associate the cached view with the current list item? For that, we use a handy method called `getTag`. This method allows us to associate arbitrary data with a view. We can leverage that method to cache the view holder itself, which in turn caches the view references. Call the `getTag` method on the current `listItem` (we let the super class decide whether a new one is created or whether it's recycled from the `convertView`) to check if the `ViewHolder` is present ❻. If it is, then we get the `CheckedTextItem` we need directly from it ❼. If it isn't there, we know that we're not dealing with a recycled view, and we must call `findViewById` to get a reference to the `CheckedTextItem` ❼, create the `ViewHolder`, and use `setTag` to stick it onto the `listItem` ❽. The ViewHolder pattern can help make your `ListView` faster and more efficient, and should always be considered when you expect to have more than a few items in the list.

CODE WITH VIEW REUSE IN MIND Because we don't persist any of this information, you may think that it seems contrived to go through the hassle of creating a custom adapter that only saves data in memory, and which is therefore going to be thrown away whenever the application is closed. You may also think that we could toggle the check box view whenever a user taps it and see the same effect, right? Wrong! That's because adapters are responsible for creating the view that represents the element at a certain position of the underlying data set, and all standard adapter classes such as `ArrayAdapter` (and also all well-implemented custom adapters) cache and reuse item views via `convertView` for performance reasons. Consequently, we'd see checked items reappearing across the list even though we never checked them. Again, even if that weren't the case, remember that state *should be* updated in the model, not the view.

Note that our custom `Adapter` is not *the* solution; it's *a* solution (a simple one). Another perfectly valid approach would be to create a `Movie` model class, and remember in these objects whether a movie is owned. We could then get rid of the `HashMap` and instead get the `Movie` object at a given position and ask the object whether it's owned by the user. In fact, we'll do that in chapter 9, when we extend MyMovies to talk to an online movie database. In any case, we have to update the model managed by our new adapter whenever the user clicks a movie item, which is achieved by implementing the `ListActivity.onListItemClick` handler we saw in listing 4.7.

DISCUSSION

Using adapters this way is a powerful approach for managing dynamic data that's completely decoupled from any views, and therefore from how it's being displayed. Even though we didn't write that much code, sometimes this is too much complexity already. If you only need to ask the user to select from multiple choices in a list (a list dialog would be a good example), then there's a much easier way than implementing your own adapter: the `ListView choiceMode` attribute. With the choice mode set to `multipleChoice`, you can receive any list items the user selected by calling `ListView.getCheckedItemIds()`. This roughly corresponds to the map of Boolean values we maintain. You can also set the choice mode programmatically using `ListView.setChoiceMode`. This is one instance where state is only maintained in the views, without a model behind it, but it's a limited approach.

There are many different kinds of adapters, some of which you'll meet in later chapters. For now it's sufficient that you've learned how to work with them, and how you can use adapters to arrive at more flexible designs by separating data from its representation on the screen. At the same time, you've probably noticed that list views, though useful, can get quite complex. This is why we'll look at some general tips coming up, but first, we'll quickly look at how header and footer views can be added to a list.

TECHNIQUE 3   **Header and footer views**

List views are a great way to cope with large data sets, but the ability to scroll alone doesn't always help—your thumbs may be sore by the time you reach the bottom of a list. It'd be nice, for instance, to have a back-to-top button at the bottom of our list, so that the user doesn't have to scroll all the way back through a hundred titles to reach the top of the list again. But our list contains movie titles, which are text views, not buttons. We need a list element that looks and behaves differently from normal entries, but our adapter is only able to create one type of list element: a movie item. Looks like we're stuck.

PROBLEM

You need dedicated list elements at the top or bottom of a list, which scroll with the list content like a normal entry, but may have entirely different layout and functionality.

SOLUTION

This is what Android's list header and footer views are for. You can set them using `ListView.addHeaderView` and `ListView.addFooterView` respectively. To see how this works, we'll build a back-to-top button for MyMovies. We first define a layout (list_footer.xml) for our footer view that contains a single button, perhaps like this:

```
<?xml version="1.0" encoding="utf-8"?>
<Button xmlns:android="http://schemas.android.com/apk/res/android"
    android:layout_width="fill_parent"
    android:layout_height="@android:attr/listPreferredItemHeight"
    android:gravity="center_vertical"
    android:text="Back to top"
    android:onClick="backToTop"
/>
```

Note how we use the `onClick` attribute in our footer view layout. This tells Android to look for a public method called `backToTop` defined in our activity, which takes a single `View` object as a parameter. This is a nifty way to wire a click handler to a component from XML (without having to write the boilerplate code to explicitly assign the handler). This is going to be our callback where we do the scrolling. We then have to inflate this layout to receive a `Button` object, and set it as our list's footer view as seen in our `Activity`'s `onCreate` method:

```
public void onCreate(Bundle savedInstanceState) {
    ...
    Button backToTop =
        (Button) getLayoutInflater().inflate(R.layout.list_footer, null);
    backToTop.setCompoundDrawablesWithIntrinsicBounds(getResources()
        .getDrawable(android.R.drawable.ic_menu_upload), null, null,
            null);
    listView.addFooterView(backToTop, null, true);
    ...
}
```

No magic involved here. We add this code to the middle of the `onCreate` method we saw in listing 4.7, directly after we declare `ListView listView = getListView()`. This way, it's included when our `ListActivity` is created, and it's set *before* we declare and set the adapter. To get an idea of what this will look like, figure 4.8 shows the list with the button at the bottom in all its glory.

We've also added an icon (we reused a framework icon that has an up-arrow on it) to the button. In case you've wondered about the allowed number of header and footer views: you can add as many header or footer views as you like. They'll stack up and appear before (for header views) or after (for footer views) the list items.

Figure 4.8   We added a button that returns us to the top of the list using a list footer view. The button icon can be set using the setCompound-DrawableWithIntrinsicBounds method.

DISCUSSION

Header and footer views are useful for displaying content that's not part of the list data, but because they're treated differently from ordinary list elements, you need to watch for some subtleties. For one, you *must* add all header and footer views before adding any data to your list (via `ListView.setAdapter`); otherwise you'll get an exception. This makes header and footer views fairly inflexible, because you can't add or remove them at will.

Moreover, even though header and footer views appear as normal list elements, remember that they're not representations of adapter data, and hence have no corresponding element in the adapter backing the list. This also means that if you want to count the list elements visible to the user, you can't rely on `Adapter.getCount` anymore. That method is oblivious to any header or footer views. Always keep in mind this asymmetry between your list view and its adapter when working with headers and footers.

We've arrived at our first MyMovies development milestone: we have an application that displays IMDB's top 100 movies, and the user can select which titles they have in their collection! List views are powerful, and now you know their ins and outs—does it feel good? In all fairness, `ListView` is a complex beast and there are many caveats regarding its use. It's likely that you'll run into one or more issues as your list item layouts grow more complex. Hence, in table 4.4 we've collected some common `ListView` related caveats and their solutions. You may be grateful for them one day!

Table 4.4   General ListView tips

ListView caveat	Solution
Don't use wrap content	Never use `wrap_content` for a list view's `height` attribute. A list is a scroll container, and by definition is infinitely large, so you should always let a `ListView fill_parent` (or let it otherwise expand itself, for example, using `layout_weight`).
Be careful with clickable list items	Generally, when you click a list item, the list item itself receives the click event—the view or container that's the root element of the item layout. If you place a button inside an item layout, the button steals the focus from the list item, which means while the button remains clickable, the list item itself can neither be focused nor clicked. You can mitigate this effect to at least let the entire list item be focusable again by setting `ListView.setItemsCanFocus(false)`, which will bring back the list highlight when selecting that item. But any click handling must still be performed on a per-element basis inside your item layout.
Pay attention to `getView` performance	List views can be performance killers. The `getView` method of an adapter is used to render a list item and is called frequently. You should avoid doing expensive operations like view inflations, or at least cache them. Reuse views, and consider the ViewHolder pattern we introduced earlier.

It's now time to move on to a topic that developers typically fear, but at the same time is fundamental to a successful mobile application: look and feel. We won't discuss graphic design here—that's probably not what you get your paycheck for, considering you're reading a book on programming—but you still need to know how to set your application up to make use of design elements. Implementing custom designs on Android requires a lot of work on the programming side. Hence, the next few sections will equip you with the knowledge to implement highly customized Android user interfaces. Pimp my Android!

4.5   Applying themes and styles

Let's not beat around the bush: a typical stock Android application looks unimpressive. With Android 3.0 (aka Honeycomb) and the tablet game, things are getting significantly better, but a vanilla pre-3.0 Android installation is visually underwhelming. Fortunately, Google has given developers the necessary tools to spice up their application UIs by means of the myriad of view attributes you can define or override for your views. As you can probably imagine, this can become a tedious and repetitive task, which is why Google added a *theme engine* to Android, and we've prepared two techniques to explore it.

4.5.1   Styling applications

First, we should get a common misconception about Android themes and styles out of the way. Yes, you can deploy custom application themes for users to download and use, but first and foremost, Android themes are a tool for developers, not end users. Many applications, such as the Firefox web browser, allow users to create their own themes and share them with others. That's because Firefox's theme engine is meant to be usable by end users, so it's not exclusively accessed by the Firefox developers themselves. That's typically not true for Android themes, because theme development is tightly coupled to the development and deployment of the application itself, and there's no mechanism to change an application's theme unless such functionality has been built into the application by the developer.

What are Android themes then, and what are styles? Let's answer that last part first.

TECHNIQUE 4   **Applying and writing styles**

It should be mentioned that you could potentially get a super-nifty looking application without writing a single style definition. You *could*. But would you want to? To understand the problem, consider this view definition:

```xml
<?xml version="1.0" encoding="utf-8"?>
<TextView xmlns:android="http://schemas.android.com/apk/res/android"
    android:text="Hello, text view!"
    android:textSize="14sp"
    android:textStyle="bold"
    android:textColor="#CCC"
    android:background="@android:color/transparent"
    android:padding="5dip"
    android:layout_width="wrap_content"
    android:layout_height="wrap_content"
    />
```

There's a lot of noise here. We've encoded a lot of information in this view definition that affects the view's appearance. Does that belong in a layout file? Layouts are about structure, not appearance. Plus, what if all our text views are supposed to use the same font size? Do we want to redefine it for every single text view? This would mean that if we were to change it, we'd have to touch the code of *all* of the text views in our application.

PROBLEM

Customizing view attributes in your layouts, especially those that affect appearance, leads to code clutter, code duplication, and generally makes them impossible to reuse.

SOLUTION

Whenever you find yourself applying several related attributes directly to a view, consider using a *style* instead. A style is a surprisingly simple concept.

> **DEFINITION**   A *style* in Android is a set of view attributes, bundled as a separate resource. Styles are by convention defined in res/values/styles.xml.

If, for instance, we create a custom style for our text views, we can define any customized attributes *once,* in a styles.xml file, like so:

```xml
<?xml version="1.0" encoding="utf-8"?>
<resources>
  <style name="MyCustomTextView" parent="@android:style/Widget.TextView">
    <item name="android:textSize">14sp</item>
    <item name="android:textStyle">bold</item>
    <item name="android:textColor">#CCC</item>
    <item name="android:background">@android:color/transparent</item>
    <item name="android:padding">5dip</item>
  </style>
</resources>
```

As you can see, we took all the styling attributes from our view definition and put them inside a `<style>` element. A style is defined in terms of *style items,* each of which refers to an attribute of the view the style is being applied to. Styles can also inherit from each other: in this case, we've inherited from the default `Widget.TextView` style, which is semantically equivalent to copying all attributes from the parent style to our own style. All attributes that are redefined in our style will overwrite any attributes of the same name that were defined in the parent style. Finally, styles can be applied to any view like this:

```xml
<?xml version="1.0" encoding="utf-8"?>
<TextView xmlns:android="http://schemas.android.com/apk/res/android"
    android:text="Hello, text view!"
    android:layout_width="wrap_content"
    android:layout_height="wrap_content"
    style="@style/MyCustomTextView"
/>
```

Note how we use the `style` attribute without the `android:` prefix. This is intentional: the `style` attribute is global and not defined under the `android` XML namespace. It's important to understand here that styles are a set of view attributes bundled together. There are no type semantics: if you define attributes in a style and then apply the style to a view that doesn't have these attributes, the style will silently fail but you won't see an error. It's up to the developer to design and apply styles in a meaningful way.

DISCUSSION

Styles are meant to alleviate two common design problems. For one, placing code for defining appearance and code for defining structure into the same file isn't a good separation of concerns. Though you're building the screen layout, the styling is most likely being done by someone who does *not* write application code. Constantly messing about with the same source code files is almost like asking for merge conflicts during commits (you *do* use a source code control system, don't you?). Even if you take on both roles, a good separation of concerns helps keep your code clean, readable, and easy to maintain.

Speaking of maintenance, this brings us to design problem number two. Defining attributes for appearance directly in your view XML—or worse, in application code—makes them impossible to reuse. This means that you'll end up copying the same style attributes to other views of the same kind, resulting in code duplication and proliferation. We've said before that this is bad, because it violates the DRY principle. Like the <merge> and <include> elements, styles in Android help you keep your view code DRY. You can put shared attributes from your views into a style resource, which can then be applied to many views while being maintained from a single point of your application.

A question that remains is: what can we style, and which styles already exist so we can inherit from them? The answer is that anything defined in the android.R.styleable and android.R.attr classes can become part of a style—may be used as a value for a style item's name attribute. Existing styles are defined in android.R.style, so anything defined in that class can be used as a value for a style's parent attribute, or even be applied directly to a view. As usual, underscores in the R class attribute names translate to dot-notation in view code, so android.R.style.Widget_TextView_SpinnerItem becomes android:style/Widget.TextView.SpinnerItem. Now you know what styles in Android are, but let's move on to themes.

TECHNIQUE 5   Applying and writing themes

We've already seen how to extract common view attributes into styles, but we're still repeating ourselves—violating the DRY principle. If we define a style for text views, we still have to apply the style manually to every TextView. This is clearly not DRY. Maybe not wet, perhaps moist, but surely not DRY. It also opens new questions: what if we forget to apply the style to one of our views?

PROBLEM

Bundling view attributes to styles is useful, but it's only half of the solution. We still need to apply styles to all views that are targeted by the style. This should be done automatically.

SOLUTION

The complete solution to this is, you guessed it, themes. Fortunately, explaining themes is simple. Themes are styles. Yes, it's as simple as that. The only difference between a theme and a style such as the one shown in the previous technique is that themes apply to activities or the entire application (which means, all activities in an application), and not to single views. The difference therefore is one of scope, not semantics or even structure.

> **DEFINITION**   A *theme* in Android is a style that applies either to a single activity or all activities (in which case it becomes the application's *global theme*).

Because themes are styles, they behave exactly the same, and are defined exactly the same: using the `<style>` tag. Because they're applied to activities, they take different style attributes than a widget style. You can identify style attributes meant for theme definitions by their `Theme_` prefix in `android.R.styleable`.

Let's proceed and apply a theme to our MyMovies app. We introduced the style concept using `TextView`, which is a good example because it takes many different attributes (we'll show you another, even better way of cutting down on `TextView` attribute bloat coming up). But our example application doesn't use many `TextView` elements, so it would seem contrived to do that. Instead, let's see if we can make our movie list look fancier. We want to add a background image to the application—something related to films would be good. It should blend with the list, letting the window background shine through. Moreover, we want to make a couple of smaller changes such as rendering a fast-scroll handle. The following listing shows how to do that using themes and styles.

Listing 4.9   The style and theme definition file for the MyMovies application

```xml
<?xml version="1.0" encoding="utf-8"?>
<resources>
  <style name="MyMoviesTheme"                                    Theme definition  ❶
      parent="@android:style/Theme.Black">
    <item name="android:listViewStyle">@style/MyMoviesListView</item>
    <item name="android:windowBackground">@drawable/film_bg</item>
  </style>

  <style name=" MyMoviesListView"
     parent="@android:style/Widget.ListView">
    <item name="android:background">#A000</item>
    <item name="android:fastScrollEnabled">true</item>        ❷ Style
    <item name="android:footerDividersEnabled">false</item>       definition
  </style>                                                         for list views
</resources>
```

The theme definition shown in listing 4.9 (which uses the style element, too) applies custom styling to all `ListView` instances in the application and sets a custom window background ❶. The custom `ListView` style that's being applied defines the attributes that all list views in this application will now share ❷.

We've defined a theme for our application, but we haven't yet applied it to anything. Recall that themes may be applied to single activities or the entire application (all activities), so we need to tell Android what we want to style. Themes are applied in the manifest file using the `android:theme` attribute. If we were to apply it to a single activity, we'd set that attribute on an activity element; otherwise we set it on the single application element, as follows:

```
<application android:theme="@style/MyMoviesTheme" ...>
    ...
</application>
```

Figure 4.9 shows how MyMovies looks now that we've slapped some styling onto it.

You can see how the window background is visible through the semitransparent list view background. You can also see the fast-scroll handle at the right side of the list. You can grab it to scroll quickly, and it'll fade away and get out of your way if the scroll has ended.

DISCUSSION

As you can define view attributes both in XML and in program code, you can also apply themes to an activity programmatically using `Activity.setTheme`. Nevertheless, this way of doing it is discouraged. In general, if something can be done in the XML, it's good practice to do it in the XML, and not in your application code. Calling `setTheme` will also only work *before* you inflate the activity's layout; otherwise the theme's styles won't be applied. This also means that you can't change a theme on-the-fly (such as through the click of a button), because you must restart the activity for it to have an effect.

Figure 4.9   The MyMovies title screen after some styling has been applied. Note how we included a transparent background image and added a fast scrolling handle.

That covers the basics of defining and using styles and themes. Still, a few things worth knowing about remain. Remember how we mentioned that `ListView` is a complex beast and that we'll come back to it? Here we are. Styling list views has a nasty pitfall that almost all developers new to Android step into, so let's get it out of the way once and for all.

TECHNIQUE 6   ## Styling ListView backgrounds

`ListView` is a complex widget, and sometimes this complexity gets in your way when trying to change its appearance. In fact, we weren't completely honest with you when we showed you the code for the list view style in listing 4.9. It's lacking a setting that will allow the style to be rendered correctly. If you try to apply a custom background, or as in our example let the background of the window or another underlying view shine through, then you may observe visual artifacts such as flickering colors when performing scrolls or clicks on the list. On a related note, if you try to set its background to a transparent color, expecting to see the widget rendered underneath the list, you'll find that Android still renders the default black background.

PROBLEM

You apply a custom background (color or image) to a `ListView`, but you don't get the desired effect or get visual artifacts when rendering the list.

SOLUTION

These problems can be attributed to a rendering optimization `ListView` performs at runtime. Because it uses fading edges (transparency) to indicate that its contents are scrollable, and this blending of colors is expensive to compute, a list view uses a color hint (by default the current theme's window background color) to produce a prerendered gradient that mimics the effect. The majority of the time a list view is rendered using the default color schemes, and in those cases this optimization is effective. Yet, you can run into the aforementioned anomalies when using custom color values for backgrounds.

To fix this problem, you need to tell Android which color it should use as the hint color using the `android:cacheColorHint` attribute. This is done as follows:

```xml
<?xml version="1.0" encoding="utf-8"?>
<resources>
  ...
  <style name="MyMoviesListView" parent="@android:style/Widget.ListView">
    <item name="android:background">#A000</item>
    <item name="android:cacheColorHint">#0000</item>
    ...
  </style>
</resources>
```

Setting the `cacheColorHint` properly (or disabling it by setting it to transparent) will fix any obscure problems you may encounter when working with a list with a custom background color.

DISCUSSION

Regarding the value for the color hint, if you use a solid list background color, set it to the same color value as the background. If you want the window background to shine through, or use a custom graphic, you must disable the cache color hint entirely by setting its value to transparent (#0000 or `android:color/transparent`). And that's that. This is a rather obscure issue, but you should keep it in mind when working with `ListView` implementations that need custom backgrounds.

Understanding the `cacheColorHint` wraps up our discussion of styles and themes, almost. We've collected one more set of tidbits about styles in Android, which we want to show you before moving to the next topic.

4.5.2 Useful styling tidbits

Ready to get even deeper into styling applications? You now know how to create and apply themes and styles, but we have some extra useful tips and tricks to round out this discussion. The paragraphs that follow cover things that haven't been mentioned yet, in no particular order, but all of which we think make your life easier when working with styles. In particular, we'll demystify color values, tell you how to work with text appearances, and also introduce some rarely seen but useful style notations.

COLOR VALUES

When working with styles, you'll often find yourself specifying color values, either directly using hexadecimal syntax or by referencing a color resource—yes, colors can be resources, too! Any color value in XML is defined using hex notation and identified by the # prefix, so let's briefly cover it now. Color values in Android are defined using the *Alpha/Red/Green/Blue* color space (ARGB), where each color is mapped to a 32-bit wide number, with the first 8 bits defining the alpha channel (the color's opacity), and the remaining 24 bits representing the three color components, with 8 bits for red, green, and blue each. Because each component may use 8 bits of information, the value range for each component is 0 to 255, or 00 to FF in the hexadecimal system. A color value of #800000FF would therefore represent blue with 50% opacity.

> **COLOR VALUE SHORTCUTS** In cases where each color channel is represented by two identical hex digits, you're allowed to use an abbreviated hex string where every hex digit pair is collapsed into a single digit. For example, the colors #FFFFFFFF and #AABBCCDD can be abbreviated to #FFFF and #ABCD, respectively. Moreover, you can always omit the alpha channel, in which case full opacity is assumed, so #FFFF can be abbreviated even further to #FFF.

Typing out these color values can get tedious. For one, you're repeating yourself, which as we've learned is a bad thing. Worse maybe, these values aren't intuitive unless you're good at mentally mapping hex values to a color space. Hence, you'll typically define these values only once, as a color resource, which you can address using a human-readable identifier. To do that, create a file named colors.xml in your res/ values folder, and add the following code to it:

```
<?xml version="1.0" encoding="utf-8"?>
<resources>
  <color name="translucent_blue">#800000FF</color>
</resources>
```

You can now reference this color from your views and styles as @color/ translucent_blue. Note that Android already defines a handful of colors for you in this way. A commonly used predefined color is android:color/transparent, which is equivalent to a color value of #00000000. When in application code, you can also use the color definitions from the Color class, but you can't reference these from XML.

One last thing about colors. Colors defined as shown here can be used as *drawables* in Android. We haven't covered drawables yet (though we touched on them in chapter 2), but for now, keep in mind that you can also assign color values to attributes that expect drawables, for example, for backgrounds or list selectors. Colors as drawables can be powerful, and we'll show you how as part of section 4.6.

TEXT APPEARANCE

We mentioned before that when working with text styles, there's a better way than defining your text styles from scratch: Android's text appearances. A *text appearance* is a style that contains elements that apply to any `TextView` in your app. Moreover, overriding these default styles will immediately affect all text styles in your application. For example, if you were to change the default text style to bold red across your entire application, you could do this:

```
<style name="MyTheme">
    <item name="android:textAppearance">@style/MyTextAppearance</item>
</style>

<style name="MyTextAppearance">
    <item name="android:textColor">#F00</item>
    <item name="android:textStyle">bold</item>
</style>
```

Plenty of text appearance attributes are available for themes, such as `textAppearance` for default text, `textAppearanceButton` for button captions and `textAppearance-Inverse` for inverted text (such as highlighted text). But you'll probably ask yourself, what's the difference between this and defining a default style for `TextView`, as seen before? The differences are subtle but important. First, the styling defined here will actually be applied to all `TextView` views, including subclasses. This isn't the case for the `textViewStyle` attribute—it won't affect text views such as `Button` or `EditText`, which both inherit from `TextView`. Second, the `textAppearance` attribute can be applied to a theme and a single `TextView` (and hence, also to a `TextView` style definition). This allows you to bundle shared text styles together and apply them en masse to different kinds of text views—think another layer of styling DRYness for your code.

By any means, if you start styling text in your application you'll want to do this using text appearances. Let them inherit from Android's default text appearance styles, and overwrite only what you need to change.

SPECIAL STYLE VALUES

You've seen how to reuse styling attributes by bundling them together into styles and by letting styles inherit from each other. You've also seen the @ notation that you use to reference existing resources. This works well if you want to address the complete resource, but what if you need only a single value? Consider a text style. For example, suppose you want to change the link color to the color Android uses for plain text, but you don't know that color's value. Furthermore, the primary text color isn't exposed as a color resource because it's variable; it changes with the theme.

The solution is to use the ? notation, which like @, only works in XML. You can use it to address style items of the *currently applied theme* by their name. To stick with the example, if you want to set your application's link color to the default text color, you could do this:

```
<style name="MyTheme">
  <item name="android:textColorLink">?android:attr/textColorPrimary</item>
</style>
```

The last thing we'd like to mention is the @null value. You can use it whenever you want to remove a value that's set by default (in a parent style). This is probably seldom required, but it makes sense if you want to get rid of a drawable that's set by default. For instance, Android will set the windowBackground attribute to a default value, but if the window background is always obscured by your own views, you can remove it by setting it to @null. This will result in a slight performance boost, because Android currently can't optimize views that are completely obscured away from the rendering chain, although this limitation may change in future versions.

Styles are a complex topic, and there's often confusion about the distinction between themes and styles. Hopefully we've solved most of these mysteries. We started by showing how styles are defined and how they're applied to views. We then showed you how you can assign styles globally to your application using themes, and even sorted out some confusion with background styling in list views. As always, we suggest you play around with view styling yourself. That's the best way to get your head around a problem. Now, let's move forward and learn about another important concept of Android's UI framework, drawables.

4.6 *Working with drawables*

To be frank, we've dodged the concept of drawables up to this point and tried shamelessly to sweep it under the rug. It's difficult to discuss all the user interface topics without touching on drawables. But we can't fool you, can we? You've already seen several occurrences of drawables: images (bitmaps) and colors. So what exactly is a drawable?

> **DEFINITION** A *drawable* in Android, defined by the Drawable class, is a graphical element displayed on the screen, but unlike a widget is typically noninteractive (apart from picture drawables, which actually allow you to record images by drawing onto a surface).

Apart from images and colors, there are drawables for custom shapes and lines, drawables that change based on their state, and drawables that are animated.

Drawables are worth covering separately, because they're powerful and ubiquitous in Android. You need them practically everywhere: as backgrounds, widget faces, custom surfaces, and generally anything involving 2D graphics. We won't cover every kind of drawable here, only the most widely used ones. Additionally we'll come back to drawables in chapter 12, where we'll discuss 2D/3D graphics rendering. For now, we'll focus on drawables that are important for styling your applications.

4.6.1 *Drawable anatomy*

Drawables always live in the res/drawables folder and its various configuration-spe-cific variants and come in two different formats: binary image files and XML. If you want to use a custom image file in your app, it's as easy as dropping it into that folder. The ADT will discover the drawable and generate an ID for it that's accessible in Java through R.drawable.*the_file_name*, (like with any other Android resource). The same is true for XML drawables, but you'll have to write these first, and we'll show you in a minute how to do that.

   If you've placed a drawable in the drawables folder, you can access it from an Activity by a call to getResources().getDrawable(id). But it's more likely that you'll use drawables in your style or view definitions, for use as backgrounds or other graphical parts of a widget, and sometimes it's difficult to identify them as such. Let's recall our list style definition from listing 4.9:

```
<style name="MyMoviesListView" parent="@android:style/Widget.ListView">
  <item name="android:background">#A000</item>
  <item name="android:fastScrollEnabled">true</item>
  <item name="android:footerDividersEnabled">false</item>
</style>
```

We're already using a drawable here. Can you see it? To be fair, it's not jumping out. It's the color we used as the list's background. For some attributes, Android allows color values where it usually expects a normal drawable, such as a bitmap image. In that case, it'll turn the color into a ColorDrawable internally. Note that for some rea-son this doesn't work everywhere. For instance, the android:windowBackground attri-bute doesn't accept color values.

   We can also define special drawables entirely in XML. When doing so, the root ele-ment is typically the drawable's class name with the *Drawable* part stripped off. For instance, to define a ColorDrawable you'd use the <color> tag, as we showed you in the previous section (we'll see two exceptions to this rule in a moment, admittedly making this a little confusing). Note that not all kinds of drawables can be used every-where; list selectors for instance don't accept a plain color value because a selector has more than one state and one color drawable isn't enough to reflect that. Curiously, a plain image would work here, though.

   Creating custom drawables is unfortunately not one of the most well-documented parts of the platform SDK. We'll cover three types of custom drawables, each of which is useful for styling your apps: shape drawables, selector drawables, and nine-patch drawables.

TECHNIQUE 7   **Working with shape drawables**

Sometimes, static images such as PNGs or JPEGs aren't flexible; they don't scale well if the area they're supposed to cover can change in size. Two examples immediately come to mind. First example is gradients. The nature of gradients is to start with one color on one end and have it blend into another color. If you define this as a static image, then stretching or squeezing the image will result in rendering problems. Another good example is dashed outlines and borders. If you define a dashed border as a background image that has the border painted on it, then the dash length will stretch along with the view you apply it to. But what if you want the dash length and dash gaps to remain static while still being able to arbitrarily resize the view? Clearly, in both cases you'd be better off if those images were generated at runtime.

PROBLEM

You want to render graphics that are difficult to scale, such as gradients or patterns, or graphics that are easier to manipulate at runtime.

SOLUTION

If you find yourself in either situation, you may want to use a *shape drawable*. A shape drawable is a declaratively defined and dynamically rendered graphical element that you can use in any place where drawables are allowed, for instance for view backgrounds.

Shape drawables are represented internally by the GradientDrawable and Shape-Drawable classes, depending on which kind you use. In XML, they're always defined using the <shape> element. We've already seen how we can change the selector drawable for our list view to a predefined drawable, but this time, let's create our own, without any help from imaging applications. A gradient list selector sounds like a cool idea for MyMovies, so let's do that. In res/drawable, create a new file (let's call it list_selector.xml) that contains a new selector as a shape drawable:

```xml
<?xml version="1.0" encoding="utf-8"?>
<shape xmlns:android="http://schemas.android.com/apk/res/android"
  android:shape="rectangle">
  <gradient android:startColor="#AFFF"
          android:endColor="#FFFF"
          android:angle="0"/>
  <stroke android:color="#CCC" android:width="1px" />
  <corners android:radius="5px" />
</shape>
```

We set the drawable's shape to rectangle because that's what we need. We could've also omitted it because that's the default shape. The subelements of the shape element define its features. For our purpose, we set a custom background gradient (<gradient>), a border line (<stroke>), and a border radius (<corners>). Now let's apply it to our list view style:

```xml
<style name="MyMoviesListView" parent="@android:style/Widget.ListView">
    . . .
    <item name="android:listSelector">@drawable/list_selector</item>
</style>
```

As you can see, the list_selector shape is applied like any other drawable. We've replaced the former value for the list selector drawable with a reference to our new gradient shape. Figure 4.10 shows how a selected list element now looks when booting up MyMovies with that change applied.

Figure 4.10   The list view selector using a custom shape drawable. Note how we used a custom gradient that goes across the selector horizontally.

Like what you see? We've only just started. There are many more options to create shape drawables, as we'll see in a moment.

Gotchas with list selectors

List views use the `android:listSelector` attribute to determine which color or image to use as the list selector. Android allows two different ways of rendering this selector: behind a list element's layout, or in front of it, as specified by `android:drawListSelectorOnTop`. Each approach has its advantages and disadvantages, of which you should be aware. The default is to draw selectors behind a list element: this requires that all views in a list element's layout have a transparent background (which is the case for most Android views unless you change it). Otherwise, they'd obscure the selector. If you render images such as photos as part of a list element, you have no choice: they'll obscure it, because a photo is always solid. This means that when using images or solid backgrounds in your list elements, you probably want to draw the selector on top. Therefore the selector must be translucent; otherwise it would itself obscure all views of a list item. Keep this in mind when designing custom list selectors.

DISCUSSION

Shape drawables are a great way of arriving at neat-looking visual elements without having to mess about with image-manipulation programs. They're customizable via the source code, and you as the developer, have full control. Did I hear the design team scream? Yes, it's their job to create nice-looking graphics, but if you want to add an outline to a widget or you need more flexibility, use the color palette assigned by the designers. That's teamwork!

We mentioned that you can create more than boxes and borders. Shape drawables can take various sizes and shapes, from rectangles and ovals to lines and rings. Table 4.5 summarizes most of the elements you can use to define shape drawables (we've omitted some of the more obscure attributes for brevity).

Table 4.5 Valid elements for defining shape drawables

Element name	Description	Attributes
`<shape>`	The root element.	`android:shape`—the type of shape, `rectangle`, `oval`, `line`, `ring`

`<gradient>`	Defines the shape's gradient background.	`android:type`—the gradient type, `linear`, `radial`, `sweep`
		`android:startColor`—the start color of the gradient
		`android:centerColor`—an optional third center color for the gradient
		`android:endColor`—the end color of the gradient
		`android:angle`—the gradient angle, if type is `linear`
		`android:centerX`/`android:centerY`—the center color position, if one is set
		`android:gradientRadius`—the gradient's radius if it's either `radial` or `sweep`.

`<solid>`	Gives the shape a solid background.	`android:color`—the background color
`<stroke>`	Defines the border/ outline of the shape.	`android:color`—the border color `android:width`—the border width `android:dashGap`—the gap width if you want the line to be dashed `android:dashWidth`—the dash width if you want the line to be dashed
`<corners>`	Defines the corner radius of the shape.	`android:radius`—the radius for all four corners `android:topLeftRadius`, `android:topRightRadius`, `android:bottomLeftRadius`, `android:bottomRightRadius`—the radius of each individual corner
`<padding>`	Defines the padding for this shape.	`android:top`, `android:bottom`, `android:left`, `android:right`—the padding for each side of the shape
`<size>`	Defines the size of the shape.	`android:width`, `android:height`—width and height of this shape

You can find the full reference at http://mng.bz/vORg

At this point, we've created a nice-looking list selector graphic, but there's a problem with it. It always looks the same. When interacting with widgets you'd normally expect some visual feedback as soon as you click or select it. But how would that work? We only have a single `listSelector` attribute, which takes exactly one value, but we'd need at least two in order to use different graphics. The answer is that no, you don't. What you need instead is a *selector drawable*.

Working with selector drawables

Sometimes, you need to display graphical elements that change along with a view's state. A good example is a button in Android. If you select one with the D-pad or trackball it receives focus and a light orange overlay is rendered. When you press it, the overlay changes its color to a darker orange, and a long press again uses a different effect. Because we can only assign one drawable at a time to be used for a background or highlight, we clearly need some sort of stateful drawable.

PROBLEM

A view exposes an attribute that takes a drawable, but you want that drawable to change with the view's state.

SOLUTION

Stateful drawables in Android are called selector drawables, and are declared using the `<selector>` element. This special kind of drawable can be thought of as a drawable switcher, if you will. Depending on which state a view is in (selected, pressed, focused, and so on), this drawable replaces one of its managed drawables with another. A true shape shifter!

Coming back to our application, we want to apply this to our list selector. Instead of always showing the same gradient, we want the gradient to change its start color from grey to a light blue whenever a list item is pressed. Because we now have two different list selectors—one for default state one for pressed state—we need to keep them in separate files (let's call them list_item_default.xml and list_item_pressed.xml). Here's a snippet for the new `list_item_pressed` drawable:

```
<?xml version="1.0" encoding="utf-8"?>
<shape xmlns:android="http://schemas.android.com/apk/res/android"
  android:shape="rectangle">
  <gradient android:startColor="#AA66CCFF"
            android:endColor="#FFFF"
            android:angle="0"/>
  <stroke android:color="#CCC" android:width="1px" />
  <corners android:radius="5px" />
</shape>
```

Nothing terribly new here; we've replaced the gradient's start color with a different one. Now that we have two drawables, we need to bring them together in a selector drawable. For that, we modify list_selector.xml from the previous technique to something like this:

```
<?xml version="1.0" encoding="utf-8"?>
<selector xmlns:android="http://schemas.android.com/apk/res/android">
  <item android:state_pressed="true"
        android:drawable="@drawable/list_item_default" />
  <item android:state_pressed="false"
        android:drawable="@drawable/list_item_pressed" />
</selector>
```

What we've done here is replace the root element of the list selector from a shape to a shape switcher—a selector. Selector drawables are defined in terms of `<item>` elements,

Figure 4.11　The new list selector in the default (left) and pressed (right) states. Note how it changes colors when in the pressed state.

each of which takes two arguments: a state, and a drawable to be displayed whenever the view to which this selector is being applied enters that state (you can also use color values as we'll see in a minute). Figure 4.11 shows the selector in both states.

You can switch all sorts of drawables using the `<selector>` tag, not just shape drawables. The most common examples are nine-patch images, which we'll cover next. In fact, Android uses this combination of selectors and nine-patches all over the place to render its system UI.

DISCUSSION

Our example was simple in that it only used two different states: pressed and not pressed, but there are plenty more states, each representing a Boolean condition. We've summarized them for you in table 4.6 (again, we only list the more commonly used ones).

Table 4.6　Common selector drawable states

State	Description
`state_focused`	The view has received the focus.
`state_window_focused`	The view's window has received the focus.
`state_enabled`	The view is enabled/activated.
`state_pressed`	The view has been pressed/clicked.

Table 4.6   Common selector drawable states *(continued)*

State	Description
state_checkable	The view can be checked/ticked (not supported by all views).
state_checked	The view has been checked/ticked (not supported by all views).
state_selected	The view has been selected (not supported by all views).

For a more exhaustive list of states, refer to http://mng.bz/Math and http://mng.bz/qzXz.

One thing to watch for is the order of your selector's state items. To find a drawable in the selector that matched a view's current state, Android walks through the list of items from top to bottom—in the order they're declared in the selector—and selects the first one that satisfies the view's current state. Why is this important? Imagine a focused and checked CheckBox view that's skinned with the following selector:

```xml
<?xml version="1.0" encoding="utf-8"?>
<selector xmlns:android="http://schemas.android.com/apk/res/android">
  <item android:state_focused="true"
        android:drawable="@drawable/my_checkbox_unchecked" />
  <item android:state_focused="true" android:state_checked="true"
        android:drawable="@drawable/my_checkbox_checked" />
</selector>
```

You may expect that Android would pick the second drawable, because it clearly declares that it's the one that should be used whenever the CheckBox is checked, right? Wrong! That's because the first item is less restrictive, and also matches the view's state: it only requires the focused state, which is true, and doesn't require any specific checked state. Because it's the first match Android finds, Android will use this for the CheckBox whenever it receives focus, regardless whether it's checked or not. The second item will therefore *never* match. What does this tell us? It tells us: always make sure that the least-restrictive state items are the *last* items in the state list. Otherwise they'll obscure more specific state items.

Here's another useful hint. We mentioned before that you may use color values in selectors using the android:color attribute. This is particularly useful when working with stateful text appearances, where you want the text color or size to change. For example, if TextView receives focus, you can assign a selector that switches colors with states to the android:color attribute of a TextView! It's in these details where it becomes apparent how flexible and awesome Android's view system is.

As with shape drawables, selector drawables are mapped to Java framework classes. When using plain drawables, a selector will become a StateListDrawable, and a ColorStateList, which curiously is *not* a Drawable, when using colors. Hence, when using selectors that switch color values, remember that you can't use them in places where drawables are expected, only for color values (but then again we learned earlier that you can turn colors into drawables easily, so this problem can be circumvented).

We're getting close—we have one kind of drawable left up our sleeves. We've mentioned nine-patch drawables before, and they're perhaps the most useful and commonly used drawables, so read carefully!

TECHNIQUE 9 Scaling views with nine-patch drawables

Nine-patch drawables are best explained by example. How about this; in our application, we'd like to add some kind of title image above the movie list view that says "IMDB Top 100". We can do this by changing the MyMovies main screen as seen in the following listing.

Listing 4.10 Extending the MyMovies layout to include a title image

```xml
<?xml version="1.0" encoding="utf-8"?>
<LinearLayout xmlns:android="http://schemas.android.com/apk/res/android"
    android:orientation="vertical"
    android:layout_width="fill_parent"
    android:layout_height="fill_parent">

    <ImageView android:src="@drawable/title"
      android:layout_width="fill_parent"
      android:layout_height="wrap_content"
      android:scaleType="fitXY" />

    <ListView android:id="@android:id/list"
        android:layout_width="fill_parent"
        android:layout_height="fill_parent"
        />
</LinearLayout>
```

1 Add ImageView and set width to fill_parent

2 Scale bitmap to fit ImageView

In listing 4.10 we've added an `ImageView` that displays our title image (stored as /res/drawable/title.9.png) **1**. The title image is a PNG image file, not an XML-based drawable. Note how we tell it to `fill_parent` across the horizontal axis. If the device is in portrait mode, this has no effect (at least on a standard screen size, which we assume for this example), because our image happens to be exactly 320 pixels wide. But if we turn the device to landscape mode, we want the `ImageView` to remain stretched across the whole screen width. Because the layout parameter only affects the `ImageView` (the widget), but not the image itself (the bitmap), we also set the `scaleType` to `fitXY`, which

means that the bitmap should be resized to fill its `ImageView` container in width and height **2**. The result is shown in figure 4.12 for both portrait and landscape mode.

Note how the text of the title image gets blurry and loses proportion in landscape mode. The white dots turned into eggs! That's because Android stretches the image to fill the screen in landscape mode, interpolating pixels until the

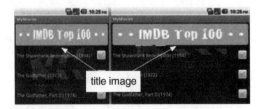

Figure 4.12   The MyMovies header image shown in portrait (left) and landscape (right) modes. In portrait mode, the image won't stretch; in landscape mode it'll stretch to fill the view horizontally, resulting in distorted proportions.

image is the same size as its container. The result looks horrible, so what can we do to avoid this problem?

PROBLEM

You want to display a static image on a view that's variable in width or height, but stretching the image results in a loss of quality.

SOLUTION

Take an educated guess... correct, nine-patch drawables are the solution. A nine-patch drawable is a PNG image that defines stretchable areas as part of its image data (the bitmap), and can be rendered across arbitrary-sized views without any noticeable loss in quality. Nine-patch PNGs must end in `*.9.png`. Without this convention, Android won't recognize the PNG as a nine-patch image. Turning a conventional image into a nine-patch image is simple:

- First, take the image you'd like to use and add a one-pixel-wide transparent border (in fact, any color will work except black).
- Second, define the stretchable areas of your image by marking the top and left edges of that border at the respective sections using a solid black stroke. The stretchable area is defined by the box these demarcations form if you extended them with imaginary lines until they intersect.
- Optionally, you may repeat this step for the right and bottom edges to pad the image, whereby any areas *not* marked with black will be used as padding.

Figure 4.13 illustrates the process of defining stretchable areas and adding padding.

The top image in figure 4.13 shows how the stretchable areas of the PNG are defined. Here, the center box indicates the area that it'll be interpolated in order to resize the image (you're allowed to have several of these boxes, not just one). In the lower image, the center box defines the image's content area. Anything else is padding; if the image's

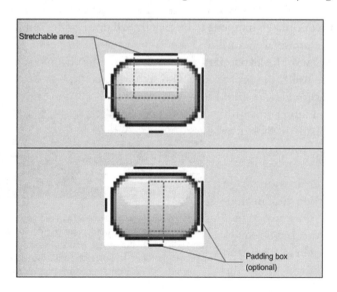

Figure 4.13
Defining stretchable areas (top) and padding boxes (bottom) in nine-patch drawables using the draw9patch tool. Whereas the stretchable area is defined using the top-left strokes, the padding area is defined using the bottom-right strokes (source: http://developer.android.com).

content outgrows this area, the image will be resized accordingly by duplicating the pixels within the content box.

> **PADDING BOX GOTCHA** Be careful if you're not explicitly defining a padding using the padding box. It is indeed optional, but if you omit it, Android will assume the padding box to be identical to the stretchable area (it copies it), which can have awkward and unexpected side effects when the image is rendered.

For our title image, we only want the small areas between the rounded corners and the text to be stretched, because they're all of the same color, and hence can be interpolated without any loss of visual quality. Figure 4.14 shows our title image again, now redefined as a nine-patch and viewed using the `draw9patch` SDK tool. Note that the thick lines going straight across the borders are merely visual guides added by that tool and are *not* part of the image itself.

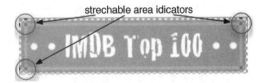

Figure 4.14 MyMovies title image defined as a nine-patch drawable; the corners demarcated by the black lines will be used for scaling (no padding has been defined).

We save this file to res/drawable/ title.9.png and restart the application. Looking at the title image again in figure 4.15, in both portrait and landscape modes, shows that we've fixed the problem. It scales!

We're pretty good at fixing things, aren't we? Wait, what? You noticed the

Figure 4.15 The title image now scales correctly in landscape mode. This is achieved by stretching only those parts of the image that are safe to stretch (they don't result in distorted imagery), as defined by the nine-patch format.

skewed background image, right? We didn't fix that, but *you* can do it, now that you know how nine-patch drawables work.

DISCUSSION

Nine-patch drawables are incredibly useful, and they're ubiquitous in Android itself. All standard widgets that come with the platform use them. They're particularly useful for widgets such as buttons and text fields, which frequently have to scale with their containing layout. If you want to restyle all standard widgets in your application, a good approach is to take the existing nine-patch drawables that are part of the Android open source project and do your modifications around them. A common example is changing the color of highlights to match the palette of an application's brand—the standard orange doesn't cut it sometimes.

Nine-patch drawables can be created using any kind of imaging software, but thankfully, for everyone without a license for fancy commercial image editing software, Google has added the aforementioned `draw9patch` tool to the SDK. The `draw9patch` tool helps you by automatically adding the one-pixel border to an existing image, rendering visual guides such as marking the resulting scaling boxes, and by computing live previews of your image scaled in all directions with the current modifications.

This section has been all about the visuals. You've seen how to organize your application's view attributes in styles and themes, as well as what drawables are and how to use them to create completely customized, beautiful user interfaces—well, if your design skills are as good as your programming skills. We've talked about scaling images (on a small scale). But what about scaling the entire user interface? Android devices come in various screen sizes, and even the most beautiful user interface will fall apart if it doesn't render correctly on all devices. Therefore, the next section is all about making your application's UI scale with the various kinds of displays and configurations that are available now, and even those that aren't available yet!

4.7 Creating portable user interfaces

When talking about portability, we can mean different things: portability with respect to software (not all SDK functions are available on all handsets) or hardware capabilities (not every Android device has a light sensor or hardware keyboard). In this section, we'll talk about portability and scalability with respect to user interfaces and screen sizes.

We started developing for the Android platform in its early Alpha days, when there wasn't a single device that would run the platform... unless you count the Nokia Internet tablets that a handful of adventurous developers flashed with prerelease versions of Android. Then came Google's G1, aka HTC Dream, and life was good—you only had one device configuration to care about. Today, there are so many different devices that we've stopped counting, and Android still grows rapidly with more manufacturers jumping on the train.

Having to support many devices, as mentioned in chapter 1, is a common criticism leveled at Android. Fortunately, the Android platform introduced support for different device configurations in a graceful way, making it almost trivial to make an application work with screens sizes that weren't around when the application was developed.

Against this backdrop, the following three techniques show you how to enable your application to gracefully scale with different screen configurations, from a simple just-works approach meant for legacy applications to more elaborate, native support approaches.

TECHNIQUE 10   Automatically scaling to different screens

All the screenshots of our example application you've seen so far have been taken from the emulator, running with the default screen configuration, the one that was standard in the pre-1.6 days. With Android 1.6 came support for new configurations, and with that support, devices using these configurations such as the HTC Tattoo, which had a QVGA screen that was shorter in height than the previous ones, as seen in figure 4.16.

Figure 4.16 **Different Android devices may come with different display configurations. Whereas the HTC Magic (left) comes with a 320x480px (160dpi) 3.4 inch screen, the HTC Tattoo has a smaller, lower-resolution 240x 320px (120dpi) 2.8 inch screen.**

The question is: if you've developed an application on Android 1.5 or earlier, and that application has already been released on the market, how do you make sure the user interface is displayed correctly on all these different devices? New devices may not only have lower or higher resolutions (fewer or more physical pixels), their displays may also have different pixel densities (fewer or more pixels spread across the same space). The latter problem may lead to rendering issues on these devices—if a UI element had been defined as being 100 pixels wide, then on a display with a higher density, that element would appear shrunken, because it occupies less physical space. This problem is illustrated in figure 4.17 using two speculative screen pixel densities of 3 and 6 dots per inch.

Android 1.6+ implements a set of algorithms that can automatically mitigate these problems. In a moment, we'll learn how to proactively solve these problems, but let's

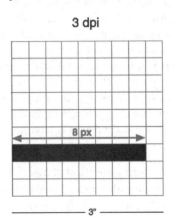
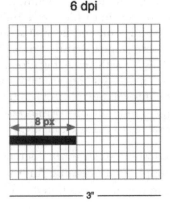

Figure 4.17 **A line that's 8 pixels long and 1 pixel high on a 3 dpi screen will be only half the height and length on a 6 dpi screen because a pixel occupies less physical space. Note that this example simplifies dots to pixels, which isn't necessarily true.**

assume for now that we're lazy and don't feel like fixing our application manually, and instead let the Android runtime take care of it somehow.

PROBLEM

Your application was developed with a specific class of displays in mind (specific size and pixel density), and you now want to target other screen configurations without having to change your view code.

SOLUTION

You can report the screen sizes and densities your application supports by means of the <supports-screens> element, which was introduced with Android 1.6. Because we haven't developed MyMovies with screen configurations that are different from the default in mind, we should tell Android about this so that it's aware of this fact. You set the configurations you support in the application manifest, as seen here:

```
<?xml version="1.0" encoding="utf-8"?>
<manifest xmlns:android="http://schemas.android.com/apk/res/android" ...>

    <uses-sdk android:minSdkVersion="4" />

    <supports-screens
        android:smallScreens="false"
        android:normalScreens="true"
        android:largeScreens="false"
        android:xlargeScreens="false"
        android:anyDensity="false"
    />

    ...
</manifest>
```

We tell Android that we only support devices that fall into the normal screens class. Note that this doesn't necessarily imply that our application isn't installable anymore on other devices. It doesn't even mean that it's doomed to break on them, but it has other implications as we'll see in a moment.

> **WARNING** The configuration from listing 4.21 is the one you'd automatically get when building for Android 1.5 or earlier (as indicated by the <uses-sdk> element). Hence, the default assumption for applications that run on Android 1.6 or newer, but which were built with an earlier SDK, is that they were developed with only the normal screen size and pixel density in mind because those were standard at that time. This is a sensible default for these applications. This is *not* the case if you're targeting an API level of 4 or higher (Android 1.6+). If you set the minSdkVersion to at least 4, all <supports-screens> attributes will default to true instead, meaning that if you want to remain in legacy-mode for one or more screen sizes, then you'll have to set the respective values to false explicitly.

What does it mean when we say normal screen? We didn't mention actual sizes in pixels or densities in dpi. That's because Android collapses all kinds of available displays into a 4x4 configuration matrix as noted in table 4.7. This matrix is organized around a central baseline configuration, which was the sole available configuration before Android 1.6 came out, and which was used by all 1.5 devices such as the G1.

Table 4.7 Screen configuration matrix with example configurations

	Low density	Medium density	High density	Extra high density*
Small screen	Sony Xperia Mini (QVGA 240x320, 2.55")			
Normal screen		baseline configuration Google G1, HTC Magic (HVGA 320x480, 3.2")	Google Nexus One (WVGA 480x800, 3.7")	
Large screen			HTC Desire HD2 (qHD 540x960, 4.3")	
Extra large screen*		Motorola Xoom tablet (WXGA 1280x800, 10.1")		

More detailed coverage at http://mng.bz/InPC
*The xlargeScreens and hxdpi configurations were added in Android 2.3 and Android 2.2, respectively.

If your application was developed for the baseline configuration (320x480, 160dpi), Android ensures that it'll continue to work on a WVGA device by entering a fallback mode. This doesn't work with all configurations though. Understanding which fallbacks Android uses for which configurations is important.

DISCUSSION

Whenever you specify `false` for any of the previously mentioned attributes, Android will enter a fallback mode for the respective screen configurations. What happens in fallback mode is different for every attribute. If `smallScreens` is set to `false`, users with a device classified as having a small screen won't see your application on the Android market anymore (although they'd still be able to install it manually). That's because it's likely that the application's user interface will break when there's suddenly less room to render it. Keep this in mind, or you may lose a significant portion of potential users because they can't even find your application in Android Market!

It's an entirely different story with large-screen devices such as tablets, because they have enough display space to render your application in its entirety. More precisely, if `largeScreens` is set to `false`, Android will render your application in *letterbox mode*, which means it'll render it using the baseline size and density and fill any unused screen space with a black background. Not beautiful, but at least functional.

This leaves the `anyDensity` flag. Here, things get more elaborate. If set to `false`, Android will enter a compatibility mode which takes care of scaling all values specified in px (absolute pixels) against the baseline density of 160 dpi in order to translate them to the device's screen density. If the density is higher, these values are scaled upward; if smaller, downward. This is done to ensure that any coordinates or dimensions specified in pixels will result in approximately the same physical positions and sizes regardless of the device's screen density (recall from figure 4.17 that measurements of screen elements defined in absolute pixels would normally have different outcomes on displays with different pixel densities).

Example: Android's auto-scaling mode

Imagine you want to display a 100px-wide image. Using the baseline configuration of 320x480 and 160 dpi, one physical pixel is 0.00625 inches wide (1/160), so this image would be 0.625 inches in width on a device using that configuration. If you now run this image on a device with a high-res 480x800 240 dpi screen, the same image would suddenly only be about 0.417 inches wide because with a higher pixel density, a single pixel takes less physical space on that screen. To counter this effect, Android multiplies the original value specified in pixels by 1.5 (240/160) which is also 0.625, and voilà, the image specified as 100 pixels wide uses the same space on both screens!

Moreover, because a density of 160 dpi is assumed, but the high-res display has significantly more pixels at a higher density, Android must report a similarly scaled-down screen size to the application, or the screen would appear to be larger, with more pixels spread across more room. Therefore, Android also downscales the screen size of the device by 0.75 (160/240) and reports a screen size of 320x533 pixels to the application, which would fall into the normal screens class.

Who said that lying can't work out well sometimes?

In addition to these measures, Android will also automatically scale all drawables it loads from the standard drawables folder, because these are assumed to have been created with the baseline configuration in mind. For instance, a 100-pixel-wide PNG image will now always take up the same room on a screen, scaling up or down depending on the size and density of the current screen (using the same logic we just discussed). This is called *prescaling* and is done when the resource in question is loaded. Scaling bitmaps comes at a cost, and we'll show you how to avoid these costly computations shortly.

To summarize, if you report in your manifest file that you don't support any but the baseline configuration, table 4.8 shows what happens.

Table 4.8   A synopsis of supports-screens settings and effects

Attribute set to false	Effect
smallScreens	On devices with small screens, your application will be filtered from Android Market. It can still be installed manually, and the same scaling logic discussed earlier will apply.
normalScreens	On devices with normal screens, this will enable Android's auto-scaling mode. Unless you specifically develop for small- or large-screen devices, this is pointless.

Table 4.8   A synopsis of supports-screens settings and effects *(continued)*

Attribute set to false	Effect
largeScreens	On devices with large screens, your application will be displayed using the baseline configuration and scaled to that accordingly. If it still doesn't occupy the entire screen, the unused space will be painted in black (letterbox mode).
xlargeScreens	Same as largeScreens.
anyDensity	On devices with pixel densities deviating from the baseline density, Android will auto-scale all images (unless specifically prepared, see next technique) and absolute pixel values to match the different configuration.

Using the appropriate supports-screens, settings can be effective, which makes it easy to forward-enable legacy applications, but it has its down sides. To do things right you need to turn to Android's alternative resources framework.

TECHNIQUE 11   Loading configuration dependent resources

The mechanisms explained in the previous technique are a great way to easily enable legacy applications to support almost all screen configurations, without having to explicitly program for it. Still, this is merely a convenience and should by no means be considered good practice for applications that you develop today.

The drawbacks are obvious: no visibility on Android Market for small-screen devices, no guaranteed full-screen mode on large screen devices, and an often noticeable loss of quality for prescaled images (coupled with a slight loss in load times). What can you do to better support various display configurations?

PROBLEM

Instead of relying on Android's image prescaling, you want to supply resources such as layouts or images created for specific screen sizes or densities, so as to eliminate any loss of visual quality introduced by Android's scaling procedures.

SOLUTION

The solution is to leverage Android's alternative resources framework. We've already touched on how this works in chapter 2, where we mentioned that you can use several different string resource files for different languages. You do this by using different resource folders with separate resource values for each permutation you need to support (for example, /res/values-en for English strings, and /res/values-de for German strings). We can leverage the same system to provide configuration-specific resources such as drawables or layouts to Android. For these resources, Android assumes that they've been designed for that specific configuration and won't attempt to prescale them.

Say for instance we were to add a custom icon to MyMovies, one that says "MyMovies" on it. The problem with this is that, on a mid- to low-resolution screen, this text will be difficult or even impossible to read. Hence, we only want to show the full text when we run on an HDPI (high dots per inch) device, and abbreviate the text to "MM" on LDPI

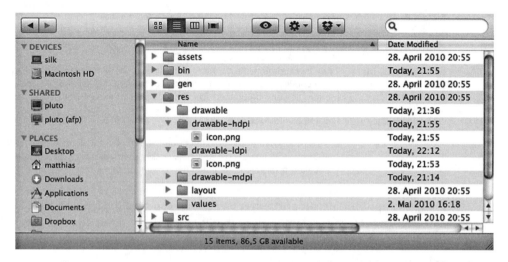

Figure 4.18   Supplying different image files for different screen configurations is done by placing them in the appropriate resource folders for a given configuration. Which folder a resource is loaded from at runtime is then determined by matching the current device configuration against the folder names.

devices (low dots per inch—we don't change anything for normal configurations). For this we need to create two variations of the standard icon and place them into the `drawable-hdpi` and `drawable-ldpi` folders respectively, as shown in figure 4.18.

We're now explicitly targeting low- and high-density devices by providing two new icon files specifically created for these screen densities. No more setup is required. Android will automatically find and load these files for you, even when you're running in fallback mode! Figure 4.19 shows how the new icons compare on both a large high-density screen, and a small low-density screen.

Figure 4.19   The two different icon files as rendered on the configurations they were made for: the icon with full text for HDPI screens (big picture), and the abbreviated version for LDPI screens (small picture).

There are plenty of ways you can leverage this technique; you could even load different strings (any kind of resource) for different screen sizes, but as you can imagine it's useful for images and layouts.

DISCUSSION

Screen densities aren't the only configuration options you can target. Much more can be encoded into resource folder names. You can load different resources based on language, SIM card country, touchscreen type, keyboard type, screen orientation, API level, and more. You can even combine them. Table 4.9 summarizes those configuration qualifiers that are relevant for screen support.

Table 4.9 Resource qualifiers relevant for screen support

Targeted attribute	Qualifiers	Examples
Screen size class	small—for small screens (about 2-3 inches) normal—for normal screens (baseline size, about 3-4 inches) large—for large screens (about 4-7 inches) xlarge—for very large screens (more than 7 inches)	/res/drawables-small /res/drawables-small-ldpi /res/layouts-normal-land
Extended screen height	long—longer screens (such as WQVGA, WVGA, FWVGA) notlong—normal aspect ratio (such as QVGA, HVGA, and VGA)	/res/drawables-long /res/drawables-large-long /res/layouts-notlong-port
Pixel density (dpi)	ldpi—low density (about 120dpi) mdpi—medium density (about 160dpi) hdpi—high density (about 240dpi) xhdpi—extra high density (about 320dpi) nodpi—disable scaling for these resources	/res/drawables-ldpi /res/drawables-large-mdpi /res/layouts-port-hdpi

For a full list plus qualifier ordering rules, see http://mng.bz/d0M9.

Keep in mind that any qualified resource folder is completely optional. If you don't have any prescaled images in the /res/drawable-hdpi folder (or if it doesn't even exist), Android will still look for an image in this folder first, but if it can't find the image in there, it'll fall back to the default drawable folder. That means it's always safe to put all your stuff in the nonqualified resource folders; that way Android will always find a resource.

> **HOW ANDROID SELECTS RESOURCE FOLDERS** If more than one folder qualifies for lookup, Android will load the resource from the folder that most closely matches the current configuration. The algorithm for this is quite refined, and is documented at http://mng.bz/7NiH.

Even though this technique can increase the size of your application when multiple versions of a given resource are bundled with it, it's a sensible choice for images, such as icons or window backgrounds that are likely to suffer a loss in quality when scaled. Consider again an icon being resized from 100 pixels to 150 pixels on an HDPI device. That's a 50% increase in pixels, and chances are that the image will look washed out when scaled. Nine-patch images on the other hand scale well by their nature, and are less problematic even when Android is in auto-scale mode.

Now that you've seen how to let Android handle everything and how to provide configuration specific resources, there's one more thing you should learn. It's last, but certainly not least: programming your application with different screen configurations up front.

TECHNIQUE 12   Programming pixel-independently

This is the last technique we're going to show you in this chapter, and it's short but important. The one big question that remains is, if we enable support for all screen densities in the `<supports-screens>` element, Android's auto-scaling logic will be disabled and we again have the problem that any values specified in absolute pixels will have different outcomes on different devices.

PROBLEM
Explicitly declaring support for screens that don't have the baseline pixel density will disable Android's auto-scaling mode, which means that any values specified in pixels won't scale to these devices.

SOLUTION
The solution is surprisingly simple: don't use absolute pixel values. Ever. The px unit is unsafe. As we've seen, any value specified in px is tailored toward the device you're developing on. So how should we specify positions and dimensions then? Android provides a set of density-independent units that, on a device using the baseline configuration, behave exactly as if specified in absolute pixels. On other screens, these same densities will be auto-scaled as seen before.

Remember how we defined our list selector's corner radius to be five pixels? Have a look at figure 4.20. On the left side you see the list selector as it's supposed to look; on the right side the corner radius appears to be *less* than the specified five pixels. Both screenshots were taken from an emulator instance running with a high-density screen configuration, but for the left image we used the *density-independent pixels* unit (dip or dp) to specify the corner radius, whereas on the right side we used the plain old px unit.

When specifying values in dip, this value will be considered to be the value in pixels you would've used to arrange the screen element on a device that uses the baseline configuration. This means that if you're running such a device, then you won't notice any difference between px and dip, but on devices with other pixel densities, Android makes sure you get the same result!

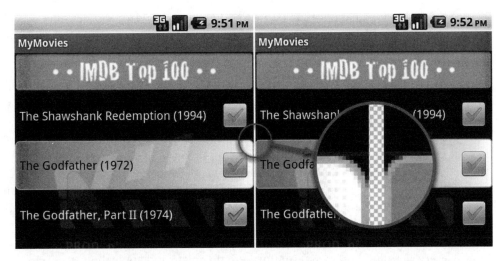

Figure 4.20 Corner radii mismatch on a high-density screen. On the left side, the radius was specified using density-independent pixels (dip), where the right side uses absolute pixels (px), resulting in a physically smaller corner radius.

DISCUSSION

Whenever possible, you should use density-independent units rather than absolute units when specifying positions or dimensions. Android defines two units you can use to auto-scale values:

- `dip` (alias `dp`)—Density-independent pixels, useful for specifying positions and dimensions in a scalable way
- `sip` (alias `sp`)—Scale-independent pixels, useful for specifying font sizes in a scalable way

You can and should use these units anywhere in your layouts or styles. If you need to specify a pixel value in your program code, but want to achieve the same effect, then you'll have to do the scaling yourself (unless you're running in fallback mode), because the SDK functions typically expect values to be in absolute pixels. The conversion is easy though. Here's one implementation of a helper function that does the scaling from dip to pixels for you:

```
public static int dipToPx(Activity context, int dip) {
    DisplayMetrics displayMetrics =
        context.getResources().getDisplayMetrics();

    return (int) (dip * displayMetrics.density + 0.5f);
}
```

With this helper you can write applications that scale across all kinds of displays, and not have to rely on Android's fallback mode anymore.

In this last section, we've taken you through three techniques that showed you how to prepare your legacy applications to run on devices with different screen configurations by leveraging Android's fallback mode. More importantly, we saw how to make newly developed applications scale to different screen sizes and densities gracefully by means of customized resources and density-/scale-independent pixel units. It's time to wrap this chapter up.

4.8   Summary

In this chapter, we focused on the user interface. We've seen how to configure views in layouts, and how view hierarchies are drawn to the screen. We've also seen how all of the supplied Android layout managers work, and how they work with attributes to create structure. This where the UI starts.

From there we looked more closely at working with ListView to uncover a few handy features, such as header and footer views, and to see how to maintain state between views and the data model exposed by an Adapter. This helped us focus on working more closely with this common and powerful widget. Also, while working with ListView we saw how to reuse styles rather than repeat look and feel values on every view, and how to go even further and create and apply themes.

Along with themes, we learned how to take the UI to the next level by working with and defining drawables. We also learned how to provide device-independent resources for different device configurations. This allowed us to create pixel-perfect layouts and images so that our application looks the way we expect on many different screen sizes.

Overall, we've now seen a good deal about the basics of building Android applications, and how to perfect the form (the UI). Now it's time to move toward function in the next chapter, where we'll depart from the UI and hone in on a new topic: background services.

Managing background
tasks with Services

5

I am the greatest. I said that even before I knew I was. Don't tell me I can't do something. Don't tell me it's impossible. Don't tell me I'm not the greatest. I'm the double greatest.

—Muhammad Ali

`Services` are a killer feature of Android. That's a bold statement, but it's accurate. It might be more accurate to say that *multitasking* is a killer feature of Android, and the way to fully implement multitasking on Android is by using `Services`. Don't take our word on this: watch TV instead. One of the most successful commercials for the popular Motorola Droid touted its ability to multitask and ridiculed "other" phones that couldn't "walk and chew gum at the same time."

Unfortunately, multitasking is one of the most often misunderstood features, even from a technical standpoint. For years, we've used desktop and laptop computers. These kinds of computers have defined how we expect multitasking to work. If

I start to load a web page in my browser and then change windows to type in a word processor, I expect that the web page will continue to load even without my attention. As programmers, we often begin a build of our code and then switch to another program while the build goes on. What would we do if the build stopped when we switched to another window? This is the multitasking world that mobile applications live in. In this chapter, we'll learn how Android's Services allow for multitasking when the traditional desktop multitasking doesn't work. First, let's understand how multitasking works on Android devices.

5.1 It's all about the multitasking

An easy way to realize how valuable multitasking is on a computing device is to live without it. For some applications, this is no big deal—everything the application does is confined to the device anyways. An example of this might be a note-taking application. If all the app does is stores notes on your device, then you probably don't care if it can multitask. But if your app stores your notes on a remote server so that they can be accessed (both read and write) from any computer/device, then multitasking starts to become nice. Why? If your app can run in the background, then it can keep the notes on the device and on the server in sync. Without this, you'll need to resync with the server every time you launch the app. That may not sound like a big deal, but this is a network operation that could be slow. The user is going to experience this slowness every time they want to use the application. In fact, it may be the first thing they experience when they launch the application. Can you say bad user experience?

The obvious solution is to let applications run in the background indefinitely, as desktop applications do. But what works fine on a desktop computer doesn't work well on a mobile device. The main problem is memory. A desktop computer has a lot of it. When it runs low, it uses virtual memory or paging to expand the available memory by using hard disk or similar storage. When an application isn't in the foreground, its real memory is often swapped out for virtual memory. When it comes back into the foreground, it'll need to get its data swapped back into real memory. This can be a slow process and make your computer seem sluggish.

On a mobile device, the amount of real memory available is low. One could imagine many apps going in and out of virtual memory. Suddenly, any time you changed apps, your device would seem to be bogged down and unresponsive. Nobody wants a device like that.

On an Android device, when you move an application into the background, it'll continue to run much like an application on a desktop computer. It's possible that it could run like this for a long time, but this is far from guaranteed. Instead, if or when memory becomes low, the Android OS will terminate your application. This may seem harsh, but it's not really. This removes the need for virtual memory and swapping, as we learned about in chapter 3. Plus, the OS will also send events to your application to let it know that this is about to happen. That gives you a chance to save the state of your application.

If this were the end of the multitasking story on Android, then you'd have to agree that Android wouldn't qualify as a multitasking OS. You might get lucky and be able to multitask for a while, but it'd be difficult to design an application around this. Even worse, there'd be nothing to talk about in this chapter! Fortunately, for all of us, Android gives you more multitasking options, and these are all built around Services. We first saw Services in chapter 2, but now it's time to take a much more detailed look at them. In this chapter, we'll look at all of the many aspects of Services.

We'll start with the basics—how to create Services and how to start them automatically when the device boots up. We'll learn about two of the most common design patterns for using Services, using them to centralize access to and cache data, and periodically executing Services to check for remote events and potentially publishing Notifications about remote events. This will naturally lead us into a discussion about scheduling Services and how to make sure these schedules are executed even when a device is asleep or low on memory. Finally, we'll learn about a new feature in Android 2.2, Cloud to Device Messaging, and see how we can use our remote servers to schedule and interact with Services. Let's get started by discussing why we'd want to use a Service.

5.2 *Why services and how to use them*

We stated this earlier, but it bears repeating: Services are the way to fully implement multitasking on Android. You'll need other technologies as well, and we'll examine those, but Services are the building blocks for any kind of multitasking on Android. Now Services aren't for running indefinitely in the background. If you need to start a task separate from your main application, consider using a Service. For example, let's say that you need to upload some large file to a remote server. This could take a long time. It's possible that the user will leave your app before this upload finishes. If the upload is tied to the app, it might still finish as long as the app runs in the background. But if the app gets terminated to free up memory, then that upload could potentially be disrupted in midstream. Another example might be building some kind of complex data structure. A common example of this would be creating a Content-Provider for Android's systemwide search. This may involve downloading some data, processing it, and then storing it on the device, probably in a SQLite database. This is a one-time task that could take a long time to execute. You don't want it tied to your application's lifecycle, or this task may never finish correctly. Services are perfect for these kinds of one-time tasks, as well as any kind of recurring task.

 GRAB THE PROJECT: STOCKPORTFOLIO You can get the source code for this project, and/or the packaged APK to run it, at the *Android in Practice* code website. Because some code listings here are shortened to focus on specific concepts, we recommend that you download the complete source code and follow along within Eclipse (or your favorite IDE or text editor).

Source: http://mng.bz/APOO, APK file: http://mng.bz/4iDX

This all sounds well and good, but let's consider a more concrete example. In this chapter, we'll develop an application called StockPortfolio. It'll allow the user to track their stock portfolio—what stocks they own, how many shares of each stock, and how much they paid for the stocks. Further, it'll allow the user to set alerts, so that if a stock's price falls too low or rises too high, they'll be notified so they can sell or buy. This is a simple application, but it benefits from multitasking via `Services` in two ways. First, it'll fetch the latest stock data in the background and cache it locally. That way, when the user launches the app, it'll immediately display accurate stock data, with no wait time for the user. Second, by running in the background, it can also compare the current stock prices to see if they're at a level where the user wants to receive a notification. This way the user can receive the notification without having the application open. All of this sounds simple enough, but such an application wouldn't be possible on some mobile devices. Even on Android, you need to be aware of some "gotchas." By the end of the chapter, you'll understand not only how to create such a `Service`, but how to get it run periodically in the background, even under low-memory situations where the OS may have to kill the `Service`.

TECHNIQUE 13   Creating a Service

This chapter is all about `Services`, and we'll cover them in great detail. But we're going to start off small and discuss the basics. `Services` have some unique characteristics, as they're designed to fill the niche of background processing given the style of multitasking supported by the Android OS. It comes as no surprise that creating and starting a `Service` isn't as simple as implementing an interface and invoking a method.

PROBLEM

You need to monitor the prices of stocks at all times, not only when the user has the application open in the foreground.

SOLUTION

The Android way of performing background processing is to use a `Service`. If all you cared about was retrieving data in the background while the user had the application open, then you could spawn a thread from your `Activity`. If you wanted it to run continuously, then you could use a `java.util.Timer`. You might also want to consider Android's `AsyncTask` as a convenient way to orchestrate the spawned thread and its interaction with the UI. (Chapter 6 has a lot more information about threads and `AsyncTasks`.) The problem with this approach is that once your application leaves the foreground, the OS could terminate it at any time.

   It might seem like this isn't the case in practice. It's easy to create an app that starts a `Timer` that continues to run when the application leaves the foreground. You could let it run on a test devise for a long time, but it will only appear as if it's never killed. This is misleading though, since it's atypical usage. Typically, users are using lots of different apps, making calls, sending emails, and so on. All of these require memory and make it more likely that the OS will terminate your application. So don't be fooled: if you need to keep running in the background, you need a `Service`. To create a `Service`, you'll need to declare it in your manifest file. The following listing shows how the `Service` for our stock portfolio, called `PortfolioManagerService`, is declared.

Listing 5.1 Declaring the `PortfolioManagerService`

```xml
<?xml version="1.0" encoding="utf-8"?>
<manifest xmlns:android="http://schemas.android.com/apk/res/android"
    package="com.manning.aip.portfolio"
    android:versionCode="1"
    android:versionName="1.0">
  <application android:icon="@drawable/icon"
      android:label="@string/app_name">
    <activity android:name=".ViewStocks"
        android:label="@string/app_name">
      <intent-filter>
        <action android:name="android.intent.action.MAIN" />
          <category android:name="android.intent.category.LAUNCHER"/>
      </intent-filter>
    </activity>
    <service android:process=":stocks_background"
        android:name="PortfolioManagerService"
        android:icon="@drawable/icon"
        android:label="@string/service_name"/>
  </application>
  <uses-sdk android:minSdkVersion="8" />
  <uses-permission android:name="android.permission.INTERNET"/>
</manifest>
```

❶ **Declare Service and process**

❷ **Service's class**

❸ **Icon and user-friendly name**

This is a straightforward manifest, so we'll focus on the `Service` declaration. `Services` are important enough in Android that they get their own tag! The first part of this declaration is significant. The first attribute that we declare ❶ is the `Service`'s process, specifying the OS-level process that the `Service` will run in. This is an optional attribute—if you don't specify it, then the `Service` will run in the same process as your application.

Having a `Service` in the same process as your main application will change the way the OS classifies your application process. This is generally good (it'll be less likely that your application process will be killed to free up memory). But it also means that your application and `Service` share the same memory allocated to the process that they run in. This can cause your application to run low on memory more often and cause more garbage collections. That can lead to a laggy/jerky user experience, as sometimes the UI will be frozen while garbage collection occurs. By putting the `Service` in its own named process, you avoid this potential problem.

All you have to do is supply a `process` attribute. Now you might notice that the value of this attribute is `:stocks_background`. The colon prefix is significant—it indicates that this separate process is private to the application. The only application that can start or interact (bind) with the `Service` is going to be your application. If we removed the colon, then the `Service` would still be in its own process, but it would be a global process. If your `Service` provides some feature that you want other applications to have access to, then you might want to do this. We'll look at global `Services` later in this chapter.

Getting back to listing 5.1, the next thing we declare is the `Service`'s name attribute ❷. This is the only attribute that's required in a `Service` declaration. It specifies the class of the Service (relative to the package of your application, like for activities). Next, we declare two more optional attributes for our Service. These are the icon and label **❸**. The Android OS allows users to see all running Services on their device and potentially stop them. The OS uses the icon and label when the user views this list of running Services, as shown in figure 5.1

Now that we've declared our Service, we still need to implement it. This is as easy as extending android.app.Service. You aren't required to do much in this extension, but you'll often want to override the Service's lifecycle methods. Here's the basic structure of the Portfolio-ManagerService.

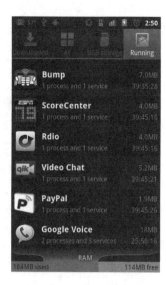

Figure 5.1   Viewing running Services

Listing 5.2   Declaring the PortfolioManagerService

```
public class PortfolioManagerService extends Service {
    @Override
    public void onCreate() {                          Start
        // ...                                         Service
    }
    @Override
    public IBinder onBind(Intent intent) {     ❶ Establish communication
        // ...                                      channel
    }
    @Override
    public void onDestroy() {                      Release resources
        // ...                                      when Service is killed
    }
}
```

The code in listing 5.2 shows the outline of our Service (we'll look at the details of its methods later). You only need to implement one method: onBind **❶**. This method allows other components—typically activities or perhaps other Services—to communicate with the Service. Remember, a Service will usually be running in its own process, so communicating with it isn't as simple as invoking its methods. Interprocess communication (IPC) is necessary. The onBind method is where the IPC channel is established.

The other methods that we chose to override in listing 5.2 are onCreate and onDestroy. These are optional. If your Service does all of its work within the onBind (an example might be uploading data to a remote server), then you may not need to override onCreate. If you need to do some processing outside the context of an onBind call, then you'll probably set that up in the onCreate method. Finally, as the name suggests, onDestroy is called when a Service is being killed. You should release any resources being used by your Service here.

DISCUSSION

You've seen all the basics of declaring and creating a Service. There are some key things to take away from this. First, the Service will run in its own process. This decouples it from the application's process, so that it won't be terminated when the application is terminated. Second, because it's in its own process, you can only communicate with it through IPC. We'll get into the mechanics of how to do this on Android later in this chapter. Before we do, one more lifecycle method is worth mentioning. Many applications will want to implement the onStartCommand (or the deprecated onStart, if you're developing for pre-Android 2.0 devices). This allows additional parameters to be passed to the Service when it's first started. If you want to expose some configuration parameters of your Service, this is a common way to do it. An example might be to let the user decide on how often to check for new stock data. This assumes that you want to manually start the Service from your application. Often you'll want to automatically start the Service with no interaction from the user. Our next technique shows how to do this.

TECHNIQUE 14   **Starting a Service automatically**

One common use for a Service is periodically downloading information and potentially raising a Notification if a given condition is met. Services are well suited for this, but the question of when to start the Service now becomes significant.

PROBLEM

We want to show the user notifications if the price of a stock goes above or below certain levels. But we don't want to require the user to launch the application just to enable Notifications. Instead, we'd like our Service to begin running automatically, right after the device has booted up.

SOLUTION

The solution is to use a BroadcastReceiver to listen for Android's BOOT_COMPLETED event. This event is fired by the OS right after the device finishes booting up, which gives us an easy way to do something when the device is booted. To make this happen we need to declare it in our manifest as shown in the following listing.

Listing 5.3   Declaring a BroadcastReceiver for the boot complete event

```xml
<?xml version="1.0" encoding="utf-8"?>
<manifest xmlns:android="http://schemas.android.com/apk/res/android"
     package="com.flexware.stocks"
     android:versionCode="1"
     android:versionName="1.0">                                        ❶ Declare
                                                                          Broadcast-
...                                                                       Receiver
     <receiver android:name="PortfolioStartupReceiver"
        android:process=":stocks_background">            Put in same
          <intent-filter>                              ❷ process as Service
```

```
              <action android:name=
                  "android.intent.action.BOOT_COMPLETED"/>
          </intent-filter>
      </receiver>
  </application>
...
</manifest>
```
⟵ **Declare
event to
❸ listen for**

In listing 5.3, we start off by declaring the `BroadcastReceiver`. This is similar to declaring a `Service` (it has many of the same attributes). We once again declare the class for the `BroadcastReceiver` by using the `name` attribute ❶. Next, we declare that we want the `BroadcastReceiver` to be in a different process from our main application ❷. If you compare this to listing 4.1, you'll see that we want it to be in the same process as our `Service`.

Going back to listing 5.3, the last important thing for us to declare about our `BroadcastReceiver` is what kind of events that it should listen to ❸. We do this using the (hopefully) now familiar intent-filter paradigm. The `BOOT_COMPLETED` event (or action) is a predefined event in Android. In fact, there may be many other `BroadcastReceivers` listening for this event as well, and they'll all get a chance to do their thing when the device boots. Now that we've declared our `BroadcastReceiver`, we need to implement it. The next listing shows its implementation.

Listing 5.4   Starting our `Service` with a `BroadcastReceiver`

```
public class PortfolioStartupReceiver extends BroadcastReceiver {
    @Override
    public void onReceive(Context context, Intent intent) {
        Intent stockService =
            new Intent(context, PortfolioManagerService.class);
        context.startService(stockService);                      ⟵❶ Start Service
    }
}
```

Our `BroadcastReceiver` couldn't be simpler. It creates a new `Intent` and uses that `Intent` to start the `Service` ❶. This will cause the `onCreate` and then the `onStartCommand` methods to be invoked on our `Service`, and then return back to the `BroadcastReceiver`. Since a `BroadcastReceiver` should return quickly, those two methods on our `Service` should execute quickly as well. So if you need to do anything time-consuming in those methods, it's better to do such things in their own thread.

About installing on the SD card

One of the most-requested features for Android 2.2 was the ability to install apps on the SD card instead of on the internal memory. This seems like a great option for users, since much more space is available on the SD card than on the internal memory. If you choose to enable this though, be careful about relying on the device boot event as we've described in this section.

(continued)

The BOOT_COMPLETED event will be fired before the SD card is mounted, before your application is available. But there's another, similar event that you can listen for: the ACTION_EXTERNAL_APPLICATIONS_AVAILABLE event. This event will be fired after the SD card is mounted. If your app is on the SD card, it can listen for this event and start services at that point.

At the time this book was written, there was an open bug in Android (8485) that could prevent an app on the SD card from receiving this broadcast.

DISCUSSSION

You may be asking why we need to run the BroadcastReceiver in a different process. The answer is that it's often desirable to share objects between a Service and the BroadcastReceiver that started it or invoked it. We want the BroadcastReceiver and Service to be in the same process, so we don't have to use IPC. We'll see this technique later in this chapter when we discuss best practices for keeping your Service running continuously. In this case, it's not absolutely necessary. We'll see other cases where a BroadcastReceiver is invoked by the system's AlarmManager or by a push notification coming from Google's Cloud to Device Messaging service and then used to start our Service using this technique.

Finally, note that starting a Service at device boot isn't useful only for Services that can trigger Notifications to be sent. It's also useful if you're prefetching and caching data in the Service. When the user first opens your app, all of their data will already be loaded and ready to use—which is a positive experience for the user.

TECHNIQUE 15   Communicating with a Service

A Service can be used to perform useful tasks in the background. We saw a simple example in chapter 2 where the Service published Notifications for the user. But you'll usually want to send data back and forth to a Service. This is the case for our StockPortfolio service.

PROBLEM

We need to tell our Service what stocks to watch. For each stock, the Service needs to know two things: the ticker symbol, and the price levels at which the user should be notified. Since our Service is going to run in a different process, passing data to it isn't as simple as invoking a method on an object. We need some type of interprocess communication (IPC). Fortunately, the Android OS provides this.

SOLUTION

To send data to our Service, we need to use Android's IPC mechanism. This mechanism allows Services to be exposed to other processes and for serialized data to be sent between the processes. This is similar to enterprise IPC mechanisms such as CORBA and Windows COM. Those systems consist of an *interface definition language*

(IDL) to describe the interface of what's being exposed and a proxy class to be used by clients of the interface. Android uses a similar pattern. It even has its own IDL, known as *Android IDL* or *AIDL*. Here's an AIDL description of the interface that we want to expose to our Service.

Listing 5.5   IStockService.aidl: The external interface into the stock portfolio service

```
package com.flexware.stocks.service;

import com.flexware.stocks.Stock;

interface IStockService{
    void addToPortfolio(in Stock stock);
    List<Stock> getPortfolio();
}
```

❶ Import another AIDL

❷ Operations that will be exposed

As you can see from listing 5.5, AIDL looks a lot like Java. It uses packages and imports, like Java. The main difference is that you can only import other AIDL definitions. You'll notice in this case that we're importing a Stock object ❶. This is the same Stock class that we'll use in the UI of our application (we'll see how this is done shortly). Our interface is simple. It only exposes two methods to the outside world ❷. Note how this method uses the Stock type and how we mark this input parameter as in. This indicates that the parameter will be passed in, but its value won't be returned to the caller. It's needed here because Stock is a complex type. If it were a Java primitive type, it wouldn't be needed.

AIDL types and parameters

Marking an input parameter as in is similar to marking it as final in Java. You can modify the value of any input parameter, but if it's marked in, then its new value won't be passed back to the caller. The in modifier is known as a *directional tag*. There are two other possible values: out and inout. The out modifier indicates that whatever data you pass in will be ignored. A blank/default value will be created by the Service, and its final value will be passed back. An inout value indicates that a value should be passed in, and that it can be modified with its new value passed back. It's important to figure out what you need. Data sent through IPC must be marshalled and unmarshalled, which can be an expensive process. A parameter marked as inout will be marshalled/unmarshalled twice. As mentioned, you don't need to specify a directional tag for primitive values. These are in only—they're always immutable values.

This small definition can be used to generate a lot of code. If you're using the command line then you'll want to use the aidl tool. If you're using Eclipse, it'll automatically generate code from any .aidl files it finds in your project. It'll put the generated Java classes in the /gen directory (the same place it puts the generated R.java file.) For this to work, it needs to resolve that import reference. You'll need another .aidl file for this:

```
package com.flexware.stocks;

parcelable Stock;
```

This file (Stock.aidl) declares the `Stock` class reference in listing 5.5. It declares the package of the class, as AIDL does in listing 5.5, but all it does is reference a `Parcelable`. This Java class can be used in your application, but it can also be turned into an `android.os.Parcel`—serialized so that instances of this class can be sent between processes. The following listing shows this `Stock` class.

Listing 5.6   The `Stock` class, a `Parcelable` class that can be sent over IPC

```
public class Stock implements Parcelable{                    ◁──┐  Implement
   // user defined                                            ❶  Parcelable interface
   private String symbol;
   private double maxPrice;
   private double minPrice;
   private double pricePaid;
   private int quantity;
   // dynamic retrieved
   private String name;
   private double currentPrice;
   // db assigned
   private int id;                                        ❷  Private constructor
   private Stock(Parcel parcel){                    ◁──┘     for Parcel
      this.readFromParcel(parcel);
   }
   public static final Parcelable.Creator<Stock> CREATOR =   ◁──┐  Static
      new Parcelable.Creator<Stock>() {                          │  factory
                                                                 │  called
      public Stock createFromParcel(Parcel source) {         ❸  CREATOR
         return new Stock(source);
      }

      public Stock[] newArray(int size) {
         return new Stock[size];
      }
   };
   public int describeContents() {
      return 0;
   }
   @Override                                                ❹  Serialize
   public void writeToParcel(Parcel parcel, int flags) {    ◁──┘  to Parcel
      parcel.writeString(symbol);
      parcel.writeDouble(maxPrice);
      parcel.writeDouble(minPrice);
      parcel.writeDouble(pricePaid);
      parcel.writeInt(quantity);
   }                                                        ❺  Deserialize
   public void readFromParcel(Parcel parcel){               ◁──┘  from Parcel
      symbol = parcel.readString();
      maxPrice = parcel.readDouble();
      inPrice = parcel.readDouble();
      pricePaid = parcel.readDouble();
```

```
            quantity = parcel.readInt();
        }
}
```

This listing shows all of the basics of making of a class that's a `Parcelable`. The interface ❶ only states that you need to implement the `writeToParcel` method ❹. As the name of this method implies, this is the method where you serialize an instance of your class into a `Parcel` ❷. As you can see from the listing, the `Parcel` class has useful methods for serializing primitives and strings. This is all you have to implement so that an instance of the class can be sent to another process. But you need to deserialize that `Parcel` back into a `Stock`. To do this, the Android runtime will look for a static field called `CREATOR` ❸ that will be of type `Parcelable.Creator`. This interface defines a factory method called `createFromParcel`. In listing 5.6, we've given our `Parcelable` class its own `readFromParcel` method ❺ that the `Creator` delegates to. Once again, the `Parcel` class has several methods to assist you in retrieving the serialized data from the `Parcel`. One key thing to notice here is that you must read values from the `Parcel` in the same order as you wrote them to the `Parcel`. For example, the `symbol` field is the first value written to the `Parcel` in the `writeToParcel` method, so it's also the first field read from the `Parcel` in the `readFromParcel` method.

Now we have a data structure that can be sent back and forth between the process where our main application runs and the process where our background service runs. In listing 5.5, we defined the operations that the background service exposes to the main application. A Java interface can be generated from the interface defined in the .aidl file. You can generate this manually using the `aidl` tool, or it'll be generated for you automatically if you're using Eclipse and the Android Developer Tools. In the following listing, you can see what this generated code looks like.

Listing 5.7   Java interface generated from AIDL interface

```
package com.flexware.stocks.service;
public interface IStockService extends android.os.IInterface
{
/** Local-side IPC implementation stub class. */           ❶ Stub
public static abstract class Stub extends android.os.Binder      class
➡       implements com.flexware.stocks.service.IStockService
{
// generated code
}
public void addToPortfolio(com.flexware.stocks.Stock stock)
➡       throws android.os.RemoteException;
public java.util.List<com.flexware.stocks.Stock> getPortfolio()
➡       throws android.os.RemoteException;
}
```

This is what you'd expect from the AIDL in listing 5.5. The interface and its two operations are directly translated. The only thing interesting is the `Stub` abstract class ❶. As the name implies, this is a classic stub class that implements the interface (but not the operations, which are still abstract), adding lots of generated boilerplate code. You'll want to extend this abstract class, implementing the IStockService methods, to leverage the generated boilerplate code. You'll also want to return your implementation class from the onBind method of your Service's class. Take a look at the following to see how this works.

Listing 5.8 The `PortfolioManagerService` class

```
public class PortfolioManagerService extends Service {                 Extend
    private final StocksDb db = new StocksDb(this);                      Service
    // Other methods omitted                                           Helper class for
    @Override                                                          persisted data
    public IBinder onBind(Intent intent) {                             Return class that
        return new IStockService.Stub() {                           ❶ extends stub class
            public void addToPortfolio(Stock stock)
                throws RemoteException {
                    db.addStock(stock);
                }

            public List<Stock> getPortfolio()
                throws RemoteException {
                    return db.getStocks();
                }
        };
    }
}
```

The PortfolioManagerService class shows you a typical Service that supports remote communication. You might recall that in chapter 2, we saw a Service that didn't support remote communication, so its onBind method returned null. Here, ❶ we're supporting IPC, so we need to return a class that extends the generated Stub class from listing 5.7. In our example, we used an anonymous inner class that extended Stub, as our implementation is simple: we're delegating to a helper class StocksDb. This class uses Android's embedded SQLite database to save the stocks that the user wants retrieved on demand. A call to addToPortfolio will execute an insert statement and a getPortfolio call will execute a simple query. The last thing we want to do is show how this is used by the main application. The following listing shows the application's main Activity and how it binds and calls the Service.

Listing 5.9 The main `Activity` binding to the `Service`

```
public class ViewStocks extends ListActivity {
                                                               Generated service
    private ArrayList<Stock> stocks;                           interface
    private IStockService stockService;
    private ServiceConnection connection = new ServiceConnection(){

        public void onServiceConnected(ComponentName className,
            IBinder service) {
          stockService = IStockService.Stub.asInterface(service);
```

```
    try {
       stocks = (ArrayList<Stock>)
              stockService.getPortfolio();
       if (stocks == null){
          stocks = new ArrayList<Stock>(0);
       }                                              ❶ Refresh UI when
       refresh();                                        data is retrieved
    } catch (RemoteException e) {
       Log.e(LOGGING_TAG, "Exception retrieving
                          portfolio from service",e);
    }
  }
  public void onServiceDisconnected(ComponentName className) {
     stockService = null;
  }
};
@Override
public void onStart(Bundle savedInstanceState) {
   super.onStart();
   bindService(new Intent(IStockService.class.getName()), connection,
     Context.BIND_AUTO_CREATE);              Bind to remote
     ... // UI code omitted                ❷ service
  }
}
```

The code in listing 5.9 is a sampling of code from a ListActivity. The first thing we do in listing 5.9 is define a ServiceConnection, a delegate that will reflect the lifecycle of our connection to our remote service. We use the generated stub to take the remote service interface (represented as an android.os.IBinder) and get an implementation of the local interface. Next, in our Activity's onStart method, we use the bindService method ❷, available on any Context object (such as an Activity or Service) to bind to the remote service. We pass in the name of the class of the service that we want to bind to, our connection delegate, and a flag indicating to automatically create the service if necessary. Invoking a service running in another process is much faster than making a call over the network, but it's still a slow operation that shouldn't be done on the main UI thread (bindService will cause this binding to happen asynchronously). The onServiceConnected method in the ServiceConnection acts as a callback to this asynchronous binding of the service. When it's called, we know that our service is bound and we can retrieve data from it and refresh the UI ❶.

Visible processes and bound Services

In our example, the application and Service each run in their own process, but there's only so much memory to be spread out among these processes. For first-generation Android devices, this is generally 16 MB per process, and 24 MB per process on second-generation devices. So when all of those 16 or 24 MB pieces of the pie have been handed out, the OS must kill some processes. Different processes are viewed as being more or less important, as we discussed in chapter 3.

DISCUSSION

Communicating with a remote service is one of the more complicated techniques that you'll see. There are several steps in the process, but they're quite straightforward. Still, you can't be blamed for wondering whether it's worth all the trouble. What makes it more complex is that you're communicating across processes. That means that a channel for communication must be created and data must be marshalled and unmarshalled as it goes between the processes. This is definitely worth it if you want to decouple the execution of your application from the user interacting with it. It's one of the features of the Android platform that give it an advantage over its competitors. One common use case for this is to use a Service to manage and cache data from remote servers.

TECHNIQUE 16   Using a Service for caching data

A Service often needs to work with the same data as your main application. Both components can retrieve and manage this data. But as we saw in the previous section, it's possible for your main app to communicate with a Service. This makes it possible to have the Service manage all of the data, and if the data comes from over the Web, the Service can cache the data from the server.

PROBLEM

You have an application that also has a background Service. Both the main application and the Service need to use data from a remote server. You want to centralize the access to this data in one place and cache it, since retrieving it over the network is slow and expensive. You want to do this from the background Service, so that it can retrieve the data even when the main application isn't being used and so that it can be exposed to the main application via IPC with the background Service.

SOLUTION

This is a common application pattern for Android apps. Part of why it's so common is because it's fairly straightforward. It builds on the other techniques that we've discussed so far. Your background Service can be started at device boot. Then it can retrieve data over the network. This can be done periodically, as needed. Finally, once the user launches your application, one of your app's activities can bind to the Service and invoke one of its methods to return the data that the Service downloaded from the network.

This simple pattern is followed by many popular Android apps. So how would we apply it to our stock portfolio application? For that application, the list of stocks that the user wants to track is managed locally, stored in a local SQLite database. To track the current price of the stock, we'll download this data over the network. To make all of this happen, we only need to modify our Service. Here's the new version.

Listing 5.10   Stock Service now with caching

```
public class PortfolioManagerService extends Service {
    private final StocksDb db = new StocksDb(this);          ❶ Keep timestamp
    private long timestamp = 0L;                                of last update
```

```
private static final int MAX_CACHE_AGE = 15*60*1000;
    // 15 minutes
@Override
public IBinder onBind(Intent intent) {
    return new IStockService.Stub() {
        public Stock addToPortfolio(Stock stock)
                        throws RemoteException {
            Stock s = db.addStock(stock);
            updateStockData();
            return s;
        }

        public List<Stock> getPortfolio() throws RemoteException {
        ArrayList<Stock> stocks = db.getStocks();
        long currTime = System.currentTimeMillis();
        if (currTime - timestamp <= MAX_CACHE_AGE){
            return stocks;
        }
        Stock[] currStocks = new Stock[stocks.size()];
        stocks.toArray(currStocks);
        try {
            ArrayList<Stock> newStocks =
                            fetchStockData(currStocks);
            updateStockData(newStocks);
            return newStocks;
        } catch (Exception e) {
            Log.e("PortfolioManagerService",
                "Exception getting stock data",e);
            throw new RemoteException();
        }
      }
    };
}
... // code for retrieving stock data omitted
```

❷ Cache data up to 15 minutes

❸ Refresh cache whenever stock added

❹ Use cached if fresh enough

❺ Get data from server

❻ Persist fresh data

The code in listing 5.10 expands on the Service first shown in listing 5.2. To allow for caching, we need a couple of things. We want to set a time limit ❷ on how stale our cache can be before we bypass it and go back to the server. To determine the freshness of our cache, we need to keep track of the last time ❶ we downloaded data from the server. Next, we need to add some cache management code to our two operations that we expose, addToPortfolio and getPortfolio. For addToPortfolio, we add the Stock to the local database, and then we call updateStockData ❸. This method will retrieve data from the network, and then update the stocks stored in our local database. We'll look at its code shortly. Because we added a new stock, we need to get information about it from the network, so we might as well get information about all of our stocks and update our cache.

For the getPortfolio method, we start by retrieving the cached data from our local database and see if this data is fresh enough. In the previous listing, we set a simple policy of allowing cached data to be used if it's less than 15 minutes old. You could imagine a much more sophisticated caching policy, where you'd be more aggressive if the current time was during stock market trading hours, but otherwise passive. This policy is good enough for our application, so we check if the current time minus the last timestamp is less than 15 minutes **4**. If so, then we return the cached data. Otherwise, we retrieve data from the network **5** and then update our cache **6** with the fresh data. We do this by calling another variant of `updateStockData`.

Listing 5.11 Updating cached stock data

```
private void updateStockData() throws IOException{
    ArrayList<Stock> stocks = db.getStocks();              ◁──● Get stocks
    Stock[] currStocks = new Stock[stocks.size()];
    currStocks = stocks.toArray(currStocks);
    stocks = fetchStockData(currStocks);                  ◁──● Get fresh data
    updateStockData(stocks);                              ◁──┐ Update
}                                                          ● cached data

private void updateStockData(ArrayList<Stock> stocks){
    timestamp = System.currentTimeMillis();
    Stock[] currStocks = new Stock[stocks.size()];
    currStocks = stocks.toArray(currStocks);
    for (Stock stock : currStocks){                      ● Update latest
        db.updateStockPrice(stock);                      ◁──┘ price of the stock
    }
    checkForAlerts(stocks);
}
```

These two methods are what the `Service` uses to refresh its cached data. The first method takes no arguments and is used when the user adds a new stock. It retrieves the full list of stocks **1** that the user is monitoring by retrieving this data from the local database. Then it uses the `fetchStockData` method **2** to get the latest information on the `Stock` from the network. Finally, it delegates to the second method **3**, which takes in a list of `Stock` objects and updates their prices in the database. This method then iterates over the list of `Stocks`, and updates the price of each `Stock` **4**.

DISCUSSION

Caching of data can make a huge difference in the performance of any application. The more expensive that data is to retrieve, the bigger the benefit of caching it will be. This is true for mobile applications, which often rely heavily on data from remote servers. The network connection speeds on mobile networks are generally never great, and are often quite slow. Storing data in a local database is a great way to cache that data. Putting all of the management of that data into a background `Service` allows its retrieval/updates to be done in the background, and not be tied to the user using the application. Having this data in the background `Service` allows that `Service` to do other things with that data. A common example of this is to create notifications based on the data that's retrieved from the server.

TECHNIQUE 17 **Creating notifications**

`Notifications` are one of the most significant features of mobile applications. They allow your application to interact with users in an asynchronous manner—the users don't have to be directly interacting with your application (have it open) in order for your application to communicate important, time-critical information. It should come as no surprise that background Services are integral to such notifications, as they're the key feature of the Android platform that enables your application to operate in an asynchronous manner.

PROBLEM

You want to alert your user when some significant events happen, even if your users aren't using your application at the time of that event. You want to provide them with detailed information about this event, and make it actionable so that they can immediately use your application to respond appropriately to the event. The event may come from a remote system, or it might be local to the device. Either way, you want to incorporate all of the various capabilities of Android to alert users, so that they can act on the event in a meaningful way.

SOLUTION

The Android platform offers a flexible and extensible notification system. The simplest type of notification offered by Android is known as a *toast notification*, or a *toast*. Toasts are often used by an Activity to alert the user to an event, but they can also be launched from a Service. Toasts are designed to display information to the user—they're not interactive. To get the kind of interactivity we desire, we need to use an android.app.Notification. A Notification allows the user to interact with your application by wrapping an Intent. It can be displayed on the status bar, create a sound, vibrate the phone, and even trigger custom colored flashing LEDs.

For our stock portfolio application, users can enter a minimum and maximum price level for each of the stocks in their portfolio. Each time we download the latest price information from the network, we want to check whether any of the stock prices have gone below the minimum price or exceeded the maximum price. The following listing shows how we can add this logic to our Service.

Listing 5.12 Checking maximum and minimum levels

```
private void updateStockData(List<Stock> stocks){
    // existing code omitted
    checkForAlerts(stocks);
}

private void checkForAlerts(Iterable<Stock> stocks){
    for (Stock stock : stocks){
        double current = stock.getCurrentPrice();
        if (current > stock.getMaxPrice()){
            createHighPriceNotification(stock);
            continue;
        }
        if (current < stock.getMinPrice()){
            createLowPriceNotification(stock);
        }
    }
}
```

1 Check for alerts after update

2 High price notification

3 Low price notification

The easiest way to add the price alert checking logic is to call it ❶ after we update our locally cached data with new data from the network. This involves iterating over each stock and creating a specific `Notification` depending on whether the current price is higher ❷ than the user's maximum or lower ❸ than the user's minimum price. Note that we've created a specific method for creating each of these different `Notifications`. Here's how we create high-price `Notifications`.

Listing 5.13 Creating a high price `Notification`

```
private static final int HIGH_PRICE_NOTIFICATION = 1;
private void createHighPriceNotification(Stock stock) {
    NotificationManager mgr = (NotificationManager)                    ┌─ Get Notification
        getSystemService(Context.NOTIFICATION_SERVICE);        ◁──────┘  service
    int dollarBill = R.drawable.dollar_icon;                              Notification  ❶
    String shortMsg = "High price alert: " + stock.getSymbol();           with ticker
    long time = System.currentTimeMillis();                                  info
    Notification n = new Notification(dollarBill, shortMsg, time);  ◁────┘
    String title = stock.getName();
    String msg = "Current price $" + stock.getCurrentPrice() +
        " is high";                                               ❷  Intent for
    Intent i = new Intent(this, NotificationDetails.class);   ◁──    launch
    i.putExtra("stock", stock);                                         ┌─ Expanded
    PendingIntent pi = PendingIntent.getActivity(this, 0, i, 0);        │  Notification
                                                                        │  info
    n.setLatestEventInfo(this, title, msg, pi);               ◁─────────┘
    n.defaults |= Notification.DEFAULT_SOUND;             ◁─────┐  Add
    long[] steps = {0, 500, 100, 200, 100, 200};            ❸  sound
    n.vibrate = steps;                            ◁──┐  Vibrate
    n.ledARGB = 0x80009500;                        ❹  phone
    n.ledOnMS = 250;
    n.ledOffMS = 500;
    n.flags |= Notification.FLAG_SHOW_LIGHTS;          ◁──┐  Flash
    mgr.notify(HIGH_PRICE_NOTIFICATION, n);             ❺  lights
}
```

The method in listing 5.12 shows many of the options available for creating `Notifications`. At its most basic, you need to create the information that will be shown on the status bar (ticker). This includes an icon (image) ❶, a short message, and when the `Notification` should be shown. We could stop here, but we want the `Notification` to be actionable. To do this, we want to start an `Activity` when the user selects the `Notification`. To do that, we need an `Intent` ❷. Note that the `Stock` object that the `Notification` pertains to is added to the `Intent` as an extra. We can do this because the `Stock` class is a `Parcelable`, the OS can easily serialize/deserialize a `Stock` object. The `Intent` then gets wrapped in a `PendingIntent`—an `Intent` that will be activated sometime in the future.

The rest of the code shows some of the other options available to you for making the user notice your `Notifications`. You can have the device play a sound ❸. In this case, we used the default sound that the user has set for `Notifications`. You could also include a sound file with your application and use it here instead. Next, we have the device vibrate ❹ when the Notification is sent. We pass in an array of longs for this. The first value in the array is how long to wait until the vibration start. After that, it's a pattern of values, alternating how long the vibration should be on and then how long it should be off. Once the end of the array is reached, the phone will stop vibrating. Finally, we can also make the LEDs on the phone flash ❺. The presence and type of these lights varies from device to device, but if you specify something that the device can't do, the OS will degrade this appropriately. In this case, we specified an ARGB hexadecimal color (green) for the LED, and then an on/off pattern. In this case, the pattern will be repeated indefinitely.

If/when the user expands the status bar to see more information about the Notification, they'll be shown the contentTitle and contentText. In listing 5.12, we specified these values using the setLatestEventInfo method. This method also takes the PendingIntent that we created, so that if the user taps on the Notification then the Intent that was wrapped by the PendingIntent will be used to start the Activity associated with it. This is a convenience method that allows you to specify these values and combines them with a predefined view. You can also specify your own custom view. The next listing shows a custom view being used to create the Notification for low prices.

Listing 5.14 Creating a low price Notification

```
private static final int LOW_PRICE_NOTIFICATION = 0;
private void createLowPriceNotification(Stock stock){
    NotificationManager mgr = (NotificationManager)
        getSystemService(Context.NOTIFICATION_SERVICE);
    int dollarBill = R.drawable.dollar_icon;
    String shortMsg = "Low price alert: " + stock.getSymbol();
    long time = System.currentTimeMillis();
    Notification n = new Notification(dollarBill, shortMsg, time);
    String pkg = getPackageName();
    RemoteViews view =                                              ❶ Get
        new RemoteViews(pkg, R.layout.notification_layout);            RemoteViews
    String msg = "Current price $" + stock.getCurrentPrice() +
        " is low";                                                 ⎫ Set text
    view.setTextViewText(R.id.notification_message, msg);          ⎭ on View
    n.contentView = view;                                          ⎫ Set View to
    Intent i = new Intent(this, NotificationDetails.class);        ⎭ be used
    i.putExtra("stock", stock);
    PendingIntent pi = PendingIntent.getActivity(this, 0, i, 0);
    n.contentIntent = pi;                                          ⎫ Set
    n.defaults |= Notification.DEFAULT_SOUND;                      ⎭ PendingIntent
    long[] steps = {0, 500, 100, 500, 100, 500, 100, 500};
    n.vibrate = steps;
    n.ledARGB = 0x80A80000;
    n.ledOnMS = 1;
    n.ledOffMS = 0;
    n.flags |= Notification.FLAG_SHOW_LIGHTS;
    mgr.notify(LOW_PRICE_NOTIFICATION, n);
}
```

The createLowPriceNotification in listing 5.13 is similar to createHighPrice-
Notification. The messaging, icons, vibration pattern, and lights are a little different, but these are the same APIs that we saw in listing 5.12. The significant difference
is that we no longer use the setLastEventInfo method on the Notification object.
Instead, we use a custom View. The tricky part about creating a View in this situation is
that we're creating it from our background Service, which is running in a separate
process from whatever application that the user is currently viewing. In fact, since this
is executing from within a Service, we can't even use the layout inflater system service, since it needs an Activity to inflate a View. Fortunately, Android has the
RemoteViews class to deal with this situation. It only needs the package name of our
application and an XML view ❶ to inflate the View. Here's the View that we're going
to inflate.

Listing 5.15   Custom XML layout used for a Notification

```
<LinearLayout
    xmlns:android="http://schemas.android.com/apk/res/android"
    android:id="@+id/notification_layout_root"
    android:orientation="horizontal"
    android:layout_width="fill_parent"
    android:layout_height="fill_parent"
    android:padding="5dp">
    <ImageView android:id="@+id/notification_icon_left"
            android:layout_width="wrap_content"
            android:layout_height="fill_parent"
            android:layout_marginRight="5dp"
            android:src="@drawable/radioactive_icon"
            />
    <TextView android:id="@+id/notification_message"
            android:layout_width="wrap_content"
            android:layout_height="fill_parent"
            android:textColor="#000"
            />
    <ImageView android:id="@+id/notification_icon_right"
            android:layout_width="wrap_content"
            android:layout_height="fill_parent"
            android:layout_marginLeft="5dp"
            android:src="@drawable/radioactive_icon"
            />
</LinearLayout>
```

❶ TextView to display message

The View for the Notification is a simple LinearLayout that flows horizontally. It has
a text message ❶ flanked by icons to its left and right. For the text message, we use a
TextView with an ID so that we can retrieve it and set its text. This needs to be done
from the setLowPriceNotification method, but that's part of our background Service. The familiar findViewById method is only available from an Activity, not from
a Service. Fortunately, the RemoteViews class has a variety of methods to work around
this. Back in listing 5.13, you can see that we used the setTextViewText method to set

the text value of the message that will be shown in our `Notification`. The `Remote-Views` class has several other similar methods to handle variations on this situation.

Once the `View` is created and ready, it's set as the `contentView` of the `Notification`. Also note that we needed to set the `contentIntent` of the `Notification` as well. We didn't have to do this in the `setHighPriceNotification` method because we used the `setLastEventInfo` method that took care of this for us.

DISCUSSION

Android provides application developers with a rich set of APIs for creating and managing and `Notifications`. We've gotten a good look at many of them in this technique. Now do you really want to play a sound, vibrate the phone for several seconds, and flash the LEDs every time you need to send a `Notification`? This is a rhetorical question on the way to the bigger question: what's the point of all these literal bells and whistles for `Notifications`? After all, if you compare it to other popular mobile platforms, you get many more capabilities, but is that necessarily a good thing? Like any other feature, it's possible to go overboard. But these rich capabilities give you many opportunities to create distinctive `Notifications` for your application, and that's valuable.

Remember that `Notifications` are usually raised while the user is using a different application, or perhaps even more commonly, while the user is not using the phone at all. Maybe it's sitting in their pocket or lying on the desk in front of them. If your `Notification` is distinctive, they'll recognize that a `Notification` is from your application without even viewing it on their phone. This makes them much more likely to react to your `Notification`, and in turn your application—which is a good thing.

The combination of background `Services` and `Notifications` is powerful and compelling. But to make it work effectively we need to understand scheduling and how this interacts with your `Service`'s lifecycle.

5.3   *Scheduling and Services*

Running in the background on a traditional desktop computer or server is fairly straightforward. It's much more complicated on a mobile operating system like Android, where memory is more scarce. Anything that's running in the background could be killed by the OS to free up memory to be used by an application that the user is interacting with. This feature of the OS is great for the user, as it ensures that their applications are always responsive, but it doesn't make life easy on application developers. If you want to run in the background indefinitely, then you can't assume that you can start a `Service` and let it go. You must assume that the OS will kill it and that you'll need to resurrect it. You need some hooks into the OS to do this, and fortunately, Android provides them. Traditionally, this has been accessing the system alarm services via Android's `android.app.AlarmManager` class. With the introduction of Android's Cloud to Device Messaging service in Android 2.2, developers have another way of doing this by sending wake-up calls from their servers to their `Service` on a specific device. In this section, we'll learn about various techniques for using these parts of the Android platform to make your background Services more robust.

TECHNIQUE 18   Using the AlarmManager

The Linux gurus out there will surely be familiar with Linux's system-level alarms and timers. These utilities are available to Android processes as well. But you don't need to read the manual. Instead, Android provides a simple Java API for setting system-level alarms, including both one-time and repeating alarms. It's the key API in Android for executing your program at some point in the future and making sure it happens even if your application or Service isn't running at that time.

PROBLEM

Your Service needs to execute code at some point in the future. But even though your Service may be currently running, you can't guarantee that it'll still be running at that point. If that was the case—or if it was okay for your code to not execute if your Service isn't running in the future—then you could use a combination of Java's Timer and TimerTask along with Android's Handler. The following listing shows such a naïve implementation.

Listing 5.16   Using a Timer and a Handler to schedule Services (DON'T DO THIS!)

```
Calendar when = Calendar.getInstance();
when.add(Calendar.MINUTE, 2);
final Handler handler = new Handler();
TimerTask task = new TimerTask(){
    @Override
    public void run() {
       handler.post(new Runnable(){
          public void run() {
             updateStockData();
          }
       });
    }
};
Timer timer = new Timer();
timer.scheduleAtFixedRate(task, when.getTime(), 15*60*1000);
```

If you can live with your Service and scheduled operations being killed by the OS, then use code like listing 5.15. This code will call the updateStockData method that we saw in listing 5.11. The first call will be two minutes from the current time. After that, it'll be called every 15 minutes, for as long as the Service is running. This is the desired behavior, except for the "for as long as the Service is running" part. Instead we'd like to change this "for as long as the device is turned on."

SOLUTION

To ensure that our code is executed at the desired time, we can't rely on the Service because the OS could kill the Service to free up memory. We must use the OS to schedule the execution, and to do this we must use the android.app.AlarmManager class. This system service is like the layout inflator or notification manager services. In our stock portfolio application, we've already created a `BroadcastReceiver` that's invoked when the device finishes booting up. Currently it starts the `Service` at that time, but here you see a new version that instead schedules the `Service` to be executed.

Listing 5.17   Using a device boot receiver to schedule `Service` execution

```
public class PortfolioStartupReceiver extends BroadcastReceiver {
    private static final int FIFTEEN_MINUTES = 15*60*1000;
    @Override
    public void onReceive(Context context, Intent intent) {
        AlarmManager mgr = (AlarmManager)                           ⊲──┐  Get
            context.getSystemService(Context.ALARM_SERVICE);          └─  AlarmManager

        Intent i = new Intent(context, AlarmReceiver.class);
        PendingIntent sender = PendingIntent.getBroadcast(context, 0,
            i, PendingIntent.FLAG_CANCEL_CURRENT);      ⊲──┐  Create Intent to
        Calendar now = Calendar.getInstance();           ❶  be scheduled
        now.add(Calendar.MINUTE, 2);
        mgr.setRepeating(AlarmManager.RTC_WAKEUP,
            now.getTimeInMillis(),FIFTEEN_MINUTES, sender);  ⊲──┐  Schedule
    }                                                        ❷  Intent
}
```

If you compare listings 5.16 and 5.4, you'll see that we've changed the implementation of the `onReceive` method. Now instead of starting the `Service`, we'll schedule it. We create an `Intent` ❶ for the `BroadcastReceiver` that will receive the alarm from the `AlarmManager`. Note that we once again wrap the `Intent` in a `PendingIntent`, similar to what we did for a `Notification`. This is because the `Intent` won't be executed now, but in the future. Then we use the `AlarmManager` ❷ to schedule the `PendingIntent` for execution. By specifying the type of alarm as `RTC_WAKEUP`, we're instructing the OS to execute this alarm even if the device has been put to sleep (that's what the *wakeup* suffix represents; the RTC part says we're measuring start time in absolute system time). We've set the alarm to first go off in two minutes from the current time, and then to go off every 15 minutes subsequently. Note that our `Intent` wasn't for the `Service` directly, but instead for a class called `AlarmReceiver`. The following listing shows this class.

Listing 5.18   `AlarmReceiver`, a `BroadcastReceiver` for handling system alarms

```
public class AlarmReceiver extends BroadcastReceiver {

    @Override
    public void onReceive(Context context, Intent intent) {
        Intent stockService =
            new Intent(context, PortfolioManagerService.class);
        context.startService(stockService);
    }

}
```

This class should look familiar. It's equivalent to the original `PortfolioStartup-Receiver` class shown in listing 5.4. All it does is create an `Intent` for the `Portfolio-ManagerService` and then immediately start that `Service`. But now we want that

Service to update the stock data and check whether it needs to send Notifications to the user. The next listing shows how we need to modify the Service.

> **WHAT'S IN THE INTENT?** You might notice that the AlarmReceiver's onReceive method has an Intent passed in to it, per the onReceive method's specification from BroadcastReceiver. This is the same Intent you created in the PortfolioStartupReceiver, wrapped in a Pending-Intent. It's not exactly the same, because it could be serialized and then deserialized. But any extended data added (using the Intent's putExtra methods) to the Intent created in listing 5.16 will be present in the Intent received in listing 5.18, and can be retrieved using the get-Extra methods.

Listing 5.19 Modified `Service` to work with system alarms

```
public class PortfolioManagerService extends Service {
    // other code omitted

    @Override
    public int onStartCommand(Intent intent, int flags, int startId) {
        updateStockData();
        return Service.START_NOT_STICKY;
    }
}
```

To get our Service to work properly with the system alarms, we need to override another of android.app.Service's lifecycle methods: the onStartCommand method. This method will be invoked each time a client context calls startService, such as in listing 5.18, even if the Service is already running. All we want to do is call our update-StockData method, since it'll take care of retrieving fresh data from the network, updating the locally cached data in our database, checking whether we need to send out Notifications, and send them out if so.

Note that this method must return an integer. The value of that integer tells the OS what to do with the Service if it's killed by the OS. The START_NOT_STICKY flag indicates that the OS can forget about this Service if it has to kill it. That makes sense in this example, since we know that we have an alarm scheduled to restart the Service later. Alternatively, we could've returned START_STICKY. This would instruct the OS to restart the Service itself.

> **SERVICE ONSTART VERSUS ONSTARTCOMMAND** If you dig around the Internet looking for examples of starting a Service periodically, you might see code that overrides onStart instead of overriding onStartCommand as we did in listing 5.18. This older lifecycle method was deprecated in Android 2.0. It has no return value, unlike onStartCommand, so it can't provide the OS any information on what to do if the Service is killed. You should always use onStartCommand, unless you need to write code specifically for devices running pre-2.0 versions of Android.

DISCUSSION

Using the `AlarmManager` sounds harmless enough. After all, it's another set of APIs that are part of the Android platform. But it's powerful. It allows us to decouple the execution of background code from the process executing that background code. Take a look at the `Service` that we've developed up to this point. It'll start up two minutes after a device boots, and will then poll data from the Internet every 15 minutes until the device shuts down. The device could even be asleep, and our alarm will still execute. To get this behavior, all we had to do was specify an alarm type (`RTC_WAKEUP`) when we scheduled the alarm.

Behind the scenes, the `AlarmManager` must obtain a *wake lock* to prevent the device from going to sleep. This wake lock is held while the `onReceive` method of the `BroadcastReceiver` that receives the alarm is executing. In this case, that `BroadcastReceiver` is our `AlarmReceiver` class shown in listing 5.17. But once its `onReceive` method returns, it again becomes possible for the device to go to sleep, and for your `Service` to stop executing. Our next technique discusses how you can prevent this from happening.

TECHNIQUE 19   Keeping Services awake

In the previous technique, we learned about the `AlarmManager`, and in particular how it can help us to resurrect our killed `Service`. But that resurrection could be short-lived. Having the alarm go off isn't good enough. We also want to make sure that we finish the work that the `Service` needs to do—retrieve fresh stock data from the Internet and send out `Notifications` if needed. To do this, we'll need to use some of Android's power management APIs, and we'll need to think carefully about Android processes.

PROBLEM

If a device is asleep, we still want our `Service` to execute. We want it to keep the device awake long enough to create `Notifications` for the user. We don't want our users to not receive `Notifications` because their device was asleep in their pocket.

SOLUTION

To solve this problem, we'll need to use Android's PowerManager API. This is another system service on Android, and it allows us to control the power state on the device. Using this API, we can acquire what Android calls a *wake lock*. Acquiring a `WakeLock` allows your application to prevent the OS from putting the device to sleep (turning off the CPU). This is a significant capability that the OS provides to developers, and you must list it as a <uses-permission> in your AndroidManifest.xml file. Obviously if you misuse this, you'll severely affect the battery life of a device. With that in mind, there are several different types of wake locks. The most common type is the `PARTIAL_WAKE_LOCK`. This turns on the CPU, but keeps the screen (and if the device has a physical keyboard, the keyboard's backlight) turned off. Considering that the screen on a device is typically the single biggest drain on the battery, it's best to use a `PARTIAL_WAKE_LOCK` when possible. It also has the advantage that it won't be affected if the user

presses the power button on the device. The other types of wake locks—SCREEN_DIM_
WAKE_LOCK, SCREEN_BRIGHT_WAKE_LOCK, and FULL_WAKE_LOCK—all turn the screen on,
but because of that, the user pressing the power button can also dismiss them. It
should come as no surprise that for a background Service, we definitely want to use
a PARTIAL_WAKE_LOCK.

At this point, the solution to our problem may seem obvious. We can add code to
our Service to acquire a WakeLock during its onStartCommand method, and then
release it after we finish checking for Notifications. But there's a big problem with
that approach. If the device is asleep, then the WakeLock acquired by the AlarmManager will be released once the onReceive method of our AlarmReceiver class finishes.
This can (and will) happen before the onStartCommand of our Service is invoked.
The device could go back to sleep before we even get a chance to acquire a WakeLock.
Therefore, we must acquire a WakeLock in the onReceive method of AlarmReceiver,
since that's the only place we're guaranteed that execution won't be suspended.
Here's the new modified version of AlarmReceiver.

Listing 5.20   Modified `AlarmReceiver`, now with power management

```
public class AlarmReceiver extends BroadcastReceiver {          Shared
    private static PowerManager.WakeLock wakeLock = null;       WakeLock
    private static final String LOCK_TAG = "com.flexware.stocks";
    public static synchronized void acquireLock(Context ctx){   Static
        if (wakeLock == null){                                  method for
            PowerManager mgr = (PowerManager)                   acquiring
                    ctx.getSystemService(Context.POWER_SERVICE);
            wakeLock =
                    mgr.newWakeLock(PowerManager.PARTIAL_WAKE_LOCK,
                        LOCK_TAG);
            wakeLock.setReferenceCounted(true);
        }
        wakeLock.acquire();
    }                                                           Static method
    public static synchronized void releaseLock(){              for releasing
        if (wakeLock != null){
            wakeLock.release();
        }
    }

    @Override
    public void onReceive(Context context, Intent intent) {
        acquireLock(context);                                   Acquire WakeLock
        Intent stockService =                                   before starting Service
            new Intent(context, PortfolioManagerService.class);
        context.startService(stockService);
    }
}
```

The AlarmReceiver has received a major makeover. It has a WakeLock instance as a
static variable. In addition, it also has two methods for acquiring and releasing the
WakeLock. We used a static WakeLock with static acquire/release methods so that this
can be shared between the AlarmReceiver instance and our background Service.

Normally, to share with a `Service` that you're starting, you'd pass it as part of the `Intent` (typically as an extra), but anything passed as part of the `Intent` must be a `Parcelable`. A `WakeLock` is a representation of a system setting, it's definitely not a `Parcelable`. So we use static variables and static methods to work around this.

Keep in mind that for this technique to work, `AlarmReceiver` and our `Service` must be running in the same process, or you'll face a tricky bug. If this is the case, then the same class loader will load them, and they'll share the static `WakeLock`. Otherwise they'll be in different class loaders and will have different copies of the `WakeLock`. Here's the declaration of `AlarmReceiver` from our AndroidManifest.xml file:

```
<receiver android:name="AlarmReceiver"
    android:process=":stocks_background" />
```

Now compare this to listing 5.1, and in particular the declaration of the `Portfolio-ManagerService`. Both components have `android:process=":stocks_background"`. Both will be run in a process outside of the main application process, and will be in the same process. With this configuration, the technique will work. Now we need to add code to `PortfolioManagerService` to release the `WakeLock` so that the device can go back to sleep. The following listing shows the modified `checkForAlerts` method, now with power management code.

Listing 5.21   Releasing the `WakeLock` after checking for alerts

```
private void checkForAlerts(Iterable<Stock> stocks){
    try{
        for (Stock stock : stocks){
            double current = stock.getCurrentPrice();
            if (current > stock.getMaxPrice()){
                createHighPriceNotification(stock);
                continue;
            }
            if (current < stock.getMinPrice()){
                createLowPriceNotification(stock);
            }
        }
    } finally {
        AlarmReceiver.releaseLock();
        stopSelf();
    }
}
```

The main thing that we've done to this method is wrap its code in a `try-finally` sequence. Inside the `finally` block, we invoke the `releaseLock` static method from `AlarmReceiver`, and release the `WakeLock` that we acquired during `AlarmReceiver`'s `onReceive` method.

DISCUSSION

It's important to think about the effect that the preceding code will have on battery life. The CPU is going to be woken up to make a network call, update a local database, and possibly create `Notifications`. Without the power management code we added, this wouldn't happen when the device is asleep. This whole process could take a few seconds, since it involves a network call. But we didn't turn on the screen, minimizing how much extra power is consumed.

Another thing to keep in mind is that a couple of other flags can be set on WakeLocks. These flags determine whether acquiring the WakeLock should cause the screen to turn on. Normally WakeLocks keep the screen from turning off, but with these extra flags they can also cause it to turn on if it's turned off. But those flags don't work with the PARTIAL_WAKE_LOCK type that we used. The PARTIAL_WAKE_LOCK is made for the "wake up, but stay in the background" kind of task like we're trying to accomplish with our Service. It's important that the Notifications that we create do more than create ticker text on the screen. The screen may be turned off, and we can't turn it on, so the user wouldn't see such Notifications. That's not a problem in our application, where our Notifications make a sound, vibrate the phone, and flash its LEDs. We didn't need to do all three of those things, but it's good that we did at least one of them.

<hr>

TECHNIQUE 20   **Using Cloud to Device Messaging**

So far in this section, we've concentrated on how we can use the Android OS to schedule execution of our Service. The main driver for this was that we wanted our service to poll an Internet server to get fresh data about stocks. But polling is inherently inefficient. Most of your polls don't result in data that requires your Service to generate a Notification, so you poll too much. On the other hand, there will always be some window of time where an event has happened that you'd like to give your user a Notification about, but your Service hasn't polled yet, so you don't know about the event yet. You don't poll enough. In our application we're polling every 15 minutes. But you can imagine that with the volatility of the stock market, this interval may be unsatisfactory to the user. We can poll more often, but this will definitely have an effect on the battery life of the device. Android's Cloud to Device Messaging service provides an elegant alternative to this.

PROBLEM

We want to immediately notify our users of important events. The less time between when the event happens and when the user sees a Notification, the more valuable our application will be to the user. But extremely frequent polling will have a negative effect on battery life, and may also overly tax the servers that our background Service is polling. Further, as we've seen, the code to make background polling robust is complicated.

SOLUTION

If you took a poll of Android developers and asked them what the most important new feature in Android 2.2 (Froyo) was, many of them would instantly say Cloud to Device Messaging (C2DM). This is Android's answer to Apple Push Notification Service (APNS), only it has many advantages over APNS. With C2DM, remote web servers can send Intents to specific applications on specific Android devices. For our sample application, we can use C2DM to allow a server to tell our background Service to refresh its cache and check for Notifications. To use C2DM requires a few steps of setup and several permissions. Here are some of the new additions to our AndroidManifest.xml.

Listing 5.22   Update manifest with C2DM permissions

```
<manifest xmlns:android="http://schemas.android.com/apk/res/android"
    package="com.flexware.stocks"
    android:versionCode="1"
    android:versionName="1.0">
  <application android:icon="@drawable/icon"
      android:label="@string/app_name">
    <!-- Code omitted -->
    <receiver android:name=".PushReceiver"
        android:permission=
          "com.google.android.c2dm.permission.SEND">     ◁────  ❶ Declare receiver
      <intent-filter>                                            ◁────
        <action android:name=                                           What
              "com.google.android.c2dm.intent.RECEIVE" />              messages
        <category android:name="com.flexware.stocks" />                receiver
      </intent-filter>                                          ❷ should get
      <intent-filter>                                            ◁────
        <action android:name=                                          Handle C2DM
            "com.google.android.c2dm.intent.REGISTRATION"/>            registration
        <category android:name="com.flexware.stocks" />        ❸ messages
      </intent-filter>
    </receiver>    </application>                                      Check for
  <uses-sdk android:minSdkVersion="8" />                 ◁────  Android 2.2
  <uses-permission android:name="android.permission.INTERNET"/>
  <permission android:name="com.example.myapp.permission.C2D_MESSAGE"
      android:protectionLevel="signature" />              ◁────  Permissions
  <uses-permission android:name=                          ❹ for C2DM
      "com.example.myapp.permission.C2D_MESSAGE"/>
  <uses-permission android:name=
      "com.google.android.c2dm.permission.RECEIVE"/>      ❺ Access
  <uses-permission android:name=                             accounts
      "android.permission.MANAGE_ACCOUNTS"/>
  <uses-permission                                            Need power
      android:name="android.permission.WAKE_LOCK"/>          management
</manifest>
```

Our manifest has a new BroadcastReceiver declared ❶, called PushReceiver. We'll take a closer look at that class momentarily. It'll handle both registration messages ❸ from the C2DM servers and app-specific messages ❷ from our app servers, routed through the C2DM servers. We also need several new permissions for C2DM ❹. Finally, we're going to access account information ❺ as well. This isn't required for C2DM, but there are advantages to using this information, as we'll see shortly. Now that we see the permissions and declarations needed, let's take a look at initiating the C2DM registration process.

Listing 5.23   Requesting C2DM registration

```
public class PortfolioStartupReceiver extends BroadcastReceiver {     ❶ Your
    private static final String DEVELOPER_EMAIL_ADDRESS = "...";   ◁──── email address
```

```
    @Override
    public void onReceive(Context context, Intent intent) {
        Intent registrationIntent =
            new Intent("com.google.android.c2dm.intent.REGISTER");
        registrationIntent.putExtra("app",
            PendingIntent.getBroadcast(context, 0,
                new Intent(), 0));
        registrationIntent.putExtra("sender", DEVELOPER_EMAIL_ADDRESS);
        context.startService(registrationIntent);
    }
}
```

As you can see in listing 5.22, we've once again modified the `PortfolioStartup-Receiver` class that gets invoked when the device boots up. Now instead of using the `AlarmManager` here to schedule the execution of our `Service`, we're going to rely on C2DM. But we need to register for C2DM messages. This is a process where we tell the C2DM servers that our app wants to receive C2DM messages. The C2DM servers will respond by providing a registration ID. The code in listing 5.22 starts this process by requesting a registration ID. Most of this is generic code, and the only thing that you must supply is the email address ❶ that you've used in conjunction with your Android apps. Once the device boots up, the receiver will send out this registration request. We need another `BroadcastReceiver` to handle the response from the C2DM servers (we saw this receiver declared in listing 5.21). In the next listing, you can see how it's implemented.

Listing 5.24   Registration and messaging receiver

```
public class PushReceiver extends BroadcastReceiver {
    @Override
    public void onReceive(Context context, Intent intent) {
        AlarmReceiver.acquireLock(context);
        if (intent.getAction().equals(
            "com.google.android.c2dm.intent.REGISTRATION")) {
                onRegistration(context, intent);
            } else if (intent.getAction().equals(
                "com.google.android.c2dm.intent.RECEIVE")) {
                    onMessage(context, intent);
        }
    }
    // code omitted
}
```

Our `PushReceiver` class is a `BroadcastReceiver`, so we must implement its `onReceive` method. Note that when we receive a message, we acquire the static `WakeLock` in a manner similar to the previous technique. There are two types of messages that it'll receive: one for registration events and one for events from your application server. To distinguish them, we look at the `Intent` that was sent from the C2DM server, and in particular at its `action` property. If we see it's a registration event, we invoke the `onRegistration` method as shown next.

Listing 5.25 Handling C2DM registration events (from `PushReceiver` class)

```
private void onRegistration(Context context, Intent intent) {
    String regId = intent.getStringExtra("registration_id");        ◄─┐
    if (regId != null) {                        Get registration ID  ❶
        Intent i =
            new Intent(context, SendC2dmRegistrationService.class);
        i.putExtra("regId", regId);
        context.startService(i);            Send registration ID to
    }                                       server and Service
}
```

To handle the registration event, we get the registration ID ❶ from the C2DM servers and send it to our own application servers. We need this ID in order for our app servers to be able to send events to the C2DM servers. The C2DM servers will use the registration ID provided by our servers to route the message to the correct device, and then to the correct `BroadcastReceiver` on that device. We could send the registration ID to our servers from this `BroadcastReceiver`, but a `BroadcastReceiver` is designed to execute quickly, so we'll offload this to an `IntentService`.

Listing 5.26 `IntentService` for sending registration info to servers

```
public class SendC2dmRegistrationService extends IntentService {

    private static final String WORKER_NAME = "SendC2DMReg";
    public SendC2dmRegistrationService() {
        super(WORKER_NAME);
    }

    @Override
    protected void onHandleIntent(Intent intent) {
        try{                                             ❶  Get regId
            String regId = intent.getStringExtra("regId");   ◄─┘  from Intent
            // TODO: Send the regId to the server
        } finally {
            AlarmReceiver.releaseLock();               ◄─┐  Make sure to
        }                                              ❷   release WakeLock
    }
}
```

This `Service` gets the registration ID ❶ that was passed in listing 5.24. Then, it sends this information to your server and releases the `WakeLock` ❷ when it's done. Your server will use this information whenever it wants to send a message to your app. In addition to the registration ID from the device, it'll also need a `ClientLogin` auth token. This is a generic Google authentication and authorization mechanism. In general, a `Client-Login` token allows a particular application to access a Google application/service in the name of a particular Google account. For C2DM, the service that you need authorization for is known as `ac2dm`, and the Google account in question is the account of the developer using C2DM. Your server will need to request this token using your email address and password. You might want to create a Google account specifically for your apps. If you use your personal Google account, then changing the password would affect your server's ability to send C2DM messages to Google's C2DM servers.

Once your server has the registration ID for a user and the `ClientLogin` auth token for your account, you can send messages to the app. As we saw in listing 5.23, messages from C2DM are processed by the `onMessage` method:

```
private void onMessage(Context context, Intent intent){
    Intent stockService =
        new Intent(context, PortfolioManagerService.class);
        stockService.putExtras(intent);
    context.startService(stockService);
}
```

This is the code to start the `PortfolioManagerService`. In this case, we've still acquired the static `WakeLock`. But as we saw in the previous technique, the `PortfolioManager-Service` will release this `WakeLock` once it finishes its work.

DISCUSSION

In this example, we use a message pushed from the server to tell our background `Service` to update its cache and generate `Notifications` as needed. But the data that we push from the server can be much richer. When your application sends data to the C2DM servers, it can send arbitrary name-value pairs. Those name-value pairs can then be accessed from your receiver using the `Intent.getXXXExtra` methods. For our application, we could have our server track the high/low price events, and it could pass this information as part of the `Intent`. That could save our background `Service` from having to wait for data from the network, so that it can issue `Notifications` quicker.

Also, it should be noted that the preceding code doesn't deal with many of the error conditions that can arise when using C2DM. Google has developed a small, open source library for working with C2DM. It's not part of Android, but can be easily obtained from Google. This library encapsulates much of the code seen here, eliminating a lot of the boilerplate.

Is C2DM right for you?

C2DM was a huge new feature added in Android 2.2. Our discussion has been brief but hopefully you can see that C2DM creates many interesting opportunities. But does that mean you should use it? Keep in mind that C2DM requires that the user's device be running Android 2.2 or later. At the time that this book was written, more than 83% of devices were running 2.2+, and this number will grow over time. Still, you'll want to carefully examine the breakdown of Android versions "in the wild" and the potential impact on your app's success when you choose what API level to require. Remember that the Android Market won't show your app to a user if their device isn't capable of running it.

5.4 Summary

In this chapter, we've talked extensively about what multitasking is, along with the various tools that Android gives you to enable it in your applications. Providing true multitasking is one of the things that sets Android apart in the mobile space. But such a powerful capability has its side effects, and Android walks a fine line between empowering applications and maintaining a quality user experience. The result is that we developers must deal with some complexity. We're hopeful that you'll agree that the result is worth this complexity. With multitasking, you can keep your application synchronized with data on your servers. This can make your app richer and more responsive.

For most of the history of Android to date, developers have walked a tightrope to get their background `Services` to be robust enough to judiciously retrieve data from the network. Some applications even go as far as to establish their own persistent connection with their servers, maintained from their background `Service`. This has its own set of pitfalls. But with the advent of Cloud to Device Messaging, the benefits of always being connected are more accessible to all applications. One of the often-overlooked features of C2DM is that it's not only for `Notifications`. You get a chance to execute code based on the message pushed to your application from your servers, and then decide if you want to show a `Notification`. You may want to synchronize data with your server, start another `Service`, and so forth. The fact that you process this message in the background gives you tremendous flexibility.

Threads and concurrency 6

This web of time—the strands of which approach one another, bifurcate, intersect or ignore each other through the centuries—embrace every possibility.

—The Garden of Forking Paths

You've seen in the previous chapter how to run parts of your application as a `Service`, which is a great way of performing tasks that don't require interaction with the user. These tasks are typically, continuously or periodically, executed routines, which is why it makes sense to have them run in the background. When we say *background*, we mean they're not visible to the user, but it must be stressed that it does *not* necessarily mean they run concurrently to an application's activities. Why is that? We have seen in the previous chapter that you can run services in separate processes, but that isn't a requirement. In fact, unless you specify a process ID explicitly, they won't.

So what happens if you don't? Recall that an application's set of activities makes up its user interface, and one golden rule about user interfaces is to *always remain responsive.* If all activities and services are executed in the same thread, and only one of these contains an operation that may block (a good example is network I/O), then your application's user interface will inevitably freeze. Say hello to the infamous

Activity Not Responding (aka ANR) dialog. Even if you haven't yet developed any Android applications, chances are you've seen this exception creeping up from the more poorly implemented applications on the Android Market. Figure 6.1 shows it in all its glory.

What a bummer! We have service objects that run in the background, but by default they're all executed on the main application thread. So unless we want to fork a separate Linux process, which brings its own overhead (AIDL and IPC, for instance), we need a means to spawn new threads if we want to run things in parallel. Fortunately, Android supports all major threading and synchronization facilities that are part of the Java class library and even adds a handful of custom helper classes to that list, making parallel code execution easy and straightforward.

Figure 6.1   If an application becomes unresponsive (for example because it's performing expensive operations on the main application thread), Android will kill it after a few seconds and raise an exception to the user.

The following sections will discuss Android's threading framework, how to use it to create concurrent applications, and problems to watch for. We'll start by looking at how basic threading is done in an Android application using ordinary Java threads. Then, we'll make our way through more elaborate techniques such as how to communicate changes to the UI from custom threads, how to implement workers using Android's `AsyncTask`, how to realize timed actions such as splash screens, and how to implement custom message queues to process events in a concurrent fashion.

6.1   Concurrency in Android

To help you understand the demand for concurrent code in an application, imagine that you want to download one or more files from the web. The easiest way to do that on Android would be to launch an `Activity` or `Service` and run the network code directly in there, perhaps as this poorly implemented `Activity` does:

```
public class PoorlyImplementedActivity extends Activity {
    private HttpClient httpClient = new DefaultHttpClient();
    public void onCreate(Bundle savedInstanceState) {
        super.onCreate(savedInstanceState) ;
        HttpGet request = new HttpGet("http://www.example.com/file");
        HttpResponse response = httpClient.execute(request);
        ...
    }
}
```

So what's the problem with this code? It's the call to `HttpClient.execute`. This is a blocking operation that may take a potentially long time to complete because it must open a network connection to a web server using HTTP and transfer data from the server to the device. When launching your application, Android will spawn a single

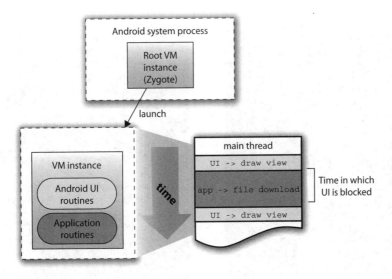

**Figure 6.2
By default, only a single thread of execution will be launched for an application (lower-right box). If this thread executes blocking operations, the UI can't update itself in between (top and bottom sections).**

system process running a single thread of execution. Any code will, by default, run in that thread. As discussed in chapter 3, this thread is called the *main application thread, main user interface thread,* or *UI thread* because Android will also draw your application's user interface elements in here.

Writing code like this may freeze your application—Android can't continue drawing your application's user interface until the download completes because both download and UI code run in the same thread. This is a fundamental problem common to all kinds of software that draw a user interface, and is by no means limited to Android. Figure 6.2 illustrates this problem for the preceding code snippet.

What can we conclude from this? Any non-blocking or fast operation is fine to execute on the main application thread that's running when an application starts. Anything else should be executed on a different thread. We'll show you how this is done in the next few techniques. Let's start simple.

TECHNIQUE 21   ## Basic threading

We want to download an image file from the web and turn it into an Android `Bitmap` object. The download is triggered by a button, and after the download has started, we want to update a text field to indicate that status. Figure 6.3 shows what this image downloader could look like.

GRAB THE PROJECT: SIMPLEIMAGEDOWNLOAD You can get the source code for this project, and/or the packaged APK to run it, at the Android in Practice code website. Because some code listings here are shortened to focus on specific concepts, we recommend that you download the complete source code and follow along within Eclipse (or your favorite IDE or text editor).

Source: http://mng.bz/l897, APK file: http://mng.bz/b134

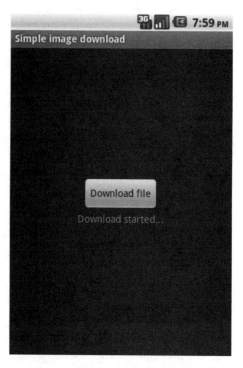

Figure 6.3 A simple image downloader application. A click on the button will trigger the download and update the status text. In order for the status text to properly update in time, the download has to be executed on a thread other than the application's main UI thread.

As we just learned, we can't run the download in our main application thread; otherwise, the entire user interface would lock up while the download is proceeding. After clicking the button that initiates the download, Android will give your application no more than a few seconds to respond to that input event. Otherwise, it'll kill it and raise the previously mentioned ANR exception. For BroadcastReceivers, Android is more forgiving and waits longer before pulling the plug, but it also monitors their execution time. In any case, this doesn't sound like a good deal, so let's see how we can use a Java thread to prevent this from happening.

PROBLEM

You must execute potentially long-running operations that, when executed on the main UI thread, may turn your application unresponsive, or even terminate it with an Activity Not Responding message.

SOLUTION

To circumvent this issue, isolate the blocking code and run it in a new thread that executes concurrently to your application's main thread. The most basic way to do so is to leverage the java.lang.Thread class. A Thread can be instantiated with a Runnable, which will carry the code that should be run (the *job*), and a call to Thread.start will then execute this code on a new thread inside your application process. Look at the

following listing, which implements our simple image downloader application without
freezing the user interface.

Listing 6.1 SimpleImageDownload.java uses java.lang.Thread to download an image file

```
public class SimpleImageDownload extends Activity {          Implement job
                                                             as Runnable
    private Runnable imageDownloader = new Runnable() {
        public void run() {
            try {
                URL url = new URL("http://www.android.com/images/froyo.png");
                Bitmap image = BitmapFactory.decodeStream(url.openStream());
                if (image != null) {
                    Log.i("DL", "Successfully retrieved file!");
                } else {
                    Log.i("DL", "Failed decoding file from stream");
                }
            } catch (Exception e) {
                Log.i("DL", "Failed downloading file!");
                e.printStackTrace();
            }
        }
    };                                                       Spawn
                                                             new
    public void startDownload(View source) {                thread
        new Thread(imageDownloader, "Download thread").start();   for job
        TextView statusText = (TextView) findViewById(R.id.status);   Set status
        statusText.setText("Download started...");           text
    }

    @Override
    public void onCreate(Bundle savedInstanceState) {
        super.onCreate(savedInstanceState);
        setContentView(R.layout.main);
    }
}
```

The layout used for the downloader activity is shown in the next listing.

Listing 6.2 The layout file main.xml defines the button and the status text view

```
<?xml version="1.0" encoding="utf-8"?>
<LinearLayout xmlns:android="http://schemas.android.com/apk/res/android"
    android:orientation="vertical"
    android:layout_width="fill_parent"
    android:layout_height="fill_parent"
    android:gravity="center">

  <Button android:id="@+id/button"
      android:layout_width="wrap_content"
      android:layout_height="wrap_content"
      android:layout_gravity="center"
      android:text="Download file"
      android:onClick="startDownload"
      />
  <TextView android:id="@+id/status"
```

```
        android:layout_width="wrap_content"
        android:layout_height="wrap_content"
        android:layout_gravity="center"
        android:text="click to start"
    />
</LinearLayout>
```

The implementation is surprisingly simple and effective—only a few additional lines of code were required, involving the creation of a job object implementing the `Runnable` interface, and finally passing that object to a new thread instance that executes that code on a new thread. Look at figure 6.4, which shows the thread and processes view of the DDMS thread tool (introduced in chapter 1) at the moment the download task is running.

You can also see from figure 6.4 that Android spawns other, internally used threads, which take care of things such as garbage collection and signal handling, but you'll never interact with these directly, so don't worry about them.

DISCUSSION

When you run the application, you'll notice that running the download thread doesn't lock up the user interface. This can be easily observed by seeing how the status text changes instantaneously *after* we fork the download thread, Consequently, the user interface still updates itself correctly and responds to user input.

An often-raised question related to the use of Java threads on Android is, how long does a thread live? Is it bound to the component (`Activity` or `Service`) that started it? What happens if the component that started it terminates *before* the thread does? Valid questions indeed. It turns out that a thread lives as long as it takes its `run` method to terminate. It's not bound to the component that started it, and can even outlive it. This has a curious implication: it means that you must be extremely cautious about keeping references to things such as an `Activity` in your thread because the `Activity` may finish before your thread terminates. The runtime will keep the `Activity` object around because you hold a strong reference to it, but its lifecycle from the perspective of the

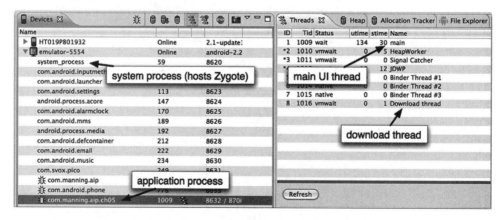

Figure 6.4   The left side shows the detected devices and the processes they're running. The process of our downloader application is highlighted. The right side shows this process's threads, including the main UI thread and the custom download thread.

framework has ended! This is a common mistake, and we're going to explore this issue further in technique 25.

Using Java threads to carry out expensive tasks is good, but often you want to update the user interface with some form of progress indication. Otherwise, the user is left in the dark about what's happening in the background. Now you may ask why we don't update the status text after the download is completed instead of logging the result. The next technique explains why that's impossible without exploring the Android threading framework a little deeper.

TECHNIQUE 22   Communicating change between threads

One of the most common patterns in user interface programming is using visual progress indicators if an application is performing expensive, long-running tasks, or is otherwise busy. Yes, we all love staring at our progress meters, don't we? To be fair, this at least gives the user the feeling that the application is keeping them up-to-date about what's happening, and the user interface remains responsive, perhaps even offering the user the option to cancel the task, should it take too long.

This approach involves at least two threads: the UI thread that updates the progress indicator and one or more threads that perform the work. Progress information is then exchanged between these threads by passing update notifications around. Figure 6.5 illustrates this.

Now, you could argue that if you split up the work to be done into many small chunks and execute both the worker code and the UI update code on the same thread, then the UI would still appear to be responsive (assuming the chunks of work are small enough to be executed swiftly in sequence). Unfortunately, that doesn't work because *by design* it's impossible to update user interface elements from outside

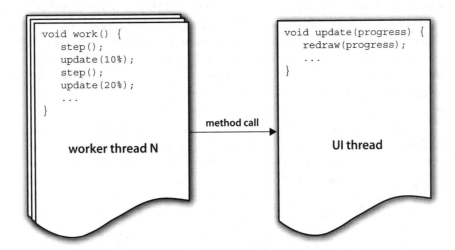

Figure 6.5 One or more worker threads update the UI thread about their progress by periodically sending progress updates. The UI thread listens for these updates and redraws the user interface accordingly (by advancing a progress meter).

the main UI thread. If you do that, Android will throw an exception. There's a good reason for this: if you're sharing state between two or more threads (and updating views using worker progress data is exactly that), you always need to synchronize this shared data using synchronization primitives such as Java's synchronize and volatile keywords, or a Lock object. The problem with making every UI routine thread-safe is that another layer of complexity is added, and performance suffers. Hence a common simplification enforced by many widgets frameworks, including Android's, is that UI elements are always updated from the UI thread. Period.

> **MORE ABOUT CONCURRENCY** Concurrency in computer programs and thread synchronization are vast and complex topics in their own right, and they range among the most difficult and complicated areas you can study about programming. Entire books have been written about this (for a Java specific perspective, we highly recommend *Java Concurrency in Practice* by Brian Goetz et al., which is available as an eBook) and going into detail here is beyond the scope of this book.

With the solution from the previous technique we're now stuck: we're not allowed to update the user interface from a worker thread directly, so there's no way we can update progress that way. Clearly, we need a way to communicate with the UI thread from another thread, so that we can send our update messages and have it react to them. Sounds like we've hit another problem.

PROBLEM

You're executing long-running tasks in separate threads, and you want to update the user interface with progress information while a task runs.

SOLUTION

You could store progress information in a shared variable and access it from both threads: the worker thread writes to it, and the UI thread periodically reads from it. But this would require us to synchronize access to it, which is always cumbersome. It turns out that there's an easier way to do these things on Android—Android's *message-passing* facilities. This approach uses message queues to allow interthread communication in a controlled, thread-safe manner. Progress information can therefore be passed from a worker to the UI thread by posting update messages to the UI thread's message queue using Android's Handler and Message classes.

A *handler* is an object that can be bound to an arbitrary thread (the *handler thread*). The handler can then be used by other threads to send messages to or even execute code on the handler thread. Binding is implicit: a handler is always bound to the thread in which it's being instantiated. If, for instance, a handler is bound to the UI thread, it'll start monitoring that thread's message queue. A second thread (the worker) can then use the handler object to send messages to the UI thread by calling its sendMessage(Message) method, or even ask it to execute a method on the UI thread by calling the post(Runnable) method. No additional synchronization is needed—it just works! We can now revisit figure 6.5 and give the update notifications a concrete shape in the form of messages (see figure 6.6).

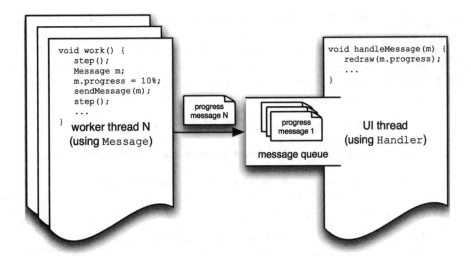

Figure 6.6   Using `Message` and `Handler`, we can bind a `Handler` instance to the UI thread and send messages to it from another thread. Any kind of data can be exchanged that way, without manual synchronization.

MESSAGE QUEUES   We've mentioned several times now that these messages are posted to a message queue. Don't worry too much about the details behind that: we'll explore this further in technique 27. For now it's sufficient to know that the main UI thread maintains a message loop from which messages can be routed to a `Handler`.

The receiving thread reacts by implementing the `handleMessage(Message)` method defined by the `Handler.Callback` interface. A common approach is to let an activity implement `Handler.Callback` and configure the handler object as the object responsible for processing a message.

This sounds like exactly what we need. We have two threads—a download thread and the main UI thread—and we want to tell the UI thread that it should update the status text view whenever the worker state changes. Against the backdrop of what we just discussed, this means that we must perform the following steps:

1 Create a `Handler` object and bind it to the UI thread.
2 Implement the `Handler.Callback` interface, for example on the `Activity`.
3 From the download thread, use the handler object to send a message containing the new status text to the UI thread.
4 In the callback method, read the status text form the message object and update the text view.

Let's rewrite our downloader app to use `Handler` and `Message`. You can find the full source code for the `Activity` in listing 6.3.

GRAB THE PROJECT: IMAGEDOWNLOADWITHMESSAGEPASSING You can get the source code for this project, and/or the packaged APK to run it, at the *Android in Practice* code website. Because some code listings here are shortened to focus on specific concepts, we recommend that you download the complete source code and follow along within Eclipse (or your favorite IDE or text editor).

Source: http://mng.bz/PnPD, APK File: http://mng.bz/vRQ1

Listing 6.3   Message passing can be used to communicate state between threads

```
public class ImageDownloadWithMessagePassing extends Activity
        implements Handler.Callback {                             ◁  Implement
                                                                     callback
    private Handler handler = new Handler(this);       ◁            ❶ interface

    private Runnable imageDownloader = new Runnable() {            Create/bind
                                                                 ❷ handler
        private void sendMessage(String what) {    ◁
            Bundle bundle = new Bundle();
            bundle.putString("status", what);                Helper to
            Message message = new Message();                 send status
            message.setData(bundle);                       ❸ message
            handler.sendMessage(message);
        }

        public void run() {                        ◁   Call
            sendMessage("Download started");       ❹  helper

            try {
                URL url = new URL("http://www.android.com/images/froyo.png");
                Bitmap image = BitmapFactory.decodeStream(url.openStream());
                if (image != null) {
                    sendMessage("Successfully retrieved file!");
                } else {
                    sendMessage("Failed decoding file from stream");
                }
            } catch (Exception e) {
                sendMessage("Failed downloading file!");
                e.printStackTrace();
            }
        }
    };

    public void startDownload(View source) {
        new Thread(imageDownloader, "Download thread").start();
    }

    @Override
    public void onCreate(Bundle savedInstanceState) {
        super.onCreate(savedInstanceState);
        setContentView(R.layout.main);
    }                                                   ❺  Handle message
                                                           by updating view
    public boolean handleMessage(Message msg) {    ◁
        String text = msg.getData().getString("status");
```

```
            TextView statusText = (TextView) findViewById(R.id.status);
            statusText.setText(text);
            return true;
        }
    }
}
```

The first step is to implement the callback interface (❶ and ❺). The callback code reads the string with the key status from the incoming message and updates the status text view with that. Before being able to send messages, we must create and bind a `Handler` object ❷. We pass a reference to the current activity to it because it implements the handler callback. Both the handler creation and the callback method will be executed on the UI thread. In our download job, we then create a helper method ❸ that prepares the message using a `Bundle` that holds the status text, and then dispatches the message via the handler object. (Think of a `Bundle` as being analogous to Java's `Map`, but able to pass key-value-pairs even across thread or process boundaries.) We then use this helper in the run method to send our status updates ❹. These steps are executed on the download thread.

DISCUSSION

Message passing is a powerful and easy way to exchange data between several threads, without having to bother about synchronization primitives. The data that's exchanged can be more complex than a string, too. Because a `Bundle` is used to wrap the data, you can pass anything from a simple number to a complex object that's either serializable or parcelable (the `Parcel` class is Android's recommended way to marshal data).

Because the callback is executed on the UI thread, and a `Bitmap` is parcelable (it implements the `Parcelable` interface), we could stick the bitmap into the bundle and pass it over to the callback, too! That way we could immediately update an `ImageView` using the downloaded image.

One thing you may have wondered about is why the receiving thread (the UI thread in this case) seems to immediately receive the message after we sent it. Recall that message passing doesn't mean we invoke the callback directly. Instead, we post the message to a message queue, which means that queue must be polled periodically by the receiving thread to check for new messages. It turns out that Android handles this for us by automatically creating a message loop for the application's UI thread. If we were to pass messages between two custom threads instead, then we'd have to handle this ourselves (we'll see how to do that in technique 27).

So we've solved the problem of passing information between threads, but our application still exposes some undesirable behavior: clicking on the button will always start a new download thread, without us having any control over how many threads run at once. If, for instance, the user were to click the download button 100 times, the user would start 100 threads. Doing so would clearly undermine the application because threads are expensive to create and handle. It would be nice to gain more control over how threads are managed.

| TECHNIQUE 23 | **Managing threads in thread pools** |

The image downloader served us well to introduce the concept of threads, but let's be honest: it starts to get dull, doesn't it? Instead, let's focus on a real application again. Remember our MyMovies application from chapter 4? Let's extend it to display a thumbnail image that plays a scene from the movie, next to the movie titles in the list view. Figure 6.7 shows how that would look compared to the previous implementation from chapter 4.

 GRAB THE PROJECT: MYMOVIESWITHIMAGES You can get the source code for this project, and/or the packaged APK to run it, at the *Android in Practice* code website. Because some code listings here are shortened to focus on specific concepts, we recommend that you download the complete source code and follow along within Eclipse (or your favorite IDE or text editor).

Source: http://mng.bz/31J4, APK File: http://mng.bz/54sf

Because it'd be tedious and resource-intensive to download 100 movie thumbnail images from the web and bundle them with our application, we instead want to save an image URL with each movie as part of our data, and then download the image on

Figure 6.7   The previous version of MyMovies without images (left), and the new-and-improved version with nifty thumbnail images (right) that are loaded on the fly.

the fly as needed. We learned in techniques 21 and 22 that this must happen asynchronously, but what implication does this have on the performance of MyMovies?

As we've learned from the previous chapters, every list item is created in the list adapter's getView method, and this method is called whenever you scroll the list to see more items. We could use this method to spawn a thread that downloads the image thumbnail because if we were to do it in place then getView would block, and our list view would behave sluggish or exit with an ANR.

But wait. If we scroll the list view quickly, with 100 movies, we'll spawn dozens of download threads because getView is called for every list item we see! Sounds like a bad plan. Obviously, we need some way to restrict the number of concurrent threads being created, and if possible, reuse them once they've completed a task.

PROBLEM

You must execute code in a separate thread, but you don't have control over the frequency at which this may happen, and you risk running into resource congestion.

SOLUTION

The solution here is to use a *thread pool*. A thread pool is a set of threads that are managed in a controlled environment, for instance by setting an upper limit on the number of threads and by forcing the application to reuse threads and distribute the workload among them.

Thread pools in Java and Android are controlled through a ThreadPoolExecutor. A ThreadPoolExecutor is an object that can schedule and manage tasks. Tasks are described by Runnable objects, and are executed in threads taken from a thread pool. This sounds complicated, but it's completely transparent to the developer. Use the executor to start a task and let the executor do the heavy lifting (see figure 6.8).

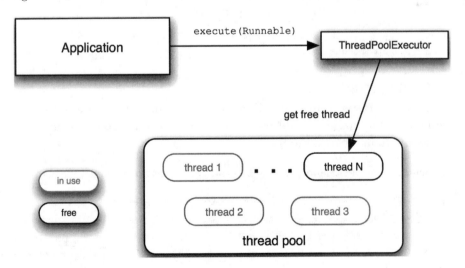

Figure 6.8   The application posts a Runnable to the executor, which then schedules it for execution. As soon as a thread becomes available, it's taken from the pool and used to execute the Runnable.

Thread pools can be configured in various ways, from the lower and upper bound of threads they run to the scheduling rules by which tasks will be distributed among all threads. A commonly used kind of thread pool is one that manages a fixed number of threads that execute tasks posted to a shared queue. If there are more tasks than threads, tasks will have to wait until a thread completes its work and becomes available.

Let's apply this technique to our MyMovies application and spice it up by downloading and displaying movie images for each list element. We only have to change two things. First, the movie_item.xml layout because we need an `ImageView` next to the movie title text view. Second, we need to change the adapter code to trigger the image download whenever `getView` is called. The new item layout is expressed in the next listing.

Listing 6.4   The new movie item layout with image thumbnails next to the title

```xml
<?xml version="1.0" encoding="utf-8"?>
<LinearLayout xmlns:android="http://schemas.android.com/apk/res/android"
    android:layout_width="fill_parent"
    android:layout_height="?android:attr/listPreferredItemHeight"
    android:gravity="center_vertical"
    >

    <ImageView android:id="@+id/movie_icon"            ◁──┐ Will hold movie
        android:layout_width="50dip"                        image thumbnail
        android:layout_height="50dip"
        android:scaleType="centerCrop"
    />

    <CheckedTextView android:id="@android:id/text1"
        android:layout_width="0px"
        android:layout_height="fill_parent"
        android:layout_weight="0.9"
        android:gravity="center_vertical"
        android:paddingLeft="6dip"
        android:paddingRight="6dip"
        android:checkMark="?android:attr/listChoiceIndicatorMultiple"
    />

</LinearLayout>
```

Nothing overly spectacular here. Note how we use the `scaleType` attribute to automatically crop the image to fit in our list element. More interesting is the new adapter code, shown in the next listing.

Listing 6.5   MoviesAdapter.java has been altered to handle image downloads

```java
public class MovieAdapter extends ArrayAdapter<String> {

    private HashMap<Integer, Boolean> movieCollection =
            new HashMap<Integer, Boolean>();

    private String[] movieIconUrls;          ◁── ❶ List of movie
                                                    image URLs

    private ThreadPoolExecutor executor;     ◁──┐ Controls
                                                ❷ thread pool
```

```
public MovieAdapter(Context context) {
    super(context, R.layout.movie_item, android.R.id.text1, context
        .getResources().getStringArray(R.array.movies));

    movieIconUrls =                                    Read image URLs into array
        context.getResources().getStringArray(R.array.movie_thumbs);
    executor =
        (ThreadPoolExecutor) Executors.newFixedThreadPool(5);
}
    ...
                                                         Create new
                                                         thread pool

@Override
public View getView(int position, View convertView, ViewGroup parent) {
    View listItem = super.getView(position, convertView, parent);

    CheckedTextView checkMark =
            (CheckedTextView) listItem.findViewById(android.R.id.text1);
    checkMark.setChecked(isInCollection(position));

    ImageView imageView = (ImageView)
        listItem.findViewById(R.id.movie_icon);            Link image position
    imageView.setTag(position);                            to image view
    downloadImage(position, imageView);

    return listItem;
}

private void downloadImage(int position, ImageView imageView) {
    final Handler handler = new ImageHandler(position, imageView);
    final String imageUrl = movieIconUrls[position];
    executor.execute(new Runnable() {                      Schedule new
        public void run() {                                download task
            try {
                URL url = new URL(imageUrl);
                Bitmap image = BitmapFactory.decodeStream(url.openStream());
                Bundle data = new Bundle();
                data.putParcelable("image", image);
                Message message = new Message();
                message.setData(data);
                handler.sendMessage(message);
            } catch (Exception e) {
                e.printStackTrace();
            }
        }
    });
}

}
```

The first thing we do is create an array that can hold the URLs of the images we need to download ❶ and an executor that manages a thread pool ❷. In the constructor, we first fill the array with the image URLs ❸, which we keep in an array XML resource (/res/values/movie_thumbs.xml), analogous to how we did it for the movie titles in chapter 4. We also leverage the Executors utility class to initialize our executor to manage a fixed thread pool of five threads ❹.

Now it gets interesting: in getView, we first get a reference to the image view that's supposed to display the image we're about to download. But hang on, the download will be asynchronous because it's run in a different thread, and we learned before that it's good to reuse list item views. We've done that here by retrieving them from the super call, during which the caching happens. This means that we could potentially trigger a download for an image view, and the image view could be reused for another movie *before* the first download completes. This is what we call a *race condition* in concurrent environments, effectively meaning a wrong image could be set for the view! That's why we leverage the setTag method ❺, which allows us to associate arbitrary metadata with a view (the position for which we're about to download an image in this case), and we'll see in a moment how this is useful to eliminate this problem. Last but not least, we trigger the image download, similar to what we've learned in the previous techniques, but this time through our executor service ❻.

You may have noticed from listing 6.5 that we're using a custom Handler implementation to set the image on the view (called ImageHandler). There's a good reason for this: it helps us eliminate the problem with the race condition we identified earlier. The next listing offers this solution.

Listing 6.6   ImageHandler.java defines the code to update the ImageViews

```
public class ImageHandler extends Handler {

    private int position;

    private ImageView imageView;

    public ImageHandler(int position, ImageView imageView) {
        this.position = position;          ❶ Remember position
        this.imageView = imageView;           and view to process
    }

    @Override
    public void handleMessage(Message msg) {       ❷ Retrieve image
        int forPosition = (Integer) imageView.getTag();    position
        if (forPosition != this.position) {       ❸ If positions
            return;                                   don't match,
        }                                             return
        Bitmap image = msg.getData().getParcelable("image");
        imageView.setImageBitmap(image);
    }
}
```

When instantiating the handler, we remember which position in the list we're about to download an image for. We also store a reference to the image view so we can change its image drawable when the download commences ❶. Whenever a download succeeds, a message is sent (as seen in listing 6.5) and this handler's handleMessage method is triggered. Before reading the downloaded image from the parcel and updating the view with it, we do a sanity check to make sure that the image view hasn't been reused for a different position than the one we triggered the download for. We do this by reading the ImageView's current position from its tag ❷ and comparing it to the position that was active when the download was initially triggered ❸. Only if these positions match do we proceed and set the image.

> **NOTE** Even though we're working in a concurrent environment, it's not necessary to synchronize the calls to `setTag` and `getTag`. Think about this for a second, and if you don't understand why, consider going back to the previous techniques and rereading them. Both `getView`, where we set the tag, and `handleMessage`, where we read it, are called on the same thread—the UI thread—so there's no way we could read stale shared state. That's the whole idea behind binding a `Handler` to the UI thread: any code executed in that `Handler` will be executed on that same thread, no synchronization required!

That was a fair amount of code. Have you followed everything and implemented it yourself? If not, why not do it now, or download the full source code from the example projects, run it, and get a feeling for how this solution behaves on a device.

DISCUSSION

The clear benefit of this solution is that only the images for those movie items that are currently visible will be downloaded from the web because `getView` will only be called for those. As the user keeps scrolling, new downloads will be triggered, reusing download threads where possible or waiting until one has finished, all without blocking UI routines—an easy and scalable solution.

The solution presented here delivers in that regard, but if you start the application and use it, you'll find that user experience is a little flaky, with the images changing rapidly, overwriting each other while the downloads commence. Also, if you click the check box on an item, the entire list is redrawn, which in this case means redownloading all images for the visible elements. That's unnecessary because the state change will merely affect the check box, not the rest of the element.

Caching images once they're downloaded can mitigate these problems. Whenever `getView` is called, instead of retriggering the download, you could query an image cache first, and when it's a hit, immediately set the image and return. We won't get into caching techniques at this point, but you can already achieve good results using simple approaches, such as a `LinkedHashMap` holding `SoftReferences` to image data, and an implementation of its `removeEldestEntry` method that removes entries from the cache if it's over capacity.

We've seen several approaches and techniques related to threading, from simple thread creation to thread pools and interthread communication using handlers, but though this gives us the maximum in flexibility, we need to write a lot of boilerplate code. Tasks such as spawning progress dialogs or otherwise updating views asynchronously while a thread is running are common, and we want to get more support from the framework here. Turns out, there is. It's called `AsyncTask`.

6.2 *Working with AsyncTask*

The previous techniques should've given you a solid understanding of how to deal with concurrent tasks on Android. We've been staying on a fairly generic level, making those techniques well-suited for a broad range of threading applications. Using handlers, threads, and thread pools directly allows for a high level of control and flexibility, which is great when you need it, but is flat out annoying when you don't.

If we look at typical scenarios like the ones from the previous techniques, some common patterns can be identified:

- One or more jobs need to run concurrently
- Before or after a job completes, you want to update the UI
- You want to report progress about a job to the UI

Google was aware of this recurring pattern and came up with a solution to simplify these things: `AsyncTask`. Let's see how it works.

TECHNIQUE 24   **Implementing jobs with AsyncTask**

According to its documentation, `AsyncTask` "enables proper and easy use of the UI thread … without having to manipulate threads and/or handlers." That's a good summary. You could also say: if running some task and updating the UI with result or progress data is all you want to do, then `AsyncTask` offers an easy-to-use (but more limited) abstraction of the concepts introduced earlier.

`AsyncTask` can be thought of as a description of a job or task, where the actual job will execute in a separate thread, but at several well-defined points will allow the developer to hook into the UI and update it. These hooks allow you to perform view updates on the user interface before the job starts, while it's progressing, and after it completes, allowing you to easily pop up progress dialogs or otherwise manipulate the UI. `AsyncTask` is also backed by a thread pool, so even that bit is handled for you.

PROBLEM

You need to perform an asynchronous job that follows a pre-process/process/post-process pattern, and are looking for a code template that allows you to report progress to the user or otherwise update the UI in each step.

SOLUTION

Like most things, `AsyncTask` is best explained by example. In the last technique, we retrieved movie thumbnail images by having a simple downloader helper method fork a new thread that downloaded the image, and then passed it to a custom handler object that updated the image on the list view. We also managed a thread pool ourselves so as to have an upper limit on the number of threads running at once. Let's rewrite this code to use an `AsyncTask` instead, effectively getting rid of the custom thread pool and the `ImageHandler`.

 GRAB THE PROJECT: MYMOVIESWITHIMAGESASYNCTASK You can get the source code for this project, and/or the packaged APK to run it, at the *Android in Practice* code website. Because some code listings here are shortened to focus on specific concepts, we recommend that you download the complete source code and follow along within Eclipse (or your favorite IDE or text editor).

Source: http://mng.bz/VAhI, APK File: http://mng.bz/CAq3

A few words before jumping into the source code. `AsyncTask` is a generic class—you instantiate it using type arguments. These are:

1 The argument type for the worker method that performs the actual task, in our case `String`, because we're running a job for an image URL

2 The type you want to use to report progress, in our case `Void`, because we don't report any progress

3 The return type for the worker method, in our case `Bitmap`, because that's what we get after decoding the image stream from the server, and it's exactly what we want to pass over to the UI thread

Figure 6.9 We'll simplify the code from the previous technique by using `AsyncTask`'s built-in user interface hooks. We'll also added a placeholder image for those images that have yet to be loaded.

By the way, you can use the `Void` type when you don't care about any of these parameters. In addition to migrating the code to use `AsyncTask`, we also want to extend the visuals a wee bit by setting a placeholder image before a download starts. As the placeholder, we're going to use Android's standard Gallery thumbnail image (`android.R.drawable.gallery_thumb`), a little white frame, as seen in figure 6.9.

Let's get our hands on some code. The following listing shows how our download logic could be implemented using `AsyncTask`.

Listing 6.7 DownladTask.java is our image downloader rewritten using `AsyncTask`

```
public class DownloadTask
    extends AsyncTask<String, Void, Bitmap> {          ←  Inherit from
                                                       ❶  AsyncTask
    private int position;
    private ImageView imageView;
    private Drawable placeholder;

    public DownloadTask(int position, ImageView imageView) {
        this.position = position;
        this.imageView = imageView;
        Resources resources = imageView.getContext().getResources();
        this.placeholder = resources.getDrawable(
                            android.R.drawable.gallery_thumb);
    }

    @Override
    protected void onPreExecute() {                    ←  Called before
        imageView.setImageDrawable(placeholder);       ❷  task runs
    }

    @Override
    protected Bitmap doInBackground(String... inputUrls) {    ←❸  Task logic
```

```
    try {
       URL url = new URL(inputUrls[0]);
       return BitmapFactory.decodeStream(url.openStream());
    } catch (Exception e) {
       e.printStackTrace();
       return null;
    }
  }

  @Override
  protected void onPostExecute(Bitmap result) {
     int forPosition = (Integer) imageView.getTag();
     if (forPosition == this.position) {
        this.imageView.setImageBitmap(result);
     }
  }
}
```

4 **Called after task completes**

We start by inheriting from AsyncTask, where we also supply the parameter types for the worker arguments (String), worker progress (Void), and worker result (Bitmap) **1**. Because we want to set a placeholder image before the download job runs, we must do that in onPreExecute **2**, which will be executed on the UI thread. The actual job is implemented in doInBackground **3**, which takes an arbitrary long list of arguments of the argument type we supplied before and returns a single value of the return type we also supplied before. Finally, we set the new image once it has been downloaded in onPostExecute **4**, which takes, as a single argument, whatever was returned from doIn-Background. Please note that in production code, you probably shouldn't use URL.openStream without first setting proper timeouts. Here, we are simplifying the call to keep the code focused on the topic at hand.

AsyncTask and thread pools

Unfortunately, AsyncTask manages threads dramatically different in different versions of Android. With Android 1.6 (Donut), AsyncTask doesn't launch a single worker thread anymore, but manages a thread pool, as seen in this example (which we tested and ran on Android 2.2). With the arrival of tablets and Android 3.0 (Honeycomb), this behavior was reverted; AsyncTask only spawns a single thread. If you want to manage a pool of threads in Honeycomb and beyond, use the executeOnExecutor method to launch a task (see http://mng.bz/PGxJ).

The question that remains is: where and how do we trigger the task? In the same place as before, Adapter.getView, which is called whenever a list item must be rendered:

```
@Override
public View getView(int position, View convertView, ViewGroup parent) {
   View listItem = super.getView(position, convertView, parent);

   ...

   ImageView imageView = (ImageView)
        listItem.findViewById(R.id.movie_icon);
   imageView.setImageDrawable(null);
```

```
        imageView.setTag(position);
        String imageUrl = this.movieIconUrls[position];

        new DownloadTask(position, imageView).execute(imageUrl);

        return listItem;
}
```

Overall, the code from listing 6.7 isn't dramatically different from our download method plus `ImageHandler` we developed previously. But there are some noteworthy improvements—first, the absence of any explicit interthread communication using handlers and messages, and second, a higher code quality achieved by having all code related to the download task in a single class.

DISCUSSION

`AsyncTask` has several other useful features. We didn't display any progress for an image download, but if you wanted, you could use `AsyncTask`'s `publishProgress` and `onProgressUpdate` methods to communicate progress (percentage of work done) between the worker thread and the UI thread.

`AsyncTask` also tracks state and, more importantly, allows you to cancel a task. This can be achieved using the `onCancelled`/`isCancelled` and `cancel` methods respectively. For instance, you can use the `cancel` method to abort the task should any precondition checks performed in `onPreExecute` not pass.

Though it provides clear benefits, nothing is perfect, and neither is `AsyncTask`. It does a good job of simplifying the execution of concurrent jobs that want to update the UI, but it has its limitations.

First is the thread pool size. Yes, `AsyncTask` internally does what we did manually in the previous technique: it manages a thread pool to run newly instantiated tasks. Unfortunately, you can't configure the size of this thread pool (we traded flexibility for convenience, remember?), and this size has even changed across different versions of the Android platform. To be frank, the `AsyncTask` example, though well-suited to explain the purpose of the class, would, in practice, not be a great fit. If you scroll the list quickly, you can observe how Android spawns more than 30 concurrent download threads (that's on Android 2.2). At least 22 will download an image to discard it again because the `ImageView` for which it was triggered will have been reused by that time, and only eight list items are ever visible at once. Have a look at figure 6.10, which shows the list of threads running when excessively scrolling the list. So although the `AsyncTask` interface may be tempting, consider whether it fits your needs!

Another limitation is error handling. By default, `doInBackground` doesn't allow you to throw exceptions because exceptions are part of a method signature in Java, and the method signature in `AsyncTask` doesn't define any. A simple workaround is to catch any exceptions in `doInBackground` and pass them to `onPostExecute`, where you can handle them on the UI thread by showing an error message.

There's another, less obvious pitfall related to `AsyncTask`, which many developers don't know about—or if they do, they don't handle properly. It's not easily fixed, and requires diving into activity lifecycle, so we've devoted the next technique to it.

ID	Tid	Status	utime	stime	Name
1	604	wait	1087	88	main
*2	605	vmwait	13	36	HeapWorker
*3	606	vmwait	0	0	Signal Catcher
*4	607	running	75	202	JDWP
5	608	native	0	0	Binder Thread #1
6	609	native	0	0	Binder Thread #2
7	644	timed-wait	0	23	AsyncTask #35
8	645	timed-wait	0	24	AsyncTask #36
9	646	timed-wait	0	35	AsyncTask #37
10	613	timed-wait	0	70	AsyncTask #4
11	647	timed-wait	0	21	AsyncTask #38
12	615	timed-wait	0	49	AsyncTask #6
13	648	timed-wait	0	28	AsyncTask #39
14	649	timed-wait	0	29	AsyncTask #40
15	650	timed-wait	0	27	AsyncTask #41
16	619	timed-wait	0	51	AsyncTask #10
17	651	timed-wait	0	33	AsyncTask #42
18	652	timed-wait	0	26	AsyncTask #43
19	653	timed-wait	0	35	AsyncTask #44
20	654	timed-wait	0	6	AsyncTask #45
21	655	timed-wait	0	4	AsyncTask #46
22	656	timed-wait	0	9	AsyncTask #47
23	657	timed-wait	0	3	AsyncTask #48
24	658	timed-wait	0	7	AsyncTask #49
25	659	timed-wait	0	5	AsyncTask #50
26	660	timed-wait	0	4	AsyncTask #51
28	631	timed-wait	0	51	AsyncTask #22

Figure 6.10 `AsyncTask` has a rather high upper limit on its internal thread pool in pre-3.0 versions of Android. If your task runs frequently, you may want to use a custom thread pool instead.

TECHNIQUE 25   Preparing for configuration changes

We all love beautiful applications. Recently, we downloaded an Android application for a popular community website from the Android Market, and after booting it up, we thought: Finally, someone who not only thinks about function, but also form! After using it for a minute or two, our excitement turned into frustration. The application was a nice-looking Android front end to that website's web service, so most screens were backed by a web service call. Apart from being slow, the application seemed to lose its memory whenever the screen was turned to landscape mode, with the progress dialog disappearing even though the call hadn't returned. Moreover, the vanishing progress dialog was often followed by an application crash, most likely due to bad synchronization between what was going on in the background and what was currently visible to the user. Form is good. Always think about form. We told you in some detail in chapter 4 how to do that. But form isn't everything: a good application should also be stable, and the two aren't mutually exclusive.

We're talking about concurrency techniques, and by their nature, concurrent programs are subject to problematic situations that can't arise in sequential programs, where everything is executed in order. One example for this is the unexpected death of a thread, or an object that's part of that thread's state. If threads depend on each other's output or state, and that state is suddenly gone or becomes invalid (we say *stale*), the program may behave erratically.

As it turns out, all Android applications suffer from such an issue by design. An activity's lifecycle can be interrupted and even destroyed at any point in time, as we learned in chapter 3. One common interruption is a screen orientation change. If the screen changes from say portrait mode to landscape mode, Android will terminate the current `Activity` and reload it using the new landscape layout.

ORIENTATION CHANGES ARE CONFIGURATION CHANGES   Note that a change in orientation isn't the only configuration change that can happen. For instance, there's a dock configuration that's triggered when someone puts their Android phone in a docking station (for example, when in a car). Any configuration change will terminate the currently visible `Activity` and restart it using the new system configuration, so always be prepared for interruptions.

That being said, consider again the poorly implemented application I mentioned earlier. Apparently, its intention was to load data from a web service in a worker thread (most likely an `AsyncTask`), and update a view with the result data. Now what happens if we start an `AsyncTask` from an `Activity` and have it update the UI in its post-execute handler, but the `Activity` gets destroyed before the task can complete (for example, flipping the screen). If not dealt with properly, you either lose the result of the worker thread, or worse, the application will crash.

You may have stumbled upon this yourself. The download task from the previous technique holds a reference to an `ImageView`. The `ImageView` holds a reference to its hosting `Activity` (all views do), which is the `Activity` it was created in. If the download task runs longer than our activity exists, manipulating the view will crash the application because the `Activity` has become stale—its window has been destroyed! To help you understand this problem, we've illustrated it in figure 6.11.

Imagine a water skier: a motorboat (the worker) drags the skier (the `Activity`) by a rope over the surface of the water. Usually, the skier holds onto the rope while skiing,

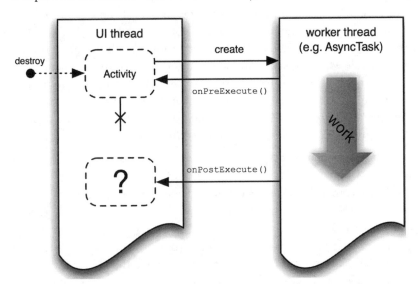

Figure 6.11 An instance of MyActivity creates a worker thread and gets destroyed while the task is running. The worker doesn't know about that, and keeps a reference to an activity instance that's considered terminated by the Android runtime.

so the connection from boat to skier is weak, but let's assume—no masochism intended!—that the skier is tied tightly to the boat using the rope, so that he can't escape. There's a strong connection between the skier and the boat, and this corresponds to our strong reference to the `Activity` object. Now what happens should the skier fall and plunge? He can't let go anymore.

As you can see from figure 6.11, any manually spawned thread, regardless whether created via `AsyncTask` or not, may outlive the `Activity` that created it. In fact, it can live as long as the entire application. If that thread keeps a strong reference to the `Activity` that created it, either directly or indirectly (through a view, for example), it risks referencing a stale object, which would've already been removed by the garbage collector if the thread didn't still hold the reference to it. We not only have a reference to a useless object, we also risk creating a memory leak because the strong reference from the task to the old `Activity` instance keeps it from being garbage collected.

This is clearly a design flaw in the Android platform because we run into a contradiction: we're not allowed to keep references to the `Activity` in a task, but we need one to do anything meaningful in the post-execute handler. This is a bit like asking a painter to paint your wall, but not allowing them to use a brush or roller. Let's try to summarize this problem more compactly.

PROBLEM

You need to perform tasks asynchronously and want to ensure that a worker thread always sees a valid instance of the `Activity` that created it, even if that `Activity` has been destroyed.

SOLUTION

I wish that I could say that Android has you covered, but I can't. Not even `AsyncTask`, which is meant to simplify the implementation of worker threads, solves this problem: although it makes sure that the `onPostExecute` callback will be called on the correct `Activity` instance when the task completes, it doesn't provide any means to get a reference to it, so you'll have to handle that yourself. You must do that whenever you want to update the UI after a task finishes because any action performed on the UI either directly or indirectly goes through the current `Activity` instance. So how do we solve that problem? Let's summarize our findings quickly:

1 We want to keep an `Activity` reference in the worker class, so that we have full access to UI operations in `onPostExecute`.

2 We learned that this reference can become stale, so we need a way of disconnecting/reconnecting that reference whenever the `Activity` gets destroyed and re-created.

3 If the `Activity` is re-created while the task is still running, that new `Activity` instance has no record of the task object created in the old `Activity` instance, so we need a way to pass a worker object from one `Activity` instance to another.

Our idea is as follows: we'll keep a reference to an `Activity` in the worker class, but we'll make sure to reset it whenever that `Activity` instance changes due to a configuration

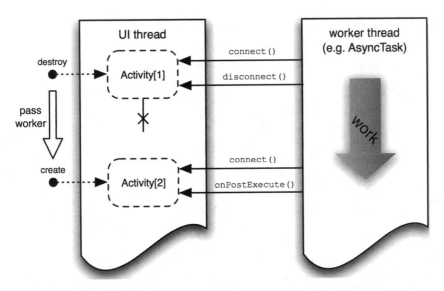

Figure 6.12 In order to not risk keeping a stale `Activity` reference, we set the reference (connect) when the `Activity` is created and remove it (disconnect) when it gets destroyed. Moreover, we pass the worker object between the two different `Activity` instances instead of re-creating it.

change. Moreover, we'll use a peculiar method that Android exposes as an optimization for quickly passing around data within the lifecycle of a single `Activity`—it goes by the unwieldy name of `onRetainNonConfigurationInstance`. In fact, you may remember that we used it in chapter 3 to pass around instance state. Figure 6.12 sketches our plan.

Sounds complicated? It's not as bad as it sounds. Look at this simple application, which will spawn a worker thread in a manner that gracefully handles configuration changes. When started, it'll start the worker, which will work for a few seconds and then post a status back to the `Activity`. Give the sample application some stress by flipping the screen back and forth, and you'll notice that this won't affect the worker.

GRAB THE PROJECT: HANDLINGACTIVITYINTERRUPTIONS You can get the source code for this project, and/or the packaged APK to run it, at the *Android in Practice* code website. Because some code listings here are shortened to focus on specific concepts, we recommend that you download the complete source code and follow along within Eclipse (or your favorite IDE or text editor).

Source: http://mng.bz/6lPJ, APK file: http://mng.bz/71bN

Let's first look at how the `Activity` is implemented, and how it manages the worker instance it's hosting.

Listing 6.8   Gracefully managing worker threads across configuration changes

```
public class WorkerActivity extends Activity {

    private Worker worker;

    @Override
    public void onCreate(Bundle savedInstanceState) {
        super.onCreate(savedInstanceState);
        setContentView(R.layout.main);

        worker = (Worker) getLastNonConfigurationInstance();
        if (worker == null) {
            worker = new Worker();
            worker.execute();
        }
        worker.connectContext(this);
    }

    @Override
    protected void onDestroy() {
        super.onDestroy();
        worker.disconnectContext();
    }

    @Override
    public Object onRetainNonConfigurationInstance() {
        return worker;
    }
}
```

- ❶ Was worker retained?
- ❷ If no, create new one
- ❸ Bind current Activity
- ❹ Unbind current Activity
- ❺ Pass worker to next Activity

We first check whether a worker object is being passed from a previous instance of this Activity class by a call to getLastNonConfigurationInstance ❶. This method can be explained quickly: it gets whatever is being returned from onRetainNonConfigurationInstance ❺, in our case, the worker. As explained in chapter 3, this method's return value is returned to the next Activity instance, as is.

If the return value of getLastNonConfigurationInstance is null, we know that the worker hasn't been retained before, so it must mean that this is a "regular" Activity start. That's when we create a new worker instance and start the task ❷. Regardless of whether the worker was restored or newly created, we call its connect-Context method ❸ (which we'll introduce in a second) to tell the worker that this is the current Activity instance.

Conversely, when our Activity is about to die, we call disconnectContext ❹ on the worker to inform it that this particular Activity instance is about to be destroyed, and that no more interactions with it should happen.

This leaves the code listing for our custom worker class. For brevity, this worker does nothing but sleep a few seconds, and then passes a String to the hosting Activity.

Listing 6.9   Worker implementation that can (dis)connect its hosting `Activity`

```
public class Worker extends AsyncTask<Void, Void, String> {

    private Activity context;

    public void connectContext(Activity context) {
        this.context = context;
```

- ❶ Bind new Activity instance

```
    }
    public void disconnectContext() {
        this.context = null;
    }

    @Override
    protected String doInBackground(Void... params) {
        try {
            Thread.sleep(3000);
        } catch (InterruptedException e) {
        }
        return "Work done!";
    }

    @Override
    protected void onPostExecute(String result) {
        if (context != null) {
            Toast.makeText(context, result, Toast.LENGTH_LONG).show();
        }
    }
}
```

**❷ Release current
Activity instance**

**❸ Only interact with
UI if Activity is valid**

What our custom `Worker` does is keep a reference to an `Activity`, making sure that its hosting `Activity` can bind to the worker ❶ and release itself ❷. That way, we don't risk keeping a reference to a destroyed `Activity`. Moreover, before trying to interact with the UI—say, by showing a `Toast`—we make sure that our `Activity` instance is still valid by checking it for null ❸. This is required in cases where our `Activity` gets destroyed without being recreated, as is the case when hitting the back button, or in out-of-memory situations.

DISCUSSION

We admit that this is a fairly obscure problem, but the solution proved to be simple. We encourage anyone to use this connect/disconnect pattern (or something equivalent) in their applications because it provides for a smoother user experience.

If you followed this technique closely, you may be asking yourself: Hang on a second, we made sure to properly handle the `Activity` reference, and everything looks okay after connecting it and before disconnecting it, but what if the task finishes *in-between*—while the configuration change is being processed? The `Activity` reference will be null at that point, so doesn't that mean the task's result data will be lost because we throw it away in `onPostExecute` whenever the `Activity` is null?

No! Finally we can say that Android has you covered here. The reason why this will work is because Android guarantees that no messages will be processed between a call to `onRetainNonConfigurationInstance` of the previous instance and `onCreate` of the new instance. This means that we can only have two situations:

1 The task finishes *before* `onRetainNonConfigurationInstance` is called, in which case it's safe to immediately proceed because the `Activity` is still alive.

2 The task finishes *after* `onRetainNonConfigurationInstance` is called, in which case the `Activity` is about to be destroyed, and the call to `onPostExecute` will be postponed until the new `Activity` instance has been fully created and is ready to process that event.

One restriction our solution has is that it only works for activities. The `Service` class doesn't define the `onRetainNonConfigurationInstance` method, so it can't keep track of task objects it hosts (at least not that way).

Another restriction is that you can't use the `Activity` instance in `doInBackground` because that method doesn't run on the UI thread, but the task thread, and it's not guaranteed that it will always see the correct `Activity` instance.

If you absolutely can't live with these restrictions, we have good news as well. The ignition Android application library (http://github.com/kaeppler/ignition) defines an implementation of `AsyncTask` called `IgnitedAsyncTask` that allows you to run jobs that are agnostic to the concrete type of their hosting `Context`, and which make sure that in all three callback methods you'll always see the correct context instance. It also saves you from writing most of the boilerplate code you've seen in this technique.

There's more good news. You have now learned everything about `AsyncTask`! Time to come back to more practical things.

6.3   *Miscellaneous techniques*

Are your eyes getting weary? We warned you that this chapter would be technical. But now you can feel prepared for any threading madness you may face in your own applications. To make for some diversity, this last section is a mixed bag: it contains two techniques that didn't quite fit elsewhere, but are both useful in their own right.

Did you ever think about adding a splash screen to your application or performing other tasks that are based on timers? What about creating custom message loops, which is useful in game development? If your answer to either question is *yes*, then you'll find it's worth sticking around a while longer.

TECHNIQUE 26   **Displaying splash screens with timers**

Sometimes it's useful to run a task, not immediately or in immediate reaction to a user interface event, but only after a certain amount of time has passed. We sometimes call this a *delayed job* or *delayed task*. Obviously, we need a separate thread for this because you can only measure how much time has passed by constantly polling for it, and we can't do this on the main UI thread because an active loop is a blocking operation. A good example for using a delayed job is a splash screen—an activity that's started when the application starts, and after a certain amount of time gets replaced by the application's landing screen.

PROBLEM

You want to execute a delayed task that executes its logic only after a certain amount of time has passed.

SOLUTION

You could use a standard Java `Thread` as seen in technique 21 and implement the polling yourself by following a *check time, sleep, repeat* approach. That's tedious though, and surely there's already something that does that for us. There is; it's part of the Java class library, and it's called `Timer`.

A `Timer` can be thought of as a task director class: it schedules jobs (implemented using `TimerTask`) for execution, and when the specified time has passed, it executes them on a separate thread. A `TimerTask` is a special kind of `Runnable`: it exposes a `run` method, but adds additional functionality such as the ability to cancel it while it's still waiting in the execution queue. Let's implement a splash screen for MyMovies using `Timer` and `TimerTask`. Figure 6.13 shows our simple splash screen in action.

Figure 6.13 A simple splash screen for the MyMovies app. We removed the title bar using the windowNoTitle theme attribute.

GRAB THE PROJECT: MYMOVIESWITHSPLASH-SCREEN You can get the source code for this project, and/or the packaged APK to run it, at the *Android in Practice* code website. Because some code listings here are shortened to focus on specific concepts, we recommend that you download the complete source code and follow along within Eclipse (or your favorite IDE or text editor).

Source: http://mng.bz/a0DD, APK File: http://mng.bz/H8LM

The ingredients we need for our recipe are:

- A splash image (such as a PNG, let's call it splash.png)
- An activity, full screen, with no title bar
- A new entry in the manifest for the splash screen activity

The splash image can be dropped in the `res/drawables` folder, as you learned already. The layout for a splash screen `Activity` is also rather minimalistic; it could be as simple as this:

```xml
<?xml version="1.0" encoding="utf-8"?>
<merge xmlns:android="http://schemas.android.com/apk/res/android">
  <ImageView android:scaleType="fitXY"
    android:layout_width="fill_parent"
    android:layout_height="fill_parent"
    android:src="@drawable/splash" />
</merge>
```

Simple and straightforward. We also need to define the new `Activity` in the manifest file. Because it'll be the first `Activity` that's launched, it'll take the place of the MyMovies `Activity`.

Listing 6.10 AndroidManifest.xml defines the new splash screen `Activity`

```xml
...
<application android:icon="@drawable/icon"
    android:label="@string/app_name"
    android:theme="@style/MyMoviesTheme">
```

```
<activity android:name=".SplashScreen"
    android:label="@string/app_name"
    android:theme="@style/SplashScreen">
  <intent-filter>
    <action android:name="android.intent.action.MAIN" />
    <category android:name="android.intent.category.LAUNCHER" />
  </intent-filter>
</activity>

<activity android:name=".MyMovies" />

</application>
...
```

Splash screen now
launched first

Former main activity
reduced to this

You may have noticed that we applied a custom style to the splash screen `Activity`. That's because activities, by default, have a title bar. We want the splash screen to be fullscreen, so add the following code to your styles.xml:

```
<style name="SplashScreen" parent="@android:style/Theme.Black">
  <item name="android:windowNoTitle">true</item>
</style>
```

So far, so good. This was all setup code; the meat is in the `Activity` code in the next listing—after all this chapter is about threading techniques.

Listing 6.11 Timer can be used to launch a screen after some time has passed

```
public class SplashScreen extends Activity {

    public static final int SPLASH_TIMEOUT = 1500;

    @Override
    protected void onCreate(Bundle savedInstanceState) {
        super.onCreate(savedInstanceState);

        setContentView(R.layout.splash_screen);

        new Timer().schedule(new TimerTask() {

            @Override
            public void run() {
                startActivity(new Intent(SplashScreen.this, MyMovies.class));
                finish();
            }
        }, SPLASH_TIMEOUT);
    }
}
```

Pretty straightforward. We schedule a new task using the `Timer` class, which will make sure that the task will be executed after `SPLASH_TIMEOUT` milliseconds have passed—in this case 1500, or 1.5 seconds. The task itself creates an `Intent` to launch our landing screen (the `MyMovies` main `Activity`). Amazingly simple and effective!

We could make the splash screen even cooler: for instance, many users like to skip them, so it'd be sensible to implement a touch listener that immediately skips to the landing screen when the splash screen is tapped. We'll leave that exercise to you this time.

DISCUSSION

The `Timer` class is more than an "execute-task-X-after-Y-seconds" scheduler. It can manage many tasks at once by queuing them up or executing a single task periodically. All tasks are always executed sequentially on a single thread. When executing a task periodically, the normal behavior (the one implemented by the `schedule` method that takes a `period` argument) is to schedule tasks for execution with *relative semantics*: the next execution of the task will be scheduled at least X milliseconds from the start time of the previous execution. We say "at least," because if the system is under heavy load, the real-world time delay can actually be more than the supplied number because the `Timer` didn't get enough time to schedule the next execution on time.

This is unlike the second scheduling strategy implemented in the `scheduleAt-FixedRate` method. This mode has *absolute semantics*, meaning that the delay of a task execution will be measured using absolute time. In this case, if the `Timer` doesn't get enough CPU time because of a busy system, it'll try to catch up and schedule missed executions directly after one another if they should normally be already running. Regardless of which strategy you choose for periodic executions, in both cases the delay at which a task will be executed is unreliable, which is why you shouldn't rely on this technique if your application has real-time requirements.

Similar to a normal `Thread`, a `Timer` thread can also be run as a *daemon thread*. Daemon threads are threads for which the application won't wait to finish when it's exiting, which makes them a sensible choice for threads that are used to control or direct other threads, or implement a certain kind of service. You shouldn't create daemon threads to perform important application logic or writing data because it could leave the application in an inconsistent state.

The classes used in this technique aren't Android-specific; they're part of the Java platform API. Because `Thread` and `ThreadPool` are useful for things such as splash screens, we thought they were worth mentioning here. Let's get back to Android specifics now. The next technique is about a more advanced way of using the previously introduced `Handler` and `Message` classes: implementing custom message loops.

TECHNIQUE 27 Implementing custom message loops

So we talked about `Handler` and `Message` in technique 22, which explained how to pass messages between two threads. Well, that's not entirely correct: we explained how you can pass messages from a *worker* thread to the *UI* thread. If you think we're nitpicking here, we're not. Using that technique alone, you wouldn't be able to send a message the other way—from the UI thread to the worker thread!

Why is that? Because of something we only mentioned briefly along the way: the main user interface thread implements a message queue, and continuously polls this queue for new messages in an endless loop. By default, only the main UI thread does that, but not any thread you create yourself (not even one managed by `AsyncTask`).

For many applications, this is sufficient because handling asynchronous user interface events such as taps or scrolls is the most common kind of event in an Android application, and the existing message loop created for you by Android already takes care of handling these. But what if you have more complex requirements? Take games for example. Games often implement custom loops to handle events specific to the game logic that may be too expensive to consume on the thread that also handles user input events. (Remember that you should always keep the UI as responsive as possible, which means that the UI thread should never do any expensive operations or other frequently executed jobs unrelated to the user interface.) But this is one example of what, in computer science, is a widely known pattern applied to many kinds of concurrent programs: the *producer-consumer scenario.*

In the producer-consumer scenario, you have two concurrent threads: a *producer thread* that generates objects and writes them to a shared message queue, and a *consumer thread* that consumes these objects. This is what happens when you use a `Handler` to update something on the UI thread: your worker (the producer) sends an object (the `Message`) to a shared message queue, which is then handled by the UI thread (the consumer). Let's see how you can apply this pattern to two arbitrary threads.

PROBLEM

You're writing an application in which several threads must exchange messages, as in a producer-consumer scenario.

SOLUTION

We've already seen how to bind a handler and use it to send messages. The interesting question that remains is how to implement a custom message loop to consume these messages outside the UI thread. In Android, message loops for threads are created using the `Looper` class. We can only say that what sounds frightening and complicated at first isn't complicated at all—the solution is simple, thanks to `Looper` doing all the heavy lifting for us.

Use cases for the producer-consumer pattern are usually application-specific, so instead of coming up with a specific example, we'll keep things simple here and write one that focuses on the pattern and leave it to you to decide how to apply it to your applications. In our simple example, we'll have two producer threads that generate random numbers and a consumer thread (running a message loop) that receives these numbers and prints a log statement if they're even.

 GRAB THE PROJECT: PRODUCERCONSUMERWITHLOOPER You can get the source code for this project, and/or the packaged APK to run it, at the *Android in Practice* code website. Because some code listings here are shortened to focus on specific concepts, we recommend that you download the complete source code and follow along within Eclipse (or your favorite IDE or text editor).

Source: http://mng.bz/9lBu, APK File: http://mng.bz/7yl3

The source code for the entire application is in the following listing.

Listing 6.12 A simple producer-consumer scenario implemented using `Looper`

```
public class ProducerConsumer extends Activity {

    private Handler handler;
```
❶ Create shared handler reference

```
private class Consumer extends Thread {

    @Override
    public void run() {

        Looper.prepare();                                   ❷ Create message
                                                              loop for consumer

        handler = new Handler() {                           ❸ Bind handler
            @Override                                         to consumer
            public void handleMessage(Message msg) {
                int number = msg.what;
                if (number % 2 == 0) {
                    Log.d("Consumer", number + " is divisible by 2");
                } else {
                    Log.d("Consumer", number + " is not divisible by 2");
                }
            }
        };
                                                            ❹ Run message
        Looper.loop();                                        loop
    }
}

private class Producer extends Thread {

    public Producer(String name) {
        super(name);
    }

    @Override
    public void run() {
        Random random = new Random();
        while (true) {                                      ❺ Generate
            int number = random.nextInt(100);                 number
            Log.d("Producer " + getName(), Integer.toString(number));
            handler.sendEmptyMessage(number);               ❻ Send number
            try {                                             to consumer
                Thread.sleep(500);
            } catch (InterruptedException e) {
            }
        }
    }
}

@Override
public void onCreate(Bundle savedInstanceState) {
    super.onCreate(savedInstanceState);

    new Consumer().start();                                 ❼ Start producers
    new Producer("A").start();                                and consumer
    new Producer("B").start();
}
}
```

The first step is to create a shared reference to the handler, which the producers will use to send their numbers to the consumer ❶. In the consumer thread, we create the message loop ❷ and bind the handler, before we start the message loop ❸ that will keep listening for incoming numbers ❹. On the producer side, we keep generating numbers between 0 and 100 in an endless loop ❺, with short periods of inactivity in between using the `Thread.sleep` method, and send the numbers to the consumer's message queue ❻. For brevity, we use `sendEmptyMessage(int)` here because an `int` is the only thing we send. Finally, we launch all three threads in `onCreate` ❼.

Figure 6.14 shows the output of our number crunching program, visible through the LogCat view of the Eclipse DDMS perspective, or by running `adb logcat` on the shell.

All right, checking whether a number is even may not be the most useful exercise. We give you that. It should be clear though, that this pattern can be used to distribute computations or other kinds of work between an army of worker threads and have them post back results to another worker (the "supervisor" collecting the results). We'll leave it to your imagination to determine what you can do with this display of sheer distributed computing power—SETI on Android perhaps?

DISCUSSION

The important things have been said about `Looper`, but we think these two points shouldn't go unnoticed:

First, the `Looper` interface allows you to register an `IdleHandler` to a looper thread's message queue. `IdleHandler` defines a single callback method that gets invoked when no more messages are currently waiting in the queue. That way, you can find out if a looper thread is sitting there and waiting, wasting precious resources. You can register an `IdleHandler` with a message queue by calling `Looper.myQueue().addIdleHandler()`.

Second, you can get a reference to the application's main looper by a call to `Looper.getMainLooper`. If you're developing a performance-critical application, this

Time	pid	tag	Message
07-04 16:21:54.223	D 296	Consumer	15 is not divisible by 2
07-04 16:21:54.269	D 296	Producer B	11
07-04 16:21:54.269	D 296	Consumer	11 is not divisible by 2
07-04 16:21:54.719	D 296	Producer A	64
07-04 16:21:54.719	D 296	Consumer	64 is divisible by 2
07-04 16:21:54.769	D 296	Producer B	65
07-04 16:21:54.769	D 296	Consumer	65 is not divisible by 2
07-04 16:21:55.227	D 296	Producer A	45
07-04 16:21:55.229	D 296	Consumer	45 is not divisible by 2
07-04 16:21:55.269	D 296	Producer B	28
07-04 16:21:55.269	D 296	Consumer	28 is divisible by 2
07-04 16:21:55.729	D 296	Producer A	21
07-04 16:21:55.729	D 296	Consumer	21 is not divisible by 2
07-04 16:21:55.776	D 296	Producer B	64
07-04 16:21:55.776	D 296	Consumer	64 is divisible by 2
07-04 16:21:56.231	D 296	Producer A	55
07-04 16:21:56.231	D 296	Consumer	55 is not divisible by 2
07-04 16:21:56.279	D 296	Producer B	65
07-04 16:21:56.279	D 296	Consumer	65 is not divisible by 2
07-04 16:21:56.729	D 296	Producer A	80
07-04 16:21:56.729	D 296	Consumer	80 is divisible by 2
07-04 16:21:56.779	D 296	Producer B	61
07-04 16:21:56.779	D 296	Consumer	61 is not divisible by 2
07-04 16:21:57.235	D 296	Producer A	98

Figure 6.14 The log output produced by the `ProducerConsumer` activity. Two producers post random numbers to the consumer's message queue, which can then be processed by the consumer.

can be useful in combination with `IdleHandler` because it lets you find out when the user interface looper is sleeping, so you can use its thread to perform other tasks and not let the resources consumed by that thread go to waste. Remember that you shouldn't use this approach for performing expensive tasks because user interface events may pile up in the UI looper's message queue while it's busy working on your custom job.

6.4   *Summary*

In this chapter, we showed you how to keep your applications responsive by doing expensive work in separate threads. We started simple, with Java's basic concurrency facilities like the `Thread` class and moved ahead to show you how to let a worker thread update the user interface using Android's message passing duo `Handler` and `Message`. We also beefed up MyMovies to asynchronously download movie thumbnails, as an example of how to manage multiple download threads in a resource sensitive way using Java's thread pools and executors.

Though this gave us a lot of flexibility, job classes are often cookie-cutter classes and contain a lot of boilerplate code, which we removed by simplifying worker thread scenarios using Android's `AsyncTask` class. We wrapped up the chapter by learning how scheduled delayed jobs can be used to implement splash screens, and how to create custom message loops to communicate freely between any number of threads, without using a single object lock or other synchronization primitives. What a ride!

The next chapter is about the most precious thing in your application: its data! Learn how to work with Android's filesystem, how to store semistructured data using shareable preference files, how to realize preference screens, and how to persist and manage data using SQLite databases. Read on.

Storing data locally

7

In this chapter

- Reading and writing files
- Setting and remembering shared preferences
- Working with SQLite databases

Data is a precious thing and will last longer than the systems themselves.

—Tim Berners-Lee

Data is essential to any application, and Android provides several local storage avenues. But Android doesn't stop there—you also have access to data from other applications on the device and the network, which we'll learn about in upcoming chapters. First, we'll focus on local data storage.

To explore local data storage we'll start with the filesystem. Don't forget: Android devices are small computers, and they have filesystems. We'll see how you can check whether the filesystem is available, how you can use it, how permissions come into play, and the differences between internal and external storage. After basic files, we'll visit SharedPreferences, which is a helpful class for storing key-value pair data. SharedPreferences uses the filesystem, but it hides some of the details and makes for a more convenient approach in some cases. Once we understand files, we'll look at more sophisticated data storage using Android's built-in database, SQLite. SQLite isn't the same as your typical server side relational database, but it's no slouch either. We'll explore how to use it, how to create a data access layer around it, and how it differs from what you may be used to.

Our first steps with local data storage will take us back to some of the concepts we discussed in chapter 1, user IDs and permissions, which always matter when working with the filesystem.

7.1 Reading and writing files

The most fundamental type of local storage in Android is the filesystem to read and write files. You can use this mechanism to persist and share data among different application components as well as across different application instances. If your application is killed, it'll lose all its nonpersistent state (as we touched on in chapter 3), but it won't lose anything stored in the filesystem.

If you're familiar with `java.io`, you already know the basics of file storage, but here we'll cover some Android specifics, additional details such as permissions and the difference between internal and external storage.

7.1.1 Internal versus external storage

The first thing to get out of the way before we start reading and writing files is understanding the difference between internal and external storage on Android. At a high level, the differences are as follows:

- *Internal storage* is on the internal device memory; it's private and always available
- *External storage* may be on removable media; it's not private and not always available

Internal storage is the easiest to work with because it's always there (it's never unmounted), and it's secure. External storage isn't guaranteed to be available, and isn't secure. Availability varies because users can dismount and remove their external storage, or mount it as USB storage that makes it unavailable to the device. To get a better idea of what a *mount point* is and how different resources are mounted with various properties, let's run the `mount` command against a device running Android 2.2, as seen in figure 7.1.

```
ccollins@crotalus:~$ adb -d shell
# mount
rootfs on / type rootfs (ro,relatime)
tmpfs on /dev type tmpfs (rw,relatime,mode=755)
devpts on /dev/pts type devpts (rw,relatime,mode=600)
proc on /proc type proc (rw,relatime)
sysfs on /sys type sysfs (rw,relatime)
none on /acct type cgroup (rw,relatime,cpuacct)
tmpfs on /mnt/asec type tmpfs (rw,relatime,mode=755,gid=1000)
none on /dev/cpuctl type cgroup (rw,relatime,cpu)
/dev/block/mtdblock3 on /system type yaffs2 (ro,relatime)
/dev/block/mtdblock5 on /data type yaffs2 (rw,nosuid,nodev,relatime)
/dev/block/mtdblock4 on /cache type yaffs2 (rw,nosuid,nodev,relatime)
/sys/kernel/debug on /sys/kernel/debug type debugfs (rw,relatime)
/dev/block/vold/179:1 on /mnt/sdcard type vfat (rw,dirsync,nosuid,nodev,noexec,relatime,uid=100
0,codepage=cp437,iocharset=iso8859-1,shortname=mixed,utf8,errors=remount-ro)
```

Figure 7.1   The mount command shows some of the locations and types of filesystems Android uses.

This partial output of the mount command shows us that Android uses several types of filesystems mounted at different locations, each with a different set of properties. First it uses rootfs for the / partition. This is a special partition that allows all other devices to attach under one tree. Another special partition is the system partition, which like / is marked ro, or *read only*. These partitions contain essential operating system files and data. You won't typically use these partitions directly; instead you'll use the other locations such as /data and /cache.

The /data and /cache mount pointsare the internal storage locations, and they're mounted using various filesystem types (the figure shows *Yet Another Flash File System 2*, yaffs2, which is designed for use on embedded flash memory devices, but the type can vary based on the device). These are writable, as indicated by the rw, or *read-write* notation.

Along with these and several other special partitions, we see the /mnt/sdcard location mounted with type vfat. That's the external location, and the fact that it's using a FAT (File Allocation Table) type of filesystem is significant. FAT is simple, and almost every operating system can read and write to it. This is why so many memory cards and cameras use it. Also, it can be mounted through a USB connection and used as a virtual drive with almost any host operating system. The simplicity it provides sacrifices security.

Many times the external location also uses a removable media format such as a Secure Digital (SD) card (hence the sdcard path name). Yet, it's important to understand that this isn't always the case. Some devices have no removable storage, and some devices have internal storage they treat as external in Android terms, and some have *both*. This means, in effect, there are two types of external storage: removable and nonremovable. Android only mounts and deals with one at a time (and most prefer the internal-external storage when available, because it's thought to be more reliable, per discussions on the group mailing lists).

We'll learn more about the security aspects and paths as we start reading and writing files, beginning with internal storage.

TECHNIQUE 28　Using internal storage

Now that we've seen the difference between internal and external storage, and discussed how internal storage is more secure and reliable, you might reasonably wonder why you wouldn't use it for everything! Like anything else, there are tradeoffs.

Internal storage space is limited, and when it's used up, no further applications can be installed. Because of this, savvy users will check how much space your application takes up, and they'll rightly scoff if you're storing a lot of data on the internal memory. It's understandable if your application is Google Earth and it takes up a few megabytes. Yet, if your fantasy football application takes up 30 megabytes, you've failed, and users will notice.

RUNNING YOUR APP ON EXTERNAL STORAGE   Android API level 8 and above (2.2) supports running applications from the external storage area. This capability is enabled in the manifest with the `android:installLocation` attribute. If this is set to `preferExternal` or `auto`, then certain application components may be placed on an encrypted separate mount point on the external storage. Other data such as databases and user private data aren't placed on the external storage. This saves the user's internal space, and users appreciate that. Performance isn't affected. The only drawback is that if the user mounts the external storage via USB, any running applications that are on external storage will be stopped. This means that applications that need to maintain running services, register alarms, or which may otherwise be affected by being stopped, shouldn't use this approach.

Due to space constraints, you must decide what data rates high enough for internal storage and what can be moved to external storage. The clearest way to make that distinction is to decide what your application can and can't live without. If you need to cache images, it might be better to do so on external storage and show placeholders when it's not available. On the other hand, the data model for your application—names, places, movies, football teams, and so on—probably needs to be on internal storage (though you should still try to keep it as slim as possible).

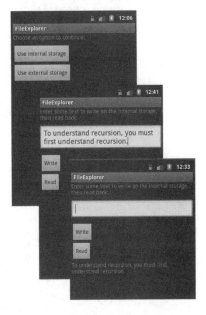

PROBLEM

You understand the different locations where you can store files and other data, and you want to use the internal storage. You also want to be able to explore and verify data that has been stored.

SOLUTION

This time we'll use a sample application to read and write data to and from the internal storage location, and then we'll use the adb shell to examine the data. Figure 7.2 shows the simple screens for FileExplorer. Once again, our sample application isn't pretty, but it gets the job done.

Figure 7.2   The FileExplorer application shows writing and reading of a text file stored on the internal storage.

    GRAB THE PROJECT: FILEEXPLORER   You can get the source code for this project, and/or the packaged APK to run it, at the *Android in Practice* code website. Because some code listings here are shortened to focus on specific concepts, we recommend that you download the complete source code and follow along within Eclipse (or your favorite IDE or text editor).

Source: http://mng.bz/FRV9, APK File: mng.bz/XuAp

The first `Activity` in FileExplorer is a screen that allows users to choose whether to work with the internal or external storage. That code is simple, so we won't show it here (it's available with the project download). If the user chooses the internal storage path, we then go to an `Activity` named `InternalStorage`. This `Activity` includes the `EditText`, `TextView`, and buttons we see in figure 7.2. There the user enters some text and clicks the Write button to store that text to a file. When they click Read, the file is read back and displayed. The code for these methods, shown in the next listing, is the interesting part.

Listing 7.1 The read and write methods of the InternalStorage.java Activity

```
public static final String LINE_SEP = System.getProperty("line.separator");

private void write() {                                                    Use      ❶
  FileOutputStream fos = null;                                     openFileOutput
  try {
    fos = openFileOutput("test.txt", Context.MODE_PRIVATE);
    fos.write(input.getText().toString().getBytes());
    Toast.makeText(this, "File written", Toast.LENGTH_SHORT).show();
    input.setText("");
    output.setText("");                                             Write data
  } catch (FileNotFoundException e) {                                to file  ❷
    Log.e(Constants.LOG_TAG, "File not found", e);
  } catch (IOException e) {
    Log.e(Constants.LOG_TAG, "IO problem", e);
  } finally {
    try {                                              ❸ Close
      fos.close();                                        FileOutputStream
    } catch (IOException e) {
    }
  }
}

private void read() {
  FileInputStream fis = null;
  Scanner scanner = null;
  StringBuilder sb = new StringBuilder();
  try {                                       Use
    fis = openFileInput("test.txt");          openFileInput    Pass FileInputStream
    scanner = new Scanner(fis);                                 to a Scanner
    while (scanner.hasNextLine()) {
      sb.append(scanner.nextLine() + LINE_SEP);
    }
    Toast.makeText(this, "File read", Toast.LENGTH_SHORT).show();
  } catch (FileNotFoundException e) {
    Log.e(Constants.LOG_TAG, "File not found", e);               Read data
  } finally {                                                    from file
    if (fis != null) {
      try {                                          Close
        fis.close();                                 FileInputStream
      } catch (IOException e) {
      }
    }
    if (scanner != null) {
```

```
        scanner.close();
    }
  }
  output.setText(sb.toString());
}
```

The easiest way to write simple files to internal storage is to use the input and output stream convenience methods provided by `Context`. This makes reading and writing files work much the same as it would with typical `java.io` code.

First, you obtain a `FileOutputStream` with `openFileOutput` ❶. This special method creates the file in the correct internal location for your application if it doesn't exist and allows you to set the permissions mode. Most often you'll keep internal files private, but you do have the option of making them `MODE_WORLD_READABLE` or even `MODE_WORLD_WRITABLE` as well. Once you have the stream, you write data to it ❷, and then make sure to close it when done ❸.

> **REMINDER: LOOK OUT FOR OVERSIMPLIFIED EXAMPLES** In our file-handling example activities you may notice a subtle potential problem. We're performing I/O operations from the main UI thread. This is almost never a good idea. Reading and writing data to and from filesystem, internal or external, can block the main UI thread. In a real implementation, you'll want to do this from a `Handler` or an `AsyncTask` (passing in the file reference). We haven't here because we want to keep each example as short and focused as possible (we learned about threading in chapter 6).

If we crack open the `adb` shell and go to the internal location /data/data/<package-name>/files, we can see the file written by the `InternalStorage` class. For example, after typing in the text seen in figure 7.2 and then pressing the Write button, we can see the file permissions details and contents via shell commands as shown in figure 7.3.

One other notable aspect of the internal storage is that the `Context` provides several other convenience methods for listing and deleting files, and for getting the internal cache directory. We'll touch on the significance of cache directories in technique 30.

DISCUSSION

Overall, internal storage is straightforward; the key is to use Android's convenience methods so files end up in the correct location or automatically created if necessary. From there, reading and writing data involves standard `java.io` operations. And, as we've seen, the shell is helpful for exploring data and troubleshooting (you can use the command-line shell or the file explorer provided by the ADT plugin in Eclipse).

Our next step is using the external storage.

```
ccollins@crotalus:~$ adb -e shell
# cd /data/data/com.manning.aip.fileexplorer/files
# ls -l
-rw-rw----  app_31    app_31         62 2010-12-08 00:33 test.txt
# cat test.txt
To understand recursion, you must first understand recursion. # ▮
```

Figure 7.3   The adb shell examines a file written to the internal storage location by FileExplorer.

Using external storage

As we've already noted, the external storage on Android (whether removable or not) is mounted with a different filesystem than the internal. It's inherently less secure, but it's also easy to use and keeps things out of the scarce internal storage space. For many application files, backup data, caches, images, and so on, you'll want to use the external storage. And you can use the external storage to store data you want to make accessible to other applications.

PROBLEM

You want to store data on the external storage. Also, you want to be able to easily determine when the external storage is and isn't available, regardless of the version of the Android SDK you're using.

SOLUTION

To see the external storage in action, we're going to continue with the FileExplorer sample application and repeat the same operations we used for the internal storage example. We'll write some text into a text box that's saved to a file, and then we'll read it back. From the UI standpoint, this looks identical to using the internal storage, as seen in figure 7.4.

The `ExternalStorage Activity` class, in the next listing, is much the same as the `Internal-Storage` class, but it has different implementations in the read and write methods.

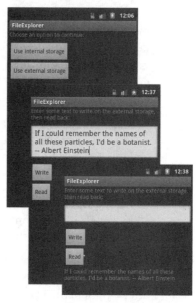

Figure 7.4   The FileExplorer application shows writing and reading of a text file on the internal storage.

Listing 7.2   The read and write methods of the ExternalStorage Activity class

```
private void write() {
    if (FileUtil.isExternalStorageWritable()) {          ❶ Is external
        File dir =                                            storage writable?
            FileUtil.getExternalFilesDirAllApiLevels(
    this.getPackageName());                              ❷ Get recommended
        File file = new File(dir, "test.txt");               file path
        FileUtil.writeStringAsFile(input.getText().toString(), file);
    Toast.makeText(this, "File written", Toast.LENGTH_SHORT).show();
        input.setText("");                               ❸
        output.setText("");
    } else {                                             Write string
        Toast.makeText(this, "External storage not writable",   as file
            Toast.LENGTH_SHORT).show();
    }
```

```
}
private void read() {                                          ④  Is external
    if (FileUtil.isExternalStorageReadable()) {          ◄──┘     storage readable?
File dir =
        FileUtil.getExternalFilesDirAllApiLevels(          ⑤  Get file
            this.getPackageName());                   ◄──┘     path again
File file = new File(dir, "test.txt");
        if (file.exists() && file.canRead()) {            ⑥  Read file
            output.setText(FileUtil.readFileAsString(file));  ◄──┘  as string
            Toast.makeText(this, "File read", Toast.LENGTH_SHORT).show();
        } else {
            Toast.makeText(this, "Unable to read file: "
                + file.getAbsolutePath(), Toast.LENGTH_SHORT).show();
        }
    } else {
        Toast.makeText(this, "External storage not readable",
            Toast.LENGTH_SHORT).show();
    }
}
```

The first thing of note in the ExternalStorage read and write methods is that we're using a FileUtil class in several places. This is an example of a small utility class that we've included in our application. It contains some useful methods that we may use for more than one Activity, and even for more than one application. We'll see the code for it next, after we get through the read and write methods.

The first thing we do with FileUtil in the write method is check whether the external storage is writable ❶ (if you're using an emulator for this example you'll have to make sure that you created an SD card for the instance you're working with). Then, if it is, we use it again to get a reference to the File that represents the recommended external path for our application ❷. That path will be /sdcard/Android/data/<packagename>/files. You might notice a pattern there—this path mirrors the internal data directory path (with a different mount point and parent). After we have the path, we create a File and write to it ❸. Later in the read method, we use a similar approach. We check whether the external storage is readable ❹, then get the path ❺ and read the data ❻. If we open the shell, we can see the file at the specified location on the external storage, as demonstrated in figure 7.5.

```
ccollins@crotalus:~$ adb -e shell
# cd /sdcard/Android/data/com.manning.aip.fileexplorer/files
# ls -l
----rwxr-x system   sdcard_rw      91 2010-12-08 00:38 test.txt
# cat test.txt
If I could remember the names of all these particles, I'd be a botanist. -- Albert Einstein# █
```

Figure 7.5   The adb shell examines a file written to the external storage location by the FileExplorer sample application.

The guts of the file I/O code can be found in `FileUtil` itself, which is shown in the next listing.

Listing 7.3 The `FileUtil` class that performs reusable file related operations

```
public final class FileUtil {

    private static final String
            EXT_STORAGE_PATH_PREFIX = "/Android/data/";       ❶ Define constants
    private static final String                                  to represent
            EXT_STORAGE_FILES_PATH_SUFFIX = "/files/";           paths
    private static final String
            EXT_STORAGE_CACHE_PATH_SUFFIX = "/cache/";

    public static final Object[] DATA_LOCK = new Object[0];    ❷ Object array
                                                                  for lock
    private FileUtil() {
    }

    public static boolean isExternalStorageWritable() {
        return Environment.getExternalStorageState().equals(  ❸ Environment
            Environment.MEDIA_MOUNTED);                           determines
    }                                                             read- and
                                                                  write-ability
    public static boolean isExternalStorageReadable() {
        if (isExternalStorageWritable()) {
            return true;
        }
        return Environment.getExternalStorageState().equals(
            Environment.MEDIA_MOUNTED_READ_ONLY);
    }

    public static File getExternalFilesDirAllApiLevels(
            final String packageName) {
        return FileUtil.getExternalDirAllApiLevels(           ❹ Get file/cache
            packageName, EXT_STORAGE_FILES_PATH_SUFFIX);          dir passing type
    }

    public static File getExternalCacheDirAllApiLevels(
            String packageName) {
        return FileUtil.getExternalDirAllApiLevels(
            packageName, EXT_STORAGE_CACHE_PATH_SUFFIX);
    }
                                                              ❺ Private method
    private static File getExternalDirAllApiLevels(              to get/create
            String packageName, String suffixType) {
        File dir = new File(Environment.getExternalStorageDirectory()
            + EXT_STORAGE_PATH_PREFIX + packageName + suffixType);
        synchronized (FileUtil.DATA_LOCK) {
            try {
                dir.mkdirs();
                dir.createNewFile();
            } catch (IOException e) {
                Log.e(Constants.LOG_TAG, "Error creating file", e);
            }
        }
        return dir;
    }
```

```
public static boolean writeStringAsFile(          ⑥ Define
    String fileContents, File file) {                writeStringAsFile
  boolean result = false;
  try {
    synchronized (FileUtil.DATA_LOCK) {
      if (file != null) {
        file.createNewFile();
        Writer out =
          new BufferedWriter(new FileWriter(file), 1024);
        out.write(fileContents);
        out.close();
        result = true;
      }
    }
  } catch (IOException e) {
    Log.e(Constants.LOG_TAG,
      "Error writing string data to file " + e.getMessage(), e);
  }
  return result;
}
public static String readFileAsString(File file) {   ⑦ Define
  StringBuilder sb = null;                              readFileAsString
  try {
    synchronized (FileUtil.DATA_LOCK) {
      if ((file != null) && file.canRead()) {
        sb = new StringBuilder();
        String line = null;
        BufferedReader in =
          new BufferedReader(new FileReader(file), 1024);
        while ((line = in.readLine()) != null) {
          sb.append(line + System.getProperty("line.separator"));
        }
      }
    }
  } catch (IOException e) {
    Log.e(Constants.LOG_TAG,
        "Error reading file " + e.getMessage(), e);
  }
  if (sb != null) {
    return sb.toString();
  }
  return null;
}
}
```

At the start, `FileUtil` defines several constants for the recommended external storage file paths ❶. We'll see why these are necessary in a moment. After that it also defines an `Object[]` array that it'll later use as a lock for synchronized blocks ❷. Because these utility methods may be accessed by different threads and could possibly touch the same files, we'll synchronize them to avoid concurrent modification problems. Then, it defines the methods we used earlier, such as those that check whether the external storage is writable and readable ❸. This is done using the `Environment` class, which has utility methods to return this information. We could call `Environment` from our activities (and sometimes that makes sense), but here we chose to put the logic in one place so as not to have to repeat it.

After the state-checking methods, we then see the methods `getExternalFiles-DirAllApiLevels` and `getExternalCacheDirAllApiLevels` methods ❹, which are wrappers around the private `getExternalDirAllApiLevels` ❺. This is all done to provide a backward-compatible way to get to the recommended paths we've already seen. If we knew we'd always be running our code on devices that support API level 8 or later, we could call `Context.getExternalFilesDir` or `Context.getExternal-CacheDir`. But we don't know that. Many users still have devices that run earlier versions of Android, so we shouldn't rely on those methods. That's why we created the utility methods that give us the same thing, for any API version. This is done using the `getExternalStorageDirectory` method (which all versions have) and then appending the recommended paths via the constants we noted earlier.

> **WHY THE RECOMMENDED PATHS?**   If you've used Android for any length of time and poked around on the external storage area of your device, you've likely seen files stuffed in all sorts of different directories. This is because the first several versions of Android had no recommended paths and each application chose what it wanted to use. This was problematic because it caused an explosion of directories, and because none of these files were deleted when applications were uninstalled. If you use the recommended path, things will be more organized, users (and other applications) will know the convention, and files can be cleaned up by the platform.

After those helper methods, we then use the `writeStringAsFile` and `readFileAs-String` methods. These don't have any Android-isms in them. Instead they use standard `java.io` and they're passed the `File` references they require. Specifically, we use `FileWriter` ❻ and `FileReader` ❼ for reading and writing file data, respectively. For either case, if we needed more control, such as specifying the file encoding, we could've used the lower-level `FileInputStream` and or `FileOutputStream` classes. Instead we chose the reader and writer because they're less verbose and we're fine with the system encoding in this case.

Even though these use less code than other Java IO classes, they aren't exactly tidy. This isn't code we'd want to repeat in multiple Android components. This is one reason we've moved these operations into a utility class.

> **HIDING APPLICATION DATA**   If you're storing images, music, or anything else that might be picked up by the Android media scanner on the external storage, you might want to also include a .nomedia file in the same directory. This file is hidden (which is why the name starts with dot), and it tells the media scanner to skip the present directory. If you don't do this, your application images will end up in the Gallery application. This may not be what you want.

Along with using the recommended external storage paths we've noted, there are also several conventions for data if you want to make it public. If you want to share a file on the external storage, you start with the same `getExternalStorageDirectory` path, and then you append the correct directory convention. These include /Music, /Movies, /Pictures, and more. We'll learn more about multimedia, and the public paths for sharing data using the external storage, in chapter 11.

DISCUSSION

Storing external data is similar to storing internal data. You need to start with Android's convenience methods to get to the correct locations, and then you'll use java.io to perform operations. The exceptions with external data are that you'll need to make sure the external paths are available before trying to use them (and have fallbacks, such as placeholder images, for when they aren't), and that everything is readable/writable (there's no security). You can also explore and troubleshoot the external storage the same way as you would the internal, starting from the /sdcard path.

With the basics of reading and writing files in general wrapped up, the next thing we need to address is cache directories.

TECHNIQUE 30 Using cache directories

Android provides cache directories on both the internal and external storage. So what makes these directories special, and why are they necessary? Fundamentally they're directories that are marked for some level of management by the platform. That management includes being deleted if an associated application is deleted and sometimes being automatically pruned if space requirements dictate it.

PROBLEM

You need to store some type of temporary data, and you'd like that data to be in a predefined recommended location so that the Android platform can help manage it.

SOLUTION

If you have data that you want to keep around for some period of time but not permanently, such as images from web service feeds, you should use the internal and external cache directories. Caching is an art, so it depends on the context—what needs to be cached and how it should be maintained—but Android tries to help by providing specific cache directories on both the internal and external file systems.

The Context.getCacheDir method will return a reference to the /data/data/<packagename/cache internal storage cache directory. Even though the cache directory can be cleaned up by the system if it needs to reclaim the space, you shouldn't rely on that behavior. Instead, your application still needs to keep an eye on the cache and not allow the directory size to grow beyond a reasonable maximum (the documentation recommends 1MB as the maximum).

Similarly, Context.getExternalCacheDir is available, for API levels 8 and above, to get a reference to the external cache directory. If you want to make sure earlier API versions will work, you can also do something similar in listing 7.3 and manually construct the same path that getExternalCacheDir creates.

DISCUSSION

Rather than creating your own special caching locations, you should try to use the platform-recommended paths because they're managed. When applications use the platform cache directories properly, the system can manage space as needed. First the system can prune files to save space as necessary, and second it completely removes such cache directories when the application referring to them is uninstalled. This helps organize and control files and allows applications to work together and share resources more efficiently.

Knowing how and where to save files, even particular types of files such as those intended for a cache, is essential. Unfortunately, it's not the only thing you need to consider. To be absolutely sure your files are saved to disk when you need them to be, you also need to be aware of how to sync them.

TECHNIQUE 31   ## Making sure files are saved with sync

Most Android devices up to version 2.2 use filesystems that don't buffer aggressively (such as YAFFS). When you save a file, it's immediately written to disk. Some newer devices (and custom ROMs), particularly those running Android 2.3, may use journaled filesystems such as ext4. These types of filesystems use more buffering, which means files aren't always immediately written to disk. The buffering allows the filesystem to be more robust (handle crashes better), and to more efficiently handle writing blocks of data, but it can also be a headache for developers at times.

PROBLEM

You need to guarantee that file data is written to disk immediately, regardless of the filesystem in use and the platform version.

SOLUTION

There are times when you need to guarantee that your file data is written to disk before moving on to other operations. For example, if you write file data in one process, and need to read that same file from another process, you'll want to make sure the data is written before trying to read it. To guarantee the file is written immediately, regardless of the filesystem involved, you can manually call sync. Syncing ensures that the buffer catches up with the physical disk. You might be surprised to learn that `FileOutput-Stream` methods such as `flush`, `write`, and even `close` don't ensure this, but it's true.

The `FileDescriptor` object in Java is where you'll find the sync method. `File-Descriptor` is a low-level handle to operations on the underlying machine-specific filesystem. You can get a `FileDescriptor` reference from `FileOutputStream`, and then sync, as shown in the next listing.

Listing 7.4 Using a `FileDescriptor` to guarantee data is written to the filesystem

```
public static boolean syncStream(FileOutputStream fos) {
    try {
        if (fos != null) {
            try {
                fos.getFD().sync();
            } catch (IOException e) {
                Log.e(Constants.LOG_TAG,
                    "Error syncing fos " + e.getMessage(), e);
            }
        }
```

```
        return true;
    }
    return false;
}
```

You don't always want to sync files immediately, because there's overhead to doing so, and it's not necessary if you're writing to a single file from one process. But it's important to know that you can (and should) when you need to guarantee the file data is written immediately.

DISCUSSION

If you use your own file storage on Android, you need to keep the filesystem and sync situation in mind. On the other hand, if you use other Android APIs such as a SQLite database, or `SharedPreferences` (both of which we'll visit in upcoming sections in this chapter), the syncing is handled for you.

Now that we've seen the differences between internal and external storage, done some basic I/O, discussed caching, and dealt with syncing, our next point of interest is the next level of abstraction with storage, the aforementioned `SharedPreferences`.

7.2 *Maintaining preferences*

Android provides an easy-to-use data storage class called `SharedPreferences` that allows you to read and write primitive key-value pairs. The not-so-secret secret is that shared preferences are files that the platform helps to manage. The preference level is an easier, less verbose wrapper around storing simple persistent items in files.

TECHNIQUE 32 Reading and writing preference data

`SharedPreferences` allow you to read and write data, and to set access modes on the files that contain them. This means you can use them to share data among different components (activities, services, and more), and even among different applications (though that should be uncommon because it requires the applications to know each others' package names and use world-writable files or shared user IDs, all of which should only be done in special circumstances).

PROBLEM

You want an easy way to store simple information, such as strings and primitive values.

SOLUTION

You can use `SharedPreferences` to easily store and retrieve data. The following listing is an example.

Listing 7.5 Using `SharedPreferences` to write and read data

```
SharedPreferences prefs = getSharedPreferences("myPrefs",
        Context.MODE_PRIVATE);
Editor editor = prefs.edit();
editor.putString("HW_KEY", "Hello World");
editor.commit();

//. . . later, or from another component
String helloWorld = prefs.getString("HW_KEY", "default value");
```

To use preferences, you first get a reference to a `SharedPreferences` object (via the `Context`), then you use an `Editor` to write data and simple `get` methods to read data.

DISCUSSION

`SharedPreferences` objects are useful and easy to work with. You can create your own, as we've done in listing 7.5, or you can use one of several convenience methods the framework supplies to make this even simpler. The default preferences are available from any component using `PreferenceManager.getDefaultSharedPreferences` `(Context c)`. This returns a preference object using the package name the context represents. You can also use `Activity.getPreferences(int mode)`, which will return an object using the class name. Remember, under the covers `SharedPreferences` are XML files that are stored at the /data/data/<PACKAGE_NAME>/shared_prefs location on the internal file system (if you need to edit them manually, or just want to check them out, that's where you can find them).

SharedPreferences also support listeners. You can attach an `OnSharedPreferenceChangeListener` that acts as a callback to notify you when preferences are changed. We'll see how that works inside a more useful example where we'll include a `PreferenceActivity`.

TECHNIQUE 33   Using a PreferenceActivity

Android takes preferences one step further than allowing them to store data and be shared among components: it can automatically wire them into onscreen selections for user preferences. To do this, Android uses a specialized activity class— `PreferenceActivity`.

PROBLEM

You need to allow users to set preferences for your application and easily persist them to `SharedPreferences` files.

SOLUTION

You've probably seen `PreferenceActivity` in action. In fact, the main Android settings screen uses it and so do many other built-in applications. Here we'll see how it works so you too can leverage it, and we'll also see how to make it more useful by having it show the current preference (rather than a description) and immediately reflect changes.

To do this, we'll be extending the MyMovies project we worked with in chapter 4. We'll create a new version of that project that changes MyMovies in several notable ways. We'll add a database to it and making it dynamic by retrieving data from the web. We'll learn more about those features soon, but first, we want to include a preference screen that allows us to enable or disable the splash screen.

 GRAB THE PROJECT: MYMOVIESDATABASE   You can get the source code for this project, and/or the packaged APK to run it, at the *Android in Practice* code website. Because some code listings here are shortened to focus on specific concepts, we recommend that you download the complete source code and follow along within Eclipse (or your favorite IDE or text editor).

Source: http://mng.bz/5M06, APK File: mng.bz/03ta

Figure 7.6 The preferences screen for MyMoviesDatabase shows the current enabled/disabled status of the splash screen.

Our `Preferences Activity` for MyMoviesDatabase, which will be accessible via the menu once we're done, is seen in figure 7.6.

There are two parts to making the preference activity screen work. There's a preference resource XML file that defines the elements, and there's a `PreferenceActivity`. This is the same arrangement as with a standard layout resource or `Activity`, but it's specialized for preferences. We'll start by examining the XML resource, shown in listing 7.6.

Listing 7.6   The preferences.xml resource file used to define the preference hierarchy

```xml
<?xml version="1.0" encoding="UTF-8"?>
<PreferenceScreen
    xmlns:android="http://schemas.android.com/apk/res/android">
        <PreferenceCategory
            android:title="Application Settings">
        <CheckBoxPreference android:title="Splash Screen"
            android:key="showsplash" android:summary="Disabled"
            android:defaultValue="false" />
        </PreferenceCategory>
</PreferenceScreen>
```

PreferenceScreen ❶ **is root**

❷ **Preferences can be grouped**

❸ **Object definition and attributes**

Every preference XML resource starts with a root `PreferenceScreen` element ❶, and then includes categories with titles ❷ and preference elements. There are several types of built-in preference objects including `DialogPreference`, `ListPreference`, `Edit-TextPreference`, and the one we're using, `CheckBoxPreference` ❸. Each preference object has a title, key, value, and summary. Most often the summary is left as static text such as "Enable or disable the splash screen." We're going to demonstrate how to make this dynamic and use it to show the current setting (such as in figure 7.6). The other half of all this is the `PreferenceActivity` class, shown in the following listing.

Listing 7.7   The Preferences.java `Activity` in the MyMoviesDatabase application

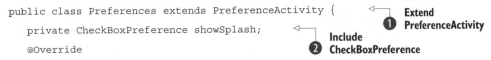

```java
public class Preferences extends PreferenceActivity {
    private CheckBoxPreference showSplash;
    @Override
```

Extend ❶ **PreferenceActivity**

❷ **Include CheckBoxPreference**

```
public void onCreate(final Bundle savedInstanceState) {
    super.onCreate(savedInstanceState);

    addPreferencesFromResource(R.layout.preferences);

    showSplash = (CheckBoxPreference)
        getPreferenceScreen().findPreference("showsplash");

    setCheckBoxSummary(showSplash);

    SharedPreferences prefs =
      PreferenceManager.getDefaultSharedPreferences(this);
    prefs.registerOnSharedPreferenceChangeListener(
        new OnSharedPreferenceChangeListener() {
            public void onSharedPreferenceChanged(
                SharedPreferences prefs, String key) {
                if (key.equals("showsplash")) {
                    setCheckBoxSummary(showSplash);
                }
            }
    });
}
private void setCheckBoxSummary(CheckBoxPreference pref) {
    if (pref.isChecked()) {
        pref.setSummary("Enabled");
    } else {
        pref.setSummary("Disabled");
    }
}
}
```

❸ Invoke addPreferences-FromResource

❹ Use findPreference

❺ Get default SharedPreferences

❻ Attach listener

❼ Update preference summary based on state

Right up front, we take the help Android provides us by extending Preference-Activity ❶. PreferenceActivity shows a hierarchical list of Preference objects to the user, and automatically saves the selections to a backing SharedPreferences file. As we saw with the XML file, preference objects such as CheckBoxPreference are used from within the activity ❷.

Here we only have the one preference, so it's simple, but the pattern is the same no matter how many you may have. We set the XML preference hierarchy in the activity with addPreferencesFromResource ❸. To obtain a reference to a specific preference object that's declared in the XML, we use findPreference ❹. This is much like findViewById, but it's for preferences.

After our initial setup, we then access the default SharedPreferences object ❺, because that's where PreferenceActivity saves data, and we attach an OnShared-PreferenceChangeListener ❻. Every time a preference is updated, this event is fired with the preferences and key that was changed. Within the listener, we check whether the key is the one we're interested in. If it is, we change the preference objects summary with an internal helper method named setCheckBoxSummary ❼. If we had multiple checkboxes, we could use this same method for each.

DISCUSSION

With a PreferenceActivity and its backing SharedPreferences file, we not only now have a preferences screen, but it updates automatically to show the user what the current state/setting is. Even though we don't have many preferences here, our users will appreciate the fact that by default the splash screen is shown only once, and after that we allow them to enable it if they want (we don't force them to look at it every time they open the application).

At this point we've seen several forms of accessing and using `SharedPreferences`, and we've kicked off the MyMoviesDatabase sample application. Next up we'll include a SQLite database to store movie selections locally and to live up to the Database part of our sample application's name.

7.3   *Working with a database*

When you need to store more complex data for your application, using a relational database is often a good choice. Databases are built for taking care of details such as inserting data with transactions and allowing multiple connections at once. Most developers are familiar with a relational database management system (RDBMS) of one form or another. They're a common and powerful way to structure and store data, built on the principles of relational algebra.

To see a database in use with an Android application, we're going to change the MyMovies application we've seen in previous chapters. We'll modify it so that it includes a local database to store movie data rather than using a flat text resource file, and we'll allow users to search for movies to add to their collection. We'll be pulling data from a web service to get movie information, and we'll store it in several database tables. We'll focus on the database aspects of this version of MyMovies, but the code download has the networking and XML parsing portions if you're interested—we'll cover those concepts in chapter 9. The finished MyMoviesDatabase product will look like figure 7.7.

To store local movie data for MyMoviesDatabase, we'll create a layered architecture to allow our application components (activities in this case) to easily save and retrieve plain Java objects to and from a database. We'll walk through the layers and look at each level up close, but first we'll touch on the database system Android provides that will ultimately store our data: SQLite.

What's SQLite? Most database systems are large server-based applications. For example many web applications use multiple servers and clusters of databases on the server side. Android can access these systems through the network, but as we noted in chapter 1, it also provides a

Figure 7.7   The MyMoviesDatabase application displays a movie list, search, and detail screens.

small open source embedded database named SQLite. SQLite is often used within applications to manage local data. Apple OS X, DropBox, Firefox, and Chrome all use it, as do many other applications and products.

SQLite uses the *Structured Query Language (SQL)*, as its name implies, to allow you to create and maintain tables and to insert and select data. Though SQLite uses SQL, it isn't meant to replace the large server offerings that Oracle, Microsoft, IBM, and others supply. Instead, it's designed to be small, fast, and easy to use for in-process data. If you've worked with SQL before, you'll be right at home with most of what SQLite offers. If you haven't, that's okay too because it's a great way to get started learning SQL without the overhead of larger systems.

Even though it's small and fast, SQLite is powerful. It supports transactions (which are atomic even after system crashes), foreign keys, functions, triggers, and more. We'll learn about many of these features as we use them in the MyMoviesDatabase application. In addition, although SQLite has many features other SQL systems have, it doesn't have them all. SQLite doesn't support certain join types (right outer, full outer), some alter statements, and it treats data types more loosely than other systems. We won't cover every facet of SQLite here, but we hope to get you started and provide information on the most common patterns you're likely to need when working with it on the Android platform. For full information on SQLite, you'll want to check the excellent online documentation: http://www.sqlite.org/.

To use SQLite we'll need to first define what we want to store, then create a database, and finally build several layers to hide the hairy details and make data persistence easy for our application components. We'll start with a tour of the database related packages Android provides.

7.3.1 *Android data packages*

Android provides two main packages for working with databases. The first, `android.database`, isn't specific to a particular underlying database type. In this package you'll find the `Cursor` interface, base implementations, several types of data and content observers, and some helper classes. The second, `android.database.sqlite`, is specific to SQLite. Therein, you'll find the SQLite cursor implementation, classes for creating and updating SQLite databases, classes for querying data, and more. Table 7.1 provides a high-level outline of these packages; for complete information see the API documentation.

If you haven't worked with cursors before, or aren't familiar with the term, don't worry; they're simple. `Cursor` objects provide a way to traverse database result sets. In essence, cursors iterate over result sets and provide access to data one row at a time. We'll see how this works as we get into code examples shortly. In addition, we'll touch on all of the other key classes involved in creating and using a SQLite database on Android.

That said, we don't intend to cover all of the classes in the Android data APIs in this chapter, nor do we plan to get into basic SQL details. We'll focus on the big picture and the main Android classes. We'll talk more about the APIs as we progress, but let's start with a grander scheme, an overall pattern that will serve as our data access layer.

Table 7.1 An overview of the Android database related packages and some of the main classes

Package	Class	Description
`android.database`	`Cursor/ AbstractCursor`	`Cursor` defines random read/write access to a result set. `AbstractCursor` provides a base implementation.
	`DatabaseUtils`	Many utility methods for creating properly escaped query strings, working with `Cursors`, and running common but simple queries.
`android.database.sqlite`	`SQLiteCursor`	A `Cursor` implementation that deals with results from a `SQLiteDatabase`.
	`SQLiteDatabase`	A wrapper that exposes SQLite database methods, including opening and closing connections, and performing queries and statements.
	`SQLiteOpenHelper`	A helper class designed to create and update databases and manage schema versions.
	`SQLiteQueryBuilder`	A helper class for creating SQLite queries.
	`SQLiteStatement`	A SQLite type of precompiled SQL statement.

7.3.2 Designing a data access layer

In the next few sections, we're going to define the tables we need and create a database. From there, we'll use SQL to insert, update, select, and delete data. But before we get to that, we'll take a step back and think about architecture and design.

We don't want to get carried away with architecture. We aren't planning a space shuttle mission; we're building a small embedded data access layer. Yet we still want to encapsulate all the details so that our application components don't have to speak SQL themselves, and so they don't have to know anything about the persistence mechanism. We'll want simple plain Java objects (which we'll call *model objects*), and a simple interface for saving and retrieving those objects. If you've used the *Data Access Object (DAO)* pattern before, this should sound familiar. We're going to create DAOs for our model objects, and we're also going to create a data manager layer to wrap around those DAOs and nicely corral all the data-handling details in one place.

We'll get our hands dirty with Android SQL statements too, but we'll do so inside our DAOs so that they're focused on what they need to do. Ultimately, we'll have a layered architecture as depicted in figure 7.8.

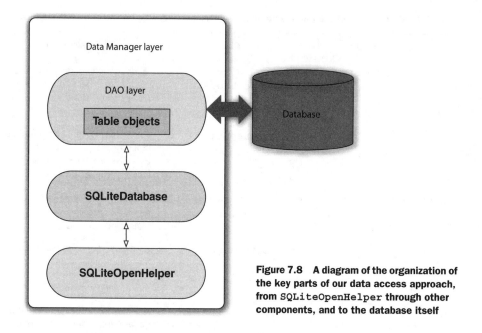

Figure 7.8 A diagram of the organization of the key parts of our data access approach, from `SQLiteOpenHelper` through other components, and to the database itself

SERVER-SIDE-ISH, BUT NOT TOO SERVER-SIDE-ISH   Scott Adams once had Dilbert's infamous boss ask him to make a web site "more webbish, but not too webbish" (http://search.dilbert.com/comic/Webbish). In the next few sections we'll outline a set of data access principles we find helpful on Android because they nicely separate responsibilities and keep code focused. But we need to keep in mind that this isn't the only way to use a database on Android. We also don't want to take the server-side patterns and analogues too far—we need to keep in mind that this isn't the server side; it's a small embedded database.

We'll start by designing our tables, then the model objects to go with those tables, and then the DAOs. Finally, we'll wrap the DAOs from within a data manager interface implementation that will be in charge of saving and retrieving data.

TECHNIQUE 34   Creating a database and model objects

Before an Android application can start using a database, it has to create one. And before we can create a database, we need to have an idea of what we want to store, and what the relationships are. To do this we'll need table definitions and model objects our main application code can use first. Then, we'll create several helper classes to define the necessary SQL statements.

PROBLEM

You want to create a database and model objects to store and retrieve, and you'd like to keep the definition of the tables separate from each other and from the main database creation code. This is useful because it helps keep each class focused on a particular function, which can make database-related code easier to understand and maintain.

SOLUTION

Android provides a lot of convenience when it comes to creating and using databases, but a few extra classes of our own can help even more. Here, we'll start by diagramming the tables we'll want our database to have. Then, we'll create model objects we can use to save and store data in those tables. From there, we'll create a separate class for each table that will hold the code needed to create and update our database schema, and we'll use the classes from an implementation of a SQLiteOpenHelper (a base class Android provides for creating and updating databases, and accessing data).

After we have our tables defined, our model objects built, and our database ready to be created with a SQLiteOpenHelper, we'll define our DAOs and data manager interface. We'll start by defining the tables we'll need.

Tables

To lay out our required tables we'll use an e*ntity relationship diagram (ERD)*. For MyMoviesDatabase we'll have only three tables, so it's a small diagram, but it still helps to visualize it, as seen in figure 7.9.

The three tables we'll use are *Movie, MovieCategory,* and *Category*. The Movie and Category tables have a unique ID named _id that's significant for Android. If you want to share your data across different Android applications, like the built-in Contacts database does, you'll need to create a ContentProvider. We'll learn about Content-Providers in the next chapter. For now, we need to keep in mind that if we want to use a ContentProvider to expose our tables later, they must have an _id column, which is the primary key (the unique ID for the table).

> **WHEN TO USE A CONTENTPROVIDER** You can also use a ContentProvider within your application to access your local database. This raises the question: when should you use a direct local database, and when you should go the extra mile and create a ContentProvider? Like many nuanced questions, there's no correct answer. ContentProviders have some nice features, but they're more complicated than direct local database access. In general, if you need to share your data with other applications you must create a Content-Provider. And, if you don't need to share data, it's usually simpler to use a database directly.

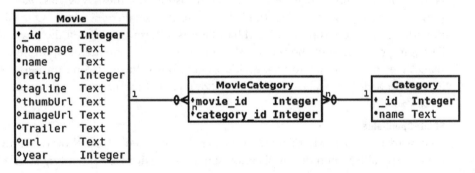

Figure 7.9   The ERD diagram for the MyMoviesDatabase database tables

The Movie table also has other attributes you might expect: homepage, name, rating, and so on. We'll use all of these attributes to sort and display movies. The Category table is even simpler than the movie table: it's _id and name. We'll display the movies' categories when we show the detail information, and we could use it for sorting and so on. The MovieCategory table is the odd man out here. It's not used for direct display purposes; rather it's a linking table. It allows us to express the many-to-many relationship we need—one movie can be in many categories, and one category can represent many movies (and we don't need to repeat the category names all over the place; our data is *normalized*).

Model objects

Along with tables, we'll create JavaBean-style model objects to represent our data entities. These will be the classes our activities and other code will use when saving, retrieving, and displaying movies. These won't match our tables exactly, but they'll be pretty close. We'll include objects for both Movie and Category. Our Movie model object is shown in the next listing.

Listing 7.8   The Movie JavaBean style model object

```
public class Movie extends ModelBase {

    private String providerId;
    private String name;
    private int year;
    private double rating;
    private String url;
    private String homepage;
    private String trailer;
    private String tagline;
    private String thumbUrl;
    private String imageUrl;
    private Set<Category> categories;

// . . . constructor, getters/setters, equals/hashCode omitted for brevity

}
```

The difference between our database tables and our model objects is the relationship between movies and categories. As we see in listing 7.8, the Movie class *has a* collection of Category as a member (and there's no MovieCategory class). Our tables on the other hand were separate. We'll handle this difference between the way our database and Java represent the relationship inside our SQL statements when we come to that. Category is similar to Movie; it's a bean, but it has only one property, String name. The ModelBase class, which both Movie and Category extend, contains only a long id.

SQLiteOpenHelper

So now that we know what data we want to store, we need to somehow tell Android to build these tables when our application starts. This is done by extending SQLiteOpen-Helper, as shown in the next listing.

Listing 7.9 The `SQLiteOpenHelper` used for creating and updating databases

```
public class OpenHelper extends SQLiteOpenHelper {          ◁─┐  Extend
                                                           ❶ SQLiteOpenHelper
    private Context context;

    OpenHelper(final Context context) {
        super(context, DataConstants.DATABASE_NAME, null,
            DataManager.DATABASE_VERSION);             ◁─┐  Provide db name
        this.context = context;                        ❷ and version
    }

    @Override
    public void onOpen(final SQLiteDatabase db) {     ◁─┐  onOpen available
        super.onOpen(db);                              ❸ if needed
    }

                                                       ❹ Override onCreate
    @Override                                              to create tables
    public void onCreate(final SQLiteDatabase db) {  ◁─┘
        CategoryTable.onCreate(db);                         ◁─┐
        CategoryDao categoryDao = new CategoryDao(db);      │
        String[] categories =                          ❻ Populate
            context.getResources().getStringArray(        Category
                R.array.tmdb_categories);                 with initial
        for (String cat : categories) {                   data
            categoryDao.save(new Category(0, cat));
        }

        MovieTable.onCreate(db);                   Create tables with  ❺
                                                   Table objects  ◁─┤
        MovieCategoryTable.onCreate(db);                        ◁─┘
    }

    @Override                                          ❼ Override
    public void onUpgrade(final SQLiteDatabase db,        onUpgrade
        final int oldVersion, final int newVersion) {  ◁─┘

        MovieCategoryTable.onUpgrade(db, oldVersion, newVersion);  ◁─┐

        MovieTable.onUpgrade(db, oldVersion, newVersion);          ◁─┤

        CategoryTable.onUpgrade(db, oldVersion, newVersion);       ◁─┘
    }
}
```

`SQLiteOpenHelper` is provided by Android for setting up databases and opening connections. To use a local database, we start by extending it ❶. Within its constructor we then provide a database name and version ❷, and we call through to the super constructor.

Then we can implement the lifecycle-style methods `OpenHelper` provides as needed. These include `onOpen` ❸ (which is optional to override, and we show for completeness, though we aren't doing anything special with it), `onCreate` ❹, and `onUpgrade` ❼. The framework will call these methods as needed, returning a connection on normal use, creating the database when it doesn't already exist, and upgrading it when the version number is higher than the current one.

Within `onCreate` we come to a pattern that we find helpful when working with Android local databases: using table-specific classes for each table we'll work with.

We'll see what these classes look like in the next few listings, but the idea here is to keep the responsibilities for defining, creating, and upgrading each table separate from the OpenHelper. This isn't required, but it prevents OpenHelper from becoming a large complicated class, and allows us to easily reuse the tables for other projects if we need to. Each table object has a static method for onCreate and onUpgrade ❺ that's called from OpenHelper's methods.

Priming a database with predefined data

Along with setting up the database in listing 7.9, inside onCreate we also read a resource file, R.array.tmdb_categories, and use the CategoryDao object to store that data in our database ❻. We do this so our database will have some initial categories as soon as it's created. Some databases need this type of seed data. Typically, you may use this approach for things such as countries, states, roles, categories, and so on. For small amounts of data this works fine. If you need to include larger amounts of already defined data with your application, then this isn't a good idea because it'll be too slow (individual insert statements for each data item). Instead, for large volumes of data, you can create your SQLite db file ahead of time (each SQLite database is stored as a single file) and ship it as part of the *assets* included with your application. You can then copy that file over to the database file your application needs (be sure to do this only once!). At runtime each application database is stored in a file at the /data/data/*<packagename>*/databases/ internal storage location.

SQLiteDatabase

Once we have a SQLiteOpenHelper, we can use it from anywhere in our application to create a SQLiteDatabase object. The SQLiteDatabase object is the keystone of Android SQLite database operations. This is where we'll create connections and perform data operations such as select, update, insert, and delete.

We'll see how this is done when we discuss the DataManager interface and implementation object our application will use to wrap up all of our data operations methods in technique 35, but for now here's an example of using our OpenHelper to obtain a SQLiteDatabase reference:

```
SQLiteOpenHelper openHelper = new OpenHelper(this.context);
SQLiteDatabase db = openHelper.getWritableDatabase();
```

The getWritableDatabase method of SQLiteOpenHelper will call onCreate the first time it's called, and thereafter will call onOpen. So this is how the helper methods get kicked off and the chain reaction is started. You can call this method as many times as you want (the instance is cached), but you should make sure to call close when you're done using a database instance.

Table classes

Having the OpenHelper implementation gets us rolling, but because it hands off to the table classes, we still haven't seen the real database dirty work. Here, we'll step into the details a bit more, starting with MovieTable in listing 7.10.

Listing 7.10   The `MovieTable` class with static methods and inner class `MovieColumns`

```
public final class MovieTable {                                    ① Define table
                                                                        name
    public static final String TABLE_NAME = "movie";

    public static class MovieColumns implements BaseColumns {       ② Include
        public static final String HOMEPAGE = "homepage";               columns
        public static final String NAME = "movie_name";                 class
        public static final String RATING = "rating";
        public static final String TAGLINE = "tagline";
        public static final String THUMB_URL = "thumb_url";
        public static final String IMAGE_URL = "image_url";
        public static final String TRAILER = "trailer";
        public static final String URL = "url";
        public static final String YEAR = "year";
    }
                                                                   ③ Include
    public static void onCreate(SQLiteDatabase db) {                   onCreate
        StringBuilder sb = new StringBuilder();
        sb.append("CREATE TABLE " + MovieTable.TABLE_NAME + " (");
        sb.append(BaseColumns._ID + " INTEGER PRIMARY KEY, ");     ④ Use SQL
        sb.append(MovieColumns.HOMEPAGE + " TEXT, ");                 CREATE
        // movie names aren't unique,                                 TABLE
        // but for simplification we constrain
        sb.append(MovieColumns.NAME + " TEXT UNIQUE NOT NULL, ");
        sb.append(MovieColumns.RATING + " INTEGER, ");
        sb.append(MovieColumns.TAGLINE + " TEXT, ");
        sb.append(MovieColumns.THUMB_URL + " TEXT, ");
        sb.append(MovieColumns.IMAGE_URL + " TEXT, ");
        sb.append(MovieColumns.TRAILER + " TEXT, ");
        sb.append(MovieColumns.URL + " TEXT, ");
        sb.append(MovieColumns.YEAR + " INTEGER");
        sb.append(");");
        db.execSQL(sb.toString());
    }

    public static void onUpgrade(SQLiteDatabase db,                ⑤ Include
            int oldVersion,                                           onUpgrade
int newVersion) {
        db.execSQL("DROP TABLE IF EXISTS "                         ⑥ Use SQL DROP TABLE
            + MovieTable.TABLE_NAME);                                 and re-create
        MovieTable.onCreate(db);
    }
}
```

The first thing we do in each of our table classes is define a constant for the table name ①. Then we include a nested inner class that implements `BaseColumns` and defines the column names with more constants ②. `BaseColumns` is provided by Android, and it defines the _id column we mentioned earlier. Once the names are out of the way, we include static `onCreate` ③ and `onUpgrade` ⑤ methods, where we use SQL commands to `CREATE` and/or update our table ④. Note that our current `onUpgrade` implementation DROPs the table and recreates it ⑥. This probably won't be what you want in production applications (you'll need to do more, such as extract the current data first, update the schema, and then reinsert the data as necessary).

The table CREATE command is fairly understandable, but remember it's not intended for any database—it's SQLite-specific. Within it, we're defining the data type. such as TEXT and INTEGER, for each of our columns, and we've used a few constraints such as UNIQUE and NOT NULL. The constraints are self-explanatory, but requiring the name to be unique is an oversimplification. Obviously, not all movies have unique names. Our database could support multiple movies with the same name, using different primary key IDs, but that would complicate our example in several areas. Because of this we've chosen to support only unique names to keep it simple.

> **SQLITE "DYNAMIC" DATA TYPES** One peculiarity of SQLite versus many other database systems is that it uses dynamic data types. That means you can declare a column of type TEXT and still put a number into it. And, you can put text into an INTEGER column as well. This is because SQLite uses *storage classes* that have affinity to particular types, but it converts any data it's handed as best it can. This can be confusing if you're not used to it, and it can affect the way sort order and operators work. For complete details, see the SQLite documentation on data types: http://www.sqlite.org/datatype3.html.

The other table classes follow the exact same pattern. CategoryTable is simple; it has only an ID and a unique category name (so we won't bother including it here). MovieCategoryTable is more complicated in that it includes foreign key references. It's shown in the next listing.

Listing 7.11 The MovieCategory class showing the declaration of foreign key references

```java
public final class MovieCategoryTable {
   public static final String TABLE_NAME = "movie_category";        ❶ Don't
                                                                        implement
   public static class MovieCategoryColumns {                          BaseColumns
      public static final String MOVIE_ID = "movie_id";
      public static final String CATEGORY_ID = "category_id";
   }

   public static void onCreate(SQLiteDatabase db) {
      StringBuilder sb = new StringBuilder();

      sb.append("CREATE TABLE " + MovieCategoryTable.TABLE_NAME + " (");
      ;
      sb.append(MovieCategoryColumns.MOVIE_ID + " INTEGER NOT NULL, ");
      sb.append(MovieCategoryColumns.CATEGORY_ID + " INTEGER NOT NULL, ");
      sb.append("FOREIGN KEY(" + MovieCategoryColumns.MOVIE_ID + ")
         REFERENCES " + MovieTable.TABLE_NAME + "("
               + BaseColumns._ID + "), ");
      sb.append("FOREIGN KEY(" +                                       ❷ Define foreign
         MovieCategoryColumns.CATEGORY_ID + ")                            key references
            REFERENCES " + CategoryTable.TABLE_NAME + "("
               + BaseColumns._ID + ") , ");
      sb.append("PRIMARY KEY ( " + MovieCategoryColumns.MOVIE_ID + ", "
         + MovieCategoryColumns.CATEGORY_ID + ")");                    ❸ Define compound
      sb.append(");");                                                    primary key
      db.execSQL(sb.toString());
```

```
    }

    public static void onUpgrade(SQLiteDatabase db, int oldVersion,
            int newVersion) {
        db.execSQL("DROP TABLE IF EXISTS " + MovieCategoryTable.TABLE_NAME);
        MovieCategoryTable.onCreate(db);
    }
}
```

The `MovieCategoryTable` class starts off the same way as our other table classes: it declares a constant for the table name, and then includes a static nested class to represent the columns (which are also constants). The difference this time is that the columns class doesn't implement `BaseColumns` ❶. This is because this table won't use the `_id` key, and won't ever need to be exposed via a `ContentProvider` (it's an internal mapping table; it doesn't represent a data entity on its own).

The next significance to the `MovieCategoryTable` is that it contains `FOREIGN_KEY` mappings with `REFERENCES` to other tables ❷. In this case the mapping table has movie ID and category ID columns that reference the Movie and Category tables. Why would we do this? Why do we want foreign keys? For referential integrity. These keys will make sure our table relationships remain meaningful. We won't be able to delete a `Movie`, for instance, and leave its `Category` reference unattached ❸. We could make do without these, and have our own checks, but it's easier to use what the database offers and fail fast if a condition we don't expect is encountered.

SQLite foreign key support

It should be noted here that not all versions of SQLite enforce foreign key constraints. Specifically Android 1.5, 1.6, and 2.1 include SQLite 3.5.9, which can parse foreign key constraint statements, but doesn't enforce them. Newer Android versions, 2.2 and 2.3, both support SQLite version 3.6.22, which does enforce foreign keys. Most of the time it doesn't hurt to include foreign key statements in any Android version; remember that they aren't always enforced. Often, such lack of enforcement won't hurt you, if you're not relying on it for conditional processing or cascading deletes, and so on. If you need to guarantee enforcement, you can query the state of the foreign key support when the database is created, and fall back to triggers.

DISCUSSION

Overall we now have an idea of what we want to store and what the relationships are. We have model objects for working with the data in our application's Java code and table objects to keep the details for each table separate from one another. We also have a `SQLiteOpenHelper` implementation that can be used to create and update our database, and to provide references to the `SQLiteDatabase` objects we'll later use to store and retrieve data.

Most of this is standard fare. Model objects are a common way to represent data (and though ours are intentionally anemic, they can also contain operations), and Android requires you to include a `SQLiteOpenHelper`. The only thing that isn't standard or required here is our use of separate table objects. These are our own creation, but we think they're a nice way to keep the code clean and focused.

With our `OpenHelper` and our table classes, we now have a database that's ready for action. What's next? We need a way to store and retrieve data, and for that we'll turn to the `DataManager` helper class and DAOs we've mentioned a few times.

TECHNIQUE 35   Creating DAOs and a data manager

Android gives you many ways to access SQL data. As we'll see, the `SQLiteDatabase` object provides both low-level methods, such as `execSql(String sql)`, various higher-level `query` and `insert` methods, access to `SQLiteStatement` for compiled SQL statements, methods to set transaction boundaries, and more. Still, we don't want to litter our main application code with low-level database-related operations. In fact, if we can help it, we don't even want our main application code to know the persistence mechanism is a database.

PROBLEM

You want to create a simple API your application can use to store and retrieve data, rather than include SQL statements and other data operations next to application logic.

SOLUTION

By creating DAOs to hide SQL details for each table, and creating a larger data manager layer that application components can use to access data, you can separate main application code from persistence details, avoid duplication, and keep code more focused. To see how this works we're going to start with a DAO for each table, and then we'll define our data manager layer.

DATA ACCESS OBJECTS

Many developers are probably familiar with the DAO pattern. DAOs are used to represent various levels of interaction with tables and the database, and definitions of the term vary. Here we'll use one DAO per table, and we'll keep each DAO focused on only its table (not the relationships between the tables). This keeps the level of abstraction of the DAO well defined and provides an interface on top of the persistence mechanism for data operations.

The DAO interface that we'll use for the MyMoviesDatabase application is shown in the next listing.

Listing 7.12   The DAO interface that defines common data operations

```
public interface Dao<T> {
    long save(T type);
    void update(T type);
    void delete(T type);
    T get(long id);
    List<T> getAll();
}
```

Our DAO interface is simple and fairly typical. The only notable thing about it is that it's parameterized. The type `T` represents the data model class it'll operate on (which will end up being our `Movie` and `Category` classes we noted earlier). With this interface and the related implementations, we'll be able to save and update our model objects with ease—hiding all the details inside the DAOs.

One thing to note here is that DAOs aren't always the right approach. DAOs are somewhat coarse-grained and can lead to more data being returned than is required in every situation. For example, if we needed to populate a selection of choices with only the name of each movie in our system, we'd have to return all the data (rather than the names). We can mitigate this by extending our interface in DAOs that need other data access methods, but the point is that DAOs aren't perfect. Also, DAOs do create a few more classes and a little more code, but we think the clean separation and ease of use they provide are often (not always) worth this overhead.

To explore our DAO implementations, we'll look at the most involved one we have for MyMoviesDatabase, the `MovieDao`. This DAO, the first part of which is seen in the following listing, touches on a lot of the different types of SQL usage an Android application might need.

Listing 7.13 The first portion of the `MovieDao` class—saving a new movie

```
public class MovieDao implements Dao<Movie> {              ← ① Implement DAO
                                                               interface for Movie
    private static final String INSERT =
        "insert into " + MovieTable.TABLE_NAME
          + "(" + MovieColumns.HOMEPAGE + ", " + MovieColumns.NAME + ", "
          + MovieColumns.RATING + ", " + MovieColumns.TAGLINE + ", "
          + MovieColumns.THUMB_URL + ", "+ MovieColumns.IMAGE_URL + ", "
          + MovieColumns.TRAILER + ", " + MovieColumns.URL + ", "
          + MovieColumns.YEAR + ")
        values (?, ?, ?, ?, ?, ?, ?, ?, ?)";              ← ② String with binding
                                                               placeholders
    private SQLiteDatabase db;
    private SQLiteStatement insertStatement;               ③ Pass SQLiteDatabase
                                                             in constructor
    public MovieDao(SQLiteDatabase db) {              ←
        this.db = db;
        insertStatement = db.compileStatement(MovieDao.INSERT);   ←
    }                                                                 Compile
                                                                      insert
    @Override                                                     ④ statement
    public long save(Movie entity) {                   ←
        insertStatement.clearBindings();
        insertStatement.bindString(1, entity.getHomepage());   Perform
        insertStatement.bindString(2, entity.getName());       insert in
        insertStatement.bindDouble(3, entity.getRating());     save
        insertStatement.bindString(4, entity.getTagline());  ⑤ method
        insertStatement.bindString(5, entity.getThumbUrl());
        insertStatement.bindString(6, entity.getImageUrl());
        insertStatement.bindString(7, entity.getTrailer());
        insertStatement.bindString(8, entity.getUrl());
        insertStatement.bindLong(9, entity.getYear());
        return insertStatement.executeInsert();
    }
}
```

To start off, MovieDAO implements our DAO interface ❶. Then, it includes a SQL insert String constant that explicitly lists each column where we'll store data and includes question marks for placeholders for the values ❷. Next, in our constructor, we pass in the SQLiteDatabase object we'll use to connect to the database and perform operations ❸, and we'll compile our insert String into a SQLiteStatement ❹.

Using a compiled statement, as opposed to a raw SQL insert, will be faster because the framework can precompute and reuse the execution plan. But you can only use compiled statements for tasks that don't return any rows or that return only one row and column (a single long or String). Because they offer good performance, yet can't return multiple rows, compiled statements are a perfect fit for insert operations.

After the constructor, we see the save method, where our insertStatement is put to work ❺. First we clear any previous bindings, and then we bind each of the placeholders in the statement with the correct value from our model object. Once the bindings are set, we call executeInsert and we pass along the ID it returns (which is the ID of the row in the Movie table for the inserted data). That's it for insert; when one table is involved it's simple.

The next part of our MovieDAO class is the update method in the next listing.

Listing 7.14   The second portion of the MovieDao class—updating a movie

```
public void update(Movie entity) {                                    ❶ Use
    final ContentValues values = new ContentValues();          ←──┐    ContentValues
    values.put(MovieColumns.HOMEPAGE, entity.getHomepage());
    values.put(MovieColumns.NAME, entity.getName());
    values.put(MovieColumns.RATING, entity.getRating());
    values.put(MovieColumns.TAGLINE, entity.getTagline());
    values.put(MovieColumns.THUMB_URL, entity.getThumbUrl());
    values.put(MovieColumns.IMAGE_URL, entity.getImageUrl());
    values.put(MovieColumns.TRAILER, entity.getTrailer());
    values.put(MovieColumns.URL, entity.getUrl());
    values.put(MovieColumns.YEAR, entity.getYear());
    db.update(MovieTable.TABLE_NAME, values,
    BaseColumns._ID + " = ?", new String[] {                          ❷ Invoke
        String.valueOf(entity.getId()) });                     ←──┐    update
}
```

For an update operation, we first set up a ContentValues object that saves key-value pairs of the column names and data we want to update ❶. ContentValues is a class that we'll see again when we deal with creating content providers in the next chapter. For now, think of it as a map for data you need to update. Once we're ready, we use the update method on our SQLiteDatabase object, passing it a table name, values, a where clause, and where clause arguments ❷.

The update is standard Android stuff, much like the delete method, shown in the next listing.

Listing 7.15   The third portion of the MovieDao class—deleting a movie

```
@Override
public void delete(Movie entity) {
    if (entity.getId() > 0) {
```

```
        db.delete(MovieTable.TABLE_NAME,
            BaseColumns._ID + " = ?", new String[]                    ❶ Invoke
            { String.valueOf(entity.getId()) });                          delete
    }
}
```

The delete method works much the same way as the update method, except it doesn't involve values. We pass it a table name, where clause, and where clause arguments ❶. After the delete method, next up are the get and getAll methods, which query the Movie table and return Movie objects using a Cursor.

Listing 7.16 The fourth portion of the `MovieDao` class—getting movies

```
@Override
public Movie get(long id) {
    Movie movie = null;
    Cursor c =
      db.query(MovieTable.TABLE_NAME,                           Query method ❶
          new String[] {                                        returns Cursor
        BaseColumns._ID, MovieColumns.HOMEPAGE,
        MovieColumns.NAME, MovieColumns.RATING, MovieColumns.TAGLINE,
        MovieColumns.THUMB_URL, MovieColumns.IMAGE_URL,
        MovieColumns.TRAILER, MovieColumns.URL, MovieColumns.YEAR },
      BaseColumns._ID + " = ?", new String[] { String.valueOf(id) },
          null, null, null, "1");
    if (c.moveToFirst()) {
        movie = this.buildMovieFromCursor(c);          Create       Move
    }                                                  Movie        to first
    if (!c.isClosed()) {                               from       ❷ position
        c.close();                                     Cursor
    }                                       Close   ❸
    return movie;                     ❹ Cursor
}

@Override
public List<Movie> getAll() {
    List<Movie> list = new ArrayList<Movie>();
    Cursor c =
          db.query(MovieTable.TABLE_NAME, new String[] {
        BaseColumns._ID, MovieColumns.HOMEPAGE,
        MovieColumns.NAME, MovieColumns.RATING, MovieColumns.TAGLINE,
        MovieColumns.THUMB_URL, MovieColumns.IMAGE_URL,
        MovieColumns.TRAILER, MovieColumns.URL, MovieColumns.YEAR },
      null, null, null, null, MovieColumns.NAME, null);
    if (c.moveToFirst()) {
        do {                                               Use do/while loop
            Movie movie = this.buildMovieFromCursor(c);  ❺ for multiple rows
            if (movie != null) {
                list.add(movie);
            }
        } while (c.moveToNext());                      Move to
    }                                            ❻ next row
    if (!c.isClosed()) {
        c.close();
    }
```

```
        return list;
    }
    private Movie buildMovieFromCursor(Cursor c) {
        Movie movie = null;
        if (c != null) {
            movie = new Movie();
            movie.setId(c.getLong(0));
            movie.setHomepage(c.getString(1));
            movie.setName(c.getString(2));
            movie.setRating(c.getInt(3));
            movie.setTagline(c.getString(4));
            movie.setThumbUrl(c.getString(5));
            movie.setImageUrl(c.getString(6));
            movie.setTrailer(c.getString(7));
            movie.setUrl(c.getString(8));
            movie.setYear(c.getInt(9));
        }
        return movie;
    }
```

7 Include
buildMovieFromCursor

8 Get methods
for typed data

The get methods are more involved than the last few we've seen. The first thing of note is that the query methods return a `Cursor` **1**. If you've done Java JDBC work, then you've probably used a `ResultSet` object. A `ResultSet` is a cursor, wrapped with some additional functionality (and some of the methods will be familiar for Java developers). Cursors are part of most databases, SQLite included. Because we aren't using JDBC with Android, we don't have `ResultSet`.

> **WHY NOT JDBC?**   There are pros and cons to JDBC. If Android supported JDBC it would be easier to have portable code or reuse code that you may already have with SQLite. But Android intentionally doesn't support JDBC, presumably because of the overhead it adds and the fact that there's already a simple to use API in place via the `android.database.sqlite` package. If you promise not to mention it to anyone we'll let you in on a secret though: Android does include a SQLite JDBC driver, and it does work, but it's undocumented and unsupported (because it may not be available on every device). Even though it's there, and we mention it because you may stumble across it, we strongly suggest that you avoid any unsupported part of the Android platform.

The query methods themselves (there are several overloaded variants on the `SQLite-Database` object) take in the table name, selection clause, and selection clause arguments. They also offer several more options, such as `order by`, `group by`, `having`, and `limit`. These SQL `select` constructs allow you to tailor your query as needed. Ultimately, after each query method is parsed, a select statement is issued, and a `Cursor` is returned.

For our get method, we use `query` **1**, and then if the Cursor it returns has a first result row **2**, we call the `buildMovieFromCursor` method **7** to create a `Movie` from the row's data **3**. Finally, we close the `Cursor` object when we're done **4**. Closing the cursor is essential. If we don't close it, we'll leak it, and potentially hang on to the calling component and cause all sorts of havoc.

Along with the get method, we also have a getAll method. The difference with getAll is that the select query it uses isn't constrained by an ID, and so it'll return all the movie rows. We handle these multiple rows with a do-while loop ❺ using the cursor's moveToNext method ❻. Inside each loop iteration we again call the buildMovie-FromCursor method. Within this method we process the row by calling the necessary typed get methods to retrieve each field of data.

Now that we have save, update, delete, get, and getAll methods ❽ for our DAO, we're nearly done. The only thing we have left is an addition to the interface that we've included to find a movie by its name.

Listing 7.17 The final portion of the MovieDao class—finding a movie by name

```
public Movie find(String name) {
    long movieId = 0L;
    String sql = "select _id from " + MovieTable.TABLE_NAME
        + " where upper(" + MovieColumns.NAME + ") = ? limit 1";
    Cursor c = db.rawQuery(sql,                         ◁──┐   Use rawQuery
    new String[]                                           ❶   to find Movie
    { name.toUpperCase() });          ◁──┐   Use upper
    if (c.moveToFirst()) {               ❷   functions
        movieId = c.getLong(0);
    }
    if (!c.isClosed()) {
        c.close();
    }                                             ❸   Call existing
    return this.get(movieId);                         get method
}                                            ◁──┘
```

The find method, which is used to search for movies already saved in the database, works much the same as our other data retrieval methods, except it uses a rawQuery ❶. We don't have to use a raw query here, but we wanted to demonstrate that this approach is available, and it's an easy way to include the limit statement in our query and use a SQLite function.

In this case, we're using the SQLite upper function to compare the database field, converted to all uppercase characters ❷, to our String (also converted to upper-case). This will make sure our comparison matches regardless of the case, and it shows that SQLite does support functions, like many other databases (for a complete list, see the documentation).

The last thing of note with the find method is that it makes two trips to the database. Our first query gets the movie ID we're interested in, and then another query is issued when we call our own previously defined get method ❸. This isn't the most efficient way to retrieve data, but we accept that. This is an easy to understand and maintain approach, and for such a small amount of data it's a reasonable trade-off. If we notice a performance issue later we can always make this code do its work with a single query, but there's no need to optimize it *before* we have a problem.

The MovieDAO is our most involved DAO class. It inserts, updates, deletes, and selects data in multiple ways. Our other DAO, CategoryDAO does much the same thing for the Category table. So are we ready to roll? Should we start using this DAO from our activities and other components? Well, not quite. First, as we've discussed, we'll create one more layer to wrap the DAOs in an easy to use data manager.

Creating a data manager

Our DAO objects represent the individual data entities our application needs, `Movie` and `Category`. Yet they intentionally don't worry about the relationships between the different tables involved. For example, if we want to save a new `Movie`, the model object comes in with a `List<Category>`, but the `MovieDAO` doesn't touch that (its only job is to handle the Movie table).

Because our DAOs are each unaware of any table other than their own, we're also going to create a `DataManager` interface, an implementation class that will wrap the multiple DAOs and take care of the remaining duties from one place. Such duties will include storing data in multiple tables and dealing with transactions. Our application components will ultimately use this class to save and retrieve data. This technique, shown in the next listing, will keep all of the SQL and logic out of our application components and views.

Listing 7.18   The `DataManager` interface defines all possible operations

```
public interface DataManager {

    public Movie getMovie(long movieId);
    public List<Movie> getMovieHeaders();
    public Movie findMovie(String name);
    public long saveMovie(Movie movie);
    public boolean deleteMovie(long movieId);

    public Category getCategory(long categoryId);
    public List<Category> getAllCategories();
    public Category findCategory(String name);
    public long saveCategory(Category category);
    public void deleteCategory(Category category);
}
```

Our data manager interface is pretty basic. It has a set of methods relating to common data operations such as `get`, `save`, and `delete` for each of our main model objects—`Movie` and `Category`. Our application components will use references to this interface to perform data operations.

The more interesting parts of this layer are within the database-backed implementation of this class, which uses our DAOs. This first portion of this is shown in the next listing.

Listing 7.19   The first part of `DataManagerImpl` implements the `DataManager` interface

```
public class DataManagerImpl implements DataManager {        ◄┐     Define
                                                              ❶ DataManagerImpl
    private static final int DATABASE_VERSION = 1;      ◄─┐
                                                          │   Specify database
    private Context context;                              ❷ version
                                                          │
    private SQLiteDatabase db;                           ◄┘
```

```
private CategoryDao categoryDao;
private MovieDao movieDao;
private MovieCategoryDao movieCategoryDao;

public DataManager(Context context) {

   this.context = context;

   SQLiteOpenHelper openHelper =
      new OpenHelper(this.context);
   db = openHelper.getWritableDatabase();

   categoryDao = new CategoryDao(db);
   movieDao = new MovieDao(db);
   movieCategoryDao = new MovieCategoryDao(db);
}
```

❸ Include needed DAOs

❹ Construct OpenHelper

Get SQLiteDatabase ❺ reference

```
// . . . remainder of class in next listing
```

The `DataManagerImpl` isn't extending or building on any Android support, it's our own invention that implements our `DataManager` interface ❶. Within it, we include a constant to define the current database version ❷ and member variables that reference each of our DAOs ❸. Also, inside its constructor we instantiate the `SQLiteOpen-Helper` class we built earlier ❹, and use it to connect to our database ❺.

Once the member variables and initial wiring are out of the way, we then move on to DAO wrapper methods.

Listing 7.20   The rest of `DataManagerImpl`, with data methods to wrap the DAOs

```
public Movie getMovie(long movieId) {
   Movie movie = movieDao.get(movieId);
   if (movie != null) {
      movie.getCategories().addAll(
         movieCategoryDao.getCategories(movie.getId()));
   }
   return movie;
}
public List<Movie> getMovieHeaders() {
   return movieDao.getAll();
}

public Movie findMovie(String name) {
   Movie movie = movieDao.find(name);
   if (movie != null) {
      movie.getCategories().addAll(
         movieCategoryDao.getCategories(movie.getId()));
   }
   return movie;
}
public long saveMovie(Movie movie) {
   long movieId = 0L;

   try {
      db.beginTransaction();
```

Wrap DAOs ❶ to get Movie

❷ Get Movie headers

❸ Wrap for saveMovie

❹ Begin transaction

```
            movieId = movieDao.save(movie);
            if (movie.getCategories().size() > 0) {
                for (Category c : movie.getCategories()) {
                    long catId = 0L;
                    Category dbCat = categoryDao.find(c.getName());
                    if (dbCat == null) {
                        catId = categoryDao.save(c);
                    } else {
                        catId = dbCat.getId();
                    }
                    MovieCategoryKey mcKey =
                        new MovieCategoryKey(movieId, catId);
                    if (!movieCategoryDao.exists(mcKey)) {
                        movieCategoryDao.save(mcKey);
                    }
                }
            }
            db.setTransactionSuccessful();
        } catch (SQLException e) {
            Log.e(Constants.LOG_TAG,
                "Error saving movie (transaction rolled back)", e);
            movieId = 0L;
        } finally {
            db.endTransaction();
        }

        return movieId;
    }
    public boolean deleteMovie(long movieId) {
        boolean result = false;
        try {
            db.beginTransaction();
            Movie movie = getMovie(movieId);
            if (movie != null) {
                for (Category c : movie.getCategories()) {
                    movieCategoryDao.delete(
                        new MovieCategoryKey(movie.getId(), c.getId()));
                }
                movieDao.delete(movie);
            }
            db.setTransactionSuccessful();
            result = true;
        } catch (SQLException e) {
            Log.e(Constants.LOG_TAG,
                "Error deleting movie (transaction rolled back)", e);
        } finally {
            db.endTransaction();
        }
        return result;
    }

    public Category getCategory(long categoryId) {
        return categoryDao.get(categoryId);
    }
```

5 Save movie

6 Save new categories

7 Save category association

8 Set transaction successful status

9 End transaction

10 Wrap for delete

```
    public List<Category> getAllCategories() {
        return categoryDao.getAll();
    }

    public Category findCategory(String name) {
        return categoryDao.find(name);
    }

    public long saveCategory(Category category) {
        return categoryDao.save(category);
    }

    public void deleteCategory(Category category) {
        categoryDao.delete(category);
    }
// . . . OpenHelper inner class in listing 7.7
}
```

At the heart of the `DataManagerImpl` class are the data management methods that use our DAO objects. These include the `getMovie` method ❶, which uses both the `MovieDao` and the `CategoryDao` to return a complete single `Movie`. The `getMovie-Headers` method, on the other hand, returns a collection of movies without the categories ❷ (these "headers" can be used to list movie data when underlying detail isn't required).

One of the most interesting aspects of the `DataManagerImpl` class, and another reason we're using a separate manager layer, can be seen in the `saveMovie` method ❸. Here we again use separate DAOs, but we do so within a transaction. A transaction ensures that if one part of our operation fails, the entire thing will be rolled back. This prevents us from ending up with an inconsistent state. For example if we are able to insert a new movie ❺ and the categories its associated with ❻, but for some reason couldn't insert its category associations ❼, we then wouldn't want anything to be saved (we don't want to save the movie or categories without the correct associations). The transaction makes sense here, at this level, but it may not be appropriate for the DAO itself (the manager has the contextual information to know a transaction is needed).

To control the transaction, we explicitly begin it ❹, set its status as successful if we don't have any exceptions ❽, and end it ❾. Note that there's no rollback method. Instead, once the `beginTransaction` method has started the process, if the `endTransaction` method is encountered before `setTransactionSuccessful` has been called, a rollback will happen implicitly (and `endTransaction` is inside a finally block, so it'll be called even if there's an earlier exception).

After the `saveMovie` method, our manager has a similar `deleteMovie` method that also has transaction support ❿. Then we include similar wrapper methods for categories (though they only need to use one DAO because they're simpler, we still use the manager as an access point). The remaining DAO wrapper methods, and the internal `OpenHelper` class which we saw earlier, round out the `DataManager` class and complete our data management layer.

Using the DataManager

How do we use our new data management layer from within the MyMoviesDatabase application? We create an instance of it inside the `Application` object that all our activities and other components have access to, and we call it as needed. For instance the `MyMovies` activity is still the main `ListView` our application needs. But instead of using an `Adapter` that's backed with `List<String>`, we change to one that uses `List<Movie>` and we get that data from our database as follows:

```
private MovieAdapter adapter;
private List<Movie> movies;
...
movies.addAll(app.getDataManager().getMovieHeaders());
adapter.notifyDataSetChanged();
```

Another alternative we might've chosen would've been to implement a `Cursor-Adapter`. A `CursorAdapter` is an adapter that can pull data from a database. Sometimes this is convenient, such as when multiple things might modify the underlying database. With a `CursorAdapter`, a `ListView` can manage the cursor and automatically update the view items as data is added. One downside with `CursorAdapter` is that database concepts such as `Cursor` leak into the logic of the activity (for example, when a list item is clicked). So usage of a `CursorAdapter` makes sense sometimes, and other times it's easier to do without it. For MyMoviesDatabase we've included both approaches in the source code for the project (see the comments in the MyMovies activity to switch between them).

DISCUSSION

We can now easily use our model objects and our `DataManager` interface implementation, which wraps our DAOs, from any of our application components. We've encapsulated all the database-related code in one place, and we've hidden the underlying details. In fact, we could change the implementation of our `DataManager` to use files, or to use web service calls (which might not be a good idea, but it's a strained theoretical example), and our main application code (our activities and so on) wouldn't need to be touched.

Behind the manager layer, we've also created separate classes to create and update our tables, and to create and open our database. We have all the layers we discussed earlier, and along the way we've touched on many of the details of working with databases on the Android platform. With our database layer in hand, we'll now move on to how to inspect and troubleshoot a SQLite database.

7.4   *Inspecting SQLite databases*

Outside of your application, there are many times when you'll want to access and inspect your SQLite database directly. You'll want to make sure your tables are there, and that they have the structure you intended. And you'll want to run test queries and experiment with the results. For these times you'll need data tools.

In the next few sections, we'll review mymovies.db using the command-line SQLite shell and a third-party GUI tool, SQLiteManager. There are many third-party

SQLite GUI tools; we've chosen SQLiteManager as an example because it's cross-platform (it's a Firefox browser extension), open source, and free.

SQLITE SHELL

SQLite comes with its own command shell, a command-line utility named *sqlite3*. This tool is the Swiss-Army knife for SQLite. To access sqlite3 on an Android device or emulator, you need to first connect with the `adb` shell, and then invoke the SQLite shell on the database you're interested in. Figure 7.10 shows this process for MyMoviesDatabase and the mymovies.db file.

From the `adb` shell session started in figure 7.10, we first navigate to the `/data/data/<packagename>/databases` file location, and then we list the contents. There we see the mymovies.db file. Next, we invoke the SQLite shell with `sqlite3 mymovies.db`. Once we're in the SQLite shell, we have access to all of the commands it provides. Some of the most useful commands to remember are shown in table 7.2.

Table 7.2   Useful sqlite3 shell commands for working with SQLite databases

sqlite3 command	Description
`.help`	List all commands and options
`.tables`	Show tables for current database
`.schema`	Show CREATE statements used to create tables for current database
`.explain`	Parse and analyze SQL statement showing execution plan

You'll also often be running direct SQL statements in the shell, such as select, insert, delete, and so on. If you want to know more about sqlite3, which is a powerful tool, you can find the complete documentation online at http://www.sqlite.org/sqlite.html.

SQLiteManager

If you'd rather use a GUI tool to inspect and manipulate your database, one of the easiest to use is the SQLiteManager Firefox extension. To use this tool, you'll need Firefox and the extension at http://mng.bz/iG6q. Once you have installed the extension, you can access SQLiteManager from the Firefox Tools menu. When you first launch it,

```
ccollins@crotalus:~$ adb -e shell
# cd /data/data/com.manning.aip.mymoviesdatabase/databases
# ls -l
-rw-rw---- app_33    app_33        13312 2010-12-20 02:55 mymovies.db
# sqlite3 mymovies.db
SQLite version 3.6.22
Enter ".help" for instructions
Enter SQL statements terminated with a ";"
sqlite> .tables
android_metadata   category        movie           movie_category
sqlite> .schema
CREATE TABLE android_metadata (locale TEXT);
CREATE TABLE category (_id INTEGER PRIMARY KEY, name TEXT UNIQUE NOT NULL);
CREATE TABLE movie (_id INTEGER PRIMARY KEY, homepage TEXT, movie_name TEXT UNIQUE NOT NULL, rating INTEGER, tagline TEXT, thumb_url TEXT,
image_url TEXT, trailer TEXT, url TEXT, year INTEGER);
CREATE TABLE movie_category (movie_id INTEGER NOT NULL, category_id INTEGER NOT NULL, FOREIGN KEY(movie_id) REFERENCES movie(_id), FOREIGN
KEY(category_id) REFERENCES category(_id) , PRIMARY KEY ( movie_id, category_id));
sqlite> select * from movie;
1||Cool Hand Luke|7||http://hwcdn.themoviedb.org/posters/013/4bc90e10017a3c57fe005013/cool-hand-luke-thumb.jpg|http://hwcdn.themoviedb.org/
posters/013/4bc90e10017a3c57fe005013/cool-hand-luke-cover.jpg|http://www.youtube.com/watch?v=l3CPz21NzUc|http://www.themoviedb.org/movie/90
|3|1967
```

Figure 7.10   Using the SQLite shell tool, sqlite3, on the mymovies.db database

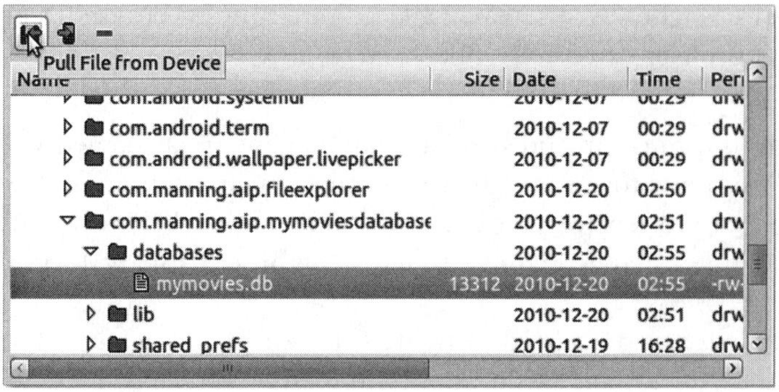

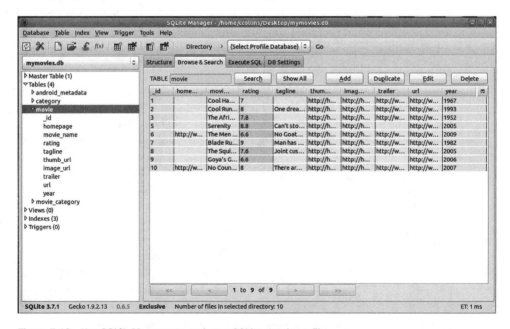

Figure 7.11
Copy the database file from a running device or emulator to the local host computer using DDMS.

it'll show a new blank window. To do anything with it, you need to point it at a SQLite database file.

There isn't a convenient (or secure) way to automatically connect to a running device or emulator and browse the database file, so to do this you'll need to copy the file to your local computer. This can be done with the adb pull command, or with the Android file explorer provided in the Eclipse ADT or DDMS tools, as seen in figure 7.11.

Once you have the database file available, it's a simple matter of opening the file with SQLiteManager. You can click and browse through the database contents, check the settings, and even execute SQL commands. Figure 7.12 shows us exploring mymovies.db.

All told, there are many ways to access and inspect SQLite databases. The SQLite shell is always available, and it's connected to live data. Other tools, such as SQLite-Manager, provide an easy-to-work-with GUI approach.

Figure 7.12   Use SQLiteManager to explore a SQLite database file.

Now that we have a working sample application complete with preferences using files, data access layer, DAOs, and database, and we've seen how to explore our data and use tools to verify the schema, run sample queries, and even explain the processing plan, our journey through local data storage on Android is complete.

7.5 *Summary*

We've covered a good bit of data storage and persistence territory. We haven't touched on every possibility, because there are too many, but we've dealt with the most common and often most useful ways to store and retrieve local data for an Android application.

We started with the filesystem, and the basics of reading and writing data to files. We then looked at the file-backed but easier-to-use SharedPreferences mechanism Android provides, and finally we topped it off with using a local SQLite database. We went into a lot of detail on the database side of things because that's the most powerful local storage mechanism Android provides. There, we separated the responsibilities for creating our database and the individual tables, and we used Data Access Objects (DAOs) for containing data logic, as well as a data manager to wrap it all up. In all, we built a layered architecture around our database and hid the gory details from our application components. Finally, we topped off our local data excursion with a look at exploring and troubleshooting databases from the command shell, and with external tools.

We did all of this in order to take the MyMovies sample application we'd seen in previous chapters to the next level. We modified it to be able to search for data, to use preferences, and to store data in a database. Now, it's not using predefined data stuck in a resources file; it's dynamic and user-defined.

Next, in chapter 8, we'll look beyond storing data locally and learn how to consume data from other applications, such as the built in Contacts manager, and we'll also learn how to share our own data—these are both the realm of the ContentProvider.

Sharing data between apps

In this chapter
- Sharing between processes
- Shared preferences files
- Accessing shared data

People have really gotten comfortable not only sharing more information and different kinds, but more openly and with more people.

—Mark Zuckerberg

You can do a lot in a single Android application. The possibilities are almost endless. But one of the differentiating features of the Android platform is that it allows—nay, encourages—applications to work together. In chapter 5, we talked extensively about how powerful multitasking is on Android. Consequently, you can assume that other applications are running at the same time as yours and vice versa. This leads to interesting possibilities. Multiple applications working together provides greater value to the user than any single application could by itself.

An essential ingredient to application integration is data sharing. There are others, such as flow of control, but not much can happen without being able to share data between apps in some way. It should come as no surprise that Android provides multiple ways to do this, empowering you the developer to share data in a way that makes the most sense for your use case. The main purpose of this chapter is to catalogue and detail the various ways there are to share data between Android apps, and describe the type of situations that you would want to apply these data sharing techniques.

8.1 Process-to-process sharing

In chapter 6, we talked about many of the Android facilities that make concurrent programming easier. Let's start off by reviewing this type of sharing so that we can contrast it to the process-to-process sharing that we'll discuss in detail. In general, concurrency is easy until you must share data. The type of concurrent programming that we've discussed so far has been multithreaded programming. When data is shared, it's shared between multiple threads running inside the same virtual machine, and the same Linux process. Figure 8.1 shows the different ways of doing this.

Now we'll focus on data being shared by different processes instead of different threads. Figure 8.2 depicts the ways that this can be done.

With threads, there's the option of threads reading from the same locations in local memory. This is the most intimate way to share data, but it can also be the most

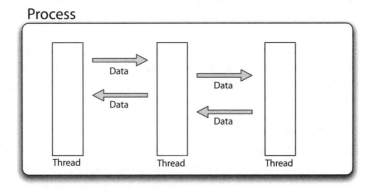

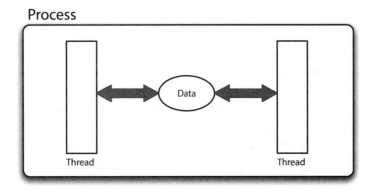

Figure 8.1 Shared data and threads, using message passing and common data

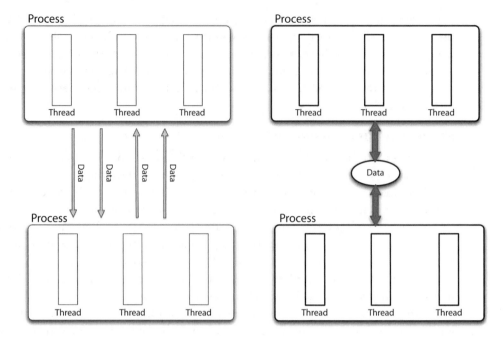

Figure 8.2   Sharing data and processes, using message (data) passing and common data

dangerous. Android's `Handler` API provides a safer way to share data between threads. When it comes to sharing data between processes (apps), we can't read from the same place in local memory. This dangerous option isn't available. Instead, we must send data across process boundaries. The first and most common way of doing this is by using `Intents`.

TECHNIQUE 36   Using Intents

By now you're familiar with `Intents`. The most common use for intents is for navigating between activities within an application. Intents can also hold data to pass to activities. This is a key feature because intents can be used to navigate to activities from other apps and share data with other apps.

PROBLEM

You need to send a request with data to another application, or you need to send a response to a request from another application. The application making the request will cede control to another application in order to accomplish this task.

SOLUTION

As we mentioned earlier, there are a number of ways to share data between applications. So it's key to understand the subtle differences between these techniques. In this case, we need another application to do something for us and we're willing to allow the other application to take control of the user interface to do this. To demonstrate the kind of situations where you'd use this technique, let's look at two sample apps.

The first app is called GoodShares and allows the user to pick a photo from their phone and then pass this photo off to our other sample app, ImageMash. This app performs an affine transformation on the image based on scale and rotation values input by the user. Figure 8.3 shows what the GoodShares app looks like.

> **An affine what?**
>
> *Affine transformation* is a term for applying some simple two-dimensional geometry to an object (image). In our example, we scale the image vertically and horizontally, and then rotate it. If you're familiar with linear algebra, an affine transform can be represented using matrix multiplication.

In the figure, the user has selected an image that they want to transform. Now pressing the Transform! button launches our second app, the ImageMash app. Figure 8.4 shows what it looks like.

As you can see in figure 8.4, the user sees the image that's being transformed. This is the image sent from the GoodShares app—it's the data that has been shared by that app. Now, the user can input the transformation values and Mash It! Figure 8.5 shows the result.

Figure 8.3 The GoodShares app, image selected

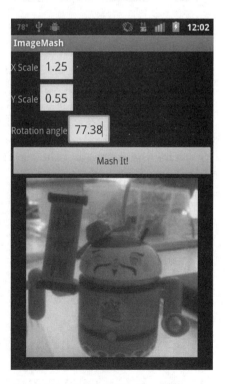

Figure 8.4 The ImageMash app with an image sent to it

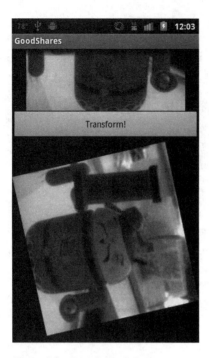

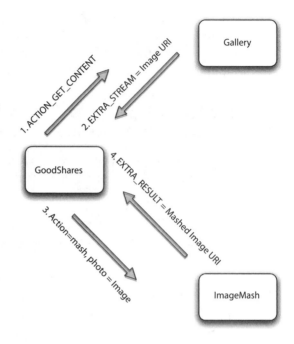

Figure 8.5   Transformed picture shown by the GoodShares app

Figure 8.6   Sending data between apps using Intents

Figure 8.5 shows the transformed picture. Note that GoodShares is displaying the transformed. The ImageMash app not only transforms the picture, it then sends the transformed picture back to the GoodShares app, which then displays it. The Image-Mash app also shares the result with the GoodShares app. All of this sharing is done using Intents. Figure 8.6 shows the Intent-based data flow.

One thing we didn't show in the preceding screenshots is how the user selects a picture to use. As you can see from figure 8.6, we use the Gallery app, using the code in the following listing.

Listing 8.1   Using Gallery to select a photo (from ShareActivity.java)

```java
public class ShareActivity extends Activity {
    Uri photoUri0;
    @Override
    public void onCreate(Bundle savedInstanceState) {
        super.onCreate(savedInstanceState);
        setContentView(R.layout.share);
        Button button = (Button) findViewById(R.id.btn0);
        button.setOnClickListener(new OnClickListener(){
            @Override
            public void onClick(View v) {
                Intent request = new
                    Intent(Intent.ACTION_GET_CONTENT);
```

❶ Use standard Intent for Get_Content

```
                    request.setType("image/*");
                    startActivityForResult(request, 0);         ◁⌐  Launch separate app,
                }                                                 ❷  give up control flow
            });
    }

    @Override
    protected void onActivityResult(int requestCode, int resultCode,
                                    Intent data) {
        if (requestCode == 0){                              Retrieve data sent ❸
            photoUri0 =                                         by Gallery
                (Uri) data.getParcelableExtra(Intent.EXTRA_STREAM);
            ImageView imgView0 = (ImageView) findViewById(R.id.pic0);
            imgView0.setImageURI(photoUri0);
        }
    }
}
```

The code in listing 8.1 is a selection of the `ShareActivity` class, which is GoodShares' main `Activity`. It's the code behind the UI shown in figure 8.3. The main thing it does is hook up an event listener to the button seen in figure 8.3.

When the button is clicked, an `Intent` is created whose action is set to `Intent.ACTION_ GET_CONTENT` ❶. This is one of many standard `Intents` in Android that launch activities for common tasks such as selecting a photo from the Gallery. We declare that we want to get an image by setting the `type` property of the `Intent`. This will cause our `Intent` to be routed to the Gallery. Then we use the `Activity`'s `start-ActivityForResult` method ❷. This will start the appropriate `Activity` (in Gallery, in a different process) and pass control flow to it. `startActivity` would do the same thing.

The key difference here is that once the other `Activity` gives up control, the control flow will return to our `Activity`. Further, the other `Activity` will be able to set a result, and our `Activity` will be able to access this result and the data associated with it. This is done in our `Activity`'s `onActivityResult` method. The Gallery app sets the response data in another `Intent` that it passes back to our app. Our app can retrieve this data from the `Intent` ❸ by using one of its `getXXXExtra` methods. This requires us to know the name of the extra (key) for the data that the Gallery app passed back, and to know its type. In this case, this is documented in the Android SDK, in the Java-Doc for `android.content.Intent`. There we see that the constant `Intent.EXTRA_STREAM` will be the key and that the value will be an `android.net.Uri` that will point to the selected image. Once we have the image, we show it to the user, as shown in figure 8.3. Then the user can tap another button to send this image to the ImageMasher app, using the code in this next listing.

Listing 8.2 Invoking the ImageMasher app (from ShareActivity.java)

```
public class ShareActivity extends Activity {
    Uri photoUri0;
    @Override
    public void onCreate(Bundle savedInstanceState) {

        Button button1 = (Button) findViewById(R.id.btn1);
```

```
button1.setOnClickListener(new OnClickListener() {
    @Override
    public void onClick(View v) {
        Intent request =
            new Intent("com.manning.aip.mash.ACTION");
        request.addCategory(Intent.CATEGORY_DEFAULT);
        request.putExtra("com.manning.aip.mash.EXTRA_PHOTO",
                            photoUri0);
        startActivityForResult(request, 1);
    }
});
}
@Override
protected void onActivityResult(int requestCode, int resultCode,
                            Intent data) {
    if (requestCode == 1){
        Uri photoUri1 = (Uri) data.getParcelableExtra(
            "com.manning.aip.mash.EXTRA_RESULT");
        ImageView imgView1 = (ImageView) findViewById(R.id.pic1);
        imgView1.setImageURI(photoUri1);
    }
  }
}
```

❶ Custom Action route to ImageMash Activity

❷ Set data to send

❸ Retrieve data sent by ImageMash

The code in listing 8.2 is similar to the code in listing 8.1. It follows the same pattern, but instead of using a commonly known action, it uses a custom action ❶ to route the Intent to our ImageMash app. In this case, we need to share some data with the other app, so we put an extra in our Intent ❷. The other app (ImageMash) will need to know what name we used for the extra so that it can retrieve it from the Intent ❸. Finally, when control returns from the other app, we can retrieve the mashed image from the Intent that it supplies. Let's take a look at what happens in between in the ImageMash app.

Interprocess communication and Parcelables

You might have noticed that in listings 8.1. and 8.2, we used the getParcelable-Extra method on the Intent object. If you've read chapter 5, then you're already familiar with Parcelables. It's Android's equivalent of a Java Serializable object. Any object that you wish to serialize, either to pass between processes or save to disk, must be a Parcelable. In the preceding examples, we passed an android.net.Uri object between processes and we can do that because it's a Parcelable. You can make your custom objects Parcelable as well. See chapter 5 for an example on how to do this.

We saw what the ImageMash app looks like in figure 8.4. For another app to invoke it, they must use the com.manning.aip.mash.ACTION action in an Intent like we did in listing 8.2. That means that we must use an Intent filter:

```
<activity android:name=".MashActivity"
          android:label="@string/app_name">
    <intent-filter>
```

```
            <action android:name="com.manning.aip.mash.ACTION" />
            <category android:name="android.intent.category.DEFAULT" />
        </intent-filter>
    </activity>
```

Now we need to handle this inbound data in our `Activity`. The following listing
shows how to do this.

Listing 8.3   Mashing the inbound image

```
public class MashActivity extends Activity {
    public static final String EXTRA_PHOTO =
        "com.manning.aip.mash.EXTRA_PHOTO";
    private static final int RESULT_ERROR = 99;
    @Override
    public void onCreate(Bundle savedInstanceState) {
        super.onCreate(savedInstanceState);
        setContentView(R.layout.main);
        Intent request = getIntent();
        if (request != null &&                                   ❶ Get URI of
        request.hasExtra(EXTRA_PHOTO)){                             inbound
            final Uri uri =                                         image
                (Uri) request.getParcelableExtra(EXTRA_PHOTO);
            ImageView image = (ImageView) findViewById(R.id.image);
            image.setImageURI(uri);

            Button button = (Button) findViewById(R.id.button);
            button.setOnClickListener(new OnClickListener(){
                @Override
                public void onClick(View v) {
                    try {                               Load image    ❷
                        Bitmap bmp = BitmapFactory.decodeStream( into memory
                            getContentResolver().openInputStream(uri));
                        Bitmap mashed = mash(bmp);
                        Uri resultUri = saveImage(mashed);
                        Intent response = new Intent();
                        response.putExtra(                ❸ Put URI to
                            "com.manning.aip.mash.EXTRA_RESULT", mashed image
                            resultUri);                      into Intent
                        MashActivity.this.setResult(Activity.RESULT_OK,
                                                    response);
                    } catch (FileNotFoundException e) {
                        Log.e("MashActivity", "Exception mashing pic", e);
                        MashActivity.this.setResult(RESULT_ERROR);
                    }
                    finish();             Release          Set result, pass
                }               ❺ control                  back Intent  ❹
            });

        }
    }
}
```

The code in listing 8.3 is from the main `Activity` in ImageMash. The code retrieves
the `Uri` of the image that we want to mash ❶ by pulling it out of the `Intent` that was
used to start the `Activity`. Then, once the user has finished setting values and taps on

the mash button, it loads the image ❷, transforms it (mashes it), and saves the image back to the SD card by using the `saveImage` method (not shown). This method returns the `Uri` to the mashed image, and we store this to a new `Intent` ❸ that we send back to the caller of this `Activity`. We then call the `setResult` method on the `Activity` ❹, saying that the result was okay and passing in the `Intent` to give back to the caller. Finally, we pass control back to the caller `Activity` by calling this `Activity`'s `finish` method ❺.

DISCUSSION

This sample app shows how `Intents` can be used to send data between apps. We've seen both how to use one of the many standard `Intents` to pass data back and forth between core apps like the Gallery, and how to do this between two custom apps. `Intents` provide a lot of flexibility. You don't need to know the name or class of the `Activity` that you want to integrate with; you need to know the name of the action (and optionally its category.) You may also need to know the names and types of parameters that are expected for inputs and uses for outputs. This is all industry standard for loosely coupled systems.

You might be wondering what happens if more than one app declares that it can handle a particular action. In that case, the Android OS will display a dialog to the user allowing them to choose which app to use. This implies that other apps could hijack `Intents` that are supposed to go to your app. If that's unacceptable, then you might want to use a different technique for sharing data, such as remote procedure calls.

TECHNIQUE 37   Making remote procedure calls

The key characteristic of the previous technique was that your app surrendered control flow to another application and waited until the user finished interacting with that application. That won't work if you want to maintain control flow within your application. In this case, you'll want to use some form of remote procedure call. We'll talk about two flavors of remote procedure calls supported by Android: synchronous and asynchronous.

PROBLEM

You need to pass data to another app so that it can perform some operation on that data and return a result back to your app. You don't want to give up control flow to this other application; you want to interact with it unseen.

SOLUTION

The key differentiator in this technique is that your application stays in control. It interacts and shares data with another application, but this process is invisible to the user. The key technology is to use an Android `Service` and there are two major variations here. Do you want the interaction to be synchronous or asynchronous? We'll examine both of these variations by modifying our GoodShares application. We'll create a remote procedure call (RPC) variant of the `Activity` shown in figure 8.3. Figure 8.7 shows what the RPC `Activity` looks like.

The key difference between the user interface shown in figure 8.3 and figure 8.7 is that you now supply the X and Y scales and the angle of rotation, instead of supplying those in the ImageMash app. Then the `Activity` calls the ImageMash app to do all of the mashing; when it gets the result back, it shows it to the user. For this to work, the ImageMash app must expose a `Service` that can be called by the GoodShares app's `Activity` shown in figure 8.7. There are a couple of ways that we can do the necessary integration.

Synchronous Integration

The first way this integration can be done is synchronously. The GoodShares app calls the ImageMash `Service` and waits for a response. After receiving a response, GoodShares updates the UI. To enable this kind of interaction, the GoodShares `Activity` must bind to the `Service` and directly invoke an operation on the `Service`. The necessary code is in the following listing.

Figure 8.7 Sharing, the RPC way

Listing 8.4 Synchronous invocation of another app's `Service`

```
public class ShareRpcActivity extends Activity {
    Uri photoUri0;
    IMashService mashService;                          Generated interface
    Button mashButton;                              ❶ representing remote Service
    int bindCount = 0;
    ServiceConnection conn = new ServiceConnection(){
        @Override
        public void onServiceConnected(ComponentName
                               className, IBinder service) {
            mashService = IMashService.Stub.asInterface(service);
            mashButton.setEnabled(true);
        }                                              Callback once
        @Override                                   ❷ Service is bound
        public void onServiceDisconnected(ComponentName className) {
            mashService = null;
            mashButton.setEnabled(false);
        }
    };

    @Override
    protected void onCreate(Bundle savedInstanceState) {
        super.onCreate(savedInstanceState);
        setContentView(R.layout.share_rpc);
```

```
mashButton = (Button) findViewById(R.id.button);
CheckBox syncBox = (CheckBox) findViewById(R.id.syncBox);
syncBox.setOnCheckedChangeListener(new OnCheckedChangeListener(){
    @Override
    public void onCheckedChanged(CompoundButton button,
                                 boolean checked) {
        if (checked){
            mashButton.setEnabled(false);
            bindService(new Intent("com.manning.aip.mash.ACTION"),
                        conn,
                        BIND_AUTO_CREATE);
            bindCount += 1;
        } else {}  }}
);
mashButton.setOnClickListener(new OnClickListener(){

    @Override
    public void onClick(View v) {
        EditText input0 = (EditText) findViewById(R.id.input0);
        float scaleX =
            Float.parseFloat(input0.getText().toString());
        EditText input1 = (EditText) findViewById(R.id.input1);
        float scaleY =
            Float.parseFloat(input1.getText().toString());
        EditText input2 = (EditText) findViewById(R.id.input2);
        float angle =
            Float.parseFloat(input2.getText().toString());
        Uri result;
        if (bindCount > 0){
            try {
                result = mashService.mash(photoUri0,
                                          scaleX,
                                          scaleY,
                                          angle);
                ImageView image =
                    (ImageView) findViewById(R.id.image);
                image.setImageURI(result);
            } catch (RemoteException e) {} }}});;}}
```

❸ Bind to remote Service

❹ Invoke remote Service

❺ Use result to update UI

The code in listing 8.4 shows how to synchronously send and receive data between two applications by using a Service. To begin with, we need an interface that represents the remote Service and describes the operations that it provides **❶**. To describe an interface to a remote Service, we use AIDL, as we learned about in chapter 5. Here's the AIDL for the ImageMash Service:

```
package com.manning.aip.mash;

import android.net.Uri;

interface IMashService{
  Uri mash(in Uri uri, float scaleX, float scaleY, float angle);
}
```

It's almost pure Java! Your app will need a copy of this AIDL file, and the Android tools will generate a stub for you that you can reference from your application. This is the key part of this subtechnique. To share data with another app's `Service` in a synchronous manner; your app must have the AIDL that describes that `Service`. Similarly, if you want to allow other apps to integrate with a `Service` in your app, you must provide an AIDL.

Going back to listing 8.4, the next thing the `Activity` needs is a `ServiceConnection` to the remote `Service` ❷. This is a callback interface to let you know when your `Activity` has bound itself to the `Service`, and that it's safe to start invoking operations on that `Service`. In our example, we initiate the binding process ❸ during the `onCreate` method of the `Activity`. We provide a check box to indicate whether we want the communication to be synchronous. If it's synchronous tapping the Mash It! button, will invoke `Service` ❹. Because the call is synchronous, the invocation returns a response and the UI is immediately updated ❺.

We've only scratched the surface of `Services`, AIDL, and so on. For much more information on these topics, you'll want to revisit chapter 5. Note that we didn't use `Intents` to share data synchronously. AIDL takes the place of an `Intent`—and provides some clear advantages over it with regards to the names and types of the data being shared.

Asynchronous integration

The alternative to synchronous invocation is an asynchronous one that's based on `Intents`. The next listing shows this asynchronous variation.

Listing 8.5 Asynchronous invocation of a remote `Service`

```
public class ShareRpcActivity extends Activity {
    Button mashButton;
    int bindCount = 0;

    @Override
    protected void onCreate(Bundle savedInstanceState) {
        mashButton = (Button) findViewById(R.id.button);
        mashButton.setOnClickListener(new OnClickListener(){
            @Override
            public void onClick(View v) {
                // get data from form widgets
                if (bindCount > 0){ // invoke synchronous        Create Intent ❶
                } else {
                    Intent request =
                        new Intent("com.manning.aip.mash.ACTION");
                    request.putExtra("com.manning.aip.mash.EXTRA_PHOTO",
                                    photoUri0);
                    request.putExtra("com.manning.aip.mash.EXTRA_SCALE_X",
                                    scaleX);
                    request.putExtra("com.manning.aip.mash.EXTRA_SCALE_Y",
                                    scaleY);
                    request.putExtra("com.manning.aip.mash.EXTRA_ANGLE",
                                    angle);                      Add data as
                    startService(request);                    ❷ extras to Intent
                }
            }
```

```
    });
    mashButton.setEnabled(true);                    Implement BroadcastReceiver  ❸
    BroadcastReceiver receiver = new BroadcastReceiver(){
        @Override
        public void
                onReceive(Context context, Intent intent) {
            Uri result = intent.getParcelableExtra(
                "com.manning.aip.mash.EXTRA_RESULT");
            ImageView image = (ImageView) findViewById(R.id.image);
            image.setImageURI(result);
        }                                                 Pull data from
    };                                                      extras  ❹
    IntentFilter filter = new IntentFilter();
    filter.addAction("com.manning.aip.mash.ACTION_RESPONSE");
    registerReceiver(receiver, filter);                   Register with  ❺
    }                                                     IntentFilter
}
```

The asynchronous path starts by creating an `Intent` and specifying its action ❶. As with `Intents` being sent to activities, the action will be used to route the `Intent` to the correct `Service`. Also similar to the `Intents` we used in technique 36, we set the data that we want to share by using the `putExtra` method ❷.

As before, this means that we need to know what names and types to use for these extras. The `Service` will need to pull them out, so we must know what it expects. Once we've properly constructed the `Intent`, we call `startService` (instead of `startActivityForResult` like we did in technique 36). This is an asynchronous invocation. The `Service` will receive it and respond by broadcasting an `Intent` with the response data in it. To receive that response, we use a `BroadcastReceiver`'s `onReceive` method ❸ as the callback method for this asynchronous invocation of `Service`. We'll receive the `Intent` sent by `Service`, and unpack the response data from it ❹. We use that to update the UI. Finally, for the `Receiver` to get the `Intent` sent by `Service`, we need to register it with an `IntentFilter` based on the action that will be used by `Service` ❺. The corresponding code in the `Service` is in the next listing.

Listing 8.6 Handling `Intents` in the ImageMash `Service`

```
public class MashService extends Service {

    @Override
    public int onStartCommand(Intent intent,       ❶  Handle
            int flags, int startId) {                   Intents          Get data  ❷
        Uri imageUri =
            intent.getParcelableExtra("com.manning.aip.mash.EXTRA_PHOTO");
        float scaleX =
            intent.getFloatExtra("com.manning.aip.mash.EXTRA_SCALE_X", 1.0f);
        float scaleY =
            intent.getFloatExtra("com.manning.aip.mash.EXTRA_SCALE_Y", 1.0f);
        float angle =
            intent.getFloatExtra("com.manning.aip.mash.EXTRA_ANGLE", 0.0f);
        try {
            Uri resultUri = stub.mash(imageUri, scaleX, scaleY, angle);
```

```
        Intent response =
          new Intent("com.manning.aip.mash.ACTION_RESPONSE");
        response.putExtra("com.manning.aip.mash.EXTRA_RESULT",
                          resultUri);                          Put data in
        sendBroadcast(response);                            4  outbound Intent
      } catch (RemoteException e) {
        Log.e("MashService", "Exception mashing image async", e);
      }
      return START_STICKY;                                 Create Intent  3
    }
}
```

This is a subset of the MashService code, only showing the part that processes inbound Intents like the one sent in listing 8.5 These are all handled by the onStart-Command method ❶. In this case, only one type of Intent is being sent in, but if there were more than one then you could check what the action is to figure out what kind of request it is. Once you know the request type, you can pull out the appropriate data from the Intent ❷. When you've processed this data and have a response to send back, you create a new Intent to do so ❸. You must put the appropriate action on this Intent, so it can be routed to the right receiver. Then you add all of the appropriate data to the Intent using the now-familiar putExtra method ❹. Finally, you broadcast this Intent using the sendBroadcast method.

DISCUSSION

There are some obvious and major differences between the synchronous and asynchronous ways of exchanging data with another app's Service. Obviously there's the synchronous versus asynchronous nature. The question of the interface is significant. In the synchronous mode, the interface is explicit and defined—in the AIDL. You know exactly how to call the Service and the response is immediate (in the sense that your thread will block until the Service gets a response—be careful about doing this on the main UI thread). In the asynchronous case, nothing is as explicit. You still must know the names and types of the data that the Service expects and produces, but this doesn't come in the form of code (AIDL). This arrangement can be more error prone. Furthermore, you also need to know the name of the action to use to send it to the Service, as well as the name of the action to use to register a BroadcastReceiver to get the response back from the Service.

Synchronous and asynchronous don't need to be mutually exclusive. For example, let's say you expose a Service for synchronous usage via AIDL. But suppose that one of your operations could take a long time. Now the Activity that binds to the Service could do so from an AsyncTask or similar, so that the UI thread isn't blocked while your Service does all of its work. So it might be okay for this operation to take a long time. But you could alternatively return a message saying that request was received, but that some or all of the response will come later. Then your Service could broadcast an Intent with more data later on as it becomes available. This is a common technique to use if your Service contains a local cache of data that's ultimately stored somewhere in the cloud.

We've now seen several useful ways to share data between apps using Intents. These techniques can be applied by any two apps with only limited knowledge of each other (actions, extras, and so forth). But if the apps have a more intimate knowledge of each other, another option is available to you: the apps can share a Context.

TECHNIQUE 38   Share data (and more) by sharing Context

This chapter is mostly about process-to-process sharing, and so technically this technique doesn't belong here because it involves sharing data between apps in a single process. In this technique, we'll have multiple apps sharing a single process. Why would we want to do that? As mentioned before, every application on Android is assigned a unique Linux user ID, and an exclusive system process will be spawned for every application you start. We also mentioned that Android does this for security reasons, to isolate code and resources of different, unrelated applications from each other.

Sometimes this behavior can get in your way. It's like allowing you to enter your kitchen but locking you out of the living room—both are distinct rooms, and they're both yours, and you should be allowed to move freely! What if you have developed two applications that depend on each other and would like to share a private configuration file, or even code? Imagine for instance that while developing an application, you want to deploy a second one, a developer dashboard that allows you to control your main application's internal settings. A good example would be controlling whether an application that connects to a web service API should contact the live servers or the staging or development servers—a feature which shouldn't be part of the final application, which is why it makes sense to outsource it to a second application. There's no security risk here. You wrote both applications, and you trust your own code, no? How can we get past this behavior in a controlled way?

PROBLEM

You have two or more applications that are closely related and depend on each other. You want them to share private resources such as files or code that must not be visible to other applications, but due to Android's strict sandboxing rules, they're not allowed to.

SOLUTION

We said before that this doesn't work for two reasons:

1 Different applications run in different Linux system processes.
2 Different applications are mapped to different Linux user IDs.

The solution is to let these applications share the same application process and the same user ID. Let's assume we have two applications (for simplicity let's call them App1 and App2) where App2 wants to reuse resources that are part of App1. More precisely, it wants to load classes that are bundled with App1 (App1's APK file) and read any settings App1 stores in SharedPreferences.

We'll keep things fairly simple, so as to not complicate the problem at hand. Hence, App1 merely does the following: it writes a small text snippet to a preference

Figure 8.8   App1 shares code and preference data with App2 by using Android's shared process and shared user ID model.

file that it wants to share with App2, and implements a custom `toString` method that should be invokable by App2. Check out the sample project, and note how App2 is able to read data that would normally be confined to App1 (see figure 8.8).

GRAB THE PROJECTS You can get the source code for these projects, and/or the packaged APK to run it, at the *Android in Practice* code website. Because some code listings here are shortened to focus on specific concepts, we recommend that you download the complete source code and follow along within Eclipse (or your favorite IDE or text editor).

Note that this time we have two sample applications that are closely related to each other. To see the desired effect, start SharedProcessApp1 first, then start SharedProcessApp2.

Source: http://mng.bz/x5a0, http://mng.bz/5141

APK Files: http://mng.bz/16sP, http://mng.bz/CXgT

App1 is the data provider in this scenario, so let's look at how to implement it first.

Listing 8.7 App1.java implements `toString()` and writes a shared preference file

```
public class App1 extends Activity {

    @Override
    public void onCreate(Bundle savedInstanceState) {          Open shared      ❶
        super.onCreate(savedInstanceState);                    preference file
        setContentView(R.layout.main);

        SharedPreferences prefs = getSharedPreferences(
                            "app1prefs", MODE_PRIVATE);
        String value = "Hello from App1 preference file!";
        prefs.edit().putString("shared_value", value).commit();    ◁——  Write value
    }                                                          ❷    to file

    @Override
    public String toString() {                              ❸  Implement custom
        return "Hello from App1 toString()!";              ◁——  toString() method
    }
}
```

We first create a shared preference file ❶, which is an XML-based configuration file that lives in App1's application data folder (see chapter 7). We create it using MODE_PRIVATE, which means that only components (such as activities or services) of App1 have access to that file. We then write a value to that file using the key shared_value ❷. We also implement a custom toString method ❸.

So far, so good. We've created a shared preference file, but it's only accessible from within App1, because it'll be created on the filesystem using the Linux user ID mapped to App1. Moreover, we created it in private mode so only that user (the application) may access it. We could've created it in world-readable mode instead, but then *any* application would be able to read it, not only ours. If you're curious, table 8.1 summarizes how the file permission masks are mapped to the different open modes (read chapter 1 again if you forgot how Linux handles file permissions).

Table 8.1 `SharedPreferences` file mode mapping

Mode*	Permission mask (u-g-o)	Permission mask (octal)
MODE_PRIVATE	rw-rw----	660
MODE_WORLD_READABLE	rw-rw-r--	664
MODE_WORLD_WRITABLE	rw-rw--w-	662

*The mode is a bitmask—these flags can be combined using the bitwise OR-operator ('|').

The same permissions apply for our toString method, which sends out a nice welcome to the world. It's trapped in App1's class loader, so no one can see it. Based on what we've observed so far, two problems need to be solved in order for App2 to be able to both call App1's toString method and access App1's preference file:

1   We somehow must get hold of the resources bundled with App1—calling `get-Resources` in App2 will only return its own!

2   We must somehow get the *right* to access these resources. Even if we find a way to reference them, they still belong to App1, not App2!

The answer to the first problem is the `createPackageContext` method defined on the `android.content.Context` class. This method allows us to create a handle to a context object that represents an application package other than the one we're currently in. Using the context object returned by that method, we can then get a reference to its class loader and load classes from that application and instantiate them. We can also use that context object to get a handle to its resource package or shared preferences. Listing 8.8 has the source code.

Listing 8.8   App2.java accesses App1's context using `createPackageContext()`

```
public class App2 extends Activity {

   private Context app1;

   @Override
   public void onCreate(Bundle savedInstanceState) {          ❶ Store ref
      super.onCreate(savedInstanceState);                        to external
      setContentView(R.layout.main);                             context

      try {
         app1 = createPackageContext(                          Load, ❷
                     "com.manning.aip.app1", CONTEXT_INCLUDE_CODE);   instantiate
         Class<?> app1ActivityCls =                            external class
                        app1.getClassLoader()
                        .loadClass("com.manning.aip.app1.App1");
         Object app1Activity = app1ActivityCls.newInstance();
         Toast.makeText(this, app1Activity.toString(),              ❸ Show result
                           Toast.LENGTH_LONG).show();                  in toast
      } catch (Exception e) {
         e.printStackTrace();
         return;
      }
                                                              ❹ Load
      SharedPreferences prefs =                                  preference file
          app1.getSharedPreferences("app1prefs", MODE_PRIVATE);
      TextView view =                                          ❺ Read value from
         (TextView) findViewById(R.id.hello);                     external file
      String shared = prefs.getString("shared_value", null);
      if (shared == null) {
         view.setText("Failed to share!");
      } else {
         view.setText(shared);
      }
   }
}
```

We first store a reference to App1, which is an object of type `Context` ❶. We can now access App1's class loader, instantiate its classes, and call methods as if these classes were part of our own application (❷ and ❸). The same works for resource or shared preferences, which we can also access through the external application context (❹ and ❺).

The code from listing 8.8 looks like what we need to solve problem 1, but it won't work yet. The reason is obvious: we haven't solved problem 2 on our list yet, which is allowing App2 to do all that. The key to this lies in two attributes we've set in the manifest files of both applications: android:process and android:sharedUserId. The former allows us to specify the system process in which an application will run (its process affinity), whereas the latter tells Android which Linux user ID it should use to install the application and to create files for. For both applications, we need to set these to identical values:

```
<?xml version="1.0" encoding="utf-8"?>
<manifest xmlns:android="http://schemas.android.com/apk/res/android"
    package="..."
    android:sharedUserId="com.manning.aip">

  <application android:process="com.manning.aip">
      <activity … />
  </application>

</manifest>
```

Try launching both applications again, and see how we succeeded! You should see both the Toast and the text view in App2 get updated with values that were bundled with App1. You can also verify that it works by switching to the DDMS perspective (or by running adb shell ps) and checking that only one new process will be spawned, even if both applications are running simultaneously!

DISCUSSION

As you can probably imagine, this opens a whole new world of possibilities. The android:process attribute is defined for components as well as for the <application> element. You can control it freely—it not only allows you to run two applications in the same process, as seen in this technique, but you could also run every service or activity of an application in its *own* system process. Before you jump to conclusions, we must say that we discourage you from doing so. Maintaining system processes is even more expensive than managing threads. Each will run their own Dalvik VM instance, which in turn means higher memory and battery consumption.

The keen eye may also have spotted a gross limitation of the way we shared code in this example. The problem with our approach is that we need to rely on the Java reflection API to instantiate classes, but remember that App2 doesn't bundle these classes itself. That's a crucial aspect: it means App1's classes aren't in App2's classpath. That means that we can't downcast these objects to any type other than Object! (Class<T>.newInstance() returns Object, which must be downcasted to call any other method than those defined on Object.) There are two solutions to this problem. One common approach is to define a set of Java interfaces that the classes you want to share must implement and bundle these in a JAR file. This interface JAR file can then be bundled with both applications, which allows you to downcast to an interface type in App2 and still call the implementation from App1. The second solution, especially if you rely on a lot of cross-application function calls, would be to use Android's RPC mechanisms, as we saw in technique 37.

Before we wrap up this technique, you should be aware of one more pitfall. If you plan to share code or resources between applications using this method, make sure you design your applications to support this technique from the get-go. If you already have an application in Android Market that didn't have a custom process affinity defined, you won't be able to publish an update to it that suddenly uses different process and user IDs. Your users would need to manually uninstall the older version first, because the Android Market updater doesn't remove preference and database files created by your applications (to not lose any user data), so the new version can't write to these files anymore. For that reason, it's always a good idea to define the `android:process` attribute for all your applications. You're then always free to add compatible applications to your portfolio at any time!

Now that we've explored the various ways to interact with another application in order to send and receive data from that application, let's look at a somewhat simpler topic. Let's look at exposing data that can be accessed in a more direct, low-level way.

8.2 Accessing common data

So far in this chapter, we've focused on having our app directly interact with another app, either by using `Intents` to communicate with another app's activities and services, or by loading another app's `Context` and using that to access its private data or even invoke its application code. You could describe the `Intent` (or AIDL) based integration as an interface-level integration (often associated with service-oriented architectures), and the shared `Context` approach as a binary-level integration. Another common form of application integration is data-level integration, akin to what Martin Fowler called the *Integration Database*. By having all apps read and write from the same data store, you avoid the need for any kind of application code to sit on top and manage the integration. This style of integration is well-suited for Android, because it includes the SQLite database. Let's take a look at how this work, starting with how to use the standard integration databases that are present on every Android device.

TECHNIQUE 39   Using standard ContentProviders

The integration database idea isn't some concept we invented for the sake of this book. It's not even some application pattern that we've extrapolated from third-party apps. It's a key part of Android itself. Not only is it used by many of the bundled Android apps, the SDK itself includes APIs for using and creating integration databases: the `android.content.ContentProvider` abstract class. Furthermore, it includes several implementations of `ContentProvider`, and you must use these for many common tasks in Android. Let's start our discussion of `ContentProviders` by examining how to use one of the standard providers in Android: the contacts provider.

PROBLEM

You need to look up one or more contacts from a user's address book. You also need to look up detailed information about a particular contact from the user's address book.

SOLUTION

For our example, we'll create a simple app that mimics a registration task. We require that the user provide us with their first and last name, along with their phone number and email address so that they can register with our service. You don't want to create too much friction for the user, so you'd like to make this as painless as possible. Chances are they already have all of this information in their address book. So the idea is to look up and suggest a contact based on information that they've typed in. Figure 8.9 shows what this will look like.

As you can see in figure 8.9, as the user types their phone number, we retrieve all of the matching phone numbers from their address book. If they see their phone number, then they can tap on it and it'll finish filling in the number for them. Figure 8.10 shows what that looks like.

As you can see, the user may only have to type in a few numbers and then make a single tap to complete their registration form. To make this work, we need to query

Figure 8.9 Auto-suggesting a contact based on a phone number

Figure 8.10 Auto-completed registration form

the contacts database, so we must use the `ContactsContract` `ContentProvider`. The next listing shows how we use this `ContentProvider` to get the list of phone numbers for the `AutoCompleteTextView` shown in figure 8.9.

Listing 8.9 Finding possible phone numbers

```
import android.provider.ContactsContract.CommonDataKinds;
public class ContactManager {
    private final ContentResolver resolver;

    public ArrayList<Contact> findByPhoneSubString(String phoneSubStr){
        String[] projection = {Phone.CONTACT_ID, Phone.NUMBER};
        String selection = Data.IN_VISIBLE_GROUP + "=1 AND " +
            Phone.NUMBER + " LIKE ?";
        String[] selectionArgs = {"%" + phoneSubStr + "%"};
        if (phoneSubStr == null){
            selection = null;
            selectionArgs = null;
        }
        Cursor phoneCursor = null;
        ArrayList<Contact> contacts = new ArrayList<Contact>();
        try{
            phoneCursor = resolver.query(Phone.CONTENT_URI,
                                    projection,
                                    selection,
                                    selectionArgs,
                                    null);
            int idCol = phoneCursor.getColumnIndex(Phone.CONTACT_ID);
            int numCol = phoneCursor.getColumnIndex(Phone.NUMBER);
            while (phoneCursor.moveToNext()){
                long id = phoneCursor.getLong(idCol);
                String phoneNum = phoneCursor.getString(numCol);
                Contact contact = new Contact();
                contact.phone = phoneNum;
                contact.id = String.valueOf(id);
                contacts.add(contact);
            }
        } finally {
            if (phoneCursor != null) phoneCursor.close();
        }
        return contacts;
    }
}
```

❶ Use ContentResolver to query

❷ Execute query

❸ Iterate over result set

If you've ever worked with databases, this is fairly straightforward. To perform a query, we need an `android.content.ContentResolver` ❶. Then, we construct a query programmatically. First we create a projection—specify which columns from the database we want. This is specified as an array of strings. Each of the strings that we're selecting are defined as constants in `ContactsContract.CommonDataKinds.Phone`. This is a pattern you'll see repeated over and over with `ContentProviders`. The names of columns will be defined as constants, as a way to document the schema of the database. Next we construct the `Where` clause for the query. Our example is exotic in that we use a `LIKE` expression as part of this `Where` clause. This will return all contacts with a phone number that contain the input string. Our Where clause contains a placeholder (a question mark); this is replaced using arguments passed in to the query. We use the percentage signs around the phone number string to indicate that the substring we've passed in can come anywhere in the full phone number. Now we can query the Content-Provider using ContentResolver ❷. Note that we passed in Phone.CONTENT_URI as the first argument to the query method. This is another constant, only this time it's a URI. If you like to think in terms of databases, you can think of the URI as a combination of database plus schema plus table. It uniquely identifies the data we're querying against. Also note that we left the final argument in the query method null. This is a sort parameter that we decided not to use. What we get back from the query is a Cursor. We can iterate over this Cursor ❸ and retrieve the data from it. We then store the values in a data structure and pass them back to the caller. This gives the user a list of phone numbers that can be thought of as suggestions for the contact that identifies them, as we saw in figure 8.9.

> **CONTACTS PROVIDER, NOW AND THEN**   This example uses the android.provider.ContactsContract provider. If you look at the android.provider package, you may also notice the Contacts provider. This was the provider to use up until Android 2.0. It's deprecated now, but still part of the SDK. If you need to support Android 1.6 or earlier and you need to work with contacts, then you'll need to work with both providers. You can check the android.os.Build.VERSION at runtime to determine what version of the OS is running on the user's phone, and pick the appropriate provider.

Once the user selects one of the phone numbers from the list of suggestions, we want to populate the rest of the data as seen in figure 8.10. The next listing does this.

Listing 8.10   Querying contact details

```
public class ContactManager {
    public Contact getContact(Contact partial){
        Contact contact = new Contact();
        contact.id = partial.id;
        contact.phone = partial.phone;
        String[] projection = new String[] {StructuredName.GIVEN_NAME,
                                            StructuredName.FAMILY_NAME,
                                            StructuredName.RAW_CONTACT_ID,
                                            StructuredName.CONTACT_ID};
        String selection = StructuredName.CONTACT_ID+ " = ? AND " +
            Data.MIMETYPE + " = '" + StructuredName.CONTENT_ITEM_TYPE +"'";
        String[] selectionArgs = new String[] {contact.id};
        Cursor nameCursor = null;
        try{
            nameCursor = resolver.query(Data.CONTENT_URI,        ◁─┐  Query first
                                        projection,                ❶  and last name
                                        selection,
                                        selectionArgs,
                                        null);
            if (nameCursor.moveToFirst()){
                contact.firstName = nameCursor.getString(
```

```
                nameCursor.getColumnIndex(
                    StructuredName.GIVEN_NAME));
            contact.lastName = nameCursor.getString(
                nameCursor.getColumnIndex(
                    StructuredName.FAMILY_NAME));


        }
    } finally {
        if (nameCursor != null) nameCursor.close();
    }
    projection = new String[] {Email.DATA1, Email.CONTACT_ID};
    selection = Email.CONTACT_ID + " = ?";
    Cursor emailCursor = null;
    try{
        emailCursor = resolver.query(Email.CONTENT_URI,       ◁──┐ Query email
                                     null,                      ❷   address
                                     selection,
                                     selectionArgs,
                                     null);
        if (emailCursor.moveToFirst()){
            contact.email = emailCursor.getString(
                emailCursor.getColumnIndex(Email.DATA1));
        }
    } finally{
        if (emailCursor != null) emailCursor.close();
    }
    return contact;
}
```

In the method shown, we start by querying for the user's first and last name ❶. Note how this is stored in a different table, represented by ContactsContract.Data. CONTENT_URI. This is a generic data table that contains many different types of data that could be associated with a given contact, including their first name (GIVEN_NAME) and last name (FAMILY_NAME). We must specify the kind of data we want to look up for this contact by specifying the Data.MIMETYPE as part of the Where clause. We then use the ID that we retrieved in listing 8.9.

Once we have the first and last name, we then query for the contact's email address ❷. Note here that as part of the projection (array of database columns), we specified Email.DATA1. This is an unusual name for the contact's email address. In Android 3.0, a new constant was added to ContactsContract.CommonDataKinds. Email: ADDRESS. Its value is the same as Email.DATA1 (it's "data1"). The preceding code was targeted at Android 2.2, so we must use Email.DATA1 instead of Email.ADDRESS. Finally, note that we again queried a different URI (table). All told, we queried three different tables to retrieve the data needed to register the user.

DISCUSSION

We mentioned earlier that one of the chief advantages of using an integration database is that you remove the need for integration code. That means that for an app to read contacts information, all it needs to do is query the appropriate ContentProvider. The ContentProvider API is a thin layer on top of a SQLite database, hence the need to work with `Cursor`s. But once you've worked with one `ContentProvider`, working with others is fairly straightforward. You get other database benefits as well. For example, note how we were able to use a `LIKE %XYZ%` clause to do a text search of the data.

This example showcased using the `ContactsContract` provider. The `android.provider` package also contains providers for the calendar and for multimedia. In chapter 11, we'll take a closer look at using a `ContentProvider` to query all of the music files on the user's device. As you'll see, it's similar to our earlier contacts example. You'll follow a similar pattern when working with any given `ContentProvider`, including custom ones. Let's take a look at how to create your own `ContentProvider` and expose it for others to use.

TECHNIQUE 40   Working with a custom ContentProvider

We saw in the previous technique how to consume a `ContentProvider`. Given that many useful Android features, such as the address book and calendar, are exposed via `ContentProvider`s, this is essential knowledge. Furthermore, once you're used to working with the standard Android `ContentProvider`s, working with any custom `ContentProvider`s from other applications is relatively straightforward. But you may also want to create your own `ContentProvider`, as another way to allow other apps to share data with your app.

PROBLEM

You want to expose data collected by your app to other apps, and even allow them to add to this data. You want to give other apps flexibility in how they query this data, and you don't want to maintain an application/service layer for doing this.

SOLUTION

You want to create your own custom `ContentProvider`. Let's look at an example of doing this. Our example is an application that allows the user to enter in movies and store them using a custom `ContentProvider`. The provider could then be used by another application that may be interested in the movies a user has an interest in. Figure 8.11 shows what the application looks like.

Tapping on any of the movies in the list shown in figure 8.11 brings up a detail view of the movie. Figure 8.12 shows this movie detail view.

The detail view gives you an idea of the kind of data we're going to store as part of our custom `ContentProvider`. Now let's look at how we implement a `ContentProvider` to allow apps (including our own!) to use this data. First, we must declare our custom `ContentProvider` in our `AndroidManifest.xml`:

```
<provider android:name =
"com.manning.aip.mymoviesdatabase.provider.MyMoviesProvider"
android:authorities = "com.manning.aip.mymoviesdatabase" />
```

Now, we need to subclass the abstract class `android.content.ContentProvider`. We must implement its query, insert, update, and delete methods to provide all of the usual CRUD (create read update delete) operations. For our example, we'll concentrate on the query features.

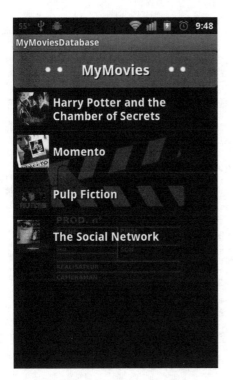

Figure 8.11 List of the user's movies

Figure 8.12 Movie detail view

Listing 8.11 The query interface to the movies ContentProvider

```
public class MyMoviesProvider extends ContentProvider {          ❶ Ref to SQLite db
    private SQLiteDatabase db;                                       where data is stored

    @Override
    public Cursor query(Uri uri, final String[] projection, String selection,
            String[] selectionArgs, String sortOrder) {
        HashSet<String> projectionCols = new HashSet<String>();
        if (projection != null) {
            projectionCols = new HashSet<String>(Arrays.asList(projection));
            if (!MyMoviesContract.Movies.MovieColumns.projectionMap.keySet().
                    containsAll(projectionCols)) {                 ❷ Is projection
                throw new IllegalArgumentException(                    valid?
                        "Unrecognized column(s) in projection");
            }
        }
        SQLiteQueryBuilder qb = new SQLiteQueryBuilder();
        switch (uriMatcher.match(uri)) {
            case MOVIES:                                           ❸ Query all
                qb.setTables(MovieTable.TABLE_NAME);                  movies
                return qb.query(db,
                            projection,
                            selection,
                            selectionArgs,
                            null,
```

```
                                    null,
                                    sortOrder);                    ④ Query particular
            case MOVIE_ID:                                            movie
                long movieId = ContentUris.parseId(uri);
                StringBuilder tables = new StringBuilder(MovieTable.TABLE_NAME)
                    .append(" as outer_movie");
                LinkedList<String> newSelectionArgs = new LinkedList<String>();
                newSelectionArgs.add(String.valueOf(movieId));
                if (selectionArgs != null) {
                    newSelectionArgs.addAll(Arrays.asList(selectionArgs));
                }
                String[] allSelectionArgs =
                    newSelectionArgs.toArray(new String[0]);    ⑤ Join category
                if (projectionCols.contains(                       table
                        MyMoviesContract.Movies.MovieColumns.CATEGORIES)) {
                    tables.append(" left outer join (select group_concat(")
                            .append(CategoryColumns.NAME)
                            .append(") as names from ")
                            .append(MovieCategoryTable.TABLE_NAME)
                            .append(", ")
                            .append(CategoryTable.TABLE_NAME)
                            .append(" where ")
                            .append(MovieCategoryTable.TABLE_NAME)
                            .append(".")
                            .append(MovieCategoryColumns.MOVIE_ID)
                            .append("= ? and ")
                            .append(MovieCategoryTable.TABLE_NAME)
                            .append(".")
                            .append(MovieCategoryColumns.CATEGORY_ID)
                            .append("=")
                            .append(CategoryTable.TABLE_NAME)
                            .append(".")
                            .append(CategoryColumns._ID)
                            .append(") mcat");
                }
                StringBuilder where = new StringBuilder()
                    .append("outer_movie.")
                    .append(MovieColumns._ID)
                    .append("= ?");
                qb.setProjectionMap(
                        MyMoviesContract.Movies.MovieColumns.projectionMap);
                qb.setTables(tables.toString());
                qb.appendWhere(where.toString());
                return qb.query(db,
                                projection,
                                selection,
                                allSelectionArgs,
                                null,
                                null,
                                sortOrder);
            case UriMatcher.NO_MATCH:
            default:
                throw new IllegalArgumentException("unrecognized URI " + uri);
        }
    }
```

The code in listing 8.11 looks verbose and complex, but it's pretty straightforward. First of all, you need a SQLite database ❶ for storing and querying this data. This is set up as part of the onCreate method of the provider (not shown here; download the full code). Next, when we process a query, we must check that the caller hasn't asked for a column that doesn't exist ❷. If they did ask for a column we haven't heard of, then we throw an exception.

Now we need to figure out what to query from our database. We use the URI that the user supplied to determine whether they're asking for all of the movies (like we saw in figure 8.8) or asking for the details of a particular movie (like we see in figure 8.9). If they're asking for all of the movies ❸, then we can use the query method parameters to directly query the SQLite database. Alternatively, if they asked for the details on a particular movie ❹, then we need to parse the URI to get the ID of that movie, so we can use it as part of the query. We must also check whether they asked for the categories associated to the movie ❺, as these are stored in a separate (join) table. If they do ask for the categories, then our query gets more complex, as we must perform a join.

DISCUSSSION

The code in listing 8.11 gets complex when creating a join. This complexity shields the users of the provider, making it seem simple for them to ask for categories and not have to make multiple calls to the ContentProvider. Compare this with our contacts example from the previous technique, where we had to make three different queries to get four pieces of data. The ContentProvider made us manually do the joins ourselves. If you're creating your own ContentProvider, you can choose the right balance between exposing the underlying database schema to your user or providing abstractions.

Once you've created a ContentProvider, the question becomes how other apps will use it. All the clients need to know is the URI(s) of the provider, plus the names and types of the columns (schema). Some variant of this information is what's needed for any kind of data sharing, whether by Intents, AIDL, or ContentProviders. You could provide this information as a set of classes with everything supplied as constants, similar to what's provided in the Android SDK. You could even package this minimal set of classes as a JAR or maybe even a library project, to make it easy for others to integrate into their apps.

8.3 *Summary*

This chapter could've easily been called "Android application integration." Being able to integrate apps together to create greater value to the end user is one of the key features of Android that sets it apart from other mobile operating systems. By default Android's security model can make your app "run in a silo." All of its data is locked away from other applications. You don't have to do anything special to get that kind of security and lockdown. But for the times when you want to allow other apps to share data and integrate with your app, you have a lot of options. There's no need to hack around the OS: the possible integration points are clearly defined.

In our first app back in chapter 2, we allowed users to share the daily deal they were looking at it with other applications. Which apps? It depended on what the user had on their device, as we used an `Intent` to do the sharing. If you've used Android much for your personal smartphone needs, then you may have noticed that this kind of sharing has become the norm. Whether it's a web page, a picture, or some plain text, users expect to be able to use other apps to share it with their friends. And this is a good thing. Now that we've examined the many ways for apps on the same device to talk to each other, let's take a deeper look at how our apps can talk to other computers over the network.

HTTP networking and web services

It's not a big truck. It's a series of tubes.

—Ted Stevens

Without a doubt, one of the most exciting technological advancements of mobile phones has been the leap from slow, limited mobile network stacks such as GPRS (General Packet Radio Service) plus WAP (the Wireless Access Protocol) to full-blown web clients. Even though the Web existed and rapidly grew back in those days, WAP was born out of sheer compromise: GPRS data connections were slow, and phones back then had small displays and weren't particular powerhouses either, making a desktop-like web experience impossible. The compromise was that WAP didn't allow you to access the entire Web, but instead locked you down to special, trimmed-down sites written in the *Wireless Markup Language (WML)*, not HTML.

As we're writing these lines, 4G data connections with transfer rates of about 100Mbit per second are on the rise. That's more than enough to stream high-definition videos to your phone. The Motorola Atrix 4G sports a 1 GHz CPU, plenty of RAM, and a high-resolution OLED screen roughly as big as your palm. That's more high-tech in a few inches than you'd find in most desktop machines available when WAP was introduced. This allows us to run the full web protocol stack plus a full-featured web browser on mobile phones today. Any given minute, you're carrying the entire World Wide Web in your pocket—think about it!

Clearly, this opens up a wide range of possibilities for mobile application development on a modern platform such as Android. You can render web pages in your application or pull live content from web services using standard web protocols such as HTTP. More and more websites make their contents available to web clients in machine-readable formats such as XML and JSON, often free of charge. Examples of websites that already expose free, public web services include (and are by no means limited to) Amazon, Twitter, eBay, Netflix, and Qype. This allows you to create your own book browser, your own Twitter client, your own movie or local reviews application. The possibilities are practically endless.

Android has a wide range of framework classes that support you here, from monitoring your phone's Wi-Fi and data connections to HTTP messaging and marshalling data from and to XML and JSON. This chapter shows you all of that in eight bite-sized techniques. We've divided this chapter into three sections: section one deals with HTTP as the web's driving protocol and how to send HTTP requests on Android. Section two then shows you how to parse XML and JSON documents, the two most commonly used data interchange formats used in web services these days. Finally, section three wraps up the chapter with more advanced networking techniques such as how to gracefully recover from network failures, and how to properly react to changes in connectivity while the user is on the move.

9.1   *Basic HTTP networking*

If you find yourself loading content from the Web, chances are it'll traverse the wire using HTTP. The *Hypertext Transfer Protocol*, an application layer protocol (OSI layer 7) that was initially created to merely transfer HTML pages from a web server to a web browser, has become the driving force behind web-based content today. It's even begun to replace more specialized protocols, such as FTP, for reliable data transfer. HTTP is a prime example of how strikingly powerful even a simple solution can be. HTTP messages are text-based, so humans can read them. HTTP is also flexible and can be adopted to many different domains by leveraging features such as HTTP header fields to transmit domain-specific metadata alongside the message payload. HTTP also has an extremely simple interface: only seven different commands are supported—the HTTP *verbs*, which can be thought of as functions. These are GET, POST, PUT, DELETE, HEAD, OPTIONS, and TRACE, of which only the first three are widely used. Success or failure in an HTTP conversation is mapped to a series of standardized status codes, which again

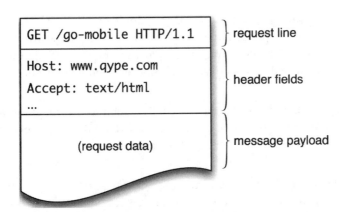

Figure 9.1 An HTTP request is a few lines of ASCII text containing instructions and options, plus an optional request body (the message payload). HTTP has become a primary means not only for requesting web pages, but also for transferring binary data or invoking web services and remote methods.

are generic enough that they can be mapped to different domain requirements easily. Figure 9.1 shows what a typical HTTP request looks like. It's all plain text; go ahead and try it. Go to the command line, `telnet` to qype.com on port 80, and type in the request line and header fields (send the request by hitting the Return key twice; this will generate the character sequence CR+LF+CR+LF, which demarcates an HTTP request).

For these reasons, HTTP has also been adopted to serve as the typical vehicle of communication between a web client and a web service, where it's sometimes used as a first-class protocol (as is the case for RESTful web services, where HTTP steers the communication). Often, HTTP is (ab)used as a mere transport (as is the case with most SOAP or XML/RPC-based web services, where HTTP usually merely carries the payload). We won't turn this into a discussion about the nature of different web services, but it's important to stress how fundamental HTTP is for mobile applications that want to connect to the Web.

First, let's focus on the basics. We'll start in technique 41 by demonstrating how to send simple HTTP requests to a web server using Java's standard HTTP networking facilities, a fast and simple approach that comes with the least overhead. We'll then introduce the more complex Apache HTTP components bundled with Android. This is your full-fledged but heavyweight HTTP solution on Android, and we'll make this more approachable by revisiting the MyMovies application (yes, again) over the course of this chapter, starting with maintaining a simple HTTP connection to a web service in technique 42. Technique 43 will then show you how to tweak HTTP connections to fit our mobile use case. Let's go unlock the Web!

TECHNIQUE 41 HTTP with HttpURLConnection

Before jumping directly to more complex solutions, it should be said that the standard Java class library already comes with a mechanism for sending and receiving HTTP messages. These classes, or more precisely, an open source implementation of them, also come with Android's Java class library. Java's HTTP implementation is simple and bare bones in its structure, and supports features such as proxy servers, cookies (to some degree), and SSL. Moreover, alternative HTTP solutions are often wrappers around the standard Java interfaces. If you don't need all the abstraction provided by, for example, the Apache `HttpClient` interfaces (which we're going to cover in the next technique) the stock Java classes may not only be sufficient for simple tasks. They also perform well, thanks to a slim, low-level implementation.

PROBLEM

You need to perform simple networking tasks via HTTP, such as downloading a file, and you want to avoid the performance penalty imposed by the more high-level, much larger and more complex Apache `HttpClient` implementation.

SOLUTION

In these cases, Java's baked in HTTP classes are a good choice. More precisely, the two classes you want to turn to are `URL` and `HttpURLConnection`, both of which can be found in the `java.net` package. These two classes work in conjunction with each other; you can't use one without the other. To send an HTTP request, you first define the `URL` the request should go to, and then use the same `URL` object to get a handle to a matching `HttpURLConnection`. `URL` therefore, acts as a factory class: you pass it the schematics (the web address) and it spits out a fitting connection object. Codewise, this may look like the following:

```
URL url = new URL("http://www.example.com/");
HttpURLConnection conn = (HttpURLConnection) url.openConnection();
conn.connect();
...
conn.disconnect();
```

Wait, you say. Can't a URL represent an address to any kind of server, not just HTTP? Correct! As it turns out, `HttpURLConnection` inherits from the more generic `URLConnection`, which represents a general-purpose data connection to *some* server using *some* protocol. Now, how does `URL` know what kind of connection to return? The simple answer is that it depends on the URL's scheme (such as `http`). A *protocol handler class* looks at the scheme and tries to find a matching connection implementation. The Java class library (and Android) already provides protocol handlers for all common schemes such as HTTP(S), FTP, MAILTO, FILE, and so on, so typically you don't have to worry about that. This also means that you're free to create your own protocol handlers that instantiate your own custom `URLConnection,` but this is something you rarely need to do, so we're not going to cover it here.

Another thing worth mentioning is that `URLConnection` uses TCP sockets and the standard `java.io` stream classes. That means I/O is blocking, so remember to never run them on the main UI thread.

Let's see how it works in a practical example. We want to extend the MyMovies application to display a message dialog with the latest news downloaded from a web server, so that the user is always up-to-date about what has changed in the latest release. For this to work, we have to place a text file containing the update notes somewhere on a web server, download and read the file, and display its text in a message dialog. Figure 9.2 shows what that will look like.

Figure 9.2 On every application start, we show a message dialog to the user with the latest update notes. The text in the dialog is fetched from a web server instead of being bundled with the APK.

GRAB THE PROJECT: MYMOVIESWITHUPDATENOTICE You can get the source code for this project, and/or the packaged APK to run it, at the *Android in Practice* code website. Because some code listings here are shortened to focus on specific concepts, we recommend that you download the complete source code and follow along within Eclipse (or your favorite IDE or text editor).

Source: http://mng.bz/mvwd, APK file: http://mng.bz/DRKz

For simplicity, we'll show the dialog on every application start, a detail that would probably annoy your users if this was a production release, but that serves our purposes well enough. The plan is to write an `AsyncTask` that establishes a connection to an HTTP server via `HttpURLConnection` and download the file containing the update notes text. We then send this text via a `Handler` object to our main activity so we can show an `AlertDialog` with that text. Let's first look at the MyMovies activity class, which contains the callback for the handler to show the pop-up dialog. Apart from the code that creates the dialog, this should all be familiar to you by now (code that didn't change from previous listings has been omitted for brevity).

Listing 9.1 MyMovies.java has been modified to show an update pop-up dialog

```
public class MyMovies extends ListActivity implements Callback {

    private MovieAdapter adapter;

    public void onCreate(Bundle savedInstanceState) {
        super.onCreate(savedInstanceState);

        setContentView(R.layout.main);

        ...

        new UpdateNoticeTask(new Handler(this)).execute();     ⟵──┐ Starts new
                                                                   │ download task
```

```
    }
    ...
    public boolean handleMessage(Message msg) {
        String updateNotice = msg.getData().getString("text");      ◁─── Reads
        AlertDialog.Builder dialog = new AlertDialog.Builder(this);       update text
        dialog.setTitle("What's new");
        dialog.setMessage(updateNotice);                            ◁─── Sets update
        dialog.setIcon(android.R.drawable.ic_dialog_info);               text
        dialog.setPositiveButton(getString(android.R.string.ok),
            new OnClickListener() {
                public void onClick(DialogInterface dialog, int which) {
                    dialog.dismiss();
                }
            });
        dialog.show();
        return false;
    }
}
```

Except for the few lines of code that spawn the dialog, this should all look familiar to you from reading the previous chapters. More interesting is the `UpdateNoticeTask` that we launch in the last line of `onCreate` because that's where the download proceeds. The source code follows.

Listing 9.2   An `AsyncTask` that downloads update text via `HttpURLConnection`

```
public class UpdateNoticeTask extends AsyncTask<Void, Void, String> {
    private static final String UPDATE_URL =
        "http://android-in-practice.googlecode.com/files/update_notice.txt";

    private HttpURLConnection connection;

    private Handler handler;

    public UpdateNoticeTask(Handler handler) {
        this.handler = handler;
    }

    @Override
    protected String doInBackground(Void... params) {                  Get instance of  ❶
        try {                                                         HttpURLConnection
            URL url = new URL(UPDATE_URL);
            connection = (HttpURLConnection) url.openConnection();   ◁
            connection.setRequestMethod("GET");
            connection.setRequestProperty("Accept", "text/plain");  ❷ Configure
            connection.setReadTimeout(10);                              request
            connection.setConnectTimeout(10);
            connection.connect();                                   ◁
            int statusCode = connection.getResponseCode();
            if (statusCode != HttpURLConnection.HTTP_OK) {          ◁  Establish
                return "Error: Failed getting update notes";        ❸ connection
            }
            return readTextFromServer();                   ◁─── Read    Handle
        } catch (Exception e) {                                 text from  non-200
            return "Error: " + e.getMessage();               ❺ response  ❹ reply
        } finally {
            if (connection != null) {
```

```
            connection.disconnect();                           Close
        }                                            ⑥         connection
    }
}

private String readTextFromServer() throws IOException {
    InputStreamReader isr =
            new InputStreamReader(connection.getInputStream());
    BufferedReader br = new BufferedReader(isr);

    StringBuilder sb = new StringBuilder();
    String line = br.readLine();
    while (line != null) {
        sb.append(line + "\n");
        line = br.readLine();
    }
    return sb.toString();
}

@Override                                                ⑦   Pass retrieved
protected void onPostExecute(String updateNotice) {          text to activity
    Message message = new Message();
    Bundle data = new Bundle();
    data.putString("text", updateNotice);
    message.setData(data);
    handler.sendMessage(message);
}
}
```

After reading the URL from the parameters, the first thing we have to do is use that URL object to retrieve an instance of a fitting URLConnection instance ❶ (an HttpURL-Connection in this case because our URL has the http:// scheme). Note that the call to openConnection doesn't yet establish a connection to the server; it merely instantiates a connection object. We then configure our HTTP request ❷. We first tell it that it should use the GET method to request the file (we could've omitted this call because GET is the default), and set an HTTP Accept header to tell the server what kind of document we expect it to return (plain text in this case). We also set proper timeouts so that the call won't block eternally when there are connectivity problems. The request is now configured and can be sent to the server by a call to connect ❸. Depending on the server reply, we either return an error message if we receive a status message that wasn't 200/OK ❹ or proceed to read the text from the response body ❺. Don't forget to close the connection when you're done processing the response ❻. Finally, we send the text we received from the server to our main Activity using the Handler, in the same manner as shown in chapter 6 ❼.

DISCUSSION

The example here was extremely simple, the simplest kind of request you can send. For these scenarios, HttpURLConnection does the job well, and it comes with practically no overhead. One problem we see with it is its class architecture. HttpURLConnection shares a large part of its interface with the general purpose URLConnection (because it inherits from it), which means that some abstraction is required for method names. If you've never used HttpURLConnection before, you've probably pondered the call to setRequestProperty, which is the way to set HTTP headers—not intuitive. This is because implementations for other protocols may not even have the concept of header fields, but would still share the same interface, so the methods in this class all have rather generic names.

Though this may sound purely cosmetic at first, it introduces another problem: URLConnection's lack of a proper separation of concerns. The request, response, and the mechanisms to send and receive them are merged into a single class, often leaving you wondering which methods to use to process which part of this triplet. This is like putting a five-course meal into a blender: you can still serve it, but it's disgusting. It also makes each part difficult to customize and even more difficult to mock out when writing unit tests, something we'll focus on in chapter 13. It's not a beaming example of good object-oriented class design.

There are more practical problems with this class. If you find yourself in a situation where you need to intercept requests to preprocess and modify them, HttpURLConnection isn't a good choice for sending HTTP requests. A good example is message signing in secure communication environments, where the sender needs to compute a signature over a request's properties and then modify the request to include the signature. That's because request payload is sent unbuffered, so there's no way to get your hands on it in a nonintrusive way. Last but not least, HttpURLConnection in Apache Harmony has bugs—serious bugs. One of the major bugs is detailed in the sidebar "HttpURLConnection and HTTP header fields."

HttpURLConnection and HTTP header fields

As you already know, the Java class library bundled with Android is based on Apache Harmony, the open source Java implementation driven by the Apache foundation. In Android releases up to and including 2.2 (FroYo, API level 8), there's a serious bug that affects HTTP messaging using HttpURLConnection: it sends HTTP header field names in lowercase. This doesn't conform to the HTTP specification, and breaks many HTTP servers because they'll drop these header fields. This can have a wide array of effects, from documents being served to you, which aren't in the format you requested (for example, the Accept header field was ignored) or requests to protected resources fail entirely because the server didn't recognize the Authorization header field. The issue has been resolved in Android 2.3 (Gingerbread, API level 9), but often you want to support older platform versions, too. A workaround is to not use HttpURLConnection at all, and use Apache HttpClient instead, which we're going to introduce in the next technique. You can find the official issue report at http://mng.bz/6T1l.

To summarize, HttpURLConnection is a simply structured, but low-level way of doing HTTP messaging. A few negative aspects about it stand out:

- Its clunky interface makes it difficult to use
- Its monolithic design and lack of object-orientation impede testability and configuration/customization
- It suffers from bugs that can turn out to be show stoppers

For simple tasks such as the file download shown here, it's fine and comes with the least overhead (it doesn't take a sledgehammer to crack a nut). But if you want to do more complex things such as request interception, connection pooling, or multipart file uploads, then don't bother with it. There's a much better way to do this in the Java world, and thanks to the engineers at Google, it's bundled with Android!

TECHNIQUE 42 HTTP with Apache HttpClient

If you find that `HttpURLConnection` doesn't cut it for you, but you don't want to add another 200 KB of library dependencies to your application, then we have good news: you don't have to. As part of the SDK, Android ships the Apache HTTP Components libraries, an open source Java implementation of the HTTP specification that rose from the Apache Jakarta and Apache Commons umbrella projects.

The Apache HTTP Components are composed of two parts: `HttpCore`, a set of low-level classes for handling HTTP connections, and `HttpClient`, a more high-level set of classes built on top of `HttpCore`, which is used to implement typical HTTP user agent software (any applications that connect to a web server). Think of `HttpCore` as the chassis, the underpinnings, whereas `HttpClient` is the final package, including chrome rims and wide-base tires. Unlike the slim and bare-bones `HttpURLConnection`, the Apache implementation is high-level, heavy, and powerful, and lets you perform complex tasks using few lines of code. It has standard, ready-to-use facilities to cope with things such as concurrent requests and connection pooling, retrying and intercepting requests, and more. Compared to `HttpURLConnection`, it also exposes much nicer, strictly object-oriented interfaces, making it easy and intuitive to use at the same time—a beautiful beast!

PROBLEM

You're implementing an HTTP user agent, such as a web service consumer, and you want a fully featured, powerful, yet easy-to-use solution to handle the HTTP communication with the server.

SOLUTION

In this technique, we'll rewrite the code from the previous technique to use Apache `HttpClient` instead of `HttpURLConnection` to perform the file download. This exercise will give you a feel for their key differences.

GRAB THE PROJECT: MYMOVIESWITHHTTPCLIENT   You can get the source code for this project, and/or the packaged APK to run it, at the *Android in Practice* code website. Because some code listings here are shortened to focus on specific concepts, we recommend that you download the complete source code and follow along within Eclipse (or your favorite IDE or text editor).

Note that all changes introduced by the techniques in the remainder of this chapter are already part of this APK, so this is the last file you need to download in this chapter.

Source: http://mng.bz/iR21, APK file: http://mng.bz/QLuf

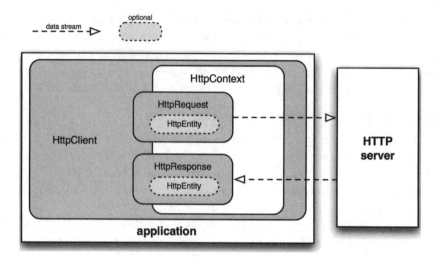

Figure 9.3   The key objects in an Apache HttpClient-based HTTP conversation. Note how each part of the client/server conversation is represented by a separate class.

Communication with an HTTP server via Apache `HttpClient` typically involves five different interfaces that are fundamental to request execution so you will deal with them frequently. These are `HttpRequest` (and its implementations `HttpGet`, `Http-Post`, and so forth) for configuring requests, `HttpClient` for sending requests, `HttpResponse` for processing a server response, `HttpContext` to maintain state of the communication, and `HttpEntity`, which represents the payload that's sent with a request or response. The library has many more classes, but you'll work with these most often. Figure 9.3 shows how these classes play together to establish and process an HTTP connection.

Unlike with `HttpURLConnection`, which is an HTTP client, connection, request and response in one single unit, here you have to think about proper scoping of the objects represented in figure 9.3. Typically you have one `HttpClient` object per application (it makes sense to encapsulate it in your `Application` class or maintain it as a static field), one `HttpContext` object per request-response group, and one `Http-Request` and `HttpResponse` respectively per request you make.

> **NOTE** `HttpContext` is used to maintain state across several request-response pairs, but don't confuse it with traditional HTTP sessions (often implemented via HTTP cookies). `HttpContext` is a mere client-side execution context; think of it as attributes you can maintain and track across several requests. If you don't know what this is useful for then chances are you won't need it. In fact, because most people don't need it, the default `execute` method of `HttpCli-ent` will create and maintain an execution context for you, so you can ignore it. For these reasons, we won't mention `HttpContext` again.

Let's rewrite our simple update notes feature to use `HttpClient` instead of `HttpURL-Connection`. We've encapsulated all HTTP-specific code to the `doInBackground` method of our task, so we'll focus on that. Here's the new code (again, we've left out the parts that didn't change from the previous listing).

Listing 9.3 `UpdateNoticeTask` rewritten to use `HttpClient` for downloading the file

```
public class UpdateNoticeTask extends AsyncTask<Void, Void, String> {
    ...
    @Override                                                      1 GET request
    protected String doInBackground(Void... params) {                from URL
        try {
            HttpGet request = new HttpGet(UPDATE_URL);      ◁────  2 Configure
            request.setHeader("Accept", "text/plain");      ◁────     request header
            HttpResponse response = MyMovies.getHttpClient()
        .execute(request);                                        3 Send
            int statusCode = response.getStatusLine().getStatusCode();  request
            if (statusCode != HttpStatus.SC_OK) {
                return "Error: Failed getting update notes";
            }
            return EntityUtils.toString(response.getEntity());  ◁──  Read
        } catch (Exception e) {                                       response
            return "Error: " + e.getMessage();                        into
        }                                                         4 string
    }

    @Override
    protected void onPostExecute(String updateNotice) {
        ...
    }
}
```

We first create a GET request from the given URL ❶ (see also listing 9.2), and configure it to expect a plain text file ❷. We then "exchange" the request object for a response object using a call to `HttpClient.execute` ❸. Note that we get this object from the main `Activity` using a static getter. We'll learn in the next technique how this shared `HttpClient` instance is set up. The call to execute will effectively open the connection and send the request using a default execution context (there's also a variant of this method that takes a custom `HttpContext`), but it won't yet retrieve the response body. To read the text from the response body (represented as an `Http-Entity` if you recall from figure 9.3), we use a helper function shipped with the library that reads from an `InputStream` into a string ❹, which means it does much the same thing we did manually in the previous technique.

DISCUSSION

It should be clear that `HttpClient` exposes a much friendlier interface than `HttpURLConnection` if you need to do HTTP messaging on Android. We also find good separation of concerns: we have separate objects for request and response, we have a client object to send and receive them, and we have the entity object that wraps the message payload. We also have helper classes at our disposal that allow us to instantly process a response by reading it into a string (as shown in the listing), a byte array, and so on. Another great feature of HttpClient is that if you *want* simple, you *get* simple. If you want to flip every bit, then you can also do that. It's a good example of the convention-over-configuration pattern: it works well out of the box with little setup required, but if your demands are high, you still have the flexibility to configure every detail. As mentioned before, this comes at a cost: it's slower and has a larger memory footprint, so choose carefully which tasks you want to perform using the swift-but-ugly HttpURLConnection, and which should use the friendly-but-heavy Apache HttpClient classes.

In this technique, we haven't paid attention to the concrete type of the HttpClient instance we used. The most commonly used one is DefaultHttpClient, which sets a couple of sane defaults for connections based on the HTTP/1.1 protocol version. These include things such as a default HTTP user agent header, a default TCP socket buffer size, a default request-retry handler that retries sending a request up to three times if it's safe to do so (if we're dealing with idempotent requests), and so forth. It also registers a handler for HTTPS (HTTP over SSL) URLs on port 443.

Although it may be tempting to use this default implementation everywhere because it's so simple to use (the constructor doesn't even take arguments, could it get any simpler?), we'd usually advise against using it in its default configuration. That's because it has a major pitfall many developers aren't aware of, severe enough that Google decided to ship an alternative implementation with Android 2.2 (API level 8) that developers are encouraged to use instead. Not all applications can rely on the recent API level 8 and hence have no access to it, so we've decided to add the following technique, which shows you how to avoid said problems by properly configuring the default implementation.

> **ATTENTION!**   As mentioned previously, the following technique contains hints and instructions that for the most part don't need to be carried out manually when using Android 2.2 (API level 8) or later because they're already part of the AndroidHttpClient class (see the previous Discussion section). If you plan to develop applications that only target Android 2.2 or newer, you may consider skipping this technique. We still encourage you to work through this section because it provides insight into HttpClient and how to tune it to suit your needs.

TECHNIQUE 43   Configuring a thread-safe HttpClient

We mentioned in the previous technique that it's common to maintain only one instance of HttpClient across an entire application. You could create a singleton accessor for it and keep a reference in your single application context, or even a static field somewhere. Doing so means that all parts of your application request the same HttpClient instance if they need to access the Web. Now imagine you're running a couple of AsyncTasks that all use this shared object to communicate with a web server. Threading and shared state? Does this ring your alarm bells? If not, go back and read chapter 6 again. Sharing state between different threads always requires synchronization through object locks or volatile fields; otherwise your application may behave erroneously. The symptoms can be anything from unexpected exceptions to connection lockups.

The evildoer here is `DefaultHttpClient`: without further customization, it'll use a `SingleClientConnManager` to handle HTTP connections. This manager doesn't manage anything because it'll hold only *one* connection object that will be used for *all* HTTP connections. If more than one thread is trying to request the connection at a time, they'll race for the single connection object and end up using it all at the same time! That's like trying to send two letters to two different recipients on a fax machine at the same time—it's not going to work.

Clearly, we need a more sensible way of handling connections if there's a risk of several threads trying to access the same `HttpClient` instance simultaneously.

PROBLEM

You're running threads that need to communicate with a web server through a single shared instance of `HttpClient`, and you must therefore make sure that connections are established in a mutually exclusive, thread-safe manner.

SOLUTION

The trick here is to tell `HttpClient` which connection manager to use—preferably a thread-safe one (one that was designed with parallel access in mind). Fortunately, we don't have to implement it ourselves; it's already part of the library, and is aptly named `ThreadSafeClientConnManager`. This connection manager doesn't handle a single connection, but a pool of them, where each connection can be taken from the pool, allocated to a thread (which then has exclusive access to it), and returned to the pool once the thread yields it. If the same or another thread claims a connection for the same route, then a connection can be immediately reused from the pool without the need to first close and reopen it, thereby avoiding the overhead of the handshake performed by HTTP when establishing a new connection. Figure 9.4 illustrates how that works.

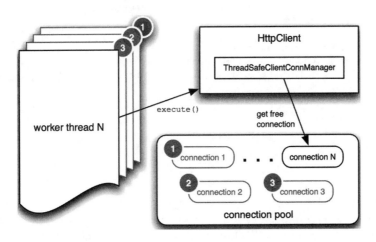

Figure 9.4   Using `ThreadSafeClient-ConnManager`, a free connection is taken from a connection pool whenever a thread wants to send an HTTP request. Once the thread closes the connection, the manager doesn't close it, but puts it back into the pool for other threads to reuse.

NOTE   Connection pooling isn't based on thread identity (the same thread getting the same connection back every time), but on *routes*. A request's route in HttpClient is defined by the series of hosts it'll traverse (the hops, such as when using proxy servers) and whether it's layered or tunneled, which is the case when doing HTTP over SSL (HTTPS). This means that a connection for a request can only be reused from the pool when the request goes to the same target host via the same intermediate hosts using the same layering or tunneling parameters.

One caveat with setting a connection manager manually is that you need to supply a set of HTTP configuration parameters and a protocol scheme registry, even if you don't want these things to be different from what DefaultHttpClient uses by default with its SingleClientConnManager.

WHERE CAN XML CONFIGURATION BE USED?   A question we've heard before is: Because Android supports defining and configuring strings, layouts, views, and more in XML files, does this mean I can configure all parts of the platform in XML rather than programmatically in code? The answer, unfortunately, is no. XML, as a means of configuration, can only be used for resources such as views and the application manifest. Anything else you'll have to write out in Java code, including your HTTP configuration.

The following shows what a minimal setup could look like, and again, we'll step through the code (here we've decided to manage the client object as a static reference in the MyMovies activity).

Listing 9.4   You can use a static initializer to set-up a thread-safe HttpClient instance

```java
public class MyMovies extends ListActivity implements Callback {     ❶ Create static
    private static final AbstractHttpClient httpClient;                   ref to client
    ...                                                    ❷ Static
    static {                                                  initializer creates object
        SchemeRegistry schemeRegistry = new SchemeRegistry();
        schemeRegistry.register(new Scheme("http", PlainSocketFactory
                .getSocketFactory(), 80));
        ...                                               Register default
        ThreadSafeClientConnManager cm =                    scheme ❸
                new ThreadSafeClientConnManager(
                    new BasicHttpParams(), schemeRegistry);      ❹ Create thread-
        ...                                                         safe manager
        httpClient = new DefaultHttpClient(cm, null);        Create
    }                                                       customized
    public static HttpClient getHttpClient() {           ❺ DefaultHttpClient
        return httpClient;
    }
    ...
}
```

Unlike the previous technique, we don't create the DefaultHttpClient using the default constructor. Instead we hold a final static reference to it ❶ and do the custom setup in the static initializer block ❷. We can pass this instance around using a public static getter method. For setting up the client object, we first must provide a scheme registry ❸. The scheme registry is responsible for resolving a URI scheme (such as http or https) and port number (80) to a TCP socket created by an appropriate socket factory. Using the scheme registry and a default set of connection manager parameters, we can create the ThreadSafeClientConnManager ❹, which we can then use to configure the HTTP client object ❺. Note how we pass a new instance of Basic-HttpParams to the manager instance, but pass null for the parameters to the new instance of DefaultHttpClient. This is an inconsistency in the library: passing null to the client constructor implies that it'll create a parameter set itself and set some sane defaults. We're not allowed to pass null to the manager though; it expects a valid HttpParams instance. If it doesn't have any values set, the manager will still fall back to the defaults. Either way, we're using the default parameter values chosen by the library here. If you find the HttpParams confusing, don't worry; we'll come back to that with some more examples.

DISCUSSION

As you can see, it only takes a couple of lines of code to get a client implementation that's safe to use in concurrent applications. Unless you're certain that no more than one thread will ever try to open a connection, you should *always* use the approach shown here because it makes sure that connection handling is properly isolated between threads using Java's synchronization mechanisms. Using this setup, you can fire away HTTP requests in one thread without having to worry about other threads doing the same thing at the same time!

As said previously, we were using default parameters for the connection manager and the client instance. But what does that mean, and what parameters are there to choose from? First, any HttpParams instance is a map of key/value pairs. Which entries are of concern for the object you pass that map to (the connection manager) is solely defined by that object itself. For example, any ClientConnManager defines the parameters it supports in the ConnManagerParams class, where you find helper methods to get and set the parameters.

ThreadSafeClientConnManager for instance sets the default values for the maximum number of total connections to 20, and the maximum number of connections per route to 2. Because we want to prepare our MyMovies application to communicate with a web service in the forthcoming techniques, let's choose more sensible numbers here:

```
HttpParams connManagerParams = new BasicHttpParams();
ConnManagerParams.setMaxTotalConnections(connManagerParams, 5);
ConnManagerParams.setMaxConnectionsPerRoute(connManagerParams,
        new ConnPerRouteBean(5));

ThreadSafeClientConnManager cm =
            new ThreadSafeClientConnManager(connManagerParams,
                    schemeRegistry);
```

We've taken the setup code from listing 9.4 and set the maximum number of both per route and total connections to the same value because all requests will go to the same host via the same port, so it makes sense to set them to the same value. We've also reduced the value to 5 because we don't want too many concurrent connections at once.

So far so good, but we can customize even more—the client object itself for instance. It always makes sense to set a default HTTP user agent, so the application can identify itself to the web service. We also want to reduce the timeouts for establishing a connection and idle time when retrieving data because this can happen frequently on a mobile device:

```
HttpParams clientParams = new BasicHttpParams();
HttpProtocolParams.setUserAgent(clientParams, "MyMovies/1.0");
HttpConnectionParams.setConnectionTimeout(clientParams, 15 * 1000);
HttpConnectionParams.setSoTimeout(clientParams, 15 * 1000);
httpClient = new DefaultHttpClient(cm, clientParams);
```

You can customize plenty more, but these are good defaults when accessing a web service. Your mileage may vary, depending on the kind of communication you plan to do. Now that you've seen how to fully customize an HTTP client instance, we can tell you: if you're targeting Android 2.2 or above, you don't have to do anything shown in this technique yourself! As we mentioned briefly before, Android bundles a custom implementation of `HttpClient` called `AndroidHttpClient` with that version. This implementation has already been optimized for mobile use, and it does all the stuff like setting proper timeouts and a thread-safe connection manager. It also supports HTTPS by default. In order to use it, you'd replace the code at ❺ in listing 9.4 with this:

```
httpClient = AndroidHttpClient.newInstance("MyMovies/1.0");
```

You can again customize it further using any of the parameters you've learned in this technique; after all, it's another implementation of `HttpClient`, so it accepts the same calls and parameters. Note that the string we pass to `newInstance` will become the HTTP User Agent header field sent with every HTTP request. This is equivalent to the call to `HttpProtocolParams.setUserAgent(clientParams, "MyMovies/1.0")` from the previous code snippet.

On top of choosing good configuration defaults, `AndroidHttpClient` also supports gzipped message payload (web services often compress their responses to conserve bandwidth for the client) and a *cURL logger*, which prints every request out in the format used by the *cURL tool*, so you can easily repeat requests on the command line. If you're not using Android 2.2 or later, but still don't want to handle all this stuff yourself, you may want look a the ignition utility library (https://github.com/kaeppler/ignition), which bundles most of these optimizations as part of its `IgnitedHttp` class (with a few other abstractions and features that make HTTP even easier to use on Android).

Looks like we're set to connect the MyMovies application to a web service. How about fetching some movie data from the live Web? Let's see how that works.

9.2   Consuming XML and JSON web services

In the first section of this chapter, you saw how to connect to the Web and download data via HTTP. This is sufficient if you want to download a file to store it on the device or display its contents as-is, as with our update notification downloader. Most mobile applications that connect to the Web do so for a different reason though: They want to retrieve data from a web service.

> **DEFINITION**   A *web service* is a set of server-side interfaces exposed on the Internet using web technologies such as HTTP for data transfer or XML and JSON for data serialization. Unlike web sites, web services are meant to be consumed by machines, not human beings.

Because the data backing a web service is always structured (it's typically served from a database-driven back end), it must be *serialized* in some way so that it can be transferred over the wire and reconstructed on the client side without losing this structure. Data serialization (also called *marshalling*) is therefore the task of turning data such as table rows or objects into some ordered, well-structured, stable format. The client can then deserialize the service response into a representation of the data it can understand (such as a Java object). Figure 9.5 illustrates how communication between a web service and a mobile client typically looks.

This process is like writing a letter to someone: you're bringing your thoughts, which are stored safely in your head (the "database"), to paper by writing one word after another on a sheet of paper: you're serializing your thoughts! You may have noticed that we made two fundamental assumptions for this process to work: first, the

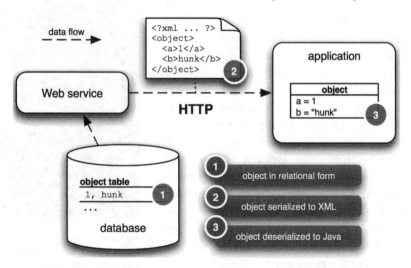

Figure 9.5   A typical data serialization/deserialization scenario in a web environment. An application requests an object from a web service via HTTP, where the object is first read from a database table, is then serialized to XML, transferred via HTTP, and finally deserialized by the application into a Java object.

sender and receiver must speak the same language, and second, they must both use the same medium to exchange information; otherwise the communication will fail. We call a format that can be used to exchange information in a way understandable by many a *common interchange format*, and the transmission medium or format the *transport*. In our analogy, the language is the common interchange format, whereas the letter is the transport. On the Web, the common interchange format is usually either XML (the Extensible Markup Language) or JSON (JavaScript Object Notation), whereas the transport is usually HTTP.

We've already seen how to transmit data using HTTP in the previous section. Now, we'll show you how to consume XML and JSON responses coming from a web service.

NOTE   We're talking about XML and JSON in the context of web services here, because we're going somewhere with this as part of the overall chapter. This does *not* mean that the techniques in this section are only meaningful in a web context! Anything related to parsing XML or JSON in this chapter can be used to parse such documents from any source, including a simple file on the device. We think it's fun to connect to a web service in order to demonstrate these techniques.

The roadmap for the remainder of this section is as follows: we'll start with XML parsers because it's the most common format used on the Web for exchanging information.

Specifically, we'll show you two different ways of parsing XML: SAX (technique 44) and XmlPull (technique 45). If you're familiar with XML APIs, note that we decided not to discuss the DOM API, because it has performance problems that make it poorly suited for a mobile device. If you need a solution that like DOM buffers the document in memory entirely, there's a much more lightweight approach: JSON, which we'll discuss in technique 46. To make things more interesting, we'll add a new feature to the MyMovies application: long pressing a list element will now fetch live data in form of a movie rating from the TMDb (The Movie Database) web service. Parsing the response will then be implemented using the three alternatives presented here. Figure 9.6 shows what it's going to look like.

To cope with this somewhat complex new feature, we had to make some small changes to the existing classes in the application:

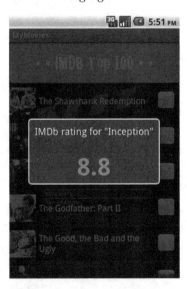

Figure 9.6   Long pressing any of the movie list elements will dispatch a call to the TMDb movie web service and retrieve information about that movie. From that information, we show the official IMDb rating in a pop-up dialog.

1   We added a `Movie` class (a POJO with ID, title, and rating fields) where the `toString` method returns the movie title.

2 We changed the list adapter to manage `Movie` objects, not strings (we changed its type from `ArrayAdapter<String>` to `ArrayAdapter<Movie>`). If you put anything that's not a string in an `ArrayAdapter`, the adapter will then use the object's `toString` method to get the label for the list item (in our case, the movie name), so nothing will change in terms of behavior.

3 We added the `OnItemLongClickListener` interface to the `MyMovies` activity where we start a new `AsyncTask` that will communicate with the TMDb web service. The source code for this task will be shown in a second.

We'll spare you the details of these changes here because they're minimal and don't contain anything new or relevant for this chapter (you can look at the full source code online if you're interested), but the new task class which connects to TMDb is worth a look.

Listing 9.5 `GetMovieRatingTask` retrieves a movies's IMDb rating from a Web service

```
public class GetMovieRatingTask extends AsyncTask<String, Void, Movie> {

    private static final String API_KEY =
                "624645327f33f7866355b7b728f9cd98";

    private static final String API_ENDPOINT =
                "http://api.themoviedb.org/2.1";

    private static final int PARSER_KIND_SAX = 0;
    private static final int PARSER_KIND_XMLPULL = 1;
    private static final int PARSER_KIND_JSON = 2;

    private int parserKind = PARSER_KIND_SAX;

    private Activity activity;

    public GetMovieRatingTask(Activity activity) {
        this.activity = activity;
    }

    @Override
    protected Movie doInBackground(String... params) {
        try {
            String imdbId = params[0];
            HttpClient httpClient = MyMovies.getHttpClient();
            String format = parserKind == PARSER_KIND_JSON ? "json" : "xml";
            String path =
                "/Movie.imdbLookup/en/" + format + "/" + API_KEY + "/";
            HttpGet request = new HttpGet(API_ENDPOINT + path);
            HttpResponse response = httpClient.execute(request);
            InputStream data = response.getEntity().getContent();

            switch (parserKind) {
                case PARSER_KIND_SAX:
                    return SAXMovieParser.parseMovie(data);
                case PARSER_KIND_XMLPULL:
                    return XmlPullMovieParser.parseMovie(data);
                case PARSER_KIND_JSON:
```

❶ Input: IMDb ID; output: Movie object

❷ Movie's address

❸ Send service request

❹ Parse response

```
                return JsonMovieParser.parseMovie(data);
              default:
                throw new RuntimeException("unsupported parser");
          }
      } catch (Exception e) {
          e.printStackTrace();
          return null;
      }
  }

  @Override                                          ❺ Show result
  protected void onPostExecute(Movie movie) {            in pop-up
      if (movie == null) {
          Toast.makeText(activity, "Error!", Toast.LENGTH_SHORT).show();
      }
      Dialog dialog = new Dialog(activity);
      dialog.setContentView(R.layout.movie_dialog);

      dialog.setTitle("IMDb rating for \"" + movie.getTitle() + "\"");

      TextView rating =
              (TextView) dialog.findViewById(R.id.movie_dialog_rating);
      rating.setText(movie.getRating());

      dialog.show();
  }
}
```

This task resolves a movie's IMDb ID (passed as a `String`) to a `Movie` object, which is a Java object with a couple of fields, such as ID, title, and rating ❶. We must first construct the path by which this movie is being addressed on the TMDb web service. For lookups by IMDb ID, the service expects a couple of parameters that are part of the URL, such as the language (`/en`) and the response format (`/xml`). We must also include the API key, which identifies our application on the web service, and the movie's ID ❷. Note that the API key is shared among all users of the application; you don't need to have a key per-user, only per-application. We then send a `GET` request to that URL, as learned in the previous techniques ❸. Now comes the interesting part: we pass the response body to one of several different parser classes, all of which have yet to be created ❹. We'll develop these parser classes in the following three techniques. If parsing succeeded, we read the relevant fields from the `Movie` object and show them in a pop-up dialog ❺.

  This entire class won't change over the course of this section, except for those two lines of code that defines the response format in the target URL and the parser invocation. That's why we won't come back to this class again; it's the glue we use to invoke our parsers (our focus here), which we'll focus on hereafter.

TECHNIQUE 44   Parsing XML with SAX

Let's forget about the web service for a minute and come back to the topic at hand. We have an XML document (wherever it comes from)—text structured into a tree using element nodes and content nodes—and we must somehow turn this textual representation into a Java object that we can then use in our application.

There are plenty of ways to do that, and different kinds of XML parsers differ in the way they process a document. Android bundles three different kinds of parser APIs (DOM, SAX, and XmlPull), each with their own pros and cons. So what *are* the differences between each of these?

> **STAX SUPPORT**   Android doesn't bundle a StAX parser (Streaming API for XML), which is now part of the official Sun JDK 6 (recall that the Android class library is based on Java 5). The StAX specification defines another pull-parser API that can be understood as the standardized successor to XmlPull, but it's functionally equivalent and because it's not part of Android, will be ignored hereafter.

One aspect by which different kinds of parsers can be classified is whether they need to load the entire XML document into memory up front. Parsers based on the Document Object Model (DOM) do that: they parse XML documents into a tree structure, which can then be traversed in-memory to read its contents. This allows you to traverse a document in arbitrary order, and gives rise to some useful APIs that can be slapped on top of DOM, such as XPath, a path query language that has been specifically designed for extracting information from trees. XPath APIs weren't part of Android before the Android 2.2 (FroYo, API level 8) release, so unless you're writing applications for Android 2.2 or later, you'd have to bundle an XPath implementation such as Jaxen with your application. Using DOM alone isn't much of a benefit because its API is clunky and it's expensive to always read everything into memory even if you don't need to. Hence, DOM parsers are, in most cases, not the optimal choice to parse XML on Android.

Which brings us to the opposite class of parsers—those that don't need to load a document up front. These parsers are *stream-based*, which means they process an XML document while still reading it from the data source (the Web or a disk). This implies that you do *not* have random access to the XML tree as with DOM because no internal representation of the document is being maintained. Stream parsers can be further distinguished from each other. There are *push parsers* that, while streaming the document, will call back to your application when encountering a new element. SAX parsers, discussed in this technique, fall into this class. Then there are *pull parsers*, which are more like iterators or cursors: here the client must explicitly ask for the next element to be retrieved (XmlPull parsers do that, and will be discussed in the next technique). Table 9.1 summarizes these parser types.

Table 9.1   The different kinds of XML parsers bundled with Android

XML API	DOM	SAX	XmlPull
Internal model	tree-based	stream-based	stream-based
Retrieval type	pull / query	push	pull
Random access	Yes	no	no

In this technique, we'll use a SAX parser on Android. SAX is an event-driven push-parser specification and operates at a low level, so it doesn't bring any unnecessary overhead. SAX has been around for ages—since XML got popular—and this reflects to some extent in its API: it's somewhat clunky, but also simple and fast.

PROBLEM

You're looking for a lightweight way to parse XML documents without having to keep them in-memory at all times. You specifically want a parser that calls back to your application whenever an element is encountered in the XML document (push).

SOLUTION

Because parsing, using the SAX (Simple API for XML) model, is event-driven, you can distinguish between the parser that fires the events and the object that receives these events. The latter is called a *SAX handler* and must implement the `ContentHandler` interface. That's what we have to do. A convenient way is to inherit from `Default-Handler` and only override those parts of its interface that we need. Figure 9.7 shows how a SAX parser works on a conceptual (and simplified) level.

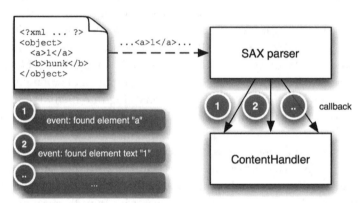

Figure 9.7   A SAX parser streams an XML document from a Java `InputStream` and calls back to a `Content-Hander` object whenever it has read an entity such as an XML element or a text node. It's in that sense, event-based, and pushes content to the handler.

Before parsing an XML document, we should have an idea of how it's structured—what kind of tags we'll find and how we want to process their values (we may, for instance, want to parse a numeric string into a Java numeric type). Because the example in this chapter fetches the XML from the TMDb service, we should take a closer look at a typical TMDb XML response to a single movie lookup request (the following listing has some details shortened for readability).

Listing 9.6   XML response format of TMDb's Movie.imdbLookup method

```
<?xml version="1.0" encoding="UTF-8"?>
<OpenSearchDescription
          xmlns:opensearch="http://a9.com/-/spec/opensearch/1.1/">
  <opensearch:Query searchTerms="tt1375666"/>
  <opensearch:totalResults>1</opensearch:totalResults>
  <movies>
    <movie>
```

```
      <popularity>3</popularity>
      <translated>true</translated>
      <adult>false</adult>
      <language>en</language>
      <name>Inception</name>
      <alternative_name>Eredet</alternative_name>
      <type>movie</type>
      <id>27205</id>
      <imdb_id>tt1375666</imdb_id>
      <url>http://www.themoviedb.org/movie/27205</url>
      <overview>In a world where technology exists to enter
   the human mind through dream invasion, a single idea within
   one's mind can be the most dangerous weapon or the most
   valuable asset.</overview>
      <rating>9.0</rating>
   ...
</movie>
   </movies>
</OpenSearchDescription>
```

Nothing overly surprising here. We get the movie's title, ID, genres, runtime, rating (that's what we're after), and a few other things. In order to parse this document using SAX, we must react to the handler events when an XML element we're interested in is encountered. In general, the SAX events you want to catch are usually related to document boundaries, element boundaries, and simple text nodes. These events and the `ContentHandler` methods they map to are summarized in table 9.2.

Table 9.2 SAX events and their method counterparts in the `ContentHander` interface

SAX event	ContentHander callback method
document start/end	startDocument, endDocument
element (tag) open/close	startElement, endElement
text found	characters

SAX defines more events—for example namespace bindings and processing instructions—but they're of no interest to us here.

The usual approach is to do setup work in `startDocument`, such as creating an empty object that will hold the data parsed from the document (a `Movie` object in our case), then collect text content in `characters` (such as a movie title) and use the text content in `endElement` to populate the respective field of the object.

We're only interested in the movie rating, and the title maybe for the sake of completeness. Here's how our SAX parser handler might look.

Listing 9.7 SAXMovieParser parses a TMDb movie document using SAX

```
public class SAXMovieParser extends DefaultHandler {         Inherit from
                                                          1  DefaultHandler
    private Movie movie;
```

```
private StringBuilder elementText;

public static Movie parseMovie(InputStream xml)
    throws Exception {
  SAXMovieParser parser = new SAXMovieParser();
  Xml.parse(xml, Encoding.UTF_8, parser);
  return parser.getMovie();
}

public Movie getMovie() {
  return movie;
}

@Override
public void startDocument() throws SAXException {
  elementText = new StringBuilder();
}

@Override
public void startElement(String uri,
      String localName, String qName,
      Attributes attributes) throws SAXException {
  if ("movie".equals(localName)) {
    movie = new Movie();
  }
}

@Override
public void characters(char[] ch, int start, int length)
    throws SAXException {
  elementText.append(ch, start, length);
}

@Override
public void endElement(String uri, String localName,
    String qName)
  throws SAXException {

  if ("name".equals(localName)) {
    movie.setTitle(elementText.toString().trim());
  } else if ("rating".equals(localName)) {
    movie.setRating(elementText.toString().trim());
  }
  elementText.setLength(0);
}
}
```

❷ Helper method to parse stream

❸ Do setup work here

❹ Create new movie object

❺ Set current value

❻ Collect character data in buffer

As said before, it's easiest to inherit from DefaultHandler ❶ because you get default implementations for every interface method (the default implementations are no-ops by the way) and must implement only those callbacks that you're interested in. It also makes sense to define a helper method to trigger the parsing ❷, which instantiates our handler object and passes it to Android's Xml.parse utility method. This method will instantiate a SAX parser for us and start parsing. When parsing commences, we know the Movie instance will have all fields set, so we can return it to the caller.

The parser callbacks used here are for one startDocument ❸ where we do some setup work. To demonstrate, we've also overridden startElement ❹ to look for a

<movie> tag, which when encountered, will create a new Movie instance. We only parse a single movie here, so this could have happened elsewhere, but if you ever need to parse a list of elements, then you should do as shown here.

The characters method ❺ will be called whenever text that's not a structural element (like a tag or preamble) is encountered. Note that this could also be whitespace between two tags, not necessarily element content, so it makes sense to do sanity checks, such as skipping whitespace characters. Moreover, two adjacent text fragments that belong to the same text node may trigger several text events instead of one, so we must collect all text fragments in a buffer until the closing tag is encountered in order to capture the entire text node. Whenever a tag is closed, endElement is called ❻. At this point we know that our text buffer must contain the text of that element, so we can use the buffer contents to set the respective fields, such as title or rating. We also reset the text buffer so it doesn't accumulate the text of all elements.

DISCUSSION

Once you come to grips with SAX's event-based approach, parsing smaller documents with it is straightforward. Moreover, because SAX is a streaming parser, it doesn't maintain an internal representation of the document, making it efficient for parsing even large documents.

At the same time, this is the biggest problem with SAX parsers, because you get little contextual information about where a parser event occurs. For instance, what if there are multiple tags with the same name in a document? In the example XML from listing 9.6 there's a tag called name (the movie title). Imagine that the category name weren't stored as an attribute, but as a tag itself (that's perfectly valid). If you then get an event about the start of an element called name, you have no idea which it is—the movie name or the category name. This means that for more complex documents with a medium to high depth, you'll have to maintain state in your handler about where you are while the document is being parsed. You could set boolean flags to remember when you're inside a category element. This can get tedious and painful to manage.

Another criticism leveled at SAX parsers is that you always receive callbacks about any kind of event—even if you're not interested. You have to implement all callbacks (although, at least you don't have to spell everything out since there's the SAX DefaultHandler and even more helpers in the android.sax package.) One way to circumvent this would be to explicitly move forward through an XML document bit by bit, and skip any entity you encounter in which you're not interested. That's what a pull parser does, which we cover in the next technique.

TECHNIQUE 45 **Parsing XML with XmlPull**

Sometimes you're interested in a specific snippet of information buried somewhere in a bigger XML document. You want to jump to the element in question, read its value, and then stop processing the document. Other times you may want to parse the entire document, but don't want to rely on callbacks—you want more control over the document traversal by explicitly asking for another element to be fetched. In both cases, Android's pull parser implementation may be what you're looking for.

PROBLEM

You're looking for a lightweight way to parse XML documents without having to keep them in memory at all times. You specifically want a parser that fetches the next token (such as an element or text) from the document explicitly rather than via callbacks (pull).

SOLUTION

Android bundles a pull parser implementation (KXML2) based on the XmlPull specification (http://www.xmlpull.org). Unlike SAX, no callback handler needs to be informed about parsing events such as processing an element. Instead, parsing is entirely in the hands of the client, which has to explicitly ask for the next token to be retrieved, a retrieval model you may be familiar with because it's the same as Java iterators or relational database cursors. The beauty of this model is its speed and simplicity: few instructions are required to parse a document. Here's a small pseudo-code snippet showing how an XML document can be parsed using XmlPull in Java:

```
int event = parser.getEventType();
while (event != XmlPullParser.END_DOCUMENT) {
   switch (event) {
   case XmlPullParser.START_DOCUMENT:
      doSetupWork();
      break;
   case XmlPullParser.START_TAG:
      readElementText(parser.nextText());
      break;
      ...
   }
   event = parser.next();
}
```

The benefit of this model is that it's easy to skip forward until a certain element is reached, read its value, and then exit early if that's all you need. You can still process the entire document element-by-element by calling the next method, which fetches the next token from the XML document. This iterator-like behavior is illustrated in figure 9.8.

To have a direct comparison to SAX, we'll implement an XmlPull counterpart to the previous example: extracting movie title and rating from a TMDb response. The

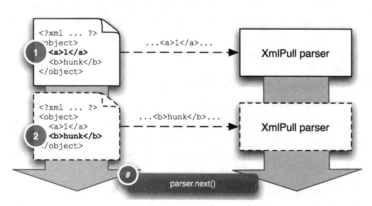

Figure 9.8   Unlike SAX, an XmlPull parser only reads the next entity from a document on-demand by a call to the **next** function. In this sense, it behaves like a Java iterator or a database cursor.

solution couldn't be more straightforward, and is shown next. `XmlPullParser` and its related classes are—unlike SAX or DOM—not part of the standard JDK 5. They're bundled with Android as a third-party library in the `org.xmlpull.v1` package.

Listing 9.8 XmlPullMovieParser parses a TMDb movie document using XmlPull

```
public class XmlPullMovieParser {

   private XmlPullParser xpp;

   public static Movie parseMovie(InputStream xml)        ❶ Helper function
         throws Exception {                                  to invoke parser
      return new XmlPullMovieParser().parse(xml);
   }
                                                           Instantiate ❷
   public Movie parse(InputStream xml) throws Exception {  new pull
      Movie movie = new Movie();                           parser

      xpp = XmlPullParserFactory.newInstance().newPullParser();
      xpp.setInput(xml, "UTF-8");

      skipToTag("name");                      ❸ Skip to name tag
      movie.setTitle(xpp.nextText());            and read value

      skipToTag("rating");
      movie.setRating(xpp.nextText());

      return movie;                                    ❹ Helper
   }                                                      to skip to
   private void skipToTag(String tagName) throws Exception {  given tag
      int event = xpp.getEventType();
      while (event != XmlPullParser.END_DOCUMENT
               && !tagName.equals(xpp.getName())) {
         event = xpp.next();
      }
   }
}
```

Similar to the SAX handler, we define a static helper method to invoke the pull parser, but here it's simplified to one line of code that instantiates and invokes our movie parser ❶. The work is done in the `parse` instance method. We first create and initialize the `XmlPullParser` object ❷. Note that you'd typically want to cache this instance somewhere instead of re-creating it every time. As with SAX, this is done by going through a factory because Java only defines the interfaces in the XML packages, whereas their implementations are library-specific. For instance, the Sun JDK ships a different SAX parser implementation than Apache Harmony and Android. Likewise, you could decide to instantiate a different `XmlPullParser` implementation here—you most likely don't want to, but it's good to know it's possible.

The rest of the `parse` method is strikingly simple. We're only interested in two fields, movie name and rating, so we can skip ahead to these tags and use their element text to populate the fields of the `Movie` object ❸. The `skipToTag` helper method ❹ enters a loop that terminates either when there's nothing more to parse (end of document reached) or when the tag that was requested has been found. The next method advances to the next token (element, text, processing instruction, and so on), determines what kind of token it is, and checks the numeric constant that it returns. Once we've found everything we want, we can quit.

DISCUSSION

Though the general performance of XmlPull is similar to that of SAX (both are significantly faster than DOM, as plenty of benchmarks indicate), XmlPull will outperform SAX on large documents where you only want to read a small piece of the entire document because you don't receive callbacks for every kind of event. Moreover, the parsing can be aborted at any point in time, allowing you to drop out early.

Another benefit over SAX is its simple and intuitive interface. It follows a strict you-get-what-you-ask-for design, often resulting in code that's easier to write and understand. It also is more convenient at times: for instance, XmlPull won't return ignorable whitespace unless you ask for it (unlike SAX), saving you calls to the `trim` method as seen in listing 9.7.

A drawback that XmlPull shares with SAX is its lack of an internal data structure to represent the document being parsed. This means you won't be able to perform random access into the document, and if documents get more complex, you'll have to maintain state about the whereabouts of the element you're currently looking at. XmlPull can support you here with the `getDepth` method, which tells you how deep you are into the XML tree. These are the trade-offs you have to take for choosing a stream-based parser.

> **NOTE** It should be mentioned that SAX can be seen as an abstraction of XmlPull because every SAX implementation can be implemented using a pull parser (and in fact, all of them are because they must first read a token from the stream before doing a callback). In that way, XmlPull can be understood as operating at an even lower level, but at the same time keeping a nice, easy interface.

Although both SAX and XmlPull have support for validating a document and even data types (given there's a schema file against which can be validated), the only data type they know on the API level is text, which means you have to transform strings to numbers or even subtrees to objects yourself. Recall the category subelement of a movie, which we may want to parse into a separate object.

We've talked to some extent about XML now. There's an entirely different solution to the problems discussed so far, one which is able to read a document into memory as a single data structure which can then be easily traversed, but without the performance penalties of the DOM. It's time to leave the realm of XML and enter the world of JavaScript. Wait, JavaScript? Enter JSON.

TECHNIQUE 46   Parsing JSON

The Ajax (Asynchronous JavaScript and XML) craze that accompanied the rise of Web 2.0 was a key element to giving modern websites a desktop application-like user experience. Interestingly, like the `XMLHttpRequest` object (never before has the invention—or rediscovery—of a single class made such a difference), AJAX made another thing popular, one which had been around for years, but the full potential of which had never been recognized: *JSON*, the *JavaScript Object Notation*.

JSON has been around since 1999, but was largely unknown outside the web development community until a few years ago. Like XML, JSON is an open, standardized data interchange format based on a subset of the JavaScript programming language. In fact, every JSON object is a valid JavaScript object, but not necessarily vice versa. It is by its nature a good choice for serializing data from a web server to a JavaScript host environment such as a web browser because a JSON server response can be executed as-is by the client using JavaScript's eval function. Because of its lean and simple, yet powerful way of representing all sorts of data, developers outside the JavaScript/ HTML world have discovered its potential to serve as a generic data representation and interchange format, particularly for use with web services that can be consumed by any client, not only web browsers. Though it's being used less often for storing data locally in a text-based form, more web services, such as Twitter, Qype, and Yahoo! FireEagle, have adopted JSON as a response format.

PROBLEM

You either want to integrate with a web service that only supports JSON, or you want to take advantage of JSON's benefits such as being able to efficiently create and manage textual representations of data structures in memory.

SOLUTION

Before looking at the JSON API bundled with Android, let's have a closer look at how JSON represents objects. If you're already familiar with JavaScript, then this will look familiar. If not, then JSON can still be quickly explained.

You can think of JSON objects as maps or object hashes. They have a single root element, and other elements (the values) are mapped to identifiers (the keys). Here's how this book could be modeled in JSON:

```
{
  "title": "Android in Practice",
  "price": 49.99,
  "authors": [
    { "name": "C. Collins" },
    { "name": "M. Galpin" },
    { "name": "M. Kaeppler" }
  ]
}
```

This simple data structure already combines all the kinds of syntax elements that JSON knows. Finally, something that's dead simple and tremendously useful at the same time—you seldom find that in computers these days!

Curly braces in JSON demarcate objects. An object is a map: it maps keys (the quotes are mandatory) to values. A value can again be an object, a string (any value put in double quotes becomes a string; you'll therefore have to escape double quotes that are part of the string itself as \"Hello!\"), or a number (with or without decimal point). Moreover, a value can also be an array of any of these. Arrays are demarcated using square brackets, and we'll see one in a second in listing 9.9.

Even though it's simple enough, you don't have to parse JSON documents yourself. Android comes with the reference JSON implementation from json.org, so you can use that straight away. Before showing you how to use it to parse JSON data, recall that we get our data from the TMDb web service, which incidentally also supports JSON. Let's look at what the response from listing 9.6 looks like when requested as JSON instead of XML (again we've left out some elements for brevity):

Listing 9.9   JSON response format of TMDb's Movie.imdbLookup method

```
[
    {
        "popularity":3,
        "translated":true,
        "adult":false,
        "language":"en",
        "original_name":"Inception",
        "name":"Inception",
        "alternative_name":"Eredet",
        "movie_type":"movie",
        "id":27205,
        "imdb_id":"tt1375666",
        "url":"http://www.themoviedb.org/movie/27205",
        "votes":52,
        "rating":9.0,
        "certification":"PG-13",
        "overview":"Dom Cobb (Leonardo DiCaprio) is a skilled thief,
    the best in the dangerous art of extraction: stealing valuable
    secrets from deep within the subconscious during the dream
    state when the mind is at its most vulnerable. ...",
        "released":"2010-07-16",
        "runtime":148,
        "version":226,
        "last_modified_at":"2010-08-19 16:04:03",
        ...
    }
]
```

As we can see, the result is an array with a single element because we've only requested a single movie. Now we need to turn this into a Movie object, so we finally need to use Android's JSON parser. Here's how that could look.

Listing 9.10   JsonMovieParser parses a TMDb movie document using JSON

```
public class JsonMovieParser {
    public static Movie parseMovie(InputStream json) throws Exception {
        BufferedReader reader = new BufferedReader(
            new InputStreamReader(json));
        StringBuilder sb = new StringBuilder();               ◁─┐  Holds server
                                                              ❶  response as string
        try {
            String line = reader.readLine();
```

```
        while (line != null) {
            sb.append(line);
            line = reader.readLine();
        }
    } catch (IOException e) {
        throw e;
    } finally {
        reader.close();
    }
    JSONArray jsonReply = new JSONArray(sb.toString());

    Movie movie = new Movie();
    JSONObject jsonMovie = jsonReply.getJSONObject(0);
    movie.setTitle(jsonMovie.getString("name"));
    movie.setRating(jsonMovie.getString("rating"));

    return movie;
    }
}
```

❷ Turn string into a JSONObject

❸ Get movie JSONObject

The JSON parser relies on the data being in memory entirely, so we have to read the response string into a buffer first ❶. We can then use this string to instantiate a JSON object (a `JSONArray` in this case, because the root element is an array), which effectively parses the JSON string into an internal key-value map ❷. We're interested in the first and only element of the array, so we get the `JSONObject` at position 0, which is the movie we're after ❸. Any such `JSONObject` has accessor methods to read its values such as strings, numbers, and other JSON objects or arrays.

DISCUSSION

You may have noticed a pattern here: our movie parser has been shrinking with every technique in this chapter! JSON is the most straightforward and simple way to parse a web service response. It's also efficient and lightweight: it's nothing more than a Java `HashMap` mapping strings to other objects. If you can use the Java `Map` interface, then you can use Android's JSON classes.

One implication of this is that the json.org parser may not be optimal if you need to access a small amount of data from a large document. You probably don't want to parse several megabytes of text into a JSON object because it'll be in memory all at once. In that sense, it's similar to what DOM is for XML; the document is kept in memory entirely. If you can't live with that, then XmlPull is probably your best bet.

JSON STREAMING PARSERS If your documents are large, but you absolutely must rely on JSON for some reason (say the data you want to access is only available in JSON), you may want to look for a stream-based JSON parser such as Jackson (http://jackson.codehaus.org) or Google's gson (http://code.google.com/p/google-gson). This means adding another dependency to your project, so choose wisely.

You should be aware of one subtlety when using Android's JSON parser: you should always know up front which values will definitely be part of the response when you parse it. That's because the get* methods of a `JSONObject` will throw an exception if you try to access a field which isn't there. For elements that can exist in some responses, but not in others (optional elements), you should use the opt* methods instead, which return null if the field you're trying to access doesn't exist. (For example, use optString instead of getString for accessing an optional string field.) We've covered a lot of ground here! You've not only seen how to connect to a real-world web service, we've also shown you how to parse a typical response using different kinds of parsers, each with their own pros and cons. You should now be well equipped for anything related to the consumption of web services in an Android application.

That only leaves a few more things to round it all up. We've talked about HTTP and the two popular data-interchange formats XML and JSON, but for a real-world application, you must be prepared to run into real-world problems, such as having to cope with network failures. The last section of this chapter contains techniques that, though maybe not as intriguing as connecting to a movie web service, are fundamental to any application dealing with HTTP networking. It's the icing on the cake, the things that make your application great instead of good, so even if "handling connection failover" sounds dusty to you, sticking around a while longer is going to be well worth it for you (and your application's users).

9.3   *How to gracefully recover from network failures*

If you've made it here, you already know everything you need to do HTTP-based networking on Android, and even how to parse the most common response formats. But this wouldn't be a good recipe book if we didn't venture past the basics, would it?

One thing we've ignored so far, and which is definitely going to happen (trust me) when taking your fancy web-enabled Android application on the streets, is network interruptions. Remember that users won't necessarily sit on their couch when using your applications. It's likely that they move around, and moving around can quickly mean roaming from one Wi-Fi network to the next, one cell-tower to another, or switching, say, from 3G to 2G because the signal strength is dropping. One tricky case is roaming from Wi-Fi to a data connection or vice versa because requests sent via the mobile carrier may be required to go through a proxy server, whereas when they may not when using Wi-Fi. This means two things:

1 We must employ a sensible logic for retrying failed requests (technique 47).
2 We must react to changes in the network configuration (technique 48).

We'll start by showing you how to implement an HTTP request-retry handler that is well suited for mobile use.

TECHNIQUE 47   Retrying requests using request-retry handlers

Pretend for a moment that you're in your office and want to go to lunch. While making your way to the street, you pull out your Android phone and fire up your favorite app and start browsing for nearby restaurants. Your phone is connected to your company Wi-Fi, but as you step outside, still searching for a good lunch spot, the connection suddenly breaks. The Wi-Fi's signal strength was too weak, so Android decided to switch over to the mobile data connection.

This is a common scenario: if your application makes heavy use of data connections, requests will fail all the time. A mobile network connection is flaky by nature. The question is this: what does that mean for your application? What happens when you try to send an HTTP request and the connection fails in between? You could catch the error and tell your user about it. But that's not trying hard, is it? If the request failed because your phone was switching over from Wi-Fi to 3G, then it's likely that the next request will succeed. So instead of bothering the user with an error dialog and asking them to try again, we can do it ourselves—using a proper request retry logic.

PROBLEM

Realizing that HTTP requests can fail when the user is on the move, you want to put a proper request-retry system in place so that when a request fails because of a flaky network, you can silently resend it.

SOLUTION

Assuming that you're going to use Apache `HttpClient`, and not Java's `HttpURLConnection`, we have good news: it ships with a simple system for retrying requests baked right in. Now, it sounds as if our problems are solved, but that's not quite true. We'll show you how the feature works, and then explain why that's often not sufficient, and how we can make it better.

`AbstractHttpClient` is the default base class that's part of the Apache `HttpClient` library. Any `HttpClient` implementation inheriting from `AbstractHttpClient`, including `DefaultHttpClient` (see techniques 42 and 43), will determine whether a request should be resent when an `IOException` occurred, and *only* then. Request failures because of other exceptions being raised will bubble up to the caller and not be retried at all. Whether a request will be retried is decided by an object of type `HttpRequestRetryHandler`. It defines a method called `retryRequest`, which is a decision method: it returns `true` if a request should be retried, or `false` if not. This method receives the exception that was raised, the number of attempts for sending that were already made, and the execution context for this request as arguments, so it can decide, based on this information, whether to retry a request.

If you don't want to provide custom decision logic for this, and if you're using `DefaultHttpClient`, then you don't have to: `DefaultHttpClient` defines a `DefaultHttpRequestRetryHandler` for you, which has a sensible default algorithm to decide this. Here are the cases in which it *won't* retry a request:

- *Execution count*—Don't retry a request if the maximum number of retries has been reached
- *Unrecoverable failures*—Don't retry a request if it failed because the host couldn't be resolved (DNS failure), the request timed out, the connection was explicitly refused by the server, or an SSH handshake failed
- *Request idempotency*—Don't retry a request if it's not idempotent (unsafe to send a second time, which is almost always the case for POST and DELETE), unless this check was disabled

You can customize the maximum number of attempts (default is 3) and whether sent requests should be retried even if that may be unsafe (default is `false`) directly in the request-retry handler; we'll show you how in a second. Customizing beyond that means you'll have to provide your own implementation.

Though these checks are fine, from a mobile point of view, there's one problem with the retry handler system in general: retries happen *immediately* after a request failed. To stick with the example of moving from Wi-Fi to 3G, which can take at least a second or more, this often means that the retry system in place is useless because it retries sending the request too quickly. You could alleviate this issue by setting the maximum number of retries to a much higher number, say 20, but what we're after is something based on time. A better solution would be to define a custom request-retry handler that reuses the decision logic from the default handler, but adds a short amount of idle time to give the phone a chance to properly recover from whatever caused the connection failure. That code follows.

Listing 9.11 MyMovies has been augmented to specify a custom request-retry handler

```
public class MyMovies extends ListActivity implements Callback,
        OnItemLongClickListener {

    private static final AbstractHttpClient httpClient;           ◁— ① Change type to AbstractHttpClient

    private static final HttpRequestRetryHandler retryHandler;    ◁┐ Declare request-retry ② handler

    static {
        ...
        httpClient = new DefaultHttpClient(cm, clientParams);

        retryHandler =
          new DefaultHttpRequestRetryHandler(5, false) {          ╱ ③ Inherit from default handler

            public boolean retryRequest(IOException ex, int execCount,
                    HttpContext context) {
                if (!super.retryRequest(ex, execCount, context)) {   ◁┐ Is resend ④ desired?
                    Log.d("HTTP retry-handler", "Won't retry");
                    return false;
                }
                try {
                    Thread.sleep(2000);                              ◁┐ Sleep before ⑤ next execution
                } catch (InterruptedException e) {
                }
                Log.d("HTTP retry-handler", "Retrying request...");
                return true;
            }
        };                                                          ⑥ Configure object to
        httpClient.setHttpRequestRetryHandler(retryHandler);        ◁— use handler
    }

    public static HttpClient getHttpClient() {
        return httpClient;
    }

    ...
}
```

We must first change the declared type of `HttpClient` to `AbstractHttpClient` **1** because the methods required to set custom handler objects aren't part of the `Http-Client` interface. We also store a static reference to our custom handler object **2** In the static initializer where we set up our client object, we now initialize the request-retry handler by inheriting from the default implementation **3**. At this point, we also pass 5 as the maximum number of attempts that should be made to retry a request (we leave the `requestSentRetryEnabled` parameter at `false`). We leave the decision whether to retry a request to the default implementation **4** because it does a good job at doing that, as mentioned earlier. We want to add an idle time of two seconds, after which we retry the request, so we let the thread sleep for this time **5**. We must also tell `HttpClient` to use our custom handler instead of the built-in one **6**.

DISCUSSION

Let's recap what we've done here: by implementing and setting a custom `HttpReques-tRetryHandler`, we've told `HttpClient` what to do should a web server drop the connection on us while we're trying to send a request. Dropping connection here means anything resulting in a Java `IOException` while the request is being processed in the network stack. In our case, we retry the request up to five times, whereas we leave it to the `DefaultHttpRequestRetryHandler` implementation to decide whether a request should be retried at all. Before we allow the request to be resent, we let the thread sleep for a brief period to give the device a chance to recover from situations such as changing the network connection from Wi-Fi to mobile network.

This code will work fine in most situations, but still has one limitation: it doesn't cope with connection failures that are purely caused by the web server. If a web server is under high load, it may decide to send a 5xx response code to the client. For instance, 503 (service unavailable) and 504 (gateway timeout) are common symptoms of systems that are under heavy load, and often indicate temporary failures. An example would be a web service where the application server waits for the database to respond, but it doesn't do in a timely manner. These timeouts can be short because a database server is expected to usually respond quickly.

In this case, it's likely that a subsequent request will succeed after waiting a second or two, so it makes sense to retry these requests as well. Unfortunately, this doesn't work with our current solution because it'll only try to recover from I/O errors, but a 5xx is a valid and complete HTTP response that, from the perspective of `HttpClient`, isn't a failure at all. If you want to write a truly robust web service connector, you'll probably want to add a second retry layer around `HttpClient` that you'll have to write yourself. This can be as simple as a loop that sleeps for a few seconds and resends the request a certain number of times.

We've mentioned in the section opening that connection failures aren't the only issue we have to deal with. If we resend a request after the network configuration changed (such as the proxy server settings) then this and all subsequent attempts could also fail. The following technique explains what to look out for and how to deal with it.

Handling network configuration changes

We explained in the previous technique that retrying failed requests is a sensible thing to do for a mobile application. One example we mentioned where it makes sense to retry requests is when the device switches over from a Wi-Fi access point to a mobile data access point (APN) because the user moved out of Wi-Fi range, or switching from one APN to another while roaming between carrier networks. There's one caveat here: retrying a failed request using the new network connection (carrier APN instead of Wi-Fi) may result in it failing again, but this time for another reason—the new APN uses different settings.

Even if the user isn't roaming between networks, an APN can still have special settings specific to that APN that your application may need to account for when sending requests over it. These include APN usernames and passwords, or proxy servers through which requests will be sent. Figure 9.9 shows Android's default interface for changing APN settings on your phone (screenshot taken from the Android emulator).

In any event, you must somehow get hold of these settings, and be notified when, for example, the proxy server changes while your application is running, so that you can update `HttpClient` to send requests through the new proxy server.

Figure 9.9   Via the Edit Access Point screen, users can configure their carrier's APN settings for mobile data connections, including proxy servers. Whenever the user saves these settings while your application is running, it's a good idea to handle them to ensure your requests won't suddenly fail.

PROBLEM

Being on the move means that network configuration may change while your application is running. To make sure that your networking code remains functional, you must handle changes to these settings.

SOLUTION

Changes to APN configuration or changes in connectivity such as connection loss are managed by a framework class called `ConnectivityManager`. In these events, `ConnectivityManager` will send a broadcast message to all subscribers, including the details of the network state change. Broadcast messages in Android are sent using broadcast `Intents`, so you need a `BroadcastReceiver` object to handle them. First, let's look at how you'd register such a receiver from an `Activity`:

```
public void onCreate(Bundle savedInstanceState) {
    ...
    registerReceiver(new ConnectionChangedBroadcastReceiver(),
        new IntentFilter(ConnectivityManager.CONNECTIVITY_ACTION));
}
```

As you can see, we have to subscribe to the CONNECTIVITY_ACTION of the Connection-Manager using an IntentFilter which makes sure that we only receive broadcast Intents of that particular kind because that's the only thing we're interested in for this technique. That's all the setup we need: from here on we'll always be informed about changes to network connectivity! The more interesting part here is our Connection-ChangedBroadcastReceiver. A BroadcastReceiver exposes only a single method, onReceive, which is where we'll deal with changing network configuration. The following listing shows how this could be implemented for the MyMovies application in case of a changing proxy server.

NOTE For an application to receive broadcast events about connectivity changes, it must request the ACCESS_NETWORK_STATE permission in AndroidManifest.

Listing 9.12 A BroadcastReceiver that handles network configuration changes

```
public class ConnectionChangedBroadcastReceiver extends BroadcastReceiver {
    public void onReceive(Context context, Intent intent) {
        NetworkInfo nwInfo = intent.getParcelableExtra(          ❶ Read network
            ConnectivityManager.EXTRA_NETWORK_INFO);                info from intent

        HttpParams httpParams = MyMovies.getHttpClient().getParams();
        if (nwInfo.getType() == ConnectivityManager.TYPE_MOBILE) {
            String proxyHost = Proxy.getHost(context);          ❷ Get current
            if (proxyHost == null) {                               proxy host
                proxyHost = Proxy.getDefaultHost();
            }
            int proxyPort = Proxy.getPort(context);             ❸ Get current
            if (proxyPort == -1) {                                 proxy port
                proxyPort = Proxy.getDefaultPort();
            }
            if (proxyHost != null && proxyPort > -1) {
                HttpHost proxy = new HttpHost(proxyHost, proxyPort);
                httpParams.setParameter(ConnRoutePNames.DEFAULT_PROXY, proxy);
            } else {
                httpParams.setParameter(ConnRoutePNames.DEFAULT_PROXY, null);
            }
        } else {
            httpParams.setParameter(ConnRoutePNames.DEFAULT_PROXY, null);
        }
    }                                                        Set current values
}                                                              on HttpClient  ❹
```

The information about what has changed is represented by a NetworkInfo object and is carried in the broadcast Intent that was sent, so we first have to retrieve it from the Intent's bundle extras ❶. If we're dealing with a mobile data connection

(TYPE_MOBILE), then we read the proxy host and port the user entered in the APN settings, or if either isn't set, use the default values (❷ and ❸). If both values are set and valid, we update our HttpClient's connection parameters to always send requests through the given proxy ❹.

And that's it! The HTTP client is now automatically updated to use the correct proxy server settings whenever the user changes it in the mobile network settings. Even if the user doesn't explicitly set it, but a default proxy is set by the carrier, our application will still work because the Intent is fired not only when the settings change, but also the first time our application starts.

DISCUSSION

The NetworkInfo object is worth looking at more closely. If you look at the class documentation, you'll find additional values carried in the Intent that you can read and potentially present to the user (such as EXTRA_REASON and EXTRA_EXTRA_INFO). But for logging, the most helpful thing is its toString method because it includes all this data already. It'll append all the information it carries into a text line useful for debug logs, which can be great when testing your application in different mobile environments. Here's how such a line looks:

```
NetworkInfo: type: mobile[UMTS], state: CONNECTED/CONNECTED, reason:
simLoaded, extra: internet, roaming: false, failover: false, isAvailable:
true
```

The type, state, and reason values are useful to monitor. Note that we decided earlier to be informed about any kind of connectivity state change (by passing ConnectivityManager.CONNECTIVITY_ACTION when registering our broadcast receiver), but then only handled changes to the proxy server settings. If you're only interested in that, then it's sufficient to register for the Proxy.PROXY_CHANGE_ACTION and Android won't notify you about other connectivity changes anymore. That's pretty much all there is to say about this matter. It's a simple solution to a problem that is, unfortunately, ignored by many developers—but not you!

9.4 Summary

This chapter was fairly technical. But trust us when we say that your users will appreciate any application that has robust networking code! Let's recap what we learned.

We started by showing you how to send HTTP requests on Android, first by using the tools Java already has: HttpURLConnection is fast, simple, and reasonably powerful, but quite an ugly duckling. That's why we quickly proceeded to Apache HttpClient, and we hope it has become clear why Google decided that HttpURLConnection alone doesn't cut it. HttpClient is easier to use, more flexible, and a true powerhouse in terms of features. But its simple and intuitive interface, driven by the convention-over-configuration paradigm, can be deceptive when used in multithreaded environments such as Android. For that reason, we showed you how to properly configure HttpClient to avoid problems in the first place.

In the second section, we moved past the necessary but boring HTTP basics and rewrote MyMovies to connect to a web service and parse its responses using different kinds of parsers (push XML, pull XML, and JSON) to give you a solid understanding of their pros and cons.

In the final section we went back to HTTP and networking, and showed you how to make your networking code even more robust by both handling network failures using request-retry handlers and by properly handling network configuration that may change while the user is on the run. Note that here again, many of these things have been implemented in the ignition utility library, so as to make your life a bit easier!

Speaking of being on the run. Our next chapter will be all about location and moving around! The ability to resolve a user's position using their phone has almost become a commodity these days, but it's an amazing and immensely powerful feature nonetheless. That's why you'll learn everything about GPS and other location-based service features on Android in chapter 10.

Location is everything

In this chapter

- Using latitude and longitude
- Finding the user's current location
- Building a map-based application

> *There isn't a parallel of latitude but thinks it would have been the equator if it had had its rights.*
>
> —Mark Twain

One of the biggest factors in the appeal of smartphones is their location-awareness. It's incredible to have a device you carry around in your pocket that can tell you exactly where you are on the planet. Thanks to brilliant engineers, science fiction is now reality. Yet, modern mobile devices take the wonder even further. Beyond pinpointing location, they provide access to a worldwide web of data, device sensors, and a market of inventions and ideas.

Developers have used Android's location capabilities to create many ingenious applications. Among them are applications that enable other phone functions based on where you are at a certain time; help you track activities when hiking, biking, or running; tell you when interesting attractions and services are nearby and where they're located; allow you to track your device remotely if it's lost or misplaced;

334

calculate current speed and other metrics; enable more precise data for ads and other commercial uses; and more.

Now it's your turn. Once you learn about the location-related APIs and capabilities that the Android platform provides, you can use them to create the next great location-aware application. To that end, in this chapter we'll start with a primer on geospatial coordinates and how location-based services work. Then we'll look at the specific `LocationProvider` implementations that Android includes. These provide multiple ways to determine location, each with potentially different capabilities. We'll access the providers, determine what is and isn't available, and set up listeners for location-based services through the `LocationManager`. We'll also explore some other location features such as converting an address into coordinates and vice versa using the `Geocoder` class.

Once we have the basic capabilities in hand, we'll build an application that uses Google APIs to determine our current location at any given time and then place markers on an interactive map. This will involve using a `MapView` and managing it from a `MapActivity`.

10.1 A brief introduction to geospatial coordinates

Before we rush headlong into building Android applications that use geospatial coordinates, we'll take a brief detour to define the related terms. We promise this won't be a long journey, just a quick walk down a side street to fill in some background for those who might not be familiar with the concepts. If you're already comfortable with geographic coordinate systems, and latitude and longitude, then you may wish to jump ahead to section 10.2 where we'll work with the location providers available in most Android devices.

10.1.1 Latitude and longitude

Though it's true that most developers are probably at least vaguely familiar with latitude and longitude, not everyone is, and there are a few subtleties when it comes to how they're expressed in different contexts. Here, we'll define these terms because they're the basis of all cartography and navigation, and they're the system used by Android location providers. We'll start with the formal definitions (derived from Wikipedia), and then break them down.

- *Latitude*—The angular distance of a location on the Earth north or south of the Equator. Latitude is an angle, and is usually measured in degrees (marked with °). The Equator has a latitude of 0°, the North Pole has a latitude of 90° N (north), and the South Pole has a latitude of 90° S (south).

  Latitude expresses locations on the Earth in terms of "up or down" if you're looking at a globe. The top of the globe is the North Pole, which is 90° north latitude. If you trace your finger down the globe and arrive at the midpoint, that's the equator—0°. If you continue to the bottom of the globe, you arrive at the South Pole, which is 90° south latitude. Latitude expresses north-south measurement, and latitude lines form parallel circles around the globe.

- *Longitude*—The angular distance of a point's meridian from the *Prime Meridian*. Longitude is an angle, and is usually measured in degrees (marked with °). Lines of longitude are often referred to as *meridians*. The Prime Meridian has a longitude of 0°; the *Antimeridian* has a longitude of 180°.

  Longitude expresses "left and right" if you're looking at a globe. This is harder to pinpoint than latitude because you have to pick a starting point (you don't have natural poles based on the axis of the Earth's rotation to start from). The Prime Meridian, by current international convention, passes through the Royal Observatory, Greenwich, in London England. (Throughout history, different societies have placed it in different locations—thankfully, we universally agree on where it is today.) This is our nonnatural starting point for longitude.

We use degrees to indicate latitude and longitude because both are based on angles. To indicate more precision, we can also use *minutes*, and further *seconds*. For example, the Tropic of Capricorn (one of the other named lines of latitude on Earth besides the Equator) is located at 23° 26' 21" S, or 23 degrees, 26 minutes, 21 seconds south. Any degree/minute/second number can also be represented in decimal form using the following formula:

```
Decimal value = Degrees + (Minutes/60) + (Seconds/3600).
```

This means 23° 26' 21" S can be written in decimal form as -23.439167. It's important to note that when using decimal form, you use positive numbers for north and east, and negative numbers for south and west. Android's tools and APIs can generally support both forms, and you can specify the format you prefer (or convert between them). The default on Android, as is natural for a computer, is the decimal form.

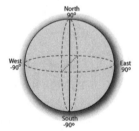

Figure 10.1 shows both latitude and longitude superimposed on a sphere representing the Earth. You can see how a combination of latitude and longitude can be used to express an exact location anywhere on the globe.[1]

Figure 10.1 Latitude and longitude represented on a globe and showing the positive and negative numbers used to represent them in decimal form

This quick voyage around geospatial coordinate systems is by no means comprehensive, but it should be enough to provide the essential background you'll need to start working with location providers and data points.

10.1.2 Potential issues to look for

So far so good: overall latitude and longitude are understandable enough. Yet, there are a few gotchas relative to conventions to look for. These are expressed in table 10.1.

Most of the time, you won't be dealing with complex calculations at either the poles or the Antimeridian. The main thing you need to keep in mind when working

---

[1] Technically, longitude becomes singular, or undefined, at the poles, but we won't worry about that unless and until we're planning an extreme expedition.

Table 10.1 Gotcha's to look for when working with latitude and longitude

Watch for	Why
Positive versus negative values	When you're expressing latitude as an integer, positive is north and negative south, and with longitude, positive is east and negative west.
Latitude is first, usually	A common convention (International Maritime Organization, and others) is to display latitude/longitude with latitude first. The Android APIs also do this, but several Android tools use the opposite! The emulator `geo fix` command and DDMS GUI both place longitude first.
Calculation complications	When you're calculating with latitude and longitude, you need to be careful around the poles, and to a lesser degree the Antimeridian. Because longitudinal lines converge at the poles (they're not parallel like latitude), they become undefined. And, the Antimeridian presents a discontinuity that you need to account for (it changes from positive to negative and you may have coordinates from each side).

with coordinates via the Android APIs is the nature of negative versus positive numbers, and the inconsistency of the tools. For example, if you're trying to locate Buenos Aires, Argentina, and you mistakenly use 34.60/58.37 instead of -34.60/-58.37, you'll end up with a location in the desert in a remote part of Iran. Buenos Aires is south of the equator, and west of the Prime Meridian, so both its latitude and longitude are negative. Also, if you use the `geo fix` command from the emulator shell and pass it the correct coordinates for Buenos Aires, -34.60/-58.37, you'll end up with a location in the middle of the Southern Ocean (because a few Android tools, inexplicably, expect longitude first).

Along with understanding latitude and longitude in general, and being aware of some of the potential problems you can run into when working with coordinates on Android, you may find a few other metrics useful.

10.1.3 Other metrics

In addition to latitude and longitude, which represent vertical and horizontal placement on a sphere, some geospatial sensors, including location providers in Android, can also represent other metrics such as elevation, bearing, and speed.

Elevation represents altitude, or distance above sea level on the Earth. Bearing is trickier because it has different definitions in different contexts. In marine navigation, *bearing* means the direction (in degrees East of true north) from one's current location to another point. *Speed* refers to the how fast something is traveling over ground.

In Android development terms, you'll access the `LocationManager` to determine which `LocationProvider` classes are available, and then you'll use the providers to query for latitude, longitude, elevation, bearing, and speed.

10.2 Location managers, providers, and listeners

To learn how to work with Android's location facilities, we're going to start by building a sample application that will take us through the basics. This application, which we'll call LocationInfo, will serve two purposes: it'll allow us to get familiar with `Location-Manager` and `LocationProvider` to see what's available, and it'll enable us to get our current location using a `LocationListener`. Once we get through our first application, we'll base a larger application on what we learn next.

The `LocationManager` class is the gateway into all the location related services on Android. It's a system service that allows you to access location providers, set up location update listeners and proximity alerts, and more. The `LocationProvider` class, on the other hand, is provides location data. `LocationListener` instances use specified providers to asynchronously return location updates to applications.

The first portion of the LocationInfo sample application shows the types of `LocationProvider` classes available, and drills down into the data each provider is capable of returning. Figure 10.2 shows what this looks like when running on an Android device.

 GRAB THE PROJECT: LOCATIONINFO You can get the source code for this project, and/or the packaged APK to run it, at the *Android in Practice* code website. Because some code listings here are shortened to focus on specific concepts, we recommend that you download the complete source code and follow along within Eclipse (or your favorite IDE or text editor).

Source: http://mng.bz/b1X5, APK file: http://mng.bz/pLh2

As we can see in figure 10.2, the available `LocationProvider` types are shown in a `ListView`. From there, each one is selectable. When a particular provider is selected, we query it to show all the data it can provide.

The second portion of LocationInfo concerns the Get Current Location via GPS button at the bottom of figure 10.2. When that button is clicked, we check to make sure the GPS is enabled. If it isn't, we prompt the user to enable it. If so, the settings

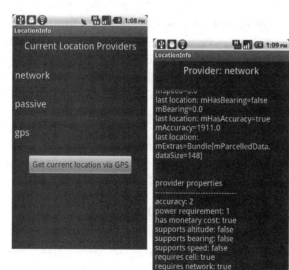

Figure 10.2   LocationInfo showing the location providers available (left) and the details of a selected provider (right)

Using a real device versus the emulator

For several of the examples in this chapter the emulator will show different results than the screen shots. Either the emulator doesn't have certain location capabilities, or it doesn't have any location information. Because of this we've been careful to say "on a device" in the screenshot descriptions in several places. We recommend you use a real device for these examples if you can. If you don't have access to a device, you can still use these examples, but you'll need to enable the relevant providers in Menu -> Settings -> Location and Security, and you'll need to send location information to the emulator using the DDMS Emulator Control -> Location Controls form.

screen is displayed. Once we know it's enabled, we check for a recent location fix. If no recent fix is available, we use a LocationListener to poll for a new location update. The screens for this portion of the application are shown in figure 10.3.

Now that we know what the LocationInfo sample application will look like, it's time to dive in and build it. We'll start with the LocationManager, which again is the gateway to the location services Android provides.

10.2.1 Checking in with the LocationManager

The LocationManager can be used to query for a list of available location providers, get a reference to a provider by name or capability criteria, get the last-known location for a named provider (which may be null, or very old), register for several types of location updates and alerts, and more.

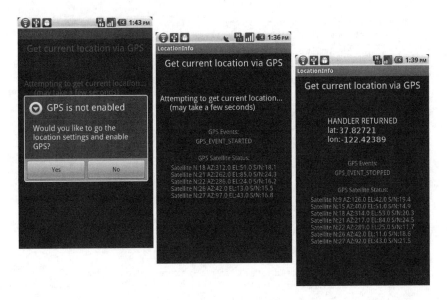

Figure 10.3 Enabling the GPS provider and then using it to get current location details

Before we can use the `LocationManager`, we need to mention that location services require special permissions in an application's manifest. We've seen permissions used in several previous applications, and we explained them in chapter 2. For the LocationInfo application, we're using the following manifest permission:

```
<uses-permission android:name="android.permission.ACCESS_FINE_LOCATION" />
```

This permission is something the user can see and agree to when they install our application. If they don't like the idea of allowing our application to get their location, they can choose not to install it. If we don't have this permission, we can't use the `Location-Manager` or any `LocationProvider` instances—if we try, we'll get a `SecurityException`.

Once the permissions are in place, we then set up the `Main Activity` of `Location-Info`, which demonstrates how you get a handle to the `LocationManager`, and then how you use it to get a list of the currently available location providers. This is seen in the following listing.

Listing 10.1 The `Main Activity` of the `LocationInfo` application

```
public class Main extends Activity implements OnItemClickListener {

    public static final String LOG_TAG = "LocationInfo";
    public static final String PROVIDER_NAME = "PROVIDER_NAME";

    private LocationManager locationMgr;                    ◁──┐    Include
    private ListView providersList;                          ❶  LocationManager
    private Button getLoc;

    @Override
    protected void onCreate(Bundle savedInstanceState) {
        super.onCreate(savedInstanceState);
        setContentView(R.layout.main);

        locationMgr = (LocationManager)                     ❷  Instantiate
            getSystemService(Context.LOCATION_SERVICE);   ◁──┘  LocationManager

        ArrayAdapter<String> adapter =
            new ArrayAdapter<String>(this,
                android.R.layout.simple_list_item_1,        ❸  Use manager to get
                locationMgr.getAllProviders());           ◁──┘  list of providers

        providersList = (ListView) findViewById(R.id.location_providers);
        providersList.setAdapter(adapter);
        providersList.setOnItemClickListener(this);        ◁──┐  Assign ListView
                                                             ❹  click listener
        getLoc = (Button) findViewById(R.id.getloc_button);
        getLoc.setOnClickListener(new OnClickListener() {
            public void onClick(View v) {
                startActivity(new Intent(Main.this, GetLocationWithGPS.class));
            }
        });
    }

    @Override                                               ❺  Implement
    public void onItemClick(AdapterView<?> parent, View view,   ListView click
            int position, long id) {                      ◁──┘  listener
        TextView textView = (TextView) view;
        String providerName = textView.getText().toString();
        Intent intent = new Intent(Main.this, ProviderDetail.class);
```

```
        intent.putExtra(PROVIDER_NAME, providerName);
        startActivity(intent);
    }
}
```

The LocationManager ❶, like other system services, is accessed via a getSystemService call using the Context.LOCATION_SERVICE constant ❷. Once you have a reference to the LocationManager, you can get a list of all the LocationProviders available ❸. In this case, we're populating an Adapter for a ListView with the list of provider names.

In order to respond when a user clicks on a provider name in the ListView, we've assigned a this click listener ❹ and overridden onItemClick locally ❺. The Intent in our click listener will launch the ProviderDetail activity with the selected provider name as extra data. The ProviderDetail activity will then instantiate the selected LocationProvider and query the last-known location and settings, as we'll see next.

10.2.2 Using a LocationProvider

As figure 10.2 demonstrates, the LocationManager returns three network providers available with the test device we used to take the screenshots. Note the provider names:

- network
- gps
- passive

The *network* provider uses the mobile network or Wi-Fi to try to determine the best location it can using information available at access points or through triangulation. It works, but it's less accurate than the *gps* provider, which uses a GPS receiver in the device to triangulate via satellites. The *passive* provider is a sort of proxy provider. It was introduced in Android 2.2 for the purpose of listening in on location updates when other applications or system services request them, rather than having to initiate a fix yourself.

> **FIXES AREN'T CHEAP** Getting a location fix isn't cheap. It can take some time, and it can consume a lot of resources. If you don't need updates right away, but instead can use an intermittent tally of location changes, consider the passive provider.

> **DON'T OVERLOOK THE NETWORK PROVIDER** Even though the GPS provider is more accurate than the network provider (and we're going to use the GPS provider for our example here because it works in the emulator), don't forget about the network provider. In many cases, especially when a device is indoors, the network provider will be the best available provider. You'll often want to use both the GPS and network providers and cascade gracefully if one or the other isn't available.

Once you select a provider to use, you'll get a reference to it via the manager, which you can use to get the last-known location and probe its capabilities. The capabilities include how accurate it is, whether it's free, how much power it uses, whether it includes altitude and bearing, and so on. A simple example of this is seen in the previously noted ProviderDetail activity, shown next.

Listing 10.2 `ProviderDetail`

```
public class ProviderDetail extends Activity {

    private LocationManager locationMgr;

    private TextView title;
    private TextView detail;

    @Override
    protected void onCreate(Bundle savedInstanceState) {
        super.onCreate(savedInstanceState);
        setContentView(R.layout.title_detail);

        locationMgr = (LocationManager)
            getSystemService(Context.LOCATION_SERVICE);

        title = (TextView) findViewById(R.id.title);
        detail = (TextView) findViewById(R.id.detail);
    }

    @Override
    protected void onResume() {
        super.onResume();

        String providerName =
            getIntent().getStringExtra("PROVIDER_NAME");      ❶ Get provider
                                                                name from Intent
        Location lastLocation =
            locationMgr.getLastKnownLocation(providerName);    ❷ Get last-
                                                                  known
        LocationProvider provider =                              location
            locationMgr.getProvider(providerName);           ❸ Get Location-
                                                               Provider by
        StringBuilder sb = new StringBuilder();                 name

        sb.append("location manager data");
        sb.append("\n------------------------------");
        if (lastLocation != null) {
            sb.append("\n");
            Printer printer = new StringBuilderPrinter(sb);
            lastLocation.dump(printer, "last location: ");
        } else {
            sb.append("\nlast location: null\n");
        }

        sb.append("\n");
        sb.append("\nprovider properties");
        sb.append("\n------------------------------");
        sb.append("\naccuracy: " + provider.getAccuracy());
        sb.append("\npower requirement: "
            + provider.getPowerRequirement());
        sb.append("\nhas monetary cost: "
            + provider.hasMonetaryCost());                   ❹ Query
        sb.append("\nsupports altitude: "                       provider
            + provider.supportsAltitude());                     capabilities
        sb.append("\nsupports bearing: "
            + provider.supportsBearing());
        sb.append("\nsupports speed: "
            + provider.supportsSpeed());
```

```
        sb.append("\nrequires cell: "
            + provider.requiresCell());
        sb.append("\nrequires network: "
            + provider.requiresNetwork());
```

Query provider capabilities ❹

```
        // . . . GpsStatus details left out of listing for brevity
        // (available only for GPS provider)

        title.setText("Provider: " + providerName);
        detail.setText(sb.toString());
    }
}
```

The first step in the `ProviderDetail` activity is to establish which provider the user selected, by name, using the `Intent` extra data ❶. Then we see a call to getting the last-known location, which we'll talk more about momentarily ❷. After that, we come to our first usage of a `LocationProvider`.

Here we get the `LocationProvider` via the manager using the name supplied ❸. Once we have the `LocationProvider`, we call the methods it provides to see what its requirements and capabilities are ❹. We're just printing out these values to demonstrate what's available, but you can see how these could be used to determine whether the provider is adequate for a certain purpose.

Getting back to the last-known location, we've seen that by using the provider name, we can query the `LocationManager` for this information without instantiating the provider itself. This is convenient and worth a check, but not something you should rely upon. The last-known location may be null or old. Nevertheless, if it's there, and it's recent, a last-known location can save you a lot of time and trouble trying to get a fix on where you are (or most recently were).

Android puts all the details about a location fix into a `Location` class. This class has all the properties you might expect: latitude, longitude, provider name, time, speed, bearing, and so on. Some items may not be populated depending on the capability of the provider. Time is a key element. Time is represented as an epoch stamp (number of milliseconds UTC since January 1, 1970). The last fix could be seconds old, in which case the device is likely still in the same vicinity. Or, it could be days or weeks old, which is probably not a reliable indicator of current location.

If the last-known location isn't present at all, or is older than you're comfortable with, you can set up a `LocationListener` to try to get a more recent fix.

10.2.3 *Using a LocationListener*

To get your current location or be notified of location changes on an ongoing basis, establish a `LocationListener`. In essence, a `LocationListener` is registered using one of several `LocationManager` methods that allow you to pass in the name of the provider you want to use, along with a callback listener (and a few other properties, such as time and distance, as needed).

TECHNIQUE 49   Checking the status of a LocationProvider

A LocationListener is simple in theory. It's a trivial class that has callback methods that specify when a location has changed, when a provider status has changed, or when that provider has been enabled or disabled. Even with that clear design, there are a few difficulties in using a listener correctly.

PROBLEM

How do you determine whether a certain provider is enabled? And if not enabled, how do you prompt the user to enable that provider because your application may require it?

SOLUTION

The LocationInfo application invokes the GetLocationWithGPS activity when the aptly named Get Current Location via GPS button seen in figure 10.2 is clicked. This activity has several key things going on within it. The first thing we'll touch on is a simple check whether the GPS provider is enabled, and if it isn't, prompting the user to enable it via the Android settings application. This is done in the onResume method with an AlertDialog and an Intent.

Listing 10.3   The onResume method checking whether the GPS provider is enabled

```
public class GetLocationWithGPS extends Activity {

    public static final String LOC_DATA = "LOC_DATA";

    private LocationManager locationMgr;
    private Handler handler;

    private TextView title;
    private TextView detail;

    // . . . onCreate method in next listing

    @Override
    protected void onResume() {
        super.onResume();

        if (!locationMgr.isProviderEnabled(            ❶ Is provider
            android.location.LocationManager.GPS_PROVIDER)) {     enabled?
            AlertDialog.Builder builder =
                new AlertDialog.Builder(this);              ❷ Use AlertDialog
            builder.setTitle("GPS is not enabled")            if not
                .setMessage(
                    "Would you like to go to the location settings
                        and enable GPS?")
                .setCancelable(true)
                .setPositiveButton("Yes",
                    new DialogInterface.OnClickListener() {
                        public void onClick(DialogInterface dialog, int id) {
                            startActivity(
                                new Intent(                    ❸ Take user
                                Settings.ACTION_SECURITY_SETTINGS));    to settings
                        }
                    })
                .setNegativeButton("No",
```

```
                    new DialogInterface.OnClickListener() {
                        public void onClick(DialogInterface dialog, int id) {
                            dialog.cancel();
                                finish();
                            }
                        });
            AlertDialog alert = builder.create();
            alert.show();
        } else {
            LocationHelper locationHelper =
                new LocationHelper(locationMgr,
                    handler, Main.LOG_TAG);
            locationHelper.getCurrentLocation(30);
        }
}
```

Set up LocationHelper for later

If you've used an Android device for any length of time, you're probably familiar with a dialog that resembles the leftmost screen in figure 10.3, where we prompt the user to enable GPS. For example, the built-in Maps application on Android has a similar dialog when trying to provide directions (navigation).

To achieve this, we check whether the provider is enabled using the `LocationMan-`ager ❶. If the provider isn't enabled, we then set up an `AlertDialog` ❷ that displays security settings screen via an `Intent`, where the user can elect to enable GPS ❸. Knowing the exact location of a device/person isn't something an application can automatically enable, for security reasons (hence the setting being in Location & Security on the main settings menu). If the user chooses to enable it (or it's already enabled), then our activity will take the other path and set up the `LocationHelper` ❹.

DISCUSSION

Checking whether a certain location provider is enabled is a straightforward task. Also, when a provider isn't enabled and your application requires it, you should fail fast. You should let the user know that you can't continue without the provider, and offer them the chance to enable it. If they don't enable said provider, you can then pare down the functionality of your application or simply quit.

If the provider in question is enabled, the next step is to utilize it to get data or perform location updates. Use `LocationListener` to get location updates.

TECHNIQUE 50   **Determining current location with a LocationListener**

Location providers return location information to interested applications through the use of registered observers with the `LocationListener` class. For our purposes, we've placed the details of using a `LocationListener` in a `LocationHelper` class. We've done this to encapsulate some of the details of getting the current location and to make reuse easier.

PROBLEM

You need to determine the current device location using a `LocationListener`, and you need that listener to attach itself, listen for a specified amount of time to get a fix, and then detach itself when no longer needed to save resources.

SOLUTION

To use a LocationListener, we're going to rely on the LocationHelper class we saw at the end of listing 10.3. We'll set up and tear down the listener, and we'll let it communicate back with our Activity using a Handler. Setting up the handler and getting ready to use the helper takes us to the onCreate method of the GetLocationWithGPS Activity, shown here.

Listing 10.4 The onCreate method and the Handler used with LocationHelper

```
@Override
  protected void onCreate(Bundle savedInstanceState) {
      super.onCreate(savedInstanceState);
      setContentView(R.layout.get_location);

      title = (TextView) findViewById(R.id.title);
      detail = (TextView) findViewById(R.id.detail);

      title.setText("Get current location via GPS");
      detail.setText("Attempting to get current location...\n
         (may take a few seconds)");

      locationMgr = (LocationManager)
         getSystemService(Context.LOCATION_SERVICE);      ❶ Setup
                                                              Handler
      handler = new Handler() {
         public void handleMessage(Message m) {            ❷ Handle
             if (m.what ==                                    location
                LocationHelper.MESSAGE_CODE_LOCATION_FOUND) {   found
                detail.setText("HANDLER RETURNED\nlat:"
                    + m.arg1 + "\nlon:" + m.arg2);         ❸ Handle
             } else if (m.what ==                             location
                 LocationHelper.MESSAGE_CODE_LOCATION_NULL) {  not found
                detail.setText("HANDLER RETURNED\nunable to get location");
             } else if (m.what ==
                 LocationHelper.
                    MESSAGE_CODE_PROVIDER_NOT_PRESENT) {
                detail.setText("HANDLER RETURNED\nprovider not present");
             }
         }
      };
  }
```

Handle provider
not present ❹

The Handler class is used to send and process Message (and Runnable) objects on a thread's MessageQueue. We initially learned about Handler in chapter 5. We'll be using it to allow our helper to pass data back to our Activity.

We set up the Handler by creating an anonymous instance that overrides handleMessage ❶. Inside handleMessage, we cope with the three possibilities we'll expect when we later use our helper to try to get the current location. These include location found and returned ❷, location not found so null ❸, and the provider itself is null ❹.

The bulk of the location work is then passed off to the LocationHelper class, which is shown next.

Listing 10.5 The LocationHelper class

```java
public class LocationHelper {

    public static final int MESSAGE_CODE_LOCATION_FOUND = 1;
    public static final int MESSAGE_CODE_LOCATION_NULL = 2;
    public static final int MESSAGE_CODE_PROVIDER_NOT_PRESENT = 3;

    private static final int FIX_RECENT_BUFFER_TIME = 30000;

    private LocationManager locationMgr;
    private LocationListener locationListener;
    private Handler handler;
    private Runnable handlerCallback;
    private String providerName;
    private String logTag;

    public LocationHelper(LocationManager locationMgr,
        Handler handler, String logTag) {
        this.locationMgr = locationMgr;
        this.locationListener = new LocationListenerImpl();
        this.handler = handler;
        this.handlerCallback = new Thread() {
            public void run() {
                endListenForLocation(null);
            }
        };

        Criteria criteria = new Criteria();
        criteria.setAccuracy(Criteria.ACCURACY_FINE);
        this.providerName = locationMgr.getBestProvider(criteria, true);

        this.logTag = logTag;
    }

    public void getCurrentLocation(int durationSeconds) {

        if (this.providerName == null) {
            sendLocationToHandler(MESSAGE_CODE_PROVIDER_NOT_PRESENT, 0, 0);
            return;
        }

        Location lastKnown = locationMgr.getLastKnownLocation(providerName);
        if (lastKnown != null &&
                lastKnown.getTime() >=
                (System.currentTimeMillis() - FIX_RECENT_BUFFER_TIME)) {
            sendLocationToHandler(MESSAGE_CODE_LOCATION_FOUND,
                (int) (lastKnown.getLatitude() * 1e6),
                (int) (lastKnown.getLongitude() * 1e6));
        } else {
            listenForLocation(providerName, durationSeconds);
        }
    }

    private void sendLocationToHandler(int msgId, int lat, int lon) {
        Message msg = Message.obtain(handler, msgId, lat, lon);
        handler.sendMessage(msg);
    }
```

- ① **Requirements**
- ② **Include callback thread**
- ③ **Establish provider**
- ④ **Retrieve current location**

```
    private void listenForLocation(String providerName,          ❺ Start listening
        int durationSeconds) {                                      for updates
      locationMgr.requestLocationUpdates(providerName, 0, 0,
          locationListener);
      handler.postDelayed(handlerCallback, durationSeconds * 1000);
    }

    private void endListenForLocation(Location loc) {              ┌──      End
      locationMgr.removeUpdates(locationListener);                 ❻     listening
      handler.removeCallbacks(handlerCallback);
      if (loc != null) {
        sendLocationToHandler(MESSAGE_CODE_LOCATION_FOUND,
            (int) (loc.getLatitude() * 1e6),
            (int) (loc.getLongitude() * 1e6));
      } else {
        sendLocationToHandler(MESSAGE_CODE_LOCATION_NULL, 0, 0);
      }
    }
  }
}
```

Our `LocationHelper` class has a lot going on. To start off, we require callers to construct an instance by passing a `LocationManager`, `Handler`, and a `String` for the log tag ❶. Then we create a `Thread` to be used as the handler's callback ❷. We do this as an instance variable because we want to be able to remove the callback when we're done. We'll see this callback in use later.

Next, we establish the GPS provider using the `Criteria` class instead of a direct name ❸. We're still pinning our hopes on the GPS provider by specifying `ACCURACY_FINE`, but you could use the lowest criteria you need. If we'd specified `ACCURACY_COARSE` then the GPS or network providers could be returned, depending on which was enabled at the time (GPS supersedes network, if both are available). We chose to stick to the GPS because it's an easier example when using various devices and the emulator.

After we have a reference to the provider, we then include the `getCurrentLocation` method that will be called by activities and possibly other Android components ❹. Callers supply a duration to this method, indicating how long they want the helper to keep trying to get a location fix. We need this because location fixes aren't immediate, and we don't want to keep trying forever.

WHAT'S WITH THE 1E6?   The `Location` object in Android stores latitude and longitude as type `double`. Other classes, such as `GeoPoint`, which we'll see in the maps API soon, use type `int`. Both represent the same location; the integer type is the microdegrees representation. The *1E6* means multiply the double value by 1 million. You can multiply or divide by 1E6 to go back and forth between the two representations.

Inside the `getCurrentLocation` method, a few key things are happening. First, if the provider is null, we return that as a result using the `sendLocationToHandler` method. Second, if we have a provider, we first check the last-known location. If there is one, and it's fairly recent, we return it. In these cases, we circumvent the rest of the logic in this class and don't even use a `LocationListener`. If the last location isn't useful to us, we then start the listener with the `listenForLocation` method ❺.

> **LAST-KNOWN LOCATION AND THE EMULATOR** When using the `adb geo fix` command, or the manual location settings in DDMS, the fix time is set to 0 and seems to be incremented by one second each time a manual update is sent. This works for listeners that are currently active, but fails miserably when you're checking the time on the last-known location. To test the effectiveness of working with the last-known location and accounting for the time of the last fix, you'll need to use a real device.

Inside `listenForLocation`, we use the location manager's `requestLocationUpdates` method. Several overloads of this method are available; the one we're using allows us to specify the provider to use, the minimum time to wait between updates (in milliseconds), the minimum distance (in meters) to wait between updates, and the `Location-Listener` to use. We'll get into the `LocationListener` implementation we're using in a bit. After the registration for location updates, we use the handler's `postDelayed` method. We pass it our earlier handler callback and the amount of time we want it to delay before firing. This is how we'll stop the listener after the specified duration is up. This is important: we don't want to leave the listener there permanently. Listening for location updates frequently (we set the time and distance stops to 0, which means update as frequently as you can) will consume the battery quickly. In this case, we want to get in, get the information we need, and get out.

The handler callback, which we saw earlier, calls the `endListenForLocation` method ❻. This method removes the `LocationListener`, removes the callback, and sends a status message back to the initial caller via the passed-in `Handler`.

To complete our LocationInfo application, we need to look at the `LocationListener` implementation we've been talking about. This inner class (placed inside `LocationHelper`) is shown next.

Listing 10.6 The `LocationListener` inner class from `LocationHelper`

```
private class LocationListenerImpl                          ❶ Implement
    implements LocationListener {                              LocationListener
  @Override
  public void onStatusChanged(String provider, int status,
      Bundle extras) {                                        Override
    Log.d(logTag, "Location status changed to:" + status);   onStatus-
    switch (status) {                                       ❷ Changed
      case LocationProvider.AVAILABLE:
        break;
      case LocationProvider.TEMPORARILY_UNAVAILABLE:
        break;
      case LocationProvider.OUT_OF_SERVICE:
        endListenForLocation(null);
    }
  }
}
```

```
@Override
public void onLocationChanged(Location loc) {        ◁─┐    Override
    if (loc == null) {                                ❸    onLocationChanged
        return;
    }
    Log.d(logTag, "Location changed to:" + loc.toString());
    endListenForLocation(loc);
}

@Override
public void onProviderDisabled(String provider) {    ◁─┐    Override
    endListenForLocation(null);                       ❹    onProviderDisabled
}

@Override
public void onProviderEnabled(String provider) {
}
}
```

LocationListener is an interface, and we've chosen to implement it with an inner class ❶. The interface defines several simple methods, the first of which is onStatusChanged ❷. For our purposes, inside this method, we log what's happening and we stop the location updates if the provider status changes to out of service. After that, we implement the onLocationChanged method ❸. This method will alert us when a new location fix has been found. In it, we also stop the location updates, and we send the newly found location along. Using this approach, we don't wait the entire duration the caller specifies if we quickly get a location update (we stop as soon as we get said update). Finally, we implement the onProviderDisabled method ❹. Here, we also stop the location updates, in case the provider is disabled while we're already listening for updates.

DISCUSSION

To boil things down, our helper class checks for the last-known location for the given provider, and if present and recent, returns it. If not, it starts a LocationListener and returns when *either* that listener gets a good fix or the duration specified runs out. All the results are returned via the Handler using a Message with constants indicating what happened, as well as data for the latitude and longitude (if present). As we said at the outset, a lot is going on in this class. That's one of the reasons we made it a helper. Recall, our Activity doesn't know about all of these details; it just has to construct a Handler, decide how long it'll wait for location updates, and then invoke getCurrentLocation.

GETTING DETAILED GPS STATUS DATA   In the earlier screenshots, you might've noticed some GPS status information. Android provides a getGpsStatus method on LocationManager that can provide details such as the number of satellites involved and the timing of fixes. From there, you can also obtain more detail about each individual satellite. None of this is central to the sample applications we're building, but we're getting this data to show you that it's possible. For more information about this, see the code download for the LocationInfo application.

Now that we've seen the `LocationManager` and `LocationProvider` classes, worked with `Location` and `Criteria`, and used a `LocationListener`, we're ready to build something that uses these features in a less abstract way. Next, we'll extend our knowledge of location awareness in Android by building an application that adds Google Maps API for Android.

10.3 *Building a map-based application*

Building upon what we've already covered in this chapter and applying some map-related concepts takes us to our next application: BrewMap. BrewMap plots the locations of breweries, brew pubs, beer stores, and beer bars onto an interactive map. Once the map is populated, you can select a location to get more information. The main screens of BrewMap are shown in figure 10.4.

 GRAB THE PROJECT: BREWMAP You can get the source code for this project, and/or the packaged APK to run it, at the *Android in Practice* code website. Because some code listings here are shortened to focus on specific concepts, we recommend that you download the complete source code and follow along within Eclipse (or your favorite IDE or text editor).

Source: http://mng.bz/43jV, APK file: http://mng.bz/YbR6

As you can see in figure 10.4, BrewMap starts off with a splash screen. Its `Main Activity` has two functions: find brew locations near me, or search. If either of those functions is used and returns data, a `MapActivity` is launched, with a `MapView` populated with beer glass icons used as map markers. If any of the markers are selected, the detail screen displays more information about that particular location.

Figure 10.4   The main screens of the BrewMap application.

BrewMap uses the Beer Mapping Project as its data source (http://beermapping .com/api/). The Beer Mapping API provides a lot of information and is free, though you need an API key to use it. The goal of the Beer Mapping Project is "to allow you to display or use our data in your own applications." We know that a beer map won't be everyone's cup of ale, so to speak, but it's a fun and complete example application that allows us to walk through Android's location and map support.

Before we get started, we need to install the Google APIs Add-On extension. Android's map support isn't included with the open source Android project, rather it's an add-in provided by Google. You'll use it by selecting Google APIs with the desired level as the Build Target when you create your project in Eclipse.

10.3.1   *Getting the Google APIs Add-On extension*

The Google APIs Add-On for Android includes the Maps library and a few other custom system components (the beta Cloud-to-Device-Messaging APIs are also part of this add-on). The Maps library for Android, which provides a Google Maps API, is our focus.

Since this is an add-on, it's not part of the default Android SDK. To install it, follow the instructions listed on the Google Projects for Android Google Code Hosting page: http://mng.bz/863c.

The installation process involves using the *Android SDK and AVD Manager* (which can be started by using the android tool on the command line) to add the Google APIs Add-On as an SDK component. This typically means browsing the Third-Party Add-ons section of the SDK management tool and checking the Google APIs by Google Inc. box for the versions of the platform you're interested in using.

Once you have the add-on installed on your development machine you'll also need to get a Maps API key. You can get a Maps API key online by pasting in the MD5 fingerprint of your Android developer's certificate. If you aren't sure what this means or where the certificate is, don't worry; it's easy. Just follow the instructions, and carefully review the terms, on the API Key Signup page: http://mng.bz/E91h.

These are extra hoops for developers for sure, but the process for both steps is relatively easy, and the powerful APIs they enable you to use are worth it. Once you have your Maps API key, you'll want to keep it handy because it'll be required in one of the layouts for the BrewMap project (the API key in the checked-in code is for one of our personal developer machines; it won't work for Android APKs built from any other computer).

We'll find out how to include the Maps Add-On in an Android project next, when we start to setup the BrewMap application.

10.3.2   *Setting up BrewMap*

After installing the Google APIs Add-On and obtaining a Maps API key, we register to use maps support in the application manifest.

Listing 10.7 The application manifest for BrewMap, showing the uses-library element

```xml
<?xml version="1.0" encoding="utf-8"?>
<manifest xmlns:android="http://schemas.android.com/apk/res/android"
    package="com.manning.aip.brewmap" android:versionCode="1"
    android:versionName="1.0">
    <uses-permission
        android:name="android.permission.INTERNET" />
    <uses-permission
        android:name="android.permission.ACCESS_FINE_LOCATION" />
    <application android:icon="@drawable/beer_icon"
        android:theme="@android:style/Theme.Black"
        android:label="@string/app_name" android:name=".BrewMapApp">
        <uses-library
            android:name="com.google.android.maps" />
        <activity android:name=".Splash" android:label="@string/app_name">
            <intent-filter>
                <action android:name="android.intent.action.MAIN" />
                <category
                    android:name="android.intent.category.LAUNCHER" />
            </intent-filter>
        </activity>
        <activity android:name=".Main" />
        <activity android:name=".MapResults" />
        <activity android:name=".BrewLocationDetails"
            android:windowSoftInputMode="adjustResize"/>
    </application>
</manifest>
```

Give permission for location ❶

Uses Google Maps ❷

Most of the BrewMap manifest should be familiar. We declare a package and version. Then, we include permissions, and define the application element. The significant parts here are the `ACCESS_FINE_LOCATION` permission for GPS support ❶, and the `includes-library` element that pulls in the Maps APIs ❷.

After the manifest, the next thing BrewMap includes is a `Main Activity` that provides click listeners for the UI elements we saw in figure 10.4 (the second screen from the left is the `Main Activity`). We aren't including the entire code for this in the text because it mostly rehashes things we've already covered. It uses an `AsyncTask` to pull XML data from the Beer Mapping project API via an XML pull parser, and includes a `ProgressDialog` to let users know what's happening. Also, it checks whether the GPS provider is enabled, and prompts users to go to the settings screen to enable it, if not. This uses the exact same code we saw in the LocationInfo project. Additionally, it uses the `LocationHelper` we created for the LocationInfo project to try to determine the current location if the user wants to find locations "near me."

TECHNIQUE 51　**Converting an address to geographical coordinates**

We now have a collection of brew location data taken from the Beer Mapping Project—we have the addresses but not the coordinates of each location. Our next problem is to turn those addresses into latitude and longitude coordinates so we can plot them on a map.

PROBLEM

You need to convert addresses into latitude and longitude coordinates, or vice versa.

SOLUTION

The only significant thing the Main Activity of BrewMap does that's different from what we've seen already is that it uses the Android Geocoder to get latitude and longitude coordinates from standard postal addresses. *Geocoding* means converting from a postal address to latitude/longitude coordinates. *Reverse geocoding* is the opposite: providing an address from coordinates. For BrewMap we need standard geocoding (not reverse), and we do it from an AsyncTask in the Main Activity. The method that does the work, doInBackground, is shown in the following listing.

Listing 10.8 Geocoding postal addresses to get latitude and longitude coordinates

```
@Override
protected List<BrewLocation> doInBackground(List<BrewLocation>... args) {
   List<BrewLocation> result = new ArrayList<BrewLocation>();
   if (args == null) {
      return result;
   }

   if (args[0] != null && !args[0].isEmpty()) {          ❶ Iterate through each
      for (BrewLocation bl : args[0]) {                       BrewLocation
         publishProgress(bl.getName());
         try {                                              Use
            List<android.location.Address> addresses =   getFromLocationName ❷
                  geocoder.getFromLocationName(
                     bl.getAddress().getLocationName(), 1);
            if (addresses != null && !addresses.isEmpty()) {
               android.location.Address a = addresses.get(0);
               bl.setLatitude(a.getLatitude());          ❷ Set latitude/longitude
               bl.setLongitude(a.getLongitude());             into BrewLocation

               if (bl.getLatitude() == 0 || bl.getLongitude() == 0) {
                  Log.d(Constants.LOG_TAG, "Skipping BrewLocation: "
                     + bl.getName()
                     + " because address was not geocoded.");
               } else {
                  result.add(bl);
               }
            }
         } catch (IOException e) {
            Log.e(Constants.LOG_TAG, "Error geocoding location name", e);
         }
      }
   }

   return result;
}
```

To perform geocoding, we iterate through each BrewLocation we get from the Beer Mapping API data source ❶ and use Geocoder's getFromLocationName method ❷. If the geocoding succeeds, we then set the latitude and longitude it returns back into the `BrewLocation` object ❸. As each `Brew-Location` is processed, we show a progress dialog that includes the name, as seen in figure 10.5.

To clarity, even though we aren't showing all the code, `BrewLocation` is a simple Java-Bean-style object that we've created to use as part of our application's model. It has getters and setters for ID, name, status, address, reviewLink, proxyLink, address, phone, and latitude and longitude. All of this information, except the latitude and longitude, comes from the Beer Mapping API data source. We need the latitude and longitude for each location so we can later plot them on a map, and this is why we need the `Geocoder`.

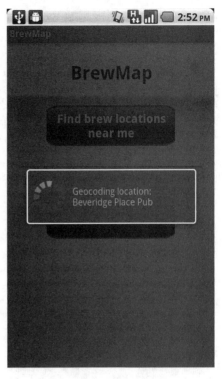

Figure 10.5 Displaying a ProgressDialog while geocoding brew locations

GEOCODE WITH CAUTION Geocoding isn't free. Each call to `Geocoder` makes a network call to a Google service to perform a lookup. Because this involves the network, it's only available when the network is available, and it can take a second or two for each invocation. Geocoding many addresses, like BrewMap potentially does in our example, should be carefully considered, and if necessary should be done off of the main UI thread with a nonblocking/nonmodal approach (BrewMap, to keep things simple, uses a modal ProgressDialog, which works, but is naive).

DISCUSSION

Geocoding is a useful service that's available to Android devices through a separate Google service. The `Geocoder` client class is part of Android, but the server side isn't. The server side is provided by the Google Geocoding API service for Google Maps. Complete geocoding documentation can be found at the APIs Google Code Hosting site: http://mng.bz/04wX.

The Geocoding API also exposes the geocoder as a web service available with several formats (so you can use it outside of Android, too). Before using the geocoding service, you should carefully review all the terms, and you should know that the service throttles requests at 2,500 per IP user in a 24-hour period. There's a commercial batch mode if you need it, but it's not free (query Google Maps API Premier for more information).

With our map data ready to go and coordinates supplied by geocoding, we're now ready to put some markers on a map and pick a place to get a drink.

10.3.3 *Working with MapActivity*

After the BrewMap application has parsed the XML data from the Beer Mapping Project API and geocoded the addresses it returns to include latitude and longitude, the next thing it does is display the locations on a map. Enter the `MapActivity`.

TECHNIQUE 52   **Creating a MapActivity with associated MapView**

`MapActivity` is an `Activity` specialization that takes care of a lot of the details associated with displaying a Google Maps–style view on Android, known as a `MapView`.

PROBLEM

You need to be able to create an interactive map that the user can move and zoom in and out with touch gestures.

SOLUTION

The `com.google.android.maps` package, which is supplied by the Maps add-on library, includes several extremely useful mapping classes that allow any Android application to leverage the power of Google Maps. Table 10.2 lists the key classes from this package.

Table 10.2 The key classes in the com.google.android.maps package

Class	Description
MapActivity	Specialized `Activity` that handles boilerplate around displaying a `MapView`
MapView	A view that displays map tiles from the Google Maps API
MapController	A manager for the panning and zooming of a `MapView`
Overlay	Base class of data that can be laid on top of a map
ItemizedOverlay	Overlay class that includes individual overlay items (often map markers)
GeoPoint	Latitude and longitude pair, represented in microdegrees

The process of including a `MapView` to display map data starts by extending `MapActivity`. For BrewMap we've named our implementation of `MapActivity` `MapResults`.

Listing 10.9 The `MapResults` activity of BrewMap that extends `MapActivity`

```
public class MapResults extends MapActivity {          ❶ Include MapView
    private MapView map;                                      variable
    private List<Overlay> overlays;         ◁──❷ Include overlays

    private BrewMapApp app;

    @Override
    public void onCreate(Bundle savedInstanceState) {
        super.onCreate(savedInstanceState);
        setContentView(R.layout.map_results);

        app = (BrewMapApp) getApplication();
```

```
map = (MapView) findViewById(R.id.map);
map.setBuiltInZoomControls(true);

List<BrewLocation> brewLocations = app.getBrewLocations();
BrewLocationOverlay brewLocationOverlay =
    new BrewLocationOverlay(this, brewLocations,
    this.getResources().getDrawable(R.drawable.beer_icon_small));
overlays = map.getOverlays();
overlays.add(brewLocationOverlay);

map.getController().setCenter(
  new GeoPoint((int) (brewLocations.get(0).getLatitude() * 1e6),
  (int) (brewLocations.get(0).getLongitude() * 1e6)));

map.getController().zoomToSpan(
    brewLocationOverlay.getLatSpanE6(),
    brewLocationOverlay.getLonSpanE6());
}

@Override
protected boolean isRouteDisplayed() {
    return false;
}
}
```

- **3** Get MapView from layout resource
- **4** Create BrewLocationOverlay
- **5** Add overlay to map
- **6** Center map
- **7** Zoom map to lat/long span

As you might expect, every `MapActivity` must be associated with a `MapView` **1**. Extending `MapActivity` handles all of the lifecycle associated with a `MapView`. Along with the `MapView`, we also include a collection of overlays that will be placed onto the map later **2**. Typically, as with many other views, you'll define where a `MapView` should be placed, and some other basic properties concerning it, in a layout resource and then reference it in code **3**. Because we're using a full screen map, the layout we've used for `MapResults` is a `LinearLayout` with a single item inside it:

```
<com.google.android.maps.MapView android:id="@+id/map"
    android:layout_width="fill_parent"
    android:layout_height="fill_parent"
    android:clickable="true"
    android:apiKey="<YOUR_KEY_HERE>" />
```

As you can see, several `MapView` properties can be defined in the layout, such as whether it's clickable, and importantly, what API key it'll use. This is where you'll need to plug in your own API key if you're building BrewMap on your own, or if you've downloaded the code and are working with the source. Alternatively, if you install the APK for this application, you don't have to worry about this (once an application is signed and exported into APK format, it uses the key it was created with, but a non-matching key can't be used to perform the build and export).

After the `MapView` reference is set up, we then include an `ItemizedOverlay` implementation **4**. An `ItemizedOverlay` includes a list of `OverlayItem` instances. Each `OverlayItem` includes a point that can be represented on the map. In our case, we've created our `ItemizedOverlay` in a separate class named `BrewLocationOverlay`, which we'll explore momentarily. Once we have the overlay class, we place it on the map using the `addOverlay` method **5**.

After we have the components we need, we then use the `MapController` to center ❻ and zoom the map to reasonable bounds ❼. `MapController` contains many useful methods. The centering is self-explanatory. The zoom-to-span is just as easy to invoke, but a little more difficult to understand. It creates a rectangle of the top-left-most and lower-right-most points, and zooms to those bounds. Without this convenient method, we'd have to iterate all the points and do the math ourselves.

DISCUSSION

Our `MapResults` class displays a zoomable and navigable map with an overlay containing all the brew locations in a given area. The finished product looks like the screenshot seen in figure 10.6.

If the map is touched anywhere, the zoom controls will be displayed. The `Itemized-Overlay` handles the placement of the map markers and their individual touch controls.

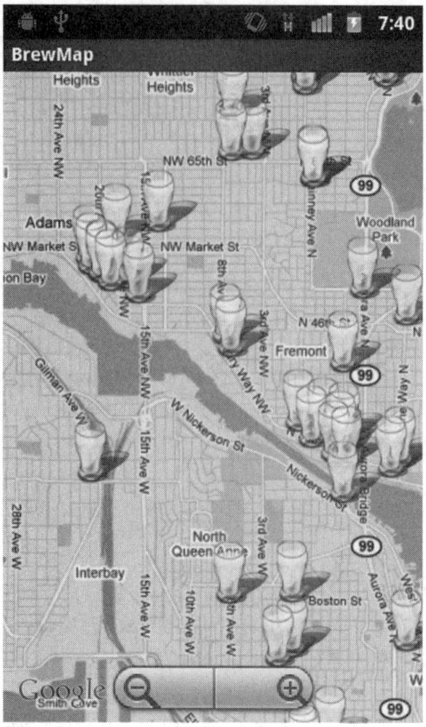

Figure 10.6   The `MapResults Activity` from the BrewMap application shows the full screen MapView with map marker results.

10.3.4   *Using a map Overlay*

Probably the most common usage of a Google Map (outside of navigation) is placing markers and routes on the map using custom or personal data sources. We noted in the previous listing that our data is being placed into an `ItemizedOverlay`, and now we need to build that class to complete our map.

TECHNIQUE 53   **Displaying OverlayItems on a MapView**

`MapView` classes display data on top of map tiles using overlays. You can use multiple overlays, and you can place any kind of data you need on a map. You have full control over what's drawn and where, if you start from the base classes. If you don't want all that control, and you just want to place some pin-style markers on a map, then there's a convenient overlay subclass just for you, `ItemizedOverlay`.

PROBLEM

You need to place map markers on a `MapView` in specified locations, and have those markers respond to touch gestures.

SOLUTION

The `Overlay` class is the base object for putting data on top of a map in Android. This class supports the base touch and tap events, and contains several `draw` methods. You can start with this class if you have special requirements, but more commonly you'll extend from `ItemizedOverlay`, which is tailor-made for placing multiple map markers, using drawables, on a `MapView`.

The `BrewLocationOverlay` class in listing 10.9 is an implementation of `ItemizedOverlay`. This is where the BrewMap application creates and draws its map markers. The code for this class is shown next.

Listing 10.10   The BrewMap `BrewLocationOverlay` class

```
public class BrewLocationOverlay                                    ❶ Extend
    extends ItemizedOverlay<OverlayItem> {                            ItemizedOverlay

    private List<BrewLocation> brewLocations;                       BrewLocations ❷
    private Context context;                                         and drawable

    public BrewLocationOverlay(Context context,
        List<BrewLocation> brewLocations, Drawable marker) {
        super(boundCenterBottom(marker));                          ❸ Call super
        this.context = context;                                       constructor
        this.brewLocations = brewLocations;
        if (brewLocations == null) {
            brewLocations = new ArrayList<BrewLocation>();
        }                                                          ❹ Invoke
        populate();                                                    populate
    }

    @Override                                                      ❺ Override
    protected OverlayItem createItem(int i) {                         createItem
        BrewLocation brewLocation = brewLocations.get(i);
        GeoPoint point =
            new GeoPoint(
                (int) (brewLocation.getLatitude() * 1e6),
                (int) (brewLocation.getLongitude() * 1e6));
        return new OverlayItem(point, brewLocation.getName(), null);
    }

    @Override                                                      ❻ Override
    public boolean onTap(final int index) {                           onTap
        BrewLocation brewLocation = brewLocations.get(index);
        AlertDialog.Builder builder = new AlertDialog.Builder(context);
        builder.setTitle("BrewLocation")
            .setMessage(brewLocation.getName()
                + "\n\nVisit the pub detail page for more information?")
            .setCancelable(true)
            .setPositiveButton("Yes", new DialogInterface.OnClickListener() {
                public void onClick(DialogInterface dialog, int id) {
                    Intent i = new Intent(context, BrewLocationDetails.class);
                    i.putExtra(BrewMapApp.PUB_INDEX, index);
                    context.startActivity(i);
                }
            })
            .setNegativeButton("No", new DialogInterface.OnClickListener() {
                public void onClick(DialogInterface dialog, int id) {
                    dialog.cancel();
                }
```

```
        });
    AlertDialog alert = builder.create();
    alert.show();
                                              ❼  Return true so as
    return true;                                  not to pass through
    }

    @Override
    public int size() {
        return brewLocations.size();
    }
}
```

As promised, the BrewLocationOverlay extends ItemizedOverlay, which takes care of many of the drawing and touch-handling details ❶. The constructor of this class requires that a collection of BrewLocations and a default marker drawable be passed in ❷. These are the data points the map will end up displaying.

Inside the constructor, we call the super class constructor and invoke boundCenterBottom ❸. The call to boundCenterBottom tells the drawing methods to draw its markers centered on a pixel in the middle of the bottom row. Then, still in the constructor, we invoke the important populate method ❹. This is an initialization method that does some internal housekeeping and should always be called on a new ItemizedOverlay. The documentation states that populate should be called as soon as the ItemizedOverlay has data, but before anything else gets called.

Once the construction is out of the way, we come to the createItem method ❺. This method creates a GeoPoint from the specified data element (using the index passed in), and then builds an individual OverlayItem. Each OverlayItem has a marker, a title, and a few other properties, and maintains its own state. This is what's drawn on screen.

In the onTap method we define what should happen when one of the overlay items is clicked ❻. The index is provided to the onTap method, so we can tell what data element has been selected, and we can react. For BrewMap we display an AlertDialog that allows the user to choose whether to go to a detail Activity. To finish up the onTap method, we return true ❼. This indicates that we don't want to pass through to any other overlays if multiple layers are present; we want the event handled here, and here alone.

The BrewLocationDetails Activity, as seen on the far right of figure 10.6, is basic (so we won't show it in the text). We pass it a pointer stating which data element was selected using Intent extra data. Then, it displays some details and allows the user to get more information using built-in applications to map, call, or browse, as seen in figure 10.7.

CREATING A MUTABLE ITEMIZEDOVERLAY   One thing to keep in mind with the BrewMap overlay is that it's not mutable. It displays a collection of data points, and then it's done. In some applications, you may need to add or remove items from the overlay dynamically. To do this, you'll need to override the removeOverlay method and make sure to call setLastFocusedIndex(-1), and again call populate. If you don't use setLastFocusedIndex(-1) and populate, you're likely to run into exceptions.

Figure 10.7 Getting more information from a selected location using intents

Working with overlays and overlay items is easy with Android. You can extend many convenience classes to perform common functions, and if you need to, you can also implement your own specialized classes at lower levels. And, though we've only used a single layer here, you can use multiple overlays on a single map to represent different sets of data.

DISCUSSION

With the completion of the BrewLocationOverlay class, we have a draggable, zoomable, populated MapView. Our map completes the BrewMap application, which allows the user to search near their current location (or a location they define) and pulls data from the Beer Mapping Project API to create data points. In all, we have a complete and useful application that can guide us to a frosty pint of beer the world over! (Well, wherever the Beer Mapping Project has data, which includes many countries.)

10.4   *Summary*

In this chapter, we've come a long way. We've stepped through the key terms and definitions involved in geospatial coordinates, and then worked through example applications that exercised related Android and Google APIs.

First, we looked at the basic concepts of using the `LocationManager` to query for location information and work with `LocationProviders`. We saw how different providers have different capabilities and requirements. Then, we used a `LocationHelper` class that we created to manage a `LocationListener` to get a fix on our current location. Once we had the basics in hand, we moved on to working with maps.

We covered how to install the Google APIs Add-On for Android, which includes the maps packages, and we discussed how to get a Maps API key. Then we built a fully functional application that included a `MapActivity` to house a `MapView`, and used data provided by an `ItemizedOverlay`. We saw how all the Maps API pieces come together to include a functional interactive map in an Android application.

11

Appeal to the senses using multimedia

Of all of our inventions for mass communication, pictures still speak the most universally understood language.

—Walt Disney

The Android Market is a vibrant and diverse bazaar of applications and games. You can find applications for listening to music, editing photos, and broadcasting videos among others with a focus on multimedia of one type or another. Obviously, if you want to build an application with a similar focus, then you'll need to master many of Android's multimedia APIs. But what if you don't? What if you're among the many developers whose applications will focus on something other than multimedia? Should you even care which APIs you'd need to play music or create a thumbnail for a video?

This is a loaded question. This chapter is all about multimedia so we're not going to start it off by telling you that it won't be applicable to you. In fact, the opposite is true. No matter what kind of applications you're developing, there's a good chance that you'll need to use some subset of Android's multimedia APIs. Multimedia is becoming increasingly important for all Android applications.

The reason for this is simple. Devices already have advanced multimedia capabilities, and each year, they're more sophisticated than before. With such innovative features in hand, multimedia has become the language that smartphone owners use to express themselves and to communicate with others. So the question of "Does my application need multimedia features?" becomes "Do the users of my app need to be able to communicate with other users?" Sure people can still use text-based communications (SMS, email, social networking update/status) or even telephony, but more and more they choose to share photos and videos. In this chapter, you'll learn how to use Android to both consume media (view pictures, listen to audio, and so on) and to produce media (capture pictures or video, and so forth). To illustrate these various techniques, we'll build an application that we'll call MediaMogul. This app will allow the user to select images, music, and video using their device to create a slideshow. It'll also allow them to capture new images and video and record audio to add to their slideshow.

Before we go into the gory details on how to do various multimedia-related tasks in Android, we need to first understand the environment that we're operating within. All of the APIs in the world would be meaningless without the hardware to back them up. This is no small statement; the world of Android devices is as diverse as the Android Market. You need to consider whether the user's device has a camera. What about a front-facing camera? Can the device record video? What about audio? Even if you're only going to play back video, there are the familiar questions of what size screen does the device have? How fast is its data connection? The answers to these questions can make you think twice about downloading a high-definition video to play on a given device. So before we go into the APIs, let's look at the various capabilities provided by Android devices and exposed via the Android SDK.

11.1 *Features too good for a feature phone*

Technology pundits often use the term feature phone, usually as a pejorative. The term is used as an antonym to *smartphone*, and any phone running Android is classified as a smartphone. But Android smartphones rarely lack in features. MP3 playback, cameras, and video playback may have once put the "features" in feature phones, but they're staples of Android smartphones as well. So how do you determine which features a given phone supports? Let's see how we can answer that question in a way that's most useful to application developers.

TECHNIQUE 54   **Detecting capabilities**

At the time this chapter was written, 200+ unique Android smartphones and 30+ Android tablets were on the market, with another 50+ such devices announced but not yet in stores. Most of these have cameras and about a dozen of the smartphones have front-facing cameras. The resolution on the cameras varies from 1–10 megapixels, but many of the front-facing cameras are so-called *VGA cameras* with a 0.3 megapixel resolution. There's a lot of variance, and you're going to have to think about these variations if you're going to use multimedia capabilities in your Android application.

PROBLEM

You're creating an application that will use multimedia. You need to make sure that your application runs properly on any device that installs it and makes the most of each devices' capabilities.

SOLUTION

Device variance is fundamental to Android. In chapter 4, we looked at how Android allows you to deal with variations in screen sizes and resolution, and this is certainly "the Android way." Instead of working around variation, Android embraces it. The same is true for hardware features. They're first class citizens in Android, and you should list exactly what features your application needs in your application's manifest file. The following listing shows an excerpt of the manifest for our MediaMogul application.

Listing 11.1 Declaring hardware requirements in the application manifest

```
<manifest xmlns:android="http://schemas.android.com/apk/res/android"
    package="com.manning.aip.media"
    android:versionCode="1"
    android:versionName="1.0">
  <!-- application section omitted -->
  <uses-feature android:name="android.hardware.camera"
      android:required="true" />
  <uses-feature android:name="android.hardware.camera.autofocus"
      android:required="true"/>
  <uses-feature android:name="android.hardware.camera.flash"
      android:required="false" />
  <uses-feature android:name="android.hardware.camera.front"
      android:required="false" />
  <uses-feature android:name="android.hardware.microphone"
      android:required="true"/>
  <uses-permission
      android:name="android.permission.CAMERA" />
  <uses-permission android:name="android.permission.RECORD_AUDIO" />
  <uses-sdk android:minSdkVersion="9" />
</manifest>
```

❶ Permission to use camera and record audio

Use the `<uses-feature>` element to declare the hardware/software features your application uses. In this example, we've declared that our application uses the camera, as well as subfeatures of the camera such as auto-focus, flash, and a front-facing camera. We've declared that some of these features are required, but some are optional. Note that if you omit the `required` attribute, it defaults to true.

Does this mean that a user whose device doesn't have a camera won't be able to install our application? Not exactly. The OS doesn't check the manifest at install-time. But the Android Market app does check the manifest and the list of features on the device and compares them. It does this to filter out apps that a user wouldn't be able to run properly. If you assume that users will only get your app from the Android Market, then they'd never see your app there if their device doesn't have necessary features.

Also note that in listing 11.1, we showed two <uses-permissions> elements ❶ from the manifest. Older versions of Android relied on uses-permissions to imply uses-feature. The CAMERA permission implied both the camera and camera. autofocus features. Similarly, the RECORD_AUDIO permission implied the microphone feature. You can still get away with specifying only these permissions and getting the uses-feature metadata for free, but it's better to explicitly list the features you need, as well as the permissions.

You might've noticed that we specified the camera.front feature to imply that we want a front-facing camera. But we set its required attribute to false, so it's optional. If a device doesn't have a front-facing camera, the Market application wouldn't filter out an app with a manifest like the one in listing 11.1. In this case, you'd want to detect whether there was a front-facing camera in your application code. There are a couple of ways to do this.

You can explicitly check for a feature by using the android.content.pm.Package-Manager. Here's an example of checking for a front-facing camera:

```
private boolean hasFrontFacingCamera(){
    PackageManager mgr = this.getPackageManager();
    for (FeatureInfo fi : mgr.getSystemAvailableFeatures()){
        if (fi.name.equals(
            PackageManager.FEATURE_CAMERA_FRONT)){
                return true;
            }
    }
    return false;
}
```

You could substitute any of the other feature names that are defined as constants in the PackageManager class if you made some other feature optional in the manifest. For the front-facing camera feature there's an even easier way.

```
private Camera getFrontFacingCamera(){
    for (int i=0;i<Camera.getNumberOfCameras()){
        Camera.CameraInfo info = new Camera.CameraInfo();
        Camera.getCameraInfo(i, info);
        if (info.facing ==
            Camera.CameraInfo.CAMERA_FACING_FRONT){
                return Camera.open(i);
            }
    }
    return null;
}
```

If getFrontFacingCamera returns null, you'll know that the device doesn't have a front-facing camera. This is consistent with the legacy behavior of the static method Camera.open(), which would return null if the device had no camera at all. At this point, we know exactly how many cameras that the user's device has. If we want to enable extra features that require a front-facing camera, then we know whether we can do this.

DISCUSSION

Web developers are all too familiar with the concept of *progressive enhancement*. The idea is to program a web application to the lowest common denominator—the most primitive web browser that you wish to support. From there you can use clever techniques to test whether more advanced features are available, and if so, then alter the user interface and/or application behavior to make use of this feature. Developing for Android devices can have some similarities with progressive enhancement. But Android is designed with these variations in mind.

We didn't pick testing for a front-facing camera code at random. One of the great things about Android is that the entire stack (hardware, network, OS, and so on) can evolve at its own pace. Device manufacturers were able to add front-facing cameras before there were Android APIs for working with front-facing cameras. The code in the two methods shown here will only compile on Android 2.3+, but there were Android smartphones running Android 2.1 that had front-facing cameras.

Multimedia input is one area where you may need to think about hardware differences between devices. Multimedia playback is more straightforward. You may want to account for screen size (see `android.view.WindowManager`) for video playback. If you're playing back audio or video over the Internet, then you may also want to consider the network speed (see the `android.net.ConnectivityManager`). Let's take a more detailed look at how to find, load, and play back multimedia resources.

11.2 Managing media

The media playback capabilities of Android devices present many intriguing opportunities for developers. But before you can start using those features to play and present any sort of media, you need some media to play. The media that you use can be found in many different places on the device. It might be an integral part of your application and thus bundled with it directly. Alternatively, it could be something that's not specific to your application—some type of media that belongs to the user. This could be media that the user loaded on the device directly (audio files are a common type). Or it could be media that the user created with the device, such as pictures or videos that the user shot with the device's camera. In all of these cases, the media will typically be stored on the external storage of the device—the SD card. There are some conventions as to where to store media on the SD card, but the truth is that it could be in a wide variety of places. Fortunately, Android provides a number of ways to find and load media from all of these various sources. Let's start with the most straightforward situation: loading media from resources or files.

TECHNIQUE 55   **Working with resources and files**

Input and output (I/O) are common tasks in most programming languages. This is certainly the case for the Java programming language that Android uses. In some places, Android augments or provides alternatives to what you find in Java. For I/O, you can use most of the Java I/O APIs that you're used to, and you can use them to load various types of media for playback. In a few places, Android provides some extra convenience methods. Let's take a look at how to use file I/O to load media.

PROBLEM

You need to find and load media for your application. The media may be part of your application, or it might be external to it on the SD card. Either way, you need to find a handle to it and use it in combination with Android's media playback APIs to present the media to the user.

SOLUTION

As we mentioned earlier, there are a few different ways that you can find and load multimedia so that it can be used for playback. Let's start with the simplest way: by using Android resources. We've seen resources used in many different places so far in the book. By now, you're probably familiar with layout, strings, and drawables (including images) as resources. Now we'll see how to use other types of files, including multimedia.

Our MediaMogul application will start off by allowing the user to pick multiple images from their device to use for the slideshow that they'll build. Figure 11.1 shows you what the final result will look like.

The user could have a lot of images to choose from. While they browse and select those images, let's play some soothing theme music in the background. The sound file that we want to use will be distributed with our application. The best place to put it is in the `/res/raw` directory. Files in this directory will have resource identifiers generated for them, but otherwise these files are opaque to the Android build tool and will be bundled with your application as-is. The following listing shows how these files can be referenced from within your application.

Figure 11.1   Grid of the user's pictures

> **GRAB THE PROJECT: LOCATIONINFO**   You can get the source code for this project, and/or the packaged APK to run it, at the *Android in Practice* code website. Because some code listings here are shortened to focus on specific concepts, we recommend that you download the complete source code and follow along within Eclipse (or your favorite IDE or text editor).
>
> Source: http://mng.bz/In6j, APK file: http://mng.bz/X0Mk

Listing 11.2   Using bundled multimedia resources

```
public class ImageBrowserActivity extends Activity {

    private MediaPlayer player;
    // other code omitted
```

❶ MediaPlayer used to play audio or video

```
@Override
public void onCreate(Bundle savedInstanceState) {
    super.onCreate(savedInstanceState);
    // other code omitted
    playThemeSong();
}

private void playThemeSong(){
    player = MediaPlayer.create(this, R.raw.constancy);
    player.start();
}
}
```

Reference to bundled MP3 ②

The code in listing 11.2 is an excerpt from an `Activity` in our app called `ImageBrowser-Activity`. This `Activity` has code for creating the UI that allows users to pick images to use in the slideshow that our app will create for them. Most of that code has been omitted from the listing so that we can concentrate on the code to play our theme music. To play music, we need an instance of `android.media.MediaPlayer` ❶. There are many ways to create an instance of this class, including using its public, no-argument constructor. In this case, we used one of a few common factory methods. This one takes a `Context` object and a resource identifier to a multimedia file that will be played. The latter parameter ❷ is `R.raw.constancy`, which was generated. By now, you can probably guess where this came from, but figure 11.2 shows you the file/directory structure that it represents.

As you can see from figure 11.2, you can add any kind of file you want to the `/res/raw` directory. The `aapt` tool will create an identifier for it as it would for any resource. As we saw in listing 11.2, this identifier can be used directly with the `Media-Player` class, providing a convenient way to use multimedia resources that are part of your application.

The code in listing 11.2 is simple, but covers many common use cases for loading multimedia that's part of an application. But it assumes there's a specific multimedia file that needs to be loaded, and provides a strong coupling between your application code and these files. If you need more flexibility, then you'll want to look at the `android.content.res.AssetManager` class. For an example of using this, let's say that instead of playing a single audio file, we have a directory of files. Perhaps we have a product manager who's having a tough time deciding what songs should be used, so we want to minimize the coupling between the songs (their names, how

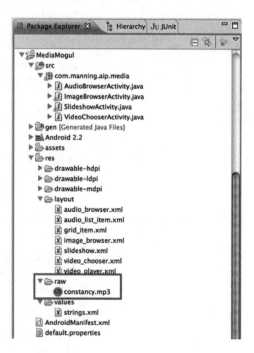

Figure 11.2 MediaMogul directory structure with theme music resource

many there are, and so forth) and our code. Here's how we can use the AssetManager to accomplish this.

Listing 11.3   Using `AssetManager` to load songs into a queue

```
public class ImageBrowserActivity extends Activity {
    private MediaPlayer player;
    // other code omitted
    @Override
    public void onCreate(Bundle savedInstanceState) {
        super.onCreate(savedInstanceState);
        // other code omitted
        playThemeMusic();
    }

    private void playThemeMusic() {
        player = new MediaPlayer();
        AssetManager mgr = getResources().getAssets();
        String audioDir = "audio";
        try {
            final LinkedList<FileDescriptor> queue =
                new LinkedList<FileDescriptor>();
            for (String song : mgr.list("audio")){
                queue.add(mgr.openFd(audioDir
                    + "/" + song).getFileDescriptor());
            }
            playNextSong(queue);
            player.setOnCompletionListener(
                    new OnCompletionListener(){
                @Override
                public void onCompletion(MediaPlayer mp) {
                    try {
                        playNextSong(queue);
                    } catch (IOException e) {
                        Log.e(LOG_TAG,
                            "Exception loading theme music",e);
                    }
                }
            });
        } catch (IOException e) {
            Log.e(LOG_TAG, "Exception loading theme music",e);
        }
    }

    private void playNextSong(LinkedList<FileDescriptor> queue)
        throws IOException {
        if (!queue.isEmpty()){
            FileDescriptor song = queue.poll();
            player.setDataSource(song);
            player.prepare();
            player.start();
        }
    }
}
```

1 Get ref to AssetManager

2 List files to iterate over

3 Enqueue FileDescriptor for each file

4 Pass FileDescriptor to MediaPlayer

AssetManager provides access to multimedia resources that are part of your application. Its API leverages Java I/O APIs. You can get a handle on the ResourceManager easily from any Context object ❶. Then you can use it to access an individual file or a directory. In listing 11.3, we use it to get a listing of all of the files in the audio directory ❷. Now we can iterate over those files without having to know the names of each file at compile time. For each file, we can get a java.io.FileDescriptor ❸ that can be used as a source for the MediaPlayer ❹, instead of using a resource identifier as we saw in listing 11.2. Now you might be wondering exactly what files will be loaded by the code in the listing 11.3. Figure 11.3 shows this structure.

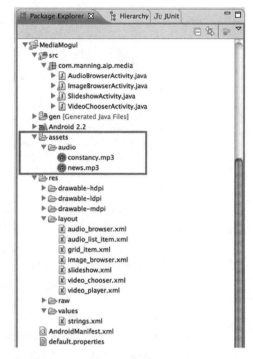

Figure 11.3 Storing multimedia files as assets

In this case the multimedia files are stored in the /assets directory, completely outside of the /res directory where resources are placed. Inside this directory, we're free to create subdirectories as we see fit to help us keep our files organized. In this example, we put our files into the audio subdirectory. If you go back to listing 11.3, we still have a strong coupling to the name of this subdirectory, but there's no coupling to any particular file. You could have one file or a hundred files (or none for that matter). They'll all get queued up and played eventually.

The two techniques discussed so far work well for resources that are bundled with your application. But you'll often want to access personal media files that the user has stored on the device. In particular, for our MediaMogul application we need to show the user pictures from their device so they can choose which ones they want to use. Such files are going to be on the device's SD card. We have a variety of ways to locate and access such multimedia, but the simplest way is to treat them as files, similar to what we did previously with the AssetManager. Here's how this simple technique works.

Listing 11.4 Adapter that accesses images from the SD card

```
import static android.os.Environment.*;
private class GridAdapter extends BaseAdapter{
    private List<File> imageFiles;
    private List<Bitmap> thumbs;
//other code omitted                                        Open public  ❶
    public GridAdapter(){                                   pictures directory
        File picturesDir =
            getExternalStoragePublicDirectory(DIRECTORY_PICTURES);
```

```
    int maxNumFiles;
    String[] nameArray = picturesDir.list();              List all files
    if (nameArray == null){                          2    in directory
       maxNumFiles = 0;
    } else {
       maxNumFiles = nameArray.length;
    }
    ArrayList<File> theFiles = new ArrayList<File>(maxNumFiles);
    if (maxNumFiles == 0) return;
    for (String fileName : nameArray){
       File file = new File(picturesDir, fileName);
       if (file.isFile()){
          theFiles.add(file);                             Add each image
       }                                            3    to local cache
    }
    imageFiles = Collections.unmodifiableList(theFiles);
    ArrayList<Bitmap> tempThumbs =
       new ArrayList<Bitmap>(imageFiles.size());
    for (int i=0;i<imageFiles.size();i++){          4    Convert files to
       tempThumbs.add(makeThumb(i));                      Bitmap and cache
    }
    thumbs = Collections.unmodifiableList(tempThumbs);
  }
}
```

The code in listing 11.4 is an excerpt from the GridAdapter class. This is an inner class inside the ImageBrowserActivity class that we saw in listings 11.2 and 11.3. As the name suggests, it's an android.widget.Adapter implementation that powers an android.widget.GridView. The GridView is used to display a grid of all of the images that the user will choose from. Those images come from the common public pictures directory ❶. The user and applications can store images anywhere they want on the SD card, but there are conventions for where these kinds of files should be stored. In listing 11.4, we used the Environment.getExternalStoragePublicDirectory method along with several constants in that class that reference these common locations. Table 11.1 shows some of those constants and the kinds of files they store.

Table 11.1   Public media directory constants

Constant	Description
DIRECTORY_PICTURES	Pictures that the user has put on the device
DIRECTORY_MUSIC	Music that the user has put on the device
DIRECTORY_MOVIES	Movies that the user has put on the device
DIRECTORY_DCIM	Pictures and videos that the user has taken with the device's camera

These are some of the common directories that you might need to access if you're using multimedia in your application. There are several other common directories, some for more specialized types of audio such as ringtones, notification sounds, and so on. Going back to listing 11.4, the getExternalStoragePublicDirectory method returns a `java.io.File`. Once we have that, it's easy to iterate over the files in the directory ❷, creating a `File` for each one that's not a directory ❸, and finally loading each image into a `Bitmap` ❹. Note that we eagerly created a cache of these `Bitmaps`. They're going to be used in a `GridView`, so we don't want to create `Bitmaps` as we scroll the `GridView`. Caching them will make scrolling smoother.

What any given user sees when they load this application will be different, depending on what images they have on their device. The code in listing 11.4 shows how to easily get to these files and then work with them as any other `File` object in Java. In this case, we loaded them into `Bitmaps`, but we could've loaded music or video files to the `MediaPlayer`.

Devices without an SD card

The previous example used the `Environment.getExternalStoragePublicDirectory` API. External storage generally equates to an SD card, usually of the microSD variety. But what happens if the device doesn't have an SD card? This is the case with third-generation Android devices such as Nexus S, as well as other Android-running devices like GoogleTV. For such devices, some portion of the internal/built-in storage will be used by Android as virtual external storage. This area can still be mounted by users and accessed as a filesystem, and then later accessed by APIs such as `getExternalStoragePublicDirectory`.

DISCUSSION

Media files are first and foremost files. Android provides several easy ways to work with them by using Java File APIs that are familiar to many developers. So far in this chapter, you've seen how these can be used with files stored in the application's `/res/` `assets` folder or the device's SD card. If you're familiar with Java's I/O capabilities, then you know that they're not limited to local files like this. You can use the network to open up a `java.io.InputStream` to read in an image or audio file from over the network. It wouldn't be too difficult to modify the code in listing 11.4 to get images from a user's Flickr account or some other photo-sharing provider. We saw some examples of this back in chapter 2, where we loaded images of eBay Daily Deal items over the network.

Another similarity you might notice between the code in chapter 2 and the code in listing 11.4 is that they both use various caching techniques when working with collections of images. In chapter 2, we cached the images that were downloaded from over the network. In this chapter, the images were local to the device, yet they were still cached in memory. To understand why, try running the MediaMogul app with a large number of images in the public picture directory. The resulting `GridView` will have many rows of data. With the images cached in memory, you'll be able to scroll this `GridView` quickly. If you don't cache in memory and instead call the `makeThumb` method each time a cell in the `GridView` is rendered, scrolling will be jerky. This method reads in the image and resizes it to fit into the `GridView`. The moral of the story is that you don't want to create images on the fly for any kind of list or grid.

There's an obvious drawback to caching images in memory—you could run out of memory. A common technique for dealing with this problem is to wait to load images in lists or grids until after the scrolling slows down. The effect of this is that a user scrolls a list, and then once the scrolling stops, the images "pop in." A single place-holder can be used for all images until the real image pops in.

So far we've talked about media files that are either part of an application or in a shared directory on the device. But media files aren't limited to these locations. Fortunately, Android provides a good way to find all such files using its `MediaStore`. In the next two sections, we'll look at different ways to work with this useful interface.

TECHNIQUE 56   **Using media ContentProviders**

If you have an Android device and use it on a regular basis, you might've noticed the Android media scanner. This service runs most noticeably when your device boots up and you see a message about it on your notification bar. If you have a large amount of storage, it can take awhile to finish its scan. It runs at other times too. In each case, it's looking for media files and creating a shared database about those files. This is both convenient and powerful. Let's see how we can access this data.

PROBLEM

You need to find all of the media of a certain type on the device, as well as metadata about that media. You need to know how to find and open each of these files. But you don't want to read all of the files on the device, and parse through the headers/meta-data of each file. Not only would it be a long process that would require you to write a lot of code, it's completely unnecessary because Android's media scanner does this for you. You need to access the data collected by the media scanner.

SOLUTION

The media scanner is exposed to applications as an Android `ContentProvider`. We talked about `ContentProviders` extensively in chapters 7 and 8, so we won't go into a lot of detail about how they work. Instead, let's concentrate on the `ContentProviders` that we should use to find media on a device.

Let's go back to our MediaMogul application. So far we've created an interface that lets the user browse pictures on their device and choose several of these pictures to be used in a slideshow. The next step in creating a slideshow will be to select music to play during the slideshow. We want to find all of the music on the device and let the user pick one of the songs. But we don't want to show them any audio file on the device, because there may be ringtones or files for creating alarms, notifications, or other sound effects used by applications. Instead, we want to make sure we only present music. Android's `MediaStore` (created by the media scanner) organizes metadata about all media files, including audio files, so it's definitely the way to go. Figure 11.4 shows this part of our application.

Figure 11.4 shows a list of songs, Each song has a radio button and a play button. The source of the data for the list is an `Adapter`, and that's where we'll need to access a `ContentProvider` to get the songs on the device. Here's the code for this `Adapter`.

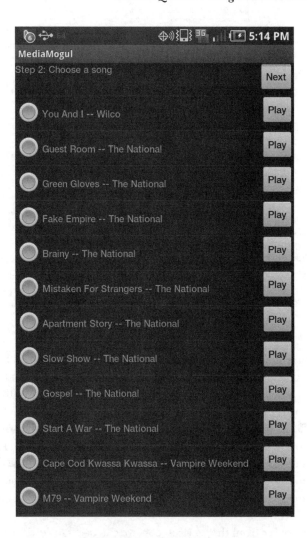

Figure 11.4   Choosing a song for the slideshow

Listing 11.5   Finding all of the music on a device

```java
import static android.provider.BaseColumns._ID;
import static android.provider.MediaStore.Audio.AudioColumns.ARTIST;
import static android.provider.MediaStore.Audio.AudioColumns.IS_MUSIC;
import static android.provider.MediaStore.Audio.Media.EXTERNAL_CONTENT_URI;
import static android.provider.MediaStore.MediaColumns.DATA;
import static android.provider.MediaStore.MediaColumns.TITLE;
private class AudioListAdapter extends BaseAdapter{
    private Cursor cursor;                                              ◁─❶ Query results
    private Activity activity = AudioBrowserActivity.this;
    //other code omitted
    public AudioListAdapter(){
        super();
        String[] columns = {TITLE,ARTIST,_ID, DATA};                   ❷ Media
        String whereClause = IS_MUSIC + " = ?";               ◁─          metadata
        String[] whereValues = {"1"};                          ❸ Limit results
                                                                  to music
```

```
    cursor = managedQuery(EXTERNAL_CONTENT_URI,
       columns,
       whereClause,
       whereValues,
       null
    );
}

@Override
public int getCount() {
    return cursor.getCount();
}

@Override
public Object getItem(int position) {
    Song song = new Song();
    cursor.moveToPosition(position);
    song.title = cursor.getString(cursor.getColumnIndex(TITLE));
    song.artist = cursor.getString(cursor.getColumnIndex(ARTIST));
    song.id = cursor.getLong(cursor.getColumnIndex(_ID));
    song.setUri(cursor.getString(
       cursor.getColumnIndex(DATA)));
    return song;
}
}
```

④ Use managed query for convenience

⑤ Move cursor to get next song

⑥ Create URI to use with MediaPlayer

The Adapter shown in listing 11.5 powers the ListView that we saw in figure 11.4. It's backed by an android.database.Cursor ①, the type of object you typically get from a ContentProvider (or from a SQLite database; see chapter 7 for details on both). We create the Cursor in its constructor by specifying what data we want from the Media-Store ContentProvider ②. In this case, we only want the internal ID of the song, its title and artist, and a URI to the song. In addition we declare that we only want music, no ringtones or sound effects ③, from the MediaStore. Finally, we create the Cursor using the managedCursor method from the Activity superclass ④. This will bind the lifecycle of the Cursor to the lifecycle of the Activity, so we don't have to worry about closing the Cursor, and so forth.

Once we've created the Cursor from the MediaStore, we can use it to retrieve a Song object for each item in the ListView ⑤. The Song object referenced in listing 11.5 is a simple datastructure encapsulating the data from the MediaStore ContentProvider. The only thing notable is that it's a Parcelable, so that we can pass an instance between activities. Most of its data is simple: strings and a long. Its uri field is the only complex part. It's an android.net.Uri object. We could've used a string (which is what we get from the Cursor), but a Uri is more convenient because it's what the MediaPlayer needs (what we'll use to play the song), and is also a Parcelable. So the setUri method on the Song class creates a Uri from a string like we get from the Cursor ⑥.

DISCUSSION

ContentProviders are a powerful feature of Android, even if they do have a crusty, implementation-leaking interface (Cursors). This technique shows a simple example of querying the MediaStore provider to get some basic information about all of the

Cursors and Adapters

Using a `Cursor` to back an `Adapter` for either a `ListView` or `GridView` is a common pattern in Android applications. It should come as no surprise that Android provides several convenience classes for this pattern. The first is the `CursorAdapter` abstract class. This class takes a `Cursor` and asks you to implement methods for creating a new view and for binding data from the `Cursor` to a `View`. It manages advancing the `Cursor` for you. If you're creating your `View` from a layout XML file, you can use a `ResourceCursorAdapter`, an abstract subclass of `CursorAdapter`. Often, you can reduce your code even further by using a `SimpleCursorAdapter`. This is a concrete subclass of `ResourceCursorAdapter`, so you must use XML for your layout. For many simple `ListView`s or `GridView`s, you can use this without any additional code by providing one or more simple objects to bind to `TextView`s or `ImageView`s, referenced by their IDs. For a more complicated example like the one in this chapter, you can provide an implementation of a `SimpleCursorAdapter.ViewBinder`.

songs on the device. You can get more information about the songs, such as the size of the files, the encoding (mp3, ogg, and so on), the year the song was released, its track number on the album it came from, and more. Take a look at `android.provider.MediaStore.Audio` for more information.

Audio isn't the only type of media on the user's device. In technique 55 we saw how we could load images from the shared pictures folder. We could've also used the `MediaStore ContentProvider` to find these pictures, plus other pictures located elsewhere on the device's external storage. Check `android.provider.MediaStore.Images` for available information about the images stored on the device. The final type of media that you can query using the `MediaStore ContentProvider` is video. By now you can probably guess that you should look at `android.provider.MediaStore.Video` to find out what kind of information Android tracks videos on the device. In the next section, we'll retrieve a video to use in our slideshow application.

TECHNIQUE 57 Using Intents and Activities

In the previous section, we saw how straightforward it is to use a `ContentProvider` to query all of the music on the device. We used this to create a `ListView`, shown in figure 11.4. In the previous section, we directly read image files from external storage to create a `GridView`. In both cases, we want the user to select one or more media files to use in a slideshow. Our UI had some nice features to it, such as multiselection of images and previewing songs without selecting them. For step 3 in our slideshow creation, we want the user to select a single video to play at the end of the slideshow. This is a common use case for applications—needing the user to select a single media file—and Android provides an easy way to do this.

PROBLEM

Your application requires the user to select a single multimedia file to be used by the application. Perhaps you have a social networking application and you want the user to select a single image or video to share with their friends. Perhaps your application is a game and you want the user to select a song to listen to while they play. Either way, you only want one file, and it seems excessive to have to create a custom UI for such a common task.

SOLUTION

Android solves this problem via two key features. First and foremost, Android's `Intent`-based architecture is the key ingredient. This allows for a loose coupling between applications. In particular, it allows for the second part of the solution, a reusable `Activity` for selecting media files. Figure 11.5 shows what this will look like.

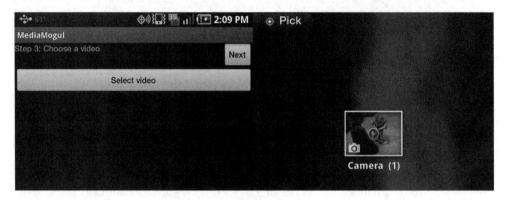

Figure 11.5   Selecting a video to be used in the slideshow

You can reuse this `Activity` only by knowing the name of its action to invoke it. The following listing shows how you can do this.

Listing 11.6   Using a common `Activity` to select a video file

```
public class VideoChooserActivity extends Activity {
    private static final int SELECT_VIDEO = 1;
    private Uri videoUri;
    @Override
    protected void onCreate(Bundle savedInstanceState) {
        super.onCreate(savedInstanceState);
        setContentView(R.layout.video_chooser);
        Button vidBtn = (Button) findViewById(R.id.vidBtn);          ①  Initiate button
        vidBtn.setOnClickListener(new OnClickListener(){
            @Override
            public void onClick(View button) {
                Intent videoChooser =
                    new Intent(Intent.ACTION_GET_CONTENT);           ②  Create Intent
                videoChooser.setType("video/*");
                startActivityForResult(                              ③  Get videos
                    videoChooser, SELECT_VIDEO);
            }                                                        ④  Start Activity
        });
        // more ui creation code omitted
```

```
    }
@Override                                                           Complete activity  ⑤
protected void onActivityResult(int requestCode, int resultCode,
    Intent data) {                                                              ⤶
    super.onActivityResult(requestCode, resultCode, data);
    if (requestCode != SELECT_VIDEO || resultCode != RESULT_OK){
        return;
    }
    VideoView video = (VideoView) findViewById(R.id.video);
    videoUri = data.getData();                                     ⟵      Get URI
    video.setVideoURI(videoUri);                                      ⑥   of video
        // video playback code omitted
    }
}
```

The `Activity` gets a handle to a button on the screen ❶. The user needs to tap on this button to initiate the video selection process. When this happens, we want to start a common `Activity` that calls the `Activity` to get the content. It can be referenced using the constant string `Intent.ACTION_GET_CONTENT` ❷. This `Activity` has an `Intent` filter saying it will handle any `Intents` that specify `Intent.ACTION_GET_CONTENT` as their action. This `Activity` can be used for different types of files and multimedia, but we only want videos. We declare that its MIME type should be `video/*` ❸—any kind of video, regardless of its format/encoding. Finally we use `Activity`'s `startActivityForResult` method to start the get content `Activity` ❹.

Now `startActivityForResult` is an asynchronous call (it returns void). But it'll cause the `Activity` to be displayed in the foreground, so it'll seem synchronous to the user. It's still asynchronous though, so we must provide a callback to get the result. The `Activity` class already defines this callback—the `Activity` class's `onActivityRe-sult` method. We override this method ❺. This method will receive an `Intent`, and we can use this `Intent`'s `getData` method to retrieve the URI of the video that the user selected ❻.

In figure 11.5, the image on the left is our application's UI. You can see the Select Video button referenced in listing 11.6. When the user taps on it, the `Activity` is started. It uses a `Gallery` widget to show files to choose from, shown on the right side of figure 11.5. This shows the videos organized by location. If it finds more than one video, they'll be shown as a stack. Tapping on a stack changes it to a grid that allows the user to choose a video. It's a nice UI, for free! Further, this is used by many Android apps, so users are familiar with the interface and how it works.

DISCUSSION

This technique is the last of three techniques that you can use in your applications to find and select multimedia files. These techniques demonstrate the different layers of abstractions available to use as a developer. At the lowest level of abstraction is direct access to the underlying filesystem. Even at this low level, Android provides some hints for finding things. At the next level of abstraction, you use a `ContentProvider` to query metadata about files stored throughout the device. You don't have to know where the files are to query about them. The third technique demonstrates the highest level of abstraction. In this case, you don't know about all of the multimedia files on the device. You only know the URI to the one file that the user selected. This is often all you need, and you could work down the levels of abstraction from there if you needed to. It has the extra benefit of abstracting away the UI/selection process for you.

Finally, we mentioned that the UI that the `Activity` used is a `Gallery` widget. This is a common widget used for working with images and videos. In fact, we could've used it for the image selection `Activity` we saw in technique 55. You'd need to provide it an `Adapter` that sends it images to show. The `Gallery` you see in figure 11.5 uses some additional styling and on top of what you get by default, but the default is still fairly attractive.

Now that we've seen the many ways that we can find and select multimedia files in Android, we need to explore some ways to work with those files. This can involve showing images, as well as playing audio and video. Some applications may not need this (for example if your application wants the user to select multimedia files so that they can be shared via a web service). Our MediaMogul definitely requires this, because we want to create a slideshow using all of the multimedia assets that the user has selected.

11.3   *Media playback*

Finding and loading multimedia files stored on the device or even over the network is more useful if you can also play those files back. Android makes this simple while still providing some sophisticated options. In fact, playing back media files is generally more straightforward than finding and loading such files. In this section, we'll discuss three techniques for working with images, audio, and video. All of the code will come from a single `Activity` in our MediaMogul application. This `Activity` will play the slideshow by using the images, song, and video that the user selected in the application. Unfortunately, a screenshot of this application doesn't do justice to the application, because even the display of the images is animated. Displaying and animating these images is the first technique that we'll discuss.

TECHNIQUE 58   **Images and simple animations**

Showing an image with an Android application is simple. We've shown examples of this throughout the book. It usually involves creating a `Bitmap` and using it as a source to an `ImageView`. We don't need a technique for this, but you can do some more interesting things with images, and creating animations is one of those. Animations come in handy when creating a slideshow similar to our MediaMogul application. Any application that needs to show multiple images can generally benefit from some type of animation to transition between these images.

PROBLEM

You have multiple images that you need to display. You want to display only a subset of them at a time, perhaps one at a time. To increase the appeal to the user, you want to use an animation to transition between these images.

SOLUTION

You might be pleasantly surprised to learn that creating animations in Android is simple. The `android.view.animation` package has a number of classes for creating different types of animations. Table 11.2 shows these convenience classes and describes their high-level functionality.

Table 11.2 Basic Android animation types

Animation class	Description
AlphaAnimation	Animate by changing the transparency of a `View`
RotateAnimation	Animate by rotating a `View`
ScaleAnimation	Animate by changing the size of a `View`
TranslationAnimation	Animate by changing the position of a `View`

In addition to these basic animation types, you can create your own animations or create animations by assembling simple animations. Several of these classes allow you to provide your own `Interpolator` and/or `Transformation` classes to customize the basic animations. Also, note that in table 11.2, each animation can be applied to any `View`, not only to an `ImageView`. You can get creative with the animation toolbox provided by Android. For our purposes, we'll use an `AlphaAnimation` to fade an `ImageView` into and out of the screen. To understand how this will work, we need to look at the layout of our UI, shown next.

Listing 11.7 Slideshow layout XML

```xml
<FrameLayout xmlns:android="http://schemas.android.com/apk/res/android"
    android:id="@+id/frame"
    android:layout_width="wrap_content"
    android:layout_height="wrap_content">
    <ImageView android:id="@+id/slide0"
        android:layout_gravity="center_vertical"
        android:layout_width="wrap_content"
        android:layout_height="wrap_content" />
    <ImageView android:id="@+id/slide1"
        android:layout_gravity="center_vertical"
        android:layout_width="wrap_content"
        android:layout_height="wrap_content" />
</FrameLayout>
```

The layout for our slideshow is simple. It's a `FrameLayout` with two `ImageViews`. We learned about `FrameLayout` in section 4.3.2. It pins all of its child views to the top left of the screen and only shows one at a time. In this case it'll pin the two `ImageViews`, which we've called `slide0` and `slide1`. It'll show only one at a time, and by default that will be `slide0`, because it's defined first. Now let's look at the `Activity` that will use this layout.

Listing 11.8 `Activity` that creates a slideshow

```java
public class SlideshowActivity extends Activity {

    private ImageView leftSlide;
    private ImageView rightSlide;
    private Handler handler = new Handler();
    private static final int TIME_PER_SLIDE = 3*1000;
    private boolean playingSlides = true;

    @Override
    public void onCreate(Bundle savedInstanceState) {
        super.onCreate(savedInstanceState);
        setContentView(R.layout.slideshow);
        leftSlide = (ImageView) findViewById(R.id.slide0);       ❶ Get ImageViews from layout
        rightSlide = (ImageView) findViewById(R.id.slide1);
        // additional code for sound and video omitted
    }
    @Override
    public void onResume() {
        super.onResume();
        final DissolveTransition animation =                     ❷ Create custom animation
            new DissolveTransition();
        handler.postDelayed(new Runnable(){
            @Override
            public void run() {                                  ❸ Start animation in 100ms
                animation.nextSlide();
            }
        }, 100);
    }
}
```

The `Activity` for creating and displaying our slideshow is appropriately titled `Slide-showActivity`. When it's first created, it creates member variables for the two `Ima-geViews` we saw defined in listing 11.7 ❶. Then when it's started/restarted, it creates an instance of a custom animation ❷ that we'll see defined in listing 11.9. Then we use a `Handler` to start running the animation on the main UI thread after a 100ms delay ❸. As you can see, most of the hard work is being done by this `DissolveTransi-tion` class. The following listing shows how this class creates the fade in/out effect that we want for our slideshow.

Listing 11.9 Custom slideshow animation

```java
private class DissolveTransition{
    private ArrayList<String> images;
    private int count = 0;
    private Bitmap currentImage = null;
    private Bitmap nextImage = null;
    public DissolveTransition() {
        images =
            getIntent().getStringArrayListExtra("imageFileNames");   ❶ Get images
        currentImage = getNextImage();                              ❷ Start with random image
        leftSlide.setImageBitmap(currentImage);
```

```
            nextImage = getNextImage();
            rightSlide.setImageBitmap(nextImage);
            count = 1;
    }
    private void nextSlide() {
        AlphaAnimation animation = new AlphaAnimation(0.0f, 1.0f);
        if ((count % 2) == 0) {
            animation = new AlphaAnimation(1.0f, 0.0f);       <---  ❸  Fade-in or
        }                                                             fade-out
        animation.setStartOffset(TIME_PER_SLIDE);
        animation.setDuration(TIME_PER_SLIDE);
        animation.setFillAfter(true);
        animation.setAnimationListener(new
                Animation.AnimationListener() {
            @Override
            public void onAnimationStart(Animation animation) {}
            @Override
            public void onAnimationRepeat(Animation animation) {}
            @Override                                                ❹  Keep
            public void onAnimationEnd(Animation animation) {  <---     looping
                if (playingSlides){
                    nextImage = getNextImage();
                    ImageView backgroundImage =
                        (count % 2 == 0) ? rightSlide :
                        leftSlide;
                    backgroundImage.setImageBitmap(
                        nextImage);
                    count++;
                    nextSlide();
                }
            }
        });
        rightSlide.startAnimation(animation);
        currentImage = nextImage;
    }
}
```

Our animation class starts by getting the array of images ❶ that have been passed in
to it, which it'll use for the slideshow. It then uses the getNextImage method to get a
random image from the list passed in to it ❷. This method isn't in the listing (check
the full source code if you're curious), but picks a random image that hasn't been previously shown. If you go back to listing 11.8, you can see that we start the animation by
calling its nextSlide method. This method is where we use AlphaAnimation. We alternate whether this animation is going to fade in (go from an alpha of 0 to 1) or fade
out (go from an alpha of 1 to 0) ❸. We then set the AlphaAnimation's animationLis-
tener object by creating an anonymous inner class that implements the Anima-
tion.AnimationListener interface. This interface defines three callbacks, for the
animation's start, end, and repeat. In this case, we only care about the end ❹. We
swap images out, and loop back by calling nextSlide. This is all it takes to create a dissolve transition like you often see in popular presentation software.

DISCUSSSION

This technique is a small foray into the world of animations. As we saw earlier, Android has several basic animations. You can use these to compose more complex ones. Any such animation is usually referred to as a *tween*. If you've ever used interactive graphics programs such as Adobe Flash, then you know that a lot can be accomplished with tweens.

Often your animations are more stateless than the one shown here. They perform a tween on a given `View` and don't care about anything else. In such cases, you can often define the tween completely using XML. You can then load the `Animation` using its resource identifier by using the `AnimationUtils` class. Once you have the `Animation` loaded, you can then apply it to any `View` object.

The code we've seen so far will show each of the images that the user selected, using the dissolve transition animation that we created in listing 11.9. Now we need to play music at the same time, and we have a slideshow. We'll also want to consider what happens when the slideshow is paused, restarted, and so forth. For that, we need to understand how to playback and control audio.

TECHNIQUE 59   **Controlling audio**

Is it an MP3 player that's also a phone? Is it a phone that can also play MP3s? At this point, it doesn't matter anymore. Users expect their device to play music, and that's certainly true of Android users. Audio playback isn't only for jukebox apps though; many apps benefit from being able to play audio, whether it's a whole song or a sound effect to let the user know about an event in their application.

PROBLEM

We want to play an audio file from within our application. This audio file could be music or any sound file. It could be local or accessed over the network. We don't care what its format is; it could be an MP3 or an Ogg file, as long as our device has the required codec. We also need to control when the audio plays and when it doesn't, based on events in our application.

SOLUTION

Earlier in this chapter in listings 11.2 and 11.3, we saw references to Android's `Media-Player` class. We used it to play theme music for our application. This is the primary way to play any kind of audio file. It's used in several other places in our MediaMogul application. One of those places is on the song selection screen shown in figure 11.4. In that interface, we have a Play button so the user can listen to a portion of the song to help them decide whether they want to use it in the slideshow. In listing 11.5, we examined the `Adapter` class used to back that list of songs. But we didn't look at the `Adapter`'s `getView` method, which is what creates the UI for each song, and in particular that Play button, as shown in the following listing.

Listing 11.10   Creating the song list UI

```
@Override
public View getView(int position, View row, ViewGroup parent) {
    // Other UI code omitted
```

```
   final Song song = (Song) getItem(position);
   final Button playBtn = holder.playBtn;
   if (playingSongs.contains(song.id)){
      playBtn.setText(R.string.pause);
   } else {
      playBtn.setText(R.string.play);
   }
   playBtn.setOnClickListener(new OnClickListener(){          ◁── ❶ Stop music
      private Handler handler = new Handler();
      MediaPlayer player = null;
      long maxTime = 15L*1000; // 15 seconds
        long timeLeft = maxTime;                              ◁── ❷ Track time
        Runnable autoStop;
        @Override
        public void onClick(View button) {
           if (player == null){
              player = MediaPlayer.create(
                 activity, song.uri);
           }                                                       ❸ Start, if not
           if (!playingSongs.contains(song.id)){             ◁──┘    playing
              player.start();
              playingSongs.add(song.id);
              autoStop = new Runnable(){                     ◁── ❹ Stop music
                 @Override
                 public void run() {
                    player.pause();
                    player.seekTo(0);
                    playingSongs.remove(
                       song.id);
                    playBtn.setText(
                       R.string.play);
                       timeLeft = maxTime;
                 }
              };
              handler.postDelayed(autoStop,
                 timeLeft);                                  ◁── ❺ Schedule stop
              playBtn.setText(R.string.pause);
           } else {
              player.pause();
              playingSongs.remove(song.id);
              timeLeft = maxTime -                                ❻ Update
                 player.getCurrentPosition();              ◁──┘    time left
              playBtn.setText(R.string.play);
              handler.removeCallbacks(autoStop);          ◁──┐
           }                                                    ❼ Remove
        }                                                          scheduled stop
      }
   });
   // radio button code omitted
   return row;
   }
}
```

A lot is going on in listing 11.10. We start by getting the Song object to correspond to a
position in our list. Take a look at listing 11.5 to see how this is done. Then we get a

handle on the Play button, which we call `playBtn`. Our `Adapter` contains a `HashSet` of all songs that are playing. You might be wondering: doesn't this imply that there could be more than one? That's exactly right: the user could tap Play on multiple files and they'll all play simultaneously. This might not be the most user friendly, but it wouldn't be hard to change the behavior to pause the current song when you tap another. But we wanted to demonstrate that the `MediaPlayer` isn't a singleton by default. Multiple `MediaPlayers` can exist at the same time, and they can all play audio. To change the preceding code so that only one song plays at a time, you could create a single `MediaPlayer` shared by all of the songs in the list.

Getting back to listing 11.10, we check whether the selected song is one of the currently playing songs and toggle the text on `playBtn` from Play to Pause, accordingly. Next, we set up the `OnClickHandler` for `playBtn`. First, we create a `Handler` that we'll use to automatically stop the music ❶. We only want to play the first 15 seconds of a song. If somebody pauses the song 5 seconds in, we want to remember that we're 5 seconds in and then only play 10 more seconds if they unpause the song. So we create a local variable to keep track of how much time is left ❷.

Next, we implement the `onClick` method of our `OnClickHandler`. We check whether a `MediaPlayer` has already been created. If not, we create one using code that specifies the song's URI. Then, we check to see if the song is already playing ❸. If it's not, we create a `Runnable` to implement the auto-stop feature ❹. This `Runnable` will execute when the song reaches the 15-second mark. In that case it'll pause the `MediaPlayer` and move it back to the beginning of the song. We then schedule this `Runnable` to execute based on how much of the 15 seconds is left ❺.

If the song is already playing when the user taps on `playBtn`, we pause the Media-Player and recalculate how much of the maximum 15 seconds is left ❻. Finally, we cancel the auto-stop `Runnable` we created earlier. We do so by using the `Handler`'s `removeCallbacks` method ❼. If the user taps to play the song again, the `Runnable` will be recreated and rescheduled based on the time remaining.

The code in listing 11.10 demonstrates how to control the `MediaPlayer` based on interactions with the user. It also demonstrates some automatic behavior to stop the song after it has played for a maximum of 15 seconds.

Often, we want to automatically manage a `MediaPlayer` based on the lifecycle of the `Activity` that's playing it. This is the case for our `SlideshowActivity` that we saw in listing 11.8. You might recall that this is the `Activity` that plays our slideshow. The user may have selected a long song to use for the slideshow, and if they leave the `Activity` for whatever reason, we don't want to continue playing music. The following listing shows how we can manage this situation.

Listing 11.11   Binding playback to the lifecycle of an `Activity`

```
public class SlideshowActivity extends Activity {
    private Song song;
    private MediaPlayer player;
    @Override
```

```
public void onCreate(Bundle savedInstanceState) {
    // other UI code omitted
    song = getIntent().getParcelableExtra("selectedSong");      ←  ❶ Get song
    player = MediaPlayer.create(this, song.uri);
    player.setOnCompletionListener(                             ←┐   Start video after
            new OnCompletionListener(){                          ❷  music stops
        @Override
        public void onCompletion(MediaPlayer mp) {
            // Code omitted
        }
    });
}
@Override
public void onResume() {
    super.onResume();                                ❸  Start or
    player.start();                                ←    unpause music
}
@Override
public void onPause(){
    super.onPause();
    if (player != null && player.isPlaying()){      ← ❹ Pause music
        player.pause();
    }
}
@Override
protected void onDestroy() {
    super.onDestroy();
    if (player != null && player.isPlaying()){
        player.stop();
    }                                              ❺  Free up
    player.release();                             ←    resources
}
// other code omitted
}
```

The code in listing 11.11 demonstrates the basics of tying media playback to the lifecycle of an `Activity`. During the `onCreate` method, we get the song that we want to play ❶ and create a `MediaPlayer` instance that's a member variable of our `Activity`. We also give it an `OnCompletionListener` ❷ to invoke when the `MediaPlayer` finishes playing the song. (We want to start playing the selected video when this happens, so we'll look at how we do that in technique 60.) Next we set our `MediaPlayer` to play in the `onResume` method of our `Activity` ❸. This will be invoked every time the `Activity` comes to the foreground. So it'll start playing the song if this is the first time the `Activity` has been started, or it'll resume/unpause the song if the `Activity` had been previously started but another `Activity` (from another application) has come to the foreground. In such a scenario, the `onPause` method of our `Activity` is called, and so that's where we want to pause our `MediaPlayer` ❹. This will prevent the Media-Player ❺ from continuing to play music when our `Activity` isn't in the foreground. Finally, when our `Activity` reaches the end of its lifecycle, its `onDestroy` method will be called and we want to make sure we free up the resources associated to our Media-Player (remember that it's reading from an open stream and sending sound to the device's audio channel, so multiple I/O resources are in use.)

DISCUSSION

In this section, we've looked at the most common way to control audio playback by using the MediaPlayer class. In the examples here, all of the audio has come from audio files local to the device. MediaPlayer is also well suited to playing back audio that comes from the network, as it'll handle buffering and stability for you. But there are a couple of other ways that you can play back audio on Android.

If you're developing a game, you'll want to look at the android.media.SoundPool class. This is perfect for playing a set of short sounds, especially if you require low latency. This is often the case in a game when you want that splash sound to play exactly when an object hits the water, for example. Android has another sound-related resource usually used for game developers: android.media.JetPlayer. This can be used to create a soundtrack for your game, and can help you sync the music to events in the game.

MediaPlayer, SoundPool, and even JetPlayer are all relatively high-level APIs offered by Android. If you need a much lower-level API, then you can use the android.media.AudioTrack API. In general if you find any of the preceding APIs too inflexible, you can probably drop down to using an AudioTrack. This is also the only way to play back audio files that use an encoding that isn't supported by the OS, but can be decoded by your application. It's also a common way to modify sound on the fly. Android 2.3 introduced another way to apply effects to audio that's being played back: the android.media.audiofx package. This includes several configurable effects for changing the equalization (bass/treble levels), adding reverb (echo), or applying virtualization (spatialize).

The number of options to audio playback in Android can seem intimidating. But MediaPlayer should be used for the vast majority of use cases. Even if you need to add an audio effect, you can use the audiofx package in conjunction with MediaPlayer. Android offers similar high-level APIs for working with video, as we'll see next.

TECHNIQUE 60   Watching video

Playing a video on your phone was unheard of a few years ago. Now it's another feature that users have come to expect. It's also another area where Android excels. Numerous Android devices sport large screens and 4G data connections, a killer combination for watching online high-definition video. It should come as no surprise that Google has made video playback simple for developers, given that the undisputed king of online video, YouTube, is part of the Google empire. Let's look at how simple it is.

PROBLEM

You want to play a video in your application. This video could be local to the device, or it could be streamed over the network. This is similar to audio playback, and as with audio playback, you don't care about the video's encoding. As long as the device has the proper codec, you want to be able to play the video.

SOLUTION

Video playback in Android is a cinch, and is similar to audio playback. In some ways it's even easier, because you generally expect the user to sit there and watch a video. You wouldn't typically play a video in the background while the user interacts with the

Figure 11.6 Video playback with controls

application (though you could) or bind its playback to events in your application (though you could do this too). Figure 11.6 shows what video playback will look like in our application.

To create a video playback as shown in figure 11.6, we'll rely on the MediaPlayer API. In listing 11.11, we mentioned that we wanted to start playing the video that the user selected after the music for the slideshow stops. Let's see how this can be done.

Listing 11.12 Playing video

```
public class SlideshowActivity extends Activity {
   private MediaController videoPlayer;
   private VideoView video;
   private boolean playingSlides = true;

   @Override
   public void onCreate(Bundle savedInstanceState) {
      // other code omitted
      player.setOnCompletionListener(new OnCompletionListener(){
         @Override
         public void onCompletion(MediaPlayer mp) {
            FrameLayout frame =
               (FrameLayout) findViewById(R.id.frame);
            frame.removeAllViews();
            playingSlides = false;
            video =
               new VideoView(SlideshowActivity.this);
            video.setLayoutParams(new LayoutParams(
```

① Remove slides from UI

② Create video player widget

```
            LayoutParams.FILL_PARENT,
            LayoutParams.FILL_PARENT));
        frame.addView(video);
        video.setVideoURI(
            (Uri) getIntent().                        ❸  Set URI of
            getExtras().get("videoUri"));                video to play
        videoPlayer = new MediaController(
            SlideshowActivity.this);                   ❹  Add media
        videoPlayer.setMediaPlayer(video);                controls
        video.setMediaController(videoPlayer);
        video.requestFocus();
        video.start();                                ❺  Play video
        }
    });
    }
// other code omitted
}
```

The code in listing 11.12 is a continuation of the code we saw in listing 11.11. When
the slideshow music finishes, we clear out the UI ❶. We also create an android.wid-
get.VideoView for playing a video ❷ and add it to the screen's layout. We then set
the source of our VideoView by getting the URI of the video that the user selected (in
figure 11.5) from the Intent that created this Activity ❸. We then create a Media-
Controller widget ❹. This will add controls to the VideoView so the user can control
the video playback. Finally, we automatically start playback ❺.

In figure 11.6 you can see that the VideoView with the MediaController controls
are activated. These provide pause/play, rewind, fast-forward, and seek functions.
These are controls that you could create yourself using the VideoView's APIs (which
are similar to the MediaPlayer APIs), but it's usually easier to rely on this built-in widget. It's used by many Android applications, for obvious reasons, so users are usually
already familiar with it.

DISCUSSION

Using a VideoView isn't the only way to play video in Android. Similar to audio playback,
there are other options. Alternatively you can create an android.view.SurfaceView.
A SurfaceView can be thought of as a canvas to draw on. Once you have one, you can
use its getHolder method to access its SurfaceHolder. You can then directly use a
MediaPlayer instance and pass the SurfaceHolder to its setDisplay method. Then you
can control video playback using the MediaPlayer instance and the video will be displayed on the SurfaceView that you created. But you won't be able to directly use the
MediaController widget that we used in listing 11.12. It's still possible to use the Media-
Controller by implementing the interface android.widget.MediaController.Medi-
aPlayerControl by using the MediaPlayer instance that you created. But this is what the
VideoView does for you automatically. It uses a MediaPlayer behind the scenes and del-
egates many of its calls to that MediaPlayer. Alternatively, you could provide your own
UI controls for the SurfaceView and MediaPlayer.

So far we've seen many different ways that you can present multimedia to your application's users, but we've only looked at multimedia from the consumption side of things.

Android devices are also capable of creating media files as well. Users will often want to create their own pictures or videos to share with other users or to use on their device. Let's look at some of the different ways to capture multimedia on Android devices.

11.4   Capturing input

Earlier in this chapter, we talked about how smartphone users use multimedia to share information. So far, we've concentrated on the consumption sides of things—viewing images, listening to audio, and watching videos from within an Android app. For the rest of this chapter we'll focus on how to capture input—how to take pictures and record audio and video from within an Android app. You might be surprised by how simple this is to do using Android. It's possible to complicate things, but we'll focus on straightforward ways to capture multimedia from your application. We'll also cover more advanced techniques and unusual situations where appropriate. We'll start with what is surely the most useful technique, taking pictures.

TECHNIQUE 61   Taking pictures

As an Android developer, there's a good chance that you use an Android device as your personal smartphone. If so, take a look at your most commonly used apps. If you're like me then you've probably put these apps on your phone's home screen. How many of them include the ability to capture a photo? For me, 7 of 17 apps on my home screen can capture input from the camera in one way or another. Of these, 6 use the technique that we're about to explore. This is the easy way to capture pictures, and it's what we'll focus on. As you'll see, it's both easy for you, the developer, and advantageous for your users.

PROBLEM

You want to allow a user to use your application to take a picture using one of the cameras on their Android device. You then want to access this picture to use it as part of your application. You want to let the user take full advantage of their device's capabilities. This may include access to a front-facing camera (if the device has one), or special photo-taking features such as panoramic photo capturing, flash photography, and so on.

SOLUTION

Wouldn't it be great if we could tell the user's device that the user wants to take a photograph with their device and it could take care of the rest? That's exactly what you can do, and that's what most applications do. Let's see how this can be done.

Listing 11.13   Taking a photograph with Android

```
import static
    android.provider.MediaStore.Images.Media.EXTERNAL_CONTENT_URI;
public class TitlePageActivity extends Activity {
    private Uri photoUri;
    private final static int TAKE_PHOTO = 1;
    private final static String PHOTO_URI = "photoUri";
    @Override
    protected void onCreate(Bundle savedInstanceState) {
```

```
        super.onCreate(savedInstanceState);
        setContentView(R.layout.title_page);
        Button takePhotoBtn = (Button) findViewById(R.id.takePhotoBtn);
        takePhotoBtn.setOnClickListener(new OnClickListener(){
            @Override
            public void onClick(View button) {              ❶ Request image
                Intent intent =                                capture
                    new Intent(
                        MediaStore.ACTION_IMAGE_CAPTURE);   ❷ Create
                photoUri = getContentResolver().insert(        MediaStore
                    EXTERNAL_CONTENT_URI, new ContentValues());  entry, get URI
                intent.putExtra(MediaStore.EXTRA_OUTPUT,
                    photoUri);                              ❸ Capture
                startActivityForResult(intent,TAKE_PHOTO);    URI
            }                                               ❹ Start Camera
        });                                                   Activity
        // ui code omitted
        if (savedInstanceState != null){
            photoUri = (Uri) savedInstanceState.get(PHOTO_URI);  ❺ Restore URI
        }                                                         from saved
    }                                                             state
    @Override
    protected void onSaveInstanceState(Bundle outState) {
        super.onSaveInstanceState(outState);
        outState.putParcelable(PHOTO_URI, photoUri);        ❻ Store URI in
    }                                                          saved state
    @Override
    protected void onActivityResult(int requestCode, int resultCode,
        Intent data) {
        super.onActivityResult(requestCode, resultCode, data);
        if (resultCode != Activity.RESULT_OK
              || requestCode != TAKE_PHOTO){
            return;
        }
        ImageView img =                                     ❼ Pass
            (ImageView) findViewById(R.id.photoThumb);          picture
        try {
            InputStream stream =                            ❽ Show
                getContentResolver().openInputStream(photoUri);  picture
            Bitmap bmp = BitmapFactory.decodeStream(stream);
            img.setImageBitmap(bmp);
        } catch (FileNotFoundException e) {
            Log.e("TitlePageActivity", "FileNotFound",e);
        }
    }
}
```

The code in listing 11.13 shows a simple `Activity` that includes a button that the user can tap on to capture a photo. When this button is tapped, we create an `Intent` to request that an image be captured ❶. The idea here is to use the system's built-in `Camera` application to capture the image, and then use the result of that `Activity` in our application. We need to tell the `Camera` where to store the picture that's taken, so we use the `ContentResolver` to insert a new row in the `MediaStore`'s images table ❷. This gives us a URI to the new row ❸ that we can then pass to the `Camera` as an extra on the `Intent`. Then we invoke `startActivityForResult` ❹, passing the `Intent` that we created plus a request code to collate with the result of this request (useful if your app may initiate other activities.)

PHOTO STORAGE LOCATIONS AND MEDIASCANNER CONNECTIONS In listing 11.13, we specify a URI corresponding to images saved in the `MediaStore`. But your application can specify any location to save the image by using the `Media-Store.EXTRA_OUTPUT` extra on the `Intent`. If you do so, you may still want this photo to show up in the Android Gallery. This is the application that we saw in figure 11.5, where we used it to browse videos on the device. It can also be used to browse photos, and like the photo-capturing `Intent` is commonly used by many applications. To make sure that the photo shows up in this application (or in a media query like the one we saw in listing 11.5), you can request that the file be scanned by the `MediaScanner Service`. To do so, you need to create an `android.media.MediaScannerConnection` instance. You'll also need to create a `MediaScannerConnection.Client` instance and listen for when the `Media-ScannerConnection` is ready. At that time, you can request that it scan your saved photo. Consult the API documentation for `MediaScannerConnection`.

The last thing we do in the `Activity`'s `onCreate` method is save the state of the `Activity`. This is necessary because we're starting a new `Activity`, namely the `Camera` application. The only state that we've created in the `Activity` is the URI that points to where the new photo will be stored on the device, identified as the instance variable `photoUri`. We check whether we have a `savedInstanceState Bundle`, and if so set the value of `photoUri` by retrieving it from `savedInstanceState` ❺. For this to work, we must make sure that we save the value of `photoUri` before the `Activity` goes into the background. The natural way to do this is to override the `Activity`'s `onSaveInstanceState` method and put the `photoUri` to the `Bundle` that's provided in that method ❻.

Once the user finishes using the `Camera` application to take a photo that they want to use in our `MediaMogul` application, our `Activity`'s `onActivityResult` method will be invoked. Here's where you can do whatever you want to do with the photo taken by the user. If you wanted to upload the picture to your server, then this would be the place to create an `AsyncTask` or invoke a `Service` to do that. For our `MediaMogul` application we'll show the image in the UI. We do this by grabbing an `ImageView` ❼ that we declared in the layout XML used by our `Activity`. We then use the `photoUri` to open an `InputStream` ❽, and pass that to the `BitmapFactory` to create a `Bitmap` we can use as the source for our `ImageView`.

Alternate ways to access photo data
If you search around for how to work with the photo-capturing `Intent` as we do in listing 11.13, you might see some other ways to access the photo in the `onActivity-Result` callback method. On some devices, the photo data can be directly accessed via the extras of the `Intent` that's passed in to `onActivityResult`. But this isn't consistent across devices.

(continued)

The Camera application is often specific to a device, and this application is what creates the Intent passed in to onActivityResult. The technique shown in listing 11.13 is completely portable. The Camera will save the photo to wherever you tell it, and so it's always safe to use this location to load the photo taken by the user.

DISCUSSION

As we mentioned in the beginning of this section, many applications use this exact technique to allow users to capture photos. Many also use another technique in conjunction. They provide the user an option to choose an existing photo or capture a new one. To do the former, you can use the ACTION_GET_CONTENT Intent to start the Gallery Activity as we did in listing 11.6. The only difference is that you'll want to specify an image/* MIME type so that the Gallery only shows images instead of videos.

Beware of Bugs!

Image capture and storage is subject to fragmentation in Android. Intents provide a loose contract between your app and the camera (and gallery) apps on the device. Unfortunately, many manufacturers don't honor this loose contract consistently, especially on older phones. As a result, you may encounter some phones where you have to resort to workarounds and hacks to properly interact with the camera.

Now you might ask why so many applications use the built-in Camera like we did in listing 11.13 instead of creating their own camera application. It's easy to capture the input from the device's camera and display it directly within your application. This avoids the overhead of starting a separate Activity (which will be in its own process) and having to save the state of your application's current Activity like we did in listing 11.13. But this approach has a number of significant drawbacks. As we mentioned, the Camera application is customized for the device that it runs on. This is necessary so that the application can take full advantage of the device's capabilities. For example, when devices first started to include front-facing cameras, the Android SDK didn't provide a way to directly access the front-facing camera. But the Camera app on these devices included a control to allow the user to switch between the rear-facing and front-facing cameras easily. If you created your own camera controls from within your application, you'd either need to re-create these device controls (which used proprietary APIs that weren't always public) or not allow the user to access the front-facing camera. Many of these Camera apps also include other hardware-specific controls, such as controlling the flash on the camera, or advanced photo taking features such as panoramic views. By handing off to the Camera application, the user can take advantage of all of these features with no extra work for you. In addition, because so many apps use the built-in Camera app, users become familiar with the application and that makes it easier for them to use.

Given all of that, there are still some cases where you may want to directly access the hardware. You can use an android.view.Surface to display a live preview of what's coming from the camera so that the user can see what the camera is pointed at. This is most useful when instead of capturing a single photo, you need to do some processing to the images being captured by the camera. A good example of this would be an application for reading QR or bar codes. Earlier, I mentioned that the six of the seven apps on my home screen that access the device's camera used the `Camera` app to take photos. The one exception was an app that scanned bar codes. Another example of apps that would want to directly access the device camera is augmented reality apps. None of these apps want to capture a specific photo.

Now let's talk about how to capture audio and video.

<table>
<tr><td>**TECHNIQUE 62**</td><td>**Recording audio and video**</td></tr>
</table>

Recording video is, in many ways, similar to taking a photo. In fact, you could go back to listing 11.13 and replace `MediaStore.ACTION_IMAGE_CAPTURE` with `Media-Store.ACTION_VIDEO_CAPTURE` as the action of the `Intent`. This would launch the `Camera` application and set it to capture a video and save wherever you specified in the `EXTRA_OUTPUT` extra. You can also specify another extra: `EXTRA_VIDEO_QUALITY` to control the quality (either 0 for low or 1 for high) of the video taken. As with photo taking, in many cases this is exactly how you'd want to capture video in your application. So why do we need to even bother with another technique? Video capture and its little brother audio capture have a few more wrinkles to them than photo capture. There are also a few more use cases beyond capture, like streaming audio or video. In addition, many of the steps for manually capturing video are shared with manually capturing a photo, so you could easily modify this technique if you needed to embed photo capture within your application. Let's look at how audio and video recording work.

PROBLEM

You want the user of your application to be able to record video or audio using their Android device, and then have this media available to your application for playback, uploading, processing, and so forth. You want to embed the video capture directly within your application, and not use the device's `Camera` application.

SOLUTION

Technique 61 showed you how to use a system `Intent` to use the `Camera` application, but now we'll handle all of the image rendering and capture within our application. Figure 11.7 shows you what this will look like.

Capturing video directly within our application, as shown in figure 11.7, involves a couple of simple steps. First we need to create a `SurfaceView` that can be used to preview the video coming from the device's camera. From there we can use the `android.media.MediaRecorder` to capture both video and audio. Capturing video doesn't automatically cause audio to be captured at the same time; you must take care of both. This is why we lumped audio and video recording together in one technique, as shown in the next listing. You could think of audio recording as a subset of video recording. These steps aren't complex, but each involves keeping numerous things in mind. Let's look at the details of the `Activity` that we'll use for audio/video recording.

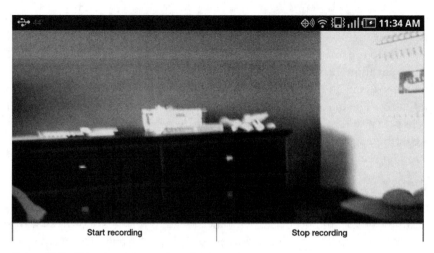

Figure 11.7   Video recording controls via the menu

Listing 11.14   Audio/video recorder `Activity`

```
public class VideoRecorderActivity extends Activity {
    private static final String LOG_TAG = "VideoRecorderActivity";
    private SurfaceHolder holder;
    private Camera camera;
    private MediaRecorder mediaRecorder;
    private File tempFile;
    private CameraPreview preview;
    private boolean isRecording = false;
    private final int maxDurationInMs = 20000;
    private final long maxFileSizeInBytes = 500000;
    private final int videoFramesPerSecond = 20;

    @Override
    protected void onCreate(Bundle savedInstanceState) {
        super.onCreate(savedInstanceState);
        requestWindowFeature(Window.FEATURE_NO_TITLE);
        preview = new SurfaceView(this);
        holder = preview.getHolder();
        holder.addCallback(cameraman);
        holder.setType(SurfaceHolder.SURFACE_TYPE_PUSH_BUFFERS);
        setContentView(preview);
        tempFile = new File(getCacheDir(), "temp.mov");
        if (tempFile.length() > 0){
            tempFile.delete();
        }
    }
    @Override
    public boolean onCreateOptionsMenu(Menu menu){
        MenuInflater inflater = new MenuInflater(this);
        inflater.inflate(R.menu.recorder_menu, menu);
        return true;
    }

    @Override
    public boolean onOptionsItemSelected(MenuItem item){
```

❶ Remove title bar

❷ View for video preview

❸ Listener to SurfaceView's lifecycle

❹ Temporary file for recording

❺ Menu to start/stop recording

```
        if (item.getItemId() == R.id.menu_rec_item){
          startRecording();
        } else if (item.getItemId() == R.id.menu_stop_item){
          stopRecording();
        }
        return true;
    }
// other code omitted
}
```

The first thing we do in this `Activity` is remove the title bar at the top of the screen ❶. We need to have the entire screen available for the preview, because the device's camera typically only supports a few different video sizes for preview. Next, we create a `SurfaceView` for the video preview ❷. We get a reference to its `SurfaceHolder` to interact with the `SurfaceView`'s underlying `Surface`. We then add a callback that will listen to `Surface`'s lifecycle events so we know when we can start displaying video from the camera. (We'll look at this callback in listing 11.15.) The last thing we do in our `Activity`'s `onCreate` method is create a temporary file ❸ where we'll save the recorded video. Finally, we create a couple of menu items ❹ that the user can use to control when the audio and video are recorded ❺. Now let's look at the `cameraman` instance variable class referenced in the following listing.

Listing 11.15   Controlling video preview during `Surface` lifecycle

```
private SurfaceHolder.Callback cameraman = new SurfaceHolder.Callback(){
    @Override
    public void surfaceCreated(SurfaceHolder holder) {         ❶ Get handle to
        camera = Camera.open();                                   device camera
        try {
            camera.setPreviewDisplay(holder);                  ❷ Set Surface
        } catch (IOException e) {                                 for preview
            camera.release();
            Log.e(LOG_TAG, "Exception setting " +
                "preview display",e);
        }
    }
    @Override
    public void surfaceChanged(SurfaceHolder holder, int format,
            int width,int height) {
        Parameters params = camera.getParameters();
        List<Size> sizes =                                     ❸ Calculate best
            params.getSupportedPreviewSizes();                    preview size
        Size optimalSize = getOptimalPreviewSize(sizes, width, height);
        params.setPreviewSize(optimalSize.width, optimalSize.height);
        camera.setParameters(params);
        camera.startPreview();                                 ❹ Start sending
    }                                                             preview to Surface
    @Override
    public void surfaceDestroyed(SurfaceHolder holder) {
        camera.stopPreview();
        camera.release();                                      ❺ Release lock
    }                                                             on camera
};
```

Our `cameraman` instance variable is an anonymous implementation of the `android.view.SurfaceHolder.Callback` interface. That interface defines three lifecycle methods: `surfaceCreated`, `surfaceChanged`, and `surfaceDestroyed`. Once the `Surface` is created, `surfaceCreated` is invoked and we get a reference to the device's camera ❶. If the device has both front- and rear-facing cameras, then this call will give us the rear-facing camera. Once we have a reference to the camera, then we can tell it to use our `SurfaceView`'s `Surface` for video preview by passing it a reference to the Surface's `SurfaceHolder` ❷.

Once the `Surface` has been sized to the screen, `surfaceChanged` will be called. Here, we want to set the size of the preview display coming from the camera. The size of the preview display depends on the size of the `Surface` that it'll draw on, but any camera will only support a finite set of preview display sizes ❸. So we want to calculate the best size to use based on the size of the `Surface`. For this, we're using a static method `getOptimalPreviewSize` (that's not shown here). This method is borrowed from the Android SDK example code, and should probably be part of the SDK itself. Once we have this calculation made, we can set the video preview display size and tell the camera to start sending the video preview ❹ to the `Surface` so that the user of our application can see it.

The last thing we need to do is some housekeeping for when the `Activity` exits the foreground. When this happens, the `Surface` will be destroyed and the `surfaceDestroyed` method will be invoked. We stop the video preview and most importantly, release the camera ❺. It's critical that this is done; otherwise your application will continue to hold a lock on the camera. If this happens, other applications will be unable to use that camera.

All of the code in listing 11.15 deals with sending video preview output to a `SurfaceView` that the user will see on their device. If you recall our two basic steps to audio/video recording, this was step ❶. What about step ❷? Look at listing 11.14 and you'll see that the recording aspects are controlled through the `Activity`'s menu, as you can see in figure 11.7.

As we saw in listing 11.14, tapping these menu items invokes the `startRecording` and `stopRecording` methods. These are the methods that will handle video recording ❷. Here's the first of these methods, the `startRecording` method.

Listing 11.16 Setting up recording of audio and video

```
private void startRecording(){
    if (isRecording){
        return;
    }
    isRecording = true;
    camera.unlock();                                              ❶ Allow access
                                                                     to Camera
    mediaRecorder = new MediaRecorder();                          ❷ Create
    mediaRecorder.setCamera(camera);                                 MediaRecorder
                                                                     instance
    mediaRecorder.setAudioSource(MediaRecorder.AudioSource.CAMCORDER);
    mediaRecorder.setVideoSource(MediaRecorder.VideoSource.CAMERA);
```

```
mediaRecorder.setOutputFormat(MediaRecorder.OutputFormat.DEFAULT);
mediaRecorder.setMaxDuration(maxDurationInMs);
Log.d(LOG_TAG, "Using tempFile=" + tempFile.getPath());                3  Set output
mediaRecorder.setOutputFile(tempFile.getPath());                          file
mediaRecorder.setVideoFrameRate(videoFramesPerSecond);
mediaRecorder.setVideoSize(preview.getWidth(), preview.getHeight());
mediaRecorder.setAudioEncoder(MediaRecorder.AudioEncoder.DEFAULT);
mediaRecorder.setVideoEncoder(MediaRecorder.VideoEncoder.DEFAULT);
mediaRecorder.setPreviewDisplay(holder.getSurface());
mediaRecorder.setMaxFileSize(maxFileSizeInBytes);
try {                                                              4  Initiate
   mediaRecorder.prepare();                                            recording
   mediaRecorder.start();
   Log.d(LOG_TAG, "Recording started");
} catch (IllegalStateException e) {
   Log.e(LOG_TAG, "State exception during recording", e);
} catch (IOException e) {
   Log.e(LOG_TAG, "IO exception during recording", e);
}
}
```

This method involves several straightforward steps to configure recording of audio
and video. First we need to unlock the Camera object ❶, so that other objects can
access it. Then we need to create a new instance of MediaRecorder ❷, the primary
class in Android for recording any kind of audio or video. Next, we pass it a reference
to the Camera object. Then, several simple methods configure things such as the audio
and video source, the format for the output file, the frame rate of the video, the
dimensions of the video, and the encoding type to use. We've mostly used default values in listing 11.16, but you can look at the API documentation to see some of the
available options. One of the most important configuration steps is to set the output
file of the MediaRecorder ❸. This is the file that we created earlier in listing 11.14.
Now we're ready to start recording audio and video, so we make calls to prepare and
start the recording ❹. When the user has finished recording, they'll use the menu to
select the Stop Recording button we saw in figure 11.7. Here's the stopRecording
method that will be invoked when this happens.

Listing 11.17   Stop recording and clean up

```
private void stopRecording(){
   if (!isRecording){
      return;
   }
   isRecording = false;
   mediaRecorder.stop();                         1  Stop
   try {                                            recording
      camera.reconnect();                                        2  Reacquire ref
   } catch (IOException e) {                                        to camera
      Log.e(LOG_TAG, "Exception reconnecting to camera", e);
   }
   camera.lock();                             3  Relock camera
}
```

The code in listing 11.17 is simple. First, we tell our `MediaRecorder` object to stop recording audio and video ❶. This will close the output file that the `MediaRecorder` is writing to, which in this case is the temporary file that we created in listing 11.14. This would be a good place to upload or scan the file (in another thread, as the code in listing 11.17 is executing on the main UI thread). Next, we reacquire our reference to the camera using the `reconnect` method ❷. This will allow us to continue to use the camera for preview or to make another recording. Finally, we relock the camera so that no other object can access it ❸. Now the recording is complete and ready to be used, and the user can interact with your application again by making another recording or proceeding to another interface in the application.

DISCUSSION

As we mentioned at the beginning of this technique, you could reuse most of this code if you wanted to manually take a photograph. You wouldn't need the `MediaRecorder` for that. Instead, you'd need to invoke the `takePicture` method on the `Camera` object. There are several callback objects that you can pass to `takePicture` to access the image data coming back from the `Camera`. Using these APIs is fairly straightforward. The tricky part is creating a good user interface overlaid on top of the camera preview that provides access to all of the photo taking options available on the device.

We also mentioned that audio recording is a subset of video recording, hence we handled them together. Listings 11.16 and 11.17 show all of the code you'd need if you only wanted audio recording. You'd still need to set audio source, output file, maximum size of the file, and the encoding format that you wanted to use. You could eliminate the video-specific configuration, such as setting the frame rate and the preview display.

11.5   *Summary*

At this point, you should be a multimedia expert! There's a lot of information in this chapter, but here are some key points to remember:

- You can assume device capabilities, but only if you explicitly state these assumptions in your application's manifest. If a feature is optional, then you'll need to test for it.

- You can package multimedia files within your application, and only your application will have access to them.

- You can access shared locations on the SD card, but multimedia can be stored anywhere. Use the `MediaStore`'s `ContentProvider` to find multimedia and use its querying capabilities to filter out inappropriate content.

- If you're playing back audio or video, make sure you bind this playback to the lifecycle of the `Activity` that's using it.

- For capturing pictures or video, it's both easier and better for the user if you rely on Android's `Intent` system to interact with the specialized `Camera` application on the device.

Multimedia is one of the many areas where rapid evolution is happening. For example, this chapter includes code examples that use APIs introduced in Android 2.2 (accessing common music and pictures folders) and 2.3 (accessing a front-facing camera). Android provides high-level APIs that make it easy to work with various forms of multimedia. Note that we never had to specify (or worse, load) a codec for playing back audio or video. If you've ever done desktop development, you should appreciate Android's simplicity. You don't need to be an expert to use image processing and animations. They're readily accessible to developers.

Accessing microphones and cameras is simple in Android. But you can also use low-level APIs, opening a world of exciting possibilities. Browsing around the Android Market, you can find examples of apps that make innovative use of the microphone and/or camera: video conferencing, shopping, fashion, health, personal finance, even silly talking animal apps. Whether you need complex or simple access to multimedia input, Android can meet your needs. There's no need to be intimidated by multimedia. Sometimes the picture that you want to show on screen isn't a static image, but something more dynamic. Fortunately, Android's graphics libraries have you covered, as we'll see in the next chapter.

2D and 3D drawing

In this chapter

- Manipulating images on the fly
- Working with 2D shapes
- Creating 3D graphics and motion

Practice what you know, and it will help to make clear what now you do not know.

—Rembrandt Van Rijn

So far, we've worked with many concepts relating to Android development. We've created UIs using the widgets and views that come with the framework, and we've put together applications using activities, services, and more. To create applications, such as games, that make extensive use of graphics, we'll need full control over the screen to be able to create our visuals. This is where Android's 2D and 3D libraries come into play.

The Android 2D library, which is based on the open source Skia library, is suitable for applications producing simple 2D visuals and a variety of effects. To go beyond simple, we can use the *OpenGL ES library*. OpenGL ES allows us to create complex 2D and 3D graphics, making full use of an underlying hardware accelerator (if present). In this chapter, we'll use both of these libraries.

402

We'll start with simple 2D lines and move on to circles, rectangles, text, images, effects, and more. Once we've splashed the 2D canvas with a few examples, we'll move on to using OpenGL ES. We'll touch on what OpenGL ES is and what versions are supported, and we'll put it to work. We'll use OpenGL ES to draw simple shapes in 2D and 3D, and we'll include coloring and textures. Along the way, we'll also learn how OpenGL ES deals with perspective and 3D scenes.

It'll be a whirlwind tour, no doubt, and we can't hope to cover every aspect of these impressive libraries here, but we'll get you started and show you how the tools work, so that you have a sketch of the basics.

12.1 Drawing with the 2D libraries

Android applications use activities and there can be only one active `Activity` at any given time. The `Activity` holds the `SurfaceView` where we place our UI elements. The `SurfaceView` is nothing more than a window that we interact with via touching (if supported) and drawing on its surface. The drawing surface is the `Canvas`.

We can draw any 2D shape we want on the `Canvas`. It supports coloring, drawing, text, geometries, images, and applying various filters and transformations. We'll review all of these as we take a look at the 2D library capabilities using the `Canvas`.

12.1.1 Introducing the Canvas

The `Canvas` class comes with a set of draw methods that allow us to do almost everything in the 2D world. To get acquainted with the `Canvas` we'll get our pencils and brushes ready and start drawing using a new project named CanvasDemo.

> **GRAB THE PROJECT: CANVASDEMO** You can get the source code for this project, and/or the packaged APK to run it, at the *Android in Practice* code website. Because some code listings here are shortened to focus on specific concepts, we recommend that you download the complete source code and follow along within Eclipse (or your favorite IDE or text editor).
>
> Source: http://mng.bz/UbW4, APK: mng.bz/CnyQ

The initial part of our CanvasDemo project is a main `Activity` that shows several plain buttons that take us to the other examples, and one "super fancy" custom button class that we'll create. We won't go into the main screen code because it's trivial, but the resulting screen is seen in figure 12.1.

From the main `Activity`, we'll build other activities that exercise many of the different `Canvas` drawing methods. We'll kick it off with an `Activity` that includes a single custom view that paints the entire content area with a random color, as seen in figure 12.2.

The code for our random color custom `CanvasView` and the `Activity` that holds it are shown next.

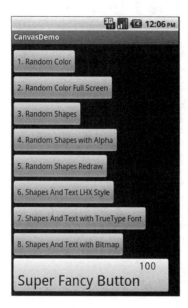

Figure 12.1   The main screen of the CanvasDemo application

Figure 12.2   This custom view draws a random color over the entire content area using a `Canvas`.

Listing 12.1   Displaying a random color using a custom `View`

```
public class Canvas2DRandomColorActivity extends Activity {

    @Override
    public void onCreate(Bundle savedInstanceState) {
        super.onCreate(savedInstanceState);
        setContentView(new CanvasView(this));        ❶ Set drawing
    }                                                    surface
    class CanvasView extends View {                  ❷ Include
        Random random = new Random();                   custom View
                                                     ❸ Define Random
        public CanvasView(Context context) {            for color values
            super(context);
        }
        @Override                                    ❹ Implement
        protected void onDraw(Canvas canvas) {          onDraw
            canvas.drawRGB(random.nextInt(256),
                random.nextInt(256), random.nextInt(256));   Draw on
        }                                            ❺ Canvas
    }
}
```

Our first `Canvas` example is short and sweet. A basic `Activity` sets the entire drawing area to use a custom `View` as the content view ❶. Next, we implement a custom `CanvasView` class ❷ with a `Random` member for obtaining random values. Then, we define the constructor and override the `onDraw` ❸ method as required. Inside the `onDraw` method ❹, we take the `Canvas` object that's passed to us and draw to it ❺ using three separate random RGB values. This fills the entire screen with a random color.

CANVAS COLOR The Android `Canvas` uses the *ARGB* color scheme (alpha, red, green, blue) and is represented as a packed `int`. Each component can have a value between 0 and 255 inclusive. For the color components, 0 means no intensity and 255 means full intensity. For the alpha component, 0 is transparent and 255 is opaque. To easily remember the int notation you can use hexadecimal format. So, an opaque green will have the following ARGB components: 255, 0, 255, 0. Converting this to hex, produces FF, 00, FF, 00. To use this format in Android, write the sequence as it is: `int color = 0xFF00FF00`.

With this first basic `Canvas` example, we're already manually drawing on the screen. A single color isn't that useful, but we'll work up to shapes and text in the next few sections. First, we want to touch on an important aspect of dealing with screen real estate with Android: going full screen.

TECHNIQUE 63 Going full screen

A lot of the screen area in our first example is taken up by the window title and the Android status bar. If we want to develop serious games or other rich graphics applications such as movie players, we'll want to go full screen.

PROBLEM

You want to use all of the screen area.

SOLUTION

To take over all of the screen area we need to decorate the window before we add our `View` to the `Activity`. This needs to happen before we set the content view, so it must occur in the activity's `onCreate` method, as follows:

```
requestWindowFeature(Window.FEATURE_NO_TITLE);
getWindow().setFlags(WindowManager.LayoutParams.FLAG_FULLSCREEN,
    WindowManager.LayoutParams.FLAG_FULLSCREEN);
```

These two calls, before setting the content view, tell the Android window manager to go full screen. Running the code will produce the same result as before, but this time there will be no window title or system bar.

DISCUSSION

This is a basic solution to a common problem. You may already know about this Android feature, but it's worth mentioning for those less familiar. This is key: this power shouldn't be taken lightly; you should only use this feature when creating a noncasual full-screen application.

When you take over the full screen, you may annoy the user. The status bar is used to quickly determine network connectivity state, see the time, respond to notifications, and more. It's part of the universal Android experience that many users want. Hiding it should only be done when your application truly requires it, and you should consider doing so carefully.

With the full screen technique out of the way, it's time to get back to the `Canvas` and see how it can be used to draw simple shapes and text.

TECHNIQUE 64   **Drawing simple shapes**

To illustrate drawing shapes and lines works, we'll attempt to paint the canvas vaguely in the style of Wassily Kandinsky, except without genius. And instead of a grammar of forms and colors, we'll again rely on random values. Some of the drawings we'll create will be attractive, depending on your taste, as seen in figure 12.3.

To create colored lines, rectangles, and circles, we'll do more with the Canvas, and we'll also introduce the Paint class. Paint is another key class that allows us to define settings for the Canvas.

PROBLEM

You want to draw lines and shapes on the screen.

SOLUTION

The Canvas is a drawing surface, as the name implies. With it, we can draw points, lines, circles, arcs, rectangles, and more. Canvas supports pixels and subpixels, but for the sake of simplicity, let's say that a point is a pixel. This will allow us to use integers in our drawing methods.

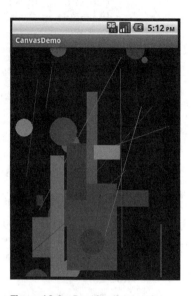

Figure 12.3 Drawing lines and shapes of varying color to a Canvas using the Paint class

Canvas uses the Paint object when drawing primitives. We need to define a Paint object before we do any drawing. Think of Paint as the brush we need to pick before we start painting. The brush defines the line thickness, the styles, the color, and more. In the following listing, our second CanvasDemo Activity modifies the custom view we've already seen and shows how these two classes work together to draw simple shapes to the screen.

Listing 12.2 Drawing random lines, circles, and rectangles to the Canvas

```
public class Canvas2DRandomShapesActivity extends Activity {

    @Override
    public void onCreate(Bundle savedInstanceState) {
        super.onCreate(savedInstanceState);

        setContentView(new CanvasView(this));
    }

    class CanvasView extends View {
        Paint paint;
        Random random = new Random();

        public CanvasView(Context context) {
            super(context);
        }
```

```
protected void onDraw(Canvas canvas) {
    canvas.drawRGB(0, 0, 0);
    for (int i = 0; i < 10; i++) {
        paint = new Paint();
        paint.setARGB(255, random.nextInt(256),
            random.nextInt(256), random.nextInt(256));
        canvas.drawLine(random.nextInt(canvas.getWidth()),
            random.nextInt(canvas.getHeight()),
            random.nextInt(canvas.getWidth()),
            random.nextInt(canvas.getHeight()), paint);
        canvas.drawCircle(random.nextInt(canvas.getWidth() - 30),
            random.nextInt(canvas.getHeight() - 30),
            random.nextInt(30), paint);
        canvas.drawRect(random.nextInt(canvas.getWidth()),
            random.nextInt(canvas.getHeight()),
            random.nextInt(canvas.getWidth()),
            random.nextInt(canvas.getHeight()), paint);
    }
  }
 }
}
```

1 Clear screen
2 Loop to draw 10 times
3 Paint class
4 Set random color
5 Draw random line
6 Draw random circle
7 Draw random rectangle

The first thing we do to draw random shapes is to color the entire screen black by using RGB values, as we did in the previous example **1**. Then, we create a loop to draw 10 times **2**. Inside our loop, we instantiate the `Paint` class we'll use **3**, and then we set a random opaque color to be used with each shape in the current iteration **4**. Next, we pick up our paintbrush and draw a line **5**, a circle **6**, and a rectangle **7**.

To determine where to draw our shapes and to find out how much space we have, we need to know the screen resolution. The coordinate system used by the `Canvas` is the Cartesian Coordinate system with the origin (0, 0) in the top-left corner of the screen. As we draw our random shapes, we use the `Canvas` `getWidth` and `getHeight` methods to constrain the dimensions. To support multiple screen resolutions, a scale factor needs to be added to each axis. The orientation also needs to be considered if our application relies on a specific resolution.

By changing the alpha value of the `Paint` instance to a random one, we can get an even more interesting result as seen in figure 12.4.

When we modify the alpha values this way, the `Canvas` handles the color blending for us. With a few simple methods and random values, we have some interesting drawings.

DISCUSSION

As you can see, `Canvas` is fairly simple to use, but provides a lot of functionality. We'll see more of the drawing methods as we progress, but the pattern

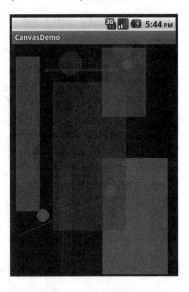

Figure 12.4 `Canvas` handles color blending when different alpha values are applied.

should already be evident. We set up the parameters our brush will use with the `Paint` object, and then we draw to the `Canvas`.

So far, our views have been drawn to the screen only once. The `onDraw` method is called once and the screen remains valid. What do we need to make our views redraw themselves when the need arises?

TECHNIQUE 65   Rendering continuously in the UI thread

When doing animations, and in other instances where state changes, we may need to update the `View`.

PROBLEM

You need a `View` to redraw itself when an update is needed.

SOLUTION

Because we've been using the `Canvas` class, redrawing our `View` is simple. All we need to do is to invalidate the screen. As an example of this, we can add the following line to the `onDraw` method in our `CanvasView`, after all the drawing is done, at the end:

```
protected void onDraw(Canvas canvas) {
    // … all drawing
    invalidate();
}
```

This tells the screen to redraw itself. Because we also do our random shape generation in the `onDraw` method, each time the screen is redrawn, the shapes will be different. If you add the invalidate line and run the updated application, you'll get a flashy screen with ever-changing shapes.

DISCUSSION

Although continuous rendering in the UI thread works for simple purposes, the presented method isn't suitable for graphics-intensive applications, such as games. To obtain better graphics performance, we need to separate the rendering thread from the state update thread. Getting into the full details of using a separate thread here (see chapter 5 for general concurrency info) is beyond the scope of our current discussion, but you should be aware that you'll want to do drawing outside of the UI thread when circumstances require it.

If we modified our custom `View` to implement the `Runnable` interface and then ran it in a separate thread, we could improve its performance. By extending the `SurfaceView` class, the `View` can obtain its holder (the container, `SurfaceHolder`); consequently, it can also get hold of the `Canvas`. Drawing on the obtained `Canvas` should be done in a synchronized manner.

Now that we've seen how to do draw some basic shapes, and how to update the `View` when needed, let's move on and throw some text into the mix.

TECHNIQUE 66   Drawing text to the screen

Almost every application that uses the screen will, at some point, need to display text. Luckily, the `Canvas` class comes with a set of `drawText` methods that make displaying text easy. To see this in action, we'll create another example that includes three colored shapes with some text, as seen in figure 12.5.

You may recognize the look of this example; it's similar to the iconic logo of the early '90s Electronic Arts game LHX Attack Chopper. Mimicking that look allows us to demonstrate some more shape examples, and we're including text for the first time.

PROBLEM

You want to draw text on the screen.

SOLUTION

At this point, we'll add another custom View to our CanvasDemo project, this time in a separate class, ShapesAndTextView. Within this class, we'll add more detail surrounding drawing shapes, and we'll meet the drawText method.

Figure 12.5 Drawing shapes and text to the screen in a custom view

Listing 12.3 The `ShapesAndTextView` class that draws shapes and text

```
public class ShapesAndTextView extends View {

    private Paint paint;
    private String text;

    public ShapesAndTextView(Context context) {
        super(context);
    }

    public void setText(String text) {
        this.text = text;
    }

    @Override
    protected void onDraw(Canvas canvas) {         ❶ Clear screen,
        canvas.drawRGB(0, 0, 0);                      paint it black
        drawShapes(canvas);
        drawText(canvas);
    }
                                                    ❷ Draw
    private void drawShapes(Canvas canvas) {           shapes
        int side = canvas.getWidth() / 5;
        paint = new Paint();
        paint.setARGB(255, 255, 0, 0);
        canvas.drawRect(side, canvas.getHeight() - 60 - side, side + side,
            canvas.getHeight() - 60, paint);
        paint.setARGB(255, 0, 255, 0);
        canvas.drawCircle(side * 2 + side / 2,
            canvas.getHeight() - 60 - side / 2, side / 2, paint);
        paint.setARGB(255, 0, 0, 255);
```

```
        paint.setStyle(Paint.Style.FILL);
        Path triangle = new Path();
        triangle.moveTo(side * 3 + 30, canvas.getHeight() - 60 - side);
        triangle.lineTo(side * 3 + 60, canvas.getHeight() - 60);
        triangle.lineTo(side * 3, canvas.getHeight() - 60);
        triangle.lineTo(side * 3 + 30, canvas.getHeight() - 60 - side);
        canvas.drawPath(triangle, paint);
    }

    private void drawText(Canvas canvas) {
        paint.setColor(Color.WHITE);
        paint.setTextSize(48);
        canvas.drawText(text, 60, 300, paint);
    }
}
```

❸ Create compound shape with Path

❹ Draw text

First, we clear the screen and paint it black ❶. Then, the drawShapes method ❷ draws a red square, a green circle, and a blue triangle . We won't go into much detail on the shape drawings in this example, as they should be familiar by now. They all use Paint to define settings and the Canvas to draw in the Cartesian coordinate system. The only new twist we've added is the use of the Path class to draw a compound geometric shape, the triangle ❸. It's also interesting to watch the triangle being drawn with the FILL effect set. We'll learn more about effects in technique 69.

After the shapes, we use the drawText method to write the "LHX Style" text to the screen ❹. Note the different ways to set the color. Along with the setARGB method, we can alternatively use setColor with predefined integers such as Color.WHITE.

Now all we need to do is to use this newly created View as the content view for an Activity, as the following snippet demonstrates:

```
public void onCreate(Bundle savedInstanceState) {
    super.onCreate(savedInstanceState);
    ShapesAndTextView view = new ShapesAndTextView(this);
    view.setText("LHX Style");
    setContentView(view);
}
```

Once we instantiate the new ShapesAndTextView view, we then set the text we want it to display and pass it as the SurfaceView for an Activity with setContentView. This displays our shape-logo and text we saw in figure 12.4.

DISCUSSION

Drawing basic geometrical shapes, such as rectangles and circles is easy, as we've seen. A triangle takes more effort, but is still simple using a Path made up of three straight lines. The Path can be used to create almost any 2D shape by including lines, curves, and arcs.

Adding text is also easy. You set up your brush with Paint, and then you drawText. But drawing text doesn't stop with plain text. Android also allows us to use custom fonts.

Using a typeface when drawing text

To demonstrate how to use a custom font, we'll modify our previous `ShapesAndTextView` class to use a free font found on the internet called *256Byte*. Our modified example is shown in figure 12.6. Custom fonts give us freedom to control the text styling we want to use when drawing on the screen, or in custom components.

PROBLEM

You want to use a custom true type font.

SOLUTION

Android supplies typefaces through its `Typeface` class, which encapsulates True Type fonts. This class exposes a factory method that creates `Typeface` instances from True Type font files (.ttf) found in the assets directory.

Figure 12.6 Drawing text on a `Canvas` using a true type font

To use a custom font, we need to place the respective .ttf file in the assets directory. Then we can create a `Typeface` from it and apply it. For an example of this, we'll copy the `ShapesAndTextView` class to a new file named `ShapesAndTextFontView` and modify it slightly.

Listing 12.4 The `ShapesAndTextFontView` custom `View` class includes a `Typeface`

```
public class ShapesAndTextFontView extends View {

    private Paint paint;                                       ❶ Declare
    private Typeface font;                                        Typeface
    private String text;

    public ShapesAndTextFontView(Context context) {
        super(context);
        font = Typeface.createFromAsset(context.getAssets(),  ❷ Load font from
            "256bytes.ttf");                                      asset directory
    }

    //onDraw, and drawShapes omitted (identical to prev listing)

    private void drawText(Canvas canvas) {
        paint.setColor(Color.WHITE);
        paint.setTextSize(40);                                 ❸ Set
        paint.setTypeface(font);                                  typeface
        canvas.drawText(text, 60, 300, paint);
    }
}
```

To use our custom font, we first declare it ❶. Then, we load it from the assets directory (the file must be included with our application) ❷. Once it's loaded, we can apply it by calling `setTypeface` on the `Paint` we're using ❸. This is simple yet offers a lot of possibilities, thanks to the world of true type fonts.

> **CANVAS USES DOUBLE BUFFERING** If you're curious about the way `Canvas` deals with creating and displaying images, you should know that it uses double buffering. *Double buffering* is a technique where two buffers are used to hold data so that one can be used to write it, and another to read it. `Canvas` uses two instances of the Android `Bitmap` class. One is used for creating the image, and another is used to display it. The image is created in memory first. When the image is done being painted, the `Canvas` displays it by copying the bitmap data from the RAM into the VRAM. This is much faster than drawing directly into the video memory.

DISCUSSION

Along with setting the typeface for a font with `Paint`, keep in mind that a normal `TextView` also has a `setTypeface` method. Underneath the covers, `TextView` will pass the typeface to the necessary `Paint` objects and draw the text the same way. This is a more common use of `setTypeface` than creating custom drawn components, but here you've learned the inner workings, and you're ready to use either approach as needed.

Our next step after working with shapes and text, including custom fonts, is to add existing images to our 2D drawings by including bitmaps.

TECHNIQUE 68 **Displaying bitmaps**

Displaying images isn't that different from displaying text with a particular font that needs to be loaded. To load an image, we follow similar steps. For our next CanvasDemo example, we'll load a `Bitmap` and use another of the `Canvas` drawing methods to display it.

For an image, we'll use a simple helicopter icon taken from Wikimedia Commons. The end result of our combined drawing of LHX-type logo and image will look like figure 12.7. By combining images and drawings, we can create a wide variety of 2D scenes for our Android applications.

PROBLEM

You need to draw image files to the screen.

SOLUTION

You can use the `Canvas` to draw colored shapes and text, as we've seen, and you can also render image files by drawing bitmaps. We'll use the `Bitmap-Factory` provided by Android to load images and obtain a handle to them. For our purposes, we'll use a PNG file. And because we won't be targeting any particular screen size here, we'll include it with our project in the res/drawable-nodpi directory.

Figure 12.7 Using the Canvas to draw custom colored shapes and include a bitmap

We'll follow the `Typeface` recipe to load the image. We'll add the `Bitmap` as a private member, and inside the `View`'s constructor, we'll load the image using one of Android's built-in methods.

Listing 12.5 Loading a PNG image via a bitmap and drawing it with the `Canvas`

```
public class ShapesAndTextBitmapView extends View {

    private Paint paint;
    private Typeface font;                                1  Declare
    private Bitmap bitmap;                                   bitmap

    public ShapesAndTextBitmapView(Context context) {
        super(context);
        bitmap = BitmapFactory.decodeResource(           2  Load bitmap using
            getResources(), R.drawable.copter);             BitmapFactory
    }

    // onDraw and drawShapes ommitted (same as prev listing)

    private void drawBitmap(Canvas canvas) {
        paint = new Paint();                             3  Draw
        canvas.drawBitmap(bitmap, 0, 0, paint);             bitmap
    }
}
```

DISCUSSION

This should almost be old hat by now. The idea is that you can control all aspects of the 2D space on the screen with `Paint` and `Canvas`, using the various draw methods. Here we're declaring the `Bitmap` we want to include ❶, loading it from resources with `BitmapFactory` ❷, and drawing it ❸. The method to draw the `Bitmap` is simple: it initializes the `Paint` object and draws the image starting from the top left of the screen. Remember that (0, 0) is top left.

So far, we've drawn basic shapes, and painted text and bitmap data. Next, we'll look more closely at some of the affects you can achieve.

TECHNIQUE 69 **Applying 2D effects**

To illustrate how to apply effects, we'll create a custom `View` class that we'll unimaginatively call `CustomButton`. It'll have scaled text with a slight inset effect in various positions and a dynamic counter. Also, we'll include a gradient running in the background, as well as a slight outset effect and slightly rounded corners. When completed, our button will look like the super fancy button we saw on the bottom of figure 12.1. (Note that we aren't making this button functional for this example, with separate pressed and unpressed states and so on; we're only working on the graphic attributes.) The main difference with our custom button won't come from any new drawing methods; we'll be relying on the effects that we can produce with `Paint`.

PROBLEM

You want to create some custom graphical effects.

SOLUTION

By composing Paint instances with a number of strategies, we can achieve a lot. To see how this works, we're going to skip around in the next example's code, between the construction and the draw areas. You can consult the full listing if you wish, but the focus is on the individual Paint tricks used to achieve the effects. We'll start by setting up the outside of the button: the border.

Listing 12.6   The `CustomButton` view class uses several `Paint` effects

```
public class CustomButton extends View {                              ❶ Include
                                                                         Paint
private Paint borderPaint;
   private PathEffect borderRadius;                                    ❷ Include
                                                                         PathEffect
// ...
   public CustomButton(Context context, AttributeSet attrs, int defStyle) {
      super(context, attrs, defStyle) {

  borderPaint = new Paint();                                          ❸ Instatiate CornerPathEffect
  borderRadius = new CornerPathEffect(5);                               with radius 5

  borderPaint.setPathEffect(borderRadius);                            ❹ Set
  borderPaint.setStyle(Style.STROKE);          ❺ Set style,              PathEffect
  borderPaint.setColor(Color.rgb(75, 75, 75));    color, and
  borderPaint.setStrokeWidth(2F);                 width
     borderPaint.setAntiAlias(true);                                  ❻ Use anti-
     // ...                                                             aliasing
  }
  // ...
}
```

The border is setup with a Paint variable ❶ and a PathEffect ❷ that we'll use for the border properties. Then, inside our overridden custom View constructor, we instantiate a CornerPathEffect ❸ with a radius of 5, and set it ❹ to make sure our border gets painted with slightly rounded corners. We also use a STROKE style with a muted gray color and a width of 2 ❺. Lastly, we use anti-aliasing to minimize the distortion of the edges ❻.

This creates the properties for our border, and we'll use the same pattern with separate Paint objects to set up our gradient and text effects. The next step sets up the gradient fill for the overall button.

Listing 12.7   Creating a gradient fill with a `Paint` object.

```
public class CustomButton extends View {                              ❶ Include
                                                                         Paint
private Paint squarePaint;

// ...
   public CustomButton(Context context, AttributeSet attrs, int defStyle) {
      super(context, attrs, defStyle) {

  squarePaint = new Paint();                                          ❷ Set style
                                                                         to FILL
  squarePaint.setStyle(Style.FILL);
```

```
squarePaint.setColor(Color.rgb(245, 245, 245));
squarePaint.setPathEffect(borderRadius);
squarePaint.setAntiAlias(true);
    // ...
  }
  // ...
}
```

❸ Path the border's radius

To achieve the gradient we include a separate `Paint` for settings ❶, and use a `FILL` pattern for the inside of our button ❷. Then, we ensure it matches the corner radius of our border; otherwise, it might protrude from underneath it slightly ❸. We'll see how the gradient is filled in when we take a look at the onDraw method coming up.

Next, we set up the text effect. This is a popular look in the Web 2.0 world, so you may already know where this is going. We'll be using black text with a slight white shadow on the bottom to give it a sharp inset look against the gradient.

Listing 12.8 Creating an inset and shadow text effect with a `Paint` object

```
public class CustomButton extends View {

private Paint textPaint;

// ...
  public CustomButton(Context context, AttributeSet attrs, int defStyle) {
    super(context, attrs, defStyle) {

  textPaint = new Paint();

  textPaint = new Paint();
  textPaint.setShadowLayer(1.0F, 0F, 2F, Color.WHITE);
  textPaint.setTextAlign(Align.CENTER);
  textPaint.setColor(Color.BLACK);
  textPaint.setStyle(Style.FILL);
  textPaint.setAntiAlias(true);
  textPaint.setTypeface(Typeface.SANS_SERIF);
    // ...
}
```

❶ Set shadow

Note that the `setShadowLayer` ❶ method, which we're using to set our white text shadow, is intrinsic to all `Paint` instances. You can cast a shadow from anything you wish to draw—paths, rectangles, text, and so on. The rest of the text effect is what you'd expect: alignment, color, style, typeface, and so forth. To complete the class we once again rely on the onDraw method, where we draw our content onto the `Canvas`.

Listing 12.9 The `onDraw` method of the `CustomButton` class

```
@Override
  public void onDraw(Canvas canvas) {
    squarePaint.setShader(new LinearGradient(0F, 0F, 0F, height,
      Color.rgb(254, 254, 254),
      Color.rgb(221, 221, 221),
        Shader.TileMode.REPEAT));

    textPaint.setTextSize(width * 0.09F);

    countPaint.setTextSize(height * 0.3F);
```

❶ Override onDraw

❷ Set Shader with LinearGradient

❸ Set sizes based on height and width

```
    Rect rect = new Rect(0, 0, width, height);
    canvas.drawRect(rect, squarePaint);
    canvas.drawText(text, (width / 2) - (width / 10) + 10,
        (height / 2) + (height / 3), textPaint);
    canvas.drawText("" + count, (int) (width * 0.92),
        height / 3, countPaint);
}
```
❹ **Draw on Canvas**

Inside the onDraw method ❶, we set the Shader strategy using a LinearGradient ❷. This makes things "pop," as the designers would say. We set this property inside onDraw, rather than in the constructor like all the other properties, because we need to know the total height of the gradient to create it properly. We also set it to repeat, so it fills the horizontal space in the shape. Then we set the text and count sizes based on the width and height of the current View ❸. Finally, we draw our button on the Canvas as a rectangle and include our text ❹.

DISCUSSION

By creating a custom View class that overrides one of the default constructors, we can set up different Paint objects for the different effects we need. Once the setup is done, we can then tweak settings based on runtime properties in the onDraw method. In total, we've used Paint to control border, gradient, and text effects, and we've drawn the result to the Canvas. In all, we have fine-grained control over all of the aspects of our custom View.

We've covered a lot of territory concerning what you can do with 2D drawing in Android. You should now have a firm handle on how to draw shapes, how to apply colors, how to include text, how to include bitmaps, and how to apply effects. Now it's time to add another dimension to the mix.

12.2 3D and OpenGL ES

Although Canvas gives us enough support to deal with 2D graphics, it comes to a halt when we want to create high-performance applications with intensive visuals. To take graphics to the next level, we need to get into the world of 3D and OpenGL ES.

Graphics processing in the Canvas happens in the CPU. The CPU can do a lot, but it's not specialized for graphics, and it's generally busy with other duties. Many modern Android devices are equipped with a dedicated GPU (graphics processing unit). A GPU can take the tasks of handling graphics over from the CPU. Using a GPU frees up precious CPU cycles and improves overall performance and capability. OpenGL ES can utilize the GPU and can create impressive 2D and 3D drawings.

We'll continue our drawing apprenticeship here by peeking into the world of OpenGL ES. We'll start with more 2D drawings, and then we'll move up to 3D. Along the way, we'll use colors and textures with 3D shapes. But before we get ahead of ourselves, we first need to step back and focus on what OpenGL ES is.

12.2.1 What is OpenGL?

OpenGL is the *Open Graphics Library*, an open cross-language, cross-platform accelerated 2D/3D graphics platform. The *ES* indicates that the flavor included with Android is the embedded systems version. This means it's optimized for use in phones, tablets, set-top boxes, consoles, and the like. It's a subset of the full desktop version, but it's still capable and powerful.

LEARNING MORE ABOUT OPENGL   We aren't going to get into the full ins and outs of OpenGL programming. That's a book in and of itself. If you're looking for more information on OpenGL development, the Neon Helium lessons at http://nehe.gamedev.net are an excellent resource. In the next few sections, we'll cover some of the same ground as the early lessons, but our purpose isn't to cover every facet of OpenGL programming, but rather to get you acquainted with using OpenGL on Android.

Technically speaking, the OpenGL API is a detailed specification maintained by the Khronos group. Each hardware manufacturer provides its own implementation for the API and has to pass rigorous tests to comply with the standard specification. Hence, there are sometimes slightly different behaviors on different devices, in rare cases when doing nonordinary tasks. OpenGL ES comes in three versions on current Android devices: 1.0, 1.1, and 2.0. Every device has support for version 1.0. Version 2.0 is supported on newer devices and isn't backward compatible with versions 1.x.

   In the overview that follows, we're going to cover OpenGL ES 1.x. We'll be doing this for several reasons. First, every Android device supports 1.x, so it's the safest best for targeting the broadest audience. Second, we want to concentrate on a series of cascading steps in the OpenGL pipeline. In OpenGL ES 1.x, the steps are fixed, whereas in OpenGL ES 2.x, the steps can be reimplemented, extra steps can be added, and we even have the possibility to alter the flow. We'll be able to focus on the fundamentals and internals better if we stick with 1.x, as v 2.0 hides some complexity behind more interfaces.

WHAT ABOUT RENDERSCRIPT?   API version 11 (3.0) introduced a new 3D graphics and compute API named Renderscript. It's portable across different system architectures and powerful, but more limited than OpenGL. Also, Renderscript is written in C, so it has a high learning curve for developers who haven't used C before. For these reasons, we won't cover Renderscript in detail, but you should be aware that it's available. Please see the documentation for more information: http://mng.bz/6i1B

TARGETING A SPECIFIC VERSION OF OPENGL ES   If you want to specify that your application supports only a particular version of OpenGL ES, you can do that in the manifest using the `<uses-feature>` element's `android:glEsVersion` attribute. This attribute lets you set the maximum version you want to support. (You must also support lower versions on down to 1.0). Also, if you don't set this attribute, it will default to 1.0. See the manifest documentation for more detail.

Devices without GPUs

Android devices with no dedicated GPU must implement OpenGL ES 1.0. In this case, the implementation is all software based and is emulated on the CPU. You can still use OpenGL on these devices, but the performance improvement won't be as great.

Now that we know a little about what OpenGL is intended to do, and which versions Android supports, it's time to move on to find out how it works.

12.2.2 *How OpenGL ES works*

OpenGL's sole purpose is to compose and draw an image on the screen—it produces pixels to fill the screen. The final image is the result of a series of calculations and processes carried out on the given input.

For example, if we want to present a simple house from a bird's perspective, we'll tell OpenGL ES everything about the scene in a geometrical context. A house consists of a cube with a pyramid on top of it. Imagine we want the final scene to appear as if we're looking down at a house at a 45 degree angle from a distance of 20 feet. The front wall is painted yellow; the other three walls have bricks. OpenGL ES will take all the information we give it and start the process of image creation.

We have to bear in mind that OpenGL ES works with triangles at a vertex level to create models:

- A *vertex* is a point in the three-dimensional space. It has the three mandatory components that position the vertex in space on the x, y, and z axes (and can have other optional components too, like color).
- A *triangle* is comprised of three vertices.
- A *mesh, model,* or *geometry* is anything consisting of one or more triangles (these terms are used interchangeably).

Everything in the OpenGL ES world is made up of triangles. For instance, a square is made up of two triangles, whereas a cube is made up of six squares. OpenGL ES takes all the triangles we provide and the data associated with them. It also takes our point of view and works out a projection. Then it applies materials to the objects, lights the scene if needed, and applies some transformations to work out the resulting image from our perspective. It also works out what to include in the final image and what to leave out. In the final step, it creates the bitmap out of pixels. All these steps are separate programs that are executed sequentially, and each step's output serves as the next step's input.

OpenGL is, in essence, a huge state machine. The commands issued to it will tell it what state it should transition to, or what values the current state's attributes should take, or issue commands that will produce an image. A pseudoflow to produce an image from some geometries might look like the following:

```
setCurrentState(READ_OBJECTS);
setValue(ObjectArray[0], triangle1);
setValue(ObjectArray[1], triangle2);
setCurrentState(CHANGE_PERSPECTIVE);
issueCommand(move_20feet_up);
issueCommand(look_down_45degrees);
setCurrentState(USE_SCREEN);
setValue(SCREEN_COLOR, black);
issueCommand(clear_screen);
issueCommand(draw_object, ObjectArray[0]);
issueCommand(draw_object, ObjectArray[0]);
```

This pseudocode tries to illustrate how we issue commands to OpenGL ES. First, we tell OpenGL ES to ready itself to be loaded up with objects. We load up its own object repository with the data describing two triangles. Then we tell OpenGL ES to switch to the state in which we can manipulate the viewport. Imagine yourself with a camera: you need to move the camera to get a good shot of the objects you want to include in your final picture. In our case, the command is to move up 20 feet and look down at a 45 degrees angle. We also set the color of the background we want to see the objects on. And finally, in the last phase we instruct it to draw the triangles (objects). OpenGL ES will do all the matrix transformations for us and will produce an image according to our instructions.

The take-away here is that OpenGL ES works with triangles defined via vertices. The input is a set of triangles and the output is an image projected onto the screen. The details are still abstract at this point, but don't worry: things will get more clear once we see some real examples in the next few sections. We'll start with wiring up our first OpenGL project.

12.2.3 *Creating an OpenGL project*

To make some OpenGL concepts more concrete, we'll build a new project that performs basic steps to draw some content to the screen. We'll add features from there once we get rolling. Our new project will be called OpenGLDemo. For starters, it'll only display a solid green screen. Then we'll create a single triangle, then make that triangle a 3D pyramid, and finally add colors and textures to the pyramid and spin it around. The end result of our work will be several different activities that show the progression, as depicted in figure 12.8.

> **GRAB THE PROJECT: OPENGLDEMO** You can get the source code for this project, and/or the packaged APK to run it, at the *Android in Practice* code web site. Because some code listings here are shortened to focus on specific concepts, we recommend that you download the complete source code and follow along within Eclipse (or your favorite IDE or text editor).
>
> Source: http://mng.bz/lhyX, APK: mng.bz/4QuG

Our OpenGLDemo project begins with a solid green screen. We know this doesn't sound like much, but it'll define our first basic renderer and clear the screen to the

Figure 12.8   OpenGLDemo's activity screens display a progression of 3D shapes.

color, our first taste of real OpenGL code. As with Canvas, we start by providing a custom View that can access the OpenGL ES driver, as shown in figure 12.9.

Listing 12.10   The OpenGLGreenScreenActivity that gets OpenGL ready for use

```
public class OpenGLGreenScreenActivity extends Activity {

    private GLSurfaceView glView;                                    ←⎯  Include
                                                              ❶  GLSurfaceView
    @Override
    public void onCreate(Bundle savedInstanceState) {                Assign ❷
        super.onCreate(savedInstanceState);                     GLSurfaceView
        requestWindowFeature(Window.FEATURE_NO_TITLE);
        getWindow().setFlags(WindowManager.LayoutParams.FLAG_FULLSCREEN,
            WindowManager.LayoutParams.FLAG_FULLSCREEN);
        glView = new GLSurfaceView(this);                         ←⎯
        glView.setRenderer(new MyOpenGLRenderer());        ←⎯❸  Set renderer
        setContentView(glView);              ←⎯   Set GLSurfaceView
    }                                        ❹  as content view

    class MyOpenGLRenderer implements Renderer {         ←⎯   Implement
                                                      ❺  MyOpenGLRenderer
        @Override
        public void onSurfaceChanged(GL10 gl,      ❻  Override
                int width, int height) {         ⎯⎯  onSurfaceChanged
            Log.d("MyOpenGLRenderer",               ←⎯
                "Surface changed. Width=" + width + " Height=" + height);
        }                                                Override ❼
        @Override                                   onSurfaceCreated
        public void onSurfaceCreated(GL10 gl, EGLConfig config) {   ←⎯
            Log.d("MyOpenGLRenderer", "Surface created");
        }
        @Override                                ❽  Override
        public void onDrawFrame(GL10 gl) {    ←⎯   onDrawFrame
            gl.glClearColor(0.0f, 0.5f, 0.0f, 1f);        ❾  Clear to color
            gl.glClear(GL10.GL_COLOR_BUFFER_BIT);             we want
        }
    }
}
```

All OpenGL-based content in an Android application is placed in a GLSurfaceView ❶. This is a View class provided by Android that acts as the conduit between the underlying OpenGL code and the Android view infrastructure and APIs. Once we declare a GLSurfaceView, we instantiate it using the context ❷ and pass an instance of class implementing the Renderer interface to it ❸.

The Renderer implementation is responsible for making calls to OpenGL to render a frame. In this case, we're using an instance of MyOpenGLRenderer, which we'll come to in a moment. Once our View is ready, we set it as the content view for the entire Activity ❹. We could use any section of the screen for this, with any layout, as with any other view. Instead, we're going to follow the approach we've used so far with drawing and take up the entire screen.

In the MyOpenGLRenderer code ❺, we're required to override several methods: onSurfaceChanged, which is called when screen size changes (such as when the device's orientation changes) ❻ and `onSurfaceCreated`, which is called when the surface is being created ❼. This can happen when the application starts, when it becomes active after being sent to the background, or when the orientation changes. Note that all these events are triggered after a context loss, so every asset (think loaded images) will be lost and need to be recreated. This is where all assets and application objects should be (re)created. And finally, the `onDrawFrame` method is also required ❽.

`onDrawFrame` is where the drawing happens. The passed-in GL10 instance enables us to issue commands to OpenGL and tell it what to do. Here, we start with `glClearColor` to set the color value from its buffer to the one provided ❾. As you've probably noticed, OpenGL prefers floats. The parameters are the color components, as in RGBA (note that the alpha channel comes last here). The first parameter is the red component, the second is green, the third is blue, and the last one is the alpha. The values can be anything between 0 and 1. A value of 0.5 means half intensity. So an opaque red would be (1, 0, 0, 1), and a half-transparent blue would be (0, 0, 1, 0.5). Once the color is taken care of, we issue the `glClear` command ❾. This tells the driver to clear the surface with the colors set.

OpenGL has many constants and each variable inside it is referenced by one constant. Think of it as a huge map or a flat database. The currently enabled buffers are referenced by the `GL10.GL_COLOR_BUFFER_BIT` constant, and the clear command will affect that. You'll notice that each constant in OpenGL is prefixed with *GL_*, as are the commands (gl).

When we launch our `OpenGLGreenScreenActivity`, we'll see a green surface that covers the entire screen (as indicated on the leftmost side of figure 12.8). The `Renderer` is in charge of rendering the screen and will do so continuously until we explicitly tell it to stop. The `onDrawFrame` method is constantly being called, similar to the `onDraw` method in the `Canvas` example with the `invalidate` call at the end. Details about frame rates and optimizations are outside the scope of this chapter, but we'll briefly mention that the frames per second (FPS) is the number representing how many times per second the `onDrawFrame` method has been called and completed.

> **RENDERING IN A SEPARATE THREAD** Unlike the `Canvas`, the OpenGL `SurfaceView` needs a separate thread to do the rendering. Luckily, we don't need to create one from scratch, as we have the `Renderer` interface. All we need to do is implement it and register the implementation with the `View`. The OpenGL framework will take care of the rest. A word of warning: you should never try to call OpenGL ES from another thread, as it's not thread-safe.

Now that we have a `GLSurfaceView` to draw on, and we've seen a simple `Renderer` implementation, let's draw something more interesting than a solid color.

TECHNIQUE 70 Drawing the first triangle

Let's define our first primitive, a basic triangle. As we create this object we'll define the bounds of the shape, and we'll make it capable of drawing itself by issuing the necessary OpenGL commands. When it's ready, we'll draw this triangle in the center of the screen as seen in figure 12.9.

Note that this first triangle is a 2D drawing. OpenGL can do 2D drawing; it's not limited to 3D. When you need higher performance, even for 2D applications, OpenGL can be the solution. We'll start with 2D when doing OpenGL drawing and work up to 3D.

PROBLEM

You need to draw simple shapes with OpenGL.

SOLUTION

OpenGL ES 1.x uses only triangles because the vertices of a triangle are *coplanar*—they're in the same plane, making calculations easy for the GPU. Remember, a triangle is defined by three vertices (points in space). Each vertex is defined by three coordinates: x, y, and z. That means that our triangle will be defined by nine values (three vertices by three components).

Figure 12.9 Using OpenGL to add a 2D triangle to the screen

The interesting part is how OpenGL ES gets this information. It gets the data in the form of arrays, and because it's not a Java API but a native C API, it expects the data in a certain order. We request Java to write the information for our triangle into a memory block outside the heap, into the system's shared memory, where it can be accessed by the GPU driver. To make sure that we use the correct data structure compatible with the system, we'll use the Java NIO API.

OpenGL ES is comfortable with floats, so we'll also use floats. Each float component takes up 4 bytes of memory so our triangle will take up 36 bytes. Let's see how we achieve the creation of the triangle with Java NIO.

Listing 12.11 The `Triangle` class

```
public class Triangle {                                    ❶ Declare
                                                             vertex buffer
    private FloatBuffer vertexBuffer;
    private float vertices[] = {
            100.0f, 150.0f, 0.0f,
            219.0f, 150.0f, 0.0f,
            160.0f, 279.0f, 0.0f                           ❷ Include
            };                                               coordinates array
    public Triangle() {
        ByteBuffer byteBuffer = ByteBuffer.allocateDirect(3 * 3 * 4);
        byteBuffer.order(ByteOrder.nativeOrder());
        vertexBuffer = byteBuffer.asFloatBuffer();         Construct triangle and
        vertexBuffer.put(vertices);                        push onto native heap  ❸
        vertexBuffer.flip();
    }
    public void draw(GL10 gl) {                             ❹ Do
        gl.glEnableClientState(GL10.GL_VERTEX_ARRAY);        drawing
```

```
        gl.glColor4f(0.0f, 1.0f, 0.0f, 0.5f);
        gl.glVertexPointer(3, GL10.GL_FLOAT, 0, vertexBuffer);
        gl.glDrawArrays(GL10.GL_TRIANGLES, 0, vertices.length / 3);
        gl.glDisableClientState(GL10.GL_VERTEX_ARRAY);
    }
}
```

We start our primitive shape class with a buffer, which will hold the coordinates of the vertices that make up the triangle on the native heap so the OpenGL driver can access it ❶. Then we include the coordinates array using the three coordinates of the three vertices ❷. Note that it's in C style, so there's no notion of a two-dimensional array. The first element is the x component of the first vertex; the second element is the y coordinate of the first vertex; the third element is the z coordinate of the same first vertex; the fourth element is the x coordinate of the second vertex, and so on.

It's important to remember the order of the vertices. The positions need to be *counterclockwise* because OpenGL has a notion of *faces* to improve rendering speed. Everything that's a front face (facing the viewer) will be rendered and everything that's facing away from the camera will be dropped. This is called *backface culling*. We made our triangle a front face using the coordinates shown in figure 12.10.

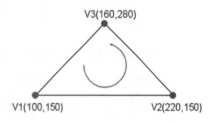

Figure 12.10 The triangle vertices and front face culling

You should note that, as figure 12.10 demonstrates, the origin of the OpenGL coordinate system is in the bottom left corner by default, not in the top left corner as with Canvas. Once we have our coordinates array and buffer, we move on to the constructor where we build the triangle and push it onto the native heap ❸.

In the constructor, we allocate a block of 32 bytes in the native heap using a Byte-Buffer, and we make sure the byte ordering is the same as the CPU. Then, we safely convert the byte buffer to a float buffer. When that's ready, we use the put method to copy the content of the array into the FloatBuffer. Lastly, we flip the buffer, which means that the cursor is repositioned to the first element to position 0. Then, we're ready to start drawing.

We pass a GL10 object to the draw method so we can issue OpenGL ES 1.0 commands ❹. First, we call glEnableClientState, which tells OpenGL that the vertices we're going to use for drawing are positions. Then, we set the color to half opaque green. And next, we use glVertexPointer, which tells OpenGL the location and data format of the array of vertex coordinates to use to render.

The first parameter to glVertexPointer tells OpenGL ES that the position of each vertex has three components. There can be a minimum of two, and in this case, OpenGL defaults to 0 for the z coordinate. The second parameter tells what type of data to expect for each coordinate. We used floats, so we'll use another constant to tell OpenGL. This way, OpenGL will know to fetch 4 bytes for each coordinate value from the memory. The third parameter is the *stride*, which lets OpenGL know how many other values are between two vertices. Imagine having to include a color component for each vertex: we'd need to skip another 16 bytes (RGBA, and each component is a float that takes up 4 bytes) until the next vertex's position starts. This is expressed by the stride attribute in bytes.

Eventually, we're ready to call drawArrays, which tells OpenGL to draw our triangle. It says that it should draw a primitive; we specify GL_TRIANGLES as the first parameter. The second parameter tells the first vertex's position in the array we've uploaded to OpenGL. This is useful for partial drawings of our meshes. The last parameter tells OpenGL the number of vertices to use for rendering. It always needs to be a multiple of 3. This command fills the GPU with the data OpenGL will use every time we issue a draw command. Finally, we clean up by disabling the state of drawing from a vertex array and closing the state. We can use this new Triangle object in an Activity as shown next.

Listing 12.12   The `OpenGLTriangleActivity` class

```
public class OpenGLTriangleActivity extends Activity {

    private GLSurfaceView glView;                              ❶ Declare triangle
    private Triangle triangle;                                   to render

    @Override
    public void onCreate(Bundle savedInstanceState) {
        super.onCreate(savedInstanceState);
        requestWindowFeature(Window.FEATURE_NO_TITLE);
        getWindow().setFlags(WindowManager.LayoutParams.FLAG_FULLSCREEN,
            WindowManager.LayoutParams.FLAG_FULLSCREEN);
        glView = new GLSurfaceView(this);
        glView.setRenderer(new MyOpenGLRenderer());
        setContentView(glView);
    }
                                                        ❷ Set viewport
    class MyOpenGLRenderer implements Renderer {              size
        @Override
        public void onSurfaceChanged(GL10 gl, int width, int height) {
            Log.d("MyOpenGLRenderer",
                "Surface changed. Width=" + width + " Height=" + height);
            gl.glViewport(0, 0, width, height);
            gl.glMatrixMode(GL10.GL_PROJECTION);                  ❸ Define
            gl.glLoadIdentity();                                    projection type
            gl.glOrthof(0, 320, 0, 480, 1, -1);
        }                                     ❹ Reset matrices
                              ❺ Map projection    to default
        @Override                  to screen
        public void onSurfaceCreated(GL10 gl, EGLConfig config) {
            Log.d("MyOpenGLRenderer", "Surface created");
            triangle = new Triangle();                         ❻ Create
        }                                                        triangle

        @Override
        public void onDrawFrame(GL10 gl) {                     ❼ Draw
                                                                 frame
```

```
        gl.glClearColor(0.0f, 0.5f, 0.0f, 1f);
        gl.glClear(GL10.GL_COLOR_BUFFER_BIT);
        triangle.draw(gl);
      }
    }
}
```

More is going on in our `Activity` for displaying our `Triangle` than changing the `View`. First, we declare the `Triangle` to draw as a member variable ❶. Then we make some additions and changes to the `Renderer` implementation.

There, we modify `onSurfaceChanged` in several ways, so we're ready to draw when the surface changes. To start, we resize the viewport when the surface is resized ❷. The viewport defines the size and resolution of the image that will be displayed. In a pixel-perfect 2D environment, it's the screen size and resolution. After that, we define the type of projection to use ❸. OpenGL works with matrices internally to calculate the final image. We tell it to use an orthogonal projection. This means that everything 3D is dropped and we'll render the scene in 2D. (More on projections later.) Then we reset the matrices to a default state ❹. For example, if we move our camera around, the new position is calculated based on values set in internal matrices. By resetting the matrices, we position the camera back to the origin. Next, we call `orthoOf`, which tells OpenGL to set up the matrices so that the viewport will be 320 pixels wide and 480 pixels high ❺.

Next in `onSurfaceCreated`, we instantiate the `Triangle` we need ❻, and then we override `onDrawFrame` ❼. The details of drawing the frame are handled internally by our `Triangle`, as we saw in the previous listing.

DISCUSSION

The resulting 2D triangle doesn't look like much, but it's a good basis to start programming OpenGL ES. With it, we've provided coordinates, set up the surface sizing and projection mode, and begun to draw shapes. Remember, for top-notch performance (and use of the GPU if present) you'll want to look at OpenGL even for 2D drawing. Our next step is to move from a 2D triangle into the realm of 3D shapes.

TECHNIQUE 71 Creating a pyramid

Next, we'll create a proper 3D object. The obvious next step is the pyramid. It has three faces (the base is ignored for now), so we need to create three triangles. We'll apply a green color to each face, and we'll spin our object in space on the screen. When we're done coding, it'll appear as shown in figure 12.11.

Because our pyramid will have three faces, we'll have more data to supply to OpenGL. To get a better grasp of what we'll be populating, let's look at the diagram in figure 12.12 before we begin.

Figure 12.11 The spinning green 3D pyramid

The three faces of our pyramid are defined as follows:

- Face 1—V1, V2, V3
- Face 2—V1, V3, V4
- Face 3—V1, V4, V2

With the knowledge for each face of the 3D shape we want to draw now in hand, we're almost ready to get to the code. First, we need to make one quick detour to talk more about projections and introduce the 3D scene.

The 3D Scene

Before we dive headlong into the code for the pyramid, we need to discuss how a 3D scene works. To do this we'll start with

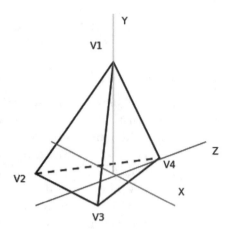

Figure 12.12   The Pyramid

another diagram, that of the 3D scene, as depicted in figure 12.13.

The diagram in figure 12.13 illustrates a typical 3D scene. The eye is where we stand and the viewport is where all the objects found in the *view frustum* are projected to. The view frustum is a pyramid with two *clipping planes*. Because our 3D world can be big, we can see only part of it at any given time (think of first person shooters, or better yet, the real world). These concepts are important because OpenGL will render only objects within the boundaries of the frustum.

When rendering objects, OpenGL works out what to *project* onto the viewport. Imagine the viewport as a window into the world. The projection of the world is a flat image shown on the surface of that window. Usually the near clipping plane coincides with the viewport, but not always—it depends on how we want to render our world.

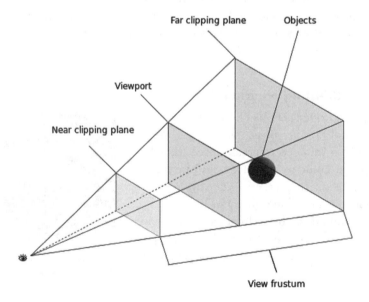

Figure 12.13   A diagram of the 3D scene

This brings us back to projections. There are two types of projections in OpenGL: *perspective* and *orthogonal*, as described in table 12.1.

Table 12.1　The two types of projections in OpenGL.

Projection	Description
Perspective projection	Used for 3D graphics. It's the scene presented in figure 12.13. Objects farther away from the viewer appear smaller, whereas objects positioned closer to the viewer appear bigger.
Orthogonal projection	Used for 2D graphics. Projection creates the objects with their original sizes on the viewport. Imagine the rays going -toward the eye being parallel.

We saw the orthogonal projection used in our last example with the 2D triangle. Next, we'll use the perspective projection with our 3D pyramid. The diagram in figure 12.14 further details the important parts of the projection perspective. Setting the aspect ratio to anything other than the viewport's width/height ratio will result in stretching or squashing the image.

Now that we have some background information about the 3D scene, we're ready to use the perspective projection and create a true 3D object in a 3D environment.

PROBLEM

You want to create a 3D object using the projection perspective.

SOLUTION

To work with the projection perspective and create a 3D pyramid we'll define a new class in much the same way we did for the triangle we saw earlier. We'll need more data and a few more settings for 3D, but we're getting close.

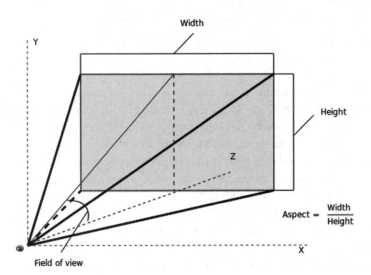

Figure 12.14　A diagram of the perspective projection

Listing 12.13   The `Pyramid` class

```
public class Pyramid {                                    ❶ Include FloatBuffer
                                                             to hold vertexes
    private FloatBuffer vertexBuffer;
    private float vertices[] = {
             0.0f, 1.0f, 0.0f,
            -1.0f, 0.0f, 0.0f,
             0.0f, 0.0f, -1.0f,

             0.0f, 1.0f, 0.0f,
             0.0f, 0.0f, -1.0f,
             1.0f, 0.0f, 0.0f,

             0.0f, 1.0f, 0.0f,
             1.0f, 0.0f, 0.0f,
            -1.0f, 0.0f, 0.0f,                           ❷ Array for
    };                                                      vertex data
                                                                        ❸ Define
    private float rotation = 0.1f;                                         rotation
                                                                ❹ Construct
    public Pyramid() {                                            object
        ByteBuffer byteBuffer =
            ByteBuffer.allocateDirect(vertices.length * 4);
        byteBuffer.order(ByteOrder.nativeOrder());
        vertexBuffer = byteBuffer.asFloatBuffer();
        vertexBuffer.put(vertices);
        vertexBuffer.flip();
    }                                                       ❺ Include all
                                                               drawing steps
    public void draw(GL10 gl) {
        rotation += 0.3f;
        gl.glRotatef(rotation, 0f, 1f, 0f);
        gl.glEnableClientState(GL10.GL_VERTEX_ARRAY);
        gl.glColor4f(0.0f, 1.0f, 0.0f, 0.5f);
        gl.glVertexPointer(3, GL10.GL_FLOAT, 0, vertexBuffer);
        gl.glDrawArrays(GL10.GL_TRIANGLES, 0, vertices.length / 3);
        gl.glDisableClientState(GL10.GL_VERTEX_ARRAY);
    }
}
```

For the `Pyramid` class we start by again including a `FloatBuffer` that will hold the coordinates of the vertices we'll use ❶, and we define all the triangles in the vertices array ❷. This is the same way we began our `Triangle` class, except we have more data in the vertices to define each separate face. Note that this time we're using floats instead of pixel sizes, because we'll work with the perspective projection and use relative distances. 1.0 is the unit distance. After the vertices, we also include a `rotation` parameter ❸. We'll rotate the pyramid so we can see it in 3D. The value represents the angle at which the pyramid is rotated from the original position.

After our initial values, we see the constructor, where we again populate the vertex buffer (the same way we did for the previous `Triangle` class) ❹. Beyond the constructor is the draw method, where the 3D settings are defined ❺. Inside draw, we first increase the rotation by 0.3 degrees. The `draw` method will be called continuously. Consequently, the angle will be constantly increased. Don't worry when it exceeds 360, as 2893 is the same calculation for the GPU as 270. Next, we call `glRotatef` to rotate the scene around the y axis (the one pointing up) by the number of degrees in the angle parameter currently. `glRotatef` takes four parameters. The first parameter tells the angle the scene will be rotated, and the other three define the vector's x, y, and z coordinates around which the rotation will take place. The vector (0, 1, 0) points upward, so the rotation will look like the pyramid is hanging on a thread and spinning. Finally, we draw the triangles onto the screen by enabling the vertex array, setting the buffer pointer, and calling `glDrawArrays`. For an in-depth explanation of the drawing see the `Triangle` class in listing 12.11, as we're using the same approach here.

To use our `Pyramid` class, we'll create a new `OpenGLPyramidActivity` class and once again reimplement the renderer.

Listing 12.14 The `OpenGLPyramidActivity` class

```
public class OpenGLPyramidActivity extends Activity {

   private GLSurfaceView glView;
   private Pyramid pyramid;

   @Override
   public void onCreate(Bundle savedInstanceState) {
      super.onCreate(savedInstanceState);
      requestWindowFeature(Window.FEATURE_NO_TITLE);
      getWindow().setFlags(WindowManager.LayoutParams.FLAG_FULLSCREEN,
         WindowManager.LayoutParams.FLAG_FULLSCREEN);
      glView = new GLSurfaceView(this);
      glView.setRenderer(new MyOpenGLRenderer());
      setContentView(glView);
   }
                                                              Set up     ❶
                                                              viewport

   class MyOpenGLRenderer implements Renderer {
      @Override
      public void onSurfaceChanged(GL10 gl, int width, int height) {
         Log.d("MyOpenGLRenderer",
            "Surface changed. Width=" + width + " Height=" + height);
         gl.glViewport(0, 0, width, height);
         gl.glMatrixMode(GL10.GL_PROJECTION);        ❷ Reset matrix
         gl.glLoadIdentity();
         GLU.gluPerspective(gl, 45.0f, (float) width / (float) height,
            0.1f, 100.0f);                                    Use
         gl.glMatrixMode(GL10.GL_MODELVIEW);          ❸ gluPerspective
         gl.glLoadIdentity();
      }                              Reset matrix  ❹

      @Override
      public void onSurfaceCreated(GL10 gl,                  ❺ Override
         EGLConfig config) {                                   onSurfaceCreated
         Log.d("MyOpenGLRenderer", "Surface created");
         pyramid = new Pyramid();
      }

      @Override
```

```
public void onDrawFrame(GL10 gl) {
    gl.glClearColor(0.0f, 0.0f, 0.0f, 1f);
    gl.glClear(GL10.GL_COLOR_BUFFER_BIT);
    gl.glLoadIdentity();
    gl.glTranslatef(0.0f, 0.0f, -10.0f);
    pyramid.draw(gl);
    }
  }
}
```

⬅ **Override**
❻ onDrawFrame

This `Activity` has several modifications but the most important is the switch from orthographic projection to perspective. Because we've moved to 3D, we want our objects to be shown in 3D.

As we walk through the code, we start by again setting up the viewport ❶. Then we enable the projection matrix and reset it ❷. Next, we set the perspective using the GLU utilities provided by Android.

GLU is inspired by the GLUT toolkit and offers convenience methods to manipulate matrices. We'll use the `gluPerspective` to set up our projection matrix with a single command ❸. Please refer to the diagram and description of the perspective. The first parameter is the GL surface; the second parameter is the field of view (fov). The field of view is expressed in degrees and represents the angle on the y axis. It's the opening of the frustum on the y axis. The closer we stand to a window, the more we can see through it; he field of view increases. The third parameter is the aspect ratio and is width/height ratio. Think of a TV set (16:9). The fourth parameter defines the near clipping plane and is always a positive value. The fifth and last parameter is the far clipping plane. Nothing after this plane will be rendered. Note that the perspective is set up using arbitrary units and these units should be used across the application. The viewport defines the resolution and OpenGL ES will work out how many pixels a triangle will contain on the resulting image. The proportions will be the same across all resolutions.

Next, after the perspective settings, we set the matrix mode ❹ and reset the model view matrix with `glLoadIdentity`. Then we create the `Pyramid` in the `onSurface-Created` method every time the surface changes ❺. Finally, we come to the `onDraw-Frame` method ❻.

In the `onDrawFrame` method, we clear the screen, reset the matrix again, and then move into the screen 10 units with `glTranslatef`. This is new. Remember that the coordinate system's origin is in the lower-left corner with the z axis pointing toward us. Translating -10 on the z axis means that we move into the screen away from us. This moves the reference point for the drawing 10 units. That will be the start point when we draw the triangles. In a 3D world, we instruct OpenGL this way: move 5 feet (units) left of the tree, draw an apple, move 10 feet toward us, draw something else, and so on. Once we're completely ready, we call the `draw` method on the `Pyramid` object, as you might expect.

DISCUSSION

Running the preceding `Activity` will produce a slowly spinning green pyramid. Still not that impressive visually, but we have our first 3D object in a full 3D environment.

From here, we can model almost anything we want. The next steps will be to add color and texture to our faces.

Coloring the pyramid

A spinning 3D shape is a start, but it can be hard to tell the different faces apart. The next obvious step to take to make our pyramid more interesting is to add a different color to each face. To do this, we'll create a new primitive object named `Coloured-Pyramid`, and a new `Activity` with renderer to display it. The end result is seen in figure 12.15.

As we've mentioned, OpenGL can carry extra data, such as color, beyond the spatial coordinates. To create our `ColouredPyramid` we'll need to add the color data, and we'll need to tell OpenGL where to find it and how to use it.

PROBLEM

You want to color vertices in a 3D shape.

SOLUTION

To add colors to a 3D shape, you can add information to the vertices being used. In the case of our pyramid example, we're working with three trian-

Figure 12.15 This spinning pyramid has a separate color for each face.

gular faces (again, leaving off the bottom), each defined in its own vertex. We'll add the color data we need in `ColouredPyramid`, as shown.

Listing 12.15 The `ColouredPyramid` class

```
public class ColouredPyramid {
    private static final int VERTEX_SIZE = (3 + 4) * 4;
    private FloatBuffer vertexBuffer;
    private float vertices[] = {
        0.0f, 1.0f, 0.0f, 1, 0, 0, 1,
        -1.0f, 0.0f, 0.0f, 1, 0, 0, 1,
        0.0f, 0.0f, -1.0f, 1, 0, 0, 1,

        0.0f, 1.0f, 0.0f, 0, 1, 0, 1,
        0.0f, 0.0f, -1.0f, 0, 1, 0, 1,
        1.0f, 0.0f, 0.0f, 0, 1, 0, 1,

        0.0f, 1.0f, 0.0f, 0, 0, 1, 1,
        1.0f, 0.0f, 0.0f, 0, 0, 1, 1,
        -1.0f, 0.0f, 0.0f, 0, 0, 1, 1,
    };

    private float rotation = 0.1f;

    public ColouredPyramid() {
        ByteBuffer byteBuffer =
```

1 Constant for vertex byte size

2 Face l, red (x, y, z, r, g, b, a)

3 Face 2, green

4 Face 3, blue

```
        ByteBuffer.allocateDirect(VERTEX_SIZE * 3 * 4);
    byteBuffer.order(ByteOrder.nativeOrder());
    vertexBuffer = byteBuffer.asFloatBuffer();
    vertexBuffer.put(vertices);
    vertexBuffer.flip();
}
public void draw(GL10 gl) {
    rotation += 1.0f;
    gl.glRotatef(rotation, 1f, 1f, 1f);
    gl.glEnableClientState(GL10.GL_VERTEX_ARRAY);
    gl.glEnableClientState(GL10.GL_COLOR_ARRAY);

    vertexBuffer.position(0);
    gl.glVertexPointer(3, GL10.GL_FLOAT, VERTEX_SIZE, vertexBuffer);
    vertexBuffer.position(3);
    gl.glColorPointer(4, GL10.GL_FLOAT, VERTEX_SIZE, vertexBuffer);

    gl.glDrawArrays(GL10.GL_TRIANGLES, 0, 3 * 3);
    gl.glDisableClientState(GL10.GL_VERTEX_ARRAY);
    gl.glDisableClientState(GL10.GL_COLOR_ARRAY);
}
}
```

❺ Include all drawing steps

The ColouredPyramid isn't that different from the original Pyramid class but let's have a look ❶. It begins with a constant that defines the size in bytes allocated for our vertex. In this case, a vertex is composed of x, y, and z coordinates and carries four color components. Each value is a float so that means 4 bytes for each component, for a total of 7. Next, we have the raw data in a vertices array. Each row in the array is (x, y, z, r, g, b, a). There's a row each for the red face ❷, the green face ❸, and the blue face ❹.

After everything is setup, we come to the all-important draw method ❺. The draw method begins by increasing the rotation value each render cycle by 1 degree. Then it uses glRotatef to rotate the scene around the vector defined by (1, 1, 1) coordinates. After that, we enable the vertex array for rendering and enable the color array. Then we set the vertex buffer position to the beginning, where the triangle coordinates start.

Next, the real drawing work begins. The line gl.glVertexPointer(3, GL10.GL_FLOAT, VERTEX_SIZE, vertexBuffer); tells OpenGL to use the vertex buffer for the triangles. Recall that the first parameter here tells OpenGL how many components each vertex has, the second tells it what type of data is being used, the third is the stride, and the fourth is the vertex data itself. This time the stride, which you'll recall lets OpenGL know how many values are between two vertices, is VERTEX_SIZE. Bear in mind that the pointer points to the beginning of the vertex buffer.

Next, we set the vertex buffer cursor to point to the first element of the first color component. Then we tell OpenGL to get the colors from the same vertex buffer. The size of a color component is 4 (RGBA) and the stride is VERTEX_SIZE, and it needs to advance 28 bytes (7*4) to get the second color. Note that the pointer points to the fourth element in the array (position 3), where the color components start.

Ultimately, we render the triangles onto the screen with `glDrawArrays`. Starting from 0, it needs to render three triangles with three vertices. When we're done, we disable the states to read from the vertex array and the color array, respectively.

The `Activity` that uses our new `ColouredPyramid` class is almost identical to the original `Pyramid` we saw in listing 12.14. The only thing we need to do is instantiate a `ColouredPyramid` instead of a `Pyramid`, as follows:

```
private ColouredPyramid pyramid;
  @Override
  public void onSurfaceCreated(GL10 gl, EGLConfig config) {
    pyramid = new ColouredPyramid();
  }
```

The resulting screen should show a spinning pyramid with one red, one green, and one blue face as we saw in figure 12.15.

DISCUSSION

Though there are a lot of moving pieces, literally and figuratively, to our spinning multi-colored pyramid, you should now have a good overview of how OpenGL can be used. You provide the raw data in arrays that represent vertexes for shapes, and you tell OpenGL exactly where to find each piece of data (what the bounds are), and how to use it. Once you're up to speed drawing basic shapes and coloring them, you can add even more detail by adding texture to surfaces.

TECHNIQUE 73 Adding texture to the pyramid

Previously, we've seen how to work with OpenGL and how to tint primitives. To display an image on the primitives, we'll need to create textures and map these textures onto the shapes composing the mesh.

To see how this can be done, we'll change our colored pyramid to a textured one by mapping a portion of an image from the android mascot onto each face. The end result will look like what's seen in figure 12.16.

PROBLEM

You want to add textures to 3D shapes to create more detail.

SOLUTION

A texture is nothing more than a bitmap. We've already seen how to load bitmaps (earlier in this chapter). To add detail to a shape or drawing with OpenGL, we can map bitmaps onto surfaces.

Before we can start slapping bitmaps onto surfaces, we first need to understand how texture mapping works, and why it's necessary. Bitmaps are

Figure 12.16 A spinning 3D textured pyramid

rectangular. If we want to map a square to a triangle, we need to tell OpenGL to cut out a triangular shape from the bitmap and to put it onto the triangle. This is *texture mapping*. Until now, we've used the x, y, and z coordinate system. For bitmaps, there's no third dimension, only the x and y coordinates. To avoid confusion, we'll use the u/v or s/t convention for the x/y in textures, as depicted in figure 12.17.

The use of u/v or s/t for the x/y in textures is a naming convention, nothing more. It's called *UV mapping* in the literature. Also note from figure 12.17 how OpenGL ES uses *normalized coordinates*, as in the perspective projection. The start is 0, and the end is 1. Half is 0.5.

To map a part of an image to a triangle, we'll cut out the triangular shape we want to apply and associate the coordinates to each vertex, as seen in figure 12.18.

Now that we know a little about what texture mapping is, and we have our bearings with regard to the terminology, let's map the faces of our pyramid. To do so, we'll create another pyramid class, `TexturedPyramid`, and build another `Activity` to display it.

We'll get to the differences in the `TexturedPyramid` class in a moment. First, we'll start with the `OpenGLTexturedPyramidActivity`, which includes the renderer. This is where the texture building happens, as seen in the next listing.

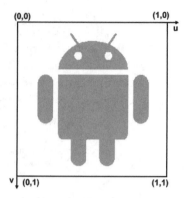

Figure 12.17   A sample image showing the texture coordinates

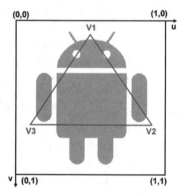

Figure 12.18   A sample of the triangle that will be cut out and the vertices to which it will map

Listing 12.16   The `OpenGLTexturedPyramidActivity`

```
public class OpenGLTexturedPyramidActivity extends Activity {

    private GLSurfaceView glView;
    private TexturedPyramid pyramid;                          ❶ Declare
    private Bitmap texture;                                     TexturedPyramid

    @Override                                                ❷ Include Bitmap
    public void onCreate(Bundle savedInstanceState) {          for texture
        super.onCreate(savedInstanceState);
        requestWindowFeature(Window.FEATURE_NO_TITLE);
        getWindow().setFlags(WindowManager.LayoutParams.FLAG_FULLSCREEN,
            WindowManager.LayoutParams.FLAG_FULLSCREEN);
        glView = new GLSurfaceView(this);
        glView.setRenderer(new MyOpenGLRenderer());
        setContentView(glView);
```

```
}

class MyOpenGLRenderer implements Renderer {

    @Override
    public void onSurfaceChanged(GL10 gl, int width, int height) {
        gl.glViewport(0, 0, width, height);
        gl.glMatrixMode(GL10.GL_PROJECTION);
        gl.glLoadIdentity();
        GLU.gluPerspective(gl, 45.0f, (float) width / (float) height,
            0.1f, 100.0f);
        gl.glMatrixMode(GL10.GL_MODELVIEW);
        gl.glLoadIdentity();
    }

    @Override
    public void onSurfaceCreated(GL10 gl, EGLConfig config) {
        texture = BitmapFactory.decodeResource(
            getResources(), R.drawable.texture);
        int textureIds[] = new int[1];
        gl.glGenTextures(1, textureIds, 0);
        gl.glBindTexture(GL10.GL_TEXTURE_2D, textureIds[0]);
        GLUtils.texImage2D(GL10.GL_TEXTURE_2D, 0, texture, 0);
        gl.glTexParameterf(GL10.GL_TEXTURE_2D,
            GL10.GL_TEXTURE_MIN_FILTER, GL10.GL_NEAREST);
        gl.glTexParameterf(GL10.GL_TEXTURE_2D,
            GL10.GL_TEXTURE_MAG_FILTER, GL10.GL_NEAREST);
        gl.glBindTexture(GL10.GL_TEXTURE_2D, 0);
        texture.recycle();
        pyramid = new TexturedPyramid(textureIds[0]);
    }

    @Override
    public void onDrawFrame(GL10 gl) {
        gl.glClearColor(0.0f, 0.0f, 0.0f, 1f);
        gl.glClear(GL10.GL_COLOR_BUFFER_BIT);
        gl.glLoadIdentity();
        gl.glTranslatef(0.0f, 0.0f, -5.0f);
        pyramid.draw(gl);
    }
}
}
```

3 Load Bitmap

4 Include array for texture ids

5 Generate IDs

6 Bind IDs

7 Load texture

8 Set texture filters

9 Unbind texture

10 Recycle image

To begin our `Activity`, we include member variables for the `TexturedPyramid` class (which we'll see next) **1** and the `Bitmap` that will hold our texture image **2**. From there, inside `onSurfaceCreated`, we set up the texture image by loading texture.png from resources **3** (this file is included with the project in the res/drawable-nodpi folder).

Powers of two are required!

To make textures work across all Android devices, the sizes (width and height) of image files used for mapping must be powers of two. They don't have to be equal, just powers of 2. (32 x 256 is fine, for example.)

After our `Bitmap` is loaded, we set up an array of ints that will contain the generated IDs for the textures ❹. Because we'll use only one texture, we create an array containing just one element. With the array ready, we then generate the texture IDs with `glGenTextures` ❺. Because OpenGL ES is a native C API, it'll give us an ID that we can use to reference the generated texture. The first parameter here tells how many textures to generate, the second parameter is the reference to the array where we want to store the generated IDs, and the last parameter represents the location to start from when inserting the IDs (it's an offset).

The next step is to bind the textures with `glBindTexture` ❻. `glGenTextures` creates names (IDs). `glBindTexture` tells OpenGL to use the texture with the ID given as the second parameter for every subsequent call. The first parameter is the target to which the texture will be bound. As you might've noticed, it's always a static constant defined in OpenGL and we'll be using `GL_TEXTURE_2D`.

Once the textures have IDs and are bound, we use `texImage2D` from the GLUtils library to upload the texture image to the VRAM ❼. This is a fairly complex task. Luckily, Android provides this helper to take care of it. The first parameter here is the texture type, which is the same `GL_TEXTURE_2D` we used to create the texture. The second is the mipmapping level, which we can ignore and set to 0. The third argument is the texture bitmap we want to upload. This can also be ignored and set to 0.

After our textures are bound and loaded into memory, we then set several texture filters ❽. Consequently, whenever a texture is too small or too big, OpenGL needs to stretch it or contract it to fit it onto the triangle. Here, we define the type of algorithm to be used for these operations. You might notice how we're setting the attributes of the OpenGL state machine. The first parameter tells what the parameter affects. In our case, it's `GL_TEXTURE_2D`. The second parameter is the attribute we need to set; it's the filter for shrinking (`TEXTURE_MIN_FILTER`) and magnifying (`TEXTURE_MAG_FILTER`). The last parameter sets the nearest pixel filter algorithm. Depending on the hardware, we can use the nicer linear filter, but that will be taxing on slow devices.

Next, we unbind the texture by binding it to ID 0, which is a special ID ❾. We can rebind it again when using it later. And, we get rid of the image, which can consume a lot of memory, by recycling it ❿. It's crucial to recycle images when no longer needed. Remember that the texture is already created and sent to the VRAM; the bitmap is just a copy of it in the heap. Disposing of it is good, as devices have limited memory.

Finally, we override `onDrawFrame` and perform the drawing steps, as we've already seen in other examples. Our renderer is now handling the loading and binding of the texture as the surface is created.

The only thing we have left is the `TexturedPyramid` class itself, as promised.

Listing 12.17   The `TexturedPyramid` class

```
public class TexturedPyramid {

    private int textureId;
    private FloatBuffer vertexBuffer;
```

❶ Hold
texture ID

```
private static final int VERTEX_SIZE = (3 + 2) * 4;
private float vertices[] = {

    0.0f, 1.0f, 0.0f, 0.5f, 0.0f,
    -1.0f, 0.0f, 0.0f, 0.0f, 1.0f,
    0.0f, 0.0f, -1.0f, 1.0f, 1.0f,

    0.0f, 1.0f, 0.0f, 0.5f, 0.0f,
    0.0f, 0.0f, -1.0f, 0.0f, 1.0f,
    1.0f, 0.0f, 0.0f, 1.0f, 1.0f,

    0.0f, 1.0f, 0.0f, 0.5f, 0.0f,
    1.0f, 0.0f, 0.0f, 0.0f, 1.0f,
    -1.0f, 0.0f, 0.0f, 1.0f, 1.0f,

};

private float rotation = 0.1f;

public TexturedPyramid(int textureId) {
    ByteBuffer byteBuffer =
        ByteBuffer.allocateDirect(
        TexturedPyramid.VERTEX_SIZE * 3 * 3);
    byteBuffer.order(ByteOrder.nativeOrder());
    vertexBuffer = byteBuffer.asFloatBuffer();
    vertexBuffer.put(vertices);
    vertexBuffer.flip();
    this.textureId = textureId;
}

public void draw(GL10 gl) {
    rotation += 1.0f;
    gl.glRotatef(rotation, 1f, 1f, 1f);

    gl.glEnable(GL10.GL_TEXTURE_2D);
    gl.glBindTexture(GL10.GL_TEXTURE_2D, textureId);

    gl.glEnableClientState(GL10.GL_VERTEX_ARRAY);
    gl.glEnableClientState(GL10.GL_TEXTURE_COORD_ARRAY);

    vertexBuffer.position(0);
    gl.glVertexPointer(3, GL10.GL_FLOAT,
        TexturedPyramid.VERTEX_SIZE, vertexBuffer);
    vertexBuffer.position(3);
    gl.glTexCoordPointer(2, GL10.GL_FLOAT,
        TexturedPyramid.VERTEX_SIZE, vertexBuffer);

    gl.glDrawArrays(GL10.GL_TRIANGLES, 0, 3 * 3);
    gl.glDisableClientState(GL10.GL_VERTEX_ARRAY);
    gl.glDisableClientState(GL10.GL_TEXTURE_COORD_ARRAY);
    }
}
```

❷ Specify new vertex size 5 components

❸ Include vertices data with UV coordinates

❹ Include draw method

As you can see, TexturedPyramid class has a few differences from the ColouredPyramid. We start with a variable to hold the texture ID for the texture bitmap we'll use on the pyramid ❶. This is set in the constructor. Then we calculate the new vertex size for five components ❷. Next, we have the vertices bearing the u/v coordinates ❸. The layout is separated in rows for each vertex. The first three elements are the x, y, and z coordinates. The fourth and fifth elements are the u/v coordinates in the texture's normalized coordinate system.

With the data ready to go, including the extra u/v coordinates, we again have the draw method ❹, where texture mapping is enabled. glEnable takes one parameter and we instruct it to enable GL_TEXTURE_2D. Note again the use of constants provided by OpenGL. glBindTexture will bind the texture with the ID passed in as a parameter in the constructor. Then we enable the use of the vertex arrays for reading out the information needed for rendering and for texture mapping that will be applied to the rendered models. Next, we set the position to 0 for rendering the objects, specify the location where to get the vertices for rendering, and then set the cursor to the fourth element, which is the first texture coordinate. This is similar to the coloring example, but this time we tell OpenGL to use the vertex buffer to get the u/v coordinates to apply the texture. The size of the texture information is two elements. The stride is VERTEX_SIZE. Finally, we draw the triangles and disable the client states.

Running the new Activity, you should see a spinning pyramid with textured faces as shown in figure 12.16.

DISCUSSION

You should now know a little about how textures can be mapped on to surfaces and drawn with OpenGL. This knowledge builds on our other examples, and hopefully the pattern should be clear. We've only scratched the surface of what OpenGL can do, but we think what we've shown you here covers the fundamentals and should get you started developing your applications with graphics in mind.

12.3   *Summary*

Drawing in Android begins with 2D lines, arcs, rectangles, circles, points, and bitmaps. This is done using the Canvas class and its myriad draw methods. To use different colors, sizes, and effects the Canvas works in conjunction with the Paint class. In this chapter, we walked through several examples of working with 2D drawing in order to draw lines and shapes, combine drawing with text and images, and even draw an example custom view with special effects. You can see how these techniques can help you include many new elements in your applications. You're only limited by what you're willing to draw.

Canvas drawing can accomplish a lot, but it's just the tip of floating triangular polyhedron, so to speak. Beyond Canvas lie 2D and 3D drawing with OpenGL ES. OpenGL ES is a rich and powerful drawing library that can take advantage of the GPU if present. In addition, if you want to step up to 3D, OpenGL is your ticket. The OpenGL ES library allows you to draw and animate shapes, and more. Here we started simple and built a 2D triangle. Then we went 3D and created a spinning pyramid, and we added colors and textures. Combining what we've seen here with our earlier discussions of working with activities, widgets, views, services, and more, you can see how the possibilities are almost unlimited.

In the next part of the book, we'll be moving past the fundamentals and core building blocks we've concentrated on up to this point. By now your foundation should be solid, and it's time to go beyond getting things done and step up to other project management techniques and working with additional form factors. This means we're moving on to tackle testing, instrumentation, automated builds, continuous integration (CI), and newer APIs and features that affect tablets.

Part 3

Beyond standard development

The third and final part of Android in Practice will continue to extend your Android programming knowledge and move into more mature and robust software development practices at the same time. Chapter 13 addresses testing, so you'll work with different kinds of tests, several different test frameworks, and you'll find out about overall testing practices. Chapter 14 covers building and managing Android projects. You'll work with build tools like Ant and Maven, and see how continuous integration can be employed with Android projects as well. Chapter 15 will wrap things up with a tour of some of the newer Android API portions that were created for tablets. Here, you'll learn how to work with drag and drop features, the Action Bar, and fragments.

Testing and instrumentation

In this chapter

- Unit testing
- Testing activities with instrumentation
- Mock objects and stubs
- Input testing with the Monkey tool

I tread paths by moonlight that others fear to speak of during day.

—Patrick Rothfuss, *The Name of the Wind*

If there's one topic that polarizes the software development community, it must be testing. Though testing is commonly understood as a true development task, as opposed to being a duty of "the QA guys," many programmers still try to avoid it like the plague. (If you don't fall into that group, feel free to skip the initial motivation that follows.)

Why is that? From our experience, there are two main reasons why programmers don't write tests: ignorance and arrogance. Ignorance, the unwitting kind, is most often found with programmers who don't come from a development background where test-oriented or test-driven development are commonplace, and who aren't familiar with the benefits of testing methodologies (unfortunately, mobile application developers often fall into that category). Even if they're familiar with the concepts, they often don't cherish the value of software tests, and therefore perceive writing tests as cumbersome, something "you know you should be doing but aren't in the mood for just now." After all, you need to get that milestone done and report progress to your senior, so why waste time writing tests, right?

The second cause is arrogance. We programmers are proud animals. Our own code is always faster, more clever, more stable, and more beautiful than everyone else's is. Most importantly, it's entirely bug free. So why write code that tests your own code, which presumably is already perfect? Or, so you think.

This boils down to the central question: why bother? Because it *will* pay off at some point, maybe earlier than you think. With a proper test suite in place, you can employ a build server to run the test suite after every commit, which allows you to discover regressions early on during development, and fixing things earlier rather than later will ultimately raise the quality of your product. Some people go further and practice *test-driven development (TDD)*, where a test is written *before* the code that it's testing even exists. That way you start with the functional requirements (the specification, or *contract*) by formulating them as a test case that initially fails, and you write and change the code under test until the test succeeds. This allows you to derive your application logic and even interfaces from your test suite, which defines how the application should work. Any deviation from that behavior introduced by a subsequent commit will then be automatically detected the next time you run the test suite (as mentioned, build servers can do that automatically for you, as we'll see in chapter 14).

Yes, writing tests takes time and effort. You have to constantly think about the two rights: writing the right tests and having them test the right things. You could rephrase that as making the correct decision about *what* should be tested, and making sure your tests correctly reflect the requirements. Green lights on the build server will give you comfort. But let's face it, they can be deceptive!

In any case, we highly encourage you to adopt some form of developer testing. Once it becomes routine, you'll be uncomfortable adding another piece to your software without backing it with a test. Comfort can be a key driver behind writing tests. Whenever you find yourself committing code that breaks the build, don't feel guilty. Instead, feel comforted, because without the help of that test, the bug might have slipped into production. Don't be ignorant. Don't be arrogant. Good developers write tests.

But this book is about Android, not about testing. If you still aren't convinced that writing tests is a good thing, we encourage you to get your hands on some books about testing and TDD. Lots of them are out there, not least because Agile development models (which heavily advertise testing practices) have become wildly popular over the last decade.

Leaving our motivation behind, here's what this chapter has to offer: the first section will lay some fundamentals by answering the basic "whats" and "hows" of Android testing. We'll then focus on the core material around testing: we explain how you can use Android's instrumentation framework to write user interface tests, and how to make your tests beautiful and expressive with the help of *domain-specific languages (DSLs)*. Toward the end of the chapter, we'll finally take you to the more advanced levels of testing. You'll learn how to use mock objects to achieve a higher decoupling of your tests, how to take alternative paths to Android UI testing, and even how to stress-test applications using UI exercisers.

You may have noticed from the table of contents that this chapter is longer than usual, but rest assured that this isn't because we plan to get you entangled in too much detail. Instead, we think that testing on Android is an area that doesn't get enough attention. When putting this chapter together, we wanted to give you an in-depth understanding of the matter and not just reiterate what can be found in the official documentation (at http://mng.bz/TM2V). So prepare for a long ride, but we promise, it'll be worth your while.

13.1 Testing the Android

This section will start by giving you a bird's eye view of Android's framework capabilities. It'll specifically answer the following questions: what kind of tests can you write for an Android application? How do you set up a test suite for your project? How are tests on Android implemented? After laying some groundwork by answering the first question, we'll show you how to set up a test project for your application in Eclipse, how tests are structured and executed, and then wrap things up the "In Practice" way by going head-first into our first technique, which is writing a simple unit test for an Android `Application` class.

13.1.1 Ways to test in Android

There are many forms of software testing and many ways to classify tests. This being a book about programming, we'll focus on developer tests—tests that you, the programmer, write and execute. Android supports two such kinds of tests, unit tests and functional tests, and two ways of running them—in the Java virtual machine, or in the emulator or device.

UNIT TESTS

Unit testing focuses on testing a specific code unit in isolation, usually a class. Ideally, a unit test tests only the behavior of the unit under test, while isolating any dependent or depending code units. This keeps the test focused and rules out unwanted side effects induced by code you're not currently testing. We can almost hear you scream for an example. Here's one. In the DealDroid application from chapter 2, we have two activities: the `DealList`, which creates the main screen of the application and the `DealDetails`, which is the screen you see when clicking a deal in the `DealList`. The `DealDetails Activity` can only be launched from the `DealList Activity`, so `DealDetails` depends on `DealList`. When writing a unit test for either class, you should test only those features that are inherent to that class—for `DealList`, the display of deal items, and for `DealDetails`, the display of deal information. If you don't obey

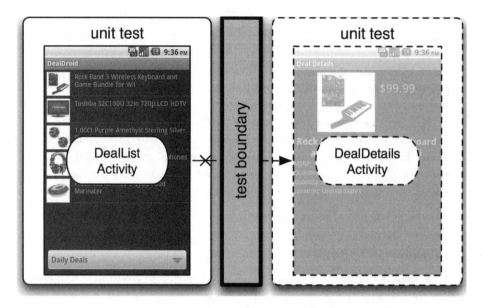

Figure 13.1   Unit tests are about focusing on a single entity while isolating it from other code units. Here we have two units, DealList and DealDetails, which although closely related, are tested in isolation.

this rule, then you may see a test for DealList fail when the cause was actually a flaw in the DealDetails class, or vice versa. Isolated testing using unit tests is a good practice. This is illustrated in figure 13.1.

Unfortunately, isolating code units from each other can be surprisingly difficult to do. Mock objects can help (we'll learn what mocks are and how to use them in section 13.3), but for classes to be properly testable using unit tests, you should think about this beforehand, ideally while writing the class. TDD can help by designing classes that are loosely coupled and therefore can easily be isolated in tests. Entire books can be written on how to achieve that, but let's not digress too far here. Note that we'll write a unit test for DealDetails in technique 75, so sit tight: a coding exercise is on its way.

FUNCTIONAL TESTS

We use the term *functional test* here because Android uses this term for a specific kind of test in its documentation. To be frank, we think it's misleading, because a unit test can also be a functional test, but one that tests an isolated piece of functionality. In general, any test that asserts that certain functionality behaves correctly with respect to a given specification is a functional test, as opposed to a nonfunctional test, which tests nonfunctional software properties such as speed or scalability. What Android calls a "functional test," we'd personally refer to as a *story test*, since Android's functional tests are mostly used for implementing user stories as tests.

That said, functional tests on Android allow you to test the behavior of your application across several code units (typically activities), and thus do full end-to-end tests of your application. In that regard, they're the opposite of unit tests, since the code

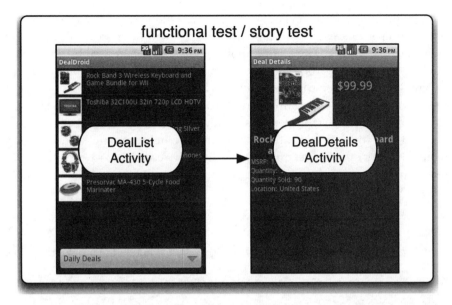

Figure 13.2 Functional tests on Android allow you to test scenarios involving several code units, such as transitioning from one screen to another when clicking a list item.

units that are part of the test don't run in isolation, but interact with each other. This way of testing is illustrated in figure 13.2.

Testing your applications using functional tests is powerful, because it allows you to translate your user stories directly to a test suite, which can then verify that the application operates as expected. If you still don't think that's a compelling argument, it's also fun to watch the screens automatically fly by while the Android emulator executes one of your functional tests!

Besides the classification into unit and functional tests, it should be said that there are also two fundamentally different ways to run tests: the standard Java way, and via Android's instrumentation infrastructure. Both have their pros and cons, which may affect the way you lay out your test projects, so let's quickly go through the differences.

TESTING THE JAVA WAY

Running tests the standard Java way means running a test on a standard JVM (not on Dalvik), as any ordinary Java application would be. This has both benefits and drawbacks. The benefits are:

- *Speed*—Tests run more quickly than instrumentation tests, since the test code doesn't have to be deployed to the emulator or device first.

- *Flexibility*—Because you don't rely on the Android runtime, you're free to use any testing framework you like, such as JUnit 4 or TestNG (we'll explore JUnit on Android in a second).

- *Mock objects*—You can make full use of sophisticated object mock libraries, even those relying on byte code manipulation, which wouldn't work on Dalvik.

Though this is all nice, the major downside of executing test code on a standard JVM is that you will *not* have access to any Android framework classes. All methods in the android.jar file against which your application (and your test code) is compiled will throw a `RuntimeException`. (See the sidebar "Help, I'm a stub!" for a more in-depth explanation of this behavior.) Without further effort, this makes running tests that directly or indirectly use Android framework classes on a standard JVM impossible, because any such test would terminate with a runtime error. We'll show you in technique 79 how you can work around this with the help of some excellent third-party libraries. Still, running tests on a JVM is perfectly reasonable when testing code that isn't bound to any framework classes. An example would be a random number generator you've written.

Help, I'm a stub!

You may have noticed that the android.jar library file linked to your Android projects doesn't actually contain the Android framework code. If you open it and look at the class files, you'll notice that every single method is implemented as:

```
throw new RuntimeException("Stub!");
```

That doesn't seem helpful, so what's the deal? The reason is simple: Android applications run on a device or the emulator, where the runtime library is already provided as part of the system image. The android.jar file you see in Eclipse will *not* be distributed with your applications. In order to compile an Android application, the compiler doesn't need access to method bodies, just type signatures, public members, and so forth. In return, this means that by removing the actual implementation, the size of the JAR file bundled with the SDK is reduced significantly while still ensuring that your application will only use classes and interfaces that will exist on a device running the same version of Android.

TESTING THE ANDROID WAY

The second (and from an Android point of view, preferred) way to run tests is to run them directly on the device. This requires a lot of work behind the scenes, because the application and test code must first be deployed to the device, making this a much slower approach. On the other hand, your tests will have full access to the Android platform functions, as any ordinary Android application does. This can be a major benefit, because it allows you to run virtually any test you like, be it framework dependent or not. The drawbacks that you should be aware of are:

- *Slow execution*—Deploying tests to the emulator or device is slow, making this a less than ideal approach for TDD, where you want quick turnaround.
- *Technology lock-in*—Running on Dalvik means you're much less flexible in terms of testing libraries, since Android only supports the somewhat aged JUnit 3, and mock libraries designed around runtime byte-code manipulation on a JVM won't work.

Still, you'll likely write most tests using this approach, because it requires less fighting against the framework. It's also the way Google's Android team writes tests. It's well suited to write UI tests (tests that involve activities).

13.1.2 Organizing tests

Now that we know what kind of tests we can write, the next step is to create an environment in which we can keep our tests. The preferred way to organize your tests is to keep them separate from your application project. That way you can isolate test from production code, and as a result, not deploy your test code with your application (Android will bundle all source code in your project folder in the APK, even its test code). This involves creating a separate test project that lives next to your application project in Eclipse, whose name by convention should end in *Test*, for example, *Deal-DroidTest* for the *DealDroid* project.

> **GRAB THE PROJECT: DEALDROIDTEST**   You can get the source code for this project at the *Android in Practice* code website. Because some code listings here are shortened to focus on specific concepts, we recommend that you download the complete source code and follow along within Eclipse (or your favorite IDE or text editor).
>
> Note that for the purpose of this chapter, we've created a branch of the Deal-Droid that changes the visibility of a few class members so that a test case can access them, and also introduces a new export feature that we're going to test. (Because this chapter focuses on test code, and not applications, there will be few APK files to download.)
>
> Source: http://mng.bz/Zk0O

The ADT plugin for Eclipse gives you a hand by providing a special wizard for creating test projects, which you can reach from the Eclipse menu via File > New > Other and selecting Android Test Project under the Android category, as seen in figure 13.3. Let's do this and create a test project for the DealDroid application.

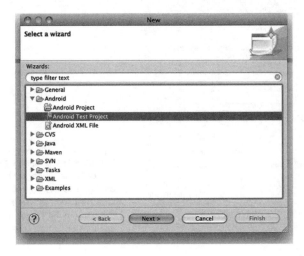

Figure 13.3   In order to create a new Android test project, you can use the wizard via File > New > Other and selecting Android Test Project.

After clicking Next, you'll see the project settings form for our new test project. Apart from the standard set of project settings, such as name and workspace location, you'll find a new setting specific to test projects: the test target. This will be our DealDroid application, so we select it from the file browser. You'll also notice how the wizard puts the test code into the `test` package with the package name of the application that we're testing as the parent package. Figure 13.4 shows how the filled-in wizard form looks for the DealDroidTest project.

Click Finish, and you'll find the new test project in your workspace. Looking at the project, you'll see that this is an ordinary Android project, so what's the deal? The differences are marginal, and it should be stressed that you could arrive at the same result by going through the standard Android project wizard (or the `android create project` command) and doing a few things manually that the test project wizard does for you. These are:

- Adding the application under test to both the build path and the project references
- Setting up the manifest so that Android knows that this project should be run as a test application

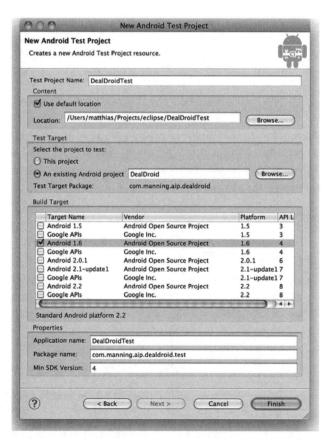

Figure 13.4 The ADT wizard to create test projects sets a few defaults, such as the Java package name, for you. Make sure that the test project uses the same build target as the application you're testing.

The second point is the interesting one. Let's look at the AndroidManifest.xml file that the ADT test project wizard generated for us:

```xml
<?xml version="1.0" encoding="utf-8"?>
<manifest xmlns:android="http://schemas.android.com/apk/res/android"
    package="com.manning.aip.dealdroid.test" ...>
  <application>
    <uses-library android:name="android.test.runner" />
  </application>
  <uses-sdk android:minSdkVersion="4" />
  <instrumentation android:targetPackage="com.manning.aip.dealdroid"
    android:name="android.test.InstrumentationTestRunner" />
</manifest>
```

As you can see, we're linking against a shared library (`android.test.runner`). That's because we're defining an `instrumentation`, a test runner defined in that shared library, which will be used to actually run our tests. We'll learn what instrumentation is in section 13.2; for now just note that it's there and that it's responsible for executing our test suite when launching this test application on a device or emulator.

Apart from these differences, the project structure is identical to that of an ordinary Android project. Since a test project is an application of its own, the test code becomes the main source code and hence goes straight into the `src` folder, where you're free to break it down into smaller subpackages. If you intend to write "classic" tests that will run on the JVM in addition to normal Android tests, it probably makes sense to put them into a different package or source folder, so that the distinction is clear to anyone looking at your test project structure.

13.1.3 *Writing and running tests*

As you may have noticed, our test project is still empty. Let's change that and write a simple test. Android comes bundled with the JUnit 3 unit testing framework, so typically, all tests are written as JUnit 3 tests. For those tests you don't intend to run on a device, you're free to link whatever testing framework as a JAR, but tests running on the device should use the JUnit classes bundled with Android, because all special test classes Android defines are derived from a JUnit 3 `TestCase`. We won't explore the JUnit testing framework in-depth here, but only cover the basics.

In JUnit, you bundle tests into *test cases*. Each test case contains the tests you'd like to perform against the unit under test (typically a class from your main application). You do so by inheriting from `junit.framework.TestCase`, and putting all tests into that class, like so:

```java
import junit.framework.TestCase;

public class MyTestCase extends TestCase {

    public void testTruth() {
        assertTrue(true);
    }

}
```

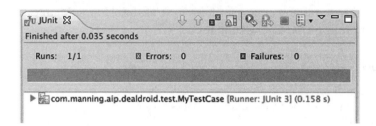

Figure 13.5
The standard JUnit test result view in Eclipse. Here you can see which tests were run, and which ones succeeded, failed, or exited in error.

This test case contains a single test that ensures that `true` evaluates to `true`. That's a fairly useless test, since it'll always succeed, but it serves our purpose of explaining the anatomy of a JUnit test case. Not every method defined in a test case needs to be a test; in fact, only those methods prefixed with `test*` (as in `testTruth`) will be executed as tests during runtime. JUnit identifies these at runtime using reflection. Any other method will be an ordinary method and not be called unless *you* explicitly call it. In order to make assertions in tests, JUnit provides helper methods starting in `assert*` (as in `assertTrue`). JUnit provides plenty of them already, such as `assertNotNull`, `assertEquals`, and so forth, and Android adds a few more in the `MoreAsserts` helper class. Using these simple building blocks, you can set up your entire test suite.

So how are these tests executed? As mentioned earlier, there are two ways: as an ordinary Java test (on a JVM), or as an Android test (on a device). If you right-click your test project (or any test class open in the current Eclipse editor), you can choose to Run As > JUnit Test or Run As > Android JUnit Test. The preceding snippet doesn't rely on any Android-specific framework code, so either will do fine. For the remainder of this chapter, we always assume that tests are run the "Android way," on the device (unless we explicitly say otherwise). The outcome of a test is displayed in the Eclipse *JUnit* view, which will open automatically when running tests. It looks something like figure 13.5.

That covers the basics of testing. If we did a good job at writing this introduction, then you know why you should write tests, what kinds of tests you can write, how to set up test projects, and even how to write and run simple JUnit tests. Hopefully you're curious for more! Let's proceed and write a real-world practical test. Since we've already set up a test project for it, the DealDroid application will be the target of our tests for the remainder of this chapter. We start with technique 74, writing a simple application unit test using Android's `ApplicationTestCase` class.

TECHNIQUE 74   A simple Android unit test

Roll up your sleeves, it's time to write our first proper test on Android. So you've learned that every Android test case is basically a JUnit `TestCase`. But Android adds some functionality on top of JUnit and provides different flavors of test cases by plugging its own test case class hierarchy underneath the JUnit `TestCase` base class. Look at figure 13.6, which shows how Android structures its test cases into different kinds.

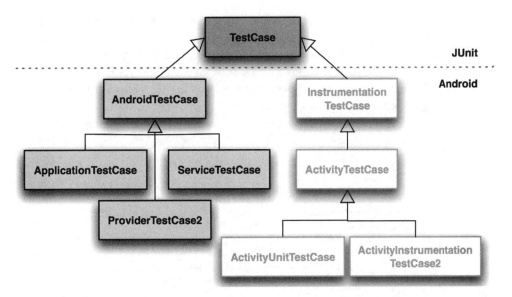

Figure 13.6 Every kind of test case on Android inherits from a JUnit 3 `TestCase`. Android further structures tests into those that require access to an instrumentation (right subtree), and those that don't (left subtree).

For the time being, we're going to focus on the left branch emerging from `TestCase` in figure 13.6, since we haven't yet introduced instrumentation code (we'll do that in technique 75). As you can see, Android defines three different kinds of test cases here:

- `ApplicationTestCase`—Used to test an `android.app.Application`
- `ServiceTestCase`—Used to test an `android.app.Service`
- `ProviderTestCase2`—Used to test an `android.content.ContentProvider` (refactoring of the older and now deprecated `ProviderTestCase`)

These inherit from `AndroidTestCase`, which contains a few helper methods, such as custom assertions to test for certain permissions being set, or even a method to inject custom `Context` objects, the latter of which is going to become important when learning about mock objects in technique 71. The difference to `InstrumentationTestCase` is that it doesn't expose access to the `Instrumentation`, and we'll see in section 13.2 what that means. In order to unit test the application object, services, and content providers, this isn't required, so we're good to go.

PROBLEM

You're writing a custom application class, content provider, or service, and you want to test it in a controlled way (isolated from other components in your application) using a unit test.

SOLUTION

Although `ApplicationTestCase`, `ServiceTestCase`, and `ProviderTestCase2` all have special helper methods tailored toward the specific kind of object they're testing, working with them is largely similar, so we're only going to look at one of them more closely as an example—ApplicationTestCase. Recall that the DealDroid defines its own application class (DealDroidApp) by deriving from android.app.Application. The application class is where you should put logic and settings that affect the entire application, so it's always a good idea to have a few tests in place that make sure everything is configured and working the way it should be.

Looking again at the DealDroidApp class, it seems that it's performing initialization logic in onCreate:

```
public class DealDroidApp extends Application {
    ...

    @Override
    public void onCreate() {
        this.cMgr = (ConnectivityManager)
            this.getSystemService(Context.CONNECTIVITY_SERVICE);
        this.parser = new DailyDealsXmlPullFeedParser();
        this.sectionList = new ArrayList<Section>(6);
        this.imageCache = new HashMap<Long, Bitmap>();
    }
    ...

}
```

This code tells us that the remainder of this class relies on certain objects to be fully initialized after onCreate has been called. This sounds like a good candidate for a test, so that we can always remain sure that this is the case. Moreover, we also want to add a test that makes sure the application remains properly configured with respect to its application icon and versioning scheme. More precisely, we want to assert that the application icon remains unchanged from the ddicon image in res/drawable, and that a developer working on DealDroid never uses a versioning scheme other than $n.m$, where n and m are digits (such as 1.0). Let's express these requirements as a test case.

Listing 13.1 ApplicationTestCase can be used to test application classes

```
public class DealDroidAppTest
    extends ApplicationTestCase<DealDroidApp> {        ◁─┐  Inherit from
                                                         ❶  ApplicationTestCase
    private DealDroidApp dealdroid;

    public DealDroidAppTest() {
        super(DealDroidApp.class);
    }

    @Override
    protected void setUp() throws Exception {
        super.setUp();                                    ❷  Use setUp
        createApplication();                                 to prepare
        dealdroid = getApplication();                        tests
    }

    public void testShouldInitializeInstances() {     ◁─❸  Run first test
        assertNotNull(dealdroid.sectionList);
        assertNotNull(dealdroid.imageCache);
```

```
        assertNotNull(dealdroid.parser);
    }

    public void testShouldStartWithEmptySections() {        ◄──4 Run second test
        assertTrue(dealdroid.sectionList.isEmpty());
        assertNull(dealdroid.currentSection);
        assertNull(dealdroid.currentItem);
    }

    public void testCorrectProjectProperties()              ◄──5 Run third test
        throws NameNotFoundException {
        PackageInfo info =
                dealdroid.getPackageManager().getPackageInfo(
                        dealdroid.getPackageName(), 0);

        assertEquals(R.drawable.ddicon, info.applicationInfo.icon);

        MoreAsserts.assertMatchesRegex("\\d\\.\\d", info.versionName);
    }
}
```

Let's review what we've done here. We've created an ordinary class, but let it inherit from ApplicationTestCase. It's a generic class, and we must pass it the application type we want to test ❶. ApplicationTestCase exposes helpers specific to testing application classes—most importantly, creating a new application instance via createApplication, which will trigger the application's onCreate handler, and getting a reference to the created application object through getApplication. We do that in the setUp method ❷. setUp is a special test lifecycle hook exposed by JUnit, which is run before *every single* test method (of which we have three here), so be careful to not perform any overly expensive tasks here. setUp is typically used to load test fixtures or reset and initialize test state. Using a test on a static variable allows you to run setUp only once if needed.

> **WARNING** Looking at our test code, you may get the idea that Deal-DroidApp.onCreate is called three times (via setUp, before every test method executes). That is *not* true: onCreate is called four times. That's because InstrumentationTestRunner always calls Application.onCreate as part of its startup routine—*before* your tests run. Keep this in mind if you do things in onCreate that may affect the outcome of your tests, like starting AsyncTasks!

We then define three tests. testShouldInitializeInstances asserts that after onCreate is called, all three instances exposed via getters (sectionList, imageCache, and parser) have been fully constructed (aren't null) ❸. The second test, shouldStartWithEmptySections, makes sure that the application is launched with a clean state, which in this case means that no deals are loaded (the section list is empty) ❹. Finally, we test that the application icon is always set to the correct drawable, and that the version name follows the *n.m* scheme ❺. JUnit doesn't provide an assertion that can test for regular expressions, but Android fortunately comes with a few custom JUnit assertions, such as the assertMatchesRegex used here, which can all be found in the android.test.MoreAsserts helper class.

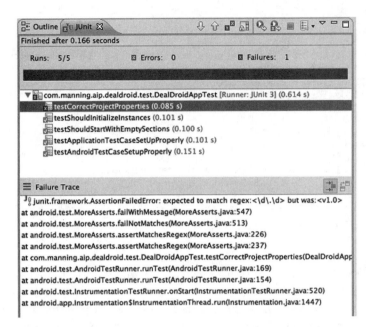

Figure 13.7 Since we've written a test for it, we can now detect changes to the application version name that aren't allowed by our rules. In that case, JUnit will report an assertion failure in the JUnit result view.

Go ahead and run this test case by right-clicking the class and selecting Run As > Android JUnit test. If everything checks out, you should see green bars in the JUnit result view! You may also want to intentionally break the test, just to see what happens. For instance, open the application's AndroidManifest.xml file and change the `android:versionName` attribute value from `1.0` to `v1.0`. Now save the file and run the test again. Whoops! We don't allow letters in the version name, so our test fails (see figure 13.7).

Just to be clear: that the test fails in this case is a *good* thing—it tells us that our test captures the correct semantics, which in this case means not allowing letters in the version name. Now go back and change the version name to what it was; after all we don't want to leave the application in a broken state, do we?

DISCUSSION

We'd like to mention one particularly irritating thing about writing tests in JUnit 3, and that's the order in which tests are executed. Looking at our test case from listing 13.1, we see that the test checking for fully initialized objects (`testShouldInitialize-Instances`) is defined *before* the test that uses one of these objects (`testShould-StartWithEmptySections`). This seems to make sense, because we can then assume that whenever we enter the latter test, the former test must've passed, right? Wrong! The order in which you define tests in your test case is entirely irrelevant. Unfortunately, JUnit 3 doesn't warrant any specific order in which it executes tests, so you should make sure to never rely on order. To alleviate this circumstance, define a special test method that contains all those assertions that you believe must pass in order for any other test to pass, and give it a meaningful name such as `testPreConditions`. That doesn't mean JUnit will give this specific test method any special treatment, but as soon as this one fails, you can tell that any other failing test may simply be failing because the preconditions weren't met, and you know where you can start looking for bugs. Google use this pattern in their test suites for the Android framework.

You've seen how to write unit tests for a few core objects, but most of what you've seen was plain JUnit functionality with a bit of Android helper sugar on top. Nevertheless, everything seen so far is essential for the things to come.

Speaking of things to come: we've mentioned `Instrumentation` a few times, but never provided any details. At this point, you may have thought: JUnit and `AndroidTestCase` are fine and good, but we haven't addressed the core issue of testing activities! After all, activities are what we're spending most of our time with when developing Android applications, and they demand more in terms of test support than being able to trigger their `onCreate` method. What about clicking buttons? Sending key events? Firing intents or testing layouts? Looks like we're ready to delve deeper into the Android testing framework. The next section explains how you can test your activities and user interfaces using Android's instrumentation framework, and how to push the boundaries of test expressiveness using DSLs.

13.2 Pulling strings: Android instrumentation

So far we've been testing the invisible parts of your application, those parts that may play a fundamental role, but aren't seen by the user. `AndroidTestCase` is sufficient for that: services, content providers, and the application object are background objects, so we don't need any support for simulating a user interacting with them. But what about activities? We have plenty of user interface interaction here: users click buttons, type text, rotate the screen, scroll lists, and so on. How would we do all that as part of an automated test?

Android's answer to this is *instrumentation*. Instead of calling methods and manipulating objects in the scope of an `Activity`, we take one step back and control the `Activity` *itself*; we orchestrate or *instrument* it. When writing normal application code, you're confined to the internal interfaces of objects such as activities or services, and you can only react to outside system events in a passive way, for instance via lifecycle hooks such as `onCreate` or keyboard listeners like `onKeyDown`. There's no way to manipulate anything from outside, to take control yourself. Instrumentation means breaking out of that restriction and being able to control activities and services from the outside. Think of puppets on strings: Instrumentation pulls the strings!

That being said, you've already seen instrumentation in action in a limited form. In technique 67 you manually created an `Application` object using `ApplicationTest-Case.createApplication`. That's instrumentation: under usual conditions, your code can be notified when the application object is created (via `Application.onCreate`), but it can't control this event directly. Closely related to this, you may recall from section 13.1 that in a test project's manifest file, you define an `InstrumentationTestRunner`, which will execute tests by using instrumentation. You may legitimately ask: if I've already seen how to use instrumentation code, what's left to know about it? Plenty, for two main reasons. The first reason is that all types of automated tests so far inherit from `AndroidTestCase`, which does *not* give any access to a full instrumentation environment, unlike `InstrumentationTestCase`, which we'll introduce in a moment. The second reason is more subtle. What we haven't told you so far is that tests executed using an `InstrumentationTestRunner` aren't executed on the main application thread, but on a separate instrumentation thread. When testing background objects such as services and content providers, that doesn't matter; they don't care on which thread they run. As explained in some detail in chapter 6, this does matter a lot when talking about user interface interaction, since UI events are *always* processed on the main application thread, and manipulating views outside that thread will fail with an error. Looks like we'd have been stuck if we only had `AndroidTestCase`, since that class has no means of executing UI actions in a test case and running them on the UI thread.

Unit testing Activities

Being able to steer user interface control flow via instrumentation opens up a new layer of complexity. You must be able to click buttons, enter text, scroll views, or open a menu item. In order to clearly separate tests that need these capabilities from those that don't, the Android framework exposes a special set of test case classes that you can use whenever you need to write tests that rely on instrumentation. These tests are derived from the aptly named `InstrumentationTestCase` base class, most notably `ActivityTestCase` (see figure 13.8). There are more kinds of instrumentation tests than just `ActivityTestCase`, but they're rather obscure and less useful than `Activity-TestCase`, so this is what we'll focus on here.

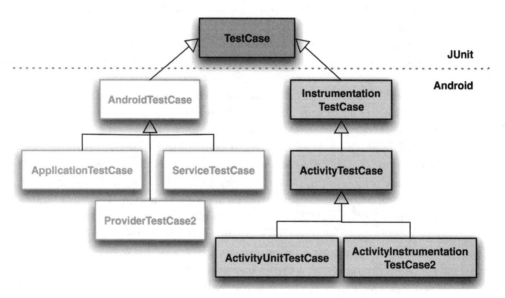

Figure 13.8 `InstrumentationTestCase` **should be used whenever tests require access to the instrumentation API. This is essential for anything related to testing Activities, especially for story driven testing via** `ActivityInstrumentationTestCase2`.

`ActivityTestCase` isn't exciting by itself, since it just handles some boilerplate code specific to testing activities, which you'd otherwise have to write yourself. The interesting distinction is between `ActivityUnitTestCase` and `ActivityInstrumentation-TestCase2`. We're going to postpone explaining the latter until we hit technique 69, and for now focus on `ActivityUnitTestCase`.

Using `ActivityUnitTestCase`, you can, unsurprisingly, unit test your activities. As explained in the introduction, unit testing an `Activity` means testing it in isolation, but what does that mean? Consider an ordinary Android application like our DealDroid. When it launches an `Activity` or transitions from one screen to the next, the runtime is busy coordinating the many components involved in these interactions: executing their lifecycle hooks (see chapter 3), drawing things on the display, and so forth. That's the opposite of running in isolation! The problem with this is twofold. First, it's slow. If you just want to test a single screen, why load or even consider other screens that may be parents of this one or branch off it? It would be more efficient to ignore them for this test. Second, and more importantly, testing in isolation minimizes effects other components may have on the component under test, and helps you focus on testing the expected input and output of your `Activity`—testing it on an interface level. Once again, let's try to turn these findings into a concise problem description.

PROBLEM

You want to test intrinsic properties of an `Activity`, and don't want it to communicate with other platform components. This implies sacrificing its execution in a fully setup runtime environment for a significant gain in test case speed.

SOLUTION

If your intention is to test things like "Given input X coming in with an `Intent`, my `Activity` should do Y," or "After creating my `Activity`, views A and B should exist and be fully initialized," then `ActivityUnitTestCase` is a perfect match. As mentioned earlier, tests defined in this kind of test case will be run "detached" from the actual system, so as to minimize dependencies on other components.

> **REMEMBER...** Again, this doesn't mean that your application won't be started as part of the test run. As explained in the previous technique, the `InstrumentationTestRunner` will always start your application by calling its `onCreate` method.

Android leverages its instrumentation capabilities to run your `Activity` in a controlled way, entirely decoupled from everything else. Note that this also means that it will *not* go through the normal runtime lifecycle; only its `onCreate` method will be called when started in a unit test (more on that in a second). This is ideally suited for testing an `Activity`'s internal state, such whether its views are setup correctly or what should happen at its interfaces. For instance, you could run a test that states that if the `Activity` isn't started using a specific kind of `Intent`, it'll output an error. That would be a test for correct input. Additionally, you could test that it constructs the correct `Intent` to launch another `Activity` (but without actually launching that other `Activity` as part of the test!). That would be a test for correct output. Most likely, you'll test that its layout and views are correctly set up.

Let's write a unit test for the `DealDetails` `Activity`. This `Activity` is well-suited for unit testing: based on the currently selected item, it displays information about that item on the screen. It also allows us to open the Android browser, in order to load the item's detail page on the eBay website. Codifying these features into assertions, we may arrive at something like this (note that we're ignoring some of the views in the `DealDetails` to keep the example compact).

Listing 13.2 `ActivityUnitTestCase` allows you to unit test a single screen

```
public class DealDetailsTest extends ActivityUnitTestCase<DealDetails> {

    private Item testItem;

    public DealDetailsTest() {
        super(DealDetails.class);
    }

    @Override
    protected void setUp() throws Exception {          ❶ Load test fixtures
        super.setUp();                                    in setUp

        testItem = new Item();
        testItem.setItemId(1);
        testItem.setTitle("Test Item");
        testItem.setConvertedCurrentPrice("1");
        testItem.setLocation("USA");
        testItem.setDealUrl("http://example.com");

        DealDroidApp application = new DealDroidApp();
        application.setCurrentItem(testItem);
        setApplication(application);
    }
                                                       ❷ Do relevant
    public void testPreConditions() {                    views exist?
        startActivity(new Intent(getInstrumentation().getTargetContext(),
                DealDetails.class), null, null);

        Activity activity = getActivity();
        assertNotNull(activity.findViewById(R.id.details_price));
        assertNotNull(activity.findViewById(R.id.details_title));
        assertNotNull(activity.findViewById(R.id.details_location));
    }
                                                       ❸ Make sure
    public void testThatAllFieldsAreSetCorrectly() {     they're updated
        startActivity(new Intent(getInstrumentation().getTargetContext(),
                DealDetails.class), null, null);

        assertEquals("$" + testItem.getConvertedCurrentPrice(),
            getViewText(R.id.details_price));
        assertEquals(testItem.getTitle(), getViewText(R.id.details_title));
        assertEquals(testItem.getLocation(),
            getViewText(R.id.details_location));
    }
                                                       ❹ Test outgoing
    public void testThatItemCanBeDisplayedInBrowser() {   Intent
```

```
        startActivity(new Intent(getInstrumentation().getTargetContext(),
                DealDetails.class), null, null);

        getInstrumentation().invokeMenuActionSync(getActivity(),
                DealDetails.MENU_BROWSE, 0);

        Intent browserIntent = getStartedActivityIntent();
        assertEquals(Intent.ACTION_VIEW, browserIntent.getAction());
        assertEquals(testItem.getDealUrl(), browserIntent.getDataString());
    }

    private String getViewText(int textViewId) {
        return ((TextView) getActivity().findViewById(textViewId)).getText()
                .toString();
    }
}
```

As seen in the previous technique, we use the `setUp` method to initialize our tests ❶. In this case, we're setting up a test fixture—a dummy deal item holding the data that we feed to the `Activity`. Moreover, we use `setApplication` to inject a custom application instance.

Next, are the actual test methods. We use the `testPreConditions` pattern again to have a separate test expressing that we need the given views to be valid before other tests can succeed ❷. In `testThatAllFieldsAreSetCorrectly`, we then make sure that given the dummy item we set up before, the respective views are actually showing that item's data on the screen ❸ (the `getViewText` method is a helper we defined to easily read the text from a `TextView`). Now it gets more interesting. In `testThatItemCan-BeDisplayedInBrowser`, we test that pressing the menu button with ID `MENU_BROWSE` will fire an `Intent` to view the current deal item via its deal URL ❹. To achieve that, we leverage instrumentation to programmatically invoke a menu action using `invoke-MenuActionSync`, and then call `getStartedActivityIntent` to check whether that triggered the `Intent` we expected. It's crucial to understand that we're not actually opening the menu, clicking the button, and launching a web browser here. If that happened, this wouldn't be a unit test, but an integration test as part of a user story. Instead, this test code makes sure that *if* someone *would* click that menu item on their device, then an `Intent` of kind `ACTION_VIEW` carrying the item's deal URL in its data field would be emitted. That's all.

We haven't explained the first line of code in each of these test methods: the call to `startActivity`. This will actually use instrumentation to mimic a launch of our `Deal-Details Activity`, without really starting it. It's an implicit call to its `onCreate` method, and it won't call any other lifecycle hooks that are involved in a full `Activity` launch, such as `onResume`, `onStart`, and so on. If you need those methods to be called, use the `getInstrumentation().callActivityOn*` helper methods.

Moreover, you must call `startActivity` in each of your test methods; otherwise a call to `getActivity` to retrieve the current activity instance will return `null`. You have to specify the `Intent` used to simulate the launch yourself: this is an example of what we mean when we say that `ActivityUnitTestCase` runs things in a controlled way. You can even inject your own context; in this case, we use the `getTargetContext` helper method that constructs a normal Android `Context` instance for us.

DISCUSSION

As you can imagine, instrumenting your activities is a powerful way to test. The key player here is the `Instrumentation` class, an instance of which is accessible from every `InstrumentationTestCase` via the `getInstrumentation()` accessor. We won't list every method it provides, but know that it allows you to start and stop activities, send key events, run actions on the main application thread, and so forth. In fact, you'll meet `Instrumentation` and a few of its more advanced features in the next technique.

Though `Activity` unit testing is a great way of testing things in isolation, sometimes you want to literally see the whole story, not just isolated fragments. In particular, wouldn't it be great if you could run entire user flows spanning several screens as part of a test? It sure is, and it's possible to do that using the not-so-well-named `ActivityInstrumentationTestCase2`.

TECHNIQUE 76   User stories as functional tests

As mentioned in the introduction, Android supports not only unit tests, but also what Android calls a *functional test*. To recap quickly: a functional test allows you to test your application (or a single component, if you like) in a fully functional runtime environment, just as if you were running the application yourself. This is fundamentally different from what we've seen before, where tests were run in a controlled environment, isolated from the rest of the system. In a functional test we're allowed to cross the boundary of one `Activity` to launch another and continue testing that new `Activity`, so we can now directly map user stories to a test suite and run full end-to-end tests of our applications.

Consider again our DealDroid application. Naturally, before we coded the Deal-Droid, the first step was to lay out the functional requirements for the application—the set of features it must support. One way to formulate functional requirements is creating *user stories*, where every feature requirement is written down as a single sentence, capturing compactly what the software must accomplish. Here's an example:

> *As a user, I want to get a list of deals and see detailed information about them.*

If you want to be picky, you could argue that this could be broken down into two user stories (get a list of deals (1), and given a deal, see detailed information about it (2)), but this serves us well enough for our example. Fortunately, this story has already been implemented for the DealDroid. The landing screen presents us with a selection of eBay offers, and clicking on one will open a new window with more detailed information about an item (see figure 13.9).

What hasn't been implemented yet is a test case that asserts in a programmatic fashion that our implementation works. Before writing the test, we must first identify the steps the user has to take in order to reach the deal details. These are:

 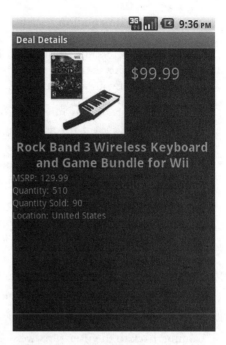

Figure 13.9   The DealDroid application as introduced in chapter 2. The user can select from a list of deals (left image) and get more information about them (right image).

1 Start the application.

2 Wait for the deal list to load.

3 Click on a deal to see the deal details. Starting the application means starting the `DealList Activity`, since that's our landing screen. If we want to test the entire flow, we therefore need to test the transition from the `DealList` to the `DealDetails Activity`. The crux of the matter is that we can't use `ActivityUnitTestCase` anymore, since it doesn't allow us to interact with any `Activity` other than the one under test.

PROBLEM

You want to run full end-to-end tests, so you can test the flows your user can take through your application. To make that happen, you need a test case that is executed in a fully functional system environment.

SOLUTION

We can realize our test scenario using `ActivityInstrumentationTestCase2`. The key difference between this class and `ActivityUnitTestCase` is that any test methods will be executed using the full system infrastructure. This allows you to simulate a user interacting with your application, such as pushing a button to open a new screen. This approach has the curious side effect that you can follow your tests being executed on the device or emulator, since you'll see all interactions happening live on the screen!

> **NOTE** Instrumentation tests like the ones discussed here are executed using a real application environment, and any call to `Activity.getApplication` will return the same application instance, even across several test cases. For story tests, this is usually what you want, but if not, bear in mind that you'll have to reset your application's state manually before running those tests.

These seemingly ghostly interactions aren't ghostly at all, but can be attributed to our old friend `Instrumentation`. Though an `ActivityUnitTestCase` was also powered by `Instrumentation` behind the scenes, its power couldn't be unleashed due to the focus on a single code unit. This time around, we'll look at some features `Instrumentation` exposes that enable us to do such useful things as:

- Create and inject custom `Activity` or `Application` objects
- Invoke `Activity` lifecycle methods directly
- Monitor whether an `Activity` has been launched in response to actions such as button clicks
- Dispatch key events
- Manually execute code on the UI thread
- Use helpers that let the test sleep until the application is idle

Coming back to the user story we want to test, there are some indispensable things on that list we'd want to use. If you've run the DealDroid yourself, you'll have noticed that when opening the `DealList`, the application displays a progress dialog while loading data from the eBay web service. Until that dialog disappears, the UI is blocked, so we need to wait for that to happen. Moreover, we must then programmatically click a list item and assert that this will result in the `DealDetails` `Activity` being launched. Let's see how `Instrumentation` allows us to do that, in the next listing.

Listing 13.3 `ActivityInstrumentationTestCase2` can test flows through the application

```
public class DealListTest extends ActivityInstrumentationTestCase2<DealList> {

    public DealListTest() {
        super("com.manning.aip.dealdroid", DealList.class);     Get reference to ❶
    }                                                           Instrumentation

    public void testDealListToDetailsUserFlow() throws Exception {
        Instrumentation instr = getInstrumentation();
        DealList dealList = getActivity();                       Get and start
                                                             ❷ Activity
        ParseFeedTask task = dealList.getParseFeedTask();
        assertNotNull("task should not be null", task);         ❸ Block until
                                                                   finished
        List<Section> taskResult = task.waitAndUpdate();
        assertNotNull("task did not return any sections", taskResult);

        instr.waitForIdleSync();                           ❹ Wait until UI thread idle

        String dealDetails = DealDetails.class.getCanonicalName();
        ActivityMonitor monitor =                              ❺ Define Activity
            instr.addMonitor(dealDetails, null, false);           monitor
```

```
View firstItem = dealList.getListView().getChildAt(0);
TouchUtils.clickView(this, firstItem);
assertTrue(instr.checkMonitorHit(monitor, 1));

        instr.removeMonitor(monitor);
    }
}
```

⑥ Click first deal item

⑦ Assert that DealDetails have launched

We've defined a single test here, `testDealListToDetailsUserFlow`, which implements our user story. We start by storing a reference to the `Instrumentation` instance powering our test case ❶ and the `DealList` `Activity` ❷. Note that `Activity-InstrumentationTestCase2`'s `getActivity` method will first check whether the `Activity` has already been started, and start it if not. Unlike an `Activity` unit test, this will call all lifecycle hooks and properly launch the `Activity`.

As mentioned before, one tricky aspect is that as soon as `DealList` starts, it'll fetch item data from the Web in a worker thread. You can stub out or proxy that task during test execution, but for a full end-to-end test, you may want to keep it. This means we have to block the instrumentation thread (the thread of the test runner) until that task has finished. That's exactly what `AsyncTask.get` is supposed to do, but in practice this method hasn't proven to be reliable, since it sometimes doesn't trigger `onPostExecute`. With several test cases testing different activities in different ways, UI processing can sometimes become flaky in instrumentation tests. That's why we've added the `waitAndUpdate` helper to the `ParseFeedTask`, which ensures that the post execution handler is called ❸:

```
public List<Section> waitAndUpdate() throws Exception {
    final List<Section> sections = this.get();
    Handler handler = new Handler(Looper.getMainLooper());
    handler.post(new Runnable() {
        public void run() {
            if (!getStatus().equals(Status.FINISHED)) {
                onPostExecute(sections);
            }
        }
    });
    return sections;
}
```

It's also time for `Instrumentation` to enter the stage: by calling `Instrumentation.waitForIdleSync` we make sure that the UI thread has settled (has stopped processing UI events) ❹. In particular, this ensures that the progress dialog has disappeared, the item list has been updated, and the `Activity` is now in an idle state in which you can interact with it. When writing an `ActivityInstrumentationTestCase2` you must always keep in mind that the application is tested in a natural environment, which means that often we must ensure that everything has settled down before advancing to the next step or assertion, just as we would as a normal user of the application.

At this point, we know that the `DealList` activity is showing a list of deals, so we can click one. Before performing the click using the `TouchUtils.clickView` helper ❻ we must first tell the `Instrumentation` which `Activity` we expect to be started after clicking that view. We do that by registering an `ActivityMonitor` **❺**. An `ActivityMonitor` is a synchronization primitive (a monitor, as the name suggests), which we can use to watch for an `Activity` being started. In our case, we don't expect a result from the `Activity` and we want it to be a nonblocking monitor, so we pass it the `null` and `false` arguments.

> **INSTRUMENTATION OBJECT MUTABILITY**   One thing you should always keep in mind is that the `Instrumentation` instance returned by `getInstrumentation` doesn't change across several test cases. It's started once and is then used throughout the entire test suite. This means that any modifications you do to it, such as adding monitors, will be visible to all tests in the same suite, not just the one in which you made the call. This can be a common source of error, for example, when you forgot to remove an `ActivityMonitor` after adding it. A good place to clean up any changes to `Instrumentation` is a test case's `tearDown` method, which is called after every test method.

With the monitor registered, we can now click a list item and wait for the system to settle (`TouchUtils.clickView` calls `waitForIdleSync`, so we don't have to do that manually here) **❻**. We can now finally check whether the `DealDetails` `Activity` hit the monitor—whether it was started **❼**. We expect it to be hit only once, hence we pass `1` here. Remember to always pair calls to `addMonitor` and `removeMonitor`. If you add a monitor and forget to remove it again, it'll stick around for an entire test suite run and can have unwanted side effects on other tests.

DISCUSSION

One thing to watch for when writing instrumentation tests is running all UI-related actions on the UI thread (we've explained that in earlier chapters in some detail), and *only* there. The problem with that is that the instrumentation test runs on its own thread, so we're not allowed to do anything that manipulates the user interface, not even something as simple as a button press. Wait, we just did that: we clicked a list item using `TouchUtils.clickView`, so surely it must work? The obvious answer is that this helper hides this technical detail from us. Without going through that helper method, we could've rewritten the list item click as:

```
instr.runOnMainSync(new Runnable() {
    public void run() {
        View firstItem = dealList.getListView().getChildAt(0);
        firstItem.performClick();
    }
});
```

`Instrumentation.runOnMainSync` will block until the UI thread is ready to process messages, and then invoke the given `Runnable` on it. That way, you can make sure that actions involving views are put where they belong: on the main application thread!

It's easy to see how powerful this way of testing is. You can pour all your user flows into test cases that use `ActivityInstrumentationTestCase2` and execute them all in sequence, simulating every possible path a user can take through your application and asserting that everything works as expected along the way. This becomes particularly powerful in combination with build automation, as we'll see in the next chapter.

One thing that may have struck you about the tests we've written so far is the gross inelegance of the syntax and functions being used. Think about it for a minute. If we hadn't talked about things such as activity monitors and `waitForIdleSync`, would you understand what this code is actually testing? We've dealt with a lot of boilerplate code here, such as explicitly waiting for the main application thread to become idle. Moreover, the assertion that the `DealDetails Activity` was started is spread over three lines of code (defining the monitor, waiting for idle sync, checking the monitor), and having to cope with synchronization primitives to do so is also not desirable. Being the esthetes we are, there's only one answer to this: We can do better than that!

TECHNIQUE 77 Beautiful tests with Robotium

Android excels in many areas, but its test framework API isn't one of them. There are two golden rules a good test framework must obey: it should make *writing* tests as easy as possible, and maybe more importantly, it should make *reading* tests as easy as possible. If tests are difficult to write, developers will refrain from doing so. If tests are difficult to read, a fellow developer may misunderstand the purpose of a test, or not understand it at all. Moreover, if you want to project user stories onto a test suite, you ideally want to have a syntax that's capable of closely matching the terms used to write these stories. That's not the case for what we've seen so far: your test's intention is often buried under a pile of ugly boilerplate code. It would be nice to have a testing API that was specifically designed to describe the steps a user can take through an Android application, such as press button, enter text, scroll list, or go back, and make assertions along the way.

When talking about syntax or instruction sets that are specific to a certain domain, such as Android testing and instrumentation, we're in the realm of *domain-specific languages (DSLs)*. DSLs come in various forms and sizes: they can be designed from scratch, like UML's Object Constraint Language (OCL), or built on top of existing languages, like Ruby's document builders. They can be short and cryptic, like regular expressions, or verbose and natural, like Cucumber (see http://cukes.info). You can even find DSLs in real life. Have you ever tried following a Texas Hold'em Poker tournament? The forced bet by the player next to the dealer is the *big blind*, and players can hold cards that are *off suite*. They can *play the river*, winning the game with *Aces up*. If you're not into Poker, you'll have no clue what these people are talking about. That's because it's domain-specific vocabulary.

DSLs are great for writing tests, because they allow you to describe what you expect to happen in a focused, natural way. The Cucumber language, for instance, is based on Ruby, and allows you to write test scenarios in something that comes close to spoken language:

```
Given I have entered 50 into the calculator
And I have entered 70 into the calculator
When I press add
Then the result should be 120 on the screen
```

Cucumber parses these instructions into test methods that can be executed like any other ordinary test case would be. Android testing isn't as advanced as that yet, but the Android community has sure been busy! In this technique, we'll see what Android testing DSLs are capable of these days.

PROBLEM

Your test cases must be understood even by nontechnical staff, or you want to arrive at test code that's generally easier to read and write, and better reflects the scenario-driven nature of your tests.

SOLUTION

One noteworthy project put forth by the Android development community in the still-manageable world of testing libraries is *Robotium*, a free and open-source third-party library released under the Apache License 2.0. It's deployed as an ordinary JAR file, so you can drop it into your test project and use it. (You can get it via its Google Code project site located at http://code.google.com/p/robotium.)

> **GRAB THE PROJECT: DEALDROIDROBOTIUMTEST**   You can get the source code for this project at the *Android in Practice* code website. Because some code listings here are shortened to focus on specific concepts, we recommend that you download the complete source code and follow along within Eclipse (or your favorite IDE or text editor).
>
> Source: http://mng.bz/5745

Robotium isn't so much a test framework on its own, as its project website suggests, but is more like an extension to the existing Android test framework. Think of Robotium as an add-on to Android's instrumentation framework that makes writing even complex test scenarios a breeze. There are no Robotium "framework" classes you'd have to extend in order to write a Robotium test—your test cases still inherit from `ActivityInstrumentationTestCase2`. Instead, you leverage the `Solo` class to steer the UI flow in a test case. Any action or step the user takes is thereby invoked on an instance of that class, using an imperative style similar to the actions we mentioned earlier (press button, go back, and so forth). This approach makes it unobtrusive, and you're free to mix calls to the Robotium `Solo` with calls to the standard Android framework classes.

> **ROBOTIUM TESTS ARE BLACK BOX TESTS**   Robotium was designed to write black box tests, much in the spirit of high-level test frameworks such as Cucumber. A *black box test* perceives the test subject as an opaque entity—assumes no knowledge of its inner structure or workings. It merely sticks in data into the test subject, and observes whether the output is what was expected. This is different from what we've seen so far, because we used implementation knowledge such as view IDs in tests.

Figure 13.10 depicts how Robotium fits into the threesome with the Android testing framework and your own test cases.

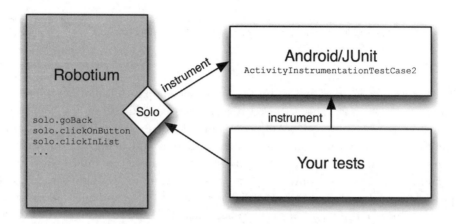

Figure 13.10 Robotium hooks into the Android testing framework by wrapping and extending existing functionality. It's then used in your own test cases by going through the `Solo` class, the central entry point into Robotium's test helpers.

Let's rewrite the test case from the previous technique using Robotium. Since Robotium exposes such a nice concise syntax, we can also make the flow more complicated this time: instead of testing the transition from the list view to the `DealDetails`, we test selecting different deal lists from the spinner box, too. Here's `Solo` in action.

Listing 13.4 Robotium uses a DSL to write functional tests as stories

```
public class DealListRobotiumTest extends
        ActivityInstrumentationTestCase2<DealList> {

    private Solo solo;

    public DealListRobotiumTest() {
        super("com.manning.aip.dealdroid", DealList.class);
    }

    @Override
    protected void setUp() throws Exception {
        super.setUp();
        solo = new Solo(getInstrumentation(), getActivity());
    }

    public void testDealListToDetailsWithListChangeUserFlow()
            throws Exception {
        DealList dealList = getActivity();
        dealList.getParseFeedTask().waitAndUpdate();

        solo.clickInList(0);
        solo.assertCurrentActivity("expected DealDetails",
            DealDetails.class);
        solo.goBack();
        solo.assertCurrentActivity("expected DealList",
            DealList.class);
        solo.pressSpinnerItem(0, 2);
        solo.scrollDown();
```

① Solo instruments an Activity

② Every command is a method on solo

```
    solo.clickInList(dealList.getItems().size() - 1);
    solo.assertCurrentActivity("expected DealDetails",
        DealDetails.class);
    }
}
```

❷ Every command is a method on solo

The first thing you do when writing a test case juiced up with Robotium is define a reference to the `Solo` ❶. This is the key object behind any Robotium test, and you use it to instrument activities by invoking command-like methods on it ❷. The commands almost need no explanation, having natural names and being free of unnecessary argument bloat: `clickInList` clicks a list item at the given index (Robotium, by default, assumes there's only one `ListView` at a time on a single screen), `goBack` presses the back button to return to the previous `Activity`, and `scrollDown` scrolls to the list's bottom. If you add words like when, and, then, and so forth, then you arrive at something that comes close to a full English sentence. On top of that, all the nasty code noise is gone: no manual `waitForIdleSync`, no `Activity` monitors, none of that super-technical hoopla distracting readers from the actual test.

DISCUSSION

Robotium came as a godsend for those who embrace clear and natural test code. The test case syntax is much nicer to read and work with, though truth be told, it's traded for a slight loss in test speediness (well, as speedy as an instrumentation test can get), due to the higher abstractions and the frequent `waits` and `sleeps` performed by the Robotium `Solo`.

Because you write black box tests using Robotium, you can't do things such as selecting views by ID. Instead, you need to write tests using only the data you can derive from what's visible on the screen, which is view text (button labels), or tree indices when using hierarchyviewer. This means you can even use Robotium to test applications that you haven't developed yourself, though it feels awkward when using it for your own projects.

There are already plans to make Robotium more powerful. One ongoing effort is to make Robotium more extensible so it's easier to build extra functionality on top of it, such as the use of existing testing languages like Cucumber. Another interesting plan is to deliver an extension to Robotium called *Remote Control (RC)*. Using the RC, a server would sit on the emulator or device, while the test code runs entirely on the client (the developer's machine) and sends commands to the server to tell it what to do. This would result in faster and more flexible test execution.

There's some traction in the world of testing libraries for Android at the moment. Another Android testing library that takes the same line as Robotium is Calculon. Unlike Robotium, Calculon doesn't go through a proxy object to instrument an `Activity`, but extends the existing framework classes with new assertions that form a DSL. In Calculon, you write sentences that start with `assertThat`, and build your test from there:

```
assertThat(R.id.button1).click().starts(MyActivity.class);
assertThat(R.id.button2).click().implies(R.id.some_view).gone();
```

Even moreso than Robotium, Calculon focuses on clear and concise expression of assertions and actions in a test case. But it's in an early stage of development and has yet to prove itself in a production environment. Calculon is also open source under the terms of the Apache License 2.0, and can be found online here: https://github.com/kaeppler/calculon.

13.3 *Beyond instrumentation: mocks and monkeys*

In the first two parts of this chapter, we showed you what makes Android tests roll, from setting up a test project to writing both simple and more complex test cases. We're not quite done yet. This last section will deal with the advanced themes of testing on Android, going beyond your typical instrumentation tests. We'll start with covering mock objects and explain why and how you should use them in tests. We'll then leave the world of Android JUnit tests and explore some alternate techniques of testing your applications that fundamentally differ from what we've seen so far, but that can be used complementary to your ordinary Android test cases.

TECHNIQUE 78   **Mock objects and how to use them**

There's a golden rule when writing tests: never let the outcome of a test depend on something that's not directly related to the entity under test, or worse, that's beyond your control. We saw this rule in practice when we wrote a unit test for the `DealDetails` activity in technique 68, where the entire test environment in which the `Activity` was executed acted as a barrier. The test couldn't possibly have failed due to the web browser crashing when we tested the "view in browser" functionality, since no actual web browser process was running! We merely tested an if-then scenario: *if* that menu item was pressed on a real device, *then* the browser would be started. That means we tested this piece of functionality without having to actually rely on the browser application, which is beyond our control. This is desirable, since we don't actually care whether the browser works; we only care that *if* the browser works, then our application should work, too.

We didn't do that in the instrumentation tests we wrote in techniques 69 and 70. Even though the entity under test was the `DealList Activity`, all sorts of entities were involved, including the `DealDetails Activity` and even a web service. There are two problems with this. First, for these kinds of instrumentation tests where everything is executed in much the same way as if an ordinary user was using the application, things can slow down. The average time for `DealListTest` test to run on an emulator on my computer was about six seconds, where most of the time was lost in the web service call. You can imagine that once your application grows large and you add more tests, the total time it takes for your test suite to run can grow significant. This is a hindrance when exercising TDD, since in that case you rely more on short feedback loops to see how a change to the source code affects the application as a whole.

Second, and much worse, it's unreliable. What if the eBay web service is down? Should our test fail? Probably not; after all we're testing *our* application, not the eBay web service, which isn't under our control. You could argue: but it was an integration test, a story test that should simulate what a user does in the application. Yes, but we could've achieved the same result by replacing the call to the web service with a static result (a list of Item objects), and testing the code that establishes the web service connection and parses Item elements in separate unit tests. That way, we keep everything well tested, but we've isolated our tests: if the unit test for the web service parser passes, and an integration test just uses its API, then we know that if we plug these things together they'll work.

This gives rise to the question: how can we remove dependencies in tests to components that aren't within our reach of control or that should be tested elsewhere? This is where *mock objects* and *stubs* come into play.

PROBLEM

You want to replace a piece of functionality in a test with a dummy, since its behavior would otherwise impact the test and potentially break it, even when the actual entity under test works correctly.

SOLUTION

Mocks and stubs act as placeholders in your tests. They expose the same API as the object they're replacing. From the test's point of view, they're identical, but their implementation has been replaced so as to not interfere with the test. Often this means returning a static result from a method, such as a test fixture bundled with the test project.

> **MANAGING TEST FIXTURES** Test fixtures often go hand in hand with mock objects, since test fixtures replace live data with some static, predefined data only meant to be used in a test. Consider the web service call in the DealDroid for instance: instead of doing that call and retrieving an XML document via HTTP, we could bundle a static XML file with our test project and use that for testing the DealList. Those files could live in your test project's res/raw folder and be loaded in a test's setUp method.

This is similar to using crash test dummies: they closely resemble human bodies (they have, for example, the same shape, size, and weight), but they're just replacements. The difference between a mock object and a stub or fake object is that whereas stubs replace method implementations to return some static or manually crafted result, mock objects also verify that method invocations have happened. This is extremely useful if you're testing object interactions where you don't actually care about the result of an invocation, but you want to make sure that it has definitely happened. An example would be the verification of a credit card-holder's name in an online payment process: you don't care if the name is John Doe or Joe Blow, but you definitely care that the name is considered when verifying the payment. For simplicity, we hereafter only refer to *mock objects*, regardless if they're true mocks or just fake objects.

To make the application of mock objects more interesting, here's a new scenario: in the DealDroid, we'd like to add a simple deal export function. This would be a simple menu item that allows us to write all items from the current deal list to a file on the device by calling an item's toString method (see figure 13.11).

Figure 13.11   A new export function has been added. By selecting it from the menu, the list of deals will be exported to a text file.

GRAB THE PROJECT: DEALDROIDWITHEXPORT   You can get the source code for this project, and/or the packaged APK to run it, at the *Android in Practice* code website. Because some code listings here are shortened to focus on specific concepts, we recommend that you download the complete source code and follow along within Eclipse (or your favorite IDE or text editor).

Source: http://mng.bz/27qZ, APK: mng.bz/1LX1

Here's how the code for the exporter helper class might look.

Listing 13.5   The new exporter exports a list of deal items to a text file

```
public class DealExporter {

    private Context context;

    private List<Item> deals;

    public DealExporter(Context context, List<Item> deals) {
        this.context = context;
        this.deals = deals;
    }

    public void export() throws IOException {
        FileOutputStream fos =
            context.openFileOutput("deals.txt", Context.MODE_PRIVATE);
        for (Item item : deals) {
            fos.write(item.toString().getBytes());
```

```
        }
        fos.close();
    }
}
```

This looks straightforward: we're writing to a text file opened using the openFileOut-put helper method, which will create a new file called deals.txt in the application's data/files folder on the device. We've also made this functionality available in the DealList by adding it to the options menu (look at the full source code for Deal-List.java for this chapter if you're interested).

Now, how would we write a unit test for the DealExporter? We're not testing an Activity, Service, or Application. We're testing a POJO, but it depends on a Context. No suitable Android test case class provides a fully set up context that we could use to call openFileOutput. Even if we had, we don't want or need to test whether Android's file I/O works; if we did that, then we'd be testing the Android platform, not our class. Long story short, we want to mock out the Context this class depends on. This involves two steps. First, defining a mock context class that implements a stubbed version of the openFileOutput method. Second, since DealExporter expects a valid FileOutputStream returned from that method, we implement a MockOutput-Stream, which doesn't write to a file, but records invocations of its write method and redirects any bytes written to standard out. Here's the DealExporterTest, including the mock objects just mentioned.

Listing 13.6   Use mock objects to decouple objects under test

```
public class DealExporterTest extends TestCase {
    private List<Item> deals = new ArrayList<Item>();
    private int itemsWritten = 0;

    private class MockOutputStream extends FileOutputStream {
        public MockOutputStream() throws FileNotFoundException {    ❶ File output
            super(FileDescriptor.out);                                  mock class
        }

        @Override
        public void write(byte[] buffer) throws IOException {      ❷ Count all
            Item currentItem = deals.get(itemsWritten++);             invocations
            assertEquals(currentItem.toString(), new String(buffer));    ◁─┐
        }                                                         Assert correct
    }                                                             file output ❸

    private class MyMockContext extends MockContext {
        @Override
        public FileOutputStream openFileOutput(String name, int mode)
            throws FileNotFoundException {
            return new MockOutputStream();                     ◁─┐ Use Context
        }                                                     ❹ mock class
    }

    @Override
    protected void setUp() throws Exception {
        super.setUp();

        Item item1 = new Item();
```

```
        item1.setTitle("test item 1");
        deals.add(item1);

        Item item2 = new Item();
        item2.setTitle("test item 2");
        deals.add(item2);                              Use Context mock  ❺
    }                                                  when exporting
    public void testShouldExportItems() throws IOException {
        new DealExporter(new MyMockContext(), deals).export();
        assertEquals(2, itemsWritten);                          Assert correct number
    }                                                    ❻      of invocations
}
```

First, we need to define a mock that'll mimic the file output. We do that by inheriting from `FileOutputStream` and configuring it to write to STDOUT (by passing the `File-Descriptor.out` object to its constructor; note that it doesn't matter what you pass here, as long as it's a valid file descriptor, since we're going to override `write` in the next step) ❶. We also override its `write` method to not write to a file, but to keep a record of the number of invocations in the `itemsWritten` field ❷, and to make sure that the data passed to this method is what we expect: a `String`-ified deal item ❸.

The next step is to use this mocked-out `FileOutputStream`. Since the `DealExporter` writes to an output stream returned by the `Context`'s `openOutputStream`, we must stub out that method to return our `MockOutputStream`. Android already provides base classes to create mock objects for `Contexts` (called `MockContext`), but all its methods throw an `UnsupportedOperationException`, so you need to implement those you want to use to do something meaningful. We do that by implementing `openFileOutput` to return a new instance of `MockOutputStream` ❹.

We haven't yet looked at the actual test we want to run. `testShouldExportItems` only needs to do two things: invoke the exporter using our `MyMockContext` ❺, and assert that the correct number of invocations have occurred ❻. That's all we require to make sure our exporter works!

DISCUSSION

In this test case we implemented a custom `MockContext` by inheriting from that class directly. This is what you want to do if you need customized behavior specific to your test. Sometimes you don't have to go that far. Often it's desirable to have a fully working `Context` that behaves differently in a test environment. Android defines a few of those specialized `Context` implementations, but they're easy to miss, since unlike `MockContext` and its brethren `MockApplication`, `MockService`, and so forth, they don't live in the `android.test.mock` package, but in the `android.test` parent package. The most notable one is `RenamingDelegatingContext`, a context wrapper you can use in instrumentation tests to redirect database or `SharedPreference` output of the wrapped `Context` to dedicated test files. This is required for making sure that a test doesn't overwrite preferences or database entries written by the actual application.

When dealing with mock objects, a general problem that arises is that of *injection*. If we want to replace an object with its dummy counterpart just for a test, then we need some way to do so. There are three basic ways to achieve that:

1 Manually using setter methods and constructors
2 Automatically using setter methods and constructors
3 Using runtime bytecode manipulation and generation

In 1 and 2, we provide setter methods or constructors that allow us to replace the object we're trying to mock out with an alternative implementation. That's what we've done manually in this technique: we've configured the `DealExporter` with a mocked-out `Context` via its constructor. This can get tedious, and there are ways to do that automatically. A common approach is to use object lifecycle frameworks capable of *dependency injection*, such as the Spring framework or Google Guice. These frameworks let you declare dependencies on other classes or interfaces, and instead of having to resolve these dependencies yourself by calling setter functions, they wire all managed objects together automatically at runtime. This is an architectural pattern often called *inversion of control (IoC)*, since objects don't handle dependencies themselves—they declare dependencies and the container then takes care of connecting them.

Against the backdrop of testing and mocking, this means you can express things like the following: if in testing mode, please use this mock implementation; otherwise, use the actual implementation. You don't need to invoke any setter manually: once your object has been initialized, the IoC container guarantees that it has all its dependencies set, mock or not! For instance, Google Guice has been adapted to Android as part of the RoboGuice project (http://code.google.com/p/roboguice/), but keep in mind that those frameworks, though comfortable to use, can leave a rather large footprint on your application, increasing startup time and memory use in general. The third and last option to inject mock objects is by leveraging runtime bytecode manipulation and generation. This is the way most established mock object libraries in the standard Java world, such as Mockito, EasyMock, or PowerMock, go. These libraries can create mock implementations of classes and interfaces at runtime, and even modify existing methods to return or do anything you want. The secret weapon here is *cglib*, a Java code generation library. Although EasyMock has at least to some degree been ported to Android as part of the *android-mock* project (http://code.google.com/p/android-mock), libraries depending on cglib don't work on Dalvik, since the code generated by cglib isn't compatible with the Dalvik virtual machine. Moreover, some of them rely on the `java.beans` package, which isn't part of the Android framework libraries.

One solution would be to write tests not as Android instrumentation tests, but as standard JUnit tests running on a JVM, and mock out all involved framework classes using one of these mock libraries. To give you an idea what this could look like, we could've implemented the mock objects from listing 13.6 using Mockito like this:

```
FileOutputStream mockOutput = mock(FileOutputStream.class);
verify(mockOutput.write((byte[]) anyObject()).times(2);
Context mockContext = mock(Context.class);
when(mockContext.openFileOutputStream(anyString(),
    anyInt())).thenReturn(mockOutput);
```

Mockito exposes a DSL for creating mock objects and assertions on them, which makes it easy to write and read tests that involve mocks. A key problem with this approach is that usually so many Android framework classes are involved that you'll find yourself almost reimplementing Android using custom mock objects. The fine people at XtremeLabs and Pivotal realized this problem early on, and came up with an entirely different answer to this: Robolectric to the rescue!

TECHNIQUE 79   ## Accelerating unit tests with Robolectric

We've seen many approaches to writing tests so far: plain JUnit tests with or without using mock object libraries, Android unit tests, Android functional tests, and tests using Android's rather limited form of mock objects. Plain JUnit tests running on a JVM have the advantage that they're quick to execute, but they require you to mock out large parts of the Android framework library, whereas instrumentation tests can leverage the platform objects, but are slow to execute and have poor support for mock objects.

If speed is what matters to you, there's a whole new way to write tests: the *Robolectric* unit test framework (http://pivotal.github.com/robolectric/). Robolectric's premise is to "de-fang the Android SDK jar" so that you can unit test your application on a standard JVM without the need to explicitly mock out every framework class used somewhere down the call tree that would otherwise crash your test case with a `RuntimeException("Stub!")`. The key idea behind Robolectric is that it automatically mocks out the Android framework classes *itself*, instead of having the developer manually do that. Robolectric can therefore be thought of as one giant Android platform mock!

PROBLEM

You want tests that execute quickly, perhaps because you're exercising TDD, but running tests on a plain JVM would require you to mock out large parts of the Android framework.

SOLUTION

Under the hood, Robolectric provides what's called a *shadow class* for some Android framework class. A shadow class looks and behaves like its Android counterpart, but is implemented purely using standard Java code designed to run on a standard JVM. For example, in any Robolectric test, an Android `Activity` instance is automatically replaced by a `ShadowActivity`, a class that implements the same methods as an ordinary `Activity` does, but is actually a big mock object. For instance, it'll support the `findViewById` method. It'll even support view inflation and return a `View` instance that has a `show` method. But Robolectric doesn't run any graphics routines to render a layout or view. It just *pretends* to. This means it's quick, while allowing you to make test assertions against views and layouts as you would in an ordinary Android test case. Similar to visibility and position of a view, checking for view state is supported as testing for behavior, such as starting new activities when clicking a view.

Any class can become a shadow of a framework class; it doesn't need to provide the full set of interface methods. All methods not implemented by the shadow class will be rewritten by Robolectric to do nothing or return `null`. This approach is called *partial stubbing* or *partial mocking*.

One cool aspect about all this is that most of the time you don't have to worry about shadow classes at all. Instead, Robolectric hooks into the class-loading procedure and

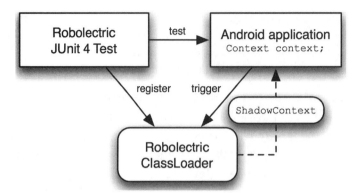

Figure 13.12   The Robolectric test runner registers a custom class loader that will intercept any requests for classes made by the application under test (requests for the `Context` class, for instance). Instead of a `Context` instance, it'll return a shadow implementation.

whenever it sees a stock Android class being requested, it silently replaces it with its shadow. Figure 13.12 depicts this.

As outlined in figure 13.12, Robolectric tests are essentially JUnit 4 tests (JUnit 3 is *not* supported) executed using the `RobolectricTestRunner`. You don't need to do any additional setup; your tests are still ordinary JUnit 4 tests, with Robolectric pulling the strings in the background.

GRAB THE PROJECT: DEALDROIDROBOLECTRICTEST   You can get the source code for this project at the *Android in Practice* code website. Because some code listings here are shortened to focus on specific concepts, we recommend that you download the complete source code and follow along within Eclipse (or your favorite IDE or text editor).

Source: http://mng.bz/zP3n

Note that this project doesn't carry the Android Eclipse project nature; it's an ordinary Java project instead.

Robolectric test projects, unfortunately, require a bit of work to set up properly. Detailed instructions on how to do that are on the Robolectric project website (http://pivotal.github.com/robolectric), but we've collected some general remarks and hints in the sidebar "Setting up Robolectric test projects."

Setting up Robolectric test projects

Unlike Android instrumentation tests, Robolectric tests run on your ordinary workstation JVM. The best strategy is to create an ordinary Java project for your Robolectric tests rather than an Android test project. Assuming you use Eclipse, this means the project will be lacking the Android project nature, so you'll have to add the dependency to the Android JAR files yourself. In Eclipse, one way to do so is through *User Libraries:*

Right click project > Build Path > Add Libraries... > User Library > User Libraries... > New > [enter a name] > Add JARs... > select both android.jar and maps.jar from your SDK home directory.

You'll also have to add the robolectric-all.jar as well as JUnit 4 to the project's build path:

(continued)

JUnit 4: Right click project > Build Path > Add Libraries... > JUnit > JUnit 4.

Robolectric: copy robolectric-all.jar to a folder in your test project, and right-click > Build Path > Add to Build Path.

As an exercise, we're now going to rewrite the `DealDetailsTest` from listing 13.2 using Robolectric and JUnit 4. At this point it probably makes sense for you to dig up that listing again and compare it directly against the Robolectric test. This will help in understanding where the differences are.

Listing 13.7 Robolectric tests can run outside a device or the emulator

```
@RunWith(RobolectricTestRunner.class)                  ◁━┐  Use
public class DealDetailsRobolectricTest {                 ❶ RobolectricTestRunner

    private DealDetails activity;

    private Item testItem;

    @Before
    public void setUp() {
        testItem = new Item();
        testItem.setItemId(1);
        testItem.setTitle("Test Item");
        testItem.setConvertedCurrentPrice("1");
        testItem.setLocation("USA");
        testItem.setDealUrl("http://example.com");

        activity = new DealDetails();                    ❷ Inject
        DealDroidApp application =                          Application object
            (DealDroidApp) activity.getApplication();       automatically
        application.setCurrentItem(testItem);

        activity.onCreate(null);                         ◁━┐ Call Lifecycle
    }                                                      ❸ methods manually

    @Test
    public void testPreConditions() {
        assertNotNull(activity.findViewById(R.id.details_price));
        assertNotNull(activity.findViewById(R.id.details_title));
        assertNotNull(activity.findViewById(R.id.details_location));
    }

    @Test
    public void testThatAllFieldsAreSetCorrectly() {
        assertEquals("$" + testItem.getConvertedCurrentPrice(),
            getViewText(R.id.details_price));
        assertEquals(testItem.getTitle(),
            getViewText(R.id.details_title));
        assertEquals(testItem.getLocation(),
            getViewText(R.id.details_location));
    }

    @Test
```

```
public void testThatItemCanBeDisplayedInBrowser() {
    activity.onOptionsItemSelected(new TestMenuItem() {
        public int getItemId() {
            return DealDetails.MENU_BROWSE;
        }
    });

    ShadowActivity shadowActivity =
        Robolectric.shadowOf(activity);
    Intent startedIntent =
        shadowActivity.getNextStartedActivity();

    assertEquals(Intent.ACTION_VIEW, startedIntent.getAction());
    assertEquals(testItem.getDealUrl(),
        startedIntent.getData().toString());
}

private String getViewText(int textViewId) {
    return ((TextView) activity.findViewById(textViewId)).getText()
        .toString();
}
}
```

4 Create menu item stub

5 Get triggered Intent from shadow

As you can see, the listing isn't dramatically different from the DealDetailsTest we've seen before, even though this time we're not using Android's testing framework *at all*. The differences on the test code level are mostly in the details. The most striking difference is that we're now dealing with a JUnit 4 test, whereas Android tests are always run using the much older JUnit 3. JUnit 4 makes heavy use of Java annotations in order to decrease the intrusiveness of the test library. In that spirit, Robolectric doesn't force us to subclass anything; instead, it provides a JUnit 4 test runner called RobolectricTestRunner via JUnit 4's @RunWith annotation **1**. Test methods don't need to start in test*, but are marked as such using the @Test annotation.

Our test setup code is still in setUp, although in JUnit 4 that method is allowed to have any name, as long as it carries the @Before annotation. You may notice that we create our DealDetails instance manually instead of having a getActivity method do that for us. On the other hand, we can call getApplication on our Activity under test, since that call will be intercepted by Robolectric to automatically create a DealDroidApp instance and invoke its onCreate method for us **2**. If you wonder how Robolectric can be clever enough to find out what our application class is: it analyzes the application manifest to find the class name. It's *that* clever!

One thing you always have to do in Robolectric tests is invoke component lifecycle methods explicitly. On a device, Android would do that for you, but Robolectric doesn't handle Android's component lifecycle management. What's called is what *you* call; hence the explicit call to activity.onCreate using a null bundle **3**.

The actual test methods remain almost unmodified, except testThatItemCan-BeDisplayedInBrowser, which nicely shows some of the main differences when testing with Robolectric. Let's reiterate what this method tests: it makes sure that when the menu item corresponding to the MENU_BROWSER menu ID is pressed, an Intent is fired that will launch the Android browser using the deal's details page on eBay.

Remember that we're not running on a device, so we can't actually bring up the options menu and press a button. What we *can* do is invoke the function that Android *would* call if the user brought up the menu. This is a safe assumption to make, as long as Android itself doesn't change significantly with respect to the way it sets up and handles an application's option menu.

That being said, we simulate a menu button press by invoking the `onOptionsItem-Selected` callback directly and pass a Robolectric `TestMenuItem` to it that identifies itself as being the Show in Browser button ❹. This is a typical pattern for Robolectric tests: we know this method will be called by Android at runtime, so we invoke it ourselves and pass to it whatever we desire, making this a quick operation.

But how do we now test that this would result in the browser being started? An ordinary Android `Activity` gives us no means of seeing which other activities were started from it. But its shadow does! Robolectric records all `Intents` fired from an `Activity` under test on its corresponding shadow. That means we can get a reference to the shadow of the `Activity` under test and check whether the `Intent` we're looking for is there. This is as simple as obtaining a reference to the shadow via `Robolectric.shadowOf` and calling `getNextStartedActivity` on the shadow ❺. We can then do an ordinary assert on the `Intent`. Note that this `Intent` has a shadow, too, which can also be retrieved via the `shadowOf` helper.

DISCUSSION

There are some strong arguments for using Robolectric. First and foremost, it's *fast*. Second, Robolectric doesn't require a device or the emulator to execute tests, since it doesn't rely on the native Android runtime. This means you won't need to manage emulators and device images (which can be difficult on headless build servers), and you get feedback from tests much more quickly. Moreover, since Robolectric can in its own way be understood as one big mock framework for Android, you often don't need other mock object libraries such as Mockito (although, you're free to use them if you like). Since Robolectric builds on JUnit 4 and standard Java, you can use whatever extra libraries you desire, without being bound by Dalvik's restrictions.

Unfortunately, there are also downsides. The building blocks of Robolectric are the shadow classes that mimic their Android counterparts; they're also Robolectric's biggest problem. First of all, at the time of this writing, there are only 75 of them. This may sound like a lot at first, but that doesn't even remotely cover the hundreds of Android framework classes that could potentially be involved in a test (directly or indirectly). That wouldn't be much of a problem if there were an easy and unobtrusive way to provide your own, but even though the Robolectric authors claim the process of adding custom shadows is easy, it's not. Instead of providing a framework API to register custom shadow classes, you need to change the library's source code to do so. The Robolectric authors therefore encourage users to check out the Robolectric source code into a subfolder of the application under test (or the corresponding test project) and change things as desired.

One thing that struck us when working with Robolectric is its requirement for the application instance to be created. This seems odd, since Robolectric never calls component lifecycle methods for you, except on the `Application` instance: Robolectric will always create an instance for you and call its `onCreate` method. This sometimes requires you to mock out things in the application class even though you aren't using them, for example when unit testing a `Service`.

Another thing to realize is that it's generally not safe to assume that a passing test means your application is working correctly. Since tests aren't executed against the Android runtime, but something that mimics it, you can never be 100% percent sure that your application will behave the same when running on an actual phone. If, for instance, Google decides to change the way `findViewById` works, then Robolectric has to follow up with its implementation of that method; otherwise, you'll end up testing against an implementation that doesn't correctly reflect how Android works. On the other hand, simple tests such as testing that views exist or are visible are relatively safe to assert via Robolectric, since its view support is exhaustive already. Those things are unlikely to change in Android, so in many cases this may sound worse than it really is.

In conclusion, you should decide for yourself whether Robolectric's benefits outweigh its disadvantages. It's an interesting alternative to Android unit testing, but may not fit everyone's need.

We've covered a lot of ground, but one thing that all approaches we've discussed so far have in common is their focus on functionality. Every test we've written so far was essentially asserting that the unit under test behaves correctly with respect to some sort of specification. As mentioned in the chapter opening, those aren't the only kinds of tests you can run; you can also test for nonfunctional properties such as speed or stability. In the last technique of this chapter, we're going to show you how you can do that with the help from a monkey. A *monkey*? If that's not the best reason to continue reading, we don't know what is.

TECHNIQUE 80   **Stressing out with the Monkey**

Isolated testing of your application's components and story-based end-to-end testing of the application as a whole are necessary to ensure an application is behaving correctly. But it doesn't end here. A bug-free application can still be slow. Also, applications may seem to work fine under normal conditions, but quickly become unresponsive or leak memory when put under load. In order to unearth these forms of nonfunctional defects, functional tests as seen so far in this chapter aren't appropriate.

Things like speed or stability are difficult to test under normal conditions—conditions typical for the users of the application, such as using only a subset of the features, typing and clicking at normal speed, and so forth. Often an application's nonfunctional defects only creep up when it's being put under pressure, so we need a convenient way of doing that. One solution would be to install your application on a phone and give it some stress by wildly pressing buttons for a while to see if you can crash it. That's not the level of convenience we had in mind though. There's a better solution: meet the Monkey.

PROBLEM

You want to stress test your application by sending a series of random input events to it, collecting information about crashes or out-of-memory situations along the way.

SOLUTION

As odd as it may sound, one of the best ways to test an application's stability and reliability is to use it in ways you typically wouldn't. Applications are always designed and developed with special paths in mind for the user to take through the application. That makes sense: you start with some form of feature description, which typically involves the user role and the interface elements being used, and then you design and implement the application according to that description. But what if the user decides to take a different path, a path that was never part of your design? Ah, surely no one would ever click that menu button when on this screen. Surely no one would ever turn the screen while the application is loading something. Or would they?

We wouldn't go as far as to compare the average user of your applications to a monkey, but you can be sure they'll use it in ways you wouldn't expect. If your application becomes even slightly unresponsive, we can almost guarantee that users will start wildly tapping at the display to get *any* sort of response from it. What they don't know is that they're making things worse, since more input events are queued up on a system that's already under heavy load. Android's *Monkey* tool allows you to simulate this kind of situation. The Monkey tool is an application and UI exerciser running on an Android device, and is capable of sending a series of pseudorandom input events to stress test your application. Since it runs directly on the device or emulator, you must invoke it remotely via adb:

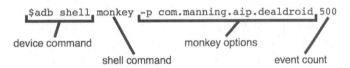

The adb shell command routes whatever you pass to it to the device's command shell (see appendix A). In this case, we're invoking the Monkey tool on the device. The Monkey tool expects two argument sets: a list of options, and the number of events it should generate (in this case 500). One option you always want to pass is the name of the application package you're targeting, which is achieved with the -p option. Before getting into more detail, let's run this command and see what happens (see figure 13.13).

It's best if you run the example yourself to get a feel for how the Monkey works, but here's what we saw: the three screen dumps in figure 13.13 were taken at random points in time while the Monkey was exercising the application, and they're in chronological order from left to right. The stress test always starts with invoking the launcher Activity–in our case, the DealList. The DealList displays a modal dialog, so any interactions with the application will have no effect until the deals have loaded, but technically the Monkey is still busy sending events. After the list of deals had been loaded, the Monkey decided to first change the screen orientation and then press the

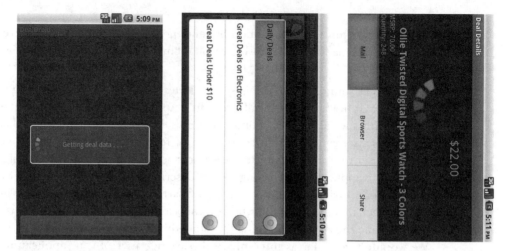

Figure 13.13   Three snapshots taken randomly while the Monkey was exercising the DealDroid application. The Monkey tool will make its way through the application in a pseudorandom manner, pressing keys and pushing buttons with no particular goal or plan in mind.

spinner box and select the first entry. After the list had changed, it selected a deal item, so the `DealDetails` were started. On that screen, the Monkey spent a few seconds in the options menu, selecting different entries.

> **PACKAGE CONFINEMENT**   Regardless of how long you run the Monkey, you'll notice that it will never leave the DealDroid application. Why is that? After all, we have a Show in Browser menu item that will bring up the website for an item, but even if the Monkey clicks that, nothing happens. That's because the `-p` option confines the Monkey to the given package; any event that would cause an `Activity` outside that package to be started will be dropped. This is great for testing your application in isolation. If you do want to include other activities and applications reachable from yours, then you must specify each such application package with an additional `-p` option. In order to allow the Monkey to open the browser, you'd have to run it as `monkey -p com.manning.aip.deal-` `droid -p com.android.browser`, but this means that it could just as well start the browser first and spend a while testing it before getting to the DealDroid.

The good news is that our application was never unresponsive, nor did it crash—the stress test succeeded. Looks like we did a good job at implementing it! Here's the shell output:

```
matthias:[~]$ adb shell monkey -p com.manning.aip.dealdroid 500
Events injected: 500
## Network stats: elapsed time=22791ms (22791ms mobile, 0ms wifi, 0ms not
    connected)
```

We fired 500 events, the whole run took round about 23 seconds, and we supposedly spent the same amount of time using a mobile data connection (that value is meaningless on the emulator, but can be useful when running on a device). It's good that

our application works so well, but for the fun of it, let's break something and throw a
RuntimeException in DealList.onCreate:

```
matthias:[~]$ adb shell monkey -p com.manning.aip.dealdroid 500
// CRASH: com.manning.aip.dealdroid (pid 1638)
// Short Msg: java.lang.RuntimeException
// Long Msg: java.lang.RuntimeException: Boom!
// Build Label: generic/google_sdk/generic/:2.2/FRF91/43546:eng/test-keys
// Build Changelist: 43546
// Build Time: 1277937122000
// java.lang.RuntimeException: Unable to start activity
    ComponentInfo{com.manning.aip.dealdroid/
    com.manning.aip.dealdroid.DealList}: java.lang.RuntimeException: Boom!
// at android.app.ActivityThread.performLaunchActivity(ActivityThread.java:2663)
//   [lengthy stack trace here]
// ... 11 more
//
** Monkey aborted due to error.
Events injected: 12
## Network stats: elapsed time=1893ms (1893ms mobile, 0ms wifi, 0ms not
    connected)
** System appears to have crashed at event 12 of 500 using seed 0
```

Once again we asked the Monkey to fire 500 events, but on event 12 it encountered a
crash: that's the exception we snuck in. We get all the usual information such as
exception class and message, as well as a stack trace (we've shortened the stack trace
here for better readability).

> **THE MONKEY EXIT CODE** If you intend to run the Monkey as part of an auto-
> mated build (see chapter 14), be careful not to rely on its exit code to deter-
> mine success or failure of the test. Typically, UNIX-compliant command-line
> tools indicate success by returning 0, and failure by returning a nonzero num-
> ber, usually -1. The Monkey always returns 0, thus indicating success even if it
> aborted due to an error in the application. This issue is known and filed as
> ticket 13562 on the official Android issue tracker.

This diagnostic output tells us that the application failed with a crash, but we don't
know which event triggered it. "Event 12" is hardly useful information; it could've
been anything. In order to get more detailed information about the events fired, you
can invoke the Monkey with the –v (verbose logging) option. This will log every event
that's fired, and also include a summary detailing the distribution of event kinds that
were used:

```
matthias:[~]$ adb shell monkey -p com.manning.aip.dealdroid -v 500
:Monkey: seed=0 count=500
:AllowPackage: com.manning.aip.dealdroid
:IncludeCategory: android.intent.category.LAUNCHER
:IncludeCategory: android.intent.category.MONKEY
// Event percentages:
//   0: 15.0%
//   1: 10.0%
//   2: 15.0%
```

```
//    3: 25.0%
//    4: 15.0%
//    5: 2.0%
//    6: 2.0%
//    7: 1.0%
//    8: 15.0%
...
```

Apparently the events fired by the Monkey aren't as random as we initially suggested. That's true: they're pseudorandom, and they can be steered to happen more often or not, depending on the type of event. *Pseudorandom* in this case means that the Monkey will use a seed in order to randomize the sequence of the events fired. You can provide this seed manually via the –s option. An equal seed means the Monkey will fire the exact same sequence of events. This means that when a test fails, you can reproduce it by rerunning the Monkey with the same seed.

> **REPRODUCIBLE TEST RUNS** In order to keep your test runs reproducible if they fail with an error, you should always use a manual seed. A good seed is the current UNIX timestamp in milliseconds, which can be obtained from the GNU date tool:

```
$adb shell monkey -p <package> -s `date +%s` -v 500
```

The back-ticks will execute the date tool and merge its output into the command. Don't forget to run with the –v flag, so that the seed used to run this session is printed to the logs:

```
:Monkey: seed=1293818128 count=500
```

This will make your life a lot easier when running the Monkey as part of an automated build, something we'll explore in chapter 14.

The Monkey can fire nine different types of events, and you can control how often they fire relative to each other. Table 13.1 summarizes the different kinds of events, their effect, and the corresponding command-line option (percentages are passed as values between 0 and 100).

Table 13.1 Kinds of events supported by the Monkey tool and the options used to steer them

Event type	Description	Option
Touch	A touchscreen press/tap (down and up)	--pct-touch
Motion	A drag gesture (down, move, up)	--pct-motion
Trackball	A trackball motion	--pct-trackball
Basic navigation	Navigation using the directional pad (DPAD)	--pct-nav
Major navigation	DPAD Center and the Menu button*	--pct-majornav
System keys	Home, Back, Call, End call, Volume up, Volume down, Mute	--pct-syskeys

Table 13.1   Kinds of events supported by the Monkey tool and the options used to steer them *(continued)*

Event type	Description	Option
Activity launch	Random launches of activities for better coverage	`--pct-appswitch`
Orientation change	A screen orientation change**	`--pct-flip`
Other	Anything else, such as keyboard keys	`--pct-anyevent`

*This doesn't include the back button as the official documentation suggests; the back button is classified as a system key instead.

**This option is undocumented at the time of this writing, but it's recognized and an integral part of a test run, so it's unlikely to disappear in future versions of the platform.

This allows us to influence a test run using the Monkey. For instance, we could decide to completely disable the menu events and increase the likelihood for orientation changes, which are known to cause instability in applications, especially if concurrency is involved (see chapter 6). So far, we've mostly looked at an application's stability. The Monkey can detect other nonfunctional defects, for instance, Application Not Responding (ANR) errors. If you followed our advice in chapter 6. then you'll never run into these problems, but let's always be prepared and remember the two virtues we mentioned in the chapter opening: don't be ignorant, and don't be arrogant! When the Monkey detects an application timeout, it exits with an error message and prints some diagnostic information. If we rewrite the standard Android HelloWorld application to get stuck in an endless loop, then exercising it with the Monkey will yield something like this:

```
matthias:[~]$ adb shell monkey -p com.aip.test 50
// NOT RESPONDING: com.android.phone (pid 3784)
ANR in com.android.phone (com.aip.test/.HelloWorld)
Reason: keyDispatchingTimedOut
...
DALVIK THREADS:
(mutexes: tll=0 tsl=0 tscl=0 ghl=0 hwl=0 hwll=0)
"main" prio=5 tid=1 SUSPENDED
  | group="main" sCount=1 dsCount=0 obj=0x4001f1a8 self=0xce48
  | sysTid=3784 nice=0 sched=0/0 cgrp=default handle=-1345006528
  | schedstat=( 5143014534 1347433116 135 )
  at com.aip.test.HelloWorld.onCreate(HelloWorld.java:~13)
...
// meminfo status was 0
** Monkey aborted due to error.
Events injected: 2
## Network stats: elapsed time=31502ms (31502ms mobile, 0ms wifi, 0ms not
     connected)
** System appears to have crashed at event 2 of 50 using seed 0
```

Since Android 2.3 (Gingerbread), the diagnostic reports printed here are fairly lengthy and in-depth, but if you dig around you'll find the stack trace that shows you where your application got stuck.

ANR TRACES ON ANDROID 2.2 AND EARLIER   Note that the Monkey spits out stack traces of all threads only on Android 2.3 or newer. On older Android versions, you can find all ANR stack traces in /data/anr/traces.txt, although that directory is only accessible on the emulator or a device with root access.

DISCUSSION

The Monkey is an indispensable tool for testing your applications for all sorts of non-functional properties such as responsiveness and stability under heavy use. One thing you should always keep in mind is that events are sent in a random fashion, so you can't rely on full coverage of all your application's elements. A passing monkey test therefore doesn't mean that your application is flawless, because it may have missed something. One way to improve coverage is to tweak the -pct-appswitch option. With higher values, the Monkey will probably see all activities in your application.

13.4   *Summary*

We've come a long way. In this chapter, we explained a few basic ideas behind testing, including how to set up test projects and write simple tests using the JUnit library that comes with Android. We then introduced the notion of instrumentation and how you can leverage it to write full end-to-end tests based on user stories. We also noticed that Android's test framework doesn't shine when it comes to ease of use and concise syntax, so we showed you how you can use open source testing libraries such as Robotium to make your tests look nicer, improving productivity in the end. We then introduced mock objects, both the Android way and the novel JVM-based approach taken by Robolectric. Having covered plenty of functional testing approaches, we wrapped everything up by showing how to Monkey-test your applications to detect nonfunctional defects such as stability or speed problems.

What a ride! This chapter should've equipped you with some solid knowledge about automated testing for your applications. But a problem remains: so far, we need to always remember to run the tests that we write. Ideally, we want to run them whenever we change a piece of code, because changes may introduce bugs. Can we automate this, too? Yes we can! The answer is to use a build system that not only generates an APK file, but also runs the automated tests for us. Enter the world of build systems and continuous integration servers.

Build management

> *A tool is but the extension of a man's hand, and a machine is but a complex tool.*
> *And he that invents a machine augments the power of a man and the well-being*
> *of mankind.*
>
> —Henry Ward Beecher

In any but the simplest software projects, there comes a point where the complexity of an application outgrows the tooling and project structure initially used to set it up. As a developer you've probably hit that problem more than once. As the number of classes and resource files in your application grows, dependencies to external libraries increase, and it all starts getting monolithic and unwieldy.

What can you do when things start to get messy? First, you could start breaking down your application into distinct modules that can be maintained and built separately, perhaps even reused for other projects. With an increasing number of library dependencies, you may also want to start employing a dependency management system, which can take care of resolving version conflicts and the like.

Shared code modules are maintained and built separately, so you need software that allows you to describe, build, and wire these projects together in order to arrive at your final executable application. At the same time, you often want to gain more control over the build process itself, so as to perform extra steps such as generating project reports and documentation, publishing and signing build artifacts, and so forth.

As application and build complexity increase, you typically also have more people working on the project at the same time. So it can be indispensable to keep a build server around; you can automatically run tests and assemble new application builds, so as to ensure that you're not accidentally breaking the project under source control by committing a defective piece of code, and to regularly archive stable builds.

What you've seen in this book so far in terms of project and build management is the simple and standard functionality you get from the ADT and its application wizard. This is enough for simple applications, but leaves a lot to be desired for larger ones, with respect to the demands we mentioned:

- Project modularization is a difficult and highly manual process. There's no notion of submodules or shared projects in Eclipse/ADT.
- Dependency management in Eclipse/ADT doesn't go beyond "A needs B" style dependencies. Transitive dependencies, versions, and version conflicts aren't handled at all.
- Extending the build process with custom steps is difficult and inflexible.
- Eclipse/ADT are visual tools with no command-line interfaces, which makes them impossible to use on a build server.
- The level of build automation gained from Eclipse/ADT is limited. For example, no hooks can be defined that can automatically trigger a build.

In order to address these deficiencies of Eclipse and the ADT, we need to look at alternative solutions to give us more flexibility, expressiveness, and control when building Android applications. Unfortunately, this also means that you'll have to leave the world of graphical interfaces behind and turn to your good old command shell.

Although it may sound scary to leave the comforting visual environment of the Eclipse IDE for this chapter, the good news is that we don't have to start from scratch. Android comes with a set of command-line tools and premade Ant tasks (we'll see in a bit what they do) that will help you create powerful build environments. And here's a promise: at the end of this chapter, your Android builds will not only be as simple to start as from within Eclipse, they'll even start all by themselves!

That being said, here's the roadmap for this chapter. It's divided into three sections, with each section following an overarching goal. Our first goal is to drive Android builds from the command line, because this is a necessity for everything that follows. As part of this section we're quickly going to look at the Android build process, along with the steps and tools that comprise it. Moreover, we'll show you how to use Android's Ant tasks to easily trigger builds from the shell prompt.

We'll then go beyond the tooling provided by the Android SDK and explore ways to arrive at project layouts that allow for better modularization and powerful dependency handling. Specifically, we'll show you how to use Maven and its Android plugin to describe and build Android applications, how to use Maven's dependency management system to enable fuss-free and simple external library management, and how to integrate Maven back into your familiar Eclipse IDE.

Last but not least, we'll show you how to employ build servers in order to assemble and test applications in a fully automated fashion. We'll see how a build server can trigger a new build with every commit we do, as well as how to have it launch multiple emulators at once in different configurations, run and test applications on them, and inform us if it finds that something doesn't check out.

Truth be told, this is going to be a long ride. Build automation is an advanced topic, but it's an essential one for companies of all sizes that create Android applications professionally. The material behind this topic is grossly under documented on the official Android website, so we hope that although this chapter contains a lot of information, it'll be more than worth your while.

14.1 *Building Android applications*

If you've haven't done much Android programming before, except to follow the examples in this book, chances are that you use Eclipse to build, test, and deploy Android applications. The ADT, the Android plugin for Eclipse, does a good job of providing these functions in a graphical environment—making them easily accessible to humans. In fact, building an Android APK from your source code in Eclipse is as simple as clicking the Save button. Doing so will trigger the tool chain responsible for turning an Android Eclipse project into something that's executable on a device.

You'd be surprised how much happens under the hood when issuing a save on a source code or resource file. We plan to build Android applications from the command line, so it's essential that you understand what's happening there. Hence, this first section of the chapter is meant to give you a solid understanding of the steps and tools required to build an application. We'll wrap it up with this chapter's first technique, which will show you how to build a typical Android application from the command line with the Apache Ant build system.

14.1.1 *The Android build process*

The process of arriving from a set of source and resource files at an executable Android application is involved. This may surprise you because this process in Eclipse is so strikingly simple. The truth is that the process involves at least seven separate steps, and several different tools, so it's worth taking a closer look at what's happening under the hood. The steps executed to build an Android APK file are shown in figure 14.1.

Even more steps may be involved, depending on your mileage. For instance, some companies may decide to obfuscate the application code as a post-processing step to the class file generation, so as to make reverse-engineering an application difficult or impossible. Let's go through each step in detail. Let us stress that we cover all this for you to better understand the process. You won't have to perform all these

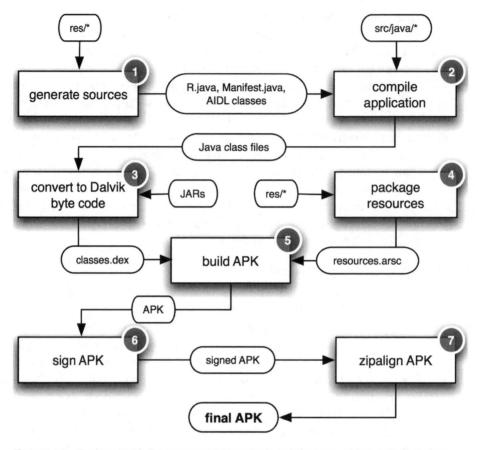

Figure 14.1   The standard build process employed by Android consists of seven distinct steps. Resources and source code are compiled into an APK file, which is then signed and byte aligned.

steps manually. In fact, in technique 81, we'll show you how Android's Ant targets greatly simplify this for you.

STEP 1: GENERATING JAVA SOURCE CODE

As you may recall from earlier chapters, Android handles resources such as pictures, layouts, strings, and so forth, by generating resource IDs and writing them to a file named R.java. This is usually done by the ADT, so every time you create a resource (say, by dropping a PNG into the res/drawables folder, and pressing F5 to refresh), the ADT will update R.java and create a new ID field for that resource. That's why you should never hand-edit that file; your changes will be overwritten. When creating an APK outside Eclipse, a build system must generate that file itself. This can be done with the aapt SDK tool (the *Android Asset Packaging Tool*), which allows you, among other things, to generate the R class from a set of resources, as well to generate the Manifest class, which is the runtime representation of the AndroidManifest.xml file.

WHERE CAN I FIND THE SDK TOOLS? Throughout this chapter we'll mention a few command-line tools that ship with the SDK. We won't cover their usage in much detail, but if you want to use them manually or toy around with them, you can find them in either `$ANDROID_HOME/tools` or `$ANDROID_HOME/platform-tools`.

Another thing to consider are remote objects defined using the AIDL, the Android Interface Definition Language, as seen in chapter 5. The interfaces to communicate with a remote service must be generated using the `aidl` tool, and they're required to compile the application. At the end of this step, we have all source code files together, and they're ready to be compiled.

STEP 2: COMPILING JAVA SOURCE CODE

The application source code from the `src/` folder, the Java source files for the R class, the `Manifest` class, and the AIDL interfaces (if any) are then compiled into Java class files. This is an invocation of the `javac` compiler; there's nothing Android-specific about this step. After this, we have a set of standard Java class files for every Java class in the application, whether hand-written or generated in the previous step. At this point, you can hook into the build lifecycle for any custom class file post-processing, such as for bytecode injection or manipulation. For instance, a common task is to minimize and obfuscate classes using ProGuard (see appendix C).

STEP 3: CONVERTING TO DALVIK BYTECODE

The Java class files from the previous step contain standard Java bytecode, and Dalvik can't read that. That's why a build system must convert all Java class files into the Dalvik Executable format (DEX) using the `dx` tool (sometimes informally referred to as *the dexer*). This includes not only your own classes, but also any classes coming from JAR files that your application depends on. The result is a single `classes.dex` file that contains the entire program code plus dependencies in a compact and efficient representation suitable to be run by the Dalvik virtual machine. We've already talked about the optimizations applied by the `dx` tool in chapter 1, when we first introduced the Dalvik VM. The application code is now ready to be packaged up, but before we do that, we need to process the application's resource files.

STEP 4: PACKAGING APPLICATION RESOURCES

We already have the application code ready for execution, but we can't build an APK yet. We must first package up the resources used by the application, similar to how we dealt with the source code. A build system would do that, again using aapt. For this particular step, aapt will process all resources in your application's `res/` and `assets/` folders by converting them into a more compact representation. Whereas binary files, such as images, remain untouched, any XML files, such as layouts or the manifest, will be rewritten using a binary format. They will be both smaller and more efficient to read at runtime. Values such as strings won't be kept in separate files at all, but are directly written to a file called `resources.arsc`, along with references to rewritten resources like layouts. The optimized `AndroidManifest.xml`, the optimized resource files, and the `resources.arsc` file are then packaged into a JAR file that's already our APK, but still without the application code.

STEP 5: ASSEMBLING THE APK

We now have both the application code and resources, and we're ready to package them together into an APK. Truth be told, steps 4 and 5 are done in a single step using aapt, but it's easier to think about them as separate steps. In any case, a build system must add the classes.dex file to the final APK, either using the aapt add command or by already including it in step 4. The point is that after this step we have the final APK containing both resources and code. To avoid confusion, there's nothing special about an APK file; it's an ordinary Java JAR file. In return, a JAR file is an ordinary ZIP file with a META-INF folder that contains some information about the package contents. If you're curious, go to your Eclipse workspace and decompress an .apk file using your archive tool of choice.

You'll see a directory structure like the one shown in figure 14.2.

At this point, we have a fully assembled APK, so aren't we done? The answer is no, because we can't do anything with it. Installing APKs to the emulator or devices requires that they be signed using a security certificate, so we must first sign our APK.

Figure 14.2   APK files are ordinary ZIP files. Uncompressing them yields a directory structure like the one above.

STEP 6: SIGNING THE APK

We said that you can't install unsigned APKs, not even to an emulator. This is done to add a layer of trust to deployed applications; it prevents users from replacing an application with another version of the same application, unless their security signatures match. The correct signature can only be written by the authority that initially created the application. Frauds tinkering with the application can't redistribute it, because they don't have the private key that was used to sign the original package.

Because an APK file is a JAR file, signing an APK is done the same way as signing a JAR: using the jarsigner tool. Like javac, the jarsigner tool has nothing to do with Android; it's part of any ordinary JDK installation. The jarsigner tool works off of a keystore file and a security certificate. The security certificate for signing APKs can be self-issued; you don't need to apply for a certificate at Google or any other trusted authority. In addition, it's always a good idea to use the same certificate to sign an application that's deployed to more than one marketplace or app store so updates remain compatible.

When signing an APK involves a keystore and certificate files, you may be wondering how Eclipse does it when you Run As > Android application. The trick is that by default, the ADT use a debug keystore that was generated for you (on MacOS- and UNIX-based systems, this file is located at ~/.android/debug.keystore). This is fine when running the application on a development machine, but for a production release, you should use a separate keystore and a security certificate that identifies your company. We won't get into the details of signing an APK using jarsigner, but if you're curious, it's fully documented on the official Android website at http://mng.bz/La8q.

STEP 7: ALIGNING RESOURCES IN THE APK

Strictly speaking, we're done after the previous step, because we have a signed APK that we can install on devices. This last step is done purely for optimization, and is entirely optional, although highly encouraged. According to Google, uncompressed resources such as PNGs or raw resources should always be aligned to 4-byte boundaries in a compressed APK, so that Android can more efficiently access these resources at runtime via memory-mapped I/O routines. This alignment of resources can be easily accomplished using the `zipalign` tool. Again, the ADT will automatically zip-align exported APKs, but in a custom build setup, you must invoke this tool manually. Calling `zipalign` should always be the last step in the build process; any modifications to the APK file after aligning it will render the alignment useless.

Equipped with the knowledge about how Android's build procedure is structured and which tools are involved, it's time to think about ways to automate this. There are many steps and moving parts, so it would be good to pour this bulky process into something that's a tad easier to handle.

14.1.2 *Moving toward automated builds*

Because remembering and performing all the different steps we've seen can become tedious and error prone, we'll look at tools that allow us to automate this process. Scripted build tools do exactly that—they take the raw application files as input, walk through the steps we explained previously, and churn out APKs. Think of an assembly line equipped with machines. We feed something in at the front (our project folder), have the machines (the platform tools) convert the different components to intermediate goods, and the final product (the APK) plops out at the end.

A build system can do even more for us, such as installing the application on a device and running the test suite. Figure 14.3 shows the typical steps a build system like Ant would perform when used in an Android environment.

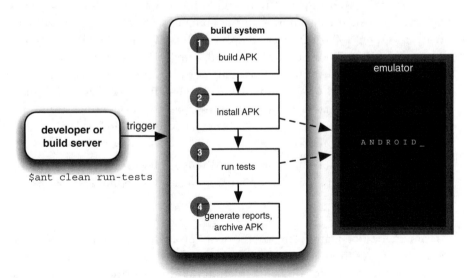

Figure 14.3   A build system such as Apache Ant can greatly simplify the build lifecycle by executing each step using a build script. A build system can usually be triggered using a simple shell command.

We're not limited to one kind of build system Fortunately, there are plenty: GNU Make, Ant, Maven, Gradle, SBT, Rake, Buildr.... the list is long. Which one is the best for you depends on your mileage, but we'll review two of the most popular ones, Ant and Maven, against the backdrop of Android.

We'll start with what's probably the simplest and also best-known build system in the Java universe: Apache Ant. A word of warning before we continue: none of the techniques about build systems that follow are meant to be in-depth introductions into the build systems themselves. Such intense cover would blow this book's scope way out of proportion. Entire books have been written on using Ant or Maven, but this isn't one of them. Instead, we'll give a quick introduction to the build system itself and its major building blocks. Then, we'll quickly advance to the Android specifics and how the build system being discussed compares to others with respect to building Android applications. We'll always point you to more detailed information about the tool being discussed.

TECHNIQUE 81   Building with Ant

Even if you've only used a bit of Java before you decided to tread the path of the Android developer, chances are you've at least heard of Apache Ant. Perhaps you've even used it. Ant (*Another neat tool*) is a build system written in Java, for Java. You can use it for more than building Java applications, but building Java applications is its primary purpose and motivation behind its development. If you've done any programming for native Linux/UNIX applications before, think of Ant as the equivalent to UNIX's `make` tool. Unlike `make`'s crude syntax found in the `Makefile` describing a build, Ant banks on XML, and the build descriptor is aptly called `build.xml`.

If you've worked with relatively simple build systems such as Ant or GNU Make before, then you already know what I'm going to say now: things can get messy if you reach a certain level of project complexity (lots of dependencies, submodules, that sort of thing). We'll explain Ant's strengths and weaknesses in more detail later. For now, let's summarize Ant by itself as being perfectly fit for simple build tasks in simple applications. Ant is also the standard and Google-official way Android applications are built from the command line. Although Ant has its shortcomings, we're not wasting your time. But before starting to assess Ant, maybe we should first look at how it works.

PROBLEM

Your application has a simple structure, there are few or no dependencies on other projects or libraries, and you're looking for an easy way to build an APK from the command line.

SOLUTION

If your application matches the profile of our problem description, which is the case for any standard Android project generated by the ADT project wizard, then Ant is the way to go. Due to its simple command-line interface, it can run directly from a shell and hence is easy to integrate back into other build environments such as Eclipse (through its Ant view) and build servers. We'll now briefly introduce Ant's basic concepts.

WHERE CAN I LEARN MORE ABOUT ANT? As mentioned in the introduction, we'll cover the build systems discussed in this chapter briefly and focus on their application to Android projects. You can find more information about Apache Ant at http://ant.apache.org/manual/.

Ant builds are based on three major building blocks: tasks, targets, and extension points, which are imported or defined using an XML-based build descriptor file called `build.xml`. A *task* in Ant describes a piece of work to be performed. This can be anything as simple as creating directories or as complex as creating a JAR file. Ant ships with a set of tasks typically useful when dealing with Java builds, but you're free to write your own. Examples for tasks are the `javac` or `jar` tasks to compile source code and create a JAR file, respectively. Tasks usually form small, atomic steps in a build, and by themselves don't add a lot of value. Ant can therefore group several tasks together into larger units called *targets*. A `distribution` target could consist of the tasks `mkdir`, `javac`, `jar`, and `copy`. Such a target would create a distribution directory, compile the source code, bundle it into a JAR, and copy it to that directory. The important thing about targets is that unlike tasks, they can be invoked from the command line by passing them to the `ant` tool as a parameter. For instance, the command

```
$ant documentation distribution
```

would first execute a target called `documentation`, and then the `distribution` target. Targets can also depend on each other: the `distribution` target could depend on `documentation`, so that the project documentation is always generated before distributing the build. In that case, you could omit the explicit invocation of the `documenta-tion` target on the command line.

The third and last building block is *extension points*. Extension points are targets, but they don't define any tasks. Instead, they're used to further group several targets into larger units. Tasks and targets are usually defined using XML in the `build.xml` file, which typically sits in the root folder of your application. Alternatively, you can write tasks in Java, package them in a JAR file, and import that JAR file in the build script. That's the way Android's Ant build scripts work.

That shall suffice for our quick overview of Ant. Build systems are best explained by example, so let's see how we can use Ant to build a Hello World style Android application. We'll call it HelloAnt.

GRAB THE PROJECT: HELLOANT You can get the source code for this project at the *Android in Practice* code website. Because some code listings here are shortened to focus on specific concepts, we recommend that you download the complete source code and follow along within Eclipse (or your favorite IDE or text editor).

Source: http://mng.bz/g3Vd

"Move along; nothing to see here!" Throughout this chapter, we won't offer sample APKs for download, because we believe it would be pointless. This chapter is about build scripts and tools, not applications. All sample applications here merely serve as sandboxes for automating builds.

The application is our standard Hello World kind of application as generated by the ADT project wizard. We extended it a little to add a dependency to an external library, the *Apache Commons Lang* library. This library includes a host of useful utility classes. For instance, HelloAnt uses its `StringUtils.` `repeat` method to repeat a greeting three times in a toast, as seen in figure 14.4.

This example may look silly, but it's to illustrate how library dependencies are handled in Ant, so bear with us. The first thing we need in order to build this application using Ant is a `build.xml` file. We could write it from scratch, but why bother if there's a simpler way. We'll generate it using the android tool.

Figure 14.4   HelloAnt uses Common Lang's `StringUtils.repeat` **method to repeat a greeting three times.**

DUDE, WHERE'S MY BUILD.XML? If you're creating applications using the ADT project wizard in Eclipse, no build.xml file will be generated for you, because the tools assume you want to build the application solely using Eclipse. But you can use the `android` command-line tool to generate an Ant build file for you, as explained in this section.

There are two ways to generate an Ant build file using the `android` tool. One way would be to create your project using the `android create` command in the first place. This is the way to scaffold Android projects outside an IDE, and it will make sure that a `build.xml` is generated for you. Most people would prefer to use the Eclipse project wizard, because it's less cumbersome. Although this leaves you without a `build.xml`, you can generate the file afterward using a trick. Navigate to your project folder in a shell and type the following:

```
$android update project -p .
```

That command is a no-op: it updates your project's base directory to be the current directory, which it already is. As a side-effect, it'll also regenerate all files that are missing, among them, a `build.xml`, as shown in the following listing. Outsmarted!

Listing 14.1   The build.xml file generated by the `android` **tool (minus comments)**

```
<?xml version="1.0" encoding="UTF-8"?>                    ❶ Project tag embraces
<project name="AntPoweredApp" default="help">                everything else

    <property file="build.properties" />                 ❷ Custom build
    <property file="default.properties" />                  properties
```

```
<path id="android.antlibs">
    <pathelement path="${sdk.dir}/tools/lib/anttasks.jar" />
    <pathelement path="${sdk.dir}/tools/lib/sdklib.jar" />
    <pathelement path="${sdk.dir}/tools/lib/androidprefs.jar" />
</path>

<taskdef name="setup"
    classname="com.android.ant.SetupTask"
    classpathref="android.antlibs" />

    <!--
    <target name="-pre-build"></target>
    <target name="-pre-compile"></target>
    <target name="-post-compile"></target>
    -->
<setup />

</project>
```

❸ Custom Ant tasks

❹ Setup task defined

❺ Build lifecycle hooks

❻ Setup task

Every Ant build script starts with the `project` tag ❶. It takes a few optional parameters, such as the project `name` and a `default` target that will be used whenever you invoke Ant without passing it any target explicitly. A third argument not being used here, `basedir`, lets you specify the path that's assumed as being the root for everything.

In Ant, parameters, constants, and variables for a build script are declared as properties. You can do that using the `property` tag ❷. Properties can be set in seven ways. The most common ways are to use the `name` and `value` attributes or read them from a Java properties file, as seen here. Of the two properties files here, `local.properties` and `default.properties`, at least the latter should look familiar to you: it's the properties file the ADT (or the `android` tool) generates for every Android project. It contains settings such as the Android version your application targets. New is `local.properties`, which contains machine-specific settings, such as the absolute path to the Android SDK, that are required to build the application. Therefore, this file shouldn't be checked into version control.

As you can see, the build file is rather short, because no tasks have been defined here. The Android SDK defines its tasks as Java classes bundled in a JAR. When running the build, Ant will resolve and load these tasks by going through the list of JAR files defined in the `android.antlibs` path element ❸. The build is then bootstrapped by declaring the `setup` task using Ant's `taskdef` element ❹. See how we reference the path to the JAR file here using the `classpathref` attribute and passing it the `id` of the path element we defined. This is a typical example of how Ant wires things together using XML.

WHERE CAN I FIND ANDROID'S ANT TASK DEFINITIONS?   If you want to take a peek at the various Ant tasks Android defines for you, and how they're implemented, download the framework source code and navigate to `sdk/anttasks`, where the task classes reside in the `com.android.ant` package. Alternatively, browse them online here: http://mng.bz/6d7s.

Android's Ant build file also defines a few empty targets for us that can be understood as hooks into the build process. These are –pre-build, -pre-compile, and –post-compile ❺. You could uncomment and implement the –post-compile hook to post-process the class files being generated for code obfuscation.

> **PRIVATE ANT TASKS** You may have wondered why these targets start with a hyphen (-). This is a common pattern to create private Ant targets—targets that can't be invoked directly from the command line. Ant has no notion of private targets, but you can trick it. Because Ant will treat any arguments starting with a hyphen as options to the ant tool itself, and not as targets, they'll become unreachable from the command line. You can still cross-reference them like any ordinary target from within your build script.

Last but not least, the build file executes the setup task we declared earlier ❻. It doesn't take any arguments, so the call is simplified to <setup />. This is where the build script setup is performed.

Building your application

Now that we've dissected the build descriptor, let's use it to build an APK from our application using Ant. The first thing you need to know is which targets are provided to you by Android. The next listing does this by running Ant with the -p flag.

Listing 14.2   Listing available targets and other project information

```
matthias:[HelloAnt]$ ant -p
Buildfile: /Users/matthias/Projects/eclipse/HelloAnt/build.xml
    [setup] Android SDK Tools Revision 9
    [setup] Project Target: Google APIs
    [setup] Vendor: Google Inc.
    [setup] Platform Version: 2.2
    [setup] API level: 8
    [setup]
    [setup] -----------------
    [setup] Resolving library dependencies:
    [setup] No library dependencies.
    [setup]
    [setup] -----------------
    [setup]
    [setup] WARNING: No minSdkVersion value set. Application will
            install on all Android versions.
    [setup]
    [setup] Importing rules file: tools/ant/main_rules.xml
Main targets:
 clean      Removes output files created by other targets.
 compile    Compiles project's .java files into .class files
 debug      Builds the application and signs it with a debug key.
 install    Installs/reinstalls the debug package onto a running
            emulator or device. If the application was previously
            installed, the signatures must match.
 release    Builds the application. The generated apk file must be signed
            before it is published.
 uninstall  Uninstalls the application from a running emulator or device.
Default target: help
```

To see all targets, including private ones, use the `-v` flag for verbose output. Alternatively, you can open a `build.xml` file in Eclipse's Ant view to get a tree-ish overview of its contents.

MAKE SURE THE TOOLS FOLDER IS ON THE PATH Ant needs to know where Android's Ant tasks are defined. Hence you must ensure that before running Android's Ant tasks, the `$ANDROID_HOME/tools` folder is part of the `$PATH` environment variable that's used to look up things on the command line.

Ant puts a task's name in square brackets when it's outputting text (in this case, that's the `setup` task introduced in listing 14.1). Look at the last line of the `setup` task: Ant indicates here that a rules file was imported. This file, `main_rules.xml`, contains all properties and `taskdefs` Android defines for a normal Android application project. It has similar rule files for Android test projects and Android library projects. The test rules will contain additional targets, such as `run-tests` to execute an instrumentation test project.

RUNNING TEST SUITES WITH ANT Note that we'll revisit test execution using Ant in section 14.3, when we talk about build servers and continuous integration. For now, it's enough to know that it's possible.

These files can be found in the `tools/ant` directory of your Android SDK installation. Go ahead and look at these files; it's helpful to understand what sort of options you can tweak to customize your build. The targets seen in listing 14.2 are the main targets, but as mentioned earlier, they consist of smaller tasks that can be mapped to the build steps we introduced in the previous section. Table 14.1 summarizes this correlation.

Table 14.1 The build steps identified in section 14.1.1 and their corresponding Ant tasks

Step #	Description	Ant tasks / targets
1	Generation of source code for R.java, Manifest.java, and AIDL interfaces	`-resource-src` `-aidl`
2	Compilation of all Java source code	`compile`
3	Conversion of class files to DEX format	`-dex`
4	Packaging of application resources	`-package-resources`
5*	Packaging of application code and resources to APK	`-package-debug-sign` (debug mode) `-package-release` (release mode)
6*	Signing of the APK file	`-package-debug-sign` (debug mode) `release` (release mode)
7*	Resource alignment in the APK file	`debug` (debug mode) `release` (release mode)

*For these steps, there's no one-to-one mapping from steps to Ant tasks or targets, because sometimes an Ant task/target may perform more than one step at a time

The setup task will always be executed, regardless of which target you run. If you don't run any target explicitly, Ant will fall back to the default target, which in case of the Android Ant scripts is the help target. Let's do a fresh build and install it to a running emulator (make sure you're running one when trying this yourself!). The following listing shows how.

Listing 14.3   Building and installing an application with Ant

```
matthias:[HelloAnt]$ ant clean install
Buildfile: /Users/matthias/Projects/eclipse/HelloAnt/build.xml
    [setup] Android SDK Tools Revision 9
    [setup] Project Target: Google APIs
    [setup] Vendor: Google Inc.
    [setup] Platform Version: 2.2
    [setup] API level: 8
    [setup]
    [setup] ------------------
    [setup] Resolving library dependencies:
    [setup] No library dependencies.
    [setup]
    [setup] ------------------
    [setup]
    [setup] WARNING: No minSdkVersion value set. Application will
            install on all Android versions.
    [setup]
    [setup] Importing rules file: tools/ant/main_rules.xml

clean:
   [delete] Deleting directory /Users/matthias/Projects/eclipse/HelloAnt/bin
   [delete] Deleting directory /Users/matthias/Projects/eclipse/HelloAnt/gen

-debug-obfuscation-check:

-set-debug-mode:

-compile-tested-if-test:

-dirs:
     [echo] Creating output directories if needed...
    [mkdir] Created dir: /Users/matthias/Projects/eclipse/
            HelloAnt/bin
    [mkdir] Created dir: /Users/matthias/Projects/eclipse/
            HelloAnt/gen
    [mkdir] Created dir: /Users/matthias/Projects/eclipse/HelloAnt/bin/
     classes

-pre-build:

-resource-src:
     [echo] Generating R.java / Manifest.java from the resources...

-aidl:
     [echo] Compiling aidl files into Java classes...

-pre-compile:

compile:
```

```
   [javac] /Users/matthias/Library/Development/android-sdk-mac_86
➥          /tools/ant/main_rules.xml:361: warning: 'includeantruntime'
➥          was not set, defaulting to build.sysclasspath=last;
➥          set to false for repeatable builds
   [javac] Compiling 2 source files to /Users/matthias/Projects/eclipse/
   HelloAnt/bin/classes

-post-compile:

-obfuscate:

-dex:
    [echo] Converting compiled files and external libraries into
➥          /Users/matthias/Projects/eclipse/HelloAnt/bin/classes.dex...

-package-resources:
    [echo] Packaging resources
    [aapt] Creating full resource package...

-package-debug-sign:
[apkbuilder] Creating HelloAnt-debug-unaligned.apk and signing
➥           it with a debug key...

debug:
    [echo] Running zip align on final apk...
    [echo] Debug Package: /Users/matthias/Projects/eclipse/HelloAnt/bin/
    HelloAnt-debug.apk

install:
    [echo] Installing /Users/matthias/Projects/eclipse/HelloAnt/bin/
    HelloAnt-debug.apk
➥   onto default emulator or device...
    [exec] 988 KB/s (154421 bytes in 0.152s)
    [exec] pkg: /data/local/tmp/HelloAnt-debug.apk
    [exec] Success

BUILD SUCCESSFUL
Total time: 18 seconds
```

If you look at the build output, you can see how Ant executes all the steps that are part of an Android build using a single command. Note that the tasks Ant performs here are precisely those we've already seen in table 14.1.

Remember how we said we've added a dependency on the Apache Commons Lang library to our application on purpose? It may not be obvious immediately how Ant handles this; after all, we didn't tell it where to look for that JAR file containing the `StringUtils` class when compiling the source code. That's because we put it in the `libs/` folder (the path libraries are automatically included from by convention). Android's Ant tasks will peek into that directory and add its contents to the classpath when compiling the application. If you want to use a different folder, you can change that by setting the `jar.libs.dir` property to a custom path.

DISCUSSION

Apache Ant offers a simple and straightforward way to build your applications from the command line. It's easy because Android comes with a basic set of tasks and targets you can execute, so you only need to apply your customizations on top of it, if required at all.

The problem with Ant is that once your project gets more complicated in terms of project structure and dependencies, Ant build files can quickly become difficult to manage. Ant has two main weaknesses that will strike you sooner or later.

First, Ant lacks any kind of built-in dependency management. Dropping JAR files into the `libs` folder is fine if there are only a few of them. If you rely on many different libraries, you can run into problems due to conflicting transitive dependencies. If, for example, your application relies on libraries A and B, and both of them rely on different versions of library C, things can quickly get messy. Moreover, you always need to maintain dependencies yourself; you need to find the correct library files on the Web and download them to your project. Your fellow developers also need them, so you need to commit them to your source code management system, something that many developers frown upon. The *Apache Ivy* project (http://ant.apache.org/ivy) addresses this issue by providing a dependency management layer that can be used by Ant, but this adds another moving part to the build environment.

Second, Ant doesn't have native support for multimodule projects. If your application has only one project folder, you're fine. But as soon as you start adding a test project, which as learned in the previous chapter you should always have, you suddenly need to maintain two builds that are unaware of each other. That may not even be the end of the line. At Qype, our Android application consists of seven projects: the application, three test projects, and three upstream library projects. Wiring all that in Ant means juggling with `includes`, `subants`, and `macrodefs`, making it a manual, complex, and tedious task. Ant has no notion of multi-part projects or builds.

Due to Ant's shortcomings related to the management of applications on the project level rather than the raw build level, alternate build systems have emerged. We're going to cover the best-known and most widely distributed one in Java world, *Apache Maven*. Maven is a lot more complex than Ant, and we'll only scratch the surface. We'll focus on its application to Android projects, but we've dedicated the entire second part of this chapter to Maven, so we hope you learn a lot.

14.2   *Managing builds with Maven*

Apache Maven was released as part of the Apache Turbine web application framework, with the purpose of providing a build environment that natively supports recurring processes in mid- to large-sized projects. Maven is written in Java, and being part of the Apache project, is free and open source software.

As opposed to Ant, Maven is modeled around the software project in its entirety, and makes describing and managing it its primary goal. Where Ant focuses on fine-grained tasks (such as `copy`) that must be manually wired together in a procedural fashion to form an overarching goal (such as building a distribution package), Maven focuses on the big picture and offers native support for recurring project management tasks such as dependency management, project modularization, build management, release and distribution management, generating documentation, and even generating entire project websites. It's much more than a build system: it's a project lifecycle management system, although for simplicity and consistency, we'll stick with the term build system for the remainder of this chapter.

> **WHICH VERSION OF MAVEN?** Throughout this chapter we're going to assume that you have Maven 3 installed (you can either download it from the project website at http://maven.apache.org or via your computer's packaging system). Maven 2 will likely work with our examples, but it was superseded by version 3 a while ago and shouldn't be used anymore.

Granularity of focus is a key difference from Ant, and this becomes particularly evident in how Maven *perceives* a project. Whereas Ant build scripts are pieced together at a fairly low level to match a project's requirements, Maven starts with the project nature in mind from the get-go. Because a web project is different from an Android project, Maven provides project scaffolding via so called *archetypes*. Using project archetypes, you can let Maven generate a default directory layout and initial POM (discussed next) to get you started. Android archetypes have been kindly provided free and open source by Akquinet (https://github.com/akquinet/android-archetypes).

At the heart of any Maven-powered project lies the *POM*, the *Project Object Model*. It tracks every aspect of your project configuration, from name, version, authors, and committers, to external library dependencies and release repositories. The POM is described using XML and kept in the project root folder in a file called pom.xml. (We'll see in a minute what a typical pom.xml looks like.) Commands are issued in the same way as Ant, but they're passed to the mvn command-line tool. Note that what's called a *target* in Ant is called *goal* in Maven. For instance, in order to clear temporary files and then recompile an application, you'd pass the clean and compile goals[1] to Maven:

```
$ mvn clean compile
```

Maven employs a powerful dependency management system. In Maven, anything that's the outcome of a successful build is called an *artifact*, and can serve as an input to another project. An artifact can be anything from a library JAR file, a source code or JavaDoc archive, to an entire Android application package. Those build artifacts can be uploaded to a Maven *repository* using the deploy goal, so as to make them visible to other developers. A repository could reside on your local machine (and in fact, there always is one, as we'll see in a bit), but it can also be hosted on a web server. Because Maven precisely defines how Maven artifacts and repositories look, any software project in the world that also uses Maven can reuse dependencies from other projects uploaded to an online Maven repository, by declaring a dependency on them in their POM. To bootstrap things, a master repository called *Maven Central* exists on the Internet. This means that if your application depends on a library that's already on Central, Maven will automatically download it to your local machine as part of the build and cache it. The relationship between a POM and different kinds of repositories is illustrated in figure 14.5.

---

[1] If you want to nitpick, this isn't exactly true: clean and compile are lifecycle phases, to which default goals are bound that will be invoked, but this is only an implementation detail.

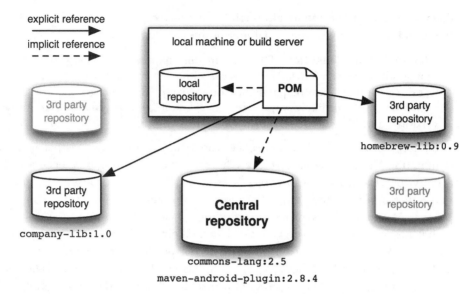

Figure 14.5 Maven always knows about the Central and local repositories, so you don't have to declare them. If you add a dependency to an artifact that hasn't been synced to Central, you must declare it in your POM using the `<repository>` tag. All artifacts downloaded from remote repositories will be cached in your local repository.

Another key design point behind Maven is its own architecture. Much like Eclipse, Maven is completely based on plugins. The Maven tool itself is only a thin core layer, with almost all extra functionality added via plugins. For instance, the `help` goal is added by the *maven-help-plugin*. Compilation, JavaDoc generation... everything is a plugin. This makes Maven extremely modular and extensible, which is important with respect to integrating Maven into the world of Android.

   That was a mouthful, so let's summarize Maven in one sentence: Maven is free and open source, it's a build system, a project lifecycle management system, a software distribution infrastructure, and a platform. To get a better grasp of Maven's popularity, here are some numbers: according to Sonatype, the company behind Maven, more than 90,000 artifacts are hosted on Central these days, with more than 40,000 companies making nearly 300 million requests every month. Not too shabby!

> **WHERE CAN I LEARN MORE ABOUT MAVEN?** The Maven build system is complex, and we can't cover all aspects here. We do our best at focusing on Android specifics while not leaving you completely in the dark in case you haven't worked with Maven before, but we suggest that you keep the Maven documentation close for the next few techniques, in case you feel that you need to catch up on some of the Maven fundamentals.
>
> Maven's User Centre is a good place to start: http://maven.apache.org/users/index.html.

With the background information out of the way, let's do some hands-on exercises to see how we can manage Android builds with help from Maven. In order to not overwhelm you with information, we'll start in technique 82 by turning a simple Hello World–style application into a Maven project. Although Maven's strengths unfold with more complex project layouts, keeping things simple here allows us to clarify what makes a Maven-powered Android application and what Maven has to offer when dealing with the typical Android application lifecycle. We'll then follow with technique 83 by introducing several Eclipse plugins that make your Maven/Android builds work fully from Eclipse. We'll wrap things up in technique 84 by showing you how to make managing your local Android libraries as Maven artifacts a breeze.

TECHNIQUE 82   **Building with Maven**

We've introduced Maven already and given you a quick overview of its architecture and strengths, but we have yet to introduce Android to the formula.

PROBLEM

Your project has grown large enough that Maven's well-established dependency management system, submodule support, and rich plugin landscape are a good choice for managing your Android builds. You now want to see what a POM for a typical Android application project looks like, and which Android specific goals are available.

SOLUTION

We already mentioned that Maven itself is a platform, to which additional functionality is added by means of plugins. It shouldn't be a surprise that the same is true when talking about Android and Maven: meet the *maven-android-plugin*.

For this first Maven technique, we'll take the simple Hello World–style application from technique 81 and build an APK with the help of Maven and its Android plugin. That means in this technique, we'll focus on how a POM for an Android project is laid out, and what kind of Maven goals are added by the plugin to make your life easier.

> **PLUGINS ARE DEPENDENCIES** Note that plugins in Maven are handled like library dependencies. There's no need to manually download or install them; you declare them in your POM, and Maven will automatically download any plugins it doesn't already have, assuming it can find them in the set of repositories it knows about.

After creating the project using the Eclipse wizard or the `android create project` command, we only need to do one thing in order to Mavenize our application: create its project descriptor, the `pom.xml` file in the root of your project folder. You can write this yourself, but usually it's easier to start with a template. For example, you can use the `mvn archetype:generate` command along with Akquinet's Android archetypes. We already have everything prepared for you, too.

> **GRAB THE PROJECT: HELLOMAVEN** You can get the source code for this project at the *Android in Practice* code website. Because some code listings here are shortened to focus on specific concepts, we recommend that you download the complete source code and follow along within Eclipse (or your favorite IDE or text editor).

Source: http://mng.bz/a9FY

Listing 14.4 contains the first part of our sample application's `pom.xml`. We've divided it in two parts to make it more readable. This first part contains everything related to the application itself and its dependencies, whereas part 2 will contain settings specific to the build. Note that in the next technique we'll also see how to get IDE support for handling POMs.

Listing 14.4   A POM file for a simple Android application (part 1)

```
<project xmlns="http://maven.apache.org/POM/4.0.0"
  xmlns:xsi="http://www.w3.org/2001/XMLSchema-instance"
  xsi:schemaLocation="http://maven.apache.org/POM/4.0.0
    http://maven.apache.org/maven-v4_0_0.xsd">
  <modelVersion>4.0.0</modelVersion>

  <groupId>com.manning.aip.maven</groupId>
  <artifactId>HelloMaven</artifactId>
  <version>1.0-SNAPSHOT</version>

  <name>HelloMaven</name>
  <description>An Android app built with Maven</description>

  <packaging>apk</packaging>

  <properties>
    <androidVersion>2.2.1</androidVersion>
    <project.build.sourceEncoding>UTF-8
      </project.build.sourceEncoding>
  </properties>

  <dependencies>
    <dependency>
      <groupId>com.google.android</groupId>
      <artifactId>android</artifactId>
      <version>${androidVersion}</version>
      <scope>provided</scope>
    </dependency>

    <dependency>
      <groupId>commons-lang</groupId>
      <artifactId>commons-lang</artifactId>
      <version>2.5</version>
    </dependency>
  </dependencies>

  ...
  [the remainder of this POM can be found in listing 14.5]

</project>
```

① **Maven metadata**

② **General project settings**

③ **Project properties**

④ **Project dependencies**

We first need to provide some metadata to Maven ①. Every POM starts with a `<project>` element, which takes a few attributes that are used by schema validators. The `<modelVersion>` tells Maven's POM interpreter which version of the POM we're using—in this case 4.0.0, which is the only model version Maven supports at this time (although that will change with Maven 3.1).

Now the project-specific configuration starts ❷ and it gets more interesting. Remember how we said that the typical result of a Maven build is an artifact, in our case an APK? Every such artifact must be uniquely identifiable around the globe, because artifacts are often kept in public Maven repositories. In order to uniquely identify artifacts, Maven uses two IDs: `groupId` and `artifactId`. The `groupId` identifies the group that governs this artifact. For example, your company id must be globally unique. As with Java packages, a good convention is to use your company's Internet domain here. A group can have many artifacts, so Maven uses a second ID, the `artifactId`. It must be unique within your group, but need not be globally unique. The combination of both IDs is therefore sufficient to uniquely identify an artifact worldwide. Because artifacts can come in many versions, you must also supply a `version`, which can be chosen freely. If you think of Maven's artifact world as a box, where every artifact has its place, then the `groupId`, `artifactId`, and `version` number form the three coordinates you need to locate a specific artifact in the box. You can also supply an artifact `name` and `description` using free form text, but those are optional and serve as documentation.

Maven by default supports eight different kinds of artifact packaging (POM, JAR, WAR, EAR, RAR, and a few more), but not the `apk` packaging; after all, we want to build an Android application, not a plain old Java archive. This new packaging format is in fact added by maven-android-plugin (we'll come back to that in a minute).

Like in Ant build files, we can also set properties using the `property` element ❸. Some properties already exist as part of Maven, and some are added from the various plugins a typical build involves, but you can also add your own. This is what we've done here with the `androidVersion` property, which will come in handy later.

Finally, we declare the dependencies our application has to other Maven artifacts ❹. First and foremost, we tell Maven that we need the `android.jar` file; otherwise compilation would fail. Fortunately, the Android and Maven community has been hard at work, and managed to get it on Maven Central, where it's archived as `com.google.android:android` (the `groupId:artifactId[:version]` notation we used is common in Maven, and we'll see it again on other occasions).

> **GOOGLE AND MAVEN—NOT QUITE A LOVE STORY** It should be stressed that although the Android artifacts are available on Maven Central under `com.google.android` since June 2010, Google Inc. isn't involved with anything related to Maven and the Android Maven artifacts. In fact, Google rejected the Maven community's plea for having artifacts as part of the official Android release process, so the community continued this effort on their own. For more background on this story, the ticket that was created for this on the Android issue tracker is filed as issue 4577 and contains the official response from Google's AOSP engineering lead Jean-Baptiste Queru.

You may have noticed that we set the `scope` to `provided`. Maven uses the `scope` element to figure out when a dependency should be visible on the class path. The default scope is `compile`, which means that this dependency is required for your application to compile and run. The `runtime` scope instead means that you don't need this dependency for compilation, but it must be loaded as soon as you execute your application. Both `compile` and `runtime` mean that Maven will package and deploy the dependency along with your application, but we don't want that to happen with `android.jar`, because that library will already be part of the devices' system images when we're running the application. That's where the `provided` scope comes in: it tells Maven that we need the dependency to compile our application, but that it should *not* be deployed with it—instead, it'll already be provided at runtime, in this case by the Android device.

Overall, our HelloMaven application is the HelloAnt application from technique 74, with some wording changed and Ant's build.xml swapped for a Maven pom.xml. That means we again need the Apache Commons Lang library for the application to compile, so we can display the "Hello Maven" toast that uses the `StringUtils` helper. Recall that Ant expects external libraries to live in `libs/`, but we explained that Maven pulls libraries from repositories. That's why we have to declare `commons-lang` as a dependency. Maven will then figure out automatically where to find it, and download it to your local repository, unless it's already there.

Until this point, we've configured the POM to give Maven all the basic information about our application, its artifact identifiers, name and description, and its dependencies. The problem is: using only that, Maven would still refuse to compile the application. It doesn't even know yet what an APK is, but we've provided that as the packaging format. The next step is therefore to hook into Maven's build phase using maven-android-plugin. It turns out this is also done in the same POM, and the following listing shows how.

Listing 14.5   A POM file for a simple Android application (part 2)

```
<project xmlns="http://maven.apache.org/POM/4.0.0"  ...

   ...
   [the beginning of this POM can be found in listing 14.4]
   <build>                                                    ❶ Set default
     <sourceDirectory>src/</sourceDirectory>                    source location

     <plugin>
        <groupId>com.jayway.maven.plugins.android.
     generation2</groupId>                                    ❷ Declare
        <artifactId>maven-android-plugin</artifactId>           Android
        <version>2.8.4</version>                                plugin

        <configuration>
          <sdk>                                  ❸ Set required
            <platform>8</platform>                 platform API level
          </sdk>
                                                                ❹ Always do
          <undeployBeforeDeploy>true</undeployBeforeDeploy>      complete
                                                                  reinstall
          <emulator>                                   ❺ Configure
            <avd>android-2.2-normal-mdpi</avd>           emulator startup
```

```
          <wait>30000</wait>                    5  Configure
        </emulator>                                emulator
      </configuration>                             startup

      <executions>
        <execution>
          <id>alignApk</id>
          <phase>install</phase>              6  Run
          <goals>                                zipalign
            <goal>zipalign</goal>
          </goals>
        </execution>
      </executions>

      <extensions>true</extensions>
    </plugin>
  </plugins>
</build>

</project>
```

Again, we're going to walk through this from top to bottom. As you can see, we've added a new element, the build element, to the POM. The build element here carries all the information that Maven needs in order to turn your Android project into a build artifact. There's two major things you configure here.

First, you must supply any configuration that specifies the input and output aspects of the build, such as where Maven can find your source code, the name of the output directory (it defaults to target/), the name of the package file that's produced, and so forth. You only need to do that if you don't follow Maven's conventions. We mentioned before that Maven makes specific assumptions about the structure of a project, including its directories. For instance, it assumes that your application sources are in a folder called src/main/java, and that your test sources are in src/test/java. That's not how a typical Android application is laid out. Tests are kept in a separate project (see chapter 13). Moreover, we don't use more than one programming language in this example, so we only need one source folder. We use the sourceDirectory element to tell Maven that our application source code is in the src/ directory ❶. Note that it'll still assume src/test/java to be the folder where our tests are, but because that folder doesn't exist, it'll silently skip it.

Second, you need to declare and configure all plugins you require to build your application here, which for us is the maven-android-plugin. The Android plugin lives in the somewhat unwieldy group called com.jayway.maven.plugins.android.generation2, and at the time of this writing, is at version 2.8.4, so that's what we declare ❷.

As you can see, we specify two blocks of configuration for the Android plugin: configuration and executions. The configuration element is used to configure a plugin. The first thing you must do is tell the plugin Android API level you're targeting ❸, level 8, which is Android 2.2.

MAVEN PROPERTIES Note that you can also use properties as values for elements using the ${...} notation we've already seen with Ant. There are also some implicit properties that you don't need to define yourself but are always available for you to use. There is env, which contains the current environment variables from the shell in which you run the mvn command; there's also a project property that contains all your project settings, and a settings property that contains the configuration from an optional settings.xml file in your Maven home directory. You can also directly access any Java system property directly that you'd otherwise read using System.getProperty.

Moreover, we tell the plugin to uninstall any already-existing APK before redeploying a new one using the undeployBeforeDeploy element ❹, so that we can't run into problems such as reinstallations failing because of different certificates being used to sign the APKs. The last aspect we configure is the emulator. Yes, maven-android-plugin can start and stop an Android emulator for you automatically, as we'll see shortly. We've set the AVD name to android-<version>-normal-mdpi, because that's a good pattern to name your AVDs. If the emulator AVD you'd like to use has a different name, you must use that instead (refer to section 1.6.2 for how to manage AVDs) ❺.

We've configured the plugin now, but we'd like to do one more thing. Remember from technique 74 how the Ant build script automatically used zipalign on any APK for us before deploying it to a device? Unfortunately, maven-android-plugin doesn't do that by default, so we must tell it to. Whenever you need to tell a plugin to do extra work as part of its default workflow, you'll use what Maven calls an execution ❻. An execution is an extension to a piece of work the plugin already does. An execution has an ID, which we called alignApk here, and hooks into a specific point in the lifecycle phase of a Maven build. (Maven employs a well-defined and quite complex build lifecycle, which we won't cover in detail here.) In our case, we'd like to invoke maven-android-plugin's zipalign goal as part of the install phase. If you don't understand what that means, maybe it'll become clearer once we start introducing the different goals the plugin supports. Recall that this step, as mentioned in section 14.1, is optional for development, but highly recommended for release builds.

We're almost done now. The last element we add is the extensions element. This is of utmost importance, because without it, the plugin can't extend Maven's default build lifecycle. Granted, we've been through a lot of dry material, but without all that, you can't do anything meaningful. That being said, what *can* you do now? Sometimes a table speaks louder than words. Table 14.2 summarizes the new goals added by maven-android-plugin.

Table 14.2 The goals exposed by maven-android-plugin

Goal*	Description
apk	Creates the APK file (by default signs it with debug keystore)
deploy	Deploys the built APK file, or another specified APK, to a connected device

Table 14.2   The goals exposed by maven-android-plugin *(continued)*

Goal*	Description
deploy-dependencies	Deploys all dependencies of packaging type apk (required by instrumentation test projects)
dex	Converts all Java class files to DEX format
emulator-start	Starts the emulator configured in the POM
emulator-stop	Stops the emulator configured in the POM
generate-sources	Generates R.java, Manifest.java, and AIDL classes
instrument	Runs the instrumentation tests on the device
pull	Copies a file or directory from the device to your local machine
push	Copies a file or directory from your local machine to the device
redeploy	Shortcut to undeploy and deploy
undeploy	Uninstalls the application from the connected device
unpack	Unzips the application JAR to target/android-classes
zipalign	Invokes the zipalign tool to byte-align resources in the APK

*Don't forget to prefix these goals with android: when passing them to mvn.

From looking at that table, cleaning and building the application, starting an emulator, and deploying the application to it sounds like a good idea, so let's do that. Go to the shell and to the HelloMaven project folder, and type:

```
$mvn clean android:emulator-start install android:deploy
```

Make sure that $ANDROID_HOME points to your SDK installation before doing this, and that you have a Java 5–compatible Java compiler installed. Note how we prefix the emulator-start and deploy goals with the android: qualifier. That's because they're goals exposed by maven-android-plugin, whereas clean and install are part of the default Maven lifecycle. Maven will understand this prefix as long as you're inside a Maven/Android project (the Android plugin is loaded).

Coming back to the command, here's what you'll see written to standard out when running Maven with these four goals (you may see a bunch of downloads happening the first time you run this command). First, we see output related to the clean and emulator-start goals:

```
[INFO] Scanning for projects...
[INFO]
[INFO] ------------------------------------------------------------------------
[INFO] Building HelloMaven 1.0-SNAPSHOT
[INFO] ------------------------------------------------------------------------
[INFO]
[INFO] --- maven-clean-plug-in:2.4.1:clean (default-clean) @ HelloMaven ---
```

```
[INFO] Deleting /Users/matthias/Projects/eclipse/HelloMaven/target
[INFO]
[INFO] ------------------------------------------------------------------
[INFO] Building HelloMaven 1.0-SNAPSHOT
[INFO] ------------------------------------------------------------------
[INFO]
[INFO] --- maven-android-plug-in:2.8.4:emulator-start (default-cli)
➥      @ HelloMaven ---
[INFO] Android emulator command: /Users/matthias/Library/Development/android-
    sdk-mac_86/tools/
➥    emulator -avd android-2.2-normal-mdpi
unknown
[INFO] Starting android emulator with script: /var/folders/0J/
    0JjfHEzqFIyzAHVWetQjWk+++TM/-Tmp-//
➥    maven-android-plug-in-emulator-start.sh
[INFO] Waiting for emulator start:30000
```

You may want to adjust the 30-second idle period where the build script waits for the emulator to start, depending on how swift your machine is. Note that if an emulator with the given AVD is already present, the emulator-start goal will do nothing:

```
[INFO] --- maven-android-plug-in:2.8.4:emulator-start (default-cli)
➥      @ HelloMaven ---
[INFO] Android emulator command: /Users/matthias/Library/Development/android-
    sdk-mac_86/tools/
➥    emulator -avd android-2.2-normal-mdpi
emulator-5554
[INFO] Emulator emulator-5554 already running. Skipping start and wait.
```

Maven then enters the build phase. This is pretty much the same as what we've seen with Ant before: source code gets compiled, resources get packaged, and the APK is bundled and zipaligned (the following snippet is shortened to only contain the log output for the goals that are being triggered):

```
[INFO] --- maven-android-plug-in:2.8.4:generate-sources
➥      (default-generate-sources) @ HelloMaven ---
[INFO] --- maven-resources-plug-in:2.4.3:resources (default-resources)
➥      @ HelloMaven ---
[INFO] --- maven-compiler-plug-in:2.3.2:compile (default-compile)
➥      @ HelloMaven ---
[INFO] --- maven-jar-plug-in:2.3.1:jar (default-jar) @ HelloMaven ---
[INFO] --- maven-android-plug-in:2.8.4:unpack (default-unpack)
v      @ HelloMaven ---
[INFO] --- maven-resources-plug-in:2.4.3:testResources
➥      (default-testResources) @ HelloMaven ---
[INFO] --- maven-compiler-plug-in:2.3.2:testCompile
➥      (default-testCompile) @ HelloMaven ---
[INFO] --- maven-surefire-plug-in:2.6:test (default-test)
➥      @ HelloMaven ---
[INFO] --- maven-android-plug-in:2.8.4:dex (default-dex)
➥      @ HelloMaven ---
[INFO] --- maven-android-plug-in:2.8.4:apk (default-apk)
➥      @ HelloMaven ---
```

```
[INFO] --- maven-android-plug-in:2.8.4:internal-pre-integration-test
    (default-internal-pre-integration-test) @ HelloMaven ---
[INFO] --- maven-android-plug-in:2.8.4:internal-integration-test
    (default-internal-integration-test) @ HelloMaven ---
[INFO] --- maven-install-plug-in:2.3.1:install (default-install)
    @ HelloMaven ---
[INFO] --- maven-android-plug-in:2.8.4:zipalign (alignApk)
    @ HelloMaven ---
[INFO] --- maven-android-plug-in:2.8.4:deploy (default-cli)
    @ HelloMaven ---
```

You can see from this snippet how the maven-android-plugin hooks into the default Maven build lifecycle at several well-defined points. For instance, android:generate-sources, the goal that generates R.java, is injected before the compile goal of the maven-compiler-plugin, because it's a prerequisite for successful compilation.

The goals being executed match almost one-to-one what we've seen from Ant (and the general build steps we introduced in section 14.1.1), but the install goal may take more explanation, especially if you were unfamiliar with Maven before. The install goal is part of the maven-install-plugin, and is responsible for copying the artifact that's being built to your local Maven repository. It can be found in *<user-home-directory>*/.m2/repository. Other Maven-managed applications could therefore reuse the APK and JAR files generated by this build by adding a respective dependency to their POM.

If everything checked out so far, the entire build should end with these lines:

```
...
[INFO] ------------------------------------------------------------------
[INFO] BUILD SUCCESSFUL
[INFO] ------------------------------------------------------------------
[INFO] Total time: 1 minute 9 seconds
[INFO] Finished at: Sun Jan 23 18:55:22 CET 2011
[INFO] Final Memory: 51M/123M
[INFO] ------------------------------------------------------------------
```

Voilà, a successful build served by Maven!

IF YOUR BUILD KEEPS FAILING   There are several reasons why the build could fail on your machine. Make sure that your environment variables (JAVA_HOME, ANDROID_HOME, and PATH) are set up, and that you use the latest Java compiler (Java 6 at the time of this writing).

Moreover, the Android dx tool can get hungry for memory when it has to process a lot of classes. If you're confronted with an OutOfMemoryError during the build, add this to the plugin configuration block:

```
<jvmArguments>
    <jvmArgument>-Xms256m</jvmArgument>
</jvmArguments>
```

That will grant the JVM Maven a little extra memory to keep it happy.

One last thing we'd like to mention is device targeting. Most plugin goals target a device. Deploying an APK, pushing a file, or running instrumentation tests require an Android device. If only one device is connected, the plugin will target that. It'll refuse to do anything though if several devices (such as your phone and an emulator) are connected, so you must tell it explicitly which device you're targeting. You do that by passing a system property to Maven using Java's standard -D option:

```
$mvn deploy -Dandroid:device=emulator-5556
```

If you'd like to know what kind of options you can pass to maven-android-plugin, you can find out via Maven's help plugin. For instance, the list of available goals (the ones we summarized in table 14.2) can be obtained by calling:

```
$mvn help:describe -Dplugin=com.jayway.maven.plugins.android.
    generation2:maven-android-plugin
```

This also works for specific goals:

```
$mvn help:describe -Dcmd=android:<goal_name>
```

> **NOTE** You can get an even more detailed description about the available goals and parameters by passing the -Ddetail property to help:describe.

That covers our hands-on introduction to Maven. If you knew Maven before stepping into this technique, but hadn't used it for Android projects, then you'll probably be pleased to see that you don't have to miss out when moving from JSE/JEE to Android. If Maven was new to you, you'll hopefully be intrigued by Maven's strengths and how you can leverage them for your applications.

DISCUSSION

Even with this simple application, it's easy to see how much work Maven can keep off your back. It does everything Eclipse and the ADT do, such as compiling source code and packaging APKs, but it does much more.

Dependencies to other projects or third party libraries are automatically managed for you, including the handling of transitive dependencies and version conflicts. Do you want to use the RoboGuice library, for example? Easy: drop a dependency declaration to it in your POM, and Maven does the rest.

Breaking up your applications into smaller submodules for better maintainability and easier reuse is another strength. Pull out the source code you want to isolate into a new project, create a POM for it, and other Maven-managed applications can declare a dependency on them. Maven also allows you to plug several Maven projects together under a parent project using a super POM. This is useful for Android projects, where you typically have a separate test project living next to your application project. Put them together under a super POM and you can build and manage them both at once (note that we won't cover multimodule builds, but examples for this have been provided on the Maven/Android plugin website at http://code.google.com/p/maven-android-plugin).

You can also extend Maven using various other plugins to add to the wealth of functionality that's already there. For instance, you can add the entire functionality of Ant to a Maven build through the maven-antrun-plugin, or leverage the maven-pro-guard-plugin to post-process your classes.

We should mention that there are also downsides to using Maven. Maven is a fairly complex build system, and its learning curve can be steep. Often it's not apparent how to achieve a certain task by looking at a POM, especially when trying to do simple imperative tasks such as "print something to standard out." Maven sometimes feels clunky here. Moreover, even though the number of libraries available as Maven artifacts in public repositories is impressive, you may still occasionally require a JAR file that isn't published as a Maven artifact. That means Maven can't directly use it, and you'll have to take things into your own hands, which in this case means downloading the file manually and turning it into a local Maven artifact using the `mvn install-file` goal. We'll see an example for this in technique 77.

> **ALTERNATIVES TO MAVEN** We should mention that there are a few promising alternatives to Maven emerging with respect to building Android applications, most notably the Android plugins for the Gradle and SBT build systems. Both are based on dynamic languages (Groovy and Scala, respectively), and follow the "build scripts are code" paradigm, which makes writing build scripts much easier and more natural. Follow them at https://github.com/jvoegele/gradle-android-plugin (Gradle) and https://github.com/jberkel/android-plugin (SBT).

Let's move forward. We've seen everything that's required to build your Maven application from the command line, which is fair enough, because that's what this section is about. But one burning question is: if we declare all our library dependencies in a POM file now and Maven takes care of locating, downloading, and wiring them all together, then how would this ever work when working in *Eclipse*? Surely we don't want to lose Eclipse support, but Eclipse knows nothing about Maven repositories. Because we no longer have a `libs/` folder that we could add to Eclipse's project build path, it seems we're missing something here to get the best of both worlds. Luckily, we thought about that and prepared a technique that shows you how to bridge that gap.

TECHNIQUE 83   The Maven Eclipse plugin

This will be a relatively short technique compared to the previous one, but important nonetheless. We've seen how to employ Maven to build things for us in a programmatic fashion on the command line, which is great for automation on a build server (as we'll see in technique 78), but we still want to be able to do our development work in Eclipse, and not lose all the features the ADT provides us. Why do we even think that would be the case? Well, let's open the HelloMaven project in Eclipse and see for ourselves (figure 14.6).

The problem is that our library dependencies (`commons-lang-2.5.jar` in this case) aren't kept in the project folder anymore. Instead, we learned in the previous

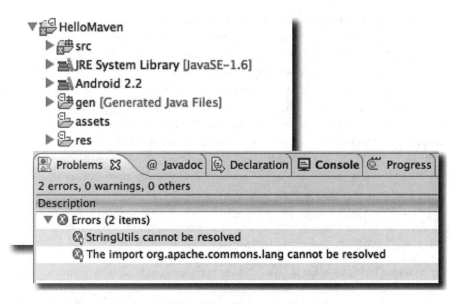

Figure 14.6   By default, Eclipse doesn't know how to resolve library dependencies defined in a Maven POM file. Apparently, something is missing to bridge this gap.

technique that Maven caches artifacts in your local Maven repository. We could add this directory to the project's build path manually, but that's an awkward solution. If we changed the version number of the library we depend on in the POM, then we'd have to manually adjust the Eclipse build path to reflect this change.

The proper solution is to use another plugin: *m2eclipse* is the official Maven plugin for Eclipse, and integrates Eclipse seamlessly with Maven-powered applications. If you're now thinking "Hold on a second, you're writing a technique that shows me how to install a plugin," hear us out. It's not that simple. The crux of the matter here is that we have three different build components that we need to get together:

1 *Eclipse/JDT*—Eclipse itself, or more precisely the JDT plugin for Eclipse, provides the core Java tooling such as source code highlighting and compiling Java source files to Java bytecode.

2 *ADT*—The Android toolkit, also an Eclipse plugin, takes over the Android-specific tasks such as converting Java bytecode to Dalvik bytecode and packaging APKs.

3 *Maven/maven-android-plugin*—Maven's functionality overlaps with the JDT and ADT (it also compiles Java code and package APKs with maven-android-plugin), but those things are already done by 1 and 2 in Eclipse. What we need to integrate is its dependency resolution system.

The m2eclipse plugin alone won't suffice here. That's because it knows how to provide Maven dependencies to the JDT so that you can compile a classic Java application that defines its library dependencies via Maven, but the ADT again has no notion of a POM and hence is oblivious to any dependencies defined by Maven.

Recall from section 13.1.1 that in step 3 when Android generates Dalvik bytecode, all JAR library dependencies become part of the `classes.dex` file. If the ADT doesn't even know that a library dependency is defined somewhere in your POM, then this can't work, and even though your application compiles fine, it'll crash with a `Class-NotFoundException` at runtime. Let's fix this.

PROBLEM

You're managing your Android projects with Maven but don't want to lose support for building them in Eclipse as well. Because Maven uses a completely different dependency resolution system than Eclipse, you must find a way to wire them together.

SOLUTION

Until recently, there was no proper way to resolve this dilemma: you'd either build an application using Maven or using the ADT, but not both. Eclipse users would typically use an "External Tools" run configuration to invoke a Maven build script from within Eclipse, but because Maven builds are a lot slower than using the ADT, this wasn't an ideal solution.

The community recognized this problem, and came up with a solution: the *m2eclipse-android-integration* plugin. This plugin won't add any new features to your Eclipse workbench—at least none that are visible. Its sole purpose is to accomplish what we mentioned earlier: wiring the ADT together with m2eclipse so that the former honors dependencies managed by the latter when building Android APK files. Because we're juggling four different Eclipse plugins now (JDT for Java, ADT for Android, m2eclipse for Maven, and m2eclipse-android-integration for the glue), we've summarized the interaction of those plugins in figure 14.7.

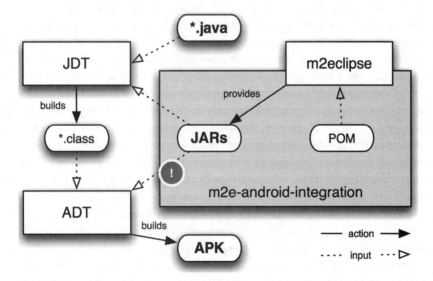

Figure 14.7 In order for the ADT to recognize dependencies managed by Maven, you need the m2eclipse-android-integration plugin. It provides the glue (specifically the edge marked as "!") that keeps the other three plugins together.

Now that you're aware of the problem, solving it is straight forward. First, we need to install m2eclipse and m2eclipse-android-integration, as explained in sidebar "Installing the plugins."

Installing the plugins

We assume that you know how to install plugins in Eclipse. If not, you can find instructions here: http://mng.bz/o3c3.

m2eclipse: This plugin is unrelated to Android, and developed by Sonatype, the company behind Maven. Its update URL is http://m2eclipse.sonatype.org/sites/m2e.

m2eclipse-android-integration: This plugin is developed by the Android community. Its update URL is http://mng.bz/bdMQ.

With the m2eclipse plugin installed, you get full support for Maven managed projects in Eclipse. Right-click any standard Android project that has a POM and select Maven > Enable Dependency Management. You should see a new dependency container called *Maven Dependencies* (for our HelloMaven project we already did that for you). In order to ensure that all settings from your POM are reflected back into the Eclipse project, you can also select Maven > Update Project Configuration. This is also useful if you changed something in the Eclipse project settings and want to revert to your configuration in the POM. Test your application by running it via Run As > Android application. Everything should run smooth as silk now!

DISCUSSION

The m2eclipse plugin adds a host of useful features to your workbench. Not only does it automatically download dependencies defined in your POM (you can follow any Maven-specific output in the Maven console), but you can edit it using a graphical user interface. Double-click the `pom.xml` and the POM editor will be launched. From there, you can get a better idea of how your project dependencies are interweaved using the Dependency Hierarchy view (see figure 14.8).

You can see from the figure that the dependencies related to the Android JAR file from Maven Central are grayed out, because they're flagged as "provided by the runtime platform" and hence won't be compiled into your application. Because we're already talking about the Android libraries and Maven Central, there's one detail we've kept from you so far. Should you ever want to use the Google Maps extension library shipped with Android (the one that identifies itself as "Google APIs" instead of "Android"), perhaps because you're using a `MapView` in your application, then we have bad news. The `maps.jar` library file is, unlike `android.jar`, not available from Maven Central. It contains proprietary code by Google, and hence is not open source. The Central repository is restricted to open source libraries, so no dice. Moreover, there are a few important things you should be aware of when compiling your applications against any Android libraries downloaded from Central. Does that mean we've maneuvered you into a dead end by settling on Maven? Not at all; it gets more complicated.

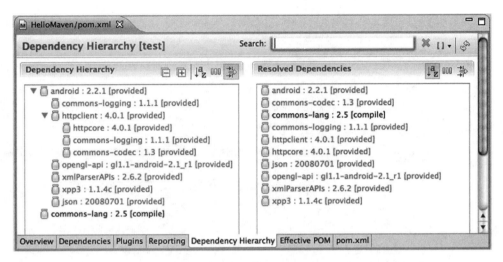

Figure 14.8   The m2eclipse plugin adds a powerful POM editor to your Eclipse workbench. From here you can keep a bird's eye view on your project dependencies, but also edit the POM using graphical tools.

TECHNIQUE 84   The Maven/Android SDK deployer

Being able to automatically pull dependencies from Maven Central (or any other online repository) is one of Maven's most redeeming features. Because Android is an open source project, the Maven community was eager to get it published on Maven Central quickly. The process to do so is complicated, though. Two major problems have to be solved, both of which affect developers.

First, not all parts of Android are open source. The most striking example is the code backing Google Maps; it's property to Google Inc. and can't be distributed freely. This means it has to be kept and distributed separately from Android's core framework classes, which is also why you can always target two different flavors of Android in your project settings. For example, you'll notice that the Vendor column for the project build target Android 2.2 is Android Open Source Project, whereas the Google APIs / 2.2 target names Google Inc. as the vendor (see figure 14.9).

That's because the latter not only includes the free and open source core framework classes, but also the proprietary extensions such as Google Maps. That's a huge problem for the Maven community, because they're not allowed to upload those extensions to Central, but any Android application that involves location and Maps needs them.

Second, the Android framework classes package other open source libraries as part of `android.jar`, such as Apache Commons HttpClient and the JSON reference implementation from json.org (see chapter 9). Because those libraries are themselves artifacts on Maven Central, it'd be wasteful to package them within another artifact (Android, in this case). Hence, the Maven community stripped out those third-party libraries from the standard `android.jar` and instead declared dependencies to them. This can be seen in the Maven dependency browser in Eclipse (see figure 14.8). So

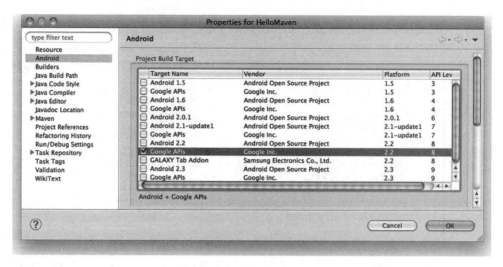

Figure 14.9   You can always choose between two flavors of Android: the fully free and open source core framework stripped of any proprietary code, and the full distribution including closed source user libraries such as Google Maps.

why is this a problem? It's a problem because sometimes, the versions of those libraries bundled with Android aren't *exactly* the same as those available on Maven Central. Google is free to make modifications to them before bundling them with Android or to package a version that's not available on Central. This has happened with the JSON library: the one on Maven Central ships with a different implementation of Json-Stringer than the one in android.jar, which means that you may run into compilation errors when using that class while building against the android.jar from Central. Clearly, we must find a way to resolve these issues.

PROBLEM

You're writing a location-aware application that uses Maps (see chapter 10), which means declaring a Maven dependency to the closed-source Google Maps library, or you don't want to rely on the Android JARs on Central, which are merely an approximation of the libraries shipped by an actual device.

SOLUTION

It seems like the artifacts from Maven Central are good enough for most purposes that involve the core framework classes, but as soon as you want to display a MapView, which almost every location-aware Android application does, you're stuck. The good news is that though you're not allowed to put the maps.jar file in an online Maven repository, you're free to install it into your local Maven repository. That way, any Maven build can depend on it and will compile fine. This solves both problems at once, because Central is completely out of the game. The only question is how?

Maven's install plugin provides an install-file goal which allows you to publish an arbitrary JAR file to your local Maven repository without needing to write a POM.

You must add the few parameters that any artifact must have (`groupId`, `artifactId`, and `version`), and Maven will turn it into a full artifact by generating the POM file for you on-the-fly. For instance, here's how you could install version 2.2 of Android's proprietary `maps.jar` to your local repository:

```
$mvn install:install-file -Dfile=/path/to/maps.jar -DgroupId=android
    -DartifactId=maps -Dversion=2.2 -Dpackaging=jar
```

You could then declare a dependency to it in your POM as follows:

```
<dependency>
  <groupId>android</groupId>
  <artifactId>maps</artifactId>
  <version>2.2</version>
  <scope>provided</scope>
</dependency>
```

That works fine. The problem is that this can be tiresome to manage. With every new platform release, you'd have to update all your development machines (your team's computers, build servers, and so on) to install the new artifacts to the local Maven cache. This is worse when your build server executes matrix builds where an application is tested against several different versions and configurations of the platform. Fortunately, the awesome Maven/Android community has us covered again: *maven-android-sdk-deployer* is a Maven installer that offers a convenient way of turning single or multiple Android platform JARs into Maven artifacts for you to use locally on your computer.

WHERE TO GET IT?   The project is on GitHub at http://mng.bz/SlaC.

If you're using Git for version control, execute `git clone` from the public repository URL. You can also download the master branch as a ZIP archive via the Downloads option.

The maven-android-sdk-deployer is nothing more than a Maven build script itself. What it does is scan your Android SDK folder for available platform versions, bundle them into Maven artifacts, and install them to your local Maven cache. For this to work, you must ensure that you've downloaded the Android platform versions you'd like to turn into Maven artifacts using the Android SDK and AVD manager. Using the latest SDK tools, you can ensure that you have all available platform versions by running `android update sdk --no-ui` from the command line (make sure the SDK's tools directory is on the `PATH`). You may need to invoke this command repeatedly until you see "There is nothing to install or update".

The `ANDROID_HOME` environment variable must be set to the root of your SDK folder. That's it for preparations. If you want to turn all downloaded Android platform versions into Maven artifacts, switch to the location where you downloaded the maven-android-sdk-deployer and type:

```
$ mvn install
```

A lengthy Maven build output should follow, ending in BUILD SUCCESSFUL. If it fails, then you probably haven't downloaded all the platform images it's trying to install. If you merely want to install a specific platform version, you can do that using the -P flag:

```
$ mvn install -P 2.3
```

This will only install Android 2.3 Gingerbread:

```
[INFO] ------------------------------------------------------------
[INFO] Reactor Summary:
[INFO] ------------------------------------------------------------
[INFO] Maven Android SDK Deployer ............... SUCCESS [1.642s]
[INFO] Android Platforms ........................ SUCCESS [0.008s]
[INFO] Android Platform 2.3 API 9 ............... SUCCESS [0.264s]
[INFO] Android Add-Ons .......................... SUCCESS [0.007s]
[INFO] Android Add-On Google Platform 2.3 API 9 .............
➡       SUCCESS [0.022s]
[INFO] ------------------------------------------------------------
[INFO] ------------------------------------------------------------
[INFO] BUILD SUCCESSFUL
[INFO] ------------------------------------------------------------
[INFO] Total time: 2 seconds
[INFO] Finished at: Sun Jan 30 12:59:14 CET 2011
[INFO] Final Memory: 16M/81M
[INFO] ------------------------------------------------------------
```

Note that maven-android-sdk-deployer installs the core Android JAR and the Maps add-on JAR into two different group IDs. Though the groupId of the Maps add-on will be com.google.android.maps, the groupId of android.jar won't be com.google. android (as seen from the artifact on Maven Central), but android. To make this more hands-on, we've supplied a slightly modified version of the HelloMaven application called HelloMavenWithMaps that renders a MapView and declares a dependency to the Maps JAR in its POM. It has also been changed to not use the Android JAR from Central anymore, but the one maven-android-sdk-deployer installs.

> **GRAB THE PROJECT: HELLOMAVENWITHMAPS**   You can get the source code for this project at the *Android in Practice* code website. Because some code listings here are shortened to focus on specific concepts, we recommend that you download the complete source code and follow along within Eclipse (or your favorite IDE or text editor).
>
> Source: http://mng.bz/1Wnt

Because the MapView related changes are miniscule, we'll spare you the details here. We covered them in chapter 10. What's important here is the change to the POM file. For your reference, the new dependencies block that now uses the installed Android artifacts follows.

Listing 14.6   Updated POM that depends on the artifacts installed by the SDK deployer

```
  ...
  <dependencies>

    <dependency>
      <groupId>android</groupId>
```

```
        <artifactId>android</artifactId>
        <version>2.2_r2</version>
        <scope>provided</scope>
    </dependency>

    <dependency>
        <groupId>com.google.android.maps</groupId>
        <artifactId>maps</artifactId>
        <version>8_r2</version>
        <scope>provided</scope>
    </dependency>

  </dependencies>
  ...
```

Even though we use the proprietary Maps JAR, Maven should now be happy, and not complain that it can't find the maps artifact.

DISCUSSION

This was a brief technique, but indispensable when you need to juggle Maven and Android JAR files. It becomes powerful when using a team repository server such as Sonatype's Nexus, to which the SDK deployer can install these artifacts automatically.

Though we could only scratch Maven on the surface in the previous techniques, you've seen everything you need to make Maven roll with Android and get all its benefits such as rich dependency management and plugins along the way. We managed to keep you around this far, through a chapter that's riddled with command line tools and lengthy build logs, so let's get more visual again! We've shown you how you can arrive at a fairly high level of build automation with the help of tools such as Ant and Maven. We're purists, so that's still not enough automation for us. After all, this still requires manual interaction, namely executing the build system. Wouldn't it be much better to have another tool that does this for us automatically? That's where build servers enter the stage.

14.3 Build servers and continuous builds

Though the power and flexibility of a build system like Maven is great by itself, there's an added benefit we've only briefly mentioned so far. If you recall from the introduction, in order to have a new APK built and tested after every commit, we need two things: the tools to build it and the machinery that kicks off the build process. We've seen at some length how to achieve the first part, but kicking off the build was done manually so far. What's missing is a tool that hooks into our version control system and decides when to trigger a new build. This is what *build servers* are for, and we'll show you how to use one of the many available that has proven itself.

Having a build server in place has countless benefits. First and foremost, it can build your application, and run its test suite, completely automated. With good test coverage, this allows you to always have a stable application package whenever the tests pass after a commit. The build server can make all output files available as downloads, so you always have a single place where people can get their hands on the latest development snapshot. While a build server is building, it produces and archives all sorts of helpful output. Test reports, visual timelines and summaries of succeeded and failed builds, the amount of time it takes for a single test or the entire build to run, changelogs and links to commits in the source code control system—all this is provided via the build server's interface. Figure 14.10 shows a snapshot of the build server we use at Qype, and a timeline of the build we recently set up for our Android application.

One of the most striking benefits is a build server's capability to alarm everyone about broken builds. A build server monitors the source code management system for changes, and can relate recent commits to a failing build. Therefore, if someone commits a change that makes a test fail, the build server can send out emails to all project members to make them aware of this. This makes it easy to detect regressions, and encourages continuous integration, a development approach where developers commit and integrate their changes to a piece of software frequently, as often as dozens of times a day, so that the feedback loop is short and direct, and the chance for diverging source trees is almost eliminated.

In this last part of the chapter, we'll show you how Android builds can be fully automated using the popular Hudson build server. Hudson has excellent support for Android builds via its rich plugin architecture, and it's free and open-source software. It's platform independent and extremely easy to set up and configure, making it a good choice for practically every environment. In this section, we again want to focus less on Hudson per se, and more on its role in relation with Android. For this purpose, we've decided to devote two techniques to building Android applications with Hudson. Technique 78 will show you how to set up Hudson's Android Emulator plugin and get things

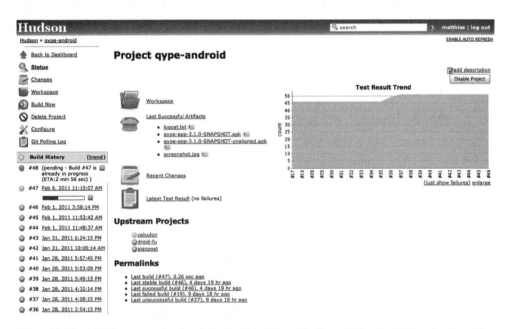

Figure 14.10   A build server not only automatically builds applications, but collects all sorts of useful information along the way, such as the time it takes for a build, test summaries, and backlinks into the source code management system.

rolling, and technique 79 will follow up by introducing *matrix builds*, a powerful way of building and testing Android applications where combinations of various platform configurations are turned into Hudson builds in a completely automatic fashion.

TECHNIQUE 85 **Continuous builds with Hudson**

Hudson, the friendly butler, is one of the most popular build servers these days. This can largely be attributed to it being open and free, highly extensible, easy to use, and a no-brainer to set up. If you think we're going to torture you with pages of installation instructions here, be relieved; we won't—it's not necessary. Hudson is great at managing itself, once started. It can update itself at the click of a button, or install new plugins that will extend its functionality. If you were wondering whether Hudson is bound to any specific kind of underlying build system, source code management (SCM) system, or even operating system, the answer is no. Hudson builds stuff, from some source, on some machine. You need to tell it what to build, where to get it, and how it's being built. Whenever you have to bridge the way to some specific technology, such as using Git for SCM or Maven for builds, you can rely on the vast supply of plugins for Hudson.

> **HUDSON OR JENKINS?**   Unfortunately, the Hudson project is splitting up as we write these lines. Oracle has claimed the name Hudson as a trademark and raised concerns about the way the project sources were moved from java.net to GitHub without getting the consent of the Hudson community beforehand. In return, this fanned fear that Oracle would use their influence to boycott or slow down other decisions that may come up, so some core committers decided to fork the project and rename it *Jenkins*, with most of the committers moving to Jenkins it seems. At this moment, both applications are almost identical, but may continue to diverge. The miniscule differences won't have any effect on the material presented here, whether you use Jenkins or Hudson.

Though Hudson isn't bound to any specific tools, we'll assume Subversion and Ant for this technique and the next. We use Subversion because that's what we used to manage the source code for this book and Hudson has out-of-the-box support for connecting to SVN repositories. We use Ant, and not Maven, because doing so will simplify things for the purpose of this technique. That's because we'd like to add a test project as part of the build here. Maven would require a multimodule project layout, which we didn't discuss. Please note that this doesn't make this technique less significant or less useful in any way. From Hudson's point of view it doesn't matter *at all* which build system you use. We could've opted for a simple shell script if we wanted.

> **ANT BUILDS AND TEST RESULTS**   There's one fundamental limitation when using Android's Ant tasks to run tests on Hudson: Hudson will consider the build to succeed even if there are test failures. That's because Android's Ant tasks print test results to standard out instead of generating proper JUnit reports. This is a shortcoming that will hopefully be addressed by Google soon. It's already compensated in other Android build solutions, such as maven-android-plugin and gradle-android-plugin.

Here, we want to focus on the Android Emulator plugin for Hudson. Because running tests should be an integral part of every build, we've added a simple HelloAntTest project containing a single Activity unit test for the HelloAnt project from technique 74, which tests for the existence of the "Hello" text view:

```java
public class SampleTestCase extends ActivityUnitTestCase<HelloAnt> {

    public SampleTestCase() {
        super(HelloAnt.class);
    }

    public void testHelloViewExists() {
        startActivity(new Intent(), null, null);
        assertNotNull(getActivity().findViewById(R.id.hello));
    }
}
```

There's nothing in there you haven't already seen in the previous chapter, so we'll spare you further details. See the sidebar about where you can find the project source code if you'd like to take a peek anyway.

> **GRAB THE PROJECT: HELLOANTTEST**   You can get the source code for this project at the *Android in Practice* code website. Because some code listings here are shortened to focus on specific concepts, we recommend that you download the complete source code and follow along within Eclipse (or your favorite IDE or text editor).
>
> Source: http://mng.bz/T10e

It's easy to see how the build server will build the HelloAnt application: it checks out the latest source code, and invokes the Ant build script. It may not be so obvious how it executes the tests. After all, we need an emulator or device to run the tests! This is where Hudson's Android Emulator plugin enters the stage.

PROBLEM

You want to automate your builds using a build server, and need a convenient way to start and shut down an emulator for the time of the build, so all instrumentation tests can be executed.

SOLUTION

Before we continue, it should be said that there are other ways to start an emulator for a build. For example, you could start it manually once and let all builds run on that emulator. This is problematic for two reasons. One, we want to make sure that the two builds don't affect each other. If one build writes a shared preference file during a test, a subsequent build will see a different initial state than the previous one. We can prevent this from happening by starting a new emulator using a fresh AVD for every build. Two, you must ensure that the emulator is always up. Because the Android emulator isn't the most stable piece of software in the world, you'd need to set up `monit` (http://mmonit.com/monit/) or equivalent tools to automatically bring it up again should it crash.

Another tool we've seen to manage emulators was the maven-android-plugin, which exposes `emulator-start` and `emulator-stop` goals. This is simplistic though, because it requires you to set a fixed wait-for-boot timeout. The Hudson plugin is smarter. It probes for a "boot completed" event to detect when the emulator is ready to receive commands. Moreover, it's build system agnostic so it doesn't matter if you build using Ant or Maven.

That being said, this technique will show you how to configure Hudson to set up a build that can automatically do these things for you:

1 Compile and package the HelloAnt application.
2 Start an emulator instance for every build.
3 Run the tests contained in HelloAntTest on that emulator.
4 Summarize and archive the outcome of a build (see figure 14.11).

If you haven't already downloaded and installed Hudson, do that now. If you're toying around, it's sufficient to download hudson.war from http://www.hudson-ci.org and start it using:

```
$java -jar hudson.war
```

That will boot up Hudson and make it available in your browser of choice at `local-host:8080`. It's *that* easy; we told you! Next, we need to install the Android emulator plugin. Hudson is completely self-contained, so you install plugins from within Hudson. This is done by going to Hudson > Manage Hudson > Manage Plugins > Available,

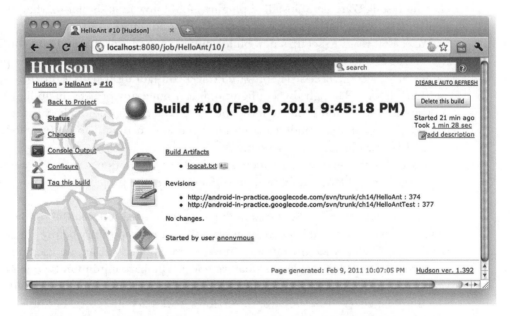

Figure 14.11 The blue ball indicates a successful build. If you don't like that and aren't suffering from dyschromatopsia, you can change the color to green by installing the Green Balls plugin, which is the first thing most people do after installing Hudson.

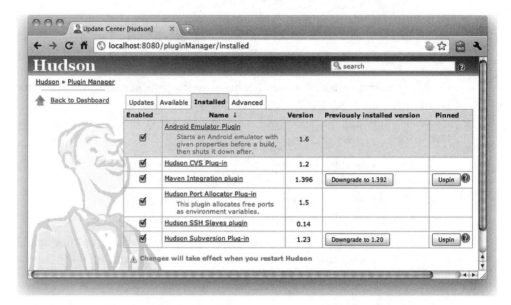

Figure 14.12   Hudson is completely self-contained. You can configure everything within Hudson itself, including the installation of new plugins. Note that plugin dependencies will automatically be resolved and installed for you.

finding and checking Android Emulator Plugin (it's listed under Build Wrappers), and clicking Install. Your list of installed plugins should now look similar to what's seen in figure 14.12. Note that you need to restart Hudson for changes to take effect.

We're now ready to set up a new build configuration. Hudson calls build configurations *jobs*, so go to Hudson > New Job. We call the job "HelloAnt", same as the project name, and select the Free-style Software Project configuration. This is the most simple and flexible one. Though this configuration can build any project, including Maven projects, for Maven you should choose the Maven2/3 configuration, because it's more convenient for Maven builds (this requires the Maven plugin to be installed). Figure 14.13 shows the job setup screen.

Proceed to the next screen, which is the build configuration screen. For a minimal setup, we must tell Hudson three things: where to get the project source code, how to run an emulator, and how to execute the build.

First, we configure the SCM system that should be used to fetch the sources. Hudson always downloads the latest version from the source repository before triggering a build, so as to always see the latest changes. As mentioned earlier, we use Subversion for version control here, so that's what we select. The bare minimum we need to provide is the path to the project on the SVN repository and the name of the folder into which it'll be checked out relative to the job's workspace directory. Because we need to build two projects (the application and the test project), we must add two locations and check them out into separate folders. This is shown in figure 14.14.

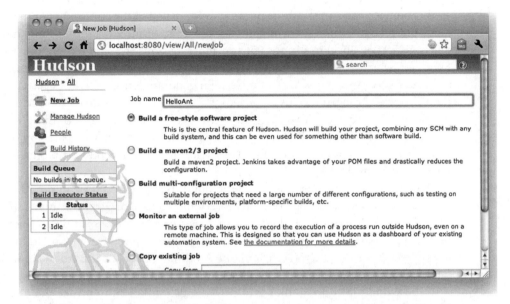

Figure 14.13 Hudson supports different kinds of job configurations. Select the Free-style configuration whenever you need utmost flexibility or no extra features specific to a particular build system.

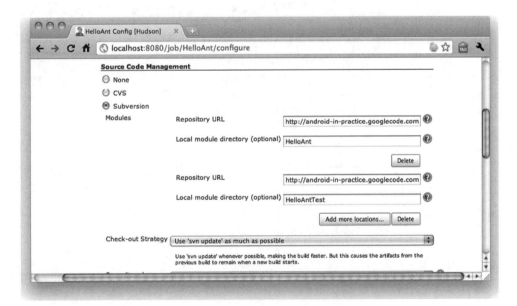

Figure 14.14 How Hudson can find your project source code is specified in the Source Code Management section. In this example, we use the book's Subversion repository.

Second, we must tell Hudson to run an Android emulator so that after assembling the application, we can run the tests. Because we've installed the Android plugin, we get a new option in the Build Environment section called Run an Android Emulator During Build. After checking it, we get two more options: we can either Run Existing Emulator, which lets us specify the Android virtual device we'd like to use (if we've already created one), or we can let the plugin generate one on-the-fly by selecting Run Emulator with Properties. This is convenient, so let's tell it to run a 2.2 emulator using the default display size. If you tick Reset Emulator State at Start-up, the plugin will invoke the emulator with the -wipe-data flag, which clears the user partition on boot. You can also decide to not Show Emulator Window if you intend to run on a headless server (see figure 14.15).

Third and last, we must configure the build. Because we chose to do a free-form build, Hudson lets us specify one or more build steps that are invocations of something like a shell script or a build tool such as Ant. Our case is simple, so under the Build section we add a single Invoke Ant build step and point it to the build file of the test project. Note that this is sufficient: the Ant build scripts generated by Android are smart enough to know that the application under test is required and must be built first, so we don't need to do that explicitly. It's also sufficient to invoke the clean and run-tests targets, because run-tests depends on the targets that compile and package everything (see figure 14.16).

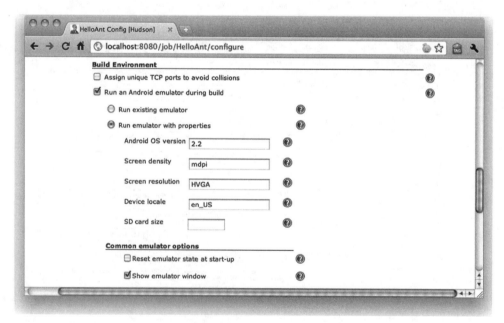

Figure 14.15   The Android plugin will add a new build environment option. Here you can specify the platform configuration that should be used to run the emulator.

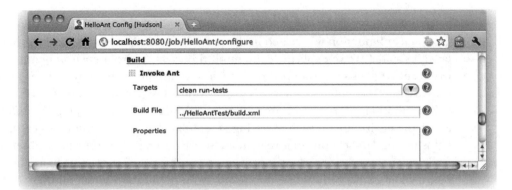

Figure 14.16   The build section is used to tell Hudson what it's supposed to do. Free-form builds are configured by specifying one or more build steps, such as an Ant invocation.

Click Save and we're ready to roll! To trigger a build manually, you can click the Build Now link in the sidebar. In a production setup, you should configure a trigger under Build Triggers, such as periodically polling the SCM system for changes. You can follow the build by clicking the link that appeared in the sidebar. All builds will appear here in reverse chronological order. If we did everything right, the final screen should look like what we saw in figure 14.11.

DISCUSSION

It should be clear that using build servers such as Hudson is mostly meaningful when maintaining a physical build machine on which the server is running. There's not much point in doing all this on your local machine beyond having the advantage of a nice interface to manage and summarize your builds. Build machines are typically headless, so the question arises of how the emulator should be started, because by default it requires a window. We've already mentioned the option that lets you disable the emulator window (when invoked directly, this would translate to the `-no-window` emulator option), but this has the disadvantage that you can't see what's going on when a build fails. You're blind to anything except the log files. Moreover, the emulator is known to be flaky when started without a window, so ideally, we'd like to have one. Fortunately, Hudson provides a plugin for XVNC, a protocol that allows you to launch virtual X11 displays. You must install both the Hudson plugin and an XVNC server such as TightXVNC for this to work. You'll then get a new option in the build configuration to run XVNC as part of the build, and even take screenshots of failed builds.

We've only run a single emulator during a build, so far. If you want to test on the baseline device configuration, then this is fine, but for a production application, it's likely that you want to run the same tests on various different combinations of platform versions and display sizes. Usually we'd have to create a new build configuration for every combination of Android parameters we'd like to test against, but as you may have guessed, there's an easier way to do that.

| TECHNIQUE 86 | **Matrix builds** |

The job configuration we created in the previous technique has one serious disadvantage: it's static. We've explicitly configured the exact Android environment we'd like to execute the tests in, from platform version to display configuration. User interface tests are highly coupled to a device's display, and a test passing on one screen size may fail on another. Moreover, there's plenty of things you could configure differently about the environment, such as having an emulator with and without SD card, which helps testing applications that rely on an SD card to fail gracefully in its absence. Yet more examples are network connectivity, geo position... all these aspects are bound to one specific emulator instance, and testing your application under all these different conditions can be tedious.

Things get even worse if you start thinking about *combinations* of configuration properties. Testing your application on either one or the other configuration may succeed, but when tested against a combination of them, it may fail. To illustrate, imagine there are two properties that affect the functionality of your application: screen size and language. You decided to support medium and small screens, as well as English and Spanish for localization. You may have decided to bundle a background image with localized text on it with your application, so you need it in four different versions: English text and small size, English text and medium size, Spanish text and small size, and Spanish text and medium size. This results in a matrix of configuration combinations, as seen in table 14.4.

Table 14.3   A 2x2 matrix of possible configurations

	en_US	es_ES
QVGA	/res/drawable-en-small/bg.png	/res/drawable-es-small/bg.png
HVGA	/res/drawable-en-normal/bg.png	/res/drawable-es-normal/bg.png

Now imagine you forgot to add the image for QVGA/es_ES. Your source code will compile fine, because as soon as there's at least one image called bg.png, there will also be an R.drawable.bg attribute. But, if your application is run using this specific configuration, it'll crash, because the runtime resource lookup will fail.

NOTE   This scenario can be avoided by always having a default configuration with a default resource to which Android can fall back. For instance, the en_US/HVGA image could be stored in /res/drawable, so although a Spanish user with a small screen device would see an untranslated text and a scaled down image, the application would at least remain operational. For more information about the algorithm Android uses to look up resources, refer to chapter 4 (section 4.7).

Clearly what we need is to be able to express which configuration axes we're interested in, and have the build server execute the job for all combinations.

PROBLEM

Your application supports various platform configurations under which its behavior will change, and you want to automatically test it on all of those without having to create separate build jobs.

SOLUTION

As of version 1.221, Hudson supports so called *multi-configuration project* jobs, often referred to as *matrix builds*. From Hudson's point of view it's a different kind of job than the one we used in the previous technique, so you can't go through the free-style software project configuration. In practice, it's exactly the same: the only difference is that you'll see a new section in your job settings called Configuration Matrix, where you can specify the axes and value sets along which you'd like to build.

Let's start from the top. Matrix builds are a separate kind of job, as explained earlier, so we need to recreate the job we created in the previous technique, but we can copy almost all configuration details; those that change we'll point out along the way. The first step is to create the matrix job, which is shown in figure 14.17.

The next screen is a free-style job, which we saw in previous techniques. You can copy all settings related to the source code management from there. What's new is the Configuration Matrix section. Here, we can define the axes and value sets we'd like to use as potential combinations of build parameters. Select Add Axis for every axis you'd like to define. In this example, we'll stick with the language and screen size example and want to execute the build for every combination of the small and medium screen sizes and English and Spanish device language. Figure 14.18 shows what our matrix configuration looks like.

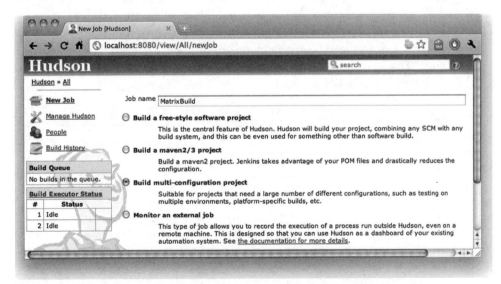

Figure 14.17   In order to create a matrix build, you must select the Multi-configuration Project job type. This is a free-style project job, but it'll make new job settings available specific to matrix builds.

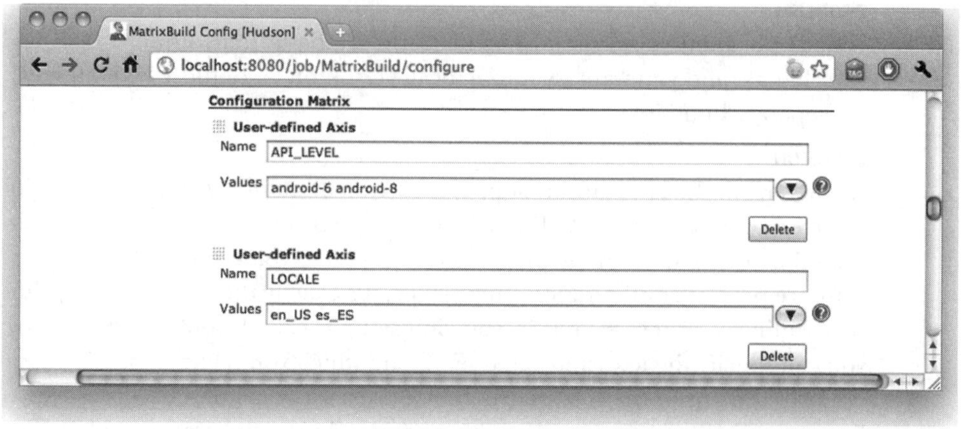

Figure 14.18 The configuration matrix defines the axes and the values each axis can take. For our example, we have an API level (platform version) and language axis. Values for each axis are entered directly, separated by a blank.

We've defined our configuration matrix now, each combination of which will automatically become its own subjob on Hudson whenever the matrix build is triggered. "But hold on a second," you may ask, "there's only one Android emulator configuration section, and we need to type the platform version and locale in there directly, so how does this work?" That's a fair question. As we saw in figure 14.15, we can't leave the emulator options for the Android emulator plugin blank. Instead, within the same build, these options shift! The solution is simple: we use variables. Hudson has built-in support for variables that can be used in build configuration, which can be made available as environment variables or directly from plugins. In this case, every Name field of a matrix axis becomes a variable that you can use throughout the rest of the build settings. This means we can put in the axes names as values for the Android emulator options, as seen in figure 14.19.

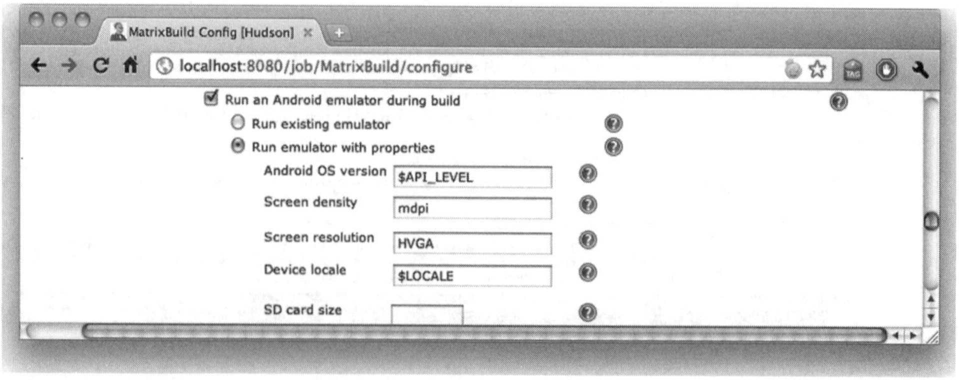

Figure 14.19 Every matrix axis can be referenced as a variable in the build settings by prefixing the axis name with the dollar sign. In this case, we're making the API level and device locale available to the Android emulator plugin through the matrix variables.

Note that those variables will also be passed to any Ant script you run automatically. If you look at the build output once we're done setting it up, you'll notice that the API_ LEVEL is made available to the Ant build script as a Java system property via the -D flag.

Speaking of the Ant build script, there's one more thing left to do. Similar to what we discussed with the Android emulator configuration, we must tell Ant which emulator instance to execute the build script against. By default, the ADB targets whichever device is currently running, and will fail if there's more than one. In the case of several emulators, you must specify the specific emulator you'd like to target using the -s flag. We don't directly invoke ADB (after all the Ant script performs the build), so we must tunnel this argument to ADB through the Ant invocation. You can do that using the adb.device.arg system property. Figure 14.20 shows the updated Ant invocation setting for our matrix build.

If you're curious, ANDROID_AVD_DEVICE isn't the only variable exported by the Android emulator plugin. You can also access the emulator's ADB and control ports through the ANDROID_AVD_ADB_PORT and ANDROID_AVD_USER_PORT variables respectively. The latter is particularly useful if your build includes build steps that involve a telnet connection to dispatch emulator commands such as mock GPS fixes (see appendix A).

We're all set now; let's save the job settings and trigger a build. The job screen has slightly changed now and displays a matrix of configurations, with each corresponding to a sub-build that you can click through (see figure 14.21).

DISCUSSION

We need not mention that matrix builds are a powerful way of automating your builds. You should be aware that this also comes at a cost: Running many emulator instances in parallel will consume a lot of system resources, and builds will take significantly longer to execute. Make sure that your build server is strong enough to handle a matrix build. A multicore machine with plenty of RAM is highly recommended; otherwise builds may fail when the Android plugin times out while waiting for an emulator to fully boot.

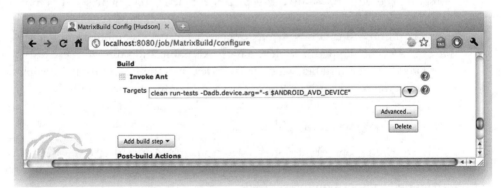

Figure 14.20 For the Ant invocation to work, we must make the specific emulator that runs the current matrix configuration available through a variable. The Android emulator plugin exports the emulator's serial number through the ANDROID_AVD_DEVICE variable, which can be passed to Ant's internal ADB task using the adb.device.arg property.

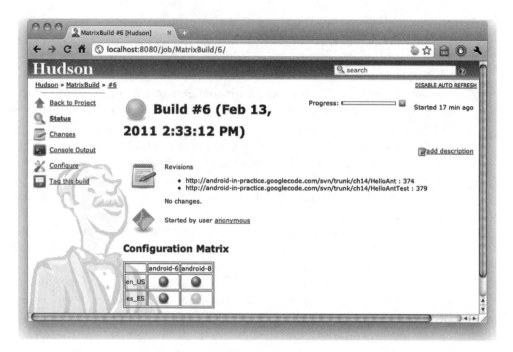

Figure 14.21   A matrix build job aggregates every subbuild in a table corresponding to the configuration matrix. The bubbles can be clicked to reach a specific subbuild.

Another thing that shouldn't be left unmentioned is sparse configuration matrixes. You may have already realized that if the number of axes and values increases, the total number of combinations will explode. Often there are combinations that don't warrant a separate build execution, and sometimes they may not even make sense. Consider, for instance, the case of having an SD versus not having one: if SD card is one axis, and language another, you don't need to rerun a build for every language and SD/no-SD combination, because they don't affect each other. Hence, matrix jobs support sparse configuration by ticking the Combination Filter check box. Here, you can enter Boolean conditions using Groovy syntax (a Java dialect); any combination that will evaluate to `false` will be skipped. You can include axis name and values in these tests, as well as the special `index` variable, which is an index into the matrix itself. To stick with our example, you could have the "no SD card" build only run once for the English language by setting a filter like this (given the two axes `SD_CARD` and `LOCALE`):

```
SD_CARD == "false" && LOCALE == "en_US"
```

This concludes our discussion on Hudson and Android. We've covered a lot of ground again with this chapter, so let's quickly summarize what you should've learned about build automation for Android.

14.4 Summary

Unlike previous chapters, you had to wade through a lot of configuration code in this chapter, and we couldn't even reward you with neat looking application screenshots! Setting up build scripts or configuring a Hudson job may not be the most enjoyable task, but we hope you agree that it was well-invested time. Let's do a short retrospective at what we achieved with the techniques in this chapter, and how.

We started out by fundamentally questioning the way we build Android applications: we quickly realized that in order to get more control of the build and a higher degree of automation, we need to step away from purely visual build environments such as Eclipse, and turn to programmatic build systems such as Ant and Maven. With a system in place that can take our project source code and assemble an APK from it solely using the command shell, we could make another leap forward by leveraging build servers such as Hudson, which can connect to our source code management systems and automatically trigger a build, including execution of the test suite, in reaction to a commit. In other words, you've seen the full range of Android build automation.

We've almost reached the end of this book. Almost! We have one more chapter up our sleeves, one that will take you yet again into something completely new. If you've followed the hype lately, then you'll have come across one particular term frequently: tablet computers! With the release of Android 3.0, aka Honeycomb, Google has added native support for tablet devices, including a completely revamped user interface and a slew of new APIs. With chapter 15, we'd like to give you an overview of what's special about Honeycomb, how developing for tablets differs from developing for ordinary smartphones, and show you the new APIs that you should know by heart.

15

Developing
for Android tablets

Everything is getting bigger. The way to go now is to program in a little more sophisticantion.

—Bill Budge

The year was 2001. Microsoft was the largest technology company in the world and they had debuted their biggest advancement to their ubiquitous operating system: Windows XP Tablet PC Edition. Touch-based computing had arrived, they claimed. We know how that turned out: XP Tablet PC Edition flopped.

In reality, XP Tablet wasn't the first attempt to bring touch-based computing to a mass market. A decade earlier engineers at Apple developed a prototype to what would one day become the Newton. It was eerily similar to those Tablet PCs that Microsoft would tout 10 years later. That variant of the Newton never saw the light of day, and instead the Newton became the forerunner to the PDA.

To say that touch-based computing was "the next big thing" for years is an understatement. One can argue that the reason these earlier attempts failed was that they tried to evolve the PC into a tablet. Two decades after the Newton-tablet prototype, it became obvious that the smartphone was the natural device for touch-base computing, and the logical ancestor to the tablet. This was the formula for Apple's iPad and for Android on tablets. The Android 3.0 Honeycomb release marked a radically new version of Android, designed with tablets in mind. So what does this mean for you, the Android developer?

If you already have an app or two on the Android Market, the immediate question to answer is "What should I do for tablets?" Truth be told, the number of tablet users out there will be far less the number of phone users. It takes awhile for a new paradigm such as tablet computing to take hold, whereas there are already millions of smartphone users. It's likely that you'll get much more return on your efforts by continuing to invest in Android application development targeting smartphones instead of tablets. This equation holds even truer for brand-new applications. You'll be able to reach a much larger audience by focusing on smartphone application development.

There are exceptions to this advice. Certain types of applications are a more natural fit for tablets than for smartphones. For example, apps that have lots of rich content to show such as newsreaders, social networking, and shopping apps will greatly benefit from all of that extra space. What might've been two or three screens of related content on a smartphone can become a single engaging screen on a tablet. Even for other types of applications, there are significant advantages to being an early mover on the Android Market. Your application can become established with little competition, putting it in a prime position as more users buy tablets and hit the Market looking for great apps to install.

Whether you're an early adopter or not, at some point you'll make the decision that it's time to create a tablet application, or you probably wouldn't be reading this chapter! In this chapter, we'll expand on the DealDroid application from chapter 2 and create a tablet application. Figure 15.1 shows you what the finished product looks like.

Figure 15.1 The DealDroid application reimaged on a tablet

Deciding to create a tablet application isn't a gradual decision; it'll be a distinct decision to start developing for tablets. This can be an exciting prospect, as many more possibilities are open to developers on a tablet compared to a smartphone. Many of the familiar constraints around screen space, memory, supporting old versions of Android, and network speeds are less of a problem on a tablet. But before you start tossing around `Fragments` full of `StackViews`, you might take inventory of what you already have in terms of Android development and figure out how to proceed from there.

15.1   Tablet prep

Tablet development isn't a matter of using some different APIs and incorporating larger artwork. You need to decide whether you want to create a separate application or expand an existing smartphone application that also works well on a tablet. In this chapter, we'll focus on the separate application route. This will allow us to take advantage of everything in Android 3.0. It's possible to leverage all or most of the techniques in this chapter while going the universal application path.

TECHNIQUE 87   **Leveraging existing code using library projects**

Because you're creating a separate application aimed squarely at Android tablets doesn't imply that your application will be completely different from what you've already created for smartphones. The applications will share a lot of functionality. In fact, they'll probably manage much of the same data. That could be data that's local to the device, or data that's stored and retrieved to a server in the cloud. The way that you access such data, and even the way that you organize it once you've loaded it into local memory will probably be the same as it was on a smartphone. Fortunately, there's a smart way to share code between Android applications.

PROBLEM

You want your new tablet application to share code with your existing smartphone application. You want there to be only one copy of this code, so you have one place to add new code, fix bugs, and so on.

SOLUTION

The key to sharing code between Android applications is to use Android library projects. This is a useful way to organize your code that was introduced at the same time as Android 2.2. It's not specific to tablets and Android 3.0; you can use library projects to share code between multiple smartphone applications as well. The smartphone-plus-tablet application use case is a perfect fit for library projects.

As we've already mentioned, library projects were introduced at the same time as Android 2.2. But they were retrofitted to even earlier versions of Android. There's a chance that you already have your code organized with them and will be able to immediately take advantage of them and start developing a tablet application that leverages your existing smartphone codebase. In that case, you can skip ahead to the next technique. Otherwise, you'll probably need to do some refactoring and reorganizing of your code.

For our tablet application, we'll bring the DealDroid application first introduced in chapter 2 to the tablet. All of the code for DealDroid was in a single Android project. We'll need to do some reorganization of this. Figure 15.2 shows how we've reorganized the code so that it can be shared with our new tablet application project.

In figure 15.2 you can see the DealsLib project and the TabletDeals project. DealsLib is our Android library project that will contain the code shared between our smartphone and tablet applications. TabletDeals is our tablet application project. We'll explore it in great detail throughout this chapter. You can see what code was placed in the library project. All of the code for retrieving and parsing data from the Internet (in the `com.manning.aip.dealdroid.xml` package) was moved to the library. There's no reason for this code to be any different on a tablet than it was on a smartphone. When XML data is parsed, the resulting model objects (in the `com.manning.aip.dealdroid.model` package) are used by the application, so these are also part of the library.

We also see several classes in the top-level package (`com.manning.aip.dealdroid`). The most interesting of these is the `DealsApp` class, which is the `Application` object for both apps. This contains a cache of data as well as the state of the application. This could've been different for the tablet application, but in this case it wasn't. So it made sense to share it between the smartphone and tablet.

Figure 15.2   Code organized for sharing with a tablet application

Finally, some resources are shared between the applications. Notably `strings.xml` and `plurals.xml` are shared. Other resources such as drawables could be shared as well.

DISCUSSION

Library projects are a powerful tool. This feature was highly requested by developers, especially those who had started writing suites of applications with lots of code shared between various applications. Often, this common code was network access and data model code, similar to our use case. Another common use case was code for authenticating a user, and then managing the resulting identity materials (tokens for authentication and/or authorization). Often this code included some UI, since you usually want to standardize what users see when they log in to your application. There's no problem with this, as you can include activities, layout XML, and more in a library project. Your library project must also have an `AndroidManifext.xml` file. You can declare activities, services, and so forth as you would in any other manifest. But, if an application is using a library project and it wants to use an `Activity` from the library project (or any other component from the library project that must be declared in the manifest), then it must still declare that `Activity` in its own `AndroidManifest.xml` file. The manifest of a library project acts more like a menu of components that you can choose from and then declare in your application's manifest file.

There are other ways to share code between projects. If you're using Eclipse (or Ant or Maven or anything else that provides dependency management), then you can roll your own library that's a collection of Java code. Your application will then depend on this other project. It could still be a source-level dependency, or a binary-level dependency where you'd compile the library project first, and maybe even package it into a JAR. The only tricky part is making sure the library code doesn't use any standard Java classes that aren't allowed in Android, and having it depend on the appropriate `android.jar`. These are both handled for you if you use an Android library project.

The other main benefit of an Android library project over the usual Java library is resource management. In our example, we're including a common `strings.xml` file. Doing so allows this file to be shared by both the smartphone and tablet versions of the application. You can also override a particular string or add extra strings by having a different `strings.xml` file in the application project. The compiler will merge the resources. This is also true for other resources like styles and `drawables`, and even layout files.

Now that we have a smart way to organize our code and share it between our smartphone and tablet applications, we can start thinking about our tablet application in more detail. As we mentioned earlier, we'll take the approach of creating an application that's only meant for tablets. We won't try to create an application that works equally well on smartphones and tablets. Fortunately, that's easy and it yields some excellent benefits.

TECHNIQUE 88   **Targeting only tablets**

Fragmentation used to be a dirty word to Android developers. The term was usually used by anti-Android pundits to claim that the Android platform was too difficult to develop for because you had to support devices with different screen sizes, and so forth.

But this was a hidden strength of Android. The "right" way to develop forced you to not make assumptions about the screen size and geometry. You were given plenty of tools to approach application design with a flexible layout in mind. So as new devices came out with 4 and 4.3 inch screens, or with smaller 2.5 inch screens, most apps worked. Even when the first tablets came out with 7 inch screens and running Android 2.2, most apps (though not all; some developers chose not to follow best practices and made unfortunate assumptions about screen size when creating their layouts) worked with no problems. This was a great selling point for these small tablets. They came to market with a huge number of apps ready to run beautifully on them.

But as larger tablets were being readied, there became some obvious advantages to designing the OS for these large tablets. This was the concept behind Android 3.0. The platform contains all of the ingredients for making applications work equally well on smartphones and tablets, but it now also allows tablet-only applications to shine. In order to do this, you must exclude devices that your tablet application isn't designed to run on.

PROBLEM

You're writing a tablet-only application. You want to take advantage of all of the platform capabilities available on tablets, and you want to take advantage of the larger screen. You don't want to adapt your application to smaller screens, regardless of what version of Android these devices are running.

SOLUTION

You may have already guessed at the solution here. We can use our `AndroidManifest.xml` file to specify all of the requirements we need for our application to work. Then the Android Market's application filters will make sure that our application won't show up for users who don't have a tablet. The next listing shows the relevant part of our manifest.

Listing 15.1 Target only tablets with the manifest

```xml
<?xml version="1.0" encoding="utf-8"?>
<manifest xmlns:android="http://schemas.android.com/apk/res/android"
    package="com.manning.aip.tabdroid"
    android:versionCode="1"
    android:versionName="1.0">
    <uses-sdk android:minSdkVersion="11" />          ❶ Require
                                                        Android 3.0+
    <supports-screens android:smallScreens="false"
        android:normalScreens="false"
        android:largeScreens="false"                 ❷ Only support
        android:xlargeScreens="true" />                 xlarge screens

</manifest>
```

For our application to only target tablets, we need to require and specify two basic things in the manifest. First, the device must be running Android 3.0 (Honeycomb) or higher ❶. Now you might be tempted to stop here. After all, as long as we have API level 11 (Android 3.0) or higher, we'll have access to all of the APIs that we'll use in the code shown in this application. But though Android 3.0 was the latest version of Android and only available on tablets at the time this book was written, there's a good chance that there is already (or will be soon) a newer version of Android that incorporates everything in Android 3.0, but works on both smartphones and tablets. We need to also specify that we only support xlarge screens ❷. This screen size was introduced with Android 2.3. It translates to screens that are at least seven inches. With these two requirements specified in your manifest, you can now be sure that any device that runs your app is a tablet with all of the optimized-for-tablet APIs introduced in Honeycomb.

Finally, one more aspect of tablet development should be mentioned. When you're developing for a smartphone, you probably assume the user will have the device in portrait mode most or all of the time. Fortunately, the OS handles orientation changes in a reasonable way, so even if you forget about landscape mode completely, your application probably works decently when the user rotates the device. It's a good idea to think about landscape mode as well, and sometimes you'll even want to create different layouts for landscape. The Android convention is to create a layout-land folder and put the optimized layout XML files there. On the other hand, you might decide not to support landscape at all and only support portrait. There are some advantages to this, though it may not please users with side-sliding keyboards.

A tablet is a different beast than a smartphone, and orientation is one place where they differ greatly. The usual orientation of a tablet is landscape, not portrait. So it's convention to put landscape-oriented layout files in the /res/layout folder and create a /res/layout-port for portrait layouts. If you're using the ADT plugin for Eclipse, its UI builder can help you get a feel for tablet development. Figure 15.3 shows an example of this.

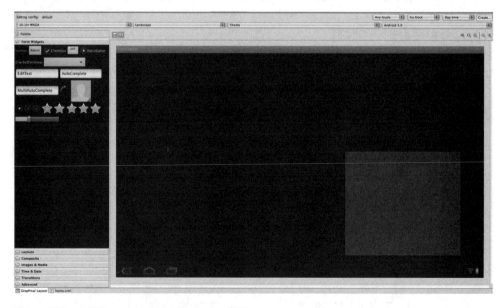

Figure 15.3 Building a tablet interface using ADT

DISCUSSION

In many ways, the approach outlined here is different from your typical Android development. Usually, you want to support as many different screen sizes as possible. Here, we're excluding all screen sizes except one. When the first wave of Android tablets running Honeycomb came out, not only did they all have similar dimensions, they had the same screen resolution: 1280x800. This presented an interesting situation for Android developers who were accustomed to developing for a range of screen sizes and resolutions. Not since the days of the G1 could your application target a single screen geometry (not quite uniform, since the physical sizes were slightly different.) But you shouldn't be tempted into dredging up the deprecated `AbsoluteLayout` or start using physical pixels for sizes within a layout.

With library projects, the latest APIs, and large layouts at our fingertips, we're ready to start developing for Android tablets. We'll start with the fundamental techniques that the developer of any tablet application should have in their arsenal. We'll also see how these techniques aren't applicable to tablets and can easily make their way back into smartphone development as well.

15.2 Tablet fundamentals

Long before Android 3.0 was released, there were Android-powered tablets. These were typically smaller than the early Honeycomb tablets, with screen sizes ranging from five to seven inches. These mini-tablets were interesting in their own right. As mentioned earlier, most Android applications ran well on them. Some looked quite good in fact, thanks to the extra space. Still, you could only describe them as adequate. It's a testament to Android that you can stretch things out without creating a horrible user experience.

Android 3.0 was designed to be far more than adequate. It didn't take the approach of getting Android to work properly on a bigger screen. It didn't bolt on extra UI components. It provided more fundamental changes to help the developer with the task of developing effectively for large screens. We'll start our examination of the essential techniques for tablet development by looking at one of the most fundamental concepts introduced in Honeycomb: `Fragments`.

> **TECHNIQUE 89** **Fragments**

Earlier, we talked about how Android 3.0 had was designed for tablets; it wasn't extra stuff bolted on top of an earlier version of Android. One key feature that demonstrates this is the `Fragment` API. This represents a new way to organize your application code that makes it much easier to handle the layout challenges created by the large screens of Android tablets. But as we'll see, the usefulness of this feature isn't limited to tablet applications.

PROBLEM

You need to modularize your application code so that it can use significantly different layouts in landscape and portrait orientations without having to duplicate code and functionality.

SOLUTION

The solution is to use Fragments to organize your code. Having different layouts for landscape and portrait orientations isn't a new thing. What makes it different on tablets is the amount of screen space you have. On a smaller-screened smartphone, it's common for the landscape and portrait layouts to have the same content and functionality. Going from one orientation to the other causes everything to be rearranged in some sensible manner. On a tablet, it's not unusual to have entirely different components on the screen depending on the layout. Let's look at a more concrete example.

Recall that our DealDroid application (see chapter 2) allowed the user to view eBay's Daily Deals. One Activity in the application showed a list of deals, while another showed the details of the deal. With a tablet, we have enough space to show all of this information in a single Activity, but only in landscape orientation. Figure 15.4 shows an example of this.

This UI pattern of showing a scrollable list on the left side of the screen with details about an individual entry of that list on the right side is common in application development for tablets. Figure 15.5 shows how tapping on an item from the list changes what's shown in the large detail area.

Going back to our problem statement of showing different components depending on the orientation of the tablet, figure 15.6 shows what happens if we rotate the tablet into a portrait orientation.

If you compare figures 15.4 and 15.5, you see that the main details part of the Activity is similar in both landscape and portrait orientations. The kinds of differences

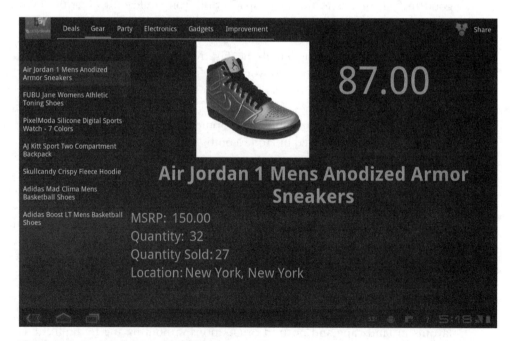

Figure 15.4   Deals list and details in landscape

Figure 15.5   Browsing items from the deals list

**Figure 15.6   Deals list
and details in portrait**

shown are similar to those we're accustomed to in smartphone applications. But the deals lists are completely different. This is what we meant by "significantly different layouts" in our problem statement. This would be an unusual phenomenon in a smartphone application, but it's par for the course in a tablet application.

The key to producing this kind of applications is to use Fragments. They allow us to modularize the UI components we've seen. The following listing contains the layout for figure 15.4.

Listing 15.2   Deals details layout XML (`/res/layout/details.xml`)

```
<?xml version="1.0" encoding="utf-8"?>
<LinearLayout xmlns:android="http://schemas.android.com/apk/res/android"
    android:orientation="horizontal"
    android:layout_width="match_parent"
    android:layout_height="match_parent"
    android:id="@+id/details_container">

    <fragment
       class="com.manning.aip.tabdroid.SectionDetailsFragment"
          android:id="@+id/section_list_fragment"
          android:visibility="gone"
          android:layout_marginTop="?android:attr/actionBarSize"
          android:layout_width="300dp"
          android:layout_height="match_parent" />

    <fragment class="com.manning.aip.tabdroid.DealFragment"
          android:id="@+id/deal_fragment"
          android:layout_width="match_parent"
          android:layout_height="match_parent" />

</LinearLayout>
```

❶ Fragment for list of deals

❷ Fragment for details of deal

Hopefully, it's reassuring to see how simple the layout file is for the details view in our application. It's a pair of Fragments. The first Fragment ❶ shows the list of deals on the right side of the screen. The second Fragment ❷ shows the details of the currently selected Fragment. The first Fragment is in the next listing.

Listing 15.3   Fragment for displaying a list of deals (SectionDetailsFragment.java)

```
public class SectionDetailsFragment extends ListFragment {
    Section section;
    int currentPosition = 0;
    DealsApp app;
    @Override
    public void onCreate(Bundle savedInstanceState){
        super.onCreate(savedInstanceState);
        app = (DealsApp) this.getActivity().getApplication();
        section = app.currentSection;

        if (savedInstanceState != null){
            currentPosition = savedInstanceState.getInt("currentPosition");
            int savedSectionPos =
                savedInstanceState.getInt("currentSection", -1);
            if (savedSectionPos >= 0){
```

❶ Declare Fragment as subclass of ListFragment

❷ Set up/restore Fragment state

```
            section = app.sectionList.get(savedSectionPos);
            app.currentSection = section;
        }
    } else if (app.currentItem != null){
        for (int i=0;i<section.items.size();i++){
            if (app.currentItem.equals(section.items.get(i))){
                currentPosition = i;
                break;
            }
        }
    }
}
@Override
public void onActivityCreated(Bundle savedInstanceState) {
    super.onActivityCreated(savedInstanceState);
    buildUi();
}
private void buildUi(){
    ListView listView = this.getListView();
    listView.setChoiceMode(ListView.CHOICE_MODE_SINGLE);
    String[] dealTitles = new String[section.items.size()];
    int i = 0;
    for (Item item : section.items){
        dealTitles[i++] = item.title;
    }
    setListAdapter(new ArrayAdapter<String>(getActivity(),
        R.layout.deal_title_list_entry, dealTitles));
    listView.setSelection(currentPosition);
    showDeal(currentPosition);
}
}
```

Build UI when ❸
Activity is created

❹ Get built-in
ListView

Create Adapter
❺ for ListView

Creating a Fragment is as simple as extending android.app.Fragment. In this case, ❶ we extend ListFragment, which is a subclass of Fragment. A ListFragment contains a single ListView and is commonly used for lists of items viewed in a split screen layout, as shown in figure 15.4. A Fragment has its own lifecycle that's tied to the lifecycle of the Activity that hosts it. The host Activity will ask the Fragment for its View by invoking the Fragment's onCreateView method. We don't have to worry about this for a ListFragment, as the superclass returns the ListFragment's ListView for us. Instead, we focus on two other lifecycle methods. The onCreate ❷ method is called right after the Activity's onCreate method is called, but before the Fragment's onCreateView method is invoked. Here, we choose to restore or set up the state of the Fragment, as you would for an Activity. Some time after the Fragment's onCreate-View is invoked, its onActivityCreated ❸ method will be invoked. As the name suggests, this happens after the Activity is created. This is where we perform all our setup for the ListView ❹ that's part of our ListFragment. It's like any other List-View so we need to provide it with a ListAdapter ❺ that provides the data and the layout of the items in the ListView.

Note that the last thing we do in the setup of the ListFragment's UI is to invoke its showDeal method. This is a method for showing a particular deal in the main deals

Fragment. As such, we also want to invoke this when an item in the list is tapped. The following listing shows the code for showing deals and tapping items.

Listing 15.4   Showing a particular deal (from SectionDetailsFragment.java)

```
@Override
public void onListItemClick(ListView l, View v, int position, long id) {
    this.currentPosition = position;                    ◁──┐   Update state and
    showDeal(position);                                    ❶  show selected deal
}

private void showDeal(int position){
    app.currentItem = app.currentSection.items.get(position);
    DealFragment fragment =
        (DealFragment) getFragmentManager().findFragmentById(    ❷  Get handle on
            R.id.deal_fragment);                           ◁──┘      DealFragment
    fragment.showCurrentItem();      ◁──❸  Invoke Fragment's method
}
```

One of the conveniences of using a ListFragment is that we only need to override its onListItemClick method to handle items from the list being tapped on. In this case, we keep track ❶ of the currently selected item in the list. Then, we invoke the same showDeal method mentioned in listing 15.3. We want to tell our other Fragment to display a different deal, so we need to get a handle ❷ on that Fragment. To do this, we use the FragmentManager instance that's available in any Fragment. If you look back at listing 15.2, you can see that we gave the Fragment an ID that we can now use to get a handle on it. Once we have a handle on it, we invoke its showCurrentItem ❸ method to tell it to redraw itself. The following listing shows this method and the rest of the DealFragment.

Listing 15.5   Fragment for displaying a deal (DealFragment.java)

```
public class DealFragment extends Fragment {        ◁──┐   Extend
    DealsApp app;                                      ❶  android.app.Fragment
    private ProgressBar progressBar;
    @Override
    public View onCreateView(LayoutInflater inflater,
        ViewGroup container,
        Bundle savedInstanceState) {                    ❷  Create view and
                                                   ◁──┘      return it to Activity
        app = (DealsApp) getActivity().getApplication();
        View dealView = inflater.inflate(R.layout.deal_details,
            container,                                  ❸  Inflate
            false);                                ◁──┘     layout XML
        progressBar = (ProgressBar) dealView.findViewById(R.id.progress);
        progressBar.setIndeterminate(true);
        Item item = app.currentItem;
        if (item != null) {
            populateDealView(dealView, item);
        }
        return dealView;
    }                                                   ❹  Bind data
    private void populateDealView(View dealView, Item item) {  ◁──┘   to layout
```

```
        ImageView icon = (ImageView) dealView.findViewById(
            R.id.details_icon);
        icon.setImageResource(R.drawable.placeholder);
        new RetrieveImageTask(icon).execute(item.picUrl);
        TextView title =
            (TextView) dealView.findViewById(R.id.details_title);
        title.setText(item.title);
        CharSequence pricePrefix =
            getText(R.string.deal_details_price_prefix);
        TextView price =
            (TextView) dealView.findViewById(R.id.details_price);
        price.setText(pricePrefix + item.convertedCurrentPrice);
        TextView msrp = (TextView) dealView.findViewById(
            R.id.details_msrp);
        msrp.setText(item.msrp);
        TextView quantity =
            (TextView) dealView.findViewById(R.id.details_quantity);
        quantity.setText(Integer.toString(item.quantity));
        TextView quantitySold = (TextView) dealView.findViewById(
            R.id.details_quantity_sold);
        quantitySold.setText(Integer.toString(item.quantitySold));
        TextView location =
            (TextView) dealView.findViewById(R.id.details_location);
        location.setText(item.location);
    }
    public void showCurrentItem(){
        Item item = app.currentItem;
        View dealView = getView();
        populateDealView(dealView, item);
    }
}
```

❺ Get current item and bind to UI

This is another example of a Fragment. This time we directly subclass ❶ the Fragment
class. We don't have to worry about managing the state of this Fragment, since it's tied
to the state of the Activity (and the ListFragment in listing 15.3). So we only override ❷ its onCreateView method. Note that this callback method gets a Layout-
Inflater passed into it. We take advantage of this by using it to inflate a layout XML file
for this view ❸. Then we need to bind ❹ the data from the currently selected deal to
the widgets in the layout XML. Finally, we expose the aforementioned showCurrentItem
method, so that other Fragments can invoke it. This method checks what the currently
selected item is and passes it to the same populateDealView that we used earlier ❺.

When the orientation of the tablet changes and we go into portrait mode, we want
to show a different layout, as seen in figure 15.6. The most straightforward way to
show a different layout is to have a different layout XML. The portrait layout XML is in
the following listing.

Listing 15.6 Layout for portrait orientation (/res/layout-port/details.xml)

```
<?xml version="1.0" encoding="utf-8"?>
<LinearLayout xmlns:android="http://schemas.android.com/apk/res/android"
    android:orientation="vertical"
    android:layout_width="match_parent"
```

```
      android:layout_height="match_parent"
      android:id="@+id/details_container"
      android:gravity="bottom">

   <fragment class="com.manning.aip.tabdroid.DealFragment"
      android:id="@+id/deal_fragment"
      android:layout_marginTop="?android:attr/actionBarSize"
      android:layout_width="match_parent"
      android:layout_height="wrap_content"
   />

   <fragment class="com.manning.aip.tabdroid.FilmstripFragment"
      android:id="@+id/section_filmstrip_fragment"
      android:layout_width="match_parent"
      android:layout_height="300dp"
      android:layout_gravity="bottom"
   />
</LinearLayout>
```

1 Use same DealFragment

2 Put new FilmstripFragment at bottom

The code in listing 15.6 isn't much different from the code in listing 15.2. It reuses **1** the same Fragment that we looked at, the DealFragment. Reuse is part of the point of Fragments. Note that we haven't shown the code for the Activity that hosts these Fragments. There's been no need. The Fragments are self-contained. For our portrait orientation we've replaced the SectionDetailsFragment with the **2** FilmstripFragment. The next listing contains the code.

Listing 15.7   Filmstrip of deal images used for selecting a deal (FilmstripFragment.java)

```
public class FilmstripFragment extends Fragment {
   @Override
   public void onCreate(Bundle savedInstanceState){
      super.onCreate(savedInstanceState);
      // manage state code omitted
   }
   @Override
   public View onCreateView(LayoutInflater inflater,
         ViewGroup container,
         Bundle savedInstanceState){
      HorizontalScrollView strip =
         (HorizontalScrollView) inflater.inflate(R.layout.filmstrip,
            container,
            false);
      fillWithPics(strip);
      return strip;
   }
   private void fillWithPics(HorizontalScrollView strip) {
      ViewGroup pics = (ViewGroup) strip.findViewById(R.id.pics);
      if (pics.getChildCount() > 0){
         pics.removeAllViews();
      }
      int i =0;
      for (Item item : section.items){
         ImageView imgView = new ImageView(getActivity());
         // code for getting image bitmap
```

1 Manage state

2 Inflate layout

3 Bind images to widgets

```
        imgView.setOnClickListener(new OnClickListener(){
          @Override
          public void onClick(View img) {                    ④ Set event
              currentPosition = pos;                            handler
              showDeal(pos);
          }
        });
    }
    showDeal(currentPosition);
}
  private void showDeal(int position){
    app.currentItem = app.currentSection.items.get(position);
    DealFragment fragment = (DealFragment) getFragmentManager()
      .findFragmentById(R.id.deal_fragment);
    fragment.showCurrentItem();                    ⎤  Invoke method on
  }                                                ⑤  DealFragment
}
```

The `FilmstripFragment` has some similarities to the `SectionDetailsFragment` from listing 15.3. They both display all of the deals in a given section and allow you to tap on a deal to change the deal's details shown by the `DealFragment` component. We follow a similar pattern to the other `Fragments`. We start by ❶ restoring state in the `onCreate` method. Then we implement ❷ the `onCreateView` method, inflating a layout XML into a `View` to return. This time we don't have a `ListView`, but a *filmstrip*–a horizontally scrolling set of images (it is a `HorizontalScrollView`; see `/res/layout-port/ filmstrip.xml`). All we need to do is populate it ❸ with `ImageViews` backed by a bitmap of the image of a deal. For each `ImageView`, we need to set an event handler ❹ for when the user taps on the image. When this happens, we once again use the `Fragment- Manager` API to get a handle on the `DealFragment` and then invoke its `showCurrentItem` method ❺.

DISCUSSION

`Fragments` provide a new way to organize application code. A `Fragment` can be self-sufficient in most regards. It manages the data that it displays and takes care of its own state. The `Fragments` shown in our examples also have a dependency on the global state of the application—the `Application` object for app. These `Fragments` could be used anywhere within our tablet app, but not outside of it. This is an intentional design decision. Alternatively, you could create `Fragments` that depend on a `Service` or `Fragments` that depend on nothing at all.

Developers were using this kind of pattern in Android well before `Fragments` were introduced. There was nothing in the Android framework to make it easy. One common pattern is to have UI components that can manage state, retrieve data, and so on. A variation of that pattern is to have the UI components interact directly with a `Ser- vice` that takes care of the heavy lifting. Though some might argue that such patterns are to be avoided, as they break the model-view-controller paradigm, they often prove valuable. Consider having a common header bar that displays some stateful information, such as the number of unread messages or new daily deals. Prior to `Fragments`, the other common alternative to mixing model code with a UI component was to have some subclass of `Activity` that managed the state. This base `Activity` would then be subclassed by all of the activities in the application. Again, there are pros and cons to these alternatives, but `Fragments` tend to be a much cleaner technique to use than any of these other approaches.

Another popular use case for the base `Activity` pattern is for handling menus. The base `Activity` can create a menu that can then show up on all activities. One common reason for this application-level menu is because the menu is often of little value to the developer. If you put anything important in the menu, then you have to put it somewhere else "on the screen" as users often don't use the menus. Hence the relegation of common utilities (such as About the App, Customer Support, Sign Out, and so forth) in the menu. Honeycomb introduces a much better alternative to the menu, the Action Bar. Our next technique is about how and when to use the Action Bar.

TECHNIQUE 90   The Action Bar

The menu concept in Android has a lot of merit. You could put many shortcuts and useful things in the menu. You could also put many contextual things in the menu. The big problem is that users may never look in the menu. The Action Bar is an evolution of the menu idea. It has many of the same use cases, but it's more effective to use because it's more visible to the end user.

PROBLEM

You want to show extra but useful functions that are contextual to the `Activity` the user is interacting with. You don't want to use the standard menu features of Android because of their usability issues.

SOLUTION

The solution is to use the Action Bar. It's located at the top of the screen, it's highly visible to the user. This solves the biggest problem of the menu system. Figure 15.7 shows an example of the Action Bar in our tablet application.

As you can see in the figure, the Action Bar is the top bar on the screen. In our example, it shows the icon of our app, several tabs, and a share button. The application icon allows the user to navigate back to the application's home screen. The tabs allow the user to change which section of eBay Daily Deals they're viewing. As figure 15.8 shows,

Figure 15.7   The Action bar in action!

Figure 15.8   Sharing a deal on the tablet

the Share button allows them to share the deal they're looking at using other applications installed on their device.

If you recall the original DealDroid application, the sharing feature was hidden away in the menu. But that application's navigation was much more limited than what we now have on the tablet edition. The Action Bar not only solves the menu problem, but it can do much more. We'll take a look at the navigation tabs shortly, but we'll start with the application and share icons on the Action Bar. Here's the code behind these features.

Listing 15.8   Action Bar app and share icons (from DetailsActivity.java)

```
@Override
public boolean onCreateOptionsMenu(Menu menu) {
    MenuInflater inflater = getMenuInflater();              ❶ Load menu
    inflater.inflate(R.menu.details_menu, menu);               data from XML
    return true;
}

@Override
public boolean onOptionsItemSelected(MenuItem item) {
    switch (item.getItemId()) {                             ❷ Menu item is
        case android.R.id.home:                                canonical home value
            Intent intent = new Intent(this, DealsMain.class);
            intent.addFlags(Intent.FLAG_ACTIVITY_CLEAR_TOP);
            startActivity(intent);                         ❸ Start home
            return true;                                       activity
```

```
        case R.id.share_action:
            shareDealUsingChooser("text/*");
            return true;
        default:
            return super.onOptionsItemSelected(item);
    }
}
```

                                                    ⟵ ❹ Menu item ID is
                                                        share_action from XML

```
private void shareDealUsingChooser(final String type) {
// omitted for brevity, same as in chapter 2
    }
private String createDealMessage() {
// omitted for brevity
    }
```

As you can see from figure 15.8, the Action Bar shows its roots as a menu. To create it, you implement the Activity's ❶ onCreateOptionsMenu lifecycle callback method. You could programmatically create the items on the Action Bar, especially if these elements depend on the state of the Activity. If not, you can use XML to specify what should be in the menu. Here's the XML for the Action Bar seen in figure 15.7:

```
<menu xmlns:android="http://schemas.android.com/apk/res/android">
   <item android:id="@+id/share_action"
       android:title="@string/deal_details_share_menu"
       android:icon="@drawable/ic_menu_share"
       android:showAsAction="ifRoom|withText" />
</menu>
```

As you can see, it specifies a single item, along with its title and its icon. In our example, both of these are externalized resources, so they could also be localized. Also note that we set the showAsAction attribute. This was introduced in Android 3.0 and gives you options on when to display the menu item as an action and how to display it. You can set this to always, but things could get messy if there isn't enough room.

Going back to listing 15.8, we define the behavior of the Action Bar (what happens when the user taps on items on it) by implementing the Activity's onOptionsItem-Selected method. This is also how we respond to the user tapping on the application icon ❷ in the left corner of the Action Bar. We identify this using the predefined resource ID home and then respond to it by clearing the Activity stack and ❸ sending the user to the home screen. Similarly, we identify tapping on the Share button by matching the ID defined in the menu XML against the ID of the selected MenuItem ❹. In this case, we invoke the shareDealUsingChooser method—the same as the one used in the DealDroid application seen in chapter 2. This will bring up the UI shown in figure 15.8.

Going back to the Action Bar, we've now defined how to create the icons on it and how to give them behavior. Now let's look at how we created the tabs seen in figure 15.7. The next listing shows this code.

Listing 15.9   Creating and managing Action Bar tabs (from DetailsActivity.java)

```
public void onCreate(Bundle savedInstanceState) {
    super.onCreate(savedInstanceState);
    setContentView(R.layout.details);
```

```
        app = (DealsApp) getApplication();                              ❶ Get ActionBar
        ActionBar bar = this.getActionBar();                                for this Activity
        TabListener listener = new TabListener(){
            @Override
            public void onTabReselected(Tab t, FragmentTransaction txn) {}
            @Override
            public void onTabSelected(Tab t, FragmentTransaction txn) {
                if (active){
                    changeTab(t.getPosition());                    Change tab based
                }                                             ❷ on selection
            }
            @Override
            public void onTabUnselected(Tab t, FragmentTransaction txn) {}
        };
        for (int i=0;i<Math.min(6, app.sectionList.size());i++){
            final Section section = app.sectionList.get(i);            ❸ Create
            Tab tab = bar.newTab();                                        new Tab
            tab.setText(chomp(section.title));
            tab.setTabListener(listener);                       Wire event
            if (app.currentSection != null &&                 ❹ listener to Tab
                    app.currentSection.equals(section)){
                bar.addTab(tab, true);
            } else {
                bar.addTab(tab);
            }
        }
        bar.setDisplayShowTitleEnabled(false);
        bar.setNavigationMode(ActionBar.NAVIGATION_MODE_TABS);
        active = true;
    }
    private void changeTab(int position){
        FragmentManager fm = getFragmentManager();
        int orientation = getResources().getConfiguration().orientation;
        if (orientation == ORIENTATION_LANDSCAPE){                 Determine
            SectionDetailsFragment fragment =                  ❺ orientation
                (SectionDetailsFragment) fm.findFragmentById(
                    R.id.section_list_fragment);
            fragment.setSection(position);                   Change section
        } else {                                          ❻ displayed by Fragment
            FilmstripFragment fragment =
              (FilmstripFragment) fm.findFragmentById(
                  R.id.section_filmstrip_fragment);
            fragment.setSection(position);
        }
    }
}
```

Starting with Android 3.0, every `Activity` can have an Action Bar and you can access it via the `Activity`'s `getActionBar` method ❶. The idea is to programmatically create tabs and add them to the Action Bar. Each tab will need a `TabListener` to respond to being tapped on, so we create a single `TabListener` to use for all of the tabs. We implement its `onTabSelected` method ❷ and invoke the `changeTab` method based on the position of the tab selected. We'll take a look at how the `changeTab` method works momentarily.

Once we have a `TabListener` instance, we're ready to create the tabs and add them to the Action Bar. We programmatically ❸ create a tab and set its title and its `TabListener` ❹. Note that we also specify which tab should be currently selected based on what section is currently selected by the user. Finally, we tell the Action Bar to not display the title of the `Activity` and to instead show the tabs and use those for navigation.

Now let's look at the `changeTab` method that's invoked via the `TabListener`'s `onTabSelected` callback method. This method first checks what orientation the device is currently in ❺. This is because the contents of the `Activity` will be different based on the orientation. It uses this knowledge along with the `Activity`'s `FragmentManager` to get a handle on the `Fragment` that's being displayed in the `Activity`. Then, we set the section on the `Fragment` ❻, so it knows which section of Daily Deals to display now.

DISCUSSION

Tabbed navigation isn't something new and unique to tablets. It's been a common way to organize web applications for many years and has been a part of Android since 1.0. These have always come via the `TabHost` and `TabWidget` classes. The `TabHost` has allowed you to create a series of tabs, each with its own `Activity` that will be displayed. The Action Bar tabs is an evolution of this idea, similar to how the other parts of the Action Bar are an evolution of the menu.

With the Action Bar and its tabbed navigation mode, you can create tabs similar to how you create tabs for a TabHost. But instead of associating a single `Activity` to a tab, you work within a single `Activity` and use Fragments. In our example, we changed the content of the `Fragment` that was there. But note that the `onTabSelected` method was passed a `FragmentTransaction` object. This would allow you to perform series of operations on the `Fragments` in the `Activity`, typically removing one or more `Fragments` and replacing them one or more other `Fragments`. The Action Bar not only improves the legacy menu system, but builds on top of `Fragments` to provide a simpler, but more flexible way to organize your application code.

The last of our essential techniques for tablet development, drag and drop, improves on how users can interact with your application.

TECHNIQUE 91   **Drag and Drop**

Product managers have been asking developers for drag and drop ever since Douglas Engelbart invented the mouse. Rich desktop application frameworks have made it an essential ingredient for decades. Drag and drop on the web struggled for years, with some JavaScript frameworks making it more accessible to developers until it finally became part of the HTML 5 specification. On mobile, the frameworks have largely ignored it until Android 3.0. Sure, it could be done via touch APIs, but this was more commonly the realm of game programming. With Honeycomb, drag and drop can be more easily used within any kind of application.

PROBLEM

You want to allow your users to more intuitively interact with your application by enabling drag and drop of various elements.

SOLUTION

To enable drag and drop in an application, we only need to use a handful of APIs introduced in Android 3.0. To demonstrate this we'll provide a simple drag and drop application. It'll display `StackViews` (a new widget introduced in Honeycomb) on a screen and allow the user to rearrange them using drag and drop. Figure 15.9 shows what this application looks like.

Figure 15.9 The Drag and Drop demo application

As you can see this is a simple grid with a couple of `StackView` widgets. Here's the code for this layout.

Listing 15.10 Drag and drop grid layout XML

```xml
<?xml version="1.0" encoding="utf-8"?>
<TableLayout
    xmlns:android="http://schemas.android.com/apk/res/android"
    android:layout_width="match_parent"
    android:layout_height="match_parent">
    <TableRow>
        <LinearLayout android:layout_width="640dp"
            android:layout_height="345dp"
            android:id="@+id/topLeft">
```

① Use LinearLayout

② Each cell is a LinearLayout container

```
            <StackView android:id="@+id/stack"
                android:layout_width="250dp"
                android:layout_height="250dp"
                android:clickable="true"
                android:loopViews="true"
                android:longClickable="true"
            />
        </LinearLayout>
        <LinearLayout android:layout_width="640dp"
            android:layout_height="345dp"
            android:id="@+id/topRight"
        />
    </TableRow>
    <TableRow>
        <LinearLayout android:layout_width="640dp"
            android:layout_height="345dp"
            android:id="@+id/bottomLeft"
        />
        <LinearLayout android:layout_width="640dp"
            android:layout_height="345dp"
            android:id="@+id/bottomRight">
            <StackView android:id="@+id/stack2"
                android:layout_width="250dp"
                android:layout_height="250dp"
                android:clickable="true"
                android:loopViews="true"
                android:longClickable="true"
            />
        </LinearLayout>
    </TableRow>
</TableLayout>
```

❸ **Place StackView within container**

Listing 15.10 shows that we're using a TableLayout ❶. There's nothing special about a TableLayout; it's an easy way to identify the various parts of the screen for a demonstration like this. Within each cell of the table we have a LinearLayout ❷. Again there's nothing special about LinearLayout; we needed some kind of container that other Views could be dragged and dropped in to. Those other Views in this case are StackViews ❸. Again, there's nothing unique about them when it comes to drag and drop. In fact, it would've been simpler to not use them, but they're visually interesting widgets so they're good for tablet applications.

The key idea in this application is to allow the user to drag and drop the Stack-Views into the various LinearLayout containers on the screen. To start dragging and dropping, the user will tap and hold (long click) a stack, causing all of the drop zones to be highlighted. Figure 15.10 shows the drop zones ready to have a stack dragged in to them.

Everything else in the application is done programmatically. The next listing shows the code for creating the UI.

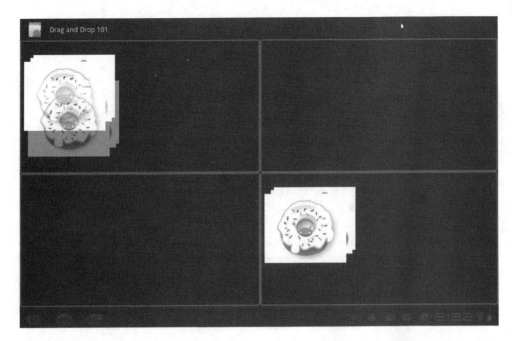

Figure 15.10 Drop zones active

Listing 15.11 Setting up the UI

```
public class DndActivity extends Activity {
    @Override
    protected void onCreate(Bundle savedInstanceState) {
        super.onCreate(savedInstanceState);
        setContentView(R.layout.grid);

        StackView stack = (StackView) findViewById(R.id.stack);
        Bitmap[] bmps = new Bitmap[5];
        Resources res = getResources();
        bmps[0] = BitmapFactory.decodeResource(res, R.drawable.donut);
        bmps[1] = BitmapFactory.decodeResource(res, R.drawable.eclair);
        bmps[2] = BitmapFactory.decodeResource(res, R.drawable.froyo);
        bmps[3] =
            BitmapFactory.decodeResource(res, R.drawable.gingerbread);
        bmps[4] =
            BitmapFactory.decodeResource(res, R.drawable.honeycomb);
        ImgAdapter adapter = new ImgAdapter(bmps, stack);
        stack.setAdapter(adapter);

        StackView stack2 = (StackView) findViewById(R.id.stack2);
        stack2.setAdapter(new ImgAdapter(bmps, stack2));

        findViewById(R.id.topLeft).setOnDragListener(
            new BoxDragListener());
        findViewById(R.id.bottomLeft).setOnDragListener(
```

① Get handle on first StackView

② Load image resources

③ Set StackView's adapter

④ Set DragListener on containers

```
        new BoxDragListener());
    findViewById(R.id.topRight).setOnDragListener(
        new BoxDragListener());
    findViewById(R.id.bottomRight).setOnDragListener(
        new BoxDragListener());
    }
}
```

The first thing we do to set up our UI is get a reference ❶ to one of the StackViews. We then load image resources that are part of the application ❷. As you can tell from figures 15.9 and 15.10 as well as the code in listing 15.11, each of the images used for the StackView is an icon representing the various releases of Android up to Honeycomb. These images are decoded into Bitmap objects and then passed in to a custom Adapter ❸ for the StackView. A StackView is an Adapter-based widget like a ListView or a GridView. We'll take a look at this custom Adapter in listing 15.12. Finally, we get a handle on each of the LinearLayout containers from listing 15.10, and we give them an OnDragListener object ❹. This is a new interface introduced in Android 3.0 and we'll look at our implementation of it in listing 15.13. For now, let's look at the custom Adapter for our StackViews.

Listing 15.12 Adapter used for the StackViews in the application

```
class ImgAdapter extends BaseAdapter{                          ◁──┐  Subclass
    private Bitmap[] bmps;                                        ❶ BaseAdapter
    private Context ctx = DndActivity.this;
    private ViewGroup owner;
    ImgAdapter(Bitmap[] bmps, ViewGroup owner){
        this.bmps = bmps;
        this.owner = owner;

    }
    @Override
    public int getCount() {
        return bmps.length;
    }
    @Override
    public Object getItem(int index) {
        return bmps[index];
    }
    @Override
    public long getItemId(int index) {
        return index;
    }
    @Override
    public View getView(int index, View recycledView, ViewGroup parent) {
        if (recycledView == null){
            recycledView = new ImageView(ctx);
        }
        ImageView imgView = (ImageView) recycledView;
        imgView.setOnLongClickListener(new OnLongClickListener(){
            @Override
            public boolean onLongClick(View view) {      ◁──❷  Listen to longClick event
                ClipData data =
                    ClipData.newPlainText("foo","bar");
```

```
                DragShadowBuilder sBuilder =
                    new DragShadowBuilder(owner);
                owner.startDrag(data, sBuilder, owner, 0);
                return true;
            }
        });
        imgView.setImageBitmap(bmps[index]);
        return imgView;
    }
}
```

③ Initiate dragging

As mentioned earlier, a `StackView` is like a `ListView` or `GridView`. It uses the same kind of `Adapter`, so we extend ❶ the `BaseAdapter` class. Everything else is like any other `Adapter`. In fact, we could use the `ImgAdapter` in listing 15.12 with a `ListView` or a `GridView`. Nothing is specific to `StackView`. The only special code is for enabling drag and drop. To do this, we set the `OnLongClickListener` ❷ for the `StackView`. This is when we want to initiate dragging. We don't want to drag and drop the individual `ImageViews` in the `StackView`; we want to drag and drop the `StackView` itself. That's why we kept a reference to the `StackView` called owner. Here, we call its `start-Drag` method ❸, a method added to `android.view.View` in Honeycomb. This is how to initiate dragging on the `StackView`. Note that one of the parameters to `startDrag` is a `DragShadowBuilder` instance. This is a class responsible for drawing a shadow of the `View` being dragged on the screen. We're using a default `DragShadowBuilder`. It will show the `View` that we passed to it in its constructor. This could be an expensive object to show, in which case you'd want to subclass `DragShadowBuilder` and provide your own custom drag shadow. Alternatively, if you use the default one but don't pass it a `View` in its constructor, then it'll draw no shadow at all.

What about `ClipData`?

You might've noticed in listing 15.13 that we also passed in a `ClipData` object to the `startDrag` method. If so, you probably also noticed that we put junk in this object. `ClipData` is useful when some more complicated piece of data is being represented by the `View` that you're dragging and dropping in your application. For example, the `View` might represent a contact object that your application is helping the user organize. `ClipData` provides a convenient way to attach a pointer to the dragged `View` that provides a references back to the complex object. You'll also need to use `Clip-Data` if you want to provide customized copy-and-paste in your application.

Once we've initiated the dragging of a `StackView` in our application, we need to deal with dropping it in one of the `LinearLayout` containers in the application. Here's how this is done by the `OnDragListener` set earlier.

Listing 15.13 Implementing the `OnDragListener` for containers

```
class BoxDragListener implements OnDragListener{
    boolean insideOfMe = false;
    Drawable border = null;
```
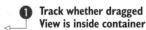 ❶ Track whether dragged View is inside container

```
Drawable redBorder = getResources().getDrawable(R.drawable.border3);
@Override
public boolean onDrag(View self, DragEvent event) {
    if (event.getAction() == DragEvent.ACTION_DRAG_STARTED){
        border = self.getBackground();
        self.setBackgroundDrawable(redBorder);
    } else if (event.getAction() == DragEvent.ACTION_DRAG_ENTERED){
        insideOfMe = true;
    } else if (event.getAction() == DragEvent.ACTION_DRAG_EXITED){
        insideOfMe = false;
    } else if (event.getAction() == DragEvent.ACTION_DROP){
        if (insideOfMe){
            View view = (View) event.getLocalState();
            ViewGroup owner = (ViewGroup) view.getParent();
            owner.removeView(view);
            LinearLayout container = (LinearLayout) self;
            if (container.getChildCount() > 0){
                container.addView(view,
                    container.getChildCount());
            } else {
                container.addView(view);
            }
        }
    } else if (event.getAction() == DragEvent.ACTION_DRAG_ENDED){
        self.setBackgroundDrawable(border);
    }
    return true;
    }
}
}
```

2 Make border red when dragging starts

3 Remove from previous owner container

4 Add to new container

5 Reset borders

Each container in our application uses an instance of the OnDragListener class shown in listing 15.13. The container needs to keep track of whether a dragged View is currently inside the container, so we use a Boolean flag to do this **1**. When dragging starts, we set the border of our container to red **2** to indicate that this container can accept a dragged View into it. Next, we keep track of the ENTERED/EXIT events by using our Boolean flag. When a drop event is fired, we need to do two things. First, we need to remove the dragged View **3** from its previous owner. Then, we need to add the dragged View to its new owner **4**. Finally, when we see that the dragging has ended, we revert border of our container **5** back to whatever it was before we turned it red. Note that we don't care what kind of View is being dragged and dropped into our container. Also note that if we had a container and we didn't want it to participate in drag and drop, we don't set its OnDragListener. Then its borders won't turn red and it won't accept a View being dropped into it.

DISCUSSION

There's a good reason why application developers are always being asked to provide drag and drop capabilities in their applications. For any kind of application, drag and drop provides a more intuitive way to interact with the application. In the past, this meant dragging and dropping with a mouse for desktop and web applications. Even with the artificial construct of a mouse, drag and drop remained intuitive.

Now we're in the age of touch computing, and smartphones have led the way. We haven't seen a lot of drag and drop in this area, and not because frameworks like Android didn't provide much for it. Drag and drop is a little awkward on a small screen. The places where you can tap to drag and or drop tend to be small, and not so easy to use. But tablets change things here significantly. The awkwardness introduced by the small screens on smartphones is gone. Tablets have large screens so you can tap on exactly what you want to interact with. Furthermore, a touch-based interface is so much more natural for dragging and dropping than a mouse-based one. Drag and drop with a mouse mimics a hand grabbing and moving something in real life. Drag and drop on a tablet doesn't have to mimic a hand because it involves a real human hand interacting with the objects on the screen.

The possibilities for creating intuitive human interfaces using drag and drop on a tablet application are endless and appealing. There are still some challenges. As drag and drop hasn't been prevalent in touch computing (smartphones), there are no well-known affordances to indicate that drag and drop is possible in an application. In our example application, we used tap and hold, or the *long click* as Android developers know it. This initiated dragging. We didn't want to initiate drag and drop from any tap on the StackView. That would've prevented the user from swiping through the images in the StackView, and it might become annoying if every time the user touched the screen, the borders on the containers went red in anticipation of drag and drop. But, we're not trying to suggest that tap and hold will become the ubiquitous way to initiate drag and drop in tablet applications. Another possibility that jumps out is to have an Edit button (perhaps on the Action Bar) as a way to turn on drag-and-drop mode, and then to allow taps to initiate dragging on an object.

15.3 Summary

As you're undoubtedly aware, Android wasn't the first smartphone platform to be extended to tablets. Android's success in touch-based computing on smartphones made it an obvious choice for tablets as well. But as you can see from this chapter, the Android team didn't rest on their laurels. Instead, a number of significant advancements were made in Android with tablets specifically in mind. The biggest of these is the introduction of Fragments. As we mentioned earlier, the need to create more self-contained components in Android didn't come from tablets. It had already existed, and many application developers had already come up with various solutions for this problem. The need for user interfaces that made better use of large screens in different orientations accentuated this missing piece to Android, and Fragments fill that void. Fragments, and the other essential parts of tablet development explained here—the Action Bar and drag and drop—are also available in earlier versions of Android via the Android Compatibility package.

Finally, it's good to note that this chapter isn't exhaustive in detailing all of the changes to Android in Honeycomb. Most of those changes were meant to help application developers build for tablets, so all of them are relevant to this chapter. But we've chosen to focus on the essential techniques that the developers of any tablet application should keep in mind. That's not meant to detract from the other features. For example, we've completely ignored several new features that are of great benefit to game developers, such as Renderscript. We've also not gone in to the improvements in `RemoteViews` that allow for improved home screen widgets and notifications. These are all important features that may be crucial to you depending on what your application is going to do. As always, the Android documentation provides great detail on these API and behavioral improvements. And with that, you've made it! You've gone from kicking the tires with Hello Android in chapter 1, through many advanced topics and over 80 techniques, to racing down the track with tablets. You should now have a very solid footing for developing Android applications, so pat yourself on the back!

appendix A
Debugging
tools of the trade

We covered many different topics in this book, hopefully in enough depth to not leave too many unanswered questions, but we wanted to talk about a few more things. The following appendixes contain useful bits and bobs about topics that we merely touched on briefly as part of a technique, or that didn't quite fit elsewhere in this book.

We have a total of four appendixes, labeled A through D. We tried to keep every topic self-contained, so that the order in which you read through them doesn't matter, although we believe the way we arranged them should be the most natural one when working through them in order.

That being said, we start in appendix A with some advanced debugging hints and tricks by revisiting the Android Debug Bridge (ADB), as well as a more recent addition to the SDK called StrictMode. In appendix B, we'll look at Android from a completely new angle, showing you alternative approaches to development that leverage web views and JavaScript, and even entirely new languages like Scala. Appendix C will shed light on a useful optimization tool that often doesn't get the attention it deserves: ProGuard. Finally, we'll look at a second tool that's similarly underappreciated: a scripted Android automation tool called Monkeyrunner. We'll start in this appendix by revisiting the ADB.

A.1 The Android Debug Bridge

When developing and debugging Android applications, you'll spend a lot of quality time with one particular tool: the *Android Debug Bridge*, or *ADB*. The ADB is a client/server application that enables you to interact with an Android device or emulator (we'll say *device* hereafter) from your command line. More specifically, it allows you to detect and enumerate connected devices and run commands directly within a device's shell. We'll now run through some typical scenarios that involve working with the adb tool.

A.1.1 Interacting with devices

If you're running an emulator or have devices connected to your development machine via USB, then you can use the ADB to discover and connect to them. For instance, if we have my Nexus One connected to my computer, and we're also running an Android emulator instance, using the adb devices command to enumerate all visible Android devices will return the following:

```
$ adb devices
List of devices attached
emulator-5554 device
HT019P801932  device
```

> **USB DEBUGGING** If your device is connected to your computer's USB port and turned on, but still refuses to show up in the list of connected devices, most likely, USB debugging has been disabled on this device. You can turn it on by going to the device's development settings via Settings > Applications > Development and checking the USB Debugging option.

> **WHEN DEVICES STILL DON'T APPEAR...** If a device still doesn't appear after enabling USB debugging, then most likely ADB has crashed. This happens every now and then, but it's nothing to worry about. In these cases, first run adb kill-server. A subsequent call to adb devices should then restart the server, and hopefully list the missing device.

The ADB identifies devices based on their serial number, which in the case of the phone used here is HT019P801932. When starting emulators, they're automatically assigned serial numbers that correspond to the port number on which they can receive commands, prefixed with emulator-. The ADB server claims ports in consecutive pairs: even port numbers designate command ports (we'll see in the next section how that works), and odd port numbers designate the ADB connection. A second emulator would therefore be assigned the serial number `emulator-5556`.

If you want to interact with a specific device via ADB, you can tell it which one you're targeting by specifying its serial number with the `-s` option:

```
$adb -s HT019P801932 [more options here]
```

In case you have only one physical device and one emulator connected, as in this example, you can simplify device targeting by using the `-d` and `-e` switches to target the single connected physical device or emulator, respectively. If only one device is present, regardless whether it's an emulator or an actual device, you don't have to use any device targeting at all; ADB will connect to the device it finds.

Once ADB knows which device it's targeting, you can trigger various commands to interact with it, such as copying files from and to it, installing and removing application packages, rebooting the device, or opening a command shell on it. To see a full list of available commands and their options, run `adb` without any arguments. It's worth noting that most commands you can directly pass to ADB are shortcuts to commands that you'd otherwise run on the device's command shell. For instance, the `adb install` command is a shortcut to the device's package manager command `pm`, and hence is equivalent to running `adb shell pm install`. For that reason, we'll now take a closer look at how to use the device shell directly.

A.1.2 *Using the device shell*

One of the ADB's most powerful features is that it lets you access an Android device's command shell. Recall from chapter 1, that Android runs on a modified Linux kernel, and it goes without saying that every honest Linux comes with a command shell. Unfortunately, Android doesn't bring the ubiquitous and powerful Bourne-Again Shell, better known as `bash`, which can be found on practically every modern Linux and MacOS X computer. Instead, a minimalistic shell is provided, with only a small subset of the OS applications that a typical GNU/Linux environment offers (for instance, `cd`, `ls`, and `mv` are available, but other often used commands such as `cp`, `more`, `less`, and `file` are absent).

You access a device's shell using the `adb shell` command, and you can do so in two ways: first by doing a one-line command, and second by launching into interactive mode, where you can send multiple commands one after another. If, for instance, you want to list all files in the current directory, you can do that as a one-line command like so (we assume a single connected device for now):

```
$adb shell ls
config
cache
sdcard
...
```

This command means: "using ADB, open a shell on the current device, execute its `ls` command, and print its output here." You can also launch into the shell by not passing a remote command:

```
$adb shell
# ls
config
cache
sdcard
...
# exit
```

You can exit out of the device shell by pressing CTRL+D. The # symbol indicates that this is the device's root account shell, which has "superuser" or "admin" access. On an emulator you'll always launch into the root account, giving you full access to files and folders. That's typically not true for phones and tablets, which you need to "root" first in order to get access to the root account. Unless you do that, you can't even peek into most folders.

Let's install the DealDroid (introduced in chapter 2) on a running emulator so we have something to toy around with (run this command from within the DealDroid directory):

```
$adb -e install -r bin/DealDroid.apk
663 KB/s (28308 bytes in 0.041s)
    pkg: /data/local/tmp/DealDroid.apk
Success
```

The -r switch will force a reinstallation in case the package already exists. Good, we've pushed an application to the emulator. Let's see what we can do now using the device shell.

A.1.3 *Controlling Android's execution environment*

Once our application is on the device, we can launch it in entirely new ways via the shell. Typically, you'd go to the application launcher and select its launcher icon. This will start the application in a standard way, which is fine in standard situations. But what if you want to see how a single `Activity` behaves with changing system configurations or when started using different `Intent` parameters? To some degree, you can test these programmatically using unit tests (see chapter 13), but this requires you to write code, and sometimes you just want to check whether something works or play around with a feature. Recall that we coded the DealDetails screen so that if no item was picked from the DealList first, we show a toast with an error message (see figure A.1).

Figure A.1   This error message is practically impossible to reproduce by running the application under normal conditions. In these cases, Android's activity manager can help to launch single screens with any Intent data you desire.

Under normal circumstances this is difficult to test manually, since usually there will be a valid item being passed to this screen. It would be useful to be able to launch an individual screen of an application using a specified set of Intent parameters, or launch it without going through another screen beforehand so that we can test and reproduce failure scenarios. This is where Android's Activity Manager kicks in.

STARTING COMPONENTS WITH ACTIVITY MANAGER

You can use the am tool, Android's Activity Manager, to start applications or even single screens in a controlled way. Coming back to our example with the DealDetails, let's start it without going through DealList first, so that no item is set:

```
$adb shell am start -n com.manning.aip.dealdroid/.DealDetails
```

The am start command will start an Activity using the Intent data you specify. Here we identified the component we want to start directly using the -n switch. This corresponds to starting an Activity from code using its class name, which is an explicit Intent. You can also fire an implicit Intent using am start, via its various other options (get a list of them by launching the command without any arguments). Not only can the Activity Manager tool start activities, it lets you start services, fire broadcast Intents, and more.

One particular command that deserves mentioning is am instrument. This is the way you start instrumentations such as an InstrumentationTestCase when not using Eclipse, and build systems such as Ant and Maven (see chapter 14) use that under the hood. It gives you a lot more flexibility regarding what will be tested, something that the ADT doesn't offer. More precisely, it allows you to only run tests that have a specific Java Annotation, that are in a specific package, or even single test methods. For instance, if we only want to run the testPreConditions test method of our Deal-DetailsTest from chapter 13, we can do so as follows:

```
$adb shell am instrument -w -e class
➥    com.manning.aip.dealdroid.test.DealDetailsTest#testPreConditions
➥    com.manning.aip.dealdroid.test/android.test.InstrumentationTestRunner

com.manning.aip.dealdroid.test.DealDetailsTest:.
Test results for InstrumentationTestRunner=.
Time: 0.295

OK (1 test)
```

> **WHERE IS THIS DOCUMENTED?**   Unfortunately, the am instrument command itself doesn't print a list of all parameters it supports, but there's a good summary of the available options in the JavaDoc comments of the InstrumentationTestRunner class: http://mng.bz/s5r7.

For this reason, Android build systems, such as the Android plug-ins for Maven and Gradle, leverage am instrument for more powerful test invocation.

MANIPULATING SYSTEM PROPERTIES

Gaining full control over how activities or services are started is great, but application behavior doesn't only change with the arguments you pass in an Intent. For instance, many applications are translated to different languages, so it's desirable to test them with the device set to a foreign language. Unfortunately, the emulator only allows us to set a handful of languages, and Portuguese, for instance, isn't available. There's a way around this, though. Android controls many different things, including system language, through a list of global system properties. These properties are available to you via Java's `System.getProperty` function. Java properties are key/value pairs, and Android's system properties can be directly read and modified through the `getprop` and `setprop` tools. If, for instance, we want to change the system locale to Portuguese (pt_PT), then we can do it like so:

```
$adb shell setprop persist.sys.language pt
$adb shell setprop persist.sys.country PT
```

Note that system properties are only read once when Android's root VM Zygote (see chapter 1) is launched. In order for this to take effect, we must restart the emulator (either manually, or using the `start` and `stop` commands).

> **SETTING CUSTOM LOCALES WITH THE DEVTOOLS** There's another way to set the system locale to any value you desire, and that's the Dev Tools application that's preinstalled on every Android emulator. This tool isn't available on phones, so you'd have to adb `pull` its APK from an emulator and install it on a phone first.

You can print out a list of active system properties by running `getprop` without arguments. You can also control the Dalvik VM via system properties. One particularly useful property is `dalvik.vm.enableassertions`. This is the equivalent of Java's `-ea` switch, which enables the use of the `assert` keyword in Java code:

```
$adb shell setprop dalvik.vm.enableassertions all
```

If, for instance, we thought that whenever a `null` item is passed to the DealDetails screen, this was a programming error rather than an expected situation we can recover from, then it would be better to place an assertion in the DealDetails as long as the application is still in development and being tested (based on listing 2.11 from chapter 2):

```
Item item = app.getCurrentItem();
assert( item != null );
```

With assertions enabled, launching this screen without selecting an item first will now make the runtime throw an `AssertionError` and terminate the application. We can then see from the logs which line of code raised the `AssertionError` and fix our application accordingly.

> **IF PROPERTIES DON'T STICK...** Again, Android can be flaky sometimes with respect to the `setprop` and `start`/`stop` commands. If you find that Android forgets properties you set that way, try putting them in a file called /data/ local.prop on the device instead. Put each property on a separate line as <key> = <value>; for example dalvik.vm.enableassertions = all.

We mentioned that `AssertionError`, like all uncaught exceptions, will get logged to the system log file. We'll come back to this in a minute, but before we look at logging in more detail, there's one last recipe to share in this section: how to manipulate an Android device's geolocation.

MANIPULATING LOCATION

We said in the beginning that ADB is a client/server application and that it operates on two ports: the command port and the ADB connection port. The former is of particular interest for developers, since we can connect to it via `telnet` and send commands directly to the device:

```
$telnet localhost 5554
Trying 127.0.0.1...
Connected to localhost.
Escape character is '^]'.
Android Console: type 'help' for a list of commands
OK
```

If only an emulator is running, then this will connect to the command port of that emulator. Using Telnet, type the text you want to send and terminate it via a carriage return (by hitting Enter). If you type `help` or `help <command>`, you'll see a list of supported commands or a single command's options, respectively. The most useful command for this is the `geo` command, since it allows you to send your device to virtually anywhere in the world by mocking a GPS fix. If, for instance, you want to reposition yourself to Mount Everest, then you'd type this into the `telnet` window:

```
geo fix 86.922 27.986 <ENTER>
OK
```

Go to the Google Maps application and see how it works! Note that the order of arguments is `longitude` first, then `latitude`. If you find yourself in open water in Google Maps, then you probably got them wrong. You can exit into the `telnet` prompt by pressing CTRL+]. Use the `quit` command to exit entirely.

A.1.4   *Accessing the system logs*

Without question, one of the most useful things for debugging is a system and application log file that you can inspect to see what's going on. This is also where uncaught exception stack traces go, so always keep an eye on it when debugging.

You can follow the system log in the DDMS perspective in Eclipse, but if you're a keyboard and console geek like us, you'll want to use Android's `logcat` command instead. Using `logcat` for debugging is documented in some detail at http://mng.bz/Tf31, but we'd like to highlight its key features and usage idioms.

As with all previous commands we've seen in this appendix, the `logcat` command is an application that sits on the device itself, but can be accessed via `adb`. If you run it without any arguments, it'll jump to the end of the system's main log file (there are two other log files, radio and events, which we're not going to cover here) and keep monitoring it, much like GNU's `tail -f` does:

```
$adb logcat
I/DEBUG    (   31): debuggerd: Jun 30 2010 14:39:19
D/qemud    (   38): entering main loop
I/Vold     (   29): Vold 2.1 (the revenge) firing up
I/Netd     (   30): Netd 1.0 starting
...
```

Android logs virtually everything, application output, garbage collector cycles, and calls to System.out.println, to this file. Note that this is a shared log file; all applications that use Android's Log class log here. Every line in the log file consists of three parts: the log level, the log tag that identifies the component that wrote the line, and the log message. For example, the call Log.i("MyActivity", "This is a log message") will appear in the system log as:

```
I/MyActivity ( 1824): This is a log message
```

Here I (info) is the log level and MyActivity is the log tag, followed by the application's process ID (1824) and the message. The logcat tool takes various options, one of the most useful being -v, which controls the log format. For instance, calling logcat -v time will enable timestamps in the log:

```
$adb logcat -v time
04-10 19:40:15.214 I/MyActivity ( 1824): This is a log message
...
```

Make yourself familiar with all options: it'll make your life a lot easier. Log levels and log tags are used to keep the log file organized, and allow for easy filtering of its contents. In fact, logcat supports filter expressions that allow you to see only those things you're interested in. Filter expressions follow the pattern tag:level, which tells logcat to only show log messages for the given log tag that have log levels with equal or higher priority as level. This approach leverages the fact that all log levels are assigned a priority. For instance, debug log output has a lower priority than error output (see table A.1 for a summary of all log levels).

Table A.1   Log levels in Android in ascending priority

Identifier	Name	Priority
V	Verbose (show everything)	1 (lowest)
D	Debug	2
I	Info	3
W	Warn	4
E	Error	5
F	Fatal	6
S	Silent (show nothing)	7 (highest)

If, for example, you only want to see errors or fatal errors, you'd call logcat like so:

```
$adb logcat *:E
```

This translates to: for all components (for all log tags), only show log messages of type E or F. (Note that the S level takes a slightly special role, since it's used to enforce that nothing is being logged, so it doesn't make sense to speak of log entries of level S.)

Filter expressions can be combined. If you want to see only error messages from other components, but still want to see your own application's debug output, you could use the following filter expression:

```
$adb logcat MyApp:D *:E
```

This will only affect log entries that have been written from your application using the log tag MyApp. One special case is standard out. If you have calls to System. out.println in your code (something we don't recommend; that's what the Log class is for), then these will appear in the log file with the log tag System.out, but unfortunately, you can't filter by that tag. Here, you'll have to fall back to solutions such as piping logcat into the grep tool, which you should be familiar with if you're on a UNIX-based computer.

This wraps up our excursion into ADB and related commands. We've seen how to connect to devices from the command line, how to use a device's command shell to get more control of how we run applications, and how to come to grips with Android's system log. This is great to manipulate, monitor, and control an application from the execution environment, but what if you want to debug the more intrinsic behavior of your application, particularly its performance—or the absence thereof? Put it in StrictMode!

A.2 StrictMode

Building an Android application is one thing, but making it fast and responsive can be challenging. With this in mind, the Android SDK added a new tool in Android 2.3: StrictMode. This tool will detect many of the things that can cause applications to be sluggish, such as network access on the main thread. It's enabled programmatically; the following listing shows it being enabled in the DealDroid application.

Listing A.1 Enabling StrictMode in DealDroid

```java
public class DealDroidApp extends Application {
// some code omitted for brevity
    @Override
    public void onCreate() {
        /* Setup StrictMode policies */
        StrictMode.setThreadPolicy(                    ❶ Configure policies
            new StrictMode.ThreadPolicy.Builder()         for main thread
                .detectAll()
                .penaltyLog()
                .penaltyDeath()
                .build());
        StrictMode.setVmPolicy(                        ❷ Configure virtual
                                                          machine policies
```

```
        new StrictMode.VmPolicy.Builder()
            .detectAll()
            .penaltyLog()
            .penaltyDeath()
            .build());
    super.onCreate();
    this.cMgr = (ConnectivityManager)
        this.getSystemService(Context.CONNECTIVITY_SERVICE);
    this.parser = new DailyDealsXmlPullFeedParser();
    this.sectionList = new ArrayList<Section>(6);
    this.imageCache = new HashMap<Long, Bitmap>();
    this.prefs = PreferenceManager.getDefaultSharedPreferences(this);
    }
}
```

To use StrictMode, you need to programmatically enable it. In this example, we've done this in our app's Application object, but you could also enable it in an individual Activity instead. If you configure like this, in the Application object, then it'll be enabled for all of your activities. We can configure two types of policies for StrictMode. The first is the policy to be used for the current thread ❶, which will be the main UI thread in this case. We've done a detectAll. This will include disk reads, disk writes, and network access. Next, we configure our virtual machine policy ❷, and again we use detectAll. This will detect several common mistakes that can cause your application to crash, such as leaking an Activity (and potentially large amounts of memory), failing to close databases/cursors, or other expensive resources.

Once we've added this code to our app, we can start it up. It'll immediately crash. In LogCat we'll see

```
StrictMode policy violation; ~duration=2689 ms:
    android.os.StrictMode$StrictModeDiskReadViolation: policy=87 violation=2
    ...
    at DealDroidApp.onCreate(DealDroidApp.java:93)
```

The StrictMode messages can be daunting at first, but you'll quickly get used to them. This says that we had a disk read violation in our application, and going further down the stack trace, we see that it happens at line 93 in our DealDroidApp class. That is the last line of the onCreate method in listing A.1. It loads the default SharedPreferences for the app. SharedPreferences are persisted to the device's internal flash memory, hence the disk read violation. You might not think this is a big deal. In this case, StrictMode says that it took 2689 ms; that's almost 3 seconds! This was run in the emulator, which makes it slow. If you decide that you want to live with this disk read, you can configure StrictMode to ignore disk reads. Or you could refactor the code. In this case, the SharedPreferences are only used by our Service, so we can easily move the reading of them out of the DealDroidApp's onCreate method and make our app start up more quickly. Finally, we should note that you should remove all StrictMode code before shipping your app. It should only be used during development.

A.3 *Summary*

In this first appendix, we've shown you a few debugging tricks that go beyond using your standard Eclipse debugger. We've shown how to get more control over your Android device and its execution environment using the ADB, and how you can profile your application's performance using StrictMode to discover no-nos such as running expensive operations on the UI thread.

The next appendix may be interesting for the adventurers among us. It enters the realm of Web development and alternative programming languages on Android.

appendix B
Extending
Android development

In this appendix

- Using WebViews
- Working with JavaScript
- Alternative programming languages

For consumers buying a smartphone, one of the appeals of Android is that it doesn't take a one-size-fits-all approach. You can pick your screen size, form factor, and more. For developers, the story is much the same. Android provides a standard set of development tools: Android SDK/NDK, ADT, and so on. This is great both for getting new developers started, and for standardization on large development teams. But you're not constrained to this standard set. The ability to do everything from the command line and the use of open build tools such as Ant allows other development environments like IntelliJ IDEA to be used for developing Android applications. You can go even further and eschew Java development completely by using web technologies, or by using alternative programming languages. Let's take a look at each of these approaches, first by examining web technologies.

B.1 Using WebViews and JavaScript

Occasionally in this book, we've mentioned how many aspects of Android development are similar to aspects of web development. Some of these are simple things, such as using the `findViewById` API as a web developer would use JavaScript's `document.getElementById` API. Others have been more substantial, such as the way visual styles are created and applied to UI elements. If your expertise is in web development and you're making the move to Android development, many things will feel familiar. But if you want to leverage your web development skills to build Android apps, another interesting option is available: WebViews.

Android provides the `android.webkit.WebView`, a `View` that shows a web page. As the name implies, it uses the popular open source WebKit library to render web content. WebKit is a C++ library, and you can think of `WebView` and its related classes as Java wrappers to that library. `WebView` provides tremendous flexibility in using web content. It's a `View`, so you can use make a `WebView` any size and put multiple `WebViews` on the screen at the same time. Or you can load a single `WebView` that uses the entire screen, turning your application into a wrapper around a web page.

The term *web page* is used loosely here. You could load a page from the Internet, or you could load a local file instead. You could even provide the `WebView` with a string of HTML to render directly. The flexibility of `WebViews` make them a powerful tool for Android developers, even those who think that writing JavaScript is for knuckle-draggers.

`WebViews` are a first-class citizen in Android, not some bolted-on technology used to fill in the gaps of the application framework. You can expose most of the APIs in Android to a web page running inside a `WebView`. Figure B.1 shows an example app that embeds a `WebView`.

This application allows the user to choose a contact from their address book and a picture from their phone that's then displayed inside the `WebView`. It shows you some of the interaction that's possible between the phone and a web page embedded within a native application using a `WebView`. The following listing shows how we achieved this kind of interactivity.

Figure B.1 Embedded web application

Listing B.1 Using a WebView in an `Activity`

```java
public class InterWebActivity extends Activity {

    private static final int REQUEST_PIC = 5;
    private static final int REQUEST_CONTACT = 4;
    private static final String LOG_TAG = "InterWebActivity";
    private WebView webView;
    private InterWebInterface webInterface;
    private static int onCreateCount = 0;
    private int onResumeCount = 0;

    @Override
    public void onCreate(Bundle savedInstanceState) {
        super.onCreate(savedInstanceState);
        setContentView(R.layout.main);
        webView = (WebView) findViewById(R.id.web);
        WebSettings settings = webView.getSettings();
        settings.setJavaScriptEnabled(true);                          ❶ Turn on
        webView.setWebChromeClient(new WebChromeClient() {               JavaScript
            @Override
            public boolean onJsAlert(WebView view, String url,
                String message,JsResult result) {
                Log.d(LOG_TAG, String.format(                         Intercept
                    "WebView JsAlert message = %s",                alerts and logs ❷
                    url, message));
                return false;
            }
            @Override
            public boolean onConsoleMessage(ConsoleMessage consoleMsg) {
                StringBuilder msg = new StringBuilder(consoleMsg
                        .messageLevel().name()).append('\t')
                        .append(consoleMsg.message()).append('\t')
                        .append(consoleMsg.sourceId()).append(" (")
                        .append(consoleMsg.lineNumber()).append(")\n");
                if (consoleMsg.messageLevel() == ERROR) {
                    Log.e(LOG_TAG, msg.toString());
                } else {
                    Log.d(LOG_TAG, msg.toString());
                }
                return true;
            }
        });                                                            ❸ Log pages
        webView.setWebViewClient(new WebViewClient() {                    being loaded
            @Override
            public boolean shouldOverrideUrlLoading(WebView view,
                String url) {
                Log.d(LOG_TAG, "Loading url=" + url);
                return false;
            }
        });                                                            ❹ Expose
        webInterface = new InterWebInterface();                          object
        webView.addJavascriptInterface(webInterface, "android");
        webView.loadUrl("file:///android_asset/interweb.html");
        onCreateCount++;
    }                                                     Load local web page ❺
```

In listing B.1, we start by enabling JavaScript ❶ in the WebView that's embedded in our Activity. We then create a WebChromeClient for the WebView. This object will allow us to intercept certain events that occur in the WebView. In this case, we'll intercept JavaScript alerts and console logs ❷ and route them to the standard Android log. Debugging embedded web pages can be challenging, because you don't have a standard Java debugger as you do normally in Android development. So you'll probably need to rely more heavily on logging than you'd like, and the easiest way to do that is to use the WebChromeClient. Next we create a WebViewClient. This is similar to a WebChromeClient, in that it also allows you to intercept other types of events that happen in the WebView—including lifecycle events such as onPageFinished and onReceivedError. In this case, ❸ we intercept a new URL being loaded. We could choose to override this. For example, if we wanted to launch an external browser instead of loading the page in the embedded WebView, you could do something like this:

```
startActivity(new Intent(Intent.ACTION_GET, Uri.parse(url)));
```

In this case, we're logging the new URL that's being loaded. Next comes one of the more interesting steps: we create a Java object and expose it to our JavaScript runtime ❹. We give it the name android, so in JavaScript we'll be able to refer to it by this name. We'll look at this object and how it's used shortly. Finally ❺, we load the web page. In this case, we load a local web page saved in the /assets folder. We could load an external page, but in this case we didn't want to go to a web server. We wanted to write our application code in HTML, CSS, and JavaScript. The following shows what this Java object does.

Listing B.2 Java object exposed to JavaScript

```
class InterWebInterface {
    String callback;

    public String getCreateCount() {
        return String.valueOf(onCreateCount);
    }

    public String getResumeCount() {
        return String.valueOf(onResumeCount);
    }

    public String getUserName() {                                    ❶ Get username from
        AccountManager mgr = AccountManager.get(InterWebActivity.this);   AccountManager
        Account gAccount = mgr.getAccountsByType("com.google")[0];
        return gAccount.name;
    }
                                                                     ❷ Start Activity to
    public void selectContact(String callback) {                        select contact
        this.callback = callback;
        Intent intentContact = new Intent(Intent.ACTION_PICK,

            ContactsContract.Contacts.CONTENT_URI);
        startActivityForResult(intentContact, REQUEST_CONTACT);
    }

    public void selectPicture(String callback) {
        this.callback = callback;
```

```
    Intent intentPicture = new Intent(Intent.ACTION_GET_CONTENT);
    intentPicture.setType("image/*");
    startActivityForResult(intentPicture, REQUEST_PIC);
}
protected void executeContactCallback(Uri contact) {
    String name = getContactDisplayName(contact);
    webView.loadUrl(String.format("javascript:contactCallback('%s')",
        name));
}

protected void executePicCallback(Uri picture) {
    String filePath = getPictureData(picture);
    File f = new File(filePath);
    String uri = Uri.fromFile(f).toString();
    webView.loadUrl(String.format("javascript:pictureCallback('%s')",
        uri));
}
}
```

❸ **Callback to JavaScript with contact**

The idea behind listing B.2 is to show that there are few limits on what kind of Android functionality you can give your JavaScript access to. In this example, we provide access to the user's name by using the AccountManager ❶. We then also allow the user to select a contact to use for whatever reason ❷. Note that this involves starting another Activity to select this, so it's an asynchronous request. When we get the result back, we need to send it back to a callback in the JavaScript ❸. To do this, we use (abuse?) the loadUrl method on WebView to execute JavaScript directly and invoke our callback method, passing in the data we got back from the external Activity. Note that we also have a similar method for passing in the file path to a picture, as well as more mundane methods that keep track of some local state in the Activity. Here's the JavaScript that makes use of this object.

Listing B.3   JavaScript application

```
<html>
  <head>
    <script type="text/javascript">
      var initCount = 0;
      function getContact(){
        window.android.selectContact("contactCallback");
      }
      function contactCallback(contact){
        document.getElementById("output").innerHTML = contact;
        status();
      }
      function status(){
        try{
          var createCount = window.android.getCreateCount();
          var resumeCount = window.android.getResumeCount();
          document.getElementById("resume").innerHTML = resumeCount;
          document.getElementById("create").innerHTML = createCount;
          document.getElementById("init").innerHTML = initCount;
        } catch (e) {
```

❶ **Call selectContact method**

❷ **Contact name passed to callback**

```
          alert("Exception during status: " + e.description)
        }
      }
      function init(){
        initCount++;
        status();
      }
      function getPicture(){
        window.android.selectPicture("pictureCallback");
      }
      function pictureCallback(url){
        alert("Loading pic with url=" + url);
        var img = document.getElementById("pic");
        img.src = url;
        img.height = "200";
        img.width = "200";
      }
    </script>
  </head>
  <body onload="init()">
    <div>
      <span id="init"></span> onloads<br/>
      <span id="resume"></span> Resumes<br/>
      <span id="create"></span> Creates
    </div>
    <input type="button" value="Select a Contact" onclick="getContact()"/>
<br/>
    <input type="button" value="Select a Pic" onclick="getPicture()"/>
    <div id="output">The Uri will go here</div>
    <img id="pic" />
  </body>
</html>
```

The code in listing B.3 shows an application that uses many native features of the Android platform, but does it all from JavaScript on a web page. It has a simple button that says "Select a Contact"; tapping it calls the selectContact method ❶ on the Java object in listing B.2. That will invoke the native contact chooser application on the Android device. When it finishes, the contactCallback function ❷ will pass the name of the contact back to it. Similarly, you can see functions for interacting with the other methods defined in the Java object shown in listing B.2.

A web application could do a lot of other things too. It could talk to a remote a server using an XMLHttpRequest object. It could use HTML 5 features such as Canvas, DOM storage, or geolocation. And all of the user interface could be done using HTML, CSS, and JavaScript. But on Android it's also possible to write a little glue code and allow the web application to have access to everything that can be accessed in a native application.

B.2 *Alternative programming languages*

When Android was first announced, its use of the Java programming language brought with it some mixed reviews. The main alternative in embedded systems is native code—something that can be compiled to machine directly, such as C, C++, or Objective-C. Compared to those languages, Java is advanced. For example, it's the only one that has garbage collection. (Objective-C 2.0 has a flavor of garbage collection, but it hasn't yet found its way into the mobile space.) Many developers consider Java to be overly verbose and restrictive, and in general "long in the tooth." There are many newer programming languages with more flexible and expressive syntax. Fortunately for aficionados of such languages, Android doesn't require Java. It requires Java bytecode. Any language that can compile to Java bytecode can then be dexed to Dalvik bytecode that can then run on an Android device. Let's look at figure B.2 to see how this works.

This figure should look familiar; it's figure 1.11 from the beginning of the book. The key here is the second rectangle. Here we have Java class files that are then dexed into a .dex file. So we can avoid writing Java code as long as whatever code we write can be converted into Java class files.

As it turns out, the Java runtime (the Java virtual machine) is a popular runtime to target for many newer programming languages. The modern JVM is high performance and provides excellent memory management, hence its popularity with modern programming languages such as Scala, Groovy, Clojure, Mirah, and Fantom. In addition to these young languages, the popular Ruby programming language has a Java-based runtime often referred to as *JRuby*. So you can add Ruby to the list of programming languages that can be compiled to Java bytecode and used to build Android applications.

As you might be able to guess from figure B.2, there's usually one tricky point to using something other than Java: the build process. Often your application code needs things such as the R class that's generated by Android. So that needs to be generated and compiled before your application code that depends on it can be compiled. Once you get this dependency managed, then you can plug into the build process visualized in figure B.2.

Now before you run off and abandon Java in favor of one of these sexier languages, there are some significant drawbacks to using an alternative language—three

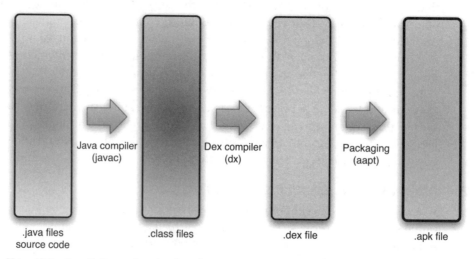

Figure B.2   **Compilation and packaging on Android**

major drawbacks. The first is that in many cases these languages have constructs that must be translated into Java before being compiled into bytecode. This is true for languages with features that have no equivalent in Java, and often the reason why you want to use these languages is because of such features. With this extra layer of interpretation going on, these languages inevitably run slower than Java. In some cases, this isn't a big deal. For example, if you have an app where most of the time you're waiting for data from the network, a slower application probably won't be noticeable. You should've already offloaded such work from the main UI thread.

The next major issue is that alternate languages often require more memory to be allocated than Java would. Again this tends to be more true when you use language features that don't translate easily to Java. For example, many languages provide *closures*, anonymous functions that can be passed around to other functions/methods. These are useful in application programming such as in Android, where you must often handle events like taps and gestures. These are often referred to as *first-class functions*, and Java doesn't have them. So for a language to provide them, it must usually perform some magic behind the scenes and create a Java object as a container for the function. Using a closure usually involves an object (a class) being defined, compiled, and then an instance of this object being created. That's a lot of hidden memory being consumed. Even worse, memory used for classes (as opposed to instances of the classes) is much harder for the garbage collector to reclaim. So not only is a lot more memory being allocated, but some of it won't become garbage that can be collected. Memory is one of the scarce resources in mobile development, so this can be a significant drawback.

The last issue to keep in mind is that alternate programming languages usually come with a runtime library. This is a standard library of classes and functions that you can always count on being there. They usually include common data structures and libraries for I/O and even networking. All of this standard library must be included with your application. This can lead to your application being much larger than you'd otherwise expect. The ProGuard tool described in appendix C can help with this. Furthermore, as Android devices become more advanced, application size becomes less of an issue as users become less likely to run out of space for apps (a common problem in the first year or so of Android). But there's another frustrating corollary to this issue. The runtime library is most likely packaged as a JAR full of class files. All of these class files will have to be dexed every time you build your application. This can cause your build times to become drastically longer. This might sound like a minor issue, but it can be a significant drag on your development process.

Given all of these potential issues with using an alternate language for Android development, many of these languages have started to include specific support for Android to make things easier for the rapidly growing number of Android developers. For example, the JRuby project has a subproject known as *Ruboto* that aims to make it easier to use Ruby for building Android apps. Another popular alternative is *Scala*. The Scala website provides many tips for tweaking the Ant build process to work with Scala. Furthermore, Scala 2.9 includes a tweak to the Scala compiler to make it easier to define static final fields such as the CREATOR fields required by Android Parcelables. There are no static fields in Scala, but some language features are functionally equivalent. But prior to Scala 2.8, the bytecode wasn't equivalent so there was a compatibility problem. The following listing shows what a Parcelable looks like in Scala.

Listing B.4   A Scala Parcelable

```scala
import android.os.{Parcelable, Parcel}

class Stock (val symbol:String, var maxPrice:Double, var minPrice:Double,
         val pricePaid:Double, var quantity:Int, var name:String,
         var currentPrice:Double) extends Parcelable{
    var id = 0

    def this(in:Parcel) = this(in.readString, in.readDouble, in.readDouble,
                  in.readDouble, in.readInt,in.readString,
                  in.readDouble)

    def describeContents = 0
    def writeToParcel(parcel:Parcel, flags:Int){
        parcel.writeString(symbol)
        parcel.writeDouble(maxPrice)
        parcel.writeDouble(minPrice)
        parcel.writeDouble(pricePaid)
        parcel.writeInt(quantity)
        parcel.writeDouble(currentPrice)
        parcel.writeString(name)
    }
}

object Stock{
    final val CREATOR = new Parcelable.Creator[Stock](){
        def createFromParcel(in:Parcel) = new Stock(in)
        def newArray(size:Int) = new Array[Stock](size)
    }
}
```

As you can see, Scala gets rid of a lot of the boilerplate you need to deal with in Java. But the lack of static members in Scala has its consequences. An object in Scala is a singleton. So its fields and methods can serve the same function as static fields and methods in Java (hence putting the CREATOR in the Stock object instead of the Stock class). As mentioned earlier, this still didn't work prior to Scala 2.9, and Scala objects couldn't be used for Parcelables. Fortunately the easy interoperability between Java and Scala meant that you could write your Parcelables in Java and everything else in Scala. But starting with Scala 2.9, the Scala compiler makes the Scala CREATOR bytecode equivalent to the Java static one, enabling you to use Scala for Parcelables.

This is only one example of how alternative languages can be used on Android and are constantly becoming easier to use on Android. These languages often provide different programming paradigms that you can take advantage of. It's another example of how the openness of Android gives you so many options as a developer. You can use the tools that you want to use. You can use web technologies if you want to. You can choose your programming language.

appendix C
ProGuard

We need not mention that decent application performance is crucial and difficult to achieve. Though you can spend hours profiling your code, there's another way to grab some low-hanging performance optimization fruit, and even improve your application's resistance to being hacked or reverse-engineered along the way. Readers with a strong Java background may already know this useful companion: meet ProGuard.

C.1   Overview

We mentioned ProGuard a few times in chapter 14 when we discussed build management and automation, but didn't explain in detail what it's good for or when and how you should use it, so that's what this section will clarify. In a nutshell, ProGuard is a Java class file processor that does two useful things for you:

- Make your application smaller and faster
- Make your application difficult to reverse-engineer

It should be mentioned that ProGuard isn't Android-specific; it was around long before Android. It ships with the SDK though, and can be found in your ANDROID_HOME/tools/proguard folder. The documentation can be found online at http://proguard.sourceforge.net/.

The desire for small and fast applications is something we don't need to explain. ProGuard can shrink and optimize your classes by processing bytecode in numerous ways, such as removing unused code, inlining method calls, merging class hierarchies, applying final and static modifiers whenever possible, and applying peephole optimizations for things such as arithmetic operations or flow control simplification.

Though every application could benefit from this, the question about reverse engineering may require some explanation. Unless you're sensitive about crafty developers being able to inspect your application's innards, there's typically no need to prevent it from being reverse engineered—converted back to its source code (this is possible by first converting the Dalvik bytecode back into Java bytecode, and then back into Java source code). There are cases where this can become problematic though:

- You've hard-coded sensitive data such as passwords in your Java classes.
- Your source code contains sensitive intellectual property that under no circumstances should be share with the world.
- You want to prevent clever developers from bypassing license or security checks by recompiling the application with the checks disabled (for example, this is important when you're charging customers for the application download using Android's licensing service).

ProGuard can assist you by obfuscating class, method, and field names, as well as removing structural information such as filename and line number tables, so that it becomes practically impossible to temper with reversed source code. This sounds all cool and useful, but it doesn't work at the snap of a finger. Therefore, we'll now show you how you set up your Android projects to be processible by ProGuard, how to trigger ProGuard in your builds, and most importantly, how to set up proper ProGuard rules for your project and where some common pitfalls lurk.

C.2   *Enabling ProGuard*

You may have wondered about the `proguard.cfg` file that you get with every project you create using the ADT project wizard (located in the project root folder). That's where you put the options and rules for how you want ProGuard to process your application. The wizard, thankfully, doesn't create an empty file, but predefines some reasonable defaults that you can build upon. We'll see in the following subsection how these rules work in detail. The only thing you have to do is to tell the ADT where the configuration resides by adding a line like this to `default.properties`:

```
proguard.config=proguard.cfg
```

If the ProGuard configuration file isn't located in the project root, you must change the path accordingly. This is enough to tell the ADT that you'd like to have your class files processed by ProGuard before building an APK, but note that ProGuard will only be active for release builds. For example, when creating an APK via right-clicking the project, then selecting Android Tools > Export Signed Application Package. This makes sense, because while developing the application, ProGuard only gets in your way. Debugging obfuscated methods is as fun as finding a needle in a haystack while blindfolded. Unfortunately, this problem also applies to analyzing error reports from a ProGuarded application that's already live, and we'll explain in section C.4 how to handle that.

We went through great lengths in chapter 14 to explain why build management using Ant or Maven is desirable, so the question now is how to run ProGuard when not using the ADT to create release builds. For Maven, there's been a ProGuard plugin for a while now, and its use in conjunction with the Maven Android plugin is documented at http://mng.bz/9uKq. These days, ProGuard is also fully integrated into the standard

Android tool chain. Android's Ant tasks define a private task called -obfuscate, which will invoke ProGuard as part of the release target. Here's what we see when running ant release for our HelloAnt project from chapter 14 (output shortened):

Listing C.1   The ProGuard output as seen for HelloAnt

```
matthias:[HelloAnt]$ ant clean release
...
-obfuscate:
    [mkdir] Created dir: /Users/matthias/Projects/eclipse/             ❶ ProGuard logs
 ➥ HelloAnt/bin/proguard                                                  kept here
     [jar] Building jar: /Users/matthias/Projects/eclipse/
 ➥ HelloAnt/bin/proguard/original.jar
[proguard] ProGuard, version 4.4
...
[proguard] Reading input...
[proguard] Reading program jar [/Users/matthias/Projects/eclipse/HelloAnt/
    bin/proguard/original.jar]
[proguard] Reading program jar [/Users/matthias/Projects/eclipse/HelloAnt/
    libs/commons-lang-2.5.jar]
[proguard] Reading library jar [/Users/matthias/Library/Development/android-
    sdk-mac_86/platforms/
 ➥ android-8/android.jar]
[proguard] Reading library jar [/Users/matthias/Library/Development/android-
    sdk-mac_86/
 ➥ add-ons/addon_google_apis_google_inc_8/libs/maps.jar]
[proguard] Initializing...
[proguard] Note: the configuration refers to the unknown class
 ➥ 'com.android.vending.licensing.ILicensingService'
[proguard] Note: there were 1 references to unknown classes.
[proguard]        You should check your configuration for typos.
[proguard] Ignoring unused library classes...
[proguard]    Original number of library classes: 2696
[proguard]    Final number of library classes:    230
[proguard] Printing kept classes, fields, and methods...               ❷ Shrinking
[proguard] Shrinking...                                                    phase
[proguard] Printing usage to [/Users/matthias/Projects/eclipse/
 ➥ HelloAnt/bin/proguard/usage.txt]...
[proguard] Removing unused program classes and class elements...
[proguard]    Original number of program classes: 139
[proguard]    Final number of program classes:    2                    ❸ Optimization
[proguard] Optimizing...                                                   phase
[proguard]    Number of finalized classes:             1
[proguard]    Number of vertically merged classes:     0   (disabled)
[proguard]    Number of horizontally merged classes:   0   (disabled)
[proguard]    Number of removed write-only fields:     0   (disabled)
[proguard]    Number of privatized fields:             0   (disabled)
[proguard]    Number of inlined constant fields:       0   (disabled)
[proguard]    Number of privatized methods:            0
[proguard]    Number of staticized methods:            0
[proguard]    Number of finalized methods:             0
[proguard]    Number of removed method parameters:     0
[proguard]    Number of inlined constant parameters:   1
[proguard]    Number of inlined constant return values: 0
```

```
[proguard]    Number of inlined short method calls:       0
[proguard]    Number of inlined unique method calls:      1
[proguard]    Number of inlined tail recursion calls:     0
[proguard]    Number of merged code blocks:               0
[proguard]    Number of variable peephole optimizations:  2
[proguard]    Number of arithmetic peephole optimizations: 0    (disabled)
[proguard]    Number of cast peephole optimizations:      0
[proguard]    Number of field peephole optimizations:     0
[proguard]    Number of branch peephole optimizations:    0
[proguard]    Number of simplified instructions:          12
[proguard]    Number of removed instructions:             20
[proguard]    Number of removed local variables:          0
[proguard]    Number of removed exception blocks:         0
[proguard]    Number of optimized local variable frames:  3
...
```

4 ⟵ **Obfuscation phase**

```
[proguard] Obfuscating...
[proguard] Printing mapping to [/Users/matthias/Projects/eclipse/
➥ HelloAnt/bin/proguard/mapping.txt]...
[proguard] Writing output...
[proguard] Preparing output jar [/Users/matthias/Projects/eclipse/
➥ HelloAnt/bin/proguard/obfuscated.jar]
[proguard]    Copying resources from program jar [/Users/matthias/Projects/
   eclipse/
➥ HelloAnt/bin/proguard/original.jar]
[proguard]    Copying resources from program jar [/Users/matthias/
➥ Projects/eclipse/HelloAnt/libs/commons-lang-2.5.jar]
[proguard] Warning: can't write resource [META-INF/MANIFEST.MF]
➥ (Duplicate zip entry [commons-lang-2.5.jar:META-INF/MANIFEST.MF])
[proguard] Printing classes to [/Users/matthias/Projects/eclipse/
➥HelloAnt/bin/proguard/dump.txt]...
```

The first thing you should know is that when invoking ProGuard from the Android tools (Ant target or ADT) is that it'll write four different log files **1**, of which three are of particular importance:

- mapping.txt—Contains the mapping from obfuscated names to their original names. *Make sure to always archive this file for every release build!* It'll become important when processing error reports from obfuscated applications (see section C.4).

- seeds.txt—A list of entry points into your application that ProGuard identified. (We'll explain in a minute why that's important.)

- usage.txt—A list of classes, fields, and methods that ProGuard removed because it thinks they're unused. This is a good reference to check how modifying your ProGuard rules will affect the shrinking phase. If something that's used is listed here, then your shrinking rules are too aggressive. If no unused code is listed here, then your shrinking rules are too coarse or lax.

LOCATING THE PROGUARD LOG FILES   Note that though the Ant ProGuard target writes these files to bin/proguard/, when ProGuard is triggered from the ADT (right-click project > Android Tools > Export Signed Application Package) instead they're written to proguard/.

HOW DOES PROGUARD KNOW WHICH FILES TO PROCESS?   How does ProGuard know which files to process, including android.jar and other library JARs? You'd normally have to tell ProGuard using the `-injars` and `-libraryjars` options. But both the ADT and the Ant tasks set these fields for you, by inspecting your project's class path and output and libs/ folder respectively.

From the code listing, you can also see that ProGuard operates in three steps: a shrinking phase ❷, an optimization phase with potentially multiple iterations ❸, and an obfuscation phase ❹. All phases are optional and can be turned off entirely using the `-dontshrink`, `-dontoptimize`, and `-dontobfuscate` switches, respectively. It's usually a better idea to run all three phases and tweak your rule set so as to suit your needs. For instance, code optimization is generally a good idea, but optimizing too aggressively may break your application, so be careful.

Let's look at how ProGuard configuration files are structured, how rules are set up, and what you need to watch for when writing rules.

C.3   *Writing ProGuard rules*

ProGuard is powerful, and contains a plethora of knobs to turn and switches to flip. One thing you should understand is that there's no single recipe for success; although some rules and options are common to many Android applications, we recommend not adopting anything in a dogmatic way—including those rules you'll see in this section—but instead adjusting and tweaking a configuration to match your application's specific requirements. One rule set may be perfect for a Twitter client, but terrible for a game.

Because ProGuard has so many options, and also uses a powerful pattern syntax to match Java code elements (like class and method names), it can be overwhelming at first. Therefore, we've put together a simple example application that we're going to process with ProGuard. The application doesn't serve any purpose other than doing a few things that will require special treatment while ProGuarding it. We start with a few basic options, which—surprise—won't be sufficient and crash our application, because ProGuard will shrink and optimize too aggressively. We'll then add more rules, bit by bit, until the application works again. We hope this will make writing ProGuard rules easier to understand and digest.

> **GRAB THE PROJECT: PROGUARDED** You can get the source code for this project at the *Android in Practice* code website. Because some code listings here are shortened to focus on specific concepts, we recommend that you download the complete source code and follow along within Eclipse (or your favorite IDE or text editor).
>
> Source: http://mng.bz/hxHs

The application is almost identical to the HelloAnt application from chapter 14, with a few customizations sprinkled in:

- The `Hello` text view is implemented using a custom widget class (called `MyButton`) that inherits from `Button`.
- The button click handler (`myClickHandler`) is wired to the view directly in the layout XML, not in Java code (something that's possible since Android 1.6).

The application is shown in figure C.1. The layout XML is in the next listing.

Listing C.2   The layout of a simple application we're going to shrink and obfuscate

```xml
<?xml version="1.0" encoding="utf-8"?>
<LinearLayout xmlns:android="http://schemas.android.com/apk/res/android"
    android:orientation="vertical"
    android:layout_width="fill_parent"
    android:layout_height="fill_parent">

  <com.manning.aip.proguard.MyButton          Custom button
      android:layout_width="fill_parent"      implementation
      android:layout_height="wrap_content"
      android:text="@string/hello"            Click handler
      android:onClick="myClickHandler"        defined in XML
      />

</LinearLayout>
```

There's nothing special about `MyButton`; it inherits from `Button` and doesn't add any new functionality. We do this to illustrate a problem with custom view classes and ProGuard shrinking rules, as we'll see in a minute. The click handler also doesn't do

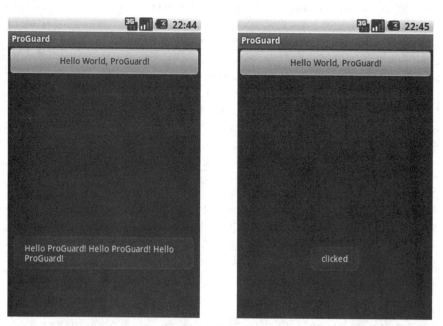

Figure C.1   Our sample application shows a toast when started. When clicking the button (a custom widget class), we show a Toast using an XML click handler.

anything interesting, apart from showing a toast. Like `MyButton`, it merely exists to illustrate a typical problem arising when using ProGuard to obfuscate method names. We've also added a method that's not used anywhere, so we want to strip this useless bloat from the final APK. Here's the full listing of our application's main `Activity`.

Listing C.3 Our application's main `Activity`

```
public class MainActivity extends Activity {

    @Override
    public void onCreate(Bundle savedInstanceState) {
        super.onCreate(savedInstanceState);
        setContentView(R.layout.main);

        String toast = StringUtils.repeat("Hello ProGuard! ", 3);
        Toast.makeText(this, toast, Toast.LENGTH_SHORT).show();
    }

    public void myClickHandler(View customView) {
        Toast.makeText(this, "clicked", Toast.LENGTH_SHORT).show();
    }

    public void unusedMethod() {
        System.out.println("I'm not used anywhere!");
    }
}
```

Let's quickly summarize what we want ProGuard to do with this application:

- We want to keep `MainActivity`, because it's the entry point into our application.
- We want to keep the `StringUtils` class and its repeat method.
- We want to keep the `myClickHandler` method.
- We want to keep our `MyButton` class.
- We want to scrap the `unusedMethod`.
- All names of classes that we keep should be obfuscated, *except* `MainActivity` and `MyButton`, because they're referenced from XML.
- All names of methods that we keep should be obfuscated, *except* `myClickHandler`, because it's referenced from XML.
- We want to apply some common optimizations (we'll have a closer look at that later).

Let's start at the top. We'll set up a minimalistic proguard.cfg file that we'll extend bit by bit to match these requirements. ProGuard shrinking and obfuscation rules are based on whitelist semantics; that means ProGuard will only refuse to shrink or obfuscate those classes that we explicitly list. That implies that we need to tell it to keep at least one class: the entry point into our application, which is `MainActivity`, and which will therefore appear in seeds.txt. We can do this by adding the following rule to proguard.cfg:

```
-keep public class * extends android.app.Activity
```

As you can see, ProGuard's rule syntax closely resembles Java syntax, which makes it easy to read. The key difference is that it supports numerous wildcards, which we won't explain here in detail (they're well documented on the ProGuard website). This particular rule uses the `-keep` option, which tells ProGuard to neither remove nor obfuscate the names of classes that inherit from `android.app.Activity`. It's important to understand here that keeping activities but still obfuscating their names would *not* be acceptable. That's because activities are always declared in the application manifest—in XML—so renaming them only in the class files would break the application.

That was easy! Let's export the signed application package and start the application. Unfortunately, you'll see this:

```
java.lang.RuntimeException: Unable to start activity ComponentInfo{
    com.manning.aip.proguard/com.manning.aip.proguard.MainActivity}:
    android.view.InflateException: Binary XML file line #6: Error inflating
    class com.manning.aip.proguard.MyButton
```

The application crashed with an exception: it failed inflating our custom button view. What went wrong? We already mentioned it: similar to our `MainActivity`, the custom view class isn't being used from Java code, but XML, so ProGuard thinks it's unused and strips it away. A peek into `usage.txt` verifies this: it lists `com.manning.aip.proguard.MyButton`. We could add a rule to keep this specific class, but clearly, this is only one instance of a larger problem that's symptomatic for Android applications: custom `View` classes should be preserved, or more precisely, any class that defines a constructor that may be invoked during a layout inflation. We can encode this requirement in ProGuard rules as follows:

```
-keepclasseswithmembers class * {
    public <init>(android.content.Context, android.util.AttributeSet);
}

-keepclasseswithmembers class * {
    public <init>(android.content.Context, android.util.AttributeSet, int);
}
```

These two rules translate to: don't remove or obfuscate any classes that define constructors (specified using the `<init>` wildcard) that may be called from a `LayoutInflater` (see also the JavaDoc comments for these constructors on `android.view.View`). You may have noticed that we didn't use the `-keep` option, but the `-keepclasseswithmembers` option. The latter is different in that it only keeps classes on the condition that they define all listed members. This is useful if you want to keep classes that may be derived from different base classes, but that all define certain fields or methods. If you were to use `-keep` instead here, then ProGuard would keep *all* classes, along with the specified constructors *if* a class defines them.

Rebuilding and starting the application shows that our application starts again. Good! Let's click our custom button.

```
java.lang.IllegalStateException: Could not find a method
➥ myClickHandler(View) in the activity class
    com.manning.aip.proguard.MainActivity for onClick handler on
➥ view class com.manning.aip.proguard.MyButton
```

Apparently, we're still doing something wrong. Looking again at usage.txt reveals that ProGuard removed myClickHandler:

```
com.manning.aip.proguard.MainActivity:
    22:23:public void myClickHandler(android.view.View)
```

We already know that it wasn't referenced from Java code, only XML, but it's part of MainActivity, which we preserved in our first rule, so why does ProGuard still remove it? That's a common misunderstanding of the -keep rule. When we set it to keep all classes that extend from Activity, we didn't supply a *class body* as part of the class specification to define which members we want to keep along with the class. If you omit this, then ProGuard will merely keep the class itself and its name, but it'll still happily remove, rename, and optimize anything *inside* it. We could do something like this instead:

```
-keep public class * extends android.app.Activity {
    <methods>;
}
```

This rule will preserve *all* activities along with *all* methods they define. This is wasteful though, and obviously, the problem with the click handler is again part of a larger problem symptomatic for Android applications: being able to reference methods from XML. A better solution would be to add a new rule instead:

```
-keepclassmembers class * extends android.app.Activity {
    public void *(android.view.View);
}
```

This rule translates to: if an Activity is *not* removed during the shrinking phase, then keep those methods (and their names) that are public, return no value, and take a single View parameter. That's exactly the requirement for click handlers to be usable from layout XML with the android:onClick attribute. Rebuilding the application shows that finally our application works as expected.

The rules we introduced here were the minimum rules to make our example application work. There are more rules and options that make sense in almost every Android application, so we'll quickly look at those now.

C.4 Useful rules and options

The rules we defined earlier are sufficient for our example application. But that's only because it doesn't, for example, define a Service. As is the case with Activity, the Service class is an Android component class that's referenced from the manifest XML, so if we were to use services, then we'd have to extend proguard.cfg with similar rules. The following rules may prove useful in Android applications.

C.4.1   *Useful rules*

In general, it's a good idea to always to keep the following Android framework classes:

```
-keep public class * extends android.app.Activity
-keep public class * extends android.app.Application
-keep public class * extends android.app.Service
-keep public class * extends android.content.BroadcastReceiver
-keep public class * extends android.content.ContentProvider
-keep public class * extends android.app.backup.BackupAgentHelper
-keep public class * extends android.preference.Preference
-keep public class com.android.vending.licensing.ILicensingService
```

Even if your application doesn't use all these classes, it doesn't hurt to define these rules, and it may save you from pondering application crashes when you add any of these classes but forget to update the ProGuard rules.

A second rule that you almost always want to define is keeping the static CREATOR field that Android uses to parcel objects (see chapter 5). That field is read at runtime via introspection, so ProGuard thinks it's unused and will remove it. You can prevent that from happening with the following rule:

```
-keepclassmembers class * implements android.os.Parcelable {
    static android.os.Parcelable$Creator CREATOR;
}
```

A similar problem arises from the use of native method invocations—methods implemented in a compiled language such as C. Only the method signatures are present in Java code, not the body, so they must be linked against native code. This means that you must prevent ProGuard from obfuscating method names, or linking them to native code will fail. Keep ProGuard from doing so by adding this rule:

```
-keepclasseswithmembernames class * {
    native <methods>;
}
```

We use -keepclasseswithmembernames here because we still want ProGuard to remove those methods if we don't invoke them, but if we do, then their names should remain intact.

The preceding rules are all fairly obvious with respect to their usage, but the last one we're going to show you here may not be. Let's look at it first:

```
-keepclassmembers enum * {
    public static **[] values();
    public static ** valueOf(java.lang.String);
}
```

This rule prevents ProGuard from shrinking and obfuscating the values and valueOf methods of any enumerations we define. These methods are special in that the Java runtime itself invokes them via reflection. This is probably also one reason why Google suggests to use Java enums conservatively. They perform worse than final static class fields. Again, if you don't use Java enums in your code, then you don't need this, but it doesn't hurt to keep this rule either.

That covers rules; let's look at a few useful options.

C.4.2 *Useful options*

So far, we've been looking at rules that tell ProGuard which classes or class members to keep. ProGuard also defines a host of options that affect the behavior of a ProGuard execution. A few general options you typically want to set are:

```
-dontusemixedcaseclassnames
-dontskipnonpubliclibraryclasses
-dontpreverify
-verbose
```

Stopping ProGuard from using mixed-case class names during obfuscation will ensure that no two class names will end up being written to the same file on case-insensitive operating systems like Windows (A.class and a.class would end up being the same file, breaking everything horribly). Moreover, ProGuard, by default, skips nonpublic (package-level) library classes from being processed, because it assumes that they're confined to the library. Some libraries expose public classes that inherit from internal, nonpublic classes, so it makes sense to sacrifice a bit of performance to get better coverage through ProGuard. We also want to skip the entire preverification step, because this is only meaningful for applications that target the Java Micro-Edition platform or Java 6. The last option, -verbose, will make ProGuard output more detailed information while processing classes.

We mentioned before that ProGuard also goes through a code optimization step. Except for a few cases, ProGuard will pull all registers and apply all optimizations it knows by default. Though personally, we never have problems with that, you should keep in mind that these optimizations are sometimes quite aggressive. For instance, ProGuard will merge class hierarchies both horizontally and vertically, so as to reduce the number of class files and hence, the final APK size. It'll also optimize loops and arithmetic operations. If you find that your code doesn't work as expected anymore, you can turn off optimizations bit by bit. The default proguard.cfg file generated by the ADT turns off all arithmetic, field, and class merging optimizations (using the ! symbol before an optimization identifier will disable that optimization):

```
-optimizations !code/simplification/arithmetic,!field/*,!class/merging/*
```

Unfortunately, Google didn't document why they decided to add this rule, but I suggest you disable it first, and see if your application still works as expected. Remember that ProGuard configurations aren't collections of cookie-cutter rules. Find what works best for you and go with that. When optimizing, ProGuard performs several iterations of the optimizations. You can tell it how many passes to do, but know that no matter how high you set this value, it'll stop by itself if it finds that there's nothing more to optimize:

```
-optimizationpasses 5
```

That covers our discussion of configuring and running ProGuard. Before we wrap up this section, we want to quickly look at one more thing: how to reverse obfuscated stack traces from error reports to their original form.

C.5   *Processing error reports*

We already mentioned the one thing about obfuscation that will sooner or later get in your way: processing error reports from an obfuscated application that's out in the wild. The first thing you usually want to do when receiving an error report is look at the stack trace. That's difficult, if not impossible, when all classes and methods suddenly have cryptic, meaningless names.

In order to demonstrate this, let's crash our application by introducing a Bomb class:

```
public class Bomb {

    public void explode() {
        throw new RuntimeException("Boom!");
    }
}
```

Let's have it explode in our onCreate method:

```
public void onCreate(Bundle savedInstanceState) {
    super.onCreate(savedInstanceState);
    setContentView(R.layout.main);

    String toast = StringUtils.repeat("Hello ProGuard! ", 3);
    Toast.makeText(this, toast, Toast.LENGTH_SHORT).show();

    new Bomb().explode();
}
```

If we now start our application, we'll see this stack trace appear in the device logs (shortened for brevity):

```
java.lang.RuntimeException: Unable to start activity ...MainActivity}:
    java.lang.RuntimeException: Boom!
...
Caused by: java.lang.RuntimeException: Boom!
    at com.manning.aip.proguard.MainActivity.onCreate(Unknown Source)
    at android.app.Instrumentation.callActivityOnCreate(
➥ Instrumentation.java:1047)
    at android.app.ActivityThread.performLaunchActivity(
➥ ActivityThread.java:2627)
    ... 11 more
```

As you can see, there's neither a line number nor a source filename next to the line in the stack trace where the error originated. That's because ProGuard by default removes this information to make reverse engineering even harder. We can prevent it from doing so by adding the following option to our proguard.cfg:

```
-keepattributes SourceFile,LineNumberTable
```

This will bring back the source filename and the line numbers in stack traces. This doesn't solve the problem with obfuscated method names. In our overly simplified example, we don't have this problem, because ProGuard refused to obfuscate the onCreate method for a simple reason: it overrides a superclass method of the same name. Because android.jar isn't targeted by ProGuard (it's merely used for code analysis; after all, android.jar isn't part of your application, it's part of the platform), it couldn't change its name. Still, in more complex scenarios you'll have to revert the stack trace to its original form, and that's what the `retrace` tool does. The `retrace` tool is a companion tool to `proguard`, and can be found in the same place in your SDK home directory. The only thing it does is read obfuscated stack traces, matching them against a ProGuard mapping file (`mapping.txt`, as seen earlier), and putting out the original stack trace:

```
$ retrace proguard/mapping.txt stacktrace.txt
```

Now it should become clear why it's so utterly important that you archive the mapping file with every application release. Without that file, you won't be able to retrace stack traces.

C.6 *Summary*

This wraps up our discussion of ProGuard. We've shown you that ProGuard can be a powerful companion to make your applications smaller, faster, and harder to reverse engineer, but it also takes a fair amount of time to configure and fine-tune it to suit your needs. It's a shame that ProGuard doesn't receive more attention in the Android documentation, but it shares this somewhat shadowy existence with another neat tool, the Monkeyrunner, which we're going to cover in appendix D.

appendix D
monkeyrunner

In this last appendix, we're going to look at another recent addition to the Android SDK toolset: the monkeyrunner. The material covered here complements what we covered in chapters 13 and 14—testing, instrumentation, and build automation—although the monkeyrunner takes a special role both technically and usage-wise, as you'll see in a minute.

D.1 Overview

Not to be confused with the monkey tool (see chapter 13), the monkeyrunner is a scripted and extensible application that allows you to control an emulator or device in a programmatic fashion. Similar to Android's instrumentation framework, it allows you to steer flow of an application by launching activities and sending input events, but it does so from outside the Android framework, much like a real-world user would. Using monkeyrunner, you can install or uninstall application packages, interact with a device's command shell, and even capture screenshots of the current screen. Think of monkeyrunner as a remote control for Android.

The monkeyrunner itself is written in Java, is part of the Android SDK, and a shell script to launch it can be found in the ANDROID_HOME/tools folder. It's a command line application and has no graphical UI. You can run monkeyrunner in two different modes: default or interactive. In default mode, monkeyrunner takes scripted programs as input and executes them:

```
$ monkeyrunner my_script.py
```

These scripts contain the instructions the monkeyrunner should execute, and we'll see in a minute what these scripts look like. When started without a script file as an argument, monkeyrunner will launch in interactive mode. This will open a shell where you can type in commands directly:

```
$ monkeyrunner
Jython 2.5.0 (Release_2_5_0:6476, Jun 16 2009, 13:33:26)
[Java HotSpot(TM) 64-Bit Server VM (Apple Inc.)] on java1.6.0_24
>>> 5 == 5
True
>>>
```

For the remainder of this section, we'll briefly look at the components that make up monkeyrunner, the functionality they expose, how we can use that functionality to write monkeyrunner scripts, and how we can extend it with custom plug-ins.

D.2 *Components and features*

The monkeyrunner consists of three major classes that you'll use in scripts. It consists of more classes, but the following three are the ones acting as facades into the monkeyrunner functionality: MonkeyRunner, MonkeyDevice, and MonkeyImage.

> **MONKEYRUNNER SOURCE CODE**   The monkeyrunner is part of the open source Android SDK, so you can find its code online. Because only the three classes we're going to cover are documented as part of the online documentation (http://mng.bz/3jBo), the monkeyrunner source code can be an invaluable source of information: http://mng.bz/kqxE.

We'll now briefly look at each of these classes and explain what they're good for.

D.2.1 *MonkeyRunner*

This class acts as a high-level controller in a monkeyrunner script. The MonkeyRunner class defines static helper methods to do such things as opening message dialogs, putting the script to sleep for some time (so as to let the device that's being controlled settle), and most importantly, connect to an emulator or device.

D.2.2 *MonkeyDevice*

The MonkeyDevice class represents a single Android device to which you've connected via MonkeyRunner.waitForConnection. It allows you to control the given device by doing things such as installing or uninstalling application and test packages, running activities or instrumentation tests, executing shell commands directly on the device, broadcasting intents, sending touch and key events, and taking screenshots. It's therefore the key class through which you control a connected device.

D.2.3 *MonkeyImage*

If you take a screenshot via MonkeyDevice, it'll be returned as a MonkeyImage. Its main purpose is to expose functionality that allows you to save these screenshots to your hard drive, and to compare two screenshots in order to detect deviations from reference screens during an end-to-end test. Let's see how all this comes together in a monkeyrunner script.

D.3   *Scripting monkeyrunner*

As mentioned earlier, the monkeyrunner is a scripted application. This means you either give it a script to run or type commands directly in interactive mode. Google didn't reinvent the wheel to come up with a proprietary scripting language, but instead leverages the popular and powerful Python language to script the monkeyrunner.

Python is an interpreted multiparadigm programming language, focusing on concise and easy-to-read code. It's therefore well suited to be used as a scripting language. Python combines concepts from the object-oriented and functional programming styles, but also allows you to write purely procedural programs if you desire. One of the more remarkable aspects of Python, especially if you're used to languages of the C family, is the absence of curly braces. Instead, lexical scopes are demarcated by indentation, which makes Python one of the few languages where whitespace is truly significant to a program's syntax. We won't explain the Python language in detail here, but will add notes and explanations to source code fragments that may not be immediately obvious to someone coming from a pure Java background.

Let's go ahead and write a monkeyrunner script that simulates a user going through our DealDroid application. You can save this file to dealdroid.py (for example), or type in each command manually in interactive mode.

Listing D.1   A simple monkeyrunner script

```
from com.android.monkeyrunner import MonkeyRunner, MonkeyDevice        ❶ Import
import commands                                                            classes
import sys

devices = commands.getoutput('adb devices').strip().split('\n')[1:]
if len(devices) == 0:
  MonkeyRunner.alert("No devices found. Start an emulator
  ➥ or connect a device.", "No devices found", "Exit")
  sys.exit(1)                                             Enumerate  ❷
elif len(devices) == 1:                                     devices
  choice = 0
else:
  choice = MonkeyRunner.choice("More than one device found.
  ➥ Please select target device.", devices, "Select target device")

device_id = devices[choice].split('\t')[0]                    ❸ Connect
                                                                selected device
device = MonkeyRunner.waitForConnection(5, device_id)    ◁

apk_path = device.shell('pm path com.manning.aip.dealdroid')
if apk_path.startswith('package:'):
    print "DealDroid already installed."                      ❹ Install
else:                                                            application
    print "DealDroid not installed, installing APKs..."
    device.installPackage('../DealDroid/bin/DealDroid.apk')

print "Starting DealDroid..."
device.startActivity(component='com.manning.aip.dealdroid/.DealList')    ◁
MonkeyRunner.sleep(7)
                                                              Start
                                                              application  ❺
```

```
device.touch(100, 450, 'DOWN_AND_UP')
MonkeyRunner.sleep(2)
device.touch(100, 250, 'DOWN_AND_UP')
MonkeyRunner.sleep(2)
device.touch(100, 150, 'DOWN_AND_UP')
MonkeyRunner.sleep(2)
device.press('KEYCODE_MENU', 'DOWN_AND_UP', None)
MonkeyRunner.sleep(1)
device.touch(280, 450, 'DOWN_AND_UP')
MonkeyRunner.sleep(2)
device.type("555-13456")
MonkeyRunner.sleep(2)
device.press('KEYCODE_BACK', 'DOWN_AND_UP', None)
MonkeyRunner.sleep(1)
device.press('KEYCODE_BACK', 'DOWN_AND_UP', None)
MonkeyRunner.sleep(1)
device.press('KEYCODE_BACK', 'DOWN_AND_UP', None)
```

6 Simulate flow through application

The first thing you must do is tell Python which classes you'd like to use. You do this using the import statement **1**. Note that you can also use the * wildcard instead of a list of classes, but as in Java, it's considered bad style to import more things than you need.

Before we can do anything meaningful, we must connect to an Android device or emulator. Therefore, we enumerate all connected devices using Python's getoutput method, which executes a shell command (the adb devices command) and returns the output as a string. Since the output of adb devices isn't suitable for putting in a list, we strip trailing whitespace, split along line breaks, and select the last two entries using Python's Array range syntax. ([x:y] means from index x to index y; when omitting x or y, the range is unbounded in the respective direction). **2** We then connect to the selected device using Monkeyrunner.waitForConnection **3**. This method will return a MonkeyDevice instance that can then be used throughout the script. Note that the arguments to this method (timeout and device ID) are optional; you can invoke it without any arguments, in which case it'll try to connect to whatever device is available, or wait indefinitely for one to appear.

Before using DealDroid, we must ensure that it's installed. We do this by first testing to see if it's installed, and install only if required **4**. To accomplish this, we leverage the shell method, which allows us to execute an arbitrary shell command on the device. Here we use the device's package manager (pm) to tell us the path of the APK for the DealDroid package. If DealDroid is installed, this will return a string such as package:/path/to/apkfile. We exploit this information to not install the package unless that string comes back empty.

NOTE For the installation to work, please make sure that DealDroid has been checked out to your hard drive and that the script is executed from within that folder. If your setup differs, make sure to change the path to the APK file accordingly.

Next, we start the application by starting its launcher activity, DealList **5**. If you're puzzled by the way we pass the component argument to the startActivity method:

this is what Python calls a *keyword argument*. In Python, you can pass parameters not only in the order in which they were defined (as is the case in Java), but in arbitrary order by spelling out their name, followed by the assignment operator and the argument. Because startActivity takes eight parameters, not all of which are always required, we can shorten this invocation by passing the component argument explicitly. The first thing DealDroid does is fetch data from the eBay web service, so we put the script to sleep for seven seconds to wait for it to finish.

At this point, the DealDroid should've settled and shown a list of deals. This is where we start simulating a user using the application ❻ by calling the touch, type, and press functions, which perform touches, text input, and button presses, respectively. Possible key or touch actions are DOWN, UP, or DOWN_AND_UP (passed as strings), whereas possible key codes are exactly those defined in android.view.KeyEvent. The outcome of running this script will be similar to what you've already seen in chapter 13, where we used instrumentation instead to steer flow in DealDroid programmatically.

You may be wondering: the monkeyrunner classes are written in Java, but we're loading and using them in a Python script. How does that work? It works because monkeyrunner uses Jython, a Java implementation of Python. Jython can load and manipulate Python scripts and run them on a JVM, and even mix and match Python and Java classes.

Speaking of Java classes, monkeyrunner can inject your custom Java classes into your scripts via its plug-in architecture, which we'll discuss next.

D.4   *Writing plugins*

The monkeyrunner supports extending its functionality by means of plugins. A monkeyrunner plugin is an ordinary JAR file that you can pass to monkeyrunner on the command line:

```
$ monkeyrunner -plugin plugin.jar script.py
```

For this to work, you'll need to create the JAR file yourself (we'll see how in a minute); there's no tool support for this in the ADT. A plugin consists of one special class, the plugin main class, which has access to the Python environment that will be used to run the monkeyrunner script. This allows you to inject custom objects, constants, and variables into a script during plugin load time, which will then be immediately available from your script. On top of that, you can add as many ordinary Java classes as you wish. A notable restriction is that you will *not* have access to any Android framework classes, only to those classes the monkeyrunner loads, including the monkeyrunner classes themselves (MonkeyRunner, MonkeyDevice, MonkeyImage, and any other classes from the com.android.monkeyrunner package). Of particular interest is ddmlib: this is the library the DDMS tool (also available as an Eclipse perspective as part of the ADT) uses to communicate with Android devices. It defines a Java API you can use to enumerate devices and interact with them directly, instead of needing to fork a shell process that invokes adb, which is a lot more cumbersome to handle. Monkeyrunner depends on ddmlib, so your plugins can use this library, too.

We're now going to write a simple Hello World style plugin for monkeyrunner. This is to show you how to set up a plug-in project, how to create a plug-in JAR file, and how to access its functionality from a monkeyrunner script.

> **GRAB THE PROJECT: DEALDROIDMONKEYRUNNER** You can get the source code for this project at the *Android in Practice* code web site. Because some code listings here are shortened to focus on specific concepts, we recommend that you download the complete source code and follow along within Eclipse (or your favorite IDE or text editor).

Source: http://mng.bz/Pufd

Before writing the plugin, we need to set up the project. Because we're writing plugins in Java, this will be an ordinary Java project, so go ahead and create one (as usual, we'll assume Eclipse as the IDE of choice). For a plugin project to compile, you must at least have the Jython and Google Guava libraries on your build path, but it also makes sense to add the monkeyrunner and ddmlib JARs. You only need the latter if you want to extend the monkeyrunner classes themselves or interact with devices directly—something we're not going to do in this simple example—but it's good to have them together if you plan to do something more advanced.

All these libraries are freely available on the internet, but it's easier and safer to use the versions that ship with the Android SDK. They can be found in `ANDROID_HOME/tools/lib`. If you find yourself bundling JARs together for a typical setup, such as writing monkeyrunner plugins, it's usually a good idea to leverage Eclipse's User Library concept to do that. Right-click the plugin project in Eclipse and go to Properties > Java build path > Libraries > Add Library... > User Library > User Libraries... and click New.... Give the new library configuration a name, for example "Monkeyrunner." Accept and select the new user library from the list, along with the previously mentioned libraries, using the Add JARs... option. When done, add the new Monkeyrunner user library to your project's build path by selecting it from the list of available user libraries. Your project layout should now look similar to what's seen in figure D.1.

We're all set now, so let's write some plugin code. The task is to simplify the calls to `touch` and `press` in script files. You almost always want to create a `DOWN_AND_UP` event, and wait a brief period of time after each input event before performing the next action. To accommodate these two points, we're going to add a helper class called

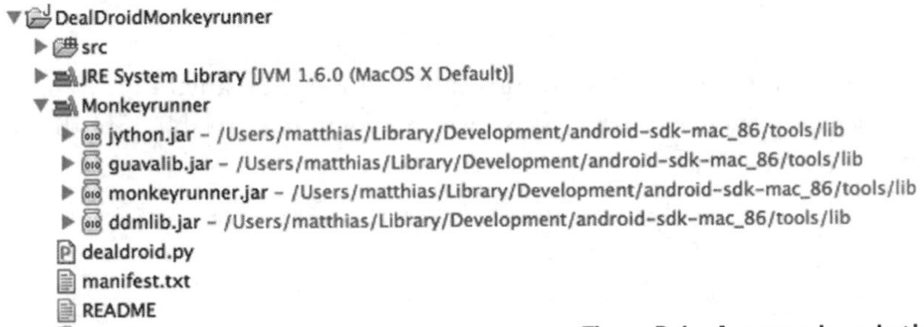

```
▼ 📂 DealDroidMonkeyrunner
  ▶ 🗂 src
  ▶ 🗁 JRE System Library [JVM 1.6.0 (MacOS X Default)]
  ▼ 🗁 Monkeyrunner
      ▶ 🔲 jython.jar – /Users/matthias/Library/Development/android-sdk-mac_86/tools/lib
      ▶ 🔲 guavalib.jar – /Users/matthias/Library/Development/android-sdk-mac_86/tools/lib
      ▶ 🔲 monkeyrunner.jar – /Users/matthias/Library/Development/android-sdk-mac_86/tools/lib
      ▶ 🔲 ddmlib.jar – /Users/matthias/Library/Development/android-sdk-mac_86/tools/lib
  📄 dealdroid.py
  📄 manifest.txt
  📄 README
  📄 run.sh
```

Figure D.1 An exemplary plug-in project layout.

MonkeyHelper. This helper class implements tap and press methods that simplify the standard touch and press invocations and also let the script sleep for two seconds after sending an event.

> **NOTE** Please note that in the sample project we didn't use an Eclipse User Library, but simply committed the JAR files that came with the SDK r12 tools to the repository. We did this strictly for your convenience, so that the project compiles straight away. Committing JAR files to the repository is something you typically wouldn't want to do in your own projects.

Listing D.2 The `MonkeyHelper` is loaded from our plug-in and available in scripts

```java
package com.manning.aip.monkeyrunner;

import org.python.core.PyInteger;
import org.python.core.PyObject;
import org.python.core.PyString;

import com.android.monkeyrunner.MonkeyDevice;
import com.android.monkeyrunner.core.TouchPressType;

public class MonkeyHelper {

    public static void tap(MonkeyDevice device, int x, int y) {
        PyObject[] args = { new PyInteger(x), new PyInteger(y),
                new PyString(TouchPressType.DOWN_AND_UP.name()) };
        device.touch(args, null);
        sleep(2000);
    }

    public static void press(MonkeyDevice device, String key) {
        String keyCode = "KEYCODE_" + key.toUpperCase();
        PyObject[] args = { new PyString(keyCode), new PyString(
                TouchPressType.DOWN_AND_UP.name()),
                new PyString("") };
        device.press(args, null);
        sleep(2000);
    }

    private static void sleep(long millis) {
        try {
            Thread.sleep(millis);
        } catch (InterruptedException e) {
        }
    }
}
```

Simplify screen tap syntax ← (annotation pointing to `tap` method)

Simplify keypress syntax ← (annotation pointing to `press` method)

We also need a plugin main class. In this case, it doesn't do anything. We merely want to introduce the MonkeyHelper class, so we're injecting a variable into the script that contains a welcome text:

```java
public class Plugin implements Predicate<PythonInterpreter> {

    @Override
    public boolean apply(PythonInterpreter python) {

        python.set("hello", "Hello, monkeyrunner!");
```

```
        return true;
    }

}
```

Every plugin main class must implement the `Predicate` interface with type `Python-Interpreter`. The `Predicate` interface is part of the Guava library, a Java utility library developed by Google. We implement its `apply` method, which is the entry point into a monkeyrunner plugin. `PythonInterpreter` is a Jython class that exposes an interface to a Python script. We can use it to read and write variables—in this case, a string variable called `hello` with a value of "Hello, monkeyrunner!". This variable will be available straight from our monkeyrunner script, as we'll see in a minute. You don't have to call the class `Plugin`; you can call it whatever you like.

That's it for our plugin code. What's left to do is roll these classes into a JAR file so that we can pass it to the monkeyrunner tool. Here's how it works: during startup, monkeyrunner will search through the plugin JAR's manifest file and look for a field called `MonkeyRunnerStartupRunner`. This manifest field must contain the fully qualified name of the class implementing `apply`; in our case, that's the `Plugin` class. We must provide a custom JAR manifest, so we create a template called `manifest.txt` containing these settings:

```
MonkeyRunnerStartupRunner: com.manning.aip.monkeyrunner.Plugin
```

Be careful: when creating a manifest file by hand, it must end with a line feed—a blank line—otherwise things will go awfully wrong. That being done, you can now create the JAR file containing our plugin classes from the project folder using:

```
$ jar cvfm bin/plugin.jar manifest.txt -C bin .
```

This will create a file called `plugin.jar` in `bin/` by including the manifest fields from `manifest.txt` and all classes from the `bin` folder. Before loading our brand new plugin, let's revise the script from listing D.1 to print out the variable we injected and use our new `MonkeyHelper` class (we left out the parts that didn't change).

Listing D.3 The revised script, now using functionality from a custom plug-in

```
from com.android.monkeyrunner import MonkeyRunner, MonkeyDevice
from com.manning.aip.monkeyrunner import MonkeyHelper      ⟵──┐  Load helper
import commands                                             ❶  class
import sys

print hello                                      ⟵──┐  Print hello
                                                 ❷  message
...

MonkeyHelper.tap(device, 100, 450)
MonkeyHelper.tap(device, 100, 250)
MonkeyHelper.tap(device, 100, 150)
MonkeyHelper.press(device, 'menu')
MonkeyHelper.tap(device, 280, 450)              ❸  Use tap and
device.type("555-13456")                           press helpers
MonkeyHelper.press(device, 'back')
MonkeyHelper.press(device, 'back')
MonkeyHelper.press(device, 'back')
```

Before using our helper class, we must import it into the script as seen before ❶. We can also access the `hello` variable set by the `Plugin` class; it's set for us before entering script execution, which is convenient ❷. The code block that was executing the screen flow now uses our new helper functions and has become less clunky. For instance, you can now specify the back key as `back` instead of `KEYCODE_BACK` ❸.

We can run this script using the following command:

```
$ monkeyrunner -plugin bin/plugin.jar dealdoid_with_plugin.py
```

If everything worked out, you should see the "Hello, monkeyrunner!" message being printed to standard out.

D.5 Summary

You can use monkeyrunner to connect to a device, install an Android application, and execute a scripted sequence of user input events. That way you can script the flows you expect your users to take and simulate them by running the script. In case you need more power or flexibility, we also showed you how monkeyrunner's functionality can be augmented by means of plugins.

The monkeyrunner can be a powerful tool to programmatically define application flows that simulate users interacting with a device. Considering its scripted nature, you can use it for whatever you want, because you're able to extend it with new functionality via Python modules or Java plug-ins.

One thing you'll quickly notice when working with monkeyrunner is that it's not reliable. It often fails with error messages from which you can't properly recover. This happens, for instance, if you're trying to dispatch input events before the device has settled, in which case *all* subsequent input events will fail. In that case, try increasing the sleep time between steps.

The obligatory and frequent use of `sleep` is the source of another hurdle. If steps are involved whose execution times are difficult to estimate, such as the web service call in our example, then your script and the device can quickly get out of sync. For these reasons, the monkeyrunner isn't well suited for use in automated test environments, such as build servers (see chapter 14). Instead, it's a tool that's executed and observed by testers manually. Given the relatively recent addition of monkeyrunner to the SDK toolbox, we haven't yet seen any plugins being released by Google or third parties, but we're hopeful that it's only a matter of time until we see the first ones emerging from the Android community. Go open source!

index

Android in Action, Third Edition
by W. Frank Ableson, Robi Sen, Chris King
   and C. Enrique Ortiz

   ISBN: 978-1-617290-50-3
   650 pages, $49.99
   October 2011

Objective-C Fundamentals
by Christopher K. Fairbairn,
   Johannes Fahrenkrug,
   Collin Ruffenach

   ISBN: 978-1-935182-53-5
   368 pages, $44.99
   September 2011

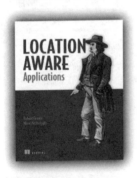

Location-Aware Applications
by Richard Ferraro
   Murat Aktihanoglu

   ISBN: 978-1-935182-33-7
   320 pages, $44.99
   July 2011

iOS 4 in Action
Examples and Solutions for iPhone & iPad
by Jocelyn Harrington, Brandon Trebitowski,
   Christopher Allen, and Shannon Appelcline

   ISBN: 978-1-617290-01-5
   504 pages, $44.99
   June 2011

For ordering information go to www.manning.com

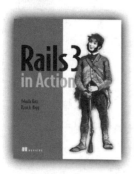